A BRASHEAR(S) FAMILY HISTORY,

Descendants of Robert and Benois Brasseur

Vol. 6

BRASHEARS/BRESHEARS FAMILIES

(Beshears, Boshears, etc)

of TN, MO, ID, WA, OK, etc

Charles Brashear, Books etc
1718 Arroyo Sierra Circle
Santa Rosa, CA 95405-7762
e-mail: <brashear@mail.sdsu.edu>

version of December 25, 2004

ISBN 0-933362-17-x

A Brashear(s) Family History: Descendants of Robert and Benois Brasseur: Vol. 6: BRASHEARS/BRESHEARS **FAMILIES (Beshears, Boshears, etc) of TN, MO, ID, WA, OK, etc**, by Charles Brashear

I am and have been for 40-something years actively engaged in research on the Brashear(s) Family, in all its branches, in all spellings of the surname. Some years ago, Troy Back and Leon Brashear gave me their blessing and permission to "update" their book, *THE BRASHEAR STORY, A FAMILY HISTORY*, but the more data I collected, the more I realized that this family history will never again fit into one volume, especially if you include the amount and kind of detail, pictures, maps, scanned documents, etc, that I like to include. This is the sixth of a planned nine volumes. See the Appendix for more details, ordering information, and blurbs on my other books.

ISBN 0-933362-17-x

Printed on demand in the United States of America by Lightning Source, Inc, LaVergne, TN

Preface

This is a "speculative" book. I'm putting together some of the documents we have, posing some questions, and suggesting some hypothetical scenarios about Basil Brashears ([Back #31]; m. Anne Belt) and his descendants. One son and one daughter--Middleton and Henrietta-- are documented.

Circumstances (such as the Rowan Co, Tax list, 1757, and land records of Spartanburg Co, SC) suggest that Basil Brashears and Anne Belt had several more children, and even suggest names, but we lack documentation for them.

This book is about Basil and Middleton Brashears and their (possible) Brashears, Breshears, Beshears, Boshears, and other descendants in Lawrence Co, Tennessee; Benton, Polk, and neighboring counties, Missouri; the Boise area of Idaho; the Okanagan Valley in Washington; eastern Oklahoma; and a few other places.

The new volume 7 in this series, "Brashears Families of SC, MO, IL, etc," will treat the "other" children of Basil Brashears and Anne Belt— that is:

- William Brashears and his wife, Sarah ______ , who lived in Spartanburg Co, SC and their sons:
  - William Brashears, who m. Mary Elizabeth Clayton and moved to Ralls Co, Missouri, and
  - Ithra Brashears, who married Hannah Elizabeth Middleton and settled in Crawford Co, IL;
- Robert Brashears of NC and his Boshears descendants in Scott and Campbell Co, TN;
- Jeremiah Brashears, who moved to Christian/Hopkins Co, KY and founded a Beshears family;

A FEW WORDS ABOUT MY CONVENTIONS:

Like Troy Back and Leon Brashear, I have marked with an **asterisk** those family lines that are followed up with later, fuller listings or, maybe, a short biographical sketch or some document. Reading genealogies quickly becomes a hopeless, confusing mess; and you just have to flip back and forth between pages, checking birth-dates, wives, etc to trace your line.

Usually, I have put several **generations** in one listing. I've indented and numbered each succeeding generation, thus:

> ^{1}1. the parents
>> ^{2}1. the children
>>> ^{3}4. the grand-children
>>>> ^{4}1. the great-grandchildren

- The **superscripts** in the outlines represent the number of generations removed from Robert Brasseur, the Immigrant Huguenot, who arrived in Virginia about 1635. The ordinal numbers indicate the sequence of that person among his/her siblings. Thus ^{2}1 indicates the second generation, first child in a family; ^{3}4 indicates the third generation, fourth child; etc. Sorry if this makes reading difficult. I hope that it's easier than flipping back and forth over dozens of pages.
- Also, I have assigned (or rather let my computer assign) a **serial number** to all members of the Brashear(s) family. In most cases, this serial number is at the beginning of a line on which the member appears. The serial number is preceded by some superscripts. Superscript ^{v1} refers to the serial number in vol 1; ^{v2} refers to the serial number in vol 2; etc. Usually, I have also given the serial number assigned by Back and Brashear in parentheses: e.g. Isaac Brashears (Back#168). I have left gaps between chapters in this numbering system, to facilitate adding family members later.
- I have also tried to **cross-reference** members of the family who married other members of the family. It's very hard for me to know when people are cousins, however, and so I apologize in advance for any cross-references I missed.
- Maybe the serial numbers will help distinguish several people of exactly the same name. I don't know how many men were named Robert Samuel Brashear(s), but it was a large number.

Whenever the family produced a famous person, as for example, Dr. Walter Brashear of Bardstown, KY, who performed the world's first amputation of a leg at the hip joint, or Dr. John Alfred Brashear, who simply made the world's finest optics for half a century, there followed a rash of namings for them. There must be a dozen John Alfred Brashears. The only way you can keep them separate is if they happened to have a known nickname, as did Robert Samuel "Old Bob" Brashear," or you nickname them with their serial number.

Much the same is true for the many Othos, Basils, Reginalds, not to mention the Johns, Josephs, Jameses, Williams, Roberts, Elizabeths, Marthas, Margarets, Nancys, etc.

- I've **boldfaced** only the people whose birth names were some form of the family name: Brashear, Brashears, Brasher, Brashers, Beshears, Boshears, etc. I have tried to give their surnames as they occur in the documents (even when obviously misspelled), sometimes with and sometimes without the "s." So if you see a man's name spelled two ways in the same document, it's likely that's the way it was in the document.

  (I have to confess that I get confused as to who uses the "s" and who doesn't— or when; in many cases a person's name appears in the records both ways. My great-grandfather's will spells his surname three ways— Brasher, Brashers, Brashears— and the county clerk filed it under the fourth possibility— Brashear!)
- Spouses are given in bold italics: e.g. ***Phoebe Nicks***. Often, a wife's maiden name and/or former name is indicated in parentheses; "née" (feminine) or "né" (masculine) (French for "born") indicates the surname at birth; thus Dorothy (née Cager/widow Munroe) Jones.
- "Nicknames" are in quotes; e.g. Robert S. "Old Bob" Brashear.
- If a person was <u>called by a name</u> other than his/her first, I've underlined that name, e.g. Howard <u>Charles</u> Brashers, who was/is called "Charles." Underlining is also used occasionally to call the reader's attention to a name or some data.
- When all I know are the names of a set of children, I've run them on in a paragraph and separated them by punctuation: e.g. (from a Bell family) Ch: Danny Joe; Karen Lynn; Stanley Farris; and Phillip Drew Bell. The exception is that all Brashear(s) family members get a bold line of their own (I think).
- When I don't know a name, either given or surname, I've offered a **blank**, e.g. Robert Brashier, III, m.1. ______; m.2. c1679, Mrs. Alice Jackson, widow of Thomas Jackson. If you know the name(s) you can fill them in with pen and ink. And, of course, I'd like to receive the data also. These blanks are NOT indexed.
- Information I have reason to believe is accurate, but have **no proof** of, is preceded and/or followed by a question mark; thus

"Bill Brashear, b. ?1845" means I'm making an informed guess at his birth date. If you take my information elsewhere, please, please, also take my doubt.

I've used some abbreviations:

HSB = *The Brashear-Brashears Family, 1449-1929,* by Henry Sinclair Brashear (1929), the first book-length history of this family

Back = *The Brashear Story, a Family History, 1637-1963,* by Troy Back and Leon Brashear (1963; 1980), the second book-length history of this family.

BFB = "Br(e)ashe(a)r(s) Family Branches," a newsletter published for more than ten years by Arzella Brashear Spear.

FHL = The Family History Library, Salt Lake City. FHL Arc or ARCfile indicates archive files in that library.

"c" in front of a number means "circa" or about: thus "c1742" should be read "about 1742."

"b." mean "was born on/at," "d." means "died on/at,"

"m." means "married," and sometimes a number is added to indicate which of multiple marriages I'm talking about, as "m.2." indicates a second marriage.

"bur" means "is/was buried at" some cemetery ("cem")

"s/o" "d/o" "gs/o" and the like mean "son of" "daughter of" etc.

I have sometimes abbreviated county names: e.g. PGCo is Prince George's Co, MD; LawrCo is Lawrence Co, TN

SCC (in land records) stands for "Sworn Chain Carrier(s)"

CCC stands for Clerk of the County Court; DC for District Clerk

DS usually mean District Surveyor; sometimes the initials of the county are added, as DSBC might mean "District Surveyor, Bullitt Co."

And in places where it struck me as awkward, or lacked clarity, I haven't used these abbreviations.

In many cases, I've followed descending families with other surnames a few generations, especially when someone in that line is an interested and active genealogist, or the lines intermarry later. Many of these people have contributed substantially to what we know about the Brashear(s) Family. As I've said before and will say again, this sort of book cannot be written by one person, because there is simply not enough time in one lifetime to go to all the places, do all the research, sort it out, organize it in a semblance of comprehension, and write it up. Any family historian is forced to rely on the research of many a cousin, most of them bearing a different surname. We all owe them heavy thanks for the money and sweat they have expended on our common family history. I'll try to acknowledge each at the spot where they contributed most.

I would also like, especially, to thank:

Georgene Humphreys, who has worked tirelessly for many years on all branches of this family;

Minnie (McGee) Fowler, who was a pioneer in the family history in Benton, Hickory, Polk, Dallas Counties, Missouri;

Glen Breshears, who sent hundreds of pages of data on Descendants of Henry Breshears Jr;

Bill Brooks, who sent data and a CD containing nearly a hundred old photos;

Norman Parks, for data on the Tennessee branches of this family;

Sybil Jobe and Wayne L. Brashear, for data on the descendants of Berry M. Brashears and Frances Pryor;

Cris McCarthy, who sent data on John Breshears and Naoma Hogg and pictures of many Idaho Breshears;

Roy Colbert, who collected a great deal of material about the Idaho and Washington branches of these families;

Charles S. Breshears and Larry Pleasants for data on the Arkansas branches of Breshears and Boshears;

And others I've tried to mention where I used their contribution.

CONTENTS

Brashears/Breshears Families

XX

1. BASIL BRASHEAR(S) and Anne Belt

Basil Brashear(s), (#[v1]288, Back #31), b. 18 March 1714, birth registered at St Barnabas Protestant Episcopal Church, Queen Anne's Parish, Prince George's Co (PGCo), Maryland, s/o Samuel Brashear Sr, the Maryland Carpenter (#[v1]232, Back #11) and Ann Jones; m. c1732, PGCo, ***Anne Belt***, d/o Benjamin Belt and Elizabeth Middleton. In the records, Basil's surname is spelled about equally with and without the "s."

Basil's Ancestry

Basil Brashear was in the fifth generation of Brashears in America. His ancestry included:

1st gen. **Robert Brasseur/Brashear,** *the Huguenot Immigrant,* (#[v1]1.), b. France, bef. 1600; to Isle of Thanet, Kent Co, England, c1620-30; to Virginia, bef. 1635; d. 1666-7, Nansemond Co, VA; m. ______. We have not found a document with a wife's name on it. Robert arrived in Virginia with at least seven children and had three more in Virginia. The wife's name was certainly NOT Florence Rey, for that was the wife of his son, Robert Jr. Nor could it be Elizabeth Fowke, for Elizabeth lived about a hundred years later and was married to other people. The Mary Brasseur named in the Nansemond land grant *may* be the wife, rather than a daughter, as we have assumed. See vol 1 for the documents we have on Robert.

2nd gen. **Benjamin Brassieur,** *the American* (#[v1]2, Back #1), also called Benois/ Benoit/ Bennet Brasseur/ Brashear, b. France, c1620; to Va with father, c1635; to Maryland, 1658; naturalized as citizen by Cecil Calvert, 1662; d. 1662, Calvert Co, Maryland; m. ***Mary Richford(?)***. We are uncertain about Mary's surname. Benois paid passage from England to Virginia for a Mary Richford, and we have thought he was "buying" a wife, a very common practice in Virginia at that time. Mary named her and Benois' eight children in her will. See Vol. 1 for details.

3rd gen. **Robert Brashier, III,** *the Improvident* (#v181, Back #2), b. 1646, Nansemond Co, Virginia; d. 1712, Prince Georges Co, Maryland; m.1. ________ (mother of the children); m.2. c1679, ***Mrs. Alice Jackson***, widow of Thomas Jackson. Again, we do not know the wife's name. But it is pretty clear that she was mother of the children. Mrs. Alice Jackson and Robert Brashier, III married c1679, AFTER the three sons, Benjamin, Sr; Samuel, Sr; and Robert, IV, were born.

4th gen. **Samuel Brashear Sr,** *the Maryland Carpenter* (#v1232, Back #11), b. 1673, Calvert Co, Maryland; d. 1740, Prince George's Co, Maryland; m. ***Ann Jones***, d/o William Jones and Dorothy (née Cager/ widow Munroe). Samuel's older brother, Benjamin Brashear Sr married Mary Jones, Ann's sister; so the two sets of children were "double cousins"—that is, their fathers were brothers (which made the children cousins) and their mothers were sisters (which made them cousins a second time). The girls' father, William Jones, "sold" (that is, he gave) a plot of land called "Cuckhold's Delight" to Benjamin and Samuel. The brothers lived the rest of their lives on this plot, and their brother, Robert, IV, lived (at least part of the time) on a plot adjoining.

<u>Children of Samuel Brashear, Sr (#v1232) and Ann Jones:</u> (References: Children's births registered at St Barnabas Protestant Episcopal Church, Queen Anne's Parish, Prince George's Co, MD; see also Will of Samuel Brashear; Queen Anne's Parish Records, Md. Historical Society, Baltimore; and Maryland Historical Magazine, v.23, p.113.)

v1281. 51. **William Jones Brashear**, (Back#25) b. 28 Jan 1694/5; apparently died young, and the name was re-used

v1282. 52. ***Samuel Brashear, Jr**, (Back #26) b. 12 Feb 1696/7, d. 1773. Prince George's Co, MD. He married his "double" cousin, **Elizabeth Brashear**, b. 30 March 1701, d. 1775, d/o Benjamin Brashear Sr and Mary Jones. They had 13 children. (See separate chapter in Vol 1.)

v1283. 53. ***Elizabeth Brashear**, (Back #27) b. 27 July 1699, m.

John Turner Jr, and had a large family. For details, see vol 1.

[v1]284. [5]4. ***John Brashear "Senior"**, Innholder ([Back #]28) b. 21 Sept 1702, Queen Anne's Parish; m. ***Ruth Walker***, d/o Charles Walker and Rebecca Isaac. John was called "senior" in the land records of Prince George's County to distinguish him from his slightly younger "double" cousin, John Brashear "Junior," s/o Benjamin Brashear Sr and Mary Jones. See vol 1.

[v1]285. [5]5. ***Robert C. (?Cager) Brashear**, ([Back #]29) b. 19 Feb 1704/5, m. ***Charity Dowell***, d/o Phillip Dowell and Mary Tydings; Charity was sister to Mary Dowell, wife of Robert's double cousin, John Brashear "Junior" of AACo. See Vol 1 and Vol 2: "Robert C. Brashear of NC, and Some Descendants in TN and KY."

[v1]286. [5]6. ***Ann Brashear**, ([Back #]30) b. 4 Jan 1707; m. 10 Feb 1731/32, PGCo, ***Thomas Brown***, b. 15 May 1709, PGCo, s/o Joseph Brown and Ann Isaac. Ann and Thomas Brown, along with their sons and several of Samuel Brashears Jr's children, moved to southwestern Pennsylvania in the early 1770s and helped to found the town of Brownsville, PA. See vol 1 and "The Brownsville Colony" in Vol 4.

[v1]287. [5]7. ***William Brashear "Junior"**, b. 1709-10; m. ***Priscilla Prather***, and moved c1748 to Frederick Co, MD. The William Brashear who married Priscilla Prather has previously been assigned, erroneously, to Benjamin Brashear and Mary Jones. See separate chapter in Vol 1 for documentation that he belongs here. He was called "Junior" in the land records to distinguish him from his slightly older "double" cousin, William Brashear "Senior," a son of Benjamin Brashear Sr and Mary Jones. See vol 1.

[v1]288. [5]8. ***Basil Brashear**, ([Back #]31) b. 18 March 1714; m. ***Anne Belt***, d/o Benjamin Belt and Elizabeth Middleton.

[v1]289. [5]9. ***Otho Brashear**, ([Back #]32) b. 18 Oct 1716; m. 6 Jan 1736 (*Queen Anne Parish Marr.* p.7) ***Mary Holmes***, d/o William Holmes and Mary Pottenger (Will of William Holmes, PGCo. 27 Oct 1740; *Md Cal. Wills*, v.8, p.132). Otho was later in North Carolina, then

disappeared.

[v1]291. [5]10. **Mary Brashear**, ([Back] #33) b. 10 June 1720

In their lifetimes, Samuel Brashear, Sr and Ann Jones gave plots of land to some of their children, always as their "separate property": to Samuel Brashear, Jr; to Elizabeth (Brashear) Turner; to John Brashear "Senior"; to Robert C. Brashear; and to William Brashear "Junior." We have not found any such deeds for William Jones Brashear, the first son; for Mary, the last child; nor for Basil and Otho Brashear. Samuel made Basil and Otho the primary legatees in his will, giving them plots of land comparable to those he had given the other children intervivos. (See vol. 1 for details.)

Under the tutelage of his father (Samuel Brashear, the Maryland Carpenter), Basil became "a very good carpenter," but Basil was the "hard luck" boy of the family.

He got a good start with considerable land and personal property in his father's will in 1740 (see vol. 1), but lost it to debt within about 7 years.

He got a new start (along with his brothers Robert C. and Otho) in the Granville District of North Carolina, but lost that to debt also in a little over a decade (see vol 2). In North Carolina, he is reported to have "mined" and transported tar to the ship-builders on Chesapeake Bay (he was one of the original "tar-heels!"), and he also had a license to keep an "ordinary," an inn for travelers. He received a Granville Land Grant and again tried farming. He was not very successful at any of these pursuits and went broke again.

He and some of his sons moved to the Spartanburg District of South Carolina and got a third start--and again Basil was charged with debt (see below).

His financial problems may have caused his sons a great deal of embarrassment and they fled, like quail being flushed. Hypothetical sons, Basil, Isaac, and Robert, seem to have followed their cousin, Robert Samuel Brashear, to middle Tennessee. The other men all lived along the Enoree and Tyger Rivers in the Spartanburg District, South Carolina, in the 1780-1800 period, then moved to Tennessee, Kentucky, Arkansas, and Missouri, with altered surnames.

Basil's Family

Considering the repeated bankruptcies of Basil (I think he was a boozer), it's not much of a surprise to me that several of his sons' families re-spelled the family name, possibly to disguise their connection to Basil, more likely to hide from Basil's creditors. The men I'm pretty sure were Middleton's sons spelled the name Breshears.

William (who m. Sarah _____) spelled the name Brashear, Bracher, Bratcher, Bradshaw, and Brasher.

Jeremiah (who m. Elizabeth _____) is the progenitor of the Beshears families who moved to Christian Co, KY, about the same times as Ithra Brashears Sr.

Berry Boshears, of Arkansas, also somehow belongs in here; but how he fits, I can't prove at the moment (I think he was a great-grandson, son of ?Absalom Brashears, a forgotten son of Middleton). The Middleton, Nathan Turner, and Alexander Brashears/ Breshears who moved to MO in the early 1830s are also great-grandsons, probably sons of another grandson, James Brashears.

We know from tax and court records that Basil Brashear(s) and Anne Belt had several children, but (at present) we can document only two: Middleton and Henrietta. However, from records in Maryland, North Carolina and South Carolina, we might posit a number of other children. Deeds and court records in Spartanburg Co, SC, establish that several of these men lived in the area where Basil's third bankruptcy took place. See below, *passim*, and Vol 7.

<u>Partially documented family of Basil Brashears and Anne Belt</u>:

[v1]701. [6]1. ***Middleton Brashears**, b. c?1732-3, (21 or over when entering land--a Granville Grant--in Orange Co, NC, 14 Jan 1754); identified as son of Basil Brashears in the will of Middleton Belt and in some North Carolina deeds. Middleton Belt, brother of Anne (Belt) Brashears, gave the child a slave in his will (Prince George's Co, MD, 1745) and John Brashear, apparently acting on behalf of Middleton Belt, gave the child a horse, called Sharper. (PGCo Land records, Book BB#1, p.385.) Basil, as father of the minor child,

took possession of the horse and slave. (See next chapter for more details on these gifts.) Circumstances suggest that Middleton had sons Basil, 1765; John, 1767; Henry, 1769; Thomas, c1771; possibly Absalom; and James. See chapters on these men, later.

V1703. 62. ***Robert Brashears**, (circumstantial evidence only), b. c1734, d. 1810, Knox Co, TN, naming daughter, Martha Morrow (b. 1754) of Mecklenburg Co, NC, in his will. This Robert probably had a son, Jeremiah W. Brashears, who was probably the ancestor of some of the Scott Co, TN, Boshears. Descendants there use names that run in Basil's family: Isaac, William, Robert, Jeremiah, Alexander, Martha, Keziah, Naomi, Mary, Ruth, etc. See Vol 7, chapter on "Robert Brashears of NC and TN."

V1702. 63. **Henrietta Brashears**, b. c?1740; m. (4th wife of) ***Philip Prather***, d. 1767, Enoree, Laurens Co, SC. Philip Prather seems to have been a very old man when a young Henrietta Brashears married him. A Laurens Co, SC, citation was granted "Henereta" Prather and Middleton Brashear on 24 Sept 1767, to administer on the Estate and Effects of Philip Prather, late of Enoree, Planter, decd. It identifies Henrietta as the widow and Middleton Brashear as a brother-in-law of Philip Prather (Brent H. Holcomb, *Probate Records of South Carolina*, v.3, p.45). This means that either Middleton married a sister of Philip Prather, or Henrietta was a Brashear. Since Philip's sisters were all about 30 years older than Middleton (b. 1703, 1705), I'm concluding that Henrietta was a sister of Middleton and therefore a daughter of Basil.

V1704. 64. ***William Brashears**, b. 5 Oct 1741 (age 79 on 5 Oct 1820, when applying for Rev. War pension, in Maury Co, TN) (frequently Bratcher in SC records, also Bracher and Bradshaw); m. ***Sarah*** _____. Circumstantial evidence suggests they had at least sons, William Brashears, b. 1770, and Ithra Brashears, b. 1780. See Vol 7, chapters on "William and Sarah Brashears," "William Brashears and Mary

Elizabeth Clayton," and "Ithra Brashears and Hannah Middleton."

[V1]705. [6]5. **Isaiah Brashears**, enlisted 25 March 1776, in Fifth Regt, ?Spartanburg Co, SC. This is possibly the Isaiah Brashear who was briefly c1805 with the Robert Samuel Brashear colony in Roane Co, TN.

[V1]706. [6]6. ***Jeremiah Brashears**, b. bef 1751 (21 or over when on 1772 Tax list, Rowan Co, NC); m. ***Elizabeth*** _____. "Jeremiah" runs in both the Belt and Brashears families as a given name. Jeremiah and Elizabeth lived on the Tygar River in Spartanburg Co, SC. His children moved to Christian and Hopkins Co, KY, and spelled their surname Beshears. See Vol 7, "Beshears Families of Christian and Hopkins Co, KY."

[V1]709. [6]7. **Benjamin Brashears**, b. bef 1755 (age 45+, 1800 census, Spartanburg Co, SC, p.177, with wife 45+, 1 fem 10-16, 1 fem 0-10. On 11 Feb 1791, Benjamin Bratcher, of Spartanburg Co, SC, bought, for £50 Sterling, 100 acres on East side of branch of Richland Creek, part of a grant to Thomas Hatteway, from John Conner and wife, Winifred, of Franklin Co, GA. Borders: conditional line with William Wood, "across the ridge to head of Fawn Br.," Clemmons, and Jesse Remes. (Spartanburg Deeds, Book C, p.89; recorded 5 Feb 1793)

[v1]710. [6]8. **Zadock Brashears**, appears in Spartanburg Co, SC deeds.

[V1]711. [6]9. **Keziah Breshears**, b. c1756, (if 16 when marrying); m. 31 Aug 1772, ***John Tucker***, wit: Janis? Woodson & William Temple Coles Jr; bondsmen: Geo. Magrene & William Breshears (Rowan County Marriages (reported in *Rowan Co Register*, v.2, No.3; see also IGI extracted record M516045/3571). We believe the witness to this marriage is William Brashears, b. 1741, son of Basil, signing for his sister; that is, Keziah is believed to be a daughter of Basil Brashear and Anne Belt.

[7]1. boy Tucker, died young

[7]2. Mary Tucker, m. Stephen Haynes,

Keziah (Brashears) Tucker did not have an especially happy life: An old book, *1770-1790 Census of the Cumberland Settlements (What is now Tennessee)*, compiled by Richard Carlton Fulcher, tells a bizarre tale: John Tucker, mentioned in Court Records in Williamson Co, TN, as "late of Robertson Co, TN," died in 1801 or 1802, intestate. "Many years ago, John Tucker was lawfully married in the state of North Carolina to Kissiah Breshears, and they had two children, a boy and a girl. The boy died when he was about 2 years old. The girl was named Mary, and she married Stephen Haynes during the lifetime of her father. She is still living (c1801-02), as is John Tucker's widow, Kissiah.

"Shortly after the birth of the second child, John Tucker left his wife and came to the part of North Carolina that is now Tennessee and never returned to his wife. Here he lived with Jane Herrod in a state of adultry for several years and had several children by her— Enoch Tucker, Henry Tucker, Hannah Tucker, Sarah Tucker, Nancy Tucker, Phoebe Tucker, and Riggs Tucker.

"Hannah married John Demor and is now living. Nancy married Nicholas Norris and is living. Phoebe married James McFarlin and is still living. Jane Herrod, Enoch Tucker, Henry Tucker, James McFarlin and Phoebe his wife, John Demor and Hannah his wife, and Sarah Cazeen whose husband is dead have all moved to the territory of Illinois. Nicholas Norris and Nancy his wife lives in Dickson Co, TN, and Riggs Tucker, a minor, lived in Robertson Co, TN.

"In 1802, Jane Herrod produced a paper purporting to be the last will of John Tucker, and Peter Spence appeared to prove the said will..."

Another possible daughter of Basil Brashear(s) and Anne Belt: **Mary Brashier/ Brashear**, b. c1755, d. 20 Jan 1840; m. ***Isaiah Lewis***. (Note that a Moses Lewis witnessed two deeds for William Brashear/Bratcher in 1795, Spartanburg Co, SC.) Isaiah and Mary Lewis lived in the Spartanburg/Pendleton area and moved to Christian Co, KY, in the early 1800's. They had at least one son, Elijah Lewis, who married Mary Moss in Christian Co, KY, in 1814. (contact: Patsy B. King, 3116 Gorton Rd, Shreveport, LA 71119.)

Belt Family Connections

Humphrey Belt, b. c1615, the Belt family's progenitor in America, landed in Jamestown, VA, 23 June 1635 on the ship "America," at the age of 20. He lived first in Henrico Co, VA; later in Lower Norfolk Co, VA. He died in Virginia c1698.

a-1. John Belt, s/o Humphrey Belt, b. 1654, Norfolk, VA, will dated 13 May 1697, entered probate 17 Nov 1698, Anne Arundel Co, MD (Bk 6, p.175); m. in AACo, Elizabeth Tydings, b. 1672(?), d. 14 Dec 1737, d/o Richard Tydings and Charity Sparrow. The Belt children were thus cousins to Charity and Mary Dowell (daughters of Philip Dowell and Mary Tydings), both of whom married Brashear men. John Belt's will names wife, Elizabeth, and sons, John, Joseph, and Benjamin Belt, daughters Elizabeth, Charity, & Sarah. The widow, Elizabeth (Tydings) Belt, m.2. 25 July 1701, All Hallows Parish, AACo, MD, John Lamb.

Family of John Belt and Elizabeth Tydings:

b-1. John Belt, Jr, b. 1678, d. 1761; m. 10 Feb 1700/01, AACo, Lucy Lawrence, (re: West River and Cliff's Meeting, Society of Friends)

b-2. *Col. Joseph Belt, b. 1680, d. 26 June 1761, PGCo; m.1. 1706, Esther Beall, m.2. 1727, Margery (Wight) Sprigg, widow of Thomas Sprigg, IV, d. 1725.

b-3. *Benjamin Belt, b. 1682, will dated 19 June 1772, prob. 28 May 1773, PGCo; m. Elizabeth Middleton, d/o William and Elizabeth Middleton.

b-4. Elizabeth Belt, b. bef 1697, AACo, Christened All Hallows Parish, AACo, 14 Dec 1703

b-5. Charity Belt, b. bef 1697, AACo, Christened All Hallows Parish, AACo, 14 Dec 1703

b-6. Sarah Belt, b. bef 1697, AACo, Christened All Hallows Parish, AACo, 14 Dec 1703; m. 11 Sept 1718, All Hallows Parish, AACo, Thomas Harwood,

b-7. Jeremiah Belt, b. 14 Dec 1698, after father's death, Christened All Hallows Parish, AACo, 14 Dec 1703; m. 21 June 1746, PGCo, Mary Sprigg, b. 15 Dec 1723, d/o Thomas Sprigg, IV and Margery Wight.

b-2. Col. Joseph Belt, b. 1680, first owner of the estate "Chevy Chase" in Maryland, d. 26 June 1761; m.1. 1706, Esther Beall, b. 1687, d. 1726, d/o Col. Ninian Beall, who arrived from Scotland in 1650 and amassed a huge estate in Maryland; m.2 Margery Wight, d/o Capt. John Wight, and widow of Thomas Sprigg, IV.

c-1. John Belt, b. 13 March 1707; m.1. 4 March 1727/8, Margaret Queen, d/o Samuel Queen, b. ?, d. 1711; m.2. Katherine Marsham, d/o Richard Marsham.

d-1. John Belt, Jr, b. 27 April 1729, d. 23 Dec 1814; m. Dinah ______, b. 19 Sept 1739, d. 12 Nov 1799. Moved to Bedford Co, PA.

d-2. ***Catherine Belt***, b. 18 March 1730, d. 1773; m. c1750, **Benjamin Brashear** (v1 536), s/o Samuel Brashear, Jr and Elizabeth Brashear. See vol 5 for their descendants.

d-3. Col. Jeremiah Belt, b. ?, d. bef 1768

d-4. Esther Belt, m. c1753, **Jeremiah Brashears, Sr** (v1 538), s/o Samuel Brashear, Jr and Elizabeth Brashear. See vol 1.

d-5. Joseph Belt, d. PGCo, 1761; m. Elizabeth ______

d-6. Marsham Belt, b. c1735, d. 1801, Fleming Co, KY; m. PGCo c1758, Elizabeth Cross, b. c1740

c-2. Mary Belt, m.1. (2nd wife of) Col. Edward Sprigg, m.2. Thomas Spindle,

c-3. Joseph Belt, Jr, m. Anne Sprigg, d/o Thomas Sprigg, IV and Margery Wight

c-4. Jeremiah Belt, m. 21 June 1746, Mary Sprigg, b. 15 Dec 1723, d/o Thomas Sprigg, IV and Margery Wight.

c-5. Rachel Belt, b. 13 Dec 1711 (reg. Queen Anne's Parish), m. 11 July 1727, (2nd wife of) Osborn Sprigg,

b-3. Benjamin Belt, b. 1682, will dated 19 June 1772, probate 28 May 1773, PGCo; m. Elizabeth Middleton, d/o William and Elizabeth Middleton.

c-1. Middleton Belt. In his will (1745, PGCo, MD), he named (among others) nephew Middleton Brashears, s/o Basil Brashears.

c-2. ***Anne Belt***, m. **Basil Brashears** (v1 288), b. 1714, s/o Samuel Brashear, Sr and Ann Jones. Volume 6 and 7 are about their descendants.

c-3. Elizabeth Belt, m. Basil Waring, III, b. 1717, d. 1776, s/o Col. Basil Waring, II and Martha Greenfield,

c-4. Joseph Belt, m. **Rachel Brashears** (v1557), d/o Samuel Brashears, III and Rachel Brashears. See Vol 1.

In the past, there has been some doubt that Anne (Belt) Brashear's mother, Benjamin Belt's wife, was a Middleton, but PGCo Deeds, Bk I, p.786, is a deed of gift from William Middleton and wife, Elizabeth, to their son-in-law, Benjamin Belt:

18 June 1719. "William Middleton and Elizabeth his wife to Benjamin Belt in consideration of 20 pounds 10 shillings Sterling ... and for diverse other good causes and considerations them hereunto moving, have given, granted, alienated, sold, assigned, transferred, enfeofed, and confirmed ... a tract of land in PGCo called "Godfather's Gift,"

"BEGINNING at a bounded oak standing on the northwest side of a branch that runs into the main branch of the Eastern [branch] of the Potomac, about four miles from the siding (?) place of the Eastern Branch, then West North West 160 perches to a bounded red oak, then North North East 64 perches to a bounded white oak near the sd branch, then North West by West 60 perches to a bounded white oak, then East North East 60 perches over the said branch, then South East 224 perches to a red oak, then South and by West 120 to a sweet gum, then North by West 100 to the first bounded tree, and containing 123 acres, together with all dwelling houses ... apurtenances," etc. Warranties (standard) not copied.

The price sounds about right for a middling piece of land (was that area GOOD?), but that phrase "for diverse other good causes..." is a giveaway. It's used primarily in family transfers. And replacing "bargained" in the string of verbs with "given" clinches it to my mind.

BASIL IN MARYLAND

The Maryland Archives, PGCo Deeds, Book F (or T?), p.561: Basil Brashears and others to Alexander Black or George Gardner (Who? when? — Book F covers c1719; Book T, 1733-39, though there are several transactions dated 1729 and 1730 in it. Both books cover times rather too early for Basil, b. 1714, s/o Samuel and Ann). Basil begins appearing in the records of Prince Georges County about 1735, i.e. about the time he came of age:

The Maryland Archives, Patents Index (cards), 1736, Bazel Brashairs, "Batchelors Fortune," 125 ac. PG Cert #44 (surveyed but not patented).

Like his brothers, John, Robert C, and Otho, Basil had his troubles with debt in Maryland: On 16 March 1740, Basil Brashears deeded to George Scoll "two negro wenches, named _____ and Sarah, and all their increase," to discharge a debt of £5/6/3. (Maryland Archives, PGCo Land Records, Bk.Y, p.260)

These following two are bonds to his brother, apparently to secure a debt:

Basil Brashears to John Brashears, Book BB, p.330
Basil Brashears to John Brashears, Bond, Book BB, p.339

Basil brought suit against Samuel Richards in 1742, and then didn't appear in court. (The Maryland Archives, Judgments, (Anne Arundel Co), Bk ? p?, 9 Nov 1742)

Basil Brashear)
vs)
Samuel Richards) Command was given to the Sheriff of Anne Arundel Co. that he should take Samuel Richards late of AA, Innholder, if he should be found in his bailiwick and him should safe keep so that he might have his body before his lordship's Justices of the Anne Arundel Court to be held at Annapolis the second Tuesday of November, then next to answer unto Basil Brashears of a plea of trespass upon the case...

[At next session, Samuel Smith, Sheriff, presented Richards, as directed. Also one Edward Rookesby offered his bond to assure the conduct and payment by Richards, should he be convicted.]

Thereupon the Prayer of the said Samuel Richards by Joshua Hopkinson, his attorney, the said Basil Brashear is adjudged to give security for cost in case he shall be nonsuited in the plea aforesaid, but the said Basil Brasher alltho solemnly called comes not but makes default, nor does he further prosecute his writ in the plea afsd against the said Samuel Richards.

THEREFORE, it is considered by the Justices here the 9th day of November, Anno Dom. 1742, afsd that the Said Basil Brashear take nothing by his writ afsd, but that he and his pledges of prosecuting be in Mercy and that the names of the pledges be sought for, etc. And that the afsd Samuel Richards go thereof without Day. And it is also considered that the afsd Samuel Richards recover against the said Basil Brashear the sum of Two hundred and thirty-one pounds of Tobacco be the court here unto him on his assent adjudged for his costs and charges by him about his defence in this behalf laid out and expended and that he have thereof his Execution against the said Basil Brashear according to the form of the Statutes, etc.

At the request of Samuel Brashears [Jr; Basil's brother], the following Bill of Sale was recorded 2 June 1744 (The Maryland Archives,, PGCo Land Records, Book BB#1, p.134): Basil Brashears sells (no mention of money; so Basil probably owed money to Samuel)

one horse called Jolly, branded on the near buttock
one black Mare called Indian, branded on the near shoulder & buttock
one Mare call Fly, branded on each thigh and a horse colt
One bay Mare called Phillis, branded on the near shoulder
one cow and calf Marked with a crop and two slits in the left ear and an underbit in the right ...
Ten head of hoggs, Marked as aforesaid
one hand mill ... two feather beds and furniture ... one Dozen and a half of Pewter plates, five pewter dishes, four pewter basons ... two iron pots and pot hooks, one iron potrack, two pair of fire tongs, one box pan and heaters ... one grid iron, one chest, two trunks, one case, one warming pan ... a cart and horse harness ... two candlesticks and pair

of snuffers ... one skillet, one frying pan,
and a parcel of carpenter's and Joyner's tools ...
/s/ Basil Brashear
in presents of Robt Brasher Jr, J. Waring

[NOTE: One of the witnesses, Basil's brother, Robert C. Brashear, was called Robert Brashear Jr in many of the records of the time to distinguish him from their uncle, Robert Brashear IV, b. c1675, who lived on land adjoining.

Imprisonment for Debt

Basil did not succeed in getting his affairs in order and was arrested for debt. He spent some time in the Prince George's County Jail, as is indicated by this news article:

from *The Maryland Gazette*, Tues, 28 April 1747: "John Cooke, Joseph Belt Jr, and John Hepburn [the Sheriff], all of Upper Marlborough, report a runaway servant, Basil Brashear, lately a prisoner in Prince George's County jail for debt. He's a very good carpenter and has probably gone to Virginia."

The practice of the times was to release a prisoner for debt into "service," that is, the court indentured him to some responsible men in the neighborhood and the "servant" was supposed to work off his debt.

Actually, it looks like Basil hastily sold out (i.e., mortgaged his holdings) and ran: At the request of John Brashear Senr the following Bond was recorded:

Know all men by these presents that I, Bazil Brashear of Prince Georges County in the province of Maryland, do stand and am firmly bound and obliged unto John Brashear Senr of the said County and province in the full and Just sum of Two Hundred pounds current money of Maryland, to which payment well and truly to be made and done I do hereby bind myself, my heirs, Exectrs and Adminrs firmly by these presents sealed with my seal and Dated the 13th day of March, Anno Domini 1746/7.

The CONDITION of the above obligation is such that if the above bound Bazil Brashear or his Heirs do well and truly make over and convey unto the said John Brashear his Heirs or Assigns by a Deed of Indenture of Special Warrantees part of "Cuckholds Delight," sixty-two acres, part of "Gleaning," eight acres, "Levings," nineteen acres, "Letchworth," ninety-five acres for and in consideration of one hundred pounds paid to him in hand without fraude or ?Covin, then the above obligation to be void and of none effect, otherwise to remain in full force and power and Virtue in Law.

Signed Sealed & Delivered
In the Presents of us Baz Brashear (Seal)
Moses Ball, Phillip Brashers
(PGCo Deeds, Book EE, p.330)

[NOTE: The use of these witnesses would suggest that this mortgage was made in Fairfax Co, VA, where Bazil's brother, Robert C. Brashear, had moved in 1742 after his bout with debt in PGCo. Moses Ball was husband of Ann Brashear, RCB's daughter, and Philip Brashears was RCB's oldest son; from 1742 to c1749, RCB and family lived in Truro Parish, Fairfax Co, VA. See vol 2.]

Basil Brashear is listed as a tithable resident of Lunenburg Co, VA, in 1748, list taken by Cornelius Cargill: one tithe. The original Lunenburg Co at that time comprised present-day Lunenburg, Mecklenburg, Charlotte, Halifax, Pittsylvania, Henry, Patrick, Franklin, parts of Campbell, parts of Bedford and about ¼ of Appomattox Counties. The precinct of Cornelious Cargill was sparsely settled. Theoretically his precinct embraced, presumably, all the territory from Butcher's Creek westward, to the Forks of Roanoke (and Dan) rivers, and from the North Carolina line northward to the boundaries of other precincts, and westward to the limits of the Colony. But probably such inhabitants as were then in the area were clustered in and about "the forks" of the river. (See USGenWeb data: http://searches.rootsweb.com/cgi-bin/ifetch2?/u1/data/va+index+1723226927+F)

BASIL IN NORTH CAROLINA

Basil led the migration to North Carolina, as early as 1749.

On 30 May 1749, Basil bought 472 acres "at a corner of William Williams' land" on Jonathans Creek, being a branch of Grassy Creek, in Granville Co, NC, near the VA/NC line, from Robert Jones Jr, attorney, of Surry Co, VA (Granville Co, NC, *Deeds*, Book A, p.94-96). Granville County once was the whole of north-central Carolina, the parent county from which dozens were later carved, including Rowan, Orange, Guilford, etc.

About 1750, Basil acquired land in Orange Co, NC, the parent county of Guilford, Rockingham, and Randolph Counties. His brothers Otho and Robert C. Brashear were his neighbors in Orange Co, NC, by 1753; their land was in present-day northeastern Guilford County. Other neighbors included Middleton Brashears, s/o Basil, and Jesse and Robert Samuel Brashears (RSB), sons of RCB.

But the quality of life was not good in north-central North Carolina from 1750 to the end of the Revolution, for the proprietor--Lord John Carteret, Earl of Granville--was the civil government. His agents levied outrageous taxes, often collected twice, or more, reneged on public acts, granted (sold) the same land to more than one party, sued for almost anything--and got it!--because they controlled the courts. Common men squabbled with each other in the courts over petty debts. And their attempt to take matters into their own hands and "regulate" them were crushed with a mini-war, the "Regulator Movement." (See vol 2 for details.) By 1780, most of the colony had evaporated, and by 1790, only one splinter group, Asa and Zaza Brasher and their sons, were left on the western edge of Guilford County.

Carolina was originally a proprietary colony, owned by eight partners, of whom Lord John Carteret, Earl of Granville, was one. However, the King decided to revoke their proprietary charters and make the colony a crown colony. Most of the partners surrendered their charters, but Granville refused. The case went to the high court of England.

In 1746, Granville won his legal arguments with the King and came out of it with clear title to the Granville District— the northern 60 miles of North Carolina, "from the Atlantic to the

South Seas," i.e. the Pacific! (Their sense of geography was somewhat skewed!)

In 1748, he opened a land office and started making "Granville Land Grants." These grants did not include fee-simple deeds, but a kind of perpetual deed/lease which involved an annual rent of 8 shillings per 100 acres, payable in two installments. Even so, land-hungry families from Maryland, Pennsylvania, Virginia, New York, Ireland, Scotland, England, and Germany flocked to the colony.

Orange County was created in 1752, then Rowan county in 1753. Guilford Co, comprising present-day Randolph, Guilford, and Rockingham Counties, was formed in 1771 from a strip of Rowan and a strip of Orange. Rockingham was separated from Guilford in 1785, and Randolph was separated in 1791.

Basil Brashear served on the Grand Jury of the newly formed Orange Co, NC, at the June, 1753, session of the Court of Pleas and Quarter Sessions. He sat on one criminal case (found a farm couple innocent of "traverse," a form of sedition) and about 12 civil cases, all of them "breach of promise" to repay loans.

At the Sept session of the same court, Robert Brashear was appointed overseer of roads in place of John West.

And on 13 Dec 1753, Brasel Brashear was granted a license to "keep an ordinary" (that is, operate an Inn for travelers) at the court house, at "Newtown Corbin," which was situated on the Eno River at present-day Hillsborough, Orange County, NC.

These appointments indicate that the Brashear men had been in the area long enough to incur such civic responsibilities— that is, be on tax rolls, jury rolls, and the like. (*Court Minutes*, part I, folio 5, page 9-obverse; f.36, p.71-obv; f.14, p.28-obv.

Part I and part II of these minutes of the Court of Pleas and Quarter Sessions (covering 1752-1766) were kept in abstract on large double-folded sheets, which I am calling "folios." Only the front sides were numbered; but the clerk kept minutes on the obverse sides as well. "28-obverse" means the record is on the back side of the page numbered 28. These records are in the State Archives at Raleigh, filed under Orange County Records: CR 073.)

The Orange County tax list for 1755 includes Robert

Brashear Sr (p. 105), Bazel Brashear & two grown sons (probably Middleton, b. c1732, and Robert, b. c1734), i.e. three white polls (p. 106), and Jesse Brashear (p. 108). These same pieces of land were included in the 1768 Rowan County Tax lists; how, I don't know. RCB's and RSB's neighbors are the same on both lists; so we can be pretty sure they didn't move. How the borders could, I don't know. (*NC Gen Soc Jrnl*, Nov 83, pp.210-211.)

Land Grants

Several of the Brashears were involved in early surveys of land grants in Orange (later Guilford) Co, NC. On 1 Dec 1753, "Othio Boshear" was chain bearer in the survey of a 404 acre grant to George Finley "on N side of Reedy Fork, joining ... the

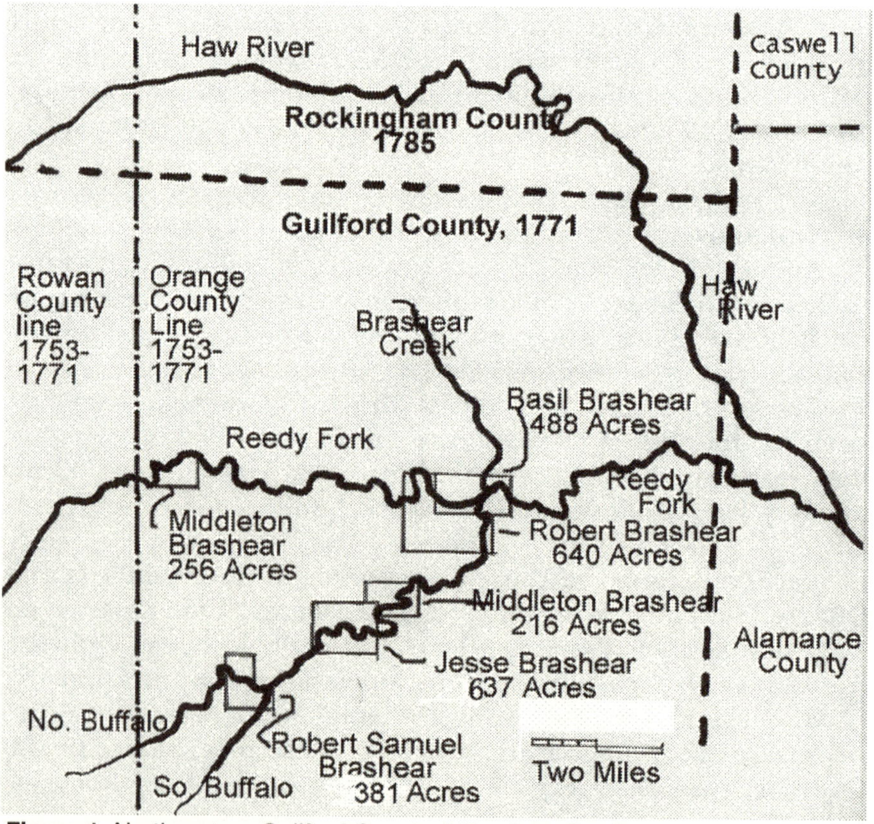

Figure 1: Northeastern Guilford County, NC, where five Brashear men received six Granville Land Grants.

line that divides the counties of Roan [Rowan] and Orange." (*Granville Grants*, Book 14, p.399) Otho, Jesse, and Bazil assisted the surveyors several times in the next few years, and even old Robert carried the chain in the survey of a grant to his son, Robert Samuel Brashears.

* * *

Basil Brashear entered a 488 acre plot of Granville land where Brashears Creek (named apparently for Basil) flows into the Reedy Fork of the Haw River. The plot also included the mouth of Buffalo Creek. This plot, however, was patented by Blake Baker, to whom Basil somehow became indebted. On 14 May 1757, a Granville Grant of 488 acres was made to Blake Baker, on both sides of the Haw River at mouth of Buffalo Creek; surveyed 9 Aug 1754, sworn chain carrier, Robt Saml Brasher; the plat reads "land surveyed for Basil Brashere." (*Granville Grants*, Book 14, p.343.) Robert C. Brashear's 640 acre grant was a big L-shaped plot of land which bordered this land on the west and south sides.

The usual procedure was for a man to get a warrant from the Granville Land office to "Enter" a certain amount of land.

The second step was to get the land surveyed. If the land around was taken and the surveyor could not find the amount of land specified in the warrant, he surveyed what was available. Thus Jesse's warrant was for 640 acres, but his survey was for 637.

Finally, the settler registered his land with the Land Office and began paying the quit-rent on a perpetual lease-deed.

This was all supposed to happen in a few months, but in practice, it often took several years. Some entries made in 1753 were not patented until 1761.

During 1760 and 1761, five Granville Land Grants were made to Brashear men on Buffalo Creek and Reedy Fork of the Haw River in Orange County, NC.

(The following descriptions are from Margaret M. Hoffman, *The Granville District of N. C., 1748-1763: Abstract of Land Grants*, Vol 2, 1987. James Watson, who appears repeatedly in the descriptions, was the County Clerk; William Churton was the County Surveyor.)

to Jesse Brashear, July 17, 1760,

637 acres in Orange Co on Buffalo Creek. Original record, signed: Jese _____? (the paper is smudged and torn) Wits: W. Churton, Rob Brasher, examined by Tho Jones and Richd Vigers. (orig. plat is missing. The metes and bounds description reveal it to be a rectangle. I have drawn a map of it and Middleton's adjoining grant). (Grant #80, Book 14, p.351, NC Archives file #402.)

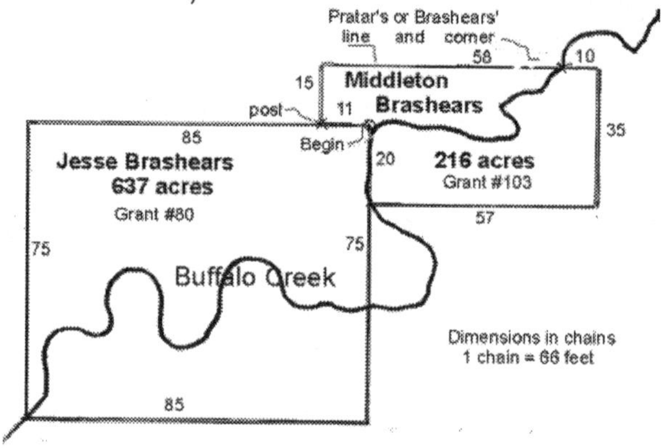

Figure 2: Granville Land Grants to Jesse and Middleton Brashears on Buffalo Creek.

On 26 Feb 1755, a Granville warrant was issued to Robert Brashear for 640 acres to be located between Brazil Brashear and Blackwood, for land Robert had "entered" 30 Dec 1754. On 5 Sept 1755, this plot was surveyed at 637 acres for Jesse Brashear; Robert Brashear and Robert Brashear Jr (Jesse's father and brother) were sworn chain carriers. A deed for 637 acres was made to Jesse, 20 Feb 1756 (*Granville Proprietary Land Office, Abstracts of Loose Papers,* Orange Co. Records, v.1, p.10, edited by Wm. D. Bennett, publ. Raleigh, NC, 1987). From this, we might conclude that Jesse was under age in Feb 1755, but had reached his majority by Sept 1755, i.e. he was born between Feb and Sept 1734.

to John Brashear, Aug 2, 1760,

140 acres in Orange Co in Parish of St. Matthews on both sides of Hico Creek. Orig rec /s/ (mark). Wits: Jas Watson, Hugh Daffin, examined by Wm Churton and Tho Jones, surveyed 27 Sept 1756, chain carriers: George Lea, Cornilas Dollerhide. Sher Haywood D. Sur. (Grant #137, Book 14,

p.348, NC Arc file #392.) NOTE: Hico Creek headwaters in present-day Caswell County, flows northeast through Person Co into Virginia and merges with the Dan River. John's land, though in the same parish, was on the other side of the watershed and some 25 miles northeast of the RCB colony on Buffalo Creek. I believe (no proof) John to be a brother of Thomas Brazier of Orange/Chatham Co, NC, i.e. sons of William B. Brashier Sr, d. Baltimore Co, MD, 1708. (For more information on this family, see *A Brazier/Brasher Saga*, by Charles Brashear and Shirley Brasher McCoy.)

to Robert Samuel Brashears, Aug 8, 1760,

381 acres in Orange County in the Parish of St. Matthews on both sides of N and S Buffelo, joining Donels corner, John McKnight, Donalds line and the mouth of S Buffaloe. Orig rec /s/ Robert Samll Brasher. Wits: Jas Watson, John Lea. Examined by W. Churton and Tho Jones, surveyed 14 July 1758. Chain carriers: Robert Brashear Sr, Jesse Brashear. W. Churton, Surveyor. (Grant #171 Book 14, p.337, NC Arc #348.) See vol 3, "Robert Samuel Brashears, and some descendants in TN, KY, MO, TX, etc" for details and a plat map of this grant.

to Middleton Brashears, Feb 11, 1761,

256 acres in Orange Co. in Parish of St. Matthews on the Reedy Fork of Haw River on the S side. Orig rec /s/ Middleton Brashear. Wits: Jas Watson, Je Cumming. Examined by Wm Matthews and W. Churton. Surveyed 12 Nov 1754. Chain carriers: Jesse Brashear, Robert Brashear. W. Churton, Surveyor. (Grant #61, Book 14, p.344, NC Arc

Figure 3: Middleton Brashear's grant on the Piney Shoals, originally warranted to Basil Brashear

#374.)

This was a grant entered by Basil Brashear, but patented by Middleton. Loose papers found recently indicate that Bazzil Brashear was issued a warrant for 640 acres on the south side of Haw River in Orange County (now Guilford Co) North Carolina, beginning against the Piney sholes. Entered 14 Jan 1754; warrant issued 17 April 1754; surveyed 12 Nov 1754 [at 256 acres]; "transferred to his son, Middleton Brashear," deed dated 3 Feb 1761. (ref: *Granville Proprietary Land Office, Abstracts of Loose Papers, Orange County Records*, Vol. 1, ed. William D. Bennet; publ 1987.)

to Robert [C.] Brashears, Dec 6, 1761,

640 acres in Orange County on both sides of the Reedy Fork of the Haw River and Buffalo, joining Bazil Brashears and both sides of the bents of the fork. Original record, signed: Rob Brasher. Wits: Jas Watson, John Hogan; surveyed 26 Oct 1761; chain carriers: Jesse Brashear, Bazil Brashear; Wm Churton, surveyor. (Grant #95, Book 14, p.341, NC Arc #362.) (An earlier survey was dated 2 Dec 1756, see *Records of the Moravians*, II:536). See vol 2, "Robert C. Brashears of NC, ... etc," for details and a map of this grant.

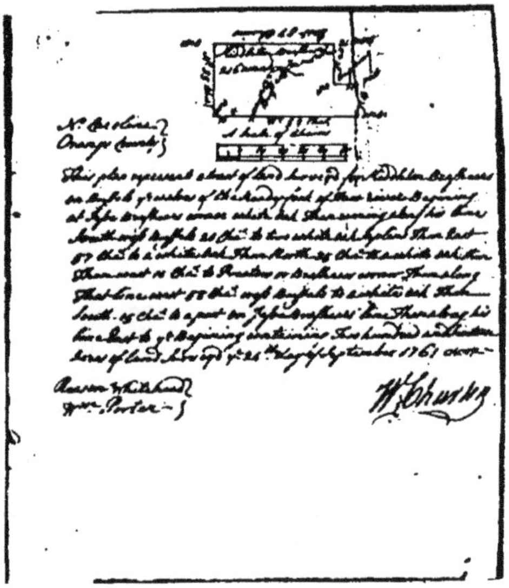

Figure 4: Middleton Brashear's grant on Buffalo Creek. The map is upside down, that is, North is at the bottom, not the top. See above the drawing of Middleton's and Jesse's adjoining grants.

to Middleton Brashears, Dec 6, 1761,

216 acres in Orange Co. on both sides of Buffilo (which is) the waters of the Reedy Fork of Haw River, joining Jesse Brashear and Pratars or Brashears corner. Original record, signed Middleton Brashear.

Wits: Jas Watson, Jas Bowie; surveryed 24 Sept 1761; chain carriers: Reason Whitehead, Wm Porter. Wm Churton, surveyor. (Grant #103, Bk 14, p.344, NC Arc #345.)

[NOTE: The Prather next door was Philip Prather, who married (as his fourth wife) Henrietta Brashears, and whose daughter, Elizabeth, married Jesse Brashears. Was Middleton also married to a Prather? In 1767 in Laurens Co, SC, Middleton is one of the executors in the estate of Philip Prather, Henrietta's deceased husband and Jesse's father-in-law.)

The metes and bounds of this grant show that the map on the certificate is upside down, that is, North is at the bottom. "This plan represents a tract of land surveyed for Middleton Brashears on Buffalo Cr, waters of the Reedy Fork of the Haw River, Beginning at Jesse Brashear's corner white oak, then running along his line South with Buffalo 20 chains to two white oak saplins,
then East 57 chains to a white oak,
then North 35 chains to a white oak,
then West 10 chains to Pratar's or Brashears corner,
then along that line west 58 cha xxgt byxxxals to white oak,
then South 15 chains to a post on Jesse Brashears' line,
then along his line East to the beginning,
containing Two hundred Sixteen Acres of land,
Surveyed this 26th day of September 1761,,...."

John Carteret, Earl of Granville, died in 1763, and his land offices were closed. There were no further grants until 1778, when North Carolina State grants begin. This only complicated an already messy situation.

During the Revolution and after, British land titles were ignored in general. Men often had to file again on their own land. Usually, pre-emption rights were honored. But some men had moved on to other parts; some were dead; some had simply given up and gone home; many Loyalists found their land had been confiscated, and they had to seek new grants.

Land records essentially started over again. Some of the old Granville lease/deed grants became North Carolina fee simple grants, often with a purchase price. To us, today, life does not seem pleasant in the Granville District before the Revolution.

The Court of Pleas & Quarter Sessions

Lord Granville's agents, especially Francis Corbin and Dr. Thomas Childs, were greatly hated for their abuses: rents were twice as high as in other parts of North Carolina; the agents charged excessive fees for routine services; the same tract of land was sometimes granted to two or three persons. And most of the money, apparently, went into Corbin's and Childs' pockets, not to the Granvilles. (Our age has no corner on graft and corruption.)

People found it hard to repay small debts; they began sueing each other, right and left. Basil had been a juror on twelve cases in the June quarter, 1753; ten years later, the August 1763 Quarter Session took 46 pages to record, about three cases per page; the November 1763 Quarter Session took 48 pages. That's an increase from 12 to about 140 cases per quarter. The county population in 1753 was 1108, and, ten years later, in 1764, the county seat was said to consist of only 30 or 40 inhabitants.

In June, 1755, Othar Brashear went to court and, in two suits, charged William Porter and George Finley with non-payment of debt. In both cases, the defendant was found not-guilty. (*Court Minutes*, folio 30, p. 59-obverse; folio 30, p. 60)

This is the last record we have of Otho... He may have returned to Prince Georges Co, Maryland, where Otho Brashear (not sure this is him; there was another Otho) got a 94 3/8 acre grant called "Brashear's Purchase" in 1769 (The Maryland Archives, PGCo Land Records, Book BC&GS, p.271, 391). Or his name may have permuted from Othar to Arthur and Brashears to Beshears. There is an Arthur Beshears, with wife Margaret, on Warrior Creek, in Old 96 District, Spartanburg Co, SC.

Jesse Brashears, son of Robert C, gave up early also. He had his 637 acre grant, and seems to have been a good citizen. In Feb 1761, for example, he served on the Grand Jury. On May 19, 1761, he was appointed constable [overseer of construction and collector of fees] on the Head of Haw River.

In the same session, Jesse and Middleton Brashear, who had entered themselves security in a case against John Pearson, brought Pearson into court, surrendered him bodily, and the court accepted other securities.

John Peterson sued Jesse in the Dec 1756 session; Jesse failed to appear and consequently lost.

In May, 1762, Jesse sued John Hallum for debt, but lost his case. (See *Court Minutes*, folio 47, p.93; f.53, p.244; f.69 p.275)

About 1762, Jesse moved first to Virginia, then to Georgia, then in 1773 to Pensacola, Spanish West Florida, where he kept an inn, after the Revolution. See "Jesse Brashears of Pensacola" in Vol. 5: *Two Brashear Families of the Lower Mississippi Valley and their Choctaw Descendants.*

Basil Brashear's story in the court records shows a life disintegrating. By 1749, he was in North Carolina, where he began acquiring property. We have already noted his land grant on Brashears Creek, his service on the Orange County Grand Jury and his license to keep a tavern in 1753. After that, his life started to repeat the pattern of his life in Maryland.

In March 1754, in John Boyd vs. Baz'l Brasher, Basil withdrew his not-guilty plea and confessed the debt. He was ordered to pay £14/17/9 in Virginia money— about $50 at 1960 rates of exchange— plus court costs of £1/1/11. (*Court Minutes*, f.17, p.33)

On 11 March 1754, he sold (?mortgaged) two lots in Newtown Corbin (as the county seat was then called; it was later renamed Hillsborough) on Eno River, 480 acres on Reedy Fork, and a Gray or White gelding, to John Watson of Suffolk, Virginia, for £40, lawful money of Great Britain. (Orange Co. *Deeds*, Book 1, p. 136) I think this was a mortgage, since Blake Baker eventually patented the 480 acres.

At the Oct 1754 Quarter Session, Basil registered his cattle mark: "a crop and two slits in the right ear and an underkeal in the left." (*Court Minutes*, f.21, p.41-obv. That's the same mark he used in Maryland). In the same session, he won judgment against Edward Southwell, £1/9 Virginia money. (*C.M.* 21:41-obv.) That seems to me a very small amount to quibble in court about!

On 2 Dec 1756, Bazil Brasher and John Hallum were chain bearers in the William Churton survey of a 640 acre grant to Robert Brashear on Reedy Fork of Haw River. (*Records of the Moravians in North Carolina*, II:536) [This may be another indication of the quality of life: I think this section had to be surveyed three times before the grant was perfected.] Robert Brashear later (Sept 1759) sued John Hallum for a 14-pound debt and won judgment against him. (*C.M.* pt 2, 33:203). This is the same John Hallum that Jesse Brashear lost to in 1762.

Dec 1755: Jacob Mitchell vs. Basil Brashear. Basil was found "not guilty in the manner and form the Plaintiff against him hath declared." (*C.M.* 40:80.)

Basil apparently pronounced the "a" in "Basil" with a kind of growling intrusive but almost silent "r", much like the British "r" of today. It came out something like "Bah-zeal", as in "I'm going to the bah to get a drink"; people consistently growled his name back at him.

June 1756: John Wade vs. Barzeel Brashear. Basil lost.
Sept 1756: Wm Little vs. Brazell Brashear. Basil confessed his debt.
Sept 1756: Blake Baker vs. Bazell Brashear. Basil failed to appear.
Sept 1757: Phillip Howard vs. Bazell Brashear. Basil lost.
Dec 1757: Caines Tinnen vs. Bazell Brashear. Basil failed to appear.
June 1757: Jacob Mason vs. Bazel Brashear. Basil failed to appear.
June 1757: Jacob Mason vs. Bazel Brashear. A separate case from the last; Basil failed to appear. Judgment: £1/5, plus costs. A small debt.
Feb 1761: Zachariah Caddle vs. Barazeel Brashear. Basil failed to appear. Judgment: £14/16, a greater than usual debt.

Basil's Second Bankruptcy

May 1763: James Watson, et al. vs. Bazel Brashear. [James Watson was the county clerk, and this seems to have been a class action in behalf of several debtors, who are not named in the summary record.] (*C.M.* pt 3, p.60).

At the same session, in Samuel Benton, et al. vs. Bazel Brashear, Basil took the insolvent debtor's oath and was released. He was bankrupt!

At both the August 1763 and May 1764 sessions, there are two cases, John Sample vs. Bazel Brashear. John Sample was one of the Justices of the Peace, and this was apparently an attempt to solve Basil's financial problems before they became criminal. It apparently didn't work. Basil failed to appear, as he did in May, 1764, in William Williams, Esq. (another Justice of the Peace) vs. Bazel Brashear, debtor.

Basil was apparently arrested for debt and thrown in jail.

At the Feb 1765 Quarter Session, the court ordered that the sheriff be allowed 10 shillings for his extraordinary services in removing the effects of Bazil Brashears. And at the Aug 1766 quarter, John Dowell, the sheriff, was allowed £13/11 for feeding Wm. Massey, James Robinson, John Ward, Moses Watkins, and Bazzel Brashears while they were in gaol [jail] awaiting trial.

I have not found a record of Basil's trial and punishment. It may be in the 1766-1787 records (which seem to be lost); it may have taken place at Raleigh. At any rate, Basil soon disappeared from the records of North Carolina. It looks like he, his sons, the whole family moved to SC, some by way of Rowan Co, NC.

At this point, records on Basil's family are very scarce: we know that Middleton left Orange/Guilford Co, NC, c1765-7 and went to Laurens District, SC.

Circumstantial evidence and tax records would suggest that some of Basil's sons (William and Jeremiah) moved first to Rowan County, NC, then to the Spartanburg area of South Carolina. Still others moved to TN.

On the 1772 Tax Lists of Rowan Co, NC, "partial--Davidson County Area" (see *Rowan County Register*, ed. Jo Linn, v.11, p.364; thanks to Marie Ownbey for a Xerox copy):

Jeremiah Brashears 1 adult poll
William Brashears 1 adult poll
[Apparently, this is the William Brashears who signed the marriage bond, 31 Aug 1772, for Keziah Brashears to marry John Tucker.]

Nearby is: John Hunt Praeter 1 adult poll
[s/o Philip Prather and his first wife, Katherine Hunt, of Maryland. (Philip Prather was brother-in-law to Middleton Brashears.) John Hunt Prather moved to Laurens District, SC, shortly after 1772, where he d. c1798.]

BASIL IN SOUTH CAROLINA: His Third Bankruptcy

Brasil Brashears was charged with debt a third time in Spartanburg Co, SC in 1785:

Sept. Court, 1785: Charles Saxon against Brazel Brashears, Debt:

Came the plaintiff by his Att. James Yancy, Gent. and the

defendant by Daniel Brown, Gent. his atto. Thereupon he the sd. defendant saith he cannot gainsay the plaintiff action but that 'tis just and true and that he owes the debt mentioned in the declaration, amounting to £8/3/2 sterling money with interest from 21st May 1784 whereupon it is considered by the Court that the plaintiff recover against the defendant the sd. sum of £8/3/2 with interest besides his Costs by him about his suit in this behalf expended and the sd. defendant in mercy.

Present: Baylis Earle, Esquire [Judge of the Court] (*Spartanburg Co, SC, Minutes of the County Court, 1785-1799*, by Brent H. Holcomb, C.A.L.S., 1980). William, probable son of Basil, once sued Baylis Earle over his administration of an estate. See vol 7. This shows that Basil and the men I am suggesting as possible sons lived in the same area.

There is another Basil Brashear in the 1790 Census, Fairfield Co, SC, with five little children. Probably a son of Middleton, he was born c1765 (age 70-80 in 1840 Census, Lawrence Co, TN). He was surely too young to be that deeply in debt by 1785. So this debtor in Spartanburg County court looks like the elder Basil.

After this trial for debt, Basil Brashear(s) disappears from the records. In 1785, he was 71 years old. He may have been infirm and died soon after.

Or, as wizened and leathery as the old man was to survive such a tumultuous life, he may have just gone into hiding.

2. MIDDLETON BRASHEARS, The Elder

son of Basil Brashears and Anne Belt

v1701. 61. Middleton Brashears, b. c?1732-3 (21 or over when entering land in the Granville District, North Carolina, 14 Jan 1754); identified as son of Basil Brashears in the will of Middleton Belt, brother of Anne (Belt) Brashears, and in some North Carolina deeds. Middleton Brashear's mother was Anne Belt, d/o Benjamin Belt and Elizabeth Middleton.

The Will of Middleton Belt (PGCo, MD, 1745) reads, in part: I, Middleton Belt, of Prince Georges Co, MD, ... to my nephew, Middleton Brashears, son of Basil Brashears, at the decease of my father, Benjamin Belt, one slave ... Witnesses: George Wills and John Brashears; Feb 25, 1745, probate 21 May 1746.

The John Brashears who was a witness to Middleton Belt's will was probably John Brashears the third, as might be suggested by this deed (The Maryland Archives, PGCo Land records, Book BB#1, p.385): "At the request of Basel Brashears the following deed was recorded, September, the sixteenth day, Anno domini Seventeen hundred forty five:

This Indenture made this 29th day of August in the year of our Lord God One thousand seven hundred and forty five between John Brashears the third of Prince George County in the province of Maryland, Planter, of the one part and Middleton Brashears of the said county of the aforesaid province, minor, of the other part--Witnesseth that the said John Brashears the Third out of the love and affection that he hath and doth bear unto the said Middleton Brashear and for diverse other causes and considerations here unto more hopefully moving hath given granted ... unto the said Middleton Brashears One Bay horse about thirteen and a half hands and branded on the off thy thus .... Aged about six years and known by the name of Sharper, To

have and to hold ...etc.
Witnesses: Anders Levens; Saml Brashears Junr
Came John Brashears and acknowledged ... August 29, 1745"

I have never seen a document that mentions a wife, much less names her. However, there is an old couple that follows Basil (b. 1765), John (b. 1767), and Henry (b. 1769), from SC to White Co, TN, then on to Lawrence Co, TN. This old couple live with Henry Brashears and Eleanor Hardin until Henry's death, then with John Brashears and Mary Berry until the old couple's death. The old man is never named in records, and the old woman is only given a first name: Elizabeth. Elizabeth is still with the John Brashears family in 1840 and is over 100 years old— that is, born in the 1730's, the right age to be wife of Middleton. It is quite possible (but unproven) that this old couple are Middleton Brashears and his wife, Elizabeth. See John's chapter for the scant records we have on this couple.

Middleton in North Carolina

As I showed above, Middleton was fairly active in land acquisitions in Orange/Guilford Co, NC, some of which identified him as a son of Basil Brashear(s). At one time, he held two Granville land grants, one he had entered himself, and one which Basil Brashears assigned "to son Middleton Brashears."

Middleton Brashear had been a far more patient man than the other Brashear men, but in Nov 1763, when it took 48 pages to record the petitions for debt, he brought suits against ten debtors at once. The first five failed to appear and Middleton was awarded an unspecified amount of money; the other five confessed their debts:

Middleton Brashear vs. Robert Brashear.	
Middleton Brashear vs. Ralph Shaw, Sr.	
Middleton Brashear vs. Wm. Runnels	
Middleton Brashear vs. Peter Shearman	
Middleton Brashear vs. Thomas Lovelotty, Sr	
Middleton Brashear vs. Henry Mines	£3/12/8 + £1/14/10 costs
Middleton Brashear vs. John Lovelotty	£3/7/9
Middleton Brashear vs. David Knight	£11/18/8

Middleton Brashear vs. Marshall Lovelotty	£7/18/8
Middleton Brashear vs. Christopher Vander Graft	£7/16/8

At the Aug 1764 quarter session, the case of Middleton Brashear vs. Ralph Shaw was referred to a jury for later trial. So many pleas were coming to quarter sessions that they could no longer be taken care of on the spot, but had to be scheduled for trial at some later date. At the Nov 1764 session, John Williams Jr sued Middleton Brashear, and Ralph Shaw entered a countersuit against him. Middleton failed to appear.

At the Feb 1765 session, Middleton sued Ralph Shaw Jr, and there were two cases of Ralph Shaw vs. Middleton Brashears, perhaps Ralph Shaw Sr and Jr. Life had degenerated to a squabble.

Figure 6: Two signatures of Middleton Brashears, from Granville Grants. He didn't always spell his own name correctly!

Middleton in South Carolina

After that, Middleton Brashears removed to Laurens Co, SC, where 23 Sept 1767, the Court of Ordinary appointed him and Henrietta Prather administrators of the estate of Philip Prather, planter, late of Enoree (*South Carolina Hist Mag*, Vol.24, p.111). Middleton's closeness to his sister, Henrietta, might suggest that he would name a son Henry.

On 6 Oct 1776, Middleton Breashear enlisted as a private in the 3rd Regiment in Spartanburg Co, SC. He was taken prisoner, 28 Dec 1778. (*Roster of South Carolina Patriots in the*

American Revolution, by Bobby Gilmer Moss, Gen. Publ. Co, 1983, p.853; see also *American Revolution Roster, Fort Sullivan, 1776–1780*, Charleston, SC, p.98.) Also in the Spartanburg Regiments were an Isaiah Breacher and a William Bratcher, probably brothers of Middleton.

Probable Family of Middleton Brashears

[V6]2. [7]1. ***Basil Brashears Sr**, b. c1765, NC (age 70-80 in 1840 Census, Lawrence Co, TN) The 1790 Census, Heads of Families, Camden Dist, Fairfield Co, SC, p.21, lists a Brasil Brashear, whose household consisted of 1 male over 16, 3 males under 16, and 3 females of all ages. Basil b. 18 May 1714 would have been 76 years old in 1790, not likely to have a bunch of young children in his household. This Basil nad his children appear in Lawrence Co, TN records.

[V6]3. [7]2. ***John Brashears/Breshears Sr**, b. NC, 1767; d. before 1 Nov 1852, Lawrence Co, TN; m. in Pendleton Dist, SC, c1790, ***Mary Berry***, b. SC, 1777, from a Guilford Co, NC family, d. Lawrence Co, TN, 1868. They had children: Isaac, Jacob, Elizabeth, Berry, John Henry, and Nancy "Polly". John's parentage has not yet been proven; he was a brother of Henry Breshears Sr, of Lawrence Co, TN.

[V6]4. [7]3. ***Henry Brashears/Breshears Sr**, b. 1769, prob. South Carolina; d. 1828, Lawrence Co, TN; m. ***Eleanor Hardin***, and had children: William, John, Jesse, Polly, Henry Jr, Eleanor, Margaret. Henry's parentage has not been proven, but note that John was born while Middleton was still in NC and Henry born when Middleton was known to be in SC.

[V6]5. [7]4. **Thomas Brashears**, b. bef. 1774 (46+ in 1820 White Co, TN). Has a son(?) 16-45 in his hh in 1820 White Co, TN; ergo b. c1775-1804. A female of same age (son's wife?) and a male child under 10 are also in the household. Any ideas anyone?

[V6]6. [7]x. <u>unknown son</u>, possibly "**James Brashears**," m. ***Mary Jane Turner***, who were probably the parents of:

[V6]7. [8]1. ***Middleton Brashears, the younger**, b. SC, 1794-5 (56 in 1850); m. ***Jane*** ____, b. 1792-94. (1820 White Co, TN; 1830 Lawrence Co, TN, p.295, line 11: 110001-110001); they moved c1833 to Missouri.

[V6]8. [8]2. ***Nathan Turner Breshears**, b. 4 April 1797, SC or GA, d. 24 Feb 1884, Dallas Co, MO; m.1. 26 Aug 1819, in Lawrence Co, TN, ***Elizabeth Catherine Keele***, b. 21 Nov 1800, Bedford, NC, d. 10 Aug 1858; m.2. ***Matilda Decker***, m.3. ***Charity Lamar***. (1830 Lawrence Co, TN, p. 295, line 7: 110001-10001); moved in 1833/34 with Middleton the younger and Alexander to Missouri.

[V6]9. [8]3. **James Brashears [Jr]**, b. [1805]; included in a FHL chart with no documentation.

The documents we do have: James G. Bashiears, age 30-40 is in the 1840 census, Lawrence Co, TN, p.128;

James Brashers has 12 acres on the 1836 Tax Lists, Lawrence Co, TN, District #7 (bordering Wayne Co and just north of Dist 6 and the middle of the county, where Alexander also had land);

James Brashears m. ***Delila Vincent***; Lawrence Co, TN Marriage License issued 25 July 1837 by Charles Hicks, Clerk. Endorsed: "Solemnized July the 24th day A.D. 1837, by S. Carrell, J.P." No further information.

[V6]10. [8]4. ***Alexander Brashears**, b. 20 April 1807, SC, m. ***Margaret "Peggy" Breshears***, b. 15 Feb 1811, SC, d/o Henry Brashears/Breshears Sr and Eleanor (Harden?). Alex and Margaret moved to MO, c1833-35. They were first cousins, which means that Alexander's father was a brother to Henry Breshears, Sr.

[V6]11. [8]5. ***Rebecca Brashers**, b. TN, c1814 (46 in 1860 Pulaski Co, AR); m. 17 Aug 1831, ****Andrew "Drury" "Drew" Boshears***, b. c1813, TN (47 in 1860 Pulaski Co, AR, Owen twp. family #155), s/o Berry Boshears Sr and wife Anna. LawrCo, TN Marr Bond, 5 Aug 1831; bondsmen: Drury (X)

Brashers and /signed/Alf (or Alx) Besher (his name is clearly Alexander Brashers in the Clerk's handwriting. See the copy, next page.) Endorsed: "I solumnised the within on the 17th 1831, Jeremiah G. ?Deredy." Not surprisingly, Rebecca and Drew named a son Alexander. See their listing in "Berry Boshears of Arkansas."

[V6]12. 7x. <u>unknown son</u> **"The Phantom Absalom Brashears"**: Circumstances, residences, family oral traditions, and naming patterns make me want to add one more son, who would be the father of at least:

[V6]13. [8]w. ***Berry Boshears**, b. 1790, SC; m. ***Anna*** _____, they lived in White Co, TN, Lawrence Co, TN, McNairy Co, TN, Tishomingo Co, MS, White Co, AR, Montgomery Co, AR, and Pulaski Co, AR.

[V6]14. [8]x. **Nancy Elizabeth Brashear**, b. 1793, SC; m. 20 Oct 1823, Lawrence Co, AL, ***Andrew Wilson***, b. 1800, SC; both died in Kendall Co, TX.

[V6]15. [9]1. *Robert Brashear Wilson, b. 3 May 1827, Lawrence Co, AL. (See chapter on John Brashear and Elizabeth "Betsy" Randall.)

[V6]16. [8]y. **Robert H. Brashear** (reported in old letters to be brother of Nancy (Brashear) Wilson and John Brashear); m. 16 April 1819, Lawrence Co, AL, ***Sally L. Rhea***,

[V6]17. [8]z. ***John Brashear**, b. 1796 (brother to Nancy (Brashear) Wilson); m.1. in Lawrence Co, AL, ***Elizabeth "Betsy" Randall***, b. 1800, and had nine children; m.2. a widow, ***Elizabeth (Baugh) Chambers***, b. 1794, SC, and had one more child, Wm Gouldsberry Brashears.

See "Basil Brashears Sr," "John Breshears Sr," "Henry Breshears Sr," "Berry Boshears of Arkansas," and "Three Brothers of Missouri: Middleton, Nathan Turner, and Alexander Breshears" for continuations.

3. BASIL BRASHEARS Sr, b. c1765

V6 2. 7 1. **Brasil (Basil) Brashears Sr**, b. 1760-70 (age 70-80 in 1840, Lawrence Co, TN); my guess is that he was born c1765; m.1. ____; m.2. ____, b. 1780-90 (50-60 in 1840 Lawrence). I believe (cannot prove) that Basil was s/o Middleton Brashears, s/o Basil Brashear(s) and Anne Belt, of Prince George's Co, MD, Orange/Guilford Co, NC, and Spartanburg Co, SC.

This is apparently the Brasil Brashear in the 1790 Heads of Families, Camden Dist, Fairfield Co, SC, p. 21; 1 m. 16+ (himself), 3 m. 0-16, 3 f. incl wife. Five children, all born 1776-1790 makes it likely he was born early 1760's at the latest. Who these five were, I have no idea, and they are all too old to be children of the (? second) wife who is 50-60 (b. c1780-90) and listed in the 1840 census, Lawrence Co, TN; therefore he must have had a first wife who died in the 1790s and he married (second) a girl about the age of his own children. Perhaps there is another generation in here, for the siblings in Lawrence Co, TN, in the 1830's seem to be b. c1805-1820. Of course, very large families, born over 30 years are not impossible; it's just that such large numbers of people usually leave more paper tracks than Basil seems to have.

I think this is also him:

1800 Census, Greenville Co, SC:

Besshares, Bazle, 20010-10100-00, p.255, l.485 , age 26-45, i.e. b. 1755–1774. Basil apparently has a wife, 16-26 years old, b. 1774-1794, and two boys and a girl under age 10, all b. 1790-1800.

Bisshares, Wm 01101-02001-00, p.255, l.484 (this William Bisshares, age 45+, b. bef 1755, is unidentified, but lives very close to Basil--next door)

Westward Migrations

Basil Brashears Sr, b. c1765; John Brashears Sr, b. c1767; Henry Breshears Sr, b. c1769, with some of their nephews, left South Carolina about 1810 and migrated to east-central Tennessee. This was a familiar migration route for men moving west at the time new land was "opening" for settlement, and they encountered some of their distant relatives in Tennessee.

Near the middle of the 1810-1820 decade, at least two of the South Carolina Breshears colony got land grants in Warren Co, TN— Berry, and Henry Sr. They are alongside Jesse Brashears, of Lee Co, VA, s/o Philip Brashears, d. 1798, Henry Co, VA, and several of his sons.

WARREN CO, TN, LAND GRANTS:

7 Aug 1811: Tennessee Land Grant #3300, 23 acres, to Jesse Brasher (Book E, p.131). Jesse Brashear was from Lee Co, VA. He was a son of Philip Brashears of Henry Co, VA. Jesse migrated to central TN about 1810 and died there some time between 1811 and 1820. His widow, Elizabeth, received his unfinished land grants. (See Vol. 2, *Robert C. Brashear, of NC, and Some Descendants in TN, KY, TX, etc.*)

4 Feb 1815: Tennessee Land Grant, 2 acres, to Littleberry Brashears. (HSB, p.29; not now listed in card index in Nashville). The same as Berry Brashears, b. 1790, SC.

7 Feb 1815: Tennessee Land Grant #11977, 40 acres, to Henry Brashears. (HSB, p. 29, and Book O, p.295 and Book 8, p.132). This is Henry Breshears Sr, b. c1769, SC, believed to be s/o Middleton Brashears.

13 May 1817: Tennessee Land Grant #10081, 10 acres, to Jesse Brashear (Book Q, p.178 and Book 8, p.618)

30 Aug 1828: Tennesse Land Grant #968, 20 acres, to William Brashears (Book B, p.394). This is William Breshears, s/o Melvry Brashears, a s/o Jesse Brashear, of Lee Co, VA.

10 March 1828: Tennessee Land Grant #305, 10 acres to Milnery Brashear (Book A, p.206-7) "Milnery" is a copyist's misreading of Melvry.

11 March 1828: Tennessee Land Grant #360, 16 acres to Milnery Brashear (Book A, p.244)

Judging from the low numbers on these 1828 grants, I'd say the land was entered very early and only registered very late.

12 March 1828: Tennessee Land Grant #413, 34 acres to Valdon Brashear (Book A, p.279) Valdon was a son of Jesse Brashears of Lee Co, VA.

9 Feb 1838: Tennessee Land Grant #5836, 25 acres to Elizabeth Brashear (Book J p.259). Widow of Jesse Brashears of Lee Co, VA.

Henry Breshears Sr, b. 1769, and at least some of his nephews did not stay long in Warren Co, but moved on to Lawrence Co, TN, about 1817. However, many of the Brashears families that had migrated from South Carolina lived in White Co, TN, in 1820. This included Basil, Sr, b. 1765, John, Sr, b. 1767, Thomas, b. c1771-2, and at least two of their nephews.

1820 Census of White County, TN (all p.369): (Identified as "my family" by Anna Locke, descendant of Berry Boshears of AR.)

Thomas Bashers, age 46+, b. bef. 1774. Believed to be a s/o Middleton.
wife, 46+, b. bef. 1774.
male, 26-45, [b. 1775-1794; looks like a son and his wife and child]
fem. 26-45, b. 1775-1794
male, 0-10, b. 1810-1820

Basil Basher, age 46+, b. bef. 1774. This is Basil, b. c1765 [Basil is 70-80 in 1840 Lawrence TN; b. 1760-70]
wife, 26-45, b. 1775-1794 [50-60 in 1840, b. 1780-1790]
fem, 10-15, b. 1805-1810
male, 0-10, b. 1810-1820 male, 0-10, b. 1810-1820
fem. 0-10, b. 1810-1820 fem. 0-10, b. 1810-1820

John Bashere, age 46+, b. bef. 1774. This is John Brashears Sr, [John is 83 in 1850 Lawrence Co, TN, b. 1767; wife, Mary, is 73, b. 1777]
wife, 26-45, b. 1775-1794
fem, 10-15, b. 1805-1810 fem, 10-15, b. 1805-1810
male, 0-10, b. 1810-1820 male, 0-10, b. 1810-1820
fem. 0-10, b. 1810-1820

Berry Bashere, age 26-45, b. 1775-1794, (he was 30, b. 1790)
wife, 26-45, b. 1775-1794
male, 10-15, b. 1805-1810 fem, 10-15, b. 1805-1810.
male, 0-10, b. 1810-1820 male, 0-10, b. 1810-1820
fem. 0-10, b. 1810-1820 fem. 0-10, b. 1810-1820
fem. 0-10, b. 1810-1820

Middleton Bashers, age 16-25, b. 1795-1804, (This is Middleton Brashears, the Younger, b. c1794; he was 56 in 1850 Stoddard Co, MO)
wife, 16-25, b. 1795-1804 fem., 0-10, b. 1810-1820

Family of Basil Brashears Sr

Possible first family of Basil Brashears Sr: (based on 1790 census)

V6 68. [8]1. son, b. 1776-1790

V6 69. [8]2. son, b. 1776-1790

V6 70. [8]3. dau, b. 1776-1790

V6 71. [8]4. son, b. 1776-1790

V6 72. [8]5. dau, b. 1776-1790

Probable second family of Basil Brashears Sr:

V6 73. [8]6. **Thomas Brashers**, b. c1806, NC, d. c1867, Tishomingo Co, MS; m. 1833, ***Mary Emily "Polly" Sullivan/Sullivant***, b. NC, c1810, d/o Samuel West Sullivan and his first wife, Sarah Bell. Lawrence Co, TN Marriage Bond, 12 Jan 1833. Bondsmen: Basil Brashers Sr and Thomas Brashers. (1840 Census, Wayne Co, TN: Thos Boshears (01001-10001). Thomas Boshears, b. NC c1806, and Emily, b. NC, c1810, are hh #426, p.118, Southern Dist, 1850 Tishomingo Co, MS Census, with seven children; 1860 census, Tishomingo Co, MS, with six. They apparently stayed in Mississippi when all the "cousins" moved to Obion Co, TN. Thomas's will dated Jan 1867, Tishomingo Co, MS.

V6 74. [9]1. **John H. Boshears**, b. TN, c1837 (13 in 1850; 24 & "at home" in 1860). John ?Henry Boshears?

V6 75. [9]2. **Sarah A. Boshears**, b. TN, c1840 (10 in 1850; not in 1860; may have married)

V6 76. [9]3. **?Rena C. Boshears**, b. TN, c1842 (18 in 1860). ?Caroline Boshears?

V6 77. [9]4. **Zilpha Jane Boshears**, b. TN or MS, c1844 (16 in 1860)

V6 78. [9]5. **James K.P. Boshears**, b. MS, c1846 (14 in 1860)

V6 79. [9]6. **Frances M. Boshears**, b. MS, c1848 (12 in 1860)

V6 80. [9]7. **Thomas J. Boshears**, b. MS, 1850 (4/12 in 1850; 10 in 1860)

[V6]81. [8]7. ***Basil Brashear Jr**, b. c1808, d. in Civil War. Basil Sr and Basil Jr, both securities of Peter Brashers when he pleaded guilty of assault and battery, Oct 1830, and was fined $2.50 (Lawrence Co, TN, Minutes of the Court, 1828-1834, p.216, 219). We had previously thought this Basil was s/o Berry Boshears, but his service record in the National Archives says he was Basil Brashear Jr. He lived for a time in Tishomingo Co, MS; then in the western edge of Pulaski Co, AR, where one of his daughters was married in his house.

[V6]82. [8]8. **Peter Brashers**, b. c1810 (40 in 1850; 20-30 in 1840 Lawrence, p.121: 11011-31002); m. 1830, ***Rebecca "Bicky" Brashers***, b. 1810. Lawrence Co, TN Marriage Bond, 9 Feb 1830, bondsmen: Peter [X] Brasher and Basil [X] Brasher. Witness: Amos Buchanan; fee not paid. Peter, b. c1810, and Rebecca, b. c1810, are hh #522, p.39, 1850 Tishomingo Co, MS Census with six children; Peter Beshear and Rebecca, both 48, are #324-503, 1860 McNairy Co, TN. Peter and Rebecca, both 68, are mother and father in household of George Bashear in 1880 Obion Co, TN.

[V6]83. [9]1. **Lewis Boshers**, b. TN, c1831 (19 in 1850)

[V6]84. [9]2. **Mary Boshers**, b. TN, c1834 (16 in 1850)

[V6]85. [9]3. **Elizabeth Boshers**, b. TN, c1836-38 (14 in 1850; 22 in 1860)

[V6]86. [9]4. **William Henry Boshers**, b. TN, c1840 (10 in 1850; Wm H., age 20 in 1860, McNairy Co, TN). The 1870 census of McNairy Co, TN, has a Henry Boshear, 26, with wife, ***Marantha***, 24; no ch. Someone, not the census-taker, has written William above the name.

[V6]87. [9]5. **Tabitha Boshers**, b. MS, c1847 (3 in 1850, 13 in 1860)

[V6]88. [9]6. **George W. Boshers**, b. MS, c1849 (1 in 1850, 10 in 1860; 24 in 1870, Obion Co, TN; 31 in 1880, Obion Co, TN); m. ***Mary A.*** _____, b. c1841 (29 in 1870, Obion Co, TN), d. c?1870-1880.

[V6]89. [10]1. **Laura Boshers**, b. c1869 (9/12 in 1870, Obion Co, TN)

[V6]90. [10]2. **Belle Boshers**, b. TN, c1871 (9 in 1880, Obion Co, TN)

[V6]91. [9]7. **Benjamin Boshers**, b. c1851 (one report says name was Perry F.) (8 in 1860, McNairy Co, TN; 29 in 1880, Obion Co, TN); m. ***Louisa*** _____, b. c1845, TN, and they are in the 1880 Census, Obion Co, TN, with two children:

[V6]92. [10]1. **Rebecca Boshears**, b. TN, c1869 (11 in 1880)

[V6]93. [10]2. **William Boshears**, b. TN, May 1880 (1/30 in 1880)

[V6]94. [8]9. Unknown. Possibly (absolutely no proof) the ***Mary Elizabeth Boshears/Brashears/Beshires**, b. c1815, who m. 1833, ***Edmund M. Shelton***. See below.

[V6]95. [8]10. **Nancy Brashers**, b. c1821 (if 16 when Marrying); m. 1837, ***Joseph Bishop***, Lawrence Co, TN Marriage Bond, 18 June 1837; bondsmen: Joseph [X] Bishop and Peter [X] Brashers.

It took practically "an arm and a leg" to get married in those days; you had to swear away several years' income to get your children married.

KNOW ALL MEN THAT WE, Thomas Brashers and Basil Brashers Sr, of the County of Giles and State of Tennessee, are held firmly bound unto the Governor of said State, for the time being, in the sum of Twelve Hundred and Fifty dollars, to be paid to his Excellency, his successors in office or assigns, to which payment well and truly to be made we bind ourselves, our heirs, executors and administrators, and each and every of us, and them jointly and severally by these presents.— Witness our hands and seals this 12th day of January 1833.

THE CONDITION of the above obligation is such, that whereas Thomas Brashers hath prayed and obtained a License to marry Polly Sulivant. Now if the said Polly be an actual resident of the aforesaid county, and there shall not appear any lawful cause why the said Thomas and Polly should not be joined together in

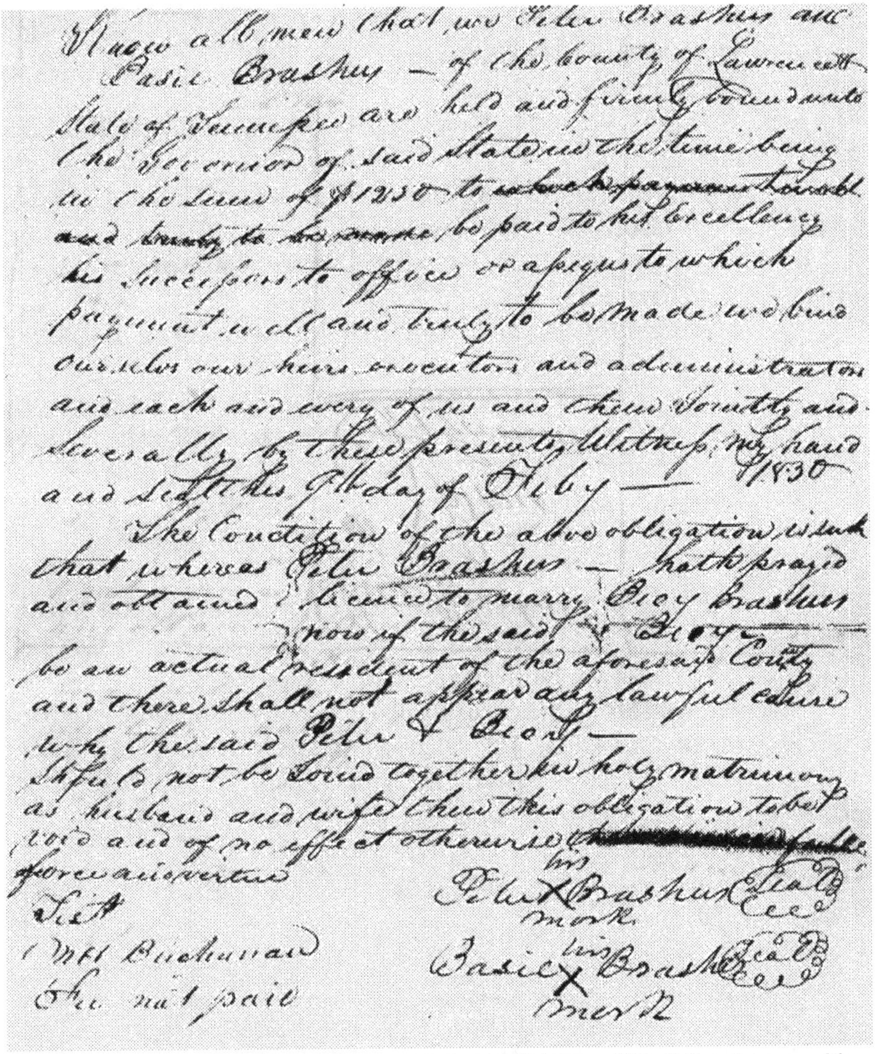
Know all men that we Peter Brashers and
Basil Brashers — of the County of Lawrence &
State of Tennessee are held and firmly bound unto
the Governor of said State and the time being
in the sum of $1250 to which payment to well
and truly to be made, be paid to his Excellency
his successors to office or assigns to which
payment well and truly to be made we bind
ourselves our heirs executors and administrators
and each and every of us and them Jointly and
Severally by these presents. Witness my hand
and seal this 9th day of Feby — 1830
The Condition of the above obligation is such
that whereas Peter Brashers — hath prayed
and obtained licence to marry Bicy Brashers
now if the said Bicy
be an actual resident of the aforesaid County
and there shall not appear any lawful cause
why the said Peter & Bicy —
Should not be Joined together in holy matrimony
as husband and wife then this obligation to be
void and of no effect otherwise in full
force and virtue
his
Peter X Brashers (Seal)
mark
Test
Wm Buchanan
Clk not paid
his
Basil X Brashers (Seal)
mark

Figure 7: Peter Brashears' license to marry Rebecca "Bicy" Brashears, with himself and Basil as bondsmen.

holy matrimony as husband and wife, then this obligation to be void and of no effect, otherwise to remain in full force and virtue.

Thomas [X] Brashers

Basil [X] Brashers

Some of the Sullivan connection:

a-x. ______ Sullivan/Sullivant

b-1. Samuel West Sullivan; m.1. Sarah Bell; m.2. Mary Osbum

c-1. Mary "Polly" Sullivan, d/o Sarah Bell, m. 1833, **Thomas Brashear**

c-2. John A. Sullivan, s/o Mary Osbum, m. Mary Reddell

c-3. James H. Sullivan, s/o Mary Osbum; m. Mary "Polly" Smith

d-1. Samuel Sullivan; m. Frances Louise Shelton, daughter of **Mary Elizabeth Boshers** and Edmund M. Shelton

b-2. Martha Sullivan; m. John A. Hail

v6 94. 89. Mary Elizabeth Boshers/Brashears/Beshires, (unidentified), b. c1815, NC; m. 30 Jan 1833, in Maury Co, TN, ***Edmund M. Shelton***, Bondsman: ***John Boshers***.

Edmund Shelton, the husband, drowned in 1850, before the census, in Giles Co, TN. Elizabeth Shelton is in the 1850 Census, Giles Co, TN with five children. (From: "Judy Sulephen" (cdjudy2@mvtel.net) and/or Judy (gladys@mvtel.net)

1. William Shelton,
2. Wesley Shelton,
3. Mary A. Shelton,
4. James F. Shelton,
5. Louis Shelton,

Her mother, ***Mary Boshears***, b. c1793, age 67, is in Elizabeth Shelton's household in 1860, Lawrence Co, TN, and "Pollie" Brashier, 77, is in her household in 1870, Lawrence Co, TN. Mary Boshears/Brashears, the mother, died in 1879, and Elizabeth Shelton moved to Izard Co, AR, to live with her daughter, Frances Louise Shelton Sullivan and her husband Samuel Sullivan.

Basil Brashears Jr and Eliza Ann Simpson

v681. 87. **Basil "Brazil" Besheārs Jr**, b. TN, c1808 (age 50 in 1860 Pulaski County AR Census, Owen Twp, taken 8 Jul, Dwelling #153), d. c1863 in Civil War; m.1. ______ and had five children (one family researcher says *Lucinda Young*, which may be a confusion with Basil Jr, s/o Basil Brashears and Margaret Horton, of Roane Co, TN. That Basil Jr m. Lucy Crunk Young, 20 Feb 1834 in Shelby Co, AL. This Basil's participation in his father's estate, as well as his own estate, are well documented. See Vol 3.); that wife d. between 1837 and 1846, in MS. Basil m.2. c1847, in MS, ***Eliza Ann Simpson***, b. MS, c1824 (age 36 in 1860 Pulaski Co, AR; 45 in 1870 Saline Co, AR), d. 5 Dec 1889, bur Cold Spring Cem, Saline Co, AR. "Brazelle Beshares" is on the Poll Tax list for White Co, AR, 1848/49.

Eliza Ann (Simpson) Breshears, m.2. 11 Aug 1864, Pulaski Co, AR, John Rhodes, but Eliza Bersheers, 45, is a widow in Union twp, Saline Co, AR, in 1870, with children William A., Edward, and Mitchell Bersheers.

On 29 Oct 1861, Bazil Beshers [Jr], age 50, enlisted as a private in Co. I, Capt. Cunningham's Company, 11th Regiment, Arkansas Infantry, Confederate States Army, for a period of one year. He was reported captured at Island No. 10, on 8 April 1862 and was on a roll of prisoners of war at Camp Douglas, Chicago, dated 4 Sept 1862. He must have been exchanged or paroled, for a company muster roll for 24 Oct 1862 says he was sick in quarters; received no pay. A muster roll for Consolidated Co. D, 11th Regt, Arkansas Volunteers, 27 Sept to 31 Dec 1862, reports him "absent sick/ present locality unknown."

He apparently died in 1863.

Children of Basil Besheārs Jr and first wife (?Lucinda Young):

V696. 91. male, b. 1825-30, indicated by MS census

V697. 92. female, b. 1825-30, indicated by MS census

V698. 93. female, b. 1830-35, indicated by MS census

V699. 94. **Peter Beshears**, b. MS, c1835-37 (15 in 1850, Mountain Twp, Montgomery Co, AR; 23 in 1860 Pulaski Co, AR); jayhawkers killed him during the Civil War.

[V6]100. [9]5. **Elizabeth Beshears**, b. 1839, MS (13 in 1850, Montgomery Co, AR; age 19 when marrying); m. 29 Aug 1858, "at the house of Bassil Boshers in Owen Township, Pulaski Co, AR, by B.W. Nowlin, JP," ***James Henry McCracens***, b. c1837

<u>Children of Basil Brashears Jr and Eliza Ann Simpson:</u>

[V6]101. [9]6. <u>Thomas Robert Simpson</u>, b. MS, 7 Oct 1846, son of Eliza Ann Simpson and Basil Beshears, born out of wedlock; Basil married Eliza, but Thomas kept the surname, Simpson, though he sometimes used the surname, Brashears. Thomas R. Simpson m. 25 Feb 1877, Pulaski Co, AR, **Sarah Jane Breshears**, b. 22 March 1856, d/o Robert Henry "Uncle Bob" Breshears. During the Civil War, he left the Confederate side and fought with the Federal Army; has a tombstone on his grave at the head of his mother's grave in the Old Brashears cemetery near Cold Springs. **Thomas R. Beshers**, age 18, b. c1846, Tippah Co, MS, enl 25 Jan 1864, Little Rock, AR, in Co. H, 4th Arkansas Cavalry, U.S. Army, as private; rose to Corporal. (*Arkansas' Damned Yankees--an Index to Union Soldiers in Arkansas Regiments,* p.25)

[V6]102. [10]1. Callep Simpson, b. c1878 (2 in 1880)

[V6]103. [10]2. Rebecca Simpson, b. c1879 (11/12 in 1880)

[V6]104. [10]3. Thomas C. Simpson, b. Nov 1884

[V6]105. [10]4. Lee A. Simpson, b. Oct 1885

[V6]106. [10]5. Robert M. Simpson, b. Dec 1888

[V6]107. [10]6. Manda E. "Anna" Simpson, b. March 1890

[V6]108. [10]7. Otie Simpson, b. March 1892

[V6]109. [9]7. **Sally Beshears**, b. MS, c1849 (1 in 1850, Mountain Twp, Montgomery Co, AR). app. d. before 1860 census.

[V6]110. [9]8. ***William Andrew "Willie" Beshears**, b. AR, 29 Dec 1851, d. 24 April 1926; m. ***Sarah Elizabeth "Aunt Sis" Crow***, b. 16 March 1851

[V6]111. [9]9. **Isaac Edward Beshears**, b. AR, c1854-6 (age 6 in 1860 Pulaski Co, AR; "Edward Bersheers" age 14 in 1870 Union twp, Saline Co, AR; Isac Breshears, in 1880, Holland twp, Saline Co); called "Uncle Ed" and he was a doctor. Uncle Ed m.1. 5 Aug 1877, Pulaski Co, AR, ***Mary Ann "Molly" Smith***, b. c1858 (22 in 1880) and had 3 children, per Anna Locke, but she didn't name them. They are fam #142-143 in 1880 census, Holland twp, Saline Co, AR, with only their first-born.

V6112. 101. **Julia Breshears**, b. Sept 1879

V6113. 910. **Michael (or Mitchel?) H./C. Beshears**, b. Nov 1859, (9/12 in 1860 Pulaski Co, AR, d. 30 March 1914; "Mitchel Bershears in 1870, Saline Co, AR, Union twp); "M.C. Brashears" m. 1 June 1879, Pulaski Co, AR, ***Susan J. Gillam***, b. c1857 (22 in 1879), security: William Brashears. "Mical Breshears" and wife are fam #139-140 in 1880 Holland twp, Saline Co, AR, with dau, Mary Lisa. Mike H. Brashear was in Big Rock twp, Little Rock, Pulaski Co, AR, in 1900 census; Rev. M.H. Brashears, d. 30 March 1914.

V6114. 101. **Mary Lisa Breshears**, b. March 1880, AR

V6115. 102. **Minnie Breshears**, b. Aug 1881, AR

V6116. 103. **Ada Breshears**, b. Jan 1883, AR

V6117. 104. **Arkansas "Arkie" Beshears**, b. Jan 1888, AR; m. ______ ***Woods***,

V6118. 105. **Thomas Brashears**, b. March 1892, AR; lived North Little Rock

V6119. 106. **Robert Brashears**, b. Sept 1894, AR; lived Chicago

V6120. 107. **Joseph Breashears**, b. Nov 1898, AR

William Andrew Beshears and Sarah Elizabeth Crow

v6110. 98. William Andrew "Willie" Beshears, (s/o Basil Beshears Jr and Eliza Ann Simpson), b. AR, 29 Dec 1851, d. 24 April 1926, at Little Rock, bur Fowler Cem at Paron, Saline Co, AR; m. 5 Nov 1876, Pulaski Co, AR, ***Sarah Elizabeth "Aunt Sis" Crow***, b. 16 March 1855, d. 11 Feb 1942, age 87, bur Fowler Cem at Paron, Saline Co, AR, d/o Robert N. Crow, b.

1830, TN and Symantha N. Miller, b. 1834, AL. William and Sarah are in the 1900 and 1910 censuses of Holland twp, Saline Co, AR. In 1894, William A. Breshears homesteaded 80 acres in Saline Co, AR; great-grandson Charles S. Breshears has the original grant, signed by President Grover Cleveland. In 1900, Sarah had had 11 children, 8 of them still living; in 1910, the same numbers were 9 and 6.

[V6]121. [10]1. **Leander "Lee" Breshears**, b. Feb 1878, AR, d. Feb 1967, age 89, bur Fowler Cem, Saline Co, AR; m. ***Johnnie Prouse Thomas***, b. 1889, AL (22 in 1910, Holland Twp, Saline Co, AR), d. 1977.

[V6]122. [11]1. **Pearl J. Breshears**, (son), b. 1 April 1913, d. 1 Oct 1925

[V6]123. [11]2. **Cleta Bell Breshears**, b. 1923; m. ______ ; ch: Brenda Darlene ______

[V6]124. [10]2. **Rhoda "Rhody" Breshears**, b. 1879, AR

[V6]125. [10]3. **Almeda Breshears**, b. 6 Feb 1881, d. 29 Jan 1958, age 76, bur Spring Valley Cem at Ferndale, Pulaski Co, AR; m. ***Henry Grimmet***, b. AR, Oct 1875, d. 1939. Her brother, Lee, was "boarder" in Henry Grimmet household in 1900.

[V6]126. [11]1. Oma Sanduski Grimmet, b. Aug 1899 (1900 Holland Twp, Saline Co)

[V6]127. [11]2. Virginia Callie Grimmet, b. 1901; m. ______ Koon.

[V6]128. [11]3. Earnest Wailon Grimmet, b. 10 April 1904, d. 1984; m. ______ (ch: Earnest Clyde Grimmet)

[V6]129. [11]4. William Olin Grmimet, b. 1906,

[V6]130. [11]5. Homer Ray Grimmet, b. 1909, d. 1936

[V6]131. [11]6. Bessie Beulah Grimmet, b. 1911, d. 1974; m. James Arthur Brown, b. 1918, d. 1993.

[V6]132. [11]7. Russie Wilma Grimmet, b. 1913, d. 1980; m. Bill White.

[V6]133. [10]4. **Maude Breshears**, b. Dec 1883, AR; m. ***P. Bowlin***,

[V6]134. [10]5. **Scott Breshears**, b. 13 Jan 1885, AR, d. 10 Nov 1966, age 71, in N. Little Rock, bur Fowler Cem at Paron, Saline Co, AR; m.1. ***Nira McCallester***, b. 1885, d. 1941; m.2. ***Mary Barnes***, no children.

[V6]135. [10]6. ***Charles William Breshears**, b. 13 Aug 1889, d. 13 Oct 1927, age 38, bur Fowler Cem at Paron,

Saline Co, AR; m. 7 Jan 1912, ***Rachel Chastain***,

[V6]136. [10]7. **James Arthur Breshears**, b. 22 Feb 1892 at Paron, AR, d. 18 Dec 1974 at Little Rock, age 82, bur Roselawn Cem at Little Rock, Pulaski Co, AR; m.1. ***Eula Mae Smith***, (1 ch); m.2. ***Ruby Inez Reed***, b. 1894,

[V6]137. [11]1. **Arthur Miller Breshears**; m. ***Ida Lucy Breshears***,

[V6]138. [12]1. **Lewis Breshears,** m. ______

[V6]139. [13]1. **Patricia Ann Breshears,**

[V6]140. [13]2. **Arthur Miller Breshears**,

[V6]141. [10]8. **Grace Breshears**, b. Sept 1894, AR; m.1. ***Harris Howard***, m.2. ______ ***Siems***,

[V6]142. [10]9. **Gaytha Breshears**, b. 4 March 1897, AR, d. 18 March 1988, age 91, bur Fowler Cem at Paron, Saline Co, AR; m. ***Olin Thomas Lambert***, (three known children, probably others in between)

[V6]143. [11]1. Charles Eudell Lambert,

[V6]144. [11]2. O.T. Lambert, b. 18 July 1918, d. 1938

[V6]145. [11]3. James Melvin Lambert, b. 15 May 1933, d. 1988; m.1. Mildred Hill; m.2. Nadja ______ .

Charles William Breshears and Rachel Chastain

[v6]135. [10]6. Charles William "Charlie" Breshears, (s/o William Andrew Beshears and Sarah Elizabeth Crow), b. 13 Aug 1889, d. 13 Oct 1927, age 38, bur Fowler Cem at Paron, Saline Co, AR; m. 7 Jan 1912, ***Rachel T. Chastain***,

[V6]146. [11]1. **Lowell Bell Breshears**, (1ch), b. 3 Feb 1913, d. 31 March 1967, bur Fowler Cem, Saline Co, AR; m.1. ***Freda DeVoe***; m.2. Mary ______ (1 ch)

[V6]147. [12]1. **Frances Ray Breshears**, b. 2 Jan 1937; m. ***Bob Foster***,

[V6]148. [13]1. Margie Foster, b. 1953

[V6]149. [13]2. Bobby Foster, b. 1955

[V6]150. [12]2. **William Harvey Breshears**, b. 1951

[V6]151. [11]2. **Doyle Adam Breshears**, b. 13 Nov 1916, Paron, AR, d. 6 Feb 1978, N. Little Rock; m. 27 July 1941, ***Juanita Mae Widener***, b. 26 March 1921, Mt. Ida, AR, d. 14 Nov 1990, N. Little Rock, AR, d/o Franklin Monroe Widener and Pearl Warneke

V6 152. 12 1. **Charles Scott Breshears**, b. 9 Jan 1943, Little Rock, AR; m. 12 June 1965, ***Sarah Virginia Grigsby***, b. 2 Sept 1943.

V6 153. 13 1. **John Scott Breshears**, b. 8 Dec 1969, Little Rock, Pulaski Co, AR; m.1. 4 July 1995, at Thorne Crown Chapel, Eureka Springs, AR, ***Brooke Michelle Johnson***, b. 14 June 1972. Scott is a chemical engineer, working on digesting tuna sludge and paper wastes into methane gas. Scott m.2. ***Katie Ann Hopkins***, b. 1979.

V6 154. 13 2. **Rebecca "Becky" Jane Breshears**, b. 29 July 1974, Little Rock, AR. Becky is a senior (1996) at Oklahoma City University in Dance Management; m. Aaron Tagerson,

4. JOHN BRASHEARS Sr, and Mary Berry

v6**3.** 7**2. John Brashears Sr**, (hypothetical s/o Middleton Brashears, who was a documented s/o Basil Brashear(s) and Anne Belt), b. probably in Guilford Co, NC, c1767 (83 in 1850); d. before 1 Nov 1852, Lawrence Co, TN; m. in Pendleton Dist, SC, c1790, ***Mary Berry***, b. SC, c1777 (73 in 1850), from a Guilford Co, NC family, d. Lawrence Co, TN, 1868.

John's parentage has not yet been proven; he was a brother of Henry Breshears Sr, of Lawrence Co, TN. I believe (cannot prove) that they and Basil, b. c1765, and a couple of others were sons of Middleton Brashears, s/o Basil Brashear(s) and Anne Belt, of Prince George's Co, MD, Orange/Guilford Co, NC, and Spartanburg/Laurens Co, SC.

Norman L. Parks, a descendant whose story changed with every letter and who refused to ever give any sort of documentation other than "family traditions," says John followed his older half-brother, Samuel Robert Brashear, to the Pendleton District, SC; there he married and had two sons. (Problems: there *was* no Samuel Robert Brashears as far as I can tell, and Robert Samuel Brashears (RSB) was 36 years older than John, not likely to be a brother.)

Then he moved, about 1800, to Roane Co, TN and worked with/for Robert Samuel Brashears in Sugar Grove Valley. There John's daughter, Elizabeth, was born. From 1807 to 1811, John lived in Hawkins Co, TN, then moved to White Co, TN, where two sons were born. He lived in Lawrence Co, TN, from 1817 to 1819; then moved back to White Co, where the last of his children was born. In 1827, he moved permanently to Lawrence Co, TN, where he died before 1 Nov 1852, when the probate of his estate was opened.

John's Paper Tracks

In 1799 and 1801, John Brashears signed petitions for creating Roane Co. (RSB's Isaac's son, John, was 15-17; so it couldn't be him).

John Brashears is on the Roane Co tax lists through 1806.

23 Jan 1806, John Brashears and Basil Brashears witnessed the deed of two slaves, Joanna and Ratliff ($450), from David Haley of Grainger Co, TN to Isaac Brashears of Roane Co. (Roane Co. Deeds Index, D:127). This Basil could be RSB's youngest son, age 25, or he could be a different Basil, brother of John; RSB's Isaac's son, John, was 20 years old—ineligible to be a legal witness?

John Brashears is in the 1810 Census, Hawkins Co, TN; the 1820 Census of White Co, TN; and the 1830, 40, and 50 censuses of Lawrence Co, TN.

1820 Census of White County, TN (p.369):
John Bashere, age 46+, b. bef. 1774, [age 83 in 1850 Lawrence, b. c1767]
wife, 26-45, b. 1775-1794 (in 1850, wife, Mary, is 73, b. c1777]
fem, 10-15, b. 1805-10. ?Elizabeth, b. 1806
fem, 10-15, b. 1805-10. ?
male, 0-10, b. 1810-20. ?Berry, b. 1814
male, 0-10, b. 1810-20. ?John Henry, b. 1816
fem. 0-10, b. 1810-20. ?

John Brashears's 1850 listing (Lawrence Co, TN, p.318) has him born in NC and 83 years old, therefore, b. c1767. His wife, Mary, (same census) was 73 years old, b. c1777, in SC. Mary Mathena Brashears, age 17, b. KY, was with them in the household; she was a granddaughter, d/o Jacob Brashears/Boshears.

Taking Care of an Older Couple

Norman Parks says that Henry Breshears, John's brother, kept an elderly half-brother, Isaac, and his wife, Elizabeth, in his household until Henry's death, in 1827. Then John took Isaac and Elizabeth into his household. He received a county subsidy for several years. I believe (can't prove, and the records have no name in them) the old man was Middleton Brashears, b. c1732-33, s/o Basil Brashears and Anne Belt.

Lawrence Co, TN Minutes Book, 1828-1834, p. 321: 3 Jan 1832: Ordered that Mrs. Mary Brashers be allowed the sum of $25 for nursing and attending to _____ Brashers and _____ Brashers, paupers of this county. (First names were left blank in the record.)

Same reference, p.592: 7 April 1832: $40 to Mary Brashers for supporting Eliz. Brashears, pauper of the county, for the ensuing year.

Same reference, p.482: 1 April 1833: Mary Brashears, $35 for supporting and taking care of Elizabeth Brashers, a pauper, for the ensuing year or portion, if said Elizabeth should die.

Lawrence Co, TN Minutes Book, 1835-46, p.38: 6 April 1835, $20 to John Brashers for boarding, clothing and taking care of Eliz. Brashers, pauper.

Same reference, p.132: 3 May 1836, that John Brashers be allowed $20 for keeping Elizabeth Brashers for one year.

Same reference, p.189: 1 May 1837, Ordered that John Brashers, Sr., be allowed $20 for keeping Elizabeth Brashers a pauper of the county for 12 months. Norman Parks says Elizabeth died in 1837, but the record indicates she kept on living.

Same reference, p.239: 2 July 1838, John Brashers, Sr., allowed $40 for keeping Hannah Pitts a pauper for the next 12 months; Jno Brashers, Sr. be allowed $20 for keeping Elizabeth Brasher a pauper for the next 12 months.

Elizabeth kept living and living; she was still in John's household in the Census of 1840 — and she was over 100 years old, born in the late 1730's, the right age to be wife of Middleton Brashears.

1840 Census of Lawrence Co, TN
p.121 John Brashers, Sr 1000100001-1010100010001 age 70-80, b. 1760-70; wife, 60-70; the elderly female in H/H is 100+, b. bef. 1740!

Lawrence County, Tenn Land Grants (from State Archives, Nashville)

#9504	10 ac.	date?	to John Brashears (Book EE, p.524)
#27966	22 ac.	15 July 1846	to John H. Brashears (Bk I, p.807)
#27968	50 ac.	15 July 1846	to John Brashears (Bk I, p.809)
#18755	272 ac.	8 April 1848	to John Brashears (Bk III, p.462)

The last two grants are the ones specified in the division of John's estate, in 1856.

1850 Census, Lawrence Co, TN:
John Brashears, 83, b. NC c1767
Mary Brashears, 73, b. SC c1777
Mary Mathena Brashears, 17, b. KY, c1833

John and Mary's Family

Children of John Brashears Sr and Mary Berry: (according to Norman Parks)

[V6]199. [8]1. ***Isaac Brashears**, b. 1795, Pendleton Dist, SC; d. 1830 (See separate chapter)

[V6]200. [8]2. ***Jacob Brashears/Boshears**, b. 1800 Pendleton Dist, SC; d. 1864, Obion Co, TN (See separate chapter)

[V6]201. [8]3. **Elizabeth Brashears**, b. 1806, Roane Co, TN; m. ***?Brian Franklin***

[V6]202. [8]4. unknown dau, b. c1805-10, indicated by 1820 White Co, TN, census; no further info

[V6]203. [8]5. ***Berry M. Brashears**, b. 1814, White Co, TN; m. 1836, ***Frances Pryor***, in Lawrence Co, TN (See separate chapter)

[V6]204. [8]6. ***John Henry Brashears**, b. 1816, White Co, TN; m. 1837, ***Rebecca*** _____ (See below)

[V6]205. [8]7. **Martha Boshears**, b. 1810-20, indicated by 1820 White Co, TN, census; m. 4 Sept 1847, Tishomingo Co, MS, ***Daniel J. Dunn***, with Patrick Dial as security. (Descendant Joyce (Dunn) DuQuette <TJDuquette@ aol.com> has the marriage license.)

[V6]206. [8]8. **Nancy "Polly" Brashears**, b. 1824, White Co, TN, d. 1914; m. 8 Sept 1847, ***Patrick Dial*** (Tishomingo Co, MS Marr. 1842-1862; Surety: Daniel J. Dunn [who m. Martha Boshears, 4 Sept 1847, with Patrick Dial as Surety].

Norman Parks says that Nancy (Boshears) Dial, youngest child of John Brashears, lived in the Parks household when he was a little boy. "I knew her as a child," says Norman. "She remembered the aged Isaac and Elizabeth Brashear, living in her father's home, being 13 years old when Elizabeth died. She knew her father was born in old Orange County, NC, a son of

Robert C. Brashear. She resolutely lived in the past, her memories reinforcing family traditions." Much of what we know, today, seems to derive from her reports," which seem to me defective. (The children of Robert C. Brashear were born 1827-c1845; he is not likely to be father of John, b. 1767. Circumstances suggest that John was born in Guilford Co, NC, 1767, moved with Middleton Brashears to Laurens Dist, SC, where Middleton was known to be, late in 1767. Brother Henry was born in SC in 1769.)

Estate Records

Lawrence Co, TN Minutes Book, 1851-1858, p. 162: "Nov 1, 1852. John Brashears has died intestate. Robert Newton appt. Admr."

Lawrence Co, TN Wills and Inventories, 1852-1856, p. 87: Dec. term 1852. Inv. and sale bill of estate of John Brashears, dec'd, Nov 20, 1852. Among buyers: Mary Brashears, Lawson Williams, William Inzer, Elijah Alsup, Berry Brashears, John H. Johnston, J.M. Halcomb, D.J. White, Shadrick Chapman, J.J. Kelton, Wm. P. Halcomb, James Dial, Wm. Pryor, John Brashears. Robert Newton, Adm. The proceedings mention 400 ac. in Lewis Co. and 250 ac. in Lawrence Co.

Same reference, p. 95: Mary Brashears, widow of John, dec'd. Provision for 1 year allotted her. 20 Nov 1852.

Same reference, p. 249: John Brashar, dec'd. Debts paid Dec 19, 1854. $144.90 left.

Mary Brashears, age 82, is #33-422, Lawrence Co, TN Census, 1860. She apparently died about 1868.

There were six heirs who reached adulthood, as is indicated by a deed in Lawrence Co, TN, when Berry Brashears and Elizabeth Franklin sold their shares in 1856:

Heirs of John Brashears, dec'd, to Wm. E. Newton, 6 March 1856. Two tracts: Grant #18755 for 273 ac. and #27968 for 50 ac. in Lawrence Co, TN. ... Heirs: Berry Brashears, Elizabeth Franklin ... "Each heir owning 1/6 said tract, being on the water of Bluewater [Creek] in range 4 & 5, Sec. 2." signed: Berry

Brashears, Prien Masterly [X] Paier, Mary Brashears. (Lawrence Co, TN Deeds, Book M, p.593. Apparently, only two of the heirs are selling their undivided share. The Mary Brashears that signed would be John's widow, who would have a 1/3 dower interest in the estate during her lifetime. She would have to sign (relinquish her dower) for any of the children to sell their shares of the estate.)

Another report on this transfer has Martha Matilda Prier signing. Martha Martela Brashears married William Pryor, 20 Oct 1846. She was a d/o Isaac Brashears, John and Mary's oldest son; she lived with John and Mary until she married, and grandmother Mary lived with William and Martha Pryor in 1860. Elizabeth (?Mrs. Brian) Franklin has not been found anywhere else in the records. If Elizabeth gave Martha her power of attorney, it has apparently been lost.

Lawrence Co, TN Minutes Book, 1828-1834, p.188: 5 July 1830, records three transfers of a plat and certificate in the name of Erasmus Tippitt for 25 acres: first, from said Tippett to Berry Brashers, was produced and proven by the oath of Franklin Buchanan, witness; second, ?? by 2/3 by ?? [can anyone ungarble the reading?] from said Brashers to Elisha Franklin and [third,] from said Franklin to Alexander Brashers, was produced and proven by oaths of Nathan McClen? and Augusten W. Bumpass, witnesses.

Since this transfer was recorded in 1830 (probably happened some time earlier), this has to be the Berry, b. 1790; because Berry, s/o John and Mary, b. 1814, is only 16 years old that year, quite ineligible to participate in such transfers, and Berry Jr is not yet born. Berry, b. 1790, had apparently left the county: he is #257 in the 1826 Tax List of Lawrence Co, TN, but he was in McNairy Co, TN for the 1830 Census. Descendants differ on where Berry Jr was born in 1832; some say in Tennessee, some say in Tishomingo Co, Mississippi, where Berry was in 1840. Berry was in Montgomery Co, Arkansas in 1850 and 1860.

However, this transfer, along with the sale of 1/6 of the estate, make it look to me like pretty positive evidence that

Berry Brashears, b. 1814, was a son of John Brashears Sr, b. 1767, and Mary Berry, and that Berry Brashears, b. 1790, was not.

Which is not to say that the families weren't close. William, s/o of Henry Breshears Sr, b. 1769, was later in Arkansas and living next door to Berry, b. 1790. Isaac Beshears Jr (m. Sidney Owl), who was a son of Isaac Brashears Sr, 1795-1830, s/o of John Brashears Sr, b. 1767, was later in Owen Twp, Pulaski Co, AR, next door to Robert and Andrew Beshears, sons of Berry, b. 1790.

We used to think, also, that John Brashears, b. 1796, was a son of John Brashears and Mary Berry. However, it's fairly clear that he is not the same John. He was a brother of Nancy Elizabeth (Brashear) Wilson, wife of Andrew Wilson.

At the moment, we cannot prove the parents of Nancy Elizabeth Brashear, b. 1793, and John Brashears, b. 1796. But I'm suspecting that Berry Brashear, b. 1790, belongs with them; they were probably siblings, children of an unknown brother of John, Sr, b. 1767 and Henry, Sr, b. 1769. Some descendants in Arkansas thought the brother's name was Absalom, but he's quite a phantom. As far as I know, his name was never entered into any record. See the chapter on "the Phantom Absalom Brashears."

John Henry Brashears and Rebecca ______

V6204. 86. John Henry Brashears, (s/o John Brashears Sr and Mary Berry, though he's young enough to be a grandson), b. 1816; m. ***Rebecca*** _____, b. c1821 (29 in 1850). He received land grants near John in 1846, Lawrence Co. He and wife are in the 1850 Lawrence Co, TN Census with six children (they may have had more later). Though unexplained, there is an exactly duplicate listing in the 1850 Census of Lewis Co, TN, fam #16-779.

V6207. 91. **Mary D. Brashears**, b. 1838

V6208. 92. **Beasley John Brashears**, b. 1839; served in Civil War; m. 21 Aug 1859, in Lawrence Co, TN, ***Permelia J. Hester***.

V6209. 93. **William G. Brashears**, b. 1842
V6210. 94. **Margaret A. Brashears**, b. 1844
V6211. 95. **Martha M. Brashears**, b. 1846
V6212. 96. **Louisa Brashears**, age 2/12, b. 1850.

5. ISAAC BRASHEARS/BESHEARS, Sr

V6199. 81. Isaac Brashears/Beshears, Sr, (s/o John Brashears, Sr and Mary Berry) was b. 1795, d. c1830, says Norman Parks. He married and had three children.

The 1825 Tax Lists of White Co, TN (ref: *Index to Early Tennessee Tax Lists*, by Byron and Barbara Sistler) lists Isaac and Jacob Brashears, among others from SC.

Isaac Breshears,
Jeremiah W. Breashears,
John Breshears,
Thomas Breshears,
Jacob Byshears,

However, the Isaac in White Co in 1825 may not be this Isaac, who seems to have been living at that time in Kentucky, where one of his children was born. The Isaac in White Co in 1825 is probably s/o the Jeremiah W. Brashears there; this Isaac later moved to Scott and Campbell Co, TN. A death certificate of a grandson of the Isaac from Scott/Campbell County says he [the grandson] was born in Sparta, White Co, TN, in Aug 1824.

When Isaac Brashears/Beshears, b. 1795, s/o John Brashears Sr and Mary Berry, died c1830, his wife having pre-deceased him, his sons Isaac and George were taken in by their uncle Jacob Boshears/Brashears in White Co, TN. In 1834, Jacob "gave" them to Hartwell Scruggs in White Co (see court record below under Jacob), while he relocated to Lawrence Co, TN. Isaac's daughter, Martha Martela Brashears, age 3, was sent by stagecoach to Lawrence Co, TN and raised from the age of 3 by her grandparents, John and Mary (Berry) Brashears. After Martha married William Pryor in 1846, Mary Mathena Brashears, one of Jacob's daughters, then lived with John and Mary.

Family of Isaac Brashears/Beshears Sr:

[V6]263. [9]1. **George W. Brashears**, b. c1820, (1840 Census, Tishomingo Co, MS; 1850 Census, Randolph Co, AR; 41 in 1860 census, Tishomingo Co, MS). Believed to be the George W. Brashears, b. c1820 (age 30 in 1850) who m. ***Rebecca*** _____, b. c1824, (26 in 1850) and was listed in 1850 Census, Randolph Co, AR, #30, 1 Oct 1850, with three children; 1860 census, Tishomingo Co, MS adds 4 more. In hh in 1860: Abram Jones, 50, and Elizabeth Jones, 14, b. MS.

[V6]264. [10]1. **Thomas Brashears**, b. c1838, TN (12 in 1850)

[V6]265. [10]2. **John Brashears**, b. c1844, AR (6 in 1850; 15 in 1860)

[V6]266. [10]3. **Frances Brashears**, (fem), b. Nov 1849, AR (11/12 in Oct 1850; 11 in 1860)

[V6]267. [10]4. **William Brashears**, b. c1852, Mississippi (8 in 1860)

[V6]268. [10]5. **Nancy Brashears**, b. c1855, MS (5 in 1860)

[V6]269. [10]6. **Robert Brashears**, b. c1857, MS (3 in 1860)

[V6]270. [10]7. **Sarah Brashears**, b. c1859, MS (11/12 in 1860)

[V6]271. [9]2. ***Martha Martela Brashears**, b. 10 Sept 1828, d. 30 March 1878, Hamilton Co, Indiana; m. 20 Oct 1846, LawrCo, TN, ***William John Pryor***, b. 28 May 1829, Lawrence Co, TN, d. 18 March 1902, Hamilton Co, Indiana

[V6]272. [9]3. ***Isaac Brashears Jr**, b. 1829, TN, (31 in 1860 Pulaski Co, AR, Owen twp); m. ***Sidney Owl***, b. TN, c1827 (33 in 1860 Pulaski, AR), d/o Lewis Owl (Indian).

Martha Martela Brashears and William John Pryor

[v6]271. [9]2. Martha Martela Brashears, (d/o Isaac Brashears/Beshears Sr) (she is Martha (and Mary) Matilda on some records) b. 10 Sept 1828, d. 30 March 1878, Hamilton Co, Indiana; m. 20 Oct 1846, Lawrence Co, TN, ***William John Pryor*** (Loose Marriage Records found in County Clerk's Office in

Lawrenceburg, most of which pre-date the marriages in Marriage Book A, 1838-1860; William Pryor and Berry Brashears (s/o John Brashears and Mary Berry) signed the marriage bond). William John Pryor, b. 28 May 1829, Lawrence Co, TN, d. 18 March 1902, Hamilton Co, Indiana, and had ten children.

After her parents died c1830, Martha Martela lived with her uncle, Jacob Brashear. When Jacob's wife, Lucy, died in 1834, Martha was sent by stage coach to Lawrence Co, TN, to live with her grandparents, John and Mary (Berry) Brashears, with whom she stayed until her marriage in 1846. The 1850 census lists William John Pryor and Martha as a neighbor to the John Brashear family. The 1860 census lists Mary Brashear [grandmother] living with William and Martha.

George Simmons, 39 North Ritter Ave, Indianapolis, IN 46219-5708, found the following information in the Indiana State Archives: William Pryor was in 3rd TN Inf, Co K, and was captured at Fort Donaldson in Feb 1862. He was imprisoned at Camp Morton, Indianapolis, until the prisoner exchange at Vicksburg, MS in Nov 1862. He was reassigned to the 48th TN Inf, Co G. He was captured Nov 16 1863 at Lawrenceberg, TN. He was sent to Camp Morton, Indianapolis, IN, and was released March 24, 1865, when he joined the Union Army (for service against the Indians in the west). Some time between his capture in 1863 and his release in 1865, Martha and the children relocated from Tenn to Indianapolis.

The family moved to Noblesville, Hamilton Co, IN and remained there till their deaths; William, d. 18 March 1902 and Martha, 30 March 1878.

Family of Martha Martela Brashears and William John Pryor (info from Ann McColley, 7901 W. Clearwater, #170, Kennewick, WA, 99336; Lawrence Co Archives, via George Simmons; Virgene Scolnik <VandA121@aol.com>).

[V6]273. [10]1. Mary Disa Pryor, b. 17 Aug 1848, Lawrence Co, TN. The 1850 and 60 census doesn't show a Mary. They show a Nancy D. Pryor, b. 1848. Was Mary a nickname? However, Virgene Scolnik assures us Mary Disa Pryor did exist. She m. on 6 June 1868, Benjamin Jefferson Davis, b. cNov 1809, after the death on 15 Nov 1867 of his first wife, Lucinda Galloway. Ben and Lucinda were parents of the Nathan Davis who m. Mary Disa's sister, Susannah. Ben Davis and Mary Disa had one child:

[V6]274. [11]1. Benjamin Jefferson Davis Jr, b. c1875, Noblesville, Hamilton Co, IN

[V6]275. [10]2. Susannah Angeline Pryor, b. 31 Dec 1849, Lawrence Co, TN, d. 6 Dec 1876, Hamilton Co, IN; m. Nathan Davis, s/o Benjamin Jefferson Davis, Sr and Lucinda Galloway. After Susannah died, Nathan m.2. Nancy Boyer.

[V6]276. [11]x. Benjamin Johnson Davis; m. Emma Rachel Hendricks

[V6]277. [12]y. Gertrude Davis; m. Joseph Eugene Linsenmann

[V6]278. [13]z. Virgene Linsenmann; m.1. Raymond Stevenson; m.2. Alvin Scolnik.

[V6]279. [10]3. John T. Pryor, b. 14 July 1850, Lawrence Co, TN, d. 27 Feb 1894, Hamilton Co, IN.

[V6]280. [10]4. William Riley Pryor, b. 20 March 1852, Lawrence Co, TN, d. Nov 28 1918, Hamilton Co, Indiana; m. 21 June 1874, Anna Marie Lewis, of New Albany, Floyd Co, IN. William was blinded in a farm accident: wheat chaff got in his eyes and an infection set in. He attended Indiana Blind School, where he met his wife, Anna, who was also blind. George Simmons' g-grandparents.

[V6]281. [11]1. William E. Pryor, b. 1886, d. 1964; m. Alta Keesling

[V6]282. [11]2. George L. Pryor, b. 1889, d. 1925, auto wreck in Arizona. Career Army.

[V6]283. [11]3. Minnie Belle Pryor, b. 1875, d. 1955

[V6]284. [11]4. Martha D. "Mattie" Pryor, b. 1877, d. 1958; m. Roy Lanham

[V6]285. [11]5. Roseanna Pryor, b. 1880, d. May 1970; m. Elmer Glaze, who d. c1905, construction worker, fell off building. Roseanna never remarried.

[V6]286. [11]6. Ora Pearlie "Pearl" Pryor, b. 1883, d. 1957; m.

Noah Matt Simmons

[V6]287. [11]7. Lewis Benjamin "Dick" Pryor, b. 2 May 1896, d. June 1961; m. Iva Irene Hiatt; had a daughter, Ann McColley. One interesting note, Dick was the last of the kids to pass on; no one living knew Dick's name was Lewis Benjamin until he died and Ann discovered some old records. Their children:

[V6]288. [12]1. Noah Lewis Pryor, m. Anna Marie Pressel; ch: Steven Noah and Richard Lewis Pryor

[V6]289. [12]2. George Paul Pryor (George's dad); m. Mary Jane Fiers

[V6]290. [13]1. George Anthony Simmons, b. 23 Feb 1943; m. Helen Diane Donofrio; no children. "Does a Calico cat and a Coon Hound count for anything?" asks George.

[V6]291. [13]2. Jane Ellen Simmons, b. 27 April 1947

[V6]292. [13]3. Ronald Tobin Simmons;

[V6]293. [14]1. Angel Marie Simmons, b. June 20 1968, m. Richard Todd Lackey, ch: Erica Nichol, Alexa Reid, and Bret Alexander Lackey.

[V6]294. [12]3. Anna Margaret Pryor; m. Thomas Leslie Davis; ch: John Matthew, Mark Simmons, and Keith Edward Davis.

[V6]295. [10]5. Berry B. Pryor, b. 18 Dec 1853, Lawrence Co, TN, d. 22 March 1877, Stringtown, Hamilton Co, Indiana

[V6]296. [10]6. James H. Pryor, b. 16 May 1855, Lawrence Co, TN. Census lists him as James H. Pryor; m. Cora Bragg

[V6]297. [10]7. Sarah Ellen Pryor, b. 13 Feb 1857, Lawrence Co, TN, d. 20 Sept 1942, bur Crownland Cem, Hamilton Co, IN. Census lists her as Sarah R.E. Pryor

[V6]298. [10]8. Joseph Allen "Jackie" Pryor, (twin) b. 26 Sept

1859, Lawrence Co, TN, d. 5 Sept 1933, Westfield, Hamilton Co, IN; m.1. Jonnie Bettie Green; m.2. Lib Denny/Dean

V6299. 109. Martha Lydia Pryor, (twin) b. 26 Sept 1859, Lawrence Co, TN

V6300. 1010. Stephen P. Pryor, b. 26 Sept 1862, Lawrence Co, TN; m. ____ Barron

Isaac Brashears Jr and Sidney Owl

v6272. 93. Isaac Brashears Jr, (s/o Isaac Brashears Sr, b. c1795, and gs/o John Brashear and Mary Berry), b. 1821, TN, (39 in 1860 Pulaski Co, AR, Owen twp); m. ***Sidney Owl***, b. TN, c1827 (33 in 1860 Pulaski, AR), d/o Lewis Owl (Indian). They are on 1849-50 Montgomery Co, AR, Poll Tax list; on 1852-55 Montgomery Co, AR, Poll Tax list; and in the 1860 Census, Owens Twp, Pulaski Co, AR, #154-137.

1860 Census, Pulaski Co, AR, Owen twp:
#154-137: **Isaac Beshears**, 39, b. TN, c1821, farmer, #200, $600; s/o Isaac Brashears, b. c1795, gs/o John Brashears Sr, b. 1767

Siony Beshears,	33, b. TN, c1827, d/o Lewis Owl, Indian
William Beshears,	15, b. MS, c1845
George Beshears,	13, b. MS, c1847
Nancy Beshears,	10, b. MS, c1850
Martha Beshears,	9, b. AR, c1851
Jacob Beshears,	7, b. AR, c1853
Clerinda Beshears,	5, b. AR, c1855
Sallie Beshears,	2, b. AR, c1858

During the Civil War, Isaac Brashears Jr served in Co. I, 11th Arkansas Infantry, Confederate States Army. His name was spelled Bershers; with him was a Robert Bershers. Isaac's sons, William and George, served in the Union Army, the 4th Arkansas Cavalry, U.S. Army.

Family of Isaac Brashears Jr and Sidney Owl:

V6301. 101. **William Boshears**, b. Tishomingo Co, MS, c1845, (15 in 1860 Pulaski Co, AR). William Brashers, age 19, b. c1845, Tishomingo Co, MS, s/o Isaac Brashears, enl 15 Feb 1864, Little Rock, AR, in

Co. H, 4th Arkansas Cavalry, U.S. Army, as a private. (*Arkansas' Damned Yankees--an Index to Union Soldiers in Arkansas Regiments*, p.23)

[V6]302. [10]2. ***George Washington Breshears**, b. Tishomingo Co, MS, c1845-47, (13 in 1860 Pulaski Co, AR), d. 13 Feb 1932, Hot Springs, Garland Co, AR; met ***Anna Burks***, whom he did not marry because they were cousins; m.1. ***Youtha Graves***; m.2. ***Sarah Adams***; m.3. ***Laura Ann Christian McCoy***. During the Civil War, George served the Union Army in the same unit as his brother, William.

[V6]303. [10]3. **Nancy Boshears**, b. MS, c1850, (10 in 1860 Pulaski Co, AR)

[V6]304. [10]4. **Martha Boshears**, b. AR, c1851, (9 in 1860 Pulaski Co, AR)

[V6]305. [10]5. ***Jacob Isaac Breshears**, b. AR, Aug 1853, (7 in 1860 Pulaski Co, AR), bur Rock Springs cem, Garland Co, AR; m. 4 Dec 1890, in Garland Co, AR, ***Bessie M. (or Betty Jane) Minton***

[V6]306. [10]6. **Clerinda Boshears**, b. AR, c1855, (5 in 1860 Pulaski Co, AR)

[V6]307. [10]7. **Sally "Sarah" Boshears**, b. AR, c1857-58, (2 in 1860 Pulaski Co, AR)

George Washington Breshears

[v6]302. [10]2. George Washington Breshears, (s/o Isaac Brashears Jr and Sidney Owl), b. MS, c1847 (13 in 1860, Pulaski Co, AR), d. 13 Feb 1932, Hot Springs, AR. In the records, his surname is often spelled Beshears.

On 28 Feb 1864, George W. Beshears enlisted at Little Rock, AR, in Co. H of the 4th Arkansas Cavalry, U.S. Army, as a private. He gave his age as 18 (he always said later that he lied about his age) and his birthplace as Tishomingo Co, MS. (*Arkansas' Damned Yankees--an Index to Union Soldiers in Arkansas Regiments*, p.24).

After the War, he was living with Eleanor (Parker) Breashears, widow of Matthew Breashears. Matthew had also served in the Union Army during the Civil War. Apparently, in the 1865-1870 period, George Washington Breshears had a child by ***Anna Burks***, a daughter of Nancy H. Brashears, d/o Berry Boshears). Annie later married Andrew J. Riley.

George W. Breshears m.1. 23 Dec 1870, in Montgomery Co, AR, ***Youtha Graves***; m.2. bef 1874, in Garland Co, AR, ***Sarah Adams***, b. AL, d/o John Adams and Salamenty Musgrove; m.3. 10 Sept 1916, in Montgomery Co, AR, ***Laura Ann Christian McCoy*** (data from Gloria Cain <Awrldtrvlr@aol.com>).

In 1982, Gerry Moyle met a Sherman Brashears in Modesto, CA, who said his grandfather or great grandfather had been in the Union Army, enlisted in Little Rock. Gerry mentioned a Geo. W. Brashear from Census and started naming the children from memory; Sherman said one of the children, William S. Brashears, was his father.

Come to find out, this line traces back to White County, TN, where a man and his wife had both died and 2 boys were being indentured to a man who bought the farm, and the girl was being sent to Lawrence Co, TN. Isaac Jr, one of the 2 boys, was supposed to have married Sidney Owl (Indian), d/o Lewis Owl, and moved from White Co, TN, to White Co, AR. ?Hot Springs Census, 1880?

Family of George Washington Breshears and Anna Burks:

[V6]308. [11]1. Elzy Riley (male), b. 1865-70, out of wedlock. In 1880, he is listed as step-son of Andrew J. Riley. He m. ______ and had at least one son:

[V6]309. [12]1. George Riley,

Family of George Washington Breshears and Youtha Graves:

[V6]310. [11]2. **Nancy D. Breshears**, b. c1872, MS, d. c1945, CA; m. 1892, in Montgomery Co, AR, John Terry, s/o Joseph Terry.

[V6]311. [12]1. Loanie Terry,

[V6]312. [12]2. Flossie Terry,

[V6]313. [12]3. Arthur Terry,

[V6]314. [12]4. Floyd Terry, b. Garland Co, AR

Family of George Washington Breshears and Sarah Adams:

[V6]315. [11]3. ***John Sidney Breshears**, b. 2 July 1874, AR, d. 11 July 1964, Hot Springs, AR; m. ***Ellen Smith***

[V6]316. [11]4. **William Mel Breshears**, b. c1877, AR; m.1. ***Mary Etta Merideth*** (4 ch); m.2. ***Mary*** _____ (1 ch)

[V6]317. [12]1. **Meadie Breshears**,

[V6]318. [12]2. **Sherman Breshears**, b. AR, d. CA. Here is the Sherman Brashears that Gerry Moyle met in Modesto, CA, in 1982.

[V6]319. [12]3. **Sherdon Breshears**, b. AR, d. CA

[V6]320. [12]4. **Albert? Breshears**,

[V6]321. [12]5. **Georgie Breshears**, (fem)

[V6]322. [11]5. ***Marion Franklin Breshears**, b. 27 July 1879, AR, d. 27 Feb 1956, Hot Springs, AR; m. 24 June 1918, in Garland Co, AR, ***Seaclia Lucille Christian***,

[V6]323. [11]6. **Samuel Clinton Breshears**, b. 5 June 1889, AR, d. March 1980; m.1. 12 Dec 1911, in Garland Co, AR, ***Donnie Graves*** (mother of the children); m.2. 9 April 1941, in Garland Co, AR, ***Lula Maland***

[V6]324. [12]1. **Euthie Breshears**,

[V6]325. [12]2. **Otis "Bill" Breshears**, b. 14 Aug 1923, d. 15 Dec 1953; m. ***Doris*** _____

[V6]326. [12]3. **Ed Breshears**,

[V6]327. [12]4. **Goldie Breshears**,

[V6]328. [12]5. **Jewell (Gerald) Breshears**,

[V6]329. [12]6. **Olas Breshears**,

[V6]330. [12]7. **Thurman? Breshears**,

[V6]331. [11]7. **Arlillian Breshears**, b. AR, d. as a very young girl.

<u>Family of George Washington Breshears and Laura McCoy</u>:

[V6]332. [11]8. **Charles Breshears,** b. 12 June 1917, Garland Co, AR; m. ***Lola Graves***

[V6]333. [12]1. **Virginia Breshears**, m. _____ ***Goslee***

[V6]334. [12]2. **Fred Breshears**,

[V6]335. [12]3. **George Breshears**,

[V6]336. [12]4. **Marshall Breshears**,

[V6]337. [12]5. **Elaine Breshears**,

[V6]338. [12]6. **Marsha Ann Breshears**,

[V6]339. [12]7. **Jimmie Carroll Breshears**, b. 16 June 1944, d. 13 June 1936

[V6]340. [11]9. **Sylvania Breshears**, b. 20 Oct 1920; m. ***Bert Graves***, b. 15 Feb 1916, d. 28 Jan 1988

[V6]341. [12]1. Bertha Launita Graves, b. 19 Nov 1937

[V6]342. [12]2. Joann Graves, b. 16 Feb 1939, d. 14 March 1939

[V6]343. [12]3. Patsy Naleen Graves, b. 4 March 1941; m. Kenneth Caldwell, Hot Springs, AR

[V6]344. [12]4. Shirley Sue Graves, b. 14 June 1943

[V6]345. [12]5. Jackie Wayne Graves, b. 30 June 1946

[V6]346. [12]6. Beverly Graves, b. 30 Oct 1948

[V6]347. [12]7. Roger Dale Graves, b. 20 June 1952

[V6]348. [12]8. Billy Paul Graves, b. 4 March 1955

[V6]349. [12]9. Ramona Jean Graves, b. 18 Feb 1958

[V6]350. [12]10. Rhonda Gayle Graves, b. 15 Aug 1963

John Sidney Breshears and Ellen Smith

[v6]315. [11]3. John Sidney Breshears, (s/o John Sidney Breshears and Ellen Smith), b. 2 July 1874, AR, d. 11 July 1964, Hot Springs, AR; m. ***Ellen Smith***

[V6]351. [12]1. **George Breshears**,

[V6]352. [12]2. **Frank Breshears**, b. 29 Jan 1916, Garland Co, AR, d. Sept 1980, Hot Springs, AR; m. 4 Oct 1934, in Garland Co, AR, ***Lucille Spears***

[V6]353. [13]1. **Monroe Breshears**; m. ***Audrey Ray***

[V6]354. [14]1. **Mary Breshears**, m. _____ ***Noakes***

[V6]355. [14]2. **James Breshears**,

[V6]356. [14]3. **Jeff Breshears**,

[V6]357. [14]4. **David Breshears**,

[V6]358. [13]2. **Gerald Breshears**,

[V6]359. [14]1. **David Breshears**,

[V6]360. [14]2. **Kenny Breshears**,

[V6]361. [13]3. **Joyce Breshears**, m. ***Lewis Neighbors***

[V6]362. [14]1. Tracy Neighbors,

[V6]363. [14]2. Lashawn Neighbors,

[V6]364. [13]4. **Laverne Breshears**, m. _____ ***Helton***

[V6]365. [14]1. Mark Helton,

[V6]366. [14]2. Tony Helton,

[V6]367. [14]3. Keith Helton,

[V6]368. [14]4. Tim Helton,

[V6]369. [14]5. Kelly Helton,

[V6]370. [13]5. **Ervin Breshears**,
[V6]371. [13]6. **Marlon Breshears**,
[V6]372. [14]1. **Jarrod Breshears**,
[V6]373. [14]2. **Shane Breshears**,
[V6]374. [13]7. **Marilyn Breshears**, m. ____ ***Rostan***
[V6]375. [14]1. Mandy Rostan,
[V6]376. [14]2. Rob Rostan,
[V6]377. [12]3. **Odis Breshears**, b. 1917; m. 4 Oct 1934, in Garland Co, AR, ***Audie Spears***
[V6]378. [13]1. **Geneva Breshears**, b. 30 Oct 1937; m. ***Sam Walker***
[V6]379. [14]1. Karen Walker, b. 9 Jan 1971
[V6]380. [14]2. Regina Walker, b. 17 Jan 1974
[V6]381. [14]3. Kristy Walker, b. 28 Oct 1975
[V6]382. [14]4. Jim Walker, b. 26 April 1977
[V6]383. [13]2. **Olen Vernon Breshears**, b. 17 Jan 1939; m. ***Joann Miller***
[V6]384. [13]3. **Lavada Breshears**, b. 30 April 1941; m. ***Edward Kizer***
[V6]385. [13]4. **Odis Breshears Jr**, b. 5 Jan 1947; m. ***Sylvia Boyette***
[V6]386. [14]1. **Bryan Kirk Breshears**, b. 21 Aug 1968
[V6]387. [14]2. **Rebecca Breshears**, b. 20 April 1971
[V6]388. [12]4. **Preston Monroe Breshears**, b. 18 July 1920, Garland Co, AR, d. 5 May 1962, (drowned in Lake Ouachita, Garland Co, AR); m.1. ***Opal Aileen Cuttler*** (1 ch); m.2. ***Gracie McGill*** (1 ch)
[V6]389. [13]1. **Anita Breshears**,
[V6]390. [13]2. **Jerry Wayne Breshears**, b. 5 April 1949, d. 5 May 1962, Lake Ouachita, Garland Co, AR
[V6]391. [12]5. **Hettie Breshears**, b. 31 Dec 1923
[V6]392. [12]6. **Ruby Breshears**, b. 13 Nov 1926
[V6]393. [12]7. **Vernon Breshears**, b. 3 April 1930
[V6]394. [12]8. **Thurston Breshears**, b. c1934

Marion Franklin Breshears and Lucille Christian

[v6]322. [11]5. Marion Franklin Breshears, (s/o George Washington Breshears and Sarah Adams), b. 27 July 1879, AR, d. 27 Feb 1956, Hot Springs, AR; m. 24 June 1918, in Garland

Co, AR, ***Seaclia Lucille Christian***, d/o C. Christian and Laura McCoy. Gloria Cain: "Seaclia, more commonly known as Lucille, was the 14-year-old daughter of Marion's step-mother. They always said the wagon broke down, they were out together after dark, and Grandma Laura made them marry. They divorced after 15 years." They had four children:

^{V6}395. ^{12}1. ***Fred Raymond Alto Breshears**, b. 24 Dec 1920; m. ***Pauline Grisham***,

^{V6}396. ^{12}2. ***Ernest Carl Breshears**, b. 28 Sept 1922; m.1. ***Lillian O. Trent*** (2 ch); m.2. ***Imogene Johnson*** (2 ch),

^{V6}397. ^{12}3. ***Mamie Esther Pauline Breshears**, b. 12 April 1925; m.1. ***Chester Lee Grisham***,

^{V6}398. ^{12}4. **Lonnie Thurman Breshears**, b. 24 Jan 1932; m.1. ***Estelle Ray***, (2 ch), d/o Willie Ray and Modean _____; m.2. c1984, ***Brenda Luker***

^{V6}399. ^{13}1. **Lonna Maria Breshears**,

^{V6}400. ^{13}2. **Theresa Breshears**,

^{v6}395. ^{12}1. Fred Raymond Alto Breshears, (s/o Marion Franklin Breshears and Lucille Christion), b. 24 Dec 1920, Garland Co, AR; m. 28 Aug 1943, in Garland Co, AR, ***Pauline Grisham***, d/o Thomas Grisham and Ada Howerton.

^{V6}401. ^{13}1. **Elaina Fay Breshears**, b. 13 July 1944, Garland Co, AR; m. ***Ides Evans***

^{V6}402. ^{14}1. Daniel Lee Evans,

^{V6}403. ^{14}2. David Ray Evans,

^{V6}404. ^{13}2. **Farrell Raymond Breshears**, b. 5 Nov 1945, Garland Co, AR; m. ***Glenda Nixon***

^{V6}405. ^{14}1. **Alan Breshears**,

^{V6}406. ^{14}2. **Keith Breshears**,

^{V6}407. ^{14}3. **Paul Breshears**,

^{V6}408. ^{14}4. **Sara Breshears**,

^{V6}409. ^{13}3. **Donald Paul Breshears**, b. 22 Sept 1947, Garland Co, AR; m. ***Jeannie*** _____

^{V6}410. ^{14}1. **Kevin Breshears**,

^{V6}411. ^{14}2. **Andy Breshears**,

^{V6}412. ^{14}3. **Jennifer Breshears**,

^{V6}413. ^{14}4. **Carrie Breshears**,

^{V6}414. ^{14}5. **Stephen Breshears**,

^{V6}415. ^{13}4. **Jerry Stephen Breshears**, b. 20 Feb 1950,

Garland Co, AR; m. ***Nancy*** ____

V[6]416. [14]1. **Chandra Breshears,**

V[6]417. [14]2. **Glenn Breshears**

V[6]418. [14]3. **Michael Breshears**

V[6]419. [14]4. **Terri Lynne Breshears**

V[6]420. [13]5. **Sharon Ruth Breshears**, b. 2 Sept 1952; m. ***Jerry Nixon***

V[6]421. [14]1. Gary Nixon,

V[6]422. [14]2. Linda Nixon,

V[6]423. [14]3. Cindy Nixon,

V[6]424. [13]6. **Martha Louise Breshears**, b. 3 Oct 1954; m. ***Larry Walker***

V[6]425. [14]1. Mindy Walker,

V[6]426. [14]2. Chuck Walker,

V[6]427. [13]7. **Paula Kay Breshears**, b. 22 July 1966, Alma, AR

V[6]396. [12]2. Ernest Carl Breshears, (s/o Marion Franklin Breshears and Lucille Christian), b. 28 Sept 1922; m.1. ***Lillian O. Trent*** (2 ch), d/o Charlie Trent and Myrtle Alexander; m.2. 1946, Hot Springs, AR, ***Imogene Johnson*** (2 ch), b. 23 Sept 1927, d. 26 Oct 1951, bur Nooner Cem, Yell Co, AR, near Perry Co Line, d/o J.Y. Johnson and Cora Cox

V[6]428. [13]1. **Charles Franklin Breshears**, b. 24 Jan 1953, permanently disabled by a childhood illness.

V[6]429. [13]2. **Jacqueline Laverne Breshears**, b. 16 Feb 1959; m. 8 April 1977, Hot Springs, Garland Co, AR, ***Daniel Michael Herring***

V[6]430. [14]1. Aubrey Layne Herring, b. 19 April 1981

V[6]431. [14]2. Whitney Herring, b. 1983

V[6]432. [13]3. **Ernest Carl Breshears Jr**, b. 27 March 1947; m.1. ***Tanya Nelson*** (no ch); m.2. ***June Miller*** (no ch); m.3. ***Elizabeth Murders*** (2 ch), d/o Clyde Murders; m.4. ***Brenda Horn*** (1 ch); m.5. ***Jacqueline Michelle Bass*** (1 ch)

V[6]433. [14]1. **Carl Anthony Breshears**, b. 9 Nov 1972

V[6]434. [14]2. **Ernest Carl Breshears III**, b. 21 Nov 1973

V[6]435. [14]3. **Carla Jean Breshears**, b. 29 Dec 1976

V[6]436. [15]1. **Quincy Breshears**, b. 1996

V[6]437. [14]4. **Austin Wayne Breshears**, b. 30 June 1994

[V6]438. [13]4. **Tony Michael Breshears**, b. 9 Aug 1951; m. 1975, ***Vicki Lynda Mooneyham***
[V6]439. [14]1. **Vanessa Laverne Breshears**, b. 1 Jan 1976
[V6]440. [15]1. Sydney Nicole Krusta, b. 8 June 1998

[V6]397. [12]3. Mamie Esther Pauline Breshears, (d/o Marion Franklin Breshears and Lucille Christian), b. 12 April 1925, Hot Springs, AR; m.1. 27 Aug 1943, Hot Springs, AR, ***Chester Lee Grisham***, s/o Thomas Grisham and Ada Howerton; m.2. 24 Jan 1948, Hot Springs, AR, ***Preston Charles Jones***

[V6]441. [13]1. Gloria Ann (Grisham) Jones, b. 23 Dec 1944, Hot Spring, AR; m. 16 Oct 1964, in Hot Springs, Garland Co, AR, ***Carmon Cain***
[V6]442. [14]1. Donna Ann Cain, b. 18 Feb 1966, Hot Springs, AR; m. 5 Sept 1987, in Sherwood, AR, Paul Don Richardson, s/o Pearl Richardson and Jane _____
[V6]443. [15]1. Kelsey Marie Richardson, b. 17 Nov 1991, Little Rock, AR
[V6]444. [15]2. Preston Drew Richardson, b. 9 March 1995, Murphreesboro, TN
[V6]445. [15]3. Logan Daniel Richardson, b. 10 Jan 1999, Little Rock, AR
[V6]446. [14]2. Paula Carol Cain, b. 18 Feb 1970; m. 4 April 1993, in Hot Springs, AR, Audon Barron
[V6]447. [15]1. Chase Alexander Barron, b. 7 Dec 1995
[V6]448. [13]2. Onia Sue Jones, b. 12 Jan 1950; m. 20 Dec 1967, Garland Co, AR, Ronnie J.R. Vaughn, s/o Jesse Vaughn and Eula Shelton
[V6]449. [14]1. Ronnie Scott Vaughn, b. 13 Feb 1969; m.1. Michelle Lawon Brooks (3 ch); m.2. April ____ (1 ch)
[V6]450. [15]1. Scott Preston Vaughn, b. 1988
[V6]451. [15]2. Jessica Desiree Vaughn, b. 1989
[V6]452. [15]3. Chad Alexander Vaughn, b. 1991
[V6]453. [15]4. Anthony Michael Vaughn, b. 1996
[V6]454. [14]2. Todd Adam Vaughn, b. 3 Feb 1971; m. Kimberly Roberts
[V6]455. [15]1. Hunter Daniel Vaughn, b. 1998

[V6]456. [14]3. Holly Sue Vaughn, b. 20 Dec 1976
[V6]457. [13]3. John Paul Jones, b. 16 Sept 1952; m. in CA, Rosita Fernandez Gonzales
[V6]458. [14]1. Michelle Jones, b. 1976
[V6]459. [14]2. Sarah Jones, b. c1978
[V6]460. [14]3. Phillip Preston Jones, b. c1980
[V6]461. [14]4. James Jones, b. c1984
[V6]462. [13]4. Brad Wayne Jones, b. 9 May 1954; m. in Hot Springs, Garland Co, AR, Deborah Palmer
[V6]463. [14]1. Heather Jones, b. 1976; m. Jason Ripley
[V6]464. [15]1. Ryan Ripley, b. c1993
[V6]465. [15]2. Skye Preston Lee Ripley, b. 1995
[V6]466. [14]2. Robin Jones, b. 1979

Jacob Isaac Breshears and Bessie M. Minton

[v6]272. [10]5. Jacob Isaac Breshears, (s/o Isaac Brashears Jr and Sidney Owl), b. AR, Aug 1853, (7 in 1860 Pulaski Co, AR), bur Rock Springs cem, Garland Co, AR; m. 4 Dec 1890, in Garland Co, AR, ***Bessie M. (or Bettie Jane) Minton***, b. 12 June 1872, Rome, GA, d. 17 Oct 1945, Garland Co, AR (data from Sharon Minton Hill (shill@cswnet.com> via Gloria Cain.) They had three children:

[V6]467. [11]1. ***Willie Andrew Breshears**, b. 22 Nov 1895; m. ***Nancie Jane Johnson***,
[V6]468. [11]2. ***Mattie Victoria Breshears**, b. 31 May 1898; m. ***William Wheeler Brogan***,
[V6]469. [11]3. ***Carl Alonzo Breshears**, b. 19 May 1902; m. ***Mary Jane McCoy***,

[v6]467. [11]1. Willie Andrew Breshears, (s/o Jacob Isaac Breshears and Bessie M. Minton), b. 22 Nov 1895 in Garland Co, AR, d. 18 Dec 1966 in Garland Co, AR; m. ***Nancie Jane Johnson***, b. 15 May 1895, d. 15 Dec 1977

[V6]470. [12]1. **Ruby Breshears**, d. 25 Dec 1936 in Phoenix, AZ; m. ***Otis Ray***
[V6]471. [13]1. Bonnie Sue Ray, b. 22 Oct 1935

[V6]472. [12]2. **Emma Jean Breshears**, d. Dec 1992; m. ***Ralph Shaw***, b. 1933

[V6]473. [13]1. Teresa Lynn Shaw

[V6]474. [13]2. Cathy Renee Shaw

[V6]475. [12]3. **Myrtle Breshears**, b. 2 April 1912, d. 26 Aug 1988; m. ***Robert Odie Bates***, b. 6 Sept 1910, d. 14 Jan 1973

[V6]476. [13]1. Bobby Joe Bates, b. 14 May 1933; m. Julia Gene Bryant, b. 6 Aug 1935

[V6]477. [14]1. Alan Clayton Bates, b. 5 Feb 1959 in Tulsa, OK, d. 5 Feb 1959 in Tulsa, OK

[V6]478. [14]2. Beverly Carol Bates, b. 24 Nov 1961; m. Richard John Esselbach III

[V6]479. [13]2. Orville Loyd Bates, b. 22 Feb 1938

[V6]480. [12]4. **Auga Argus Breshears**, b. 28 July 1916 in AR, d. 21 Sept 1957 in CA; m. ***Verna Mae Minton***, b. 29 Nov 1923 in Garland Co, AR

[V6]481. [13]1. **Carolyn Breshears**; m. ***James Willington***

[V6]482. [13]2. **Larry Breshears**

[V6]483. [13]3. **Sammy Argus Breshears**, b. 28 Dec 1946 in Mt. Pine, Garland Co, AR; m.1. ***Siglinda Schidt***, b. in Ansbouch, Germany; m.2. ***Marlene Wuyerski***, b. in Belair, Maryland; m. ***Sandra Calbert***, b. in Idabell, OK; m. ***Vicki Lynn Coony***, b. 4 Jan 1950 (3 ch); m.5. ***Carol Ann Baker***, b. Dec 4

[V6]484. [14]1. **Tonya Louise Breshears**, b. in Ukiah, CA

[V6]485. [14]2. **Larry William Breshears**, b. 16 Aug 1974 in Oroville, CA

[V6]486. [14]3. **Mark Anthony Breshears**, b. 15 April 1977 in Ft. Bragg, CA

[V6]487. [12]5. **Velma Breshears**, b. 2 May 1920; m. ***Charles C. Hubble***, b. 23 Jan 1913 in Kinta, OK, d. 14 June 1985

[V6]488. [13]1. Freda May Hubble, b. 30 May 1937, d. 17 May 1938

[V6]489. [13]2. Billy Ray Hubble, b. 10 March 1939; m. Sharon Cavognars

[V6]490. [14]1. Richard Charles Hubble, b. 15 Aug 1954

in Damron Hospital, Stockton, CA; m. Kim Weulkins

V6491. [14]2. Deniece Hubble, b. 1 Aug 1961; m. Edmon Castler

V6492. [15]1. Greg Castler, b. 9 Jan 1983

V6493. [15]2. Amanda Castler, b. 9 May 1984

V6494. [13]3. Pauline Louise Hubble, b. 17 Oct 1951; m.1. Dennis Ester; m.2. Joe Luztr

V6495. [12]6. **Etta A. Breshears**, b. 2 Dec 1923 in Garland Co, AR, d. 7 July 1982; m. ***Gilbert Herman Meeks***, b. 4 April 1910 in AR, d. 30 Sept 1978

V6496. [13]1. Willie Mae Meeks, b. 4 April 1940; m. L.B. Tapp, b. 12 Feb 1937 in Molalia, Oregon

V6497. [13]2. Bonnie Fay Meeks, b. 4 Dec 1941 in Hot Springs, Garland Co, AR; m.1. James David Sawyer; m.2. Elvis Lee Warren, d. 7 July 1974

V6498. [13]3. Harold Dean Meeks, b. 29 Feb 1944; m. Eleaner Kay Jackson, b. 11 Jan 1946

V6499. [13]4. Timothy Otis Meeks, b. 27 March 1952 in Stockton, CA

V6500. [13]5. Mack Ray Meeks, b. 5 June 1956 in Ukiah, CA

V6501. [12]7. **Lessie Breshears**, (twin), b. 3 Sept 1925; m.1. ***Otha Faulkner***; m.2. ***Hubert Bright, Jr***

V6502. [13]1. Shirley Bright

V6503. [13]2. Benny Bright

V6504. [12]8. **Bessie Breshears**, (twin), b. 3 Sept 1925; m. ***Cecil Bert Minton***, b. 28 May 1918 in Avant, Garland Co, AR

V6505. [12]9. **Otas Breshears**, b. 22 June 1929; m. ***Ruby Franklin***

V6506. [13]1. **Annette Breshears**

V6507. [13]2. **Jeanette Breshears**

V6468. [11]2. Mattie Victoria Breshears, (d/o Jacob Isaac Breshears and Bessie M. Minton), b. 31 May 1898 in Hot Springs, Garland Co, AR, d. April 1983 in Tyro, AR; m. ***William Wheeler Brogan***, b. 1 March 1881 in Brigsville, AR

[V6]508. [12]1. Willadean Brogan, b. 26 Nov 1921 in Pangburn, Cleburne Co, AR; m.1. Oswald Guinn; m.2. L.C. Henslee

[V6]509. [13]1. Eudelle Guinn

[V6]510. [13]2. Mattie Lee Henslee

[V6]511. [13]3. Linda Henslee

[V6]512. [13]4. Marvin Edward Henslee

[V6]513. [12]2. Sybil Brogan, b. 25 March 1925 in Hot Springs, Garland Co, AR; m.1. Arvil Danley; m.2. William Rogers

[V6]514. [13]1. Barbara Danley

[V6]515. [13]2. Roger Danley

[V6]516. [12]3. Bert Brogan, b. 9 May 1927 in Little Ax, OK, d. 1983 in Tyro, AR; m. Mary Elizabeth Wilkerson

[V6]517. [13]1. Sherman Wayne Brogan

[V6]518. [12]4. Ernestine Brogan, b. 15 July 1932 in Appleton, Pope Co, AR; m.1. Raymond Rainwater; m.2. Bill Deal

[V6]519. [13]1. Buddy Rainwater

[V6]520. [13]2. Rebecca Rainwater

[V6]521. [13]3. Donald Ray Rainwater

[V6]522. [13]4. Debbie Rainwater

[V6]523. [12]5. Sherman Colan Brogan, b. 6 May 1933 in Appleton, Pope Co, AR; m. Evelyn Othela Mabry

[V6]524. [13]1. Bobby Mark Brogan

[V6]525. [13]2. Sabrina Lynn Brogan

[V6]526. [13]3. Tamara Lovis Brogan

[V6]527. [12]6. Kenneth Ray Brogan, b. 10 April 1935 in Lost Corner, Benton Co, AR; m. Wanda Sue

[V6]528. [13]1. Michael Brogan

[V6]529. [13]2. Gary Brogan

[V6]530. [12]7. Dallas Mae Brogan, b. 12 Aug 1937 in Dansby, Lee Co, AR, d. 1982; m.1. Fidel Pena; m.2. D.L. McClain

[V6]531. [13]1. Paul Pena

[V6]532. [13]2. William McClain, b. bef. 1921, d. 1942 in WW II; m. Rachel ____

^{V6}**469.** ^{11}**3. Carl Alonzo Breshears**, (s/o Jacob Isaac Breshears and Bessie M. Minton), b. 19 May 1902 in Garland Co, AR, d. 17 Nov 1983 in Hot Springs, Garland Co, AR; m. ***Mary Jane McCoy***, b. 13 June 1906 in Garland Co, AR, d. 29 March 1983 in Hot Springs, Garland Co, AR

^{V6}533. ^{12}1. **Leona Breshears**, b. 13 June 1925; m. ***Ira McTragite***

^{V6}534. ^{13}1. Lois McTragite

^{V6}535. ^{13}2. Laverne McTragite

^{V6}536. ^{13}3. Shirley McTragite

^{V6}537. ^{13}4. Barbra McTragite

^{V6}538. ^{12}2. **Manuel Alonzo Breshears**, b. 15 March 1927; m. ***Rachel Fay White***

^{V6}539. ^{13}1. **Brenda Breshears**; m.1. ***Scottie Garner***; m.2. _____ ***Miller***

^{V6}540. ^{14}1. Stoney Garner

^{V6}541. ^{14}2. Scooter Garner

^{V6}542. ^{14}3. Robbie Miller

^{V6}543. ^{13}2. **Rita Fay Breshears**; m. _____ ***Nolen***

^{V6}544. ^{13}3. **Carol Breshears**; m. _____ ***Eichler***

^{V6}545. ^{14}1. Don Carol Breshears Eichler

^{V6}546. ^{13}4. **Tommy Breshears**

^{V6}547. ^{13}5. **Robbie Breshears**

^{V6}548. ^{13}6. **Linda Breshears**; m. _____ ***Screnwedge***

^{V6}549. ^{13}7. **Tina Breshears**; m. _____ ***Owen***

^{V6}550. ^{12}3. **Juanita Emagene Breshears**, b. 16 March 1930; m. ***Charles L. Dewey Thornton***, d. 26 Nov 1967

^{V6}551. ^{13}1. Linda Sue Thornton, b. 2 May 1950; m.1. Donnie Green; m.2. Ray Raines

^{V6}552. ^{14}1. Darrell Green, b. 17 Feb 1967 in Hot Springs, Garland Co, AR; m. Tiffney Wallace

^{V6}553. ^{15}1. Duston Green

^{V6}554. ^{15}2. Buddy Green

^{V6}555. ^{14}2. Buddy Green, b. 14 Aug 1969 in Hot Springs, Garland Co, AR

^{V6}556. ^{13}2. Billy Ray Thornton, b. 6 Oct 1951; m. Mina Sonders

^{V6}557. ^{14}1. Veronica Thornton, b. 14 Feb 1976 in Denver, Colorado

[V6]558. [14]2. Billie Thornton, b. 18 July 1990
[V6]559. [13]3. Judy Gail Thornton, b. 9 Nov 1954; m. Steven H. Rascoe, b. 1955
[V6]560. [13]4. Terry Lynn Thornton, b. 5 Nov 1959; m.1. Renee Darling (3 ch); m.2. Tammie ____ (3 ch)
[V6]561. [14]1. Brandon Thornton
[V6]562. [14]2. Zackrie Thornton
[V6]563. [14]3. Jada Lynn Thornton, b. 13 Feb 1980
[V6]564. [14]4. Cody Thornton
[V6]565. [14]5. Steven Thornton
[V6]566. [14]6. Chad Thornton
[V6]567. [13]5. Diane Denice Thornton, b. 24 Jan 1964; m.1. Johnnie Bradshaw; m.2. Thomas B. Brock
[V6]568. [14]1. Buckley Bradshaw
[V6]569. [14]2. Matthew Bradshaw
[V6]570. [14]3. John Bradshaw
[V6]571. [12]4. **Bernice Lola Breshears**, b. 30 May 1932, d. 25 June 1993 in Hot Springs, Garland Co, AR; m. ***Stanley Cook***
[V6]572. [13]1. Sheila Cook; m. _____ Pennington
[V6]573. [13]2. Quinton Cook; m. Jan Chapman
[V6]574. [13]3. Carolyn Cook; m. _____ Strange
[V6]575. [13]4. Carol Cook
[V6]576. [13]5. Carla Cook
[V6]577. [13]6. Jeff Cook
[V6]578. [12]5. **Charles Harold Breshears**, b. 1 Jan 1934 in AR; m.1. ***Peggy Allen*** (2 ch); m.2. ***Bessie Velma Kern*** (3 ch)
[V6]579. [13]1. **Ronald Breshears**
[V6]580. [13]2. **Roy Charles Breshears**, b. 11 Nov 1975 in McGehee, Desha Co, AR
[V6]581. [13]3. **Shirley Breshears**
[V6]582. [13]4. **Patricia Jane Breshears**, b. 16 Aug 1957 in Marianna, Lee Co, AR; m. ***Rerall William Johnson***
[V6]583. [14]1. William Grover Johnson, b. 9 Sept 1977 in Hot Springs, Garland Co, AR
[V6]584. [14]2. Robert Wesley Johnson, b. 26 Sept 1978 in Hot Springs, Garland Co, AR

V6585. [13]5. **Kathy Bernice Breshears**, b. 24 June 1959; m.1. ***Eddie Figby***; m.2. ***Scott*** ____

V6586. [12]6. **William J. Breshears**, b. 10 March 1935

V6587. [12]7. **Carl Raymond Breshears**, (twin), b. 18 April 1940; m. ***Gladys Yarber***

V6588. [13]1. **Raymond Dale Breshears**, b. 07 Nov 1964

V6589. [12]8. **Carol Breshears**, (twin), b. 18 April 1940, d. 31 Aug 1940

6. JACOB BRASHEARS/BOSHEARS Sr

[v6]**200.** [8]**2. Jacob Beshears/Boshears/Brashears Sr**, (s/o John Brashears Sr and Mary Berry), b. 1800, also lived in White County, Tennessee. He married at the age of 17, but his wife, ***?Lucy*** _____, died c1834, and he contracted with a neighbor to keep his children, presumably while he relocated. His brother, Isaac, had also died, leaving 2 boys and a girl, whom Jacob was supposed to take care of. Jacob left Isaac's sons, Isaac Jr and George, and his own daughters with a man in White Co, TN, while he relocated. He remarried and retrieved his daughters and nephews before the 1840 Census of Lawrence Co, TN. George and Isaac, orphans of Jacob's brother, Isaac, seem to have been in Tishomingo Co, MS, with him.

> Memorandum of a contract made and entered into between Hartwell Scruggs of the one part and Jacob Beshears of the other part, both of the County of White and State of Tennessee; the said Beshears sells to the said Scruggs one bay filly, one blind Mare, two beds and furniture, and some other household and kitchen furniture, all that the said Beshears had, and all the farming tools that he had at this time and what corn he has now in the crib and one cow and calf and two heifers. For this property, the said Scruggs binds himself to keep and support six children, two boys George and Isaac Beshears and four daughters, Lucy, Martha, Elizabeth, and Mary Beshears. The said Scruggs to keep the four girls until they become free or married. If the said Beshears takes a notion to marry he then takes the two boys George and Isaac Beshears if he wants them. As witness our hands and seals... (White Co, TN, Court Minutes for 19 Dec 1834; thanks to Faye Breshears for a xerox copy; for some reason, we did not get the list of witnesses.)

After making this deal, says Norman Parks, Jacob and his two older sons, Thomas J, age 17, and Henry, age 10, removed to Lawrence Co, TN. The two sons rode one horse, double. In Lawrence Co, Jacob m.2. a 14-year-old girl, ***Gillia*** _____, in 1840. (She's 37 in 1850; 34 in 1860)

Jacob Brashers is on the 1836 Tax List of Lawrence Co, TN, no acres mentioned; District #5 (south-central section of the county)

1840 Census of Lawrence Co, TN: p.121: Jacob Brashers (000111-11211) 30-40, b. 1800-1810. He apparently has his daughters back, as well as a new one. His son, Thomas J. and his wife, may be in the household also.

About 1840-41, Jacob and Gillia moved to Tishomingo Co, MS (1850 Census #498, p. 37, between T.J. Brashers and Henry Brashers), where two(?) more children were born, Melinda and Jacob Jr. In the fall of 1855, Jacob moved to Obion Co, TN (1860 Census, p.178, Dist #4) and lived on Madrid Bend of the Mississippi River, now in Lake County. He died there in 1864.

Family of Jacob Beshears Sr and his first wife, ?Lucy:

V6640. 91. ***Thomas Jefferson Brashers**, b. c1817 (33 in 1850); d. 1877; m.1. ***Nancy ?Law***; m.2. ***Mrs. Sarah (Brashears) Gibson***, d/o Middleton Brashears the Younger, of Stoddard Co, MO, and widow of John Gibson. Seven children, see below.

V6641. 92. ***Henry Boshears**, b. c1822 (28 in 1850), d. 1865; m. 24 Aug 1840, in Lawrence Co, TN, ***Tabitha Stewart***, b. c1826, TN; Eleven children, see below.

V6642. 93. **Lucinda Beshears**,

V6643. 94. **Elizabeth "Betts" Beshears**, b. c1830 (20 in 1850), d. 1878; m. ***Wiley Smith***

V6644. 101. Will Smith, b. c1858

V6645. 102. Martha Smith, b. c1861

V6646. 103. Nancy Smith, b. c1864; m. _____ Russell

V6647. 11x. Pearl Russell; m. _____ Kelty

V6648. 104. Sally Smith, b. c1865

V6649. 105. John Smith, b. c1868

V6650. 95. **Martha "Marth" Beshears**, b. c1831 (19 in 1850); m. 1856, ***James McCue***

[V6]651. [10]1. John McCue,
[V6]652. [10]2. Wash McCue,
[V6]653. [10]3. Bill McCue,
[V6]654. [10]4. Mary McCue,
[V6]655. [10]5. Mattie "Matt" McCue, b. c1871; m. ____ Everett
[V6]656. [11]x. Iona May Everett
[V6]657. [10]6. Sarah McCue,
[V6]658. [9]6. **Mary Mathena Brashears**, b. c1833, KY; lived with grandparents, John and Mary Brashears, of Lawrence Co, TN, in 1850.

Family of Jacob Beshears and his second wife, Gillia:
[V6]659. [9]7. **Mary Ann Beshears**, b. c1838 (12 in 1850)
[V6]660. [9]8. ***Jacob Beshears Jr**. b. TN c1840 (10 in 1850); b. MS 1842 acc. Norman Parks
[V6]661. [9]9. **Melinda Beshears**, b. 1841 (9 in 1850, Census says "Adaline")

Thomas Jefferson Brashers and Nancy Law/ Sarah Brashears

[V6]640. [9]1. **Thomas Jefferson Brashers**, (s/o Jacob Beshears Sr), b. c1817, TN; m.1. ***Nancy ?Law***, b. 1808-13, SC/VA (in H/H in 1860: Jane Law, age 92, probably Nancy's mother; in H/H 1870: Jane P. Law, age 103). Nancy d. 1860-68, Obion Co, TN or Randolph Co, AR; Thomas Jefferson Brashers m.2. 1 Nov 1868, Randolph Co, AR, ***Mrs. Sarah (Brashears) Gibson*** (d/o Middleton Brashears the Younger, of Stoddard Co, MO, and widow of John Gibson). Thomas and Nancy lived in Alabama during the 40's when their children were born, then alongside Jacob (next door in both 1850 and 1860). FGS by Jerri Kennedy, based on 1850 Tishomingo MS (#497, p.37); 1860 Obion TN (p.177, Dist #4); 1870 Randolph AR (#245, Current River Twp). Thomas J. Brashers, d. c1877, says Norman Parks. In 1850, his sister, **Martha Brasher**, b. c1831 (19 in 1850, Tishomingo Co, MS) was in his household
Children of Thomas J. Brashers and his first wife, Nancy ?Law:
[V6]662. [10]1. **Nancy Brasher**, b. c1838-9, AL (11 in 1850)
[V6]663. [10]2. **Alfred/Alford Brasher**, b. c1840, AL (10 in 1850);

m. ***Susan C.*** ______, b. c1842, TN; 1860 Obion Co, TN & 1870 Randolph Co, AR: Alfred Boshears, 32, b. 1838, MS; Susan, 28, b. 1842, TN, w/ three children.

[V6]664. [11]1. **Julia Boshears**, b. 1860, TN

[V6]665. [11]2. **Jennie Boshears**, b. 1863, TN

[V6]666. [11]3. **Nancy Boshears**, b. 1867, TN

[V6]667. [10]3. **Elijah Brasher**, b. c1843, AL (7 in 1850); Norman Parks has "Elizabeth Brasher," but my reading of the original census is pretty clear.

[V6]668. [10]4. **William H. Brasher**, b. c1846, AL (4 in 1850); may have been with his ?uncle Peter Brasher, 1860, McNairy Co, TN; may have made home in Clay Co, AR after 1870; may have died in Civil War, says Norman

[V6]669. [10]5. **Sarah E. Brasher**, b. c1847 (3 in 1850), Tishomingo Co, MS

[V6]670. [10]6. **Tabitha Brasher**, b. c1850 (not in 1850 census), Tishomingo Co, MS

Child of Thomas Jefferson Brashers and his second wife, Mrs Sarah Gibson:

[V6]671. [10]7. **Martha Brashers**, b. c1870, AR (age 3/12 in 1870, Randolph Co, AR)

Thomas J. Brashers settled with his father in Alabama in 1840, moved with his father, Jacob, to Obion Co, TN, in 1855. All of Jacob's children (except Lucinda, Mrs. Nathan Pryor, who stayed in Lawrence) moved with him to Obion Co, TN. In 1867, Thomas J. Brashers, his son, Alfred Brashers, and all of the children of Thomas's brother, Henry Brashers, moved to Randolph Co, AR.

1870 Census, Randolph Co, AR, #245, Current River Twp:

Thomas Beshears,	56, b. TN
Sarah	46, wife, should be 36, if same as in 1850 Stoddard MO
Martin J. Gibson,	13, "step-son", b. TN
Wm. Gibson	7, "step-son" b. AR
Jane P. Law	103, (no rel given, but prob mo/o his first wife) b. TN
Martha Beshears	3/12, "dau" b. AR

(H/H #246, next door: Thomas J. Gibson, 21, b. TN, and Mary Gibson, 27, b. TN)

Henry Boshears
and Tabitha Stewart

^{v6}641. ^{9}2. **Henry Brashears/Boshiers/Boshears**, (s/o Jacob Beshears, Sr), b. c1822, TN; d. 1865, Obion Co, TN; m. 24 Aug 1840, in Lawrence Co, TN, ***Tabitha Stewart***, b. c1826, TN, d. 1882 Clay Co, AR (she's called "Faithy" in 1850 Census, Tishomingo MS, #499, p.37; next door to Jacob and T.J.). Tabitha was d/o William Pemberton Stewart and Martha Green... per "Rosebud" <lynrose@lightspeed.net>. We believe she m.2. William C. Greyston (see 1870 Randolph, AR). FGS by Jerri Kennedy, based on 1850 Tishomingo, MS; 1860 Obion, TN; 1870 Randolph, AR; Marr. rec. Lawrence Co, TN and Butler Co, MO; Goodspeed "History of Northeastern Arkansas" 1890 (Goodspeed reports 14 ch; we know of only 11; grandchildren added by Norman Parks):

Family of Henry Boshears and Tabitha Stewart:

^{V6}672. ^{10}1. **Rebecca J. Boshears**, b. c1842, MS (8 in 1850); never married

^{V6}673. ^{10}2. **Bazzle Boshears**, b. c1844, MS (6 in 1850); no record after 1860

^{V6}674. ^{10}3. **Sarah Boshears**, b. c1846, MS (4 in 1850); no record after 1860

^{V6}675. ^{10}4. **Martha P. Boshears**, b. c1848, MS (2 in 1850); no record after 1860

^{V6}676. ^{10}5. ***Zacheriah Taylor Boshears**, b. c1849, MS (1 in 1850); moved to Texas and had large family.

^{V6}677. ^{10}6. ***Henry Clay Boshears**, b. 25 Jan 1850, Corinth, MS; m. 1869, in Maynardsville, Clay Co, AR, ***Margaret Maynard***, b. 22 Dec 1849, Clay Co, AR

^{V6}678. ^{10}7. **Ishmael Boshears**, b. c1852 (29 in 1880, Clay Co, AR, p.24a, #163-166), MS; m. ***Lucinda*** _____, b. c1850, AR (30 in 1880). They are #163-166 in 1880, Clay Co, AR, p.24a)

^{V6}679. ^{11}1. **Frances P. Boshears**, b. 1870 (10 in 1880)

^{V6}680. ^{11}2. **James A. Boshears**, b. 1874 (6 in 1880)

^{V6}681. ^{11}3. **Harriett M. Boshears**, b. Dec 1879 (per 1880)

^{V6}682. ^{11}4. **Henry A. Boshears**, b. 1881

^{V6}683. ^{11}5. **Marie? Boshears**, b. 1883

[V6]684. [10]8. **Thomas/Cyrus/Josiah Boshears**, b. c1854, Tishomingo Co, MS ("Josiah", 25 in 1880, Clay Co, AR, #104-105); m. ***Hetty A. ?Cole***, b. c1857 (23 in 1880). In 1880, Jane Cole, sister-in-law, 25, is in Josiah's h/h.

[V6]685. [11]1. **Margaret Boshears**, b. 1878 (2 in 1880)

[V6]686. [11]2. **James Henry Boshears**, b. 1880 (1 in 1880)

[V6]687. [11]3. **Eugene Boshears**, b. 1881

[V6]688. [11]4. **Kizzie Boshears**, b. 1883

[V6]689. [11]5. **Charley Boshears**, b. 1890

[V6]690. [11]6. **Ella Boshears**, b. 1893

[V6]691. [11]7. **Ross Boshears**, b. 1895

[V6]692. [10]9. ***James A. Boshears**, b. c1856, Obion Co, TN; m. 18 Aug 1878, Butler Co, MO, ***Lucy Sysco***, b. c1862 (18 in 1880), KY.

[V6]693. [10]10. **Larsen "Larry" A. Boshears**, b. c1858, TN; m.1. 15 April 1877, Butler Co, MO, ***Mrs. Amanda Williams***; m.2. 1880, ***Jennie Montgomery***, d/o Daniel and Polly Montgomery. Jennie d. 1885, Clay Co, AR. Norman Parks gives children of Larry Boshears, b. 1859, as Birdell Boshears, b. 1912, and Cabitha Boshears, b. 1915. This looks just a generation too late.

[V6]694. [10]11. **Nancy M. E. Boshears**, b. c1861, TN; m. _____ ***Blanton***

[V6]695. [11]1. Frank Blanton,

[V6]696. [11]2. Birdell Blanton,

Zachary Taylor Boshears

[v6]676. [10]5. **Zachary Taylor Boshears**, (s/o Henry Boshears and Tabitha Stewart), b. 1849, settled 30 miles east of Dallas and built up a large land holding, several thousand acres that are still in the family, says Norman Parks; m.1. ***Nancy M. George***, b. c1835 (35 in 1870), d/o _____ George and Elizabeth _____. Elizabeth George, b. 15 May 1810, d. 10 Dec 1885, bur beside grandson, William G. Boshars, in New Salem Cem, Kaufman Co, TX, where the double tombstone says Nancy was mother of William and daughter of Elizabeth. Nancy and Taylor got a divorce, the first known divorce in the family. Taylor Boshears, 20, and first wife Nancy, 35, with first child, William G., are in the 1870 Census, McNairy Co, TN. Nancy and William's names are spelled "Boshars" on the tombstone.

Taylor had six wives, did banking, shipped huge loads of cattle to St. Louis, sometimes riding personally with the train-load shipments.

Children of Zachary Taylor Boshears:

[V6]697. [11]1. **William G. Boshars**, b. 16 Sept 1866 (3 in 1870, McNairy Co, TN), d. 15 Sept 1886, age 20, minus one day; s/o the first wife, Nancy M. George.
[V6]698. [11]2. **Pearl Boshears**, b. 1887; probably d/o the second wife. Note separation of birth dates of children.
[V6]699. [11]3. **Walter Boshears**, b. 1893
[V6]700. [11]4. **Irwin Boshears**, b. 1895
[V6]701. [11]5. **Walton Boshears**, b. 1897
[V6]702. [11]6. **Ethel Boshears**, b. 1899
[V6]703. [11]7. **T.B. Boshears**, b. 1903
[V6]704. [11]8. **Georgia Boshears**, b. 1904
[V6]705. [11]9. **Birdell Boshears**, b. 1905
[V6]706. [11]10. **H.B. Boshears**, b. 1907
[V6]707. [11]11. **Alice Boshears**, b. 1908
[V6]708. [11]12. **Taylor Boshears Jr**, b. 1910
[V6]709. [11]13. **Larry Boshears**, b. 1911
[V6]710. [11]14. **T.B. Boshears, II**, b. 1912
[V6]711. [11]15. **Golda Boshears**, b. 1915, twin
[V6]712. [11]16. **Gelia Boshears**, b. 1915, twin

Henry Clay Boshears and Margaret Maynard

[v6]677. [10]6. **Henry Clay Boshears**, (s/o Henry Boshears and Tabitha Stewart), b. 25 Jan 1850, Corinth, MS (6/12 in 1850), d. 22 Jan 1895, Kaufman Co, TX; m. 1869, in Maynardsville, Clay Co, AR, ***Margaret Maynard*** (see 1870 Randolph Co, AR census), b. 22 Dec 1849, Clay Co, AR, d. 3 April 1925, Terrell, TX, both bur New Salem Cem, Kaufman Co, TX. Much data from B.G. "Bo" Boshear, 902 River Oaks Drive, Greenville, TX 75402 (bgboshear@argontech.net>)

[V6]713. [11]1. **James A. Boshears**, b. 1870, d. 1937; m. 1893, in Elmo, Kaufman Co, TX, ***Willie Oller***, b. 1878

[V6]714. [11]2. **Margarete Boshears**, b. 16 Jan 1872, d. 27 April 1954; m. ***R.M. Carroll***

[V6]715. [11]3. **Ada Boshears**, b. c1874; m. ***Jake Lindsay***

[V6]716. [11]4. **R. Lee Boshears**, b. c1876; m. ***Monnie Lee Dupall***

[V6]717. [11]5. **Jefferson "Jeff" Boshear**, b. 10 Feb 1878, d. 2 July 1966, Wills Point, Van Zandt Co, TX; m. 25 Dec 1898, in Elmo, Kaufman Co, TX, ***Lenora Althea Adams***, b. 17 June 1881, Kaufman Co, TX, d. 25 Oct 1961, Wills Point, Van Zandt Co, TX, d/o Jordan Adams and Caroline Bryson. Jeff and Lenora both bur White Rose Cem, Wills Point, Van Zandt Co, TX. Jeff and his children dropped the "s" at the end of the surname.

[V6]718. [12]1. **Dewey Edward Boshear**, b. 18 Sept 1899, Elmo, Kaufman Co, TX, d. 22 Sept 1972, Terrell, TX; m. 19Aug 1919, in Van Zandt Co, TX, ***Lola Jeffie Feazell***, b. 15 Dec 1902, Italy, Ellis Co, TX, D. 21 May 1981, Presbyterian Hosp, Dallas, TX, d/o James Feazell and Lula Howell. Dewey and Lola both bur White Rose Cem, Wills Point, Van Zandt Co, TX

[V6]719. [13]1. **Dewey Dewitt Boshear**, b. 11 May 1920, Kaufman Co, TX, d. Jan 1987, Gladewater, TX; m.1. ***Marie Galloway***, in Wills Point, Van Zandt Co, TX; m.2. ***Grace Ione Rodgers***, b. ?, d. 31 May 1966, Gladewater, TX (1 ch); m.2. ***Jessie*** _____, (1 ch)

[V6]720. [14]1. **Linda Kay Boshear**, b. 28 Sept 1947, Dallas, TX, d. 1 March 1991, Gregg Co, TX; m. ***Tommy Arnold***

[V6]721. [15]1. Tammy Ione Arnold. b. 23 April 1970

[V6]722. [15]2. Shawn Wesley Arnold, b. 24 Oct 1972, d. 31 Oct 1993, Upsher Co, TX

[V6]723. [14]2. **Larry Robert Boshear**, b. 8 Aug 1968

[V6]724. [13]2. **Jeff Clinton Boshear**, b. 15 Jan 1924, d. 12 Feb 1992, Kaufman Co, TX, bur White Rose Cem, Wills Point, Van Zandt Co, TX

[V6]725. [13]3. **Barbour Gene "B.G." "Bo" Boshear**, b. 12 Oct 1931, Wills Point, Van Zandt Co, TX; m.1. 1 May 1954, Dallas, TX, ***Dorothy Lenear Armstrong***, b. 9 Aug 1925, Evant, TX, d. 18 May 1999, Greenville, TX, d/o Arthur Armstrong and Sallie Wiley (1 ch); m.2. 28 Dec 1985, South Padre Island, TX, ***Beverly Mae Gehrke***, b. 26 July 1943, Springfield, IL, d/o Walter Gehrke and Lillian Barnard

[V6]726. [14]1. **Kimberly Ann Boshear**, b. 26 Jan 1960, Wills Point, Van Zandt Co, TX; m. 15 Sept 1979, Westview Meth Ch, Greenville, TX, ***Dean Edward Converse***, b. 4 Aug 1959, s/o Billy Converse and Katherine Long

[V6]727. [15]1. Cody Edward Converse, b. 23 May 1985, Greenville, TX

[V6]728. [15]2. Courtney Ann Converse, b. 20 Dec 1989, Greenville, TX

[V6]729. [12]2. **Ollie Mable Boshear**, b. 20 March 1902, Elmo, Kaufman Co, TX, d. 6 Oct 1986; m. ***Albert Houston Henderson***, b. 24 Dec 1896, Green Co, AL, d. 5 Jan 1949, Dallas, TX, both bur White Rose Cem, Wills Point, Van Zandt Co, TX

[V6]730. [13]1. Arthur Edmond Henderson, b. 28 April 1927, Wills Point, Van Zandt Co, TX; m. Jeanne Hale, b. 4 April 1928, Dallas, TX

[V6]731. [14]1. Dee Becka Henderson, b. 5 May 1950, Dallas, TX; m. James Douglas Stokes, b. 14 July 1949,

Dallas, TX

[V6]732. [15]1. Amy Christine Stokes, b. 4 Dec 1974

[V6]733. [14]2. Arthur Edmond Henderson Jr, b. 13 May 1959, San Angelo, TX

[V6]734. [13]2. Anna Lou Henderson, b. 8 May 1929, Wills Point, Van Zandt Co, TX; m.1. John W. "Bill" Clark, b. 18 April 1925; m.2. Don R. Alford, b. 25 Oct 1936, d. 15 April 1998, Dallas, TX

[V6]735. [14]1. Theresa A. Kulwiki Clark, b. 13 Aug 1954

[V6]736. [14]2. Lana Clark, b. 12 April 1961; m. _____ Rains

[V6]737. [15]1. Mollie D'Ann Rains, b. 18 May 1991

[V6]738. [14]3. Jana Clark, b. 12 April 1961; m. _____ Bailey

[V6]739. [15]1. Jamie Lea Bailey, b. 28 March 1990

[V6]740. [12]3. **Willie Catherine Boshear**, b. 6 July 1906, Kaufman Co, TX, d. 3 Feb 1998, Dallas, TX, bur White Rose Cem, Wills Point, Van Zandt Co, TX; m.1. ***Leonard "Slim" Mann***; m.2. 6 Nov 1967, ***Lester Cleo Morrison***, b. 1905, d. 16 March 1981

[V6]741. [11]6. **Zettie Mae Boshears**, b. 1882

[V6]742. [11]7. **John Blanton Boshears**, b. 4 Jan 1885, d. 21 July 1934; m. ***Minnie Lee Dupree***, b. 21 Feb 1885

[V6]743. [12]1. **Auston V. Boshears**, b. 1908

[V6]744. [13]1. **Mary Lou Boshears**; m. _____ ***Casafi***, of Mesquite, TX, and had three sons, per Auston's obit.

[V6]745. [12]2. **Verna Cleo Boshears**, b. 1913; m. _____ ***Standifer***, of Dallas, per Auston's obit.

[V6]746. [12]3. **Edna Ruth Boshears**, b. 1916; m. ***C.E. Prewitt***, of San Diego, CA, per Auston's obit

[V6]747. [12]4. **Horace Douglas "Dick" Boshears**, b. 11 Nov 1919, d. 8 April 1994; m. ***Helen Harrison***, b. 25 March 1922, d. 3 May 1992. Lives Dallas,

TX, per Auston's obit.

V6748. 131. **Patricia Helen Boshears**, b. 18 Nov 1950; m. ____ ***Rogers***

V6749. 141. Ray Boshears Rogers, b. 12 May 1972

V6750. 125. **Walter Bently Boshear**, b. 1921; lives Farmington, NM, per Auston's obit.

V6751. 126. **Ina Nevada Boshear**, b. 1926; m. ____ ***Shipley***, of Forney, TX, per Auston's obit.

V6752. 118. **Don Carlos Boshears**, b. 29 Oct 1890, d. 1 Jan 1968; m. 1910, ***Lottie L. Lindsay***, b. 25 June 1893, d. Feb 1960, bur together, Locust Grove Cem, Hiram Community, Kaufman Co, TX.

James A. Boshears and Lucy Sysco

v6692. 109. **James A. Boshears**, (s/o Henry Boshears and Tabitha Stewart), b. c1856, Obion Co, TN, d. c1899, when Delcie, the youngest child was one year old; m. 18 Aug 1878, Butler Co, MO, ***Lucy Sysco***, b. c1862 (18 in 1880), KY, d. c1908, when Delcie was about ten. In 1880, Clay Co, AR, they are h/h #104-105, next door to Josiah Boshears and ____ Mansker. (Thanks to Beth Peck Cooper for the census data.)

V6753. 111. **Jefferson B. Boshears**, b. 23 Feb 1880, Clay Co, AR, d. 19 Dec 1936, Brenham, Washington Co, TX, bur Prairie Lea Cem, Brenham, TX (stone and grave lost); m. ***Nellie Krummel*** (Crummel, Crumble), b. 3 March 1887 (or 1884) Birch Tree, Shannon Co, MO, d. 6 July 1975, Jacksonville, Duval Co, FL. After Jeff died, Nellie m.2. A.H. Henderson; they lived in Atwater, CA. (data from Niki Scoggins <ndscoggins@worldnet.att.net>)

V6754. 121. **Flossie Ann Boshears** (she spelled her surname Boshea much of the time), b. 7 Dec 1906, Corning, Clay Co, AR, d. 27 June 1976, Los Angeles, CA; m. bef 1926, at Wills Point, Van Zandt Co, TX, ***George D. Herron***. They moved to CA c1938; divorced c1946; Flossie m.2. ***Archie Jack "Art" Silva***.

[V6]755. [13]1. Myra Jo Herron, b. 26 Dec 1926, Grand Saline, Van Zandt Co, TX, d. 2 June 1968, Palos Verdes, L.A. Co, CA; m. ______ (Niki Scoggins' mother)

[V6]756. [13]2. Barbara Ann Herron, b. 25 Aug 1934, Dallas, TX, Dallas, TX, d. 5 April 1945 of Leukemia in L.A. Co, CA. Family story has it that George Herron worked for the railroad and was transferred to AZ, but Flossie refused to leave the grave of her baby in L.A. So George and Flossie were divorced, c1946.

[V6]757. [13]3. Billie Lee Herron, b. 7 Sept 1938

[V6]758. [13]4. Jackie Ann Silva, b. 6 Dec 1947

[V6]759. [13]5. William Ray Silva, b. 21 May 1949, Oakland, CA, d. 28 Sept 1978, L.A., CA

[V6]760. [12]2. **Edna Faye Boshears**, b. 20 Aug 1908, Clay Co, AR, d. 28 April 1981, Brenham, Washington Co, TX, bur Prairie Lea Cem, Brenham, TX; m. 3 Nov 1928, Brenham, TX, ***Jack William Montgomery***, s/o Jessie James Montgomery and Ella Wilkes

[V6]761. [13]x. Bonnie Gail Montgomery; m. _____ West <kwwave@aol.com>

[V6]762. [12]3. **Jessie Boshears**, b. 14 Oct 1910, Peach Orchard, Clay Co, AR, d. 3 Jan 1989, Brenham, Washington Co, TX, bur Prairie Lea Cem, Brenham, TX; m. 10 Aug 1927, Washington Co, TX, ***John Lee Giese***

[V6]763. [12]4. **Pearl Boshears**, b. 1916, bur Prairie Lea Cem, Brenham, TX

[V6]764. [12]5. **Nellie Inez Boshears**, b. 18 May 1829, Brenham, TX; m. 29 June 1947, in Brenham, TX, ***Vernon Kindle Jones***, b. 18 Dec 1916, Cosby, Cocke Co, TN, d. 3 Dec 1992, Jacksonville, Duval Co, FL

[V6]765. [11]2. **Eirey (or Eivy) Boshears**, b. 1882; m. 28 Jan 1900, ***James L. Daley*** (info from Bonnie Montgomery West)

[V6]766. [11]3. **Lawrence Boshears**, b. 1886

[V6]767. [11]4. **Taylor Boshears**, b. 26 Oct 1893, d. Jan 1963 (per SS Death Index)

[V6]768. [11]5. **Delcie Boshears**, b. 1898, d. 1968, Piggott, AR; m. 16 July 1914 in Datto, Clay Co, AR (by Henry Gilbert, JP), ***Jimmie Johnson***, b. 1889, d. 1967, Piggott, AR. (On the Marriage Bond, Affidavit, License, and Certificate, "Henry" was first written for Jimmie's name, then a line was drawn through it and "Jimmie" written above. Was the JP day-dreaming and wrote his own name first, then had to correct it? Delcie's name is entered as Elsie and Elsey, and her age as 18; she was probably fibbing by two years. Data from Troy Lewis, grandson, and his wife, Lola (tllllola@tc3net.com). Delcie is said to have had two sets of twins, one year part. Lucille is the only one of the four to survive.

[V6]769. [12]1. Willie Johnson (fem, oldest)

[V6]770. [12]2. Arlie Johnson,

[V6]771. [12]3. Ethel Lucille Johnson,

[V6]772. [12]4. Fred Johnson,

[V6]773. [12]5. J.C. Johnson,

[V6]774. [12]6. Edmond Johnson,

[V6]775. [12]7. Vernon Johnson,

[V6]776. [12]8. Christine Johnson,

JACOB BOSHEARS Jr and Martha Ann McGuire

[v6]660. [9]8. **Jacob Boshears Jr**, (s/o Jacob Brashears Sr, s/o John Brashears Sr and Mary Berry), was b. in Tishomingo Co, MS in 1842 and moved with his father to Obion (area now Lake) Co, TN in 1855. He married ***Martha Ann McGuire***, b. 1840, LA, d. of TB April or May, 1880, d/o _____ McGuire and Hannah Tipton, sister of the William A. Tipton who founded Tiptonville in 1860.

Jacob farmed for his father on land rented by Jacob Sr from 1861 to 1874. He moved to Texas and made one crop on a land grant near Sugar Loaf Mountain, northwest of Fort Worth, in 1874. "He went too early," said Norman Parks, "for his plows, so well suited to the soils of Mississippi and Tennessee, were unequal to "that terrible Texas sod." Just two years later, the modern steel curved-shield plow was introduced. Jacob returned to his Tennessee farm in 1875, where he died, nearly the same time as his wife, Martha Ann, in 1880. His daughter, Victoria, ran the farm in 1880 and 1881, before marrying J.W. Parks at the end of 1881."

Norman also wrote a sketch of his family history:

"Jake (Jacob) was a handsome, vigorous man with a black beard and a shock of black hair. He died of "quinsey throat" (a swelling of the throat from cold and irritation) at the prime of life (perhaps 40), begging the doctor by motions to open his windpipe so he could breathe. He walked to the window minutes before dying. It was a needless death since it seems anybody could have opened a breathing passage without serious injury.

"Jake was a small farmer and apparently did not accumulate any property, except tools and livestock. However, he appears to have had some resources, since, according to my brother, Harris, he lent $750 in gold to Mr. Beckham shortly before the famous "Beckham Massacre" by Negro Union soldiers from Island No. 10. The slaughter took place on the Beckham farm on the State Line. My father, a small boy, saw the Negroes pass by on their way back to the island fort.

"He was a man of some feeling and resolution, according to this story my father told. Irregulars (generally robbers posing as army men) raided his barn to carry off his horses. He sat in his corn crib with his gun aimed at the leader, fully resolved to shoot him the minute he put the bridle on his horse. The man's life was saved when another one of the gang talked the leader out of taking the animal because Boshears needed it to carry on farming for his young family.

"Martha (McGuire) Boshears was a sweet, frail woman with dark brown eyes and prominent forehead, somewhat like that of my sister Maude. She suffered from slow tuberculosis, finally succumbing in April or May of 1880, perhaps at the age of 40. Jake died one or two weeks later very suddenly, leaving a young family of four and his crop barely planted. My mother, Victoria (naturally named after Queen Vic of England), was 19. Her picture at that age shows her to be a beautiful girl with shapely features, dark serious eyes, and long hair hanging down her back. Jessie was 12, Willis was 9, and Ida was 5. Victoria made the crop, taking the plow in her own hand, while Willis and Jessie did the hoeing. In carrying on her family and maintaining the independence of it, Victoria showed the courage, confidence, reliance, and will that made her a very loved person in the Madrid Bend area later in life.

"Perhaps early in 1881 (I do not know the date) she was married to Joe Wiley Parks. The newlyweds began life with a large family. In addition to Jessie, Willis, and Ida, there was my dad's blind mother (Malinda), a maiden sister (Adaline), and a brother, John. Beginning his married life with a household of eight, my father never had a smaller number until in his advanced years, since there was always one or more relatives needing sheltering and care. Jessie married young to a ne'er-do-well and she and her young son, Wiltz, spent most of their time in my father's home. Jessie died there about 1890 or 1891. Her child was in and out of our home, depending on the whims of his wanderlust father. It finally reached a crisis and Victoria laid down the law— he must, for the child's own sake, either keep him himself or give the Parks family legal custody. He chose the former course and finally wandered away permanently with the child.

"Uncle Will first married a lovely widow with two children, Maggie and Bea. Maggie throughout her life, and her husband, and Bea's one son, whom they adopted, considered themselves close relatives of us and spent weeks every year visiting us. Maggie and Claude Baird's daughter, Gladys, lived in Caruthersville.

"[Uncle Will's son] Murph was born perhaps in 1897 or 1898 and Maude in 1900 (Nov). On their mother's death, the two children lived in our home until Uncle Will married Lee Adams. I have a lovely family picture made in 1904, shortly after my mother's death. Maude is in the picture, a cute, chubby, black-headed girl of four. She could never adjust to life with her mother-in-law [I think he means step-mother]. There was a constant clash of temperaments, and finally Uncle Will "gave" her to Aunt Ida. So she grew up in our family, and I loved her exactly as another sister. Indeed, nobody could ever know she was not born in our family.

"Murph had a similar clash in personality, but being older

and being a boy, he made it better, since he could be out of the house a great deal. However, he spent much of his younger years shifting between our home and Uncle Will's The last year before his marriage to Azalea Alexander was spent in our home, while he attended school at Tiptonville.

"Aunt Ida married George Crafton, a man held in high regard by my own family as a gentle and kindly person, but she lived with him only three days before returning to my father's home. Why the marriage failed, nobody ever knew unless it was my mother, and if she did, she kept it in confidence (which I suspect was the case). When a neighbor was so bold as to ask her, my mother shut her up gently but firmly by replying, "If Ida wants me to know, she will tell me." Neither my father nor any other member of my family ever mentioned the subject to her.

"When my mother died in 1904, when I was less than seven months old, Aunt Ida took over my rearing, and nobody ever had a better mother. She ran the household with a keen eye to economy and cleanliness, and divided the work duties among the children. ... She was the greatest natural nurse I ever saw. She had healing in her hands (somewhat like my mother did) and whenever a neighbor got sick, the first thing the husband would think of was to "send for Ida." When Uncle Will was stricken with pneumonia in November of 1925 after gathering corn in Kentucky on a wet, cold day, Aunt Ida rushed to his bedside. [Lee Adams] did not "jibe" with my family and members did not feel welcome to visit in her home. I suppose this was the first time Aunt was in Uncle Will's home in 20 years. I did visit a few times, once when he lived in Kentucky Bend just north of the State Line (he had a wonderful phonograph with round cylinder records which I liked to hear), once when he lived in Tiptonville before Forrest was old enough to go to school, and once when he moved back to his farm. Carrie and to some extent Buster visited our home when young. Part of this [breech], I think, was Lee's feeling that my family rated her notches below the first wife, and this is hard for a second wife to take."

Martha Ann Boshears, 40, b. LA, c1840, is in the 1880 Lake Co, TN, census, with children Victory, 18; Jesse (dau) 12; Willis, 8; and Ida May, 5.

Family of Jacob Boshears Jr and Martha Ann McGuire:

^{V6}777. ^{10}1. **Victoria Boshears**, b. TN, July 1861 (18 in 1880), d. 1904; m. 1882, ***Joe Wiley Parks***, b. 1856, d. 1932.

^{V6}778. ^{11}1. Harris R. Parks, b. 1883

^{V6}779. ^{11}2. Maude M. Parks, b. 1884

^{V6}780. ^{11}3. Carrie Parks, b. 1887

^{V6}781. ^{11}4. Wilford Parks, b. 1889

^{V6}782. ^{11}5. Fred T. Parks, b. 1893

^{V6}783. ^{11}6. Eulah W. Parks, b. 1896

^{V6}784. ^{11}7. Bernice Parks, b. 1899

^{V6}785. ^{11}8. Norman L. Parks, b. 1904, age 88 in 1992. Norman wrote a history of several of his families, *Like Old Man River*.

^{V6}786. ^{10}2. **Buddy Boshears**, b. 1864, d. as a child

^{V6}787. ^{10}3. **Jessie Boshears**, b. TN, 1868 (12 in 1880), d. 1892; m. ***Wiltz W. Davis***.

^{V6}788. ^{11}1. James Davis

^{V6}789. ^{10}4. **Norman Boshears**, b. 1870, d. as a child

^{V6}790. ^{10}5. **Willis "Will" Boshears**, b. TN, April 1872/73 (8 in 1880), d. 29 Nov 1925, m.1. ***Emma (Hairslip) Connelly*** (mother of first two children; she had been married before and had two daughters: Maggie and Bea Connelly), m.2. ***Rachel Lee Adams*** (mother of other children), b. 1861, d. 1938.

^{V6}791. ^{11}1. **Murph Boshears**, b. 1898; m. ***Azalea Alexander***.

^{V6}792. ^{11}2. **Maude Boshears**, b. 1900, d. 1981; m. ***Frank*** _____.

^{V6}793. ^{11}3. **Carrie Boshears**, b. 1907

^{V6}794. ^{11}4. **Mary Boshears**, b. 14 July 1908, d. 29 Feb 1910

^{V6}795. ^{11}5. **Willis Boshears, Jr**, b. 1909, d. 1982

^{V6}796. ^{11}6. **Henry Welton Boshears**, b. 29 Aug 1911, d. 22 Dec 1913

^{V6}797. ^{11}7. **Forrest Boshears**, b. 1913, d. 1991

^{V6}798. ^{11}8. **Lucille Boshears**, b. 1915, d. 1991

^{V6}799. ^{11}9. **Fred Boshears**, b. 1917, d. 1976

^{V6}800. ^{11}10. **Eva Love Boshears**, b. 1919

[V6]801. [11]11. **Margrette Boshears**, b. 1921
[V6]802. [11]12. **Miles Boshears**, b. 1924, d. 1957
[V6]803. [11]13. **John F. Boshears**, b. 1926, d. 1970
[V6]804. [10]6. **Ida May Boshears**, b. TN, 6 Feb 1875 (5 in 1880), d. 25 Nov 1935; m. ***George Crafton***. Ida lived with George only a few days, then returned to her brother-in-law's house. When her sister, Victoria (Boshears) Parks, d. in 1904, Ida moved into the Parks house to take care of the children.

7. BERRY M. BRASHEARS and Frances Pryor

v6**203.** 85. **Berry M. Brashears**, (s/o John Brashears, Sr and Mary Berry), b. 1814, probably in White Co, TN; m. 13 Aug 1836, Lawrence Co, TN, "by justice of peace Daniel Bentley," ***Frances "Fanny" Pryor***, b. Jan 1819 (31 in 1850), d/o Thomas (or Thomson) Pryor and Dicey ?Tripp, gd/o Richard Pryor and Mourning Thomson. They are ancestors of Sybil Jobe's husband. Sybil has about 60 pages of typed data on this branch of the family, which she has shared with us. Additional data on William James and Henry Newton Brashears came from Wayne L. Brashear. Many thanks; we could not have done this chapter without them. They did virtually all of the research; I am responsible for the formatting and wording.

The Pryor and Tripp Connections

Sybil Jobe's data shows that Thomas (or Thomson) and Dicey Pryor had 10 children, four of whom married Brashears/Boshears.

1. Nathan C. Pryor; m. 23 Aug 1842 in Lawrence Co, TN, **Lucinda Boshears,** d/o James and Elizabeth Boshears, a different family from the Brashear(s).
2. Henry N. Pryor,
3. Thompson Pryor,
4. Frances Pryor, b. Jan 1819; m. 13 Aug 1836, Lawrence Co, TN, **Berry M. Brashears**, (s/o John Brashear, b. 1867, NC, and Mary Berry)
5. Jonathan T. Pryor; m. 19 Dec 1839, Lawrence Co, TN, ***Ester Boshers***, d/o James and Elizabeth Boshears, a different family from the Brashear(s).
6. M. Elizabeth Pryor; m. 10 Feb 1859, Joseph Harland
7. William J. Pryor; m. 20 Oct 1846 in Lawrence Co, TN, **Martha Martela Brashears**, (d/o Isaac Brashears Sr, b. c1795)

8. Martha Pryor; m. Eli Cooper, 4 March 1851, Lawrence Co, TN
9. Johanna (Hannah) A. Pryor; m. Henry Lucas 19 Feb 1853
10. Angeline Pryor,

Some researchers think that Dicey may have been a Tripp, d/o Reuben Tripp. Reuben Tripp and Thomas Pryor were certainly close acquintances: Lawrence County Court Record, p.502: "April 1822 - Levied on 16 acres of land lying on the head of shoal creek about 3 miles east of Lawrenceburg where Rueben Tripp and Thomas Pryer now live, supposed to be the property of David Crockett. Sheriff ordered the land sold."

Thomas Pryor received a Tennessee Land Grant for 160 acres (Deed Book A, p.89-90). On May 23, 1824, Reubin Tripp made a deed of conveyance for 160 acres of land to Thomas Pryor (Deed Book A, p.189-190).

Thomas Pryor may have had a wandering eye. On Monday, 1 Nov 1819, he appeared in Lawrence Co, TN county court with Mary Tripp and posted bond "to indemnify the county from the costs of a bastard child of the said Mary Tripp. ... Mary Tripp's fine paid." (*County Court Minutes*, v.1, 1 Nov 1819).

What was the connection between these two families? Was Thomas married to one of the Tripp girls? Was Thomas the father of Mary Tripp's illegitimate child? Did he marry her? Was Dicey a Tripp or was she a second wife? We have found no marriage records for Thomas Pryor in Lawrence County.

Thomas (Thomson) Pryor died before 1838. An inventory of his estate appears in *Lawrence Co Wills and Probate Deeds, 1829-1855*, p.167: "December 23, 1838, Inventory of Thompson (sic) Pryor deceased: 2 horses, 7 head of cattle, from 6 to 13 hed of sheep supposed; a lot of hogs number unknown, and doubtful whether they can be counted, 3 beds, furniture, 1 bedstead, one loom, one table, 3 spinning wheels, 1 press over, one pot, one sad iron, farming tool and some other small article, some corn in the field, some fodder, and some wheat."

In the same book, p.291, Dicy Prior, Sept 1843, was appointed "guardian of William J., Johana A., Martha, and Angeline Prior," her four youngest children. After Thomas (Thomson) died, Dicey m.2. 21 May 1843, LawrCo, TN, Payton Manuel. She was still living in 1880, when she appears in the census as mother-in-law of Berry M. Brashears.

Berry's Family

The first known public record of Berry M. Brashears is his marriage to Frances "Fanny" Pryor, 13 Aug 1836 in Lawrence County, TN. The Brashears and Pryor families had been in Lawrence County when it was formed from Maury and Hickman Counties in May 1818.

Goodspeed's *History of Lawrence County Tennessee* (1888, p.751) states:

"On Sugar Creek and vicinity there settled Jacob Brashears, John Miller, John and William Brashears, George Brenn, Joseph Baldwin, and others. All of the families had settled in the county previous to 1818. By actual enumeration in 1818, the enrollment shows a voting population of 458. The first permanent settlers came in 1815."

The Goodspeed History goes on to say, p.751:

"Many deer, wolves, bears, wildcats, and turkeys were found in the county and the settlers' food was mostly of game. Among the most noted hunters was David Crockett, who was one of the justices chosen for the county at its organization."

In 1848, John Brashears [Berry's father] sold 72 acres of land to John H. Brashears [Berry's brother] in Lawrence County, TN for $45.00. Berry Brashears and William J. Prior were witnesses. (Deed Book L, p.305). Berry Brashears is also named as an heir of John Brashears in an 1856 deed to William Newton. He owned one sixth of the land. (Deed Book M, p.593-594).

The Federal Census shows Berry and Fanny Brashears living in Lawrence County, TN in 1850; Wayne County, TN in 1860; Giles County, TN in 1870 and 1880. They probably did not move from Lawrence County to Giles County for he petitioned the Tennessee State Legislature in 1879 to move the boundaries between the two counties so that his land would be back in Lawrence County. The petition was granted, but he is still listed in Giles County in the census. (Tennessee State Archives).

In the mid-1880's, some of the grown children of Berry and Fanny moved to east Texas. Whether Berry went along is not known. Perhaps he was dead by then, but no records of his land sale, or a will, or an inventory has yet been found. Fanny went to Texas. She and her youngest son, Nathan, were in the household of J.W. and Tealie Penny in the 1900 census of Collin County, TX. She is not listed with any of her children in Texas or Tennessee in the 1910 Census. She probably died between 1900 and 1910. She is probably buried in Old Grounds Cemetery near Blue Ridge, Collin Co, TX.

Berry and Frances are in the 1850 Census, Lawrence Co, TN, p. 380 with 6 children; more were born later.

[V6]851. [9]1. **Ethalinda F. Brashears**, b. c1838, Lawrence Co, TN (12 in 1850); m. 3 March 1856, in Lawrence Co, TN, ***Coleman C. Parham***, who apparently died young. Ethalinda and two children were living with her parents in 1860.

[V6]852. [10]1. Jemima J. Parham, b. c1857

[V6]853. [10]2. Tennessee Parham, b. c1859

[V6]854. [9]2. **John T. (or F.) Brashears**, b. c1840, Lawrence Co, TN (10 in 1850); m. ***Sarah J.*** ______, b. c1844 (36 in 1880, Giles Co, TN). John was a farmer. His middle initial is variously interpreted as "F," "T," and "J." He and Sarah had six children.

[V6]855. [10]1. **John W. Brashears**, b. c1872, d. 1955

[V6]856. [10]2. **Julia H. Brashears**, b. c1873

[V6]857. [10]3. **Cora A. Brashears**, b. c1874

[V6]858. [10]4. **Ida L. Brashears**, b. 1875

[V6]859. [10]5. **Robert G. Brashears**, b. 1876

[V6]860. [10]6. **Walter Brashears**, b. c1879

[V6]861. [9]3. ***William James Brashears**, b. 14 Jan 1842, TN (8 in 1850), d. 26 April 1928, Giles Co, TN; m.1. 5 May 1867, Giles Co, TN (Bk.2, p.107, J.M. Parker, JP), ***Nancy A. Chapman***; m.2. 31 Dec 1874, Giles Co, TN, (Bk.2, p.1??, J.M. Parker, JP) ***Elizabeth E. Owens***; m.3. ***Nellie*** ______. (see below). Sybil Jobe has Elizabeth as first wife, Nellie as second.

[V6]862. [9]4. ***Henry Newton Brashears**, b. c1845, TN (5 in 1850), d. 4 Dec 1914; m. 5 March 1869, Giles City, TN, ***Mary Ann Brownlow***, b. c1847; m.2. ***Sara Allen***, (see below)

[V6]863. [9]5. ***Reuben T. Brashears**, b. 21 Oct 1849, TN (2 in 1850), d. 10 Dec 1917. *See separate chapter.*

[V6]864. [9]6. **Sarah E. Brashears**, b. c1850, TN (4/12 in 1850). ***possibly the Sarah Brashears who married on

8 May 1868 (Tennessee Marriages, Giles County, TN, 1851-1900), ***Joseph L. Wales.*** She's last seen with Berry and Frances in the 1860 census for Wayne Co, TN, but is not with them in the 1870 census. In the 1870 census in Williamson Co, TX, Wayne Brashear found Joseph Wales, 27 and wife, Sarah E., 26. These census ages are probably in error. The copyist could have mis-read a correct but sloppy "0" as an erroneous "6".

[V6]865. [9]7. ***Dicey Ann Brashears**, b. c1854, d. 1930, Collin Co, TX

[V6]866. [9]8. ***Martilla "Teallie" Brashears**, b. 1 April 1856, TN, d. 1 June 1895, Collin Co, TX; m. about 1878, probably in Giles Co, TN, ***John W. Penny***,

[V6]867. [9]9. **Nathan T. Brashears**, b. Oct 1859, Wayne Co, TN, d. 4 Dec 1922, McKinney, Collin Co, TX, bur Blue Ridge, TX. Evidently, he never married. Nathan and his mother were living with his sister, Tealie Penny, in 1900.

BLUE RIDGE MAN DIES IN HOSPITAL AFTER OPERATION :

NATHAN T. BRASHEARS of Blue Ridge, aged 61 years [b. c1861] died in the McKinney City Hospital at 9:40 o'clock Monday night following an operation. Deceased was a native of Tennessee but had lived in Collin County for several years. He leaves two sisters and several nephews and nieces to mourn his death. The remains were taken to Blue Ridge Tuesday where interment was made at 1 p.m.

— *Courier Gazette*, McKinney, TX, Monday, December 5, 1922 (Thanks to Nova Wade <davon104@aol.com> for the copy.

Jonnie Vee (Brashears) Robertson has a funeral card for him. It reads: "In Loving Remembrance of Nathan T. Brashears, Died Dec 4, 1922, Age 61 Years.

Gone but Not Forgotten.
A precious one from us has gone
A voice we loved is stilled;
A place is vacant in our home,
Which never can be filled.
God in his wisdom has recalled,

The boon his love had given,
And though the body slumbers here,
The soul is safe in heaven."

Berry's Blacksmith Records

Deed of Trust (mortgage) from Berry Beshears to A. M. Perkins. Berry Beshears of Lawrence Co, sold to A.M. Perkins, one horse, two head cattle, two sows, nine pigs, one bedstead, one trunk, one pair fire irons, five chairs ... also states indebted to Stephen Matthers in the sum of $50 on note dated Dec 31, 1838, due Dec 5, 1839. This instrument dated 30 Jan 1839, Attest: J.D. Perkins, Allen Anthony (LawrCo, TN, Deeds, F:237). Berry was buying the blacksmith tools of Jacob Bryant.

Five months later, Berry and his ?partner mortgaged their blacksmith books and equipment: Deed of Trust... Berry Beshears and Isaac Perkins, June 1, 1839, of one part, and Smith Voss of the other part, all of the County of Lawrence, State of Tennessee, witnesseth that Isaac Perkins and Berry Brashers has procured the said Andrew Perkins and Stephen Matthews to go security for the sum of $46.67, payable to Jacob Bryant due the 15th of December next (1839) for that purpose and for the consideration of One Dollar to me in hand paid by the said Andrew Perkins and Stephen Matthews has and does by these present bargain, sell and convey to the said Smith Voss, his heirs or assigns, forever, all of their blacksmith shop books with all of the accounts in said book from 1st Jan 1839 to this date; CONDITION: that if the debt and interest are paid by the 25th day of Dec 1839 to the said Voss or his assigns, [the deed is null and void; otherwise, Voss] may at any time thereafter, if not paid by the executors, sell the same book with the accounts therein to the highest bidder after giving 10 days notice, which proceeds shall go to satisfaction of said debts with the interest of same debt, the date above written.

/s/ Berry Brashears, I.D. Perkins

Attest: Wm A. Edminton(?) and Alfred Ratliff
(LawrCo TN, Deeds, Bk.F, p.423)

His business apparently recovered from debt and prospered. He was still a blacksmith when the Civil War started.

Berry's Civil War Records

Evidently, Berry M. Brashears put his blacksmith skills to good use during the Civil War. He and his family were living in Wayne County, TN, in 1861, and he joined (or was conscripted by) the Confederate 19th Cavalry (Col. Biffle's), B Company, a unit of Gen. Nathan Bedford Forrest's cavalry. Berry was about 48 years old, married with 6 children living at home, but the cavalry probably needed blacksmiths to keep their horses shod. He enlisted 8 Sept 1863 with Capt. Reynolds for a period of 3 years. (Civil War Records of Berry Brashears, Card No. 48467496).

Tennesseans in the Civil War, pages 95-96, tells that Biffle's Regiment Was in the battle at Chickamauga, Sept19-20, 1863. A diary kept by Pvt. Stephen A. Jordan of Co. "G" said that, from Chickamauga, the Regiment went to Cleveland [TN], on to Loudon County and Monroe County. They had several fights between Philadelphia (Loudon County) and Sweetwater (Monroe County) and were in a battle at Cleveland, Oct 19. They moved into east Tennessee and southwest Virginia and remained there until March 1864.

Colonel Biffle was next reported in the Army of Tennessee in Georgia, where they made raids against General Sherman's railroad communications during the summer of 1864. They were with Wheeler's main force at the battle near Franklin, TN, on Sept 2, 1864, where General Kelly was killed.

Biffle's Regiment remained in Wayne and Maury Counties, TN, until Oct 8, 1864, when they crossed the Tennessee River south of Lawrenceburg (Lawrence County, TN) and moved into Mississippi. On Oct 20th, they moved into Alabama and became part of the Tennessee campaign to regain Tennessee for the Confederacy. On Feb 13th, 1865, all Tennessee troops were ordered to Verona, Mississippi for consolidation into six regiments. Biffle's Regiment was placed in Brigadier General Tyree H. Bell's Brigade.

On May 3, just prior to the surrender and parole, Biffle's Regiment reported 22 officers, 281 men present; 257 effectives; aggregate present and absent 508. It was paroled in May 1865 at Gainsville, Alabama as part of Bell's Brigade.

Ironically, Berry's second son, William J. Brashears, served with the Union forces in the Civil War, according to his obituary in the *Pulaski Citizen*, (Giles County, TN) 2 May 1928.

8. WILLIAM JAMES BRASHEARS and Elizabeth ________/ Nellie ________,

V6861. 93. **William James "W.J." Brashears**, (s/o Berry M. Brashears and Frances Pryor), b. 14 Jan 1842, TN (8 in 1850), d. 26 April 1928, Giles Co, TN; m.1. 5 May 1867, Giles Co, TN (Bk.2, p.107, J.M. Parker, JP; IGI M519221/0832), ***Nancy A. Chapman*** (4 ch); m.2. 31 Dec 1874, Giles Co, TN, (Bk.2, p.1??, J.M. Parker, JP; IGI M519221/3544) ***Elizabeth E. Owens*** (4 ch); m.3. ***Nellie*** ________ (no ch of record; "Nellie" may be a nickname for Elizabeth). Sybil Jobe has Elizabeth as first wife, Nellie as second.

According to his obituary, W.J. died at the home of his youngest son, B.F. Brashears in Giles Co, TN. He was a Union soldier in the Civil War. He was survived by his "second" wife, Nellie, and 6 children: B.F., Will, and T.W. Brashears, all of Giles County, Mrs. W.C. Hannah of Tanner, AL, Mrs. B.F. Newton of Decatur AL, Mrs. T.C. Hannah of Dallas TX. W.J. and Nelly are buried in Scotts Hill Cemetery, Giles Co. (Census Records of Giles County TN; "Giles County Historical Society Bulletin," 23 Oct 1988, p.79).

<u>Family of William James Brashears and Nancy A. Chapman:</u>

V6868. 101. **Janie B. "Nannie" Brashears**, b. 1866 (14 in 1880); m. ***T.C. Hannah***. In 1928, they lived in Dallas, TX

V6869. 102. **James R. Brashears**, b. c1868 (11 in 1880); possible marriage: 8 June 1889, Young Co, TX, to ***Lula May Scott*** (Texas Marriages, 1814-1909)

V6870. 103. **Samuel Brashears**, b. c1869 (8/12 in 1870); not in 1880 census

V6871. 104. ***William Henry "Willis" Brashears**, b. 11 Jan 1873 (7 in 1880), d. 1946; m.1. ______ ; m.2. ***Birl Fry***, b. 8 Oct 1882; living in 1928 in Giles Co, TN.

Family of William James Brashears and Elizabeth E. Owens:

V6872. 105. **Pauline Frances "Fanny" Brashears**, b. c1876 (4 in 1880); m. ***W.C. Hannah***. In 1928, they lived in Tanner, AL.

V6873. 106. **Thomas W. Brashears**, b. 1878 (2 in 1880); m.1. ***Sally Howell***, (1ch); m.2. c1903 (had been married 7 yrs in 1910), ***Myrtle*** ______, b. c1885, TN (24 in 1910); m.3. ***Zana F. Boaz Parks***, b. c1895, d. 15 May 1980, Pulaski, Giles Co, TN. Thomas was a blacksmith, like his father.

V6874. 11x. **Kenneth Brashears**, b. c1907 (ch. of 2nd marr; 3 in 1910 census, Pulaski, Giles Co, TN)

V6875. 107. **Nettie Brashears**, b. Feb 1882; m. ***Ben F. Newton***, living in 1928 in Decatur, AL.

V6876. 108. ***Berry Franklin Brashears**, b. 11 Oct 1885 in Giles Co TN; m. ***Eliza F. Simpson***, b. 29 Oct 1887; living in 1928 in Giles Co, TN.

William Henry "Willis" Brashears and Birl Fry

V6870. 103. **William Henry "Willis" Brashears**, (s/o William James Brashears and Nancy A. Chapman; his mother may have died at his birth), b. 11 Jan 1873, Giles Co, TN, d. 28 Aug 1946; bur Maplewood Cemetery, Giles Co, TN; m.1. _______, (2 ch); m.2. ***Birl Fry***, b. 8 Oct 1882, d. 13 Aug 1961 (9 ch). (Cemetery Records; information (1989) from daughter, Maxie Bobo, Pulaski, TN).

V6877. 111. **Noah Brashears**, b. Oct 1900; living in Giles Co, TN (1989).

V6878. 112. **John Brashears**; living in Giles Co, TN (1989)

V6879. 113. **Sally Brashears**, b. 1905; m. _______ ***Hamby***,

V6880. 114. **Willa Mae Brashears**; m. _______ ***Warren***, Lives (1989) in Nashville, TN.

V6881. 115. **Margaret Brashears**; m. ______ ***Simpkins***, Lives (1989) in New Jersey.

V6882. 116. **Maxie Brashears**; m. _______ ***Bobo***, Lives (1989) in Pulaski, TN

V6883. 117. **Kathleen Brashears**, Lives (1989) in Pulaski, TN

V6884. 118. **Frank Brashears**, - deceased before 1989

[V6]885. [11]9. **Lee Brashears**, Lives (1989) in Pulaski, TN

[V6]886. [11]10. **Mary Brashears**; m. ______ ***Williams***,

[V6]887. [11]11. Infant daughter **Brashears**, b.&d. 1916; bur Scotts Hill Cem, Giles Co, TN.

Berry Franklin Brashears and Eliza F. Simpson

[V6]876. [10]7. **Berry Franklin Brashears**, known as "Uncle Bud" Brashears, (s/o William James Brashears and Elizabeth E. Owens), b. 11 Oct 1885 in Giles Co TN, d. April 1967, Pulaski, Giles Co, TN; m. ***Eliza F. Simpson***, b. 29 Oct 1887; d. 22 Feb 1960; both bur Maplewood Cemetery, Giles Co, TN. They had 9 children (See *Giles Co Historical Society Bulletin*, Oct 23, 1988, p.79)

[V6]888. [11]1. **Geanie (or Jenie) Brashears**, b. c1906, TN (4 in 1910); m. ***Raymond Grubbs***,

[V6]889. [11]2. **Will Tom Brashears**, b. 25 Nov 1907 in Giles Co, TN (3 in 1910), d. there 3 June 1982; m.1. ***Kathleen Young***, (3 ch), b. 5 Dec 1912, d. 3 June 1953, Giles Co, TN, d/o Henry and Annie (Odeneal) Young. Will and Kathleen are buried in Maplewood Cemetery; m.2. ***Tavie Cates Newton***,

[V6]890. [12]1. **Charles Henry Brashears**, b. 9 Dec 1928, d. 22 Feb 1978; bur Maplewood Cem, Giles Co, TN; m. ***Edna Dean Arthur***, d/o Clarence and Hattie (McKelvey) Arthur. They had 4 children:

[V6]891. [13]1. **Donna Carol Brashears**,

[V6]892. [13]2. **Charles Henry Brashears, Jr**,

[V6]893. [13]3. **Kathy Brashears**, m. ______ ***Spivey***,

[V6]894. [13]4. **Sherrel Ann Brashears**; m. ______ ***Tatum***,

[V6]895. [12]2. **Peggy Brashears**, m. ______ ***Rogers***,

[V6]896. [12]3. **Shirley Brashears**,

[V6]897. [11]3. **John D. Brashears**, b. 1908 (18 months in 1910), d. 1973; m. ***Wilma Abernathy***, b. 1903, d/o Hardy Abernathy

[V6]898. [11]4. **Leslie Brashears**; m. ***Ella Mae Adcock***,

[V6]899. [11]5. **Luna Jewel Brashears**; m. ______ ***Tankersley***,

V6900. 116. **Billy Brashears**; m. ***Mary*** _______, and has 1 son.
V6901. 117. **Doris Brashears**; m. ***Ima Jean*** _______,
V6902. 118. **L.V. "Pete" Brashears**; m. ***Edna Dean***,
V6903. 119. **Geraldine Brashears**; m. _______ ***Estes***,

OBIT: "**Charles Henry Brashears**, 49, Rebel Acres, Pulaski, died of a gunshot wound, apparently accidentally self-inflicted, suffered at the grocery store he operated Wednesday, February 22, 1978. Funeral services were held at 11am Fri., February 24 at Carr & Erwind Chapel with burial in Maplewood Cemetary, the Rev. Clarence K. Stewart and the Rev. R.E. Wilsford officiating. A native of Giles County, Mr. Brashears was the son of Mr. and Mrs. Will Tom Brashears, Pulaski. In addition to his parents, he is survived by a son, Charles Henry Brashears Jr., three daughters, Sherrel Ann Tatum, Kathy Spivey, and Donna Carol Brashears, Pulaski two sister, Peggy Rogers and Shirley Brashears, Pulaski, and two grandchildren." (*Obituaries of Giles County Tennessee*, Vol 1 A-J)

9. HENRY NEWTON BRASHEARS and Mary Ann Brownlow/ Sarah Ann Allie

v6862. 94. **Henry Newton Brashears**, (s/o Berry M. Brashears and Frances Pryor), b. c1845 (5 in 1850, 15 in 1860, 34 in 1880), Lawrence Co, TN, d. 4 Dec 1914, Dougherty, Murray Co, Oklahoma; m. 5 March 1869, Giles Co, TN, ***Mary Ann Brownlow***, b. c1842 (38 in 1880, Giles Co, TN, with 6 ch), d/o Joseph L. Brownlow and Judith Sims. About 1885-90. After Henry was widowed, he m.2. c1885, ***Sarah Ann Allie***, gggrandmother of the late Cheryl Holder, who sent much data. In 1880, Henry was living next door to his brother, William James Brashears, in Giles Co, TN. In 1988 and 1991, Wayne Brashears interviewed Lillian Killman, oldest daughter of Berry Francis Brashears and acquired much good data and a couple of photos.

Henry N. Brashears, some of his siblings and their spouses,

along with their mother, Fannie, removed to North Texas and Indian Territory. They traveled in covered wagons, stopping in Arkansas for a spell.

Dovie said Henry was a minister, liked fishing and was "strict." Cheryl Holder's mother thinks Henry was a Church of Christ minister. She says this particular church didn't keep good records in a central location, so it would be hard to find records of his ordination.

Figure 8: Henry Newton Brashears and his grandson, Maynard Brashear Smith, about 1911, in Ok City. Cheryl Holder's mother had the badge Henry is wearing: it said "Oklahoma Special Police." Photo from Lillian Killman, via Wayne Brashear

Cheryl Holder sent for her grandmother's social security application, which gives Henry's name as Henry Newin Brashears and Sarah's as Sarah Ann Allie. "I have absolutely no information on her other than my great-grandmother states Sarah was Cherokee and born in TN. I have found no marriage record for them either in TN or Indian Territory where they moved to. Henry and Sarah had, per my ggrandmother, 3 children. (data from Cheryl Holder. Additional data from Peggy (Brashears) McGee, 51 Northwood Ct, Danville, CA 94506, <Peggymcgee@aol.com>); and Wayne L. Brashear (CityJazz @aol.com).

In the 1900 and 1910 US Census of Harris Co, TX, Henry and wife, "Maggie" are listed. Descendant: Oma B. (Brashears) Ford. 13005 Palm Place, Cerritos, CA 90701.

<u>Family of Henry Newton Brashears and Mary Ann Brownlow</u>:

V6904. 101. **Laura <u>Alice</u> Brashears**, b. 1869, TN (10 in 1880). Alice Killman:"She went by her middle name of Alice. I was named after her. Her youngest daughter, Vernie, who was born about 1910, now living in Middleton, Texas (1992). Children were named"

V6905. 111. Pearl ______ ; Alice Killman: "She married twice and "Stone" was the last name of one of her husbands."

V6906. 112. Bill "Bud"______ , b. c1902; Alice Killman: "Bill was a year older than me. He had just one girl and they lived in Odessa, TX. The daughter still lives there."

V6907. 113. Vernie______ , b. c1910; m. William Ingram, b. 19 Sept 1902.

V6908. 102. ***Ozrow W. Brashears**, b. 1872 [or 23 Oct 1870], Nashville, Davidson Co, TN (8 in 1880), d. 17 Nov 1960, Ada, Pontotoc Co, OK, bur Stonewall Cem, Pontotoc Co, OK; m. 24 Nov 1894, Pontotoc Co, OK, ***Ada Nancy Hanson***, b. 13 Nov 1874, TX,

V6909. 103. ***Joseph B. Brashears**, b. 1 April 1869, TN; m. 9 Aug 1892, Hickory, OK, ***Ada Paralee Kirk***, b. 3 Oct 1876,

V6910. 104. ***William Patrick Brashears**, b. 6 June 1876, TN, (4 in 1880) d. 7 Jan 1966, Oroville, Butte Co, CA; m. ***Lester Marie Blackwell***, b. Blue Ridge, Collin Co, TX (2 ch; div); m.2. ***Mona M.G. Browne*** (5 ch)

V6911. 105. ***Berry Francis (or Franklin) Brashears**, b. ?24 Nov 1879, TN (3 in 1880); m. ***Oma G. Johnson***, b. TX, c1884

V6912. 106. **Pauline Brashears**, b. 1880, TN (3 months old in 1880), d. about 18 months old.

Family of Henry Newton Brashears and Sarah Ann Allie:

V6913. 107. **Claude Brashears**, b. 15 Oct 1888, Durant, Bryan Co, OK. On 5 June 1917, he registered for the draft in Gainsville, TX. Dovie searched and searched for him, but never found a trace.

V6914. 108. **Dovie Gertrude Brashears**, b. 22 Nov 1891, (22 Oct 1890, per her Soc Sec Appl), in Indian Territory (near Stonewall, OK), d. 17 Oct 1981, Graham, Young Co, TX; m.1. c1908-09, ***Thomas Douglas Smith Sr***, b. 2 July 1886, TX; m.2. Feb 1915, Gainsville, TX, ***John A. Young***, b. 1881, d.

1968, Graham, Young Co, TX. See notes below.

[V6]915. [11]1. Maynard Brashear Smith/Young, b. 26 Sept 1909, OK City, d. 25 Nov 1975, Bedford, Tarrant Co, TX; adopted by Dovie's second husband; m. c1935, Wanda Ilean Beals, b. 1909, d. 1981

[V6]916. [12]x. Wanda Louise Smith, b. 1937; m.1. Charles Durrel Poynor, b. 1932; m.2. Frank Rich, b. 1930

[V6]917. [13]1. Charles Timothy Poynor, b. 1954; m. Tammy Tingesdahl, b. 1958. Ch: Valerie Ann and Samantha Lynn Poynor.

[V6]918. [13]2. Cheryl Ilean Poynor, b. 1958; m. Michael Wayne Holder, b. 1953. Ch: John, b. 1991, and Desiree Nichole Holder, b. 1993. Cheryl was a researcher in this line.

[V6]919. [13]3. James Vincent Rich,

[V6]920. [10]9. **Malinda "Lindy" Margaret Brashears**, b. 12 Jan 1892, per Soc Sec application; in Indian Terriortory (near Colegate, OK, per her daughters), d. 12 April 1973, Blue Ridge, Collin Co, TX. In 1900 census, Collin Co, TX, she is age 8, "boarder," with a couple named Covington. She m. ***David Crockett White***, See notes below.

[V6]921. [11]1. Elise White, b. c1918 (76 in 1994); m. ______ Becknoll, and living then in McKinney, TX

[V6]922. [11]2. Mary White, b. c1924 (70 in 1994); m. E.C. Green, and living then in Blue Ridge, TX

[V6]923. [11]3. Howard White,

Notes on Dovie Gertrude Brashears:
Cheryl Holder: Dovie studied nursing and became quite a good nurse. She worked at the Graham Hospital in Young Co, TX. Surprisingly, there is no record of her being either a registered or licensed nurse in TX and she did in fact work as a registered nurse.

She met John A. Young at the Rose Croix school of Nursing in Ardmore OK. He was treated for burns he received in the oil fields. He sent her postcards from Petrolia TX. In 1924 they became members of the United Methodist church in Graham TX. They were living in Graham in 1920 according to the census.

Maynard was raised as John's own son, and took the name of Young. At one time John was going to make this permanent and had gone to the courthouse to do so, however he returned without accomplishing this. John and Dovie became wealthy in the "oil boom," however all the wealth was lost in the crash.

Cheryl says her father, Charles Durrel Poynor, says that Dovie often spoke of Pawnee Co, OK and seemed to have close ties there. He says Dovie often spoke of her Cherokee heritage and her mother Sarah Allen was either full or part Cherokee.

She says that Dovie said that Henry, her father, would not allow her to wear face powder. So she decided to get some powder from the flour barrel and wear that. She was punished severely and recalled that experience and while doing so was still indignant that her papa would not let her wear powder.

She never went a day without it as an adult. Even in the nursing home in her old age. She says Dovie loved her father, Henry, with all heart. though he was strict. She treasured family and from what Malinda's nieces told, she missed her brother Claude dearly.

Notes on Malinda “Lindy” Margaret Brashears: Alice Killman: I called her "Aunt Lindy." Saw her one time when Alice was about 6 years old. "Grandpa (Henry Newton Brashears) brought both of the girls (Dovie & Lindy) to our house for a visit. I remember, mainly, partly, because she had a beautiful bracelet and she let me wear it." Believes that her father let some people by the name of "White" have her when she was very young. She lived in Texas.

Cheryl Holder: Her mother died three days after Malinda was born having bleed to death. Malinda is buried in Blue Ridge TX. Her birth date may be Dec 1892.

Mary Green: She was raised by the Covington family in Melissa TX. She was raised a Methodist. Dovie and Malinda had searched and searched for Claude but never found him and were quite disappointed.

A stray:

V6924. 10?. **Willie May Brashears**, b. c1877 (age 23 at marriage); m. 23 Dec 1900, ***J.M. McKellogg***, of Rolf. From: CIHolder @aol.com— I have a marriage certificate for J.M. Mckelog(z) of Rolf and Willie May Brashears of Wynewood he aged 22 and she aged 23 on the 21st of Dec 1900. They married on the 23rd of Dec 1900. My great grandmother Dovie mentioned a Willie May, but I do not know how they might be related. Dovie was dau of Henry and Sarah and granddaughter of Berry and Francis Brashears. If anyone would like a copy of it or has knowledge of who Willie May belongs to please let me know.— Cheryl

Ozrow W. Brashears and Ada Nancy Hanson

v6908. 102. **Ozrow W. Brashears**, (s/o Henry Newton Brashears and Mary Ann Brownlow), b. 1872 [or 23 Oct 1870], Nashville, Davidson Co, TN (8 in 1880), d. 17 Nov 1960, Ada, Pontotoc Co, OK, bur Stonewall Cem, Pontotoc Co, OK; m. 24 Nov 1894, Pontotoc Co, OK, ***Ada Nancy Hanson***, b. 13 Nov 1874, TX, d. 22 March 1959, Harden City, Ponotoc Co, OK.

Wanda Schneider: Ozrow was about 17 in 1887 and went by wagon from TN to Blue Ridge, TX. I ,Wanda Schneider, granddaughter, remember seeing him read his Bible every day. No one knows how many times he must have read the Bible completely. He would go for walks down the lane and would always walk with his hands clasped behind his back. He and his wife Ada lived with their daughter Pearl Phillips for many years. She and her husband, Roland Phillips, lived in the country near Harden City, Pontotoc Co. OK. I used to go and stay with them (grandparents) during the summer months when they lived in Tupelo, Coal Co, OK to help him with grandmother as she was bedridden most of those years.

Alice Killman: Orzow had a saw mill. Of course, he farmed too. He did a lot of that work all around the area (Stonewall, OK). Marvin continued until he was old enough that he was not able to, in Tupelo, with it. I guess it's still there, their sawmill.

From "The Stonewall Weekly" newspaper extracts, 1909 from Cheryl Holder, "O. W. Brashears gave us a pleasant call Sat. He has been manager of Dr. Sullivan's mill on Boggy for several years, but will leave for Coalgate before long."

Alice Killman: We went out there (Oklahoma) because my oldest brother was having trouble. Ozrow lost a baby named Arthur. The grave is in Frisco, OK were Oma G. Johnson (Alice's mother) is buried (In 1945, Alice Killman and her husband put a concrete slab over the graves to protect them in the old rundown cemetery).

Wanda Schneider: My Mother said Alice Killman told her the same thing about a baby named Arthur and buried at Frisco but my grandparents never told me or my mother that.

Family of Ozrow W. Brashears and Ada Nancy Hanson:

[V6]925. [11]1. **Henry Marvin "Bush" Brashears**, b. 23 Feb 1899, Frisco, I.T. (Pontotoc Co, OK), d. 13 Dec 1984, bur Stonewall cem, Pontotoc Co, OK; m. ***Bertha Holland***, b. 16 Oct 1906, d. 31 July 1997.

[V6]926. [12]1. **Marvella Brashears**, m. ***Jesse Loyd***.

[V6]927. [13]1. Lavonda Loyd; m. James Richard "Dicky" Goode. Ch: James Richard Goode, Jr; and Kellie Lynn Goode

[V6]928. [13]2. Jackie Loyd; m.1. Robert Mayberry. Ch: Kyle Emory Mayberry; Chad Lee Mayberry; m.2. Larry Johnston,

[V6]929. [12]2. **Wayne Keith Brashears**, m. Rosemary Ethridge.

[V6]930. [13]1. **Becky Brashears**, m. Leroy Laxton. Ch: Brandon Lee; and Lindsey Ann Laxton

[V6]931. [13]2. **Beverly Brashears**,

[V6]932. [13]3. **Paul Keith Brashears**,

[V6]933. [12]3. **Donald Paul Brashears**, b. 13 Jan 1942, Ada, Pontotoc Co, OK, d. 27 Aug 1984, Stonewall, Pontotoc Co, OK; m.1. ***Shirley Hisaw*** (3 ch); m.2. Charlotte ______ (2 ch)

[V6]934. [13]1. **Dawn Jean Brashears**,

[V6]935. [13]2. **Rana Leann Brashears**,

[V6]936. [13]3. **Todd Kent Brashears**,

[V6]937. [13]4. **Amber Rachelle Brashears**,

[V6]938. [11]2. **Robert Malley Brashears,** b. 1 May1901, Stonewall, I.T., d. 3 Oct 1986, Ada, Pontotoc Co, OK; m. 28 July 1927, Tupelo, Coal Co, OK, ***Jewel Jennings***, b. 11 Feb 1902, d. 12 Aug 1989. Wanda Schneider: Robert was a school teacher in various towns of OK and later a Superintendent. Pearl, his sister, said she and Robert helped each other with their college education.

[V6]939. [12]1. **Geneva Brashears**, m. ***Edgar O'Neal***,

[V6]940. [13]1. Gary Ed O'Neal; m. Linda ______ . Ch: Todd and Jennifer O'Neal

[V6]941. [13]2. Sharon O'Neal;

[V6]942. [13]3. Ricky O'Neal

[V6]943. [12]2. **Bobbie Nell Brashears**, (she is a school teacher); m. ***J. Roma Hipp***. Ch: Hipp

[V6]944. [11]3. **Pearl Marie Brashears**, b. 12 May 1905 (twin), Wooley Pontotoc Co, OK, d. 27 July 2001, Norman, Cleveland Co, OK, bur Stonewall, Pontotoc Co, OK; m. 19 Jan 1926, Egypt, Pnototoc Co, OK, Roland Terry Phillips, b. 28 Jan 1901, Jonesboro, AR, d. 26 Sep 1996, Norman, OK. Wanda Schneider: "She taught school in Eureka in 1925 and 1926. Graduated from Tupelo School (same place as now but different building) in 1925. Attended East Central College 1924-1926 during summer and taught school during winter. Twin to Earl Lee. Played piano in church many years. She would take the young people from church to various church activities.

[V6]945. [12]1. R.V. Phillips, m. Margie Jean Fields

[V6]946. [13]1. Linda Jean Phillips, b. & d. 2 Aug 1948, Ada, Pontotoc Co, OK

[V6]947. [13]2. Ronnie Vernon Phillips,

[V6]948. [12]2. Billy Ray Phillips, b. 6 Oct 1928 Burr Valley, Ponototoc Co, OK, d. 3 Sept 1996, Enid, OK; m.1. c1949, in Pontotoc Co, OK, Billie Ray Ray; m.2. Zelma Barnes,

[V6]949. [13]1. Judith Elaine Phillips, b. & d. 25 July 1950, Ada, Pontotoc Co, OK

V6950. [13]2. Justin Wayne Phillips, b. & d. 25 July 1950, Ada, Pontotoc Co, OK

V6951. [13]3. Donna Gale Phillips,

V6952. [13]4. Vicky Lynn Phillips,

V6953. [13]5. Cathy Phillips,

V6954. [12]3. Ada Janelle Phillips, b. 2 July 1931, Pleasant Hill, OK, d. c1977, Healdton, OK. Wanda Schneider: "She attended East Central College, Ada, OK, married Floyd Wilbur Barton 2 Nov 1951, Sulphur, Murray Co, OK, moved to Healdton in 1953. Worked for the OK Natural Gas Co. Member of BPW Club. Floyd Wilbur Barton had children by his first wife. Evelyn, also. Ada Janelle is buried at Memorial Park, Ada, Pontotoc Co, OK."

V6955. [12]4. Charles Doyle Phillips, m. Anna Faye Bailey. Ch: Charoletta Faye; Charles Doyle, Jr; and Cary Don Phillips,

V6956. [12]5. Wanda Sue Phillips, m. Ellis Schneider, Jr. Wanda Schneider if a very active researcher in Brashears families.

V6957. [13]1. Wanda Gwen Schneider, b. 5 March 1956, San Diego, CA, d. 11 Nov 1960, Pauls Valley, OK. Wanda Schneider: "Died of heart problems and pnenomia, buried in Highland Cemetery, Stonewall, Pontotoc Co, OK."

V6958. [13]2. Bobbie Karen Schneider,

V6959. [13]3. Terry Ellis Schneider,

V6960. [12]6. Glenda Kay Phillips, m. Johnny Dale Cradduck. Ch: Roger Earl; and Kim Marie Cradduck,

V6961. [11]4. **Earl Lee Brashears**, b. 12 May 1905 (twin), Wooley, Pontotoc Co, OK, d. 14 Nov 1987, Ft Worth, Tarrant Co, TX; m. ***Nettie Mae Holland***, b. 19 Nov 1908, Georgia, d. 20 Oct 2001, Ft Worth.

V6962. [12]1. **Ozrow Doyle Brashears**, (twin) b.& d. 8 March 1932, Tupelo, Coal Co, TX, bur Pontotoc Co, OK

V6963. [12]2. **Newton Royal Brashears**, (twin) b. 8 March

1932, d. 1998 TX; m. ***Jewelene Tankersly***,

^{V6}964. ^{13}1. **Kathy Louette Brashears**,

^{V6}965. ^{13}2. **Julie Lynn Brashears**,

^{V6}966. ^{13}3. **Kristi Lee Brashears**,

^{V6}967. ^{12}3. **Barbara Earlene Brashears**, m. Jesse William Pearce, Jr

^{V6}968. ^{13}1. Kenneth Wayne Pearce,

^{V6}969. ^{11}5. **Floyd Talmadge Brashears**, b. 8 Sept 1909, OK, d. 22 June 1970, Dallas, TX; m. ***Esther Bray***,

^{V6}970. ^{12}1. **Wynell Brashears**, m. ***Frank Shirley***

^{V6}971. ^{13}1. Brenda Shirley,

^{V6}972. ^{13}2. Tommy Shirley,

^{V6}973. ^{13}3. Mark Shirley,

^{V6}974. ^{11}6. **Eugene Ozrow Brashears**, b. 12 Dec 1911, OK, d. 30 May 1962, Stonewall, Pontotoc Co, OK; m. ***Velma Lee Jones***, b. 8 Oct 1913, Tupelo, Coal Co, OK, d. 1 Sept 1984. Wanda Schneider: Eugene died of a heart attack at the home of Pearl and Roland Phillips on Jones Oil Co. Lease land in Harden City, OK.

^{V6}975. ^{12}1. **Betty Imogene Brashears**, m.1. ***Robert Widdle***, m.2. ***Raymond Linker***, b. 7 Jan 1927, d. 17 April 1976,

^{V6}976. ^{13}1. Larry Eugene Widdle,

^{V6}977. ^{13}2. Patrician Ann Linker,

^{V6}978. ^{13}3. Raymond Foster Linker,

^{V6}979. ^{13}4. Linda Gail Linker, b. 26 Sept 1954, Tokyo, Japan, d. 14 April 1955, San Bruno, San Mateo Co, CA

^{V6}980. ^{13}5. Ronald Paul Linker, b. 12 Feb 1957, San Francisco, CA, d. 20 Nov 1975, San Bruno, San Mateo Co, CA

^{V6}981. ^{13}6. Michael Stephen Linker,

^{V6}982. ^{12}2. **Gerald Dale Brashears**, m. ***Beverly*** ______,

^{V6}983. ^{13}1. **Christopher Don Brashears**,

^{V6}984. ^{12}3. **Glen Dale Brashears**, m. ***Jo Murray***,

^{V6}985. ^{13}1. **Bill Dale Brashears**, m. ***Karen Eileen Kinney***,

^{V6}986. ^{13}1. **Ben Michael Brashears**,

^{V6}987. ^{13}2. **Joe Lynn Brashears**, m. ***Mary Taylor***,

[V6]988. [13]3. **Brenda Leigh Brashears**,
[V6]989. [12]4. **Jimmy Brashears**,
[V6]990. [12]5. **Clifton Darrell Brashears**,
[V6]991. [11]7. **Louis Quitman Brashears**, b. 28 May 1913, Debb's Corner, OK, d. 27 June 1984. Ada, Pontotoc Co, OK, bur Stonewall, Pontotoc Co, OK; m. ***Lois Edna Holland***,
[V6]992. [12]1. **Jerry Ted Brashears**,
[V6]993. [12]2. **David Lee Brashears**,
[V6]994. [12]3. **Pamela Diane Brashears**,

Joseph B. Brashears and Ada Paralee Kirk

[v6]909. [10]3. **Joseph B. Brashears**, (s/o Henry Newton Brashears and Mary Ann Brownlow), b. 1 April 1869, TN (6 in 1880), d. 15 Dec 1954, Dougherty, Murray Co, OK. Wayne Brashear reports that his sisters called him "Uncle Ras" or "Rassie." The 1880 census gives his middle initial as "R." In some other listings, it is "B." His tombstone says J.B. Rassie Brashears. He m. 9 Aug 1892, Hickory, OK, ***Ada Paralee Kirk***, b. 3 Oct 1876, Blue Ridge, Collin Co, TX, d/o Dan Kirk and Malissa Dotson. They are in the 1920 census, Atoka Co, OK, Wilson twp, and the 1930 census of Murray Co, OK. A short autobiography of Joe B. Brashears appears in *OK Indian-Pioneer Histories*, S-149. (See below.)

Family of Joe B. "Rassie" Brashears and Ada Paralee Kirk:
[V6]995. [11]1. **Virgie Brashears**, b. before 1903
[V6]996. [11]2. **Minnie Brashears**, b. before 1903
[V6]997. [11]3. **Ruby Brashears**, b. c1905, OK (15 in 1920)
[V6]998. [11]4. **Cletus O. Brashears**, b. c1908, OK (11 in 1920)
[V6]999. [11]5. **Willie Brashears**, b. 10 Dec 1910, d. 16 Sept 1999, buried near Rassie and Paralee. See Obit below.
[V6]1000. [11]6. **Viola Brashears**, b. c1914, OK (5 in 1920)
[V6]1001. [11]7. **Joe C. Brashears**, b. c1918, OK (1 8/12 in 1920)

OBIT: Ardmorerite Sunday Newspaper, Ardmore, OK, 19 Sep 1999: Dougherty - Graveside rites for **Willie Brashears**, 88,

Sulphur, will be 10:30 a.m. Monday at Dougherty Cemetery with the Rev. Eddie Malphrus officiating. Born Dec 10, 1910, at Dougherty to Joseph Razzie and Ada Paralee Kirk Brashears, he died Sept. 16, 1999, at Oklahoma City. He was preceded in death by four sisters, Ruby, Virgie, Cletus and Viola; and one brother, J.C. Brashears. Brashears had lived in the Murray County area all of his life. He had worked as a farmer. Survivors include nieces and nephews. Services are under the direction of Clagg Funeral Home. (Barbara Giddens, email WQ8AwB18fqO, was source)

Indian-Pioneer History, S-149
"Life of a Cowboy in Territorial Days"
Joe B. Brashears: My parents were Henry Brashears and Mary Brownlow Brashears, born in Tennessee (dates unknown). There were seven children. Father was a farmer. I was born in Tennessee, April 1, 1870.

When I was thirteen years old, I ran away from home and went to Texas. I got a job on a ranch belonging to Dan Harrison. I helped drive a herd of about twenty-eight hundred head of cattle to the Osage Country, in 1883. I went back to Texas and, in a few months, we drove about nineteen hundred to the Osage country.

This time, as we got to Twelve Mile Prairie, in the Chickasaw Nation; it was time to camp for the night. In the meantime, my father had moved to the Territory and was living on Twelve Mile Prairie. I asked my boss if I might spend the night with Father, and he said that I could. Father's house was not far from where we camped, so I went over there for the night.

During the night, our cattle stampeded. I hurriedly jumped on my horse and rode toward Blue River to get ahead of them. The river was high and it was early in the Spring, so I knew the water was cold. But I plunged my horse into the racing water and some of the cattle followed me. Then I turned my horse and swam back to the bank, shooting. We finally got them to milling, but the next morning, we found three hundred dead steers. I received thirty dollars per month and my board.

One day not long after I came here, I went to see Frank Byrd. I was sitting in the house taking with Frank when

Governor Harris of the Chickasaw rode up. I asked him if he would give me a job. He replied that they were just ready to begin the Spring roundup and I could go to work.

That afternoon, I rode to Blue Prairie where the roundup was to be held. It was just about sundown when I got there, and the boys were all sitting near the chuck wagon waiting for supper. I got off my horse, staked him and went to the merry circle.

The boys didn't say much, but they laughed a great deal among themselves. I wondered why they were so amused, but after supper I found out the cause of their merriment. Two of them arrested me, and took me to the center of the circle. I was very much perplexed about what I had done to be treated in such a manner.

They had a judge and jury and held court. I was charged with riding too near the chuck wagon. They found me guilty and sentenced me to fifty stripes with a leather belt. I was tied to a barrel, face down and the punishment was administered amid shouts of laughter. To me, it wasn't so funny, but I wasn't hurt.

The next evening, Governor Harris came to the ranch and tied his team to the wheel of the chuck wagon. Alas, the boss had committed a crime, and he must be brought to justice. I was appointed judge and the Governor was given a fair and impartial trial by the high court. I decided he should be rolled in a blanket and rolled to the creek, where he must be plunged into the water.

My orders were fulfilled, and Governor Harris took it all as it was meant, in fun. We had some fine times on his ranch. I worked here for three years, then I went to work for Frank Byrd. I hauled the first machinery for his mill from Coalgate with seven yoke of oxen. It took five days to make the trip.

I attended several Pashofah dances near Stonewall. The sick Indian was placed in a hut and guards stood near. If anything came near the dancers, it was shot. It was thought to be the evil spirit which was causing the Indian's illness.

One night, I was forced to ride through Robber's Roost. I was alone, and there were so many murders committed there that I was very frightened before I entered the Roost. However, I had a six shooter, and I could use it if it became necessary.

Just after I passed the spring, a man reached up and

grabbed the bridle reins. My horse reared twice, and he held to the reins. I had a loaded riding quirt and I struck him a blow with it. He fell to the ground, stunned, and I rode away in a gallop. I didn't even remember that I had a gun. I gave it to a man for a night's lodging a few days later. If I couldn't remember to use it in case of necessity, I decided there was no need to carry it.

We drove our cattle to Davis to ship them, before the Frisco was built through Scullin, Mill Creek, and Ada.

I married Paralee Kirk in 1892 at Hickory. I have lived in Murry County forty years.

William Patrick Brashears and Lester Blackwell/ Mona Browne

V6910. 105. **William Patrick Brashears**, (s/o Henry N. Brashears and Mary Ann Brownlow), b. 6 June 1876, TN, d. 7 Jan 1966, Oroville, Butte Co, CA; m. 1903, ***Lester Marie Blackwell***, (2 ch; div), b. 31 March 1886, Blue Ridge, Collin Co, TX, d. 26 Oct 1943, Los Angeles, CA, d/o Lemuel D. Blackwell and Martha Jane Haney; m.2. 24 Oct 1928, in San Diego, CA, ***Mona M. G. Browne*** (5 ch), b. 27 Oct 1906, Ireland, d. 12 July 2003, Oroville, Butte Co, CA. Additional data from Wayne L. Brashear. There was 12 years between his marriage to Lester and Mona. He and Mona met while she was working in a restaurant in Los Angeles on Jefferson. They lived in Hawthorne, CA before moving to Oroville, CA. Mona Browne: Pat lived a long time in Stonewall OK. He was a paving plant superintendent and farmer.

1910 Census Sentinal, Washita Co, OK, district #262, Sheet #8 (22 Apr 1910):
W.P. Brashears, head, 35, b. TN, married 7 yrs, laborer, cement work, father born TN, mother born TN.
Lester Brashears, wife, 24, b. TX, married 7 yrs, mother of 2 children, 2 living, father born NC, mother born NC.
Alton Brashears, son, 5, b. OK, father born TN, mother born TX.
Dorothy Brashears, daughter, 2, b. OK, father born TN, mother born TX.
Dollie Womack, boarder, 18, single, b. TN, operator, telephone co. They're renting a house on Main St.

1930 Census Inglewood, Los Angeles Co, CA, District 1008, Sheet #5A (8 Apr 1930):

William P. Brashears, head, renting, 52, married, 27 when first married, b. TN, father b. TN, mother b. TN, occupation paving, not a veteran.

Mona M. G. Brashears, wife, 22, married, 20 when first married, b. Ireland, father b. Ireland, mother b. England, year of immigration unknown, naturalization or alien unknown.

Donald H. Brashears, son, 1 ?/12, b. CA, father b. TN, mother b. Ireland.

Family of William Patrick Brashears and Marie Louise Blackwell:

V6 1002. 11 1. **Alton Harold Blackwell Brashear**, (he took the "s" off the surname), b. 31 July 1904, Romulus, Pottawatomie Co, OK, d. 2 Jan 1956, Los Angeles, CA. Alton played ragtime piano accompaniment for silent movies prior to coming to Los Angeles (probably in Kansas). m. ***Dorothy Violetta Pettit***,

Figure 9: Alton Blackwell Brashear as a baby. Photo from Alice Killman, via Wayne Brashear; thanks.

V6 1003. 12 1. **Wayne Lloyd Brashear**, b. 1942; m. ***Shirley Jeanette Jensen***, Wayne has collected a great deal of data on this branch of the family, which he has shared with us.

V6 1004. 13 1. **Debra Louise Brashear**, b. 1967, m. ***Stephen Todd Bingham***,

V6 1005. 14 1. Rachel Jeanette Bingham,

V6 1006. 14 2. Michelle Louise Bingham,

V6 1007. 14 3. Christopher Todd Bingham,

V6 1008. 13 2. **David Alton Brashear**, b. 1970, m. ***Tamara Lynn Tucker***,

V6 1009. 14 1. **Emily Ruth Brashear**,

V6 1010. 14 2. **Natalie Mae Brashear**,

V6 1011. 14 3. **Joshua Wayne Brashear**,

V6 1012. 13 3. **Michael Wayne Brashear**, b. 1975, m. ***Katlyn Alison Krist***, d/o Craig Alan Krist and Gwynis Lynn Holdsworth

V6 1013. [14]1. **Hunter Michael Brashear**,

V6 1014. [13]4. **Mark Raymond Brashear**, b. 1976, m. ***Katherine "Katie" Theresa Reid***,

V6 1015. [13]5. **Daniel Matthew Brashear**, b. 1979, m. ***Justin Renee Ford***,

V6 1016. [12]2. **Carol Yvonne Brashear**, b. 1946, m. ***Frederick Granger Williams***,

V6 1017. [11]2. **Dorothy Brashears**, (d/o William Patrick Brashears and Marie Louise Blackwell), b. 28 May 1907, OK, d. 4 March 1994, San Bernardino, CA; m.1. ______ probably in OK, before moving to CA with her mother; m.2. ______ ; m.3. ***Howard Wilson***. Dorothy V. Brashear: Married 1st husband and probably divorced before coming to CA. She married for money only. No children by 1st marriage. She came to CA with her mother, Lester (apparently Alton had come first). 2nd or possibly 3rd husband was Howard Wilson. Dorothy was 40 or 41 when she had her first child. The second child was born about a year later.

V6 1018. [12]1. Leroy Wilson, b. c1947-48

V6 1019. [12]2. Ward "Bunny" Wilson, b. c1948-49

Family of William Patrick Brashears and Mona M.G. Browne, all b. Los Angeles, CA

V6 1020. [11]3. **Donald Henry Brashears**, b. c1887, Los Angeles, CA, d. 1966, age 89 (father of Peggy (Brashears) McGee)

V6 1021. [11]4. **Betty Jean Brashears**,

V6 1022. [11]5. **Sally Brashears**,

V6 1023. [11]6. **Claude William Brashears**, b. 15 March 1934, Los Angeles, CA, d. 29 April 1987, Butte Co, CA

V6 1024. [11]7. **Jeanette Brashears**,

Berry Francis Brashears and Oma G. Johnson

[v6]**911.** [10]6. **Berry Francis (or Franklin) Brashears**, (s/o Henry N. Brashear and Mary Ann Brownlow), b. Giles Co, TN, 24 Nov 1879 (23 at marriage in 1902), TN, d. 18 Dec 1955, Oklahoma City, bur OK City; m. 10 July 1902, in Chickasaw Nation, Stonewall, Pontotoc Co, OK, (Bk F, p.399), ***Oma G. Johnson***, b. TX, 25 March 1885, Montague Co, TX (18 at time of marriage), d. 22 Feb 1918, Tupelo, Coal Co, OK, bur Stonewall, OK. (Data from Wanda Schneider, <Waschn @yahoo.com>

Alice Killman: "Father never talked about his aunts and uncles. He would clam up when something bothered him." She believes that his mother died when he was very young. He is buried in the same plot with Claude in Oklahoma City, OK.

Laura Alice Brashears: Berry, when he was young, was very close to [his sister] Pauline and when she died it was very hard on him. He was just a year older than she and he carried her around on his back. Pauline died when she was 14 or 15 months old. Berry never mentioned her to Alice Killman.

1910 Census: Pontotoc Co., Stonewall Township, OK, Dist 058, No. 0190.
Berry F. Brashears, head, 30, married 8 yrs, b. TN, father b. TN, mother b. TN, farmer, general farming, renting.
Oma G. Brashears, wife, 25, married 8 yrs, 4 children born, 3 living, b. TX, father b. TX, mother b. TX.
Alice V. Brashears, daughter, 6, b. OK, father b. TN, mother b. TX, attended school in the past year.
Raymond H. Brashears, son, 4, b. OK, father b. TN, mother b. TX.
Hobert D. Brashears, son, 1, b. OK, father b. TN, mother b. TX.

1920 Census: Bryan Co. OK, Vol.7, Ed.15, Sheet 4, Line 31 shows his family living on East Mulberry St in Durant, OK. No wife is listed. The children are
Ilas (Alice?) Brashears 16,
Raymund (Raymond?) Brashears 14,
Hobart Brashears 11,
Claud (Claude) Brashears, 7
Oman Brashears 1 11/12,
Omie (Oma?) Brashears 1 11/12. All were born in OK.

Family of Berry Francis Brashears and Oma G. Johnson:

[V6]1025. [11]1. **Alice Virginia Brashears,** b. 25 Sept 1903, Stonewall, Pontotoc Co, OK, d. 11 March 2000,

Torrance, Los Angeles Co, CA; m. 31 Aug 1927, in Altus, Jackson Co, OK, ***Samuel Love Killman***, b. 28 Dec 1897, Burleson, Johnson Co, TX, d. 23 Nov 1971, Torrance, CA.

V6 1026. 12 1. Harvey Killman,

V6 1027. 12 2. Virginia Killman, b. 1930, d. 1988

V6 1028. 12 3. Betty Jo Killman,

V6 1029. 11 2. **Raymond Henry Brashears**, b. 16 Aug 1905, Stonewall, Pontotoc Co, OK, d. 15 May 1983, Tulsa, OK; m. cNov 1933, in OK City, ***Mary Helen Farny***,

V6 1030. 11 3. **"Sweet Sister" Brashears**, b. 3 May1907 and died same, Stonewall, OK

V6 1031. 11 4. **Hobart Delos Brashears,** b. 5 Feb 1909, Colgate, Coal Co, OK, d. 31 Dec 1984, Torrance, Los Angeles Co, CA; m. c1930, in Altus, Jackson Co, OK, ***Lorene Chestine***, Alice Killman: He was named after the city of Hobart where the family had lived for a while. He was born in Colgate while the family was there a short time, as Berry was hired out doing winter farming. Married to Lorene Chestine a short time. They met in Altus, OK.

V6 1032. 11 5. **Claude Francis Brashears**, b. 7 May 1912, Franks, Pontotoc Co, OK, d. 30 Dec 1981, Del City, OK; m. c1935, in OK City, ***Gladys ______,***

V6 1033. 11 6. **"Baby" Brashears**, b. 22 May 1916 and died same, Franks, Pontotoc Co, OK

V6 1034. 11 7. **Oman Berry Brashears**, (twin), b. 22 Feb 1918, Tupelo, OK; m. 1939, in OK City, ***Gladys Lundy***, d. c28 Dec 1989; m.2. ***May*** ______,

V6 1035. 11 8. **Oma Bertha Brashears**, (twin), b. 22 Feb 1918, Tupelo, OK; m. 13 Feb 1937 in Norman, OK, ***Menten Hayward Ford***,

10. DICEY ANN BRASHEARS and James M. Brookins

[v6]**865.** [9]7. **Dicey Ann Brashears**, (d/o Berry M. Brashears and Frances Pryor), b. 11 Aug 1854 in Tennessee, d. 16 Aug 1927 in Blue Ridge, Collin Co, TX; m. 24 July 1870, in Giles Co, TN (*Tn Marr, Giles Co, TN, 1851-1900*), ***James M. Brookins***, b. 2 Dec 1853, AL, d. 30 Aug 1930, McAlester, OK, s/o Assurbus Brookins and Lucinda Teel. Dicey and J.M. are buried in Blue Ridge Cem, Collin Co, TX.

1880 Census Giles Co, TN, No. 5 civil district, 17/18 Jun 1880:
James Brookins, 25, farmer, b. Alabama, father b. Georgia, mother b. (?).
Dicea A. Brookins, 25, wife, keeping house, b. TN, father b. (?), mother b. TN.
James H. Brookins, 8, son, b. TN, father b. AL, mother b. TN.
Thomas C. Brookins, 5, b. TN, father b. AL, mother b. TN.
Berry D. Brookins, 2, son, b.TN, father b. AL, mother b. TN.
Rosia A. Brookins, 3/12, b. TN, father b. AL, mother b. TN.

1900 census Collin Co, TX, District 24, Sheet No. 13 (15 Jun 1900):
James Brookins, head, 30, b. Feb 1850, farmer, father born TN, mother born NC.
Dicy Brookins, wife, 30, b. Aug 1850, had 9 children, 8 living, father b. TN, mother b. Unknown.
Effie B. Brookins, daughter, 14, b. Feb 1886, father born TX, mother born TN.
Joseph Brookins, son, 12, b. Sep 1888, father born TX, mother born TN.
Bulah Brookins, daughter, 8, b. Sep 1891, father born TX, mother born TN.
Utha Brookins, daughter, 5, b. Aug 1885, father born TX, mother born TN.
Rosa Woods, dau, 20, married, b. Mar 1880, no ch, father b. TN, mother b. TN.
Thomas Walker, boarder, 20, single, b. Apr 1880, father b. TX, mother b. Unknown.

1910 census: Collin Co. TX, Sup Dist 2, Enumeration Dist 24, Sheet 13; says she had 9 children with 8 living. Lists: James 47?, Dicy 46?, Effie B. 14, Joseph 12, Bulah 8, Utha 5.

1920 census McAlester, Pittsburg Co, OK, 15 Jan 1920:
James R. Brookins, head, 66, b. AL, father b. AL, mother b. AL, farmer.
Dicy Brookins, wife, 64, b. AL, father b. TN, mother b. TN.
Floyd Brookins, grandson, 18, b. TX, father b. TN, mother b. TX, no job.

<u>They had 9 children, 8 of whom survived:</u>

[V6]1101. [10]1. James <u>Henry</u> Brookins, b. 1872 in, TN; m.15 May 1893 in Collin Co, TX (Bk 9, p.3), Edna Dunlap

[V6]1102. [10]2. Thomas <u>Clayton</u> Brookins, b. 1875 in, TN; m.1. 10

Feb 1895 in Collin Co, TX (Bk9, p.471), Almer Kemp, (4 ch), b. Sept 1874, GA, d. 10 Feb 1895, Collin Co, TX; m.2. 3 March 1907 in Collin Co, TX, Zella K. Sutton (1 ch)

[V6]1103. [11]1. Charley Brookins (13 in 1910 Census); m. 12 Oct 1915 in Collin Co, TX, Jewel Maddox.

[V6]1104. [11]2. Lizzie Brookins (11 in 1910 Census); m. 26 Nov 1916 in Collin Co, TX (Bk18, p.246), A.M. Antone. Two ch in 1900 Census, Collin Co, TX: Charley Antone, b. 3 May 1897, and Lizzie Antone, b. 1 June 1898.

[V6]1105. [11]3. Mattie Brookins (9 in 1910 Census)

[V6]1106. [11]4. Elmer Brookins (7 in 1910 Census)

[V6]1107. [11]5. Thelma Brookins (age 2 in 1910)

[V6]1108. [10]3. Berry D. Brookins, b. Dec 1877, in Tennessee; m. 7 Sept 1897 in Collin Co, TX (Bk10, p.494), M.E. "Lizzie" Driggers, b. Jan 1881, TX. They lived at Terral, OK and later at Duncan, OK. They had 3 sons and a daughter. In 1900, Collin Co, TX, they had Mary Herley, grandmother, age 77, b. Jan 1823, TN. Next door, William T. Driggers, age 23, b. Dec 1876, his wife, Irene, and three ch.

[V6]1109. [11]1. Hozy Brookins, b. Aug 1898; m. Lillian ______, lived in Crowley, TX.

[V6]1110. [12]1. Douglas Brookins

[V6]1111. [12]2. B.F. Brookins

[V6]1112. [11]2. Roy Brookins, b. Dec 1899; m. Ethel and had 3 children. They moved to Colorado.

[V6]1113. [11]3. Eura Brookins

[V6]1114. [11]4. Joe Brookins - lived in, OK City.

[V6]1115. [10]4. Rosa A. Brookins, b. March1880 in TN; m. 7 May 1899 in Collin Co, TX (Bk.11, p.326), W. R. Woods.

[V6]1116. [10]5. Effie B. Brookins, b. Feb 1886 in Texas; m. 21 Aug 1904 in Collin Co, TX. (Bk.13, p.512), W.T. White.

[V6]1117. [10]6. Joseph Lawson Brookins, b. Sept 1888 in, TX; m. 11 Nov 1906 in Collin Co.(Bk.14, p.323), Cordia Crouch, b. c1888, KY, d/o William Crouch.

[V6]1118. [10]7. Beulah May Brookins, b. Sept 1891 in TX; m. 26 Sept 1909 in Blue Ridge, TX (Bk.15, p. 369), Heba

I. Aston.

V6 1119. 10 8. Utha Bell Brookins, b. 14 Aug 1894 in TX, d. 29 Nov 1902; bur Old Grounds Cem, Blue Ridge, Collin Co, TX. The inscription on her tombstone reads, "We Had a Little Treasure Once,/ She Was Our Joy and Pride,/ We Loved Her Ah, Perhaps too Well,/ for Soon She Slept, died."

Diane Brookins (email 25 Aug 2003 to Wayne Brashear): James M. was my husband's great-grandfather, but he did not have any contact with him, probably because he and some of the family moved to OK.

J. M. did own the Blue Ridge Hotel about 1915 to 1917. It was managed by his son-in-law and daughter, Tom and Effie White. I have a picture of it that came out of a newspaper well after it was abandoned. Have been trying to find a pic when it was open, but no success as yet.

Interestingly, James M. married Sara Sprague in McAlester, OK on 19 Nov 1928 about year after Dicey died. No one in the family now alive and able to remember, was aware of this marriage. I had a lot of doubters, even after I produced a marriage record. Later, someone found some papers where she got the house they were living in on North Katy street in McAlester. I have often wondered if she was a close friend of Dicey and J. M.

One of James M's children was named Berry D. Brookins. The "D" was for DeCaster or DeCasta or Decastro, it's been spelled all these ways. Several of subsequent Brookins had that middle name and we can't figure out where it came from. I talk with Berry's namesake and great-grandson frequently.

Not sure when James M. went to McAlester. He is on the 1880 Giles Co, TN census. In Collin Co, TX in 1900 and 1910 and is in McAlester, OK by 1920. He may have moved after he sold the hotel, but it is possible he kept it, as his daughter was running it for him.

Another J. M.'s sons, James Henry, called Henry, also went to McAlester. His first wife, Edna Dunlap died of tuberculosis in TX. He later married Hailey Graves Cougler, who had several children and she and Henry had two more, Eunice and Jennie Laura. I can find Henry in 1900 and 1920, but have not been successful in finding him in 1910 which I would like to do.

Several family members worked at the prison in McAlester. One worked only until the first electrocution. When the lights dimmed, he left.

Family records show Dicey with seven names. Dicy Ann Matilda Hawkins Cannella Ann Josephine Brashears (Brashers). Cousins from the TX and OK group both had this info written down.

James M's parents were Assurbus (sometimes Ascerbus and Asarvus) Brookins and Lucinda Teel. I just recently found Assurbus' parents were Robert N. Brookin and Martha Ruffin Claiborne. They went from Georgia to Alabama. Robert N. is a direct bloodline to Col Francis Vivion Brooking of Amelia Co, VA, who served in the Continental Army. The "g" probably came off as a result of Alabama accent. There were some relatives in Arkansas who added the "g," but left the "s" and are known as Brookings. But not all of them made the change.

There is a Dovie Brashears who apparently lived for a time with Henry and his family. Her married name was Young. A relative recently found mention of her.

Diane Brookins (email 1 Jan 2004): I hunted a long time for James Brookins in Giles Co, TN in 1870 as I figured you just didn't show up suddenly and marry a young girl back then. I could never find him for a long time, although I did find his widowed mother and the rest of the family living a short distance from Dicey. His mother is listed as Brackens on the index.

A relentless search, page by page, said the only possibility was a James Brooks, 16, living with the Annanias and Delany Kilpatric family (1870 census Giles Co, TN, p0191 on Rootsweb.com). Then I sent away for his marriage license and the person who signed on his marriage bond was none other than A. B. Kilpatric. So that proved to me he was the James Brooks living with them. I was told that the Kilpatric name is related to either the Brookins or Brashears, in some way, and I find them living near each other on census records, but can't make a direct connection although I have tried hard.

Since the 1900 census said Dicey had 9 children and 8 alive, I believe she may have lost a child that we have no record of. James Henry was born 21 Aug 1873, so she may have had a child previous to him. None of the relatives are aware of this ninth child.

11. MARTILLA "TEALLIE" BRASHEARS and John W. Penny

v6866. 98. **Martilla "Teallie" Brashears**, (d/o Berry M. Brashears and Frances Pryor), b. 1 April 1856, TN (23 in 1880 Giles Co, TN); m. about 1878, probably in Giles Co, TN, ***John W. Penny***, b. Nov 1832 in Tennessee, d. between World War I and 1925 and is buried in the Old Grounds Cem. Tealie died about 1925 and is buried in Elm Grove Cem, Collin Co, TX.

1900 census Collin Co, TX, District 23, Sheet No. 6 (7 Jun 1900):
John W. Penney, head, 67, married 22 yrs, b. Nov 1832, b. TN, father b. NC, mother b. NC, farming, owns property.
Martela I. Penney, wife, 41, married 22 yrs, b. May 1859, mother of 9 children, 4 living, b. TN, father b. TN, mother b. TN.
Berry W. Penney, son, 20, single, b. Sep 1879, TN, father b. TN, mother b. TN.
John L. Penney, son, 14, b. May 1886, b. TN, father b. TN, mother b. TN.
Rubin A. Penney, 4, son, b. Apr 1896, b. TX, father b. TN, mother b. TN.
Onits [Otis] Penney, son, 2, b. Jan 1898, b. TX, father b. TN, mother b. TN.
Nathan Brashears, brother-in-law, 38, single, b. Oct 1861, TN,
Francis, mother-in-law, 78, widow, b. Jan 1822, TN

Martilla Brashears and John Penny had 9 ch, but only 4 sons survived:

V61151. 101. Berry W. Penny, b. 1879 in Giles Co, TN, d. 1964, Collin Co, TX; m. 31 Aug1910 in Collin Co, TX (Bk 15, p.567), Vicktory Smith, b. 1890, d. 1958. Both are buried in Blue Ridge Cem.

V61152. 111. Flossie Penny; m. 3 Sept 1932, T.L. Williams,

V61153. 112. Malcome Penny; m. 16 Dec 1939, Collin Co, TX (Bk24, p.435), Faustine Hartness

V61154. 102. Lindsey J. Penny, b. 28 May 1886; m. 6 March 1910 in Collin Co, TX (Bk15, p.485), Myrtle Randles, b. 15 Sept 1891, d. 1 Dec 1957. Both are buried in Elm Grove Cem. (Tombstone Inscriptions)

V6 1155. 11 1. Lee Penny; m. Billie Marlow

V6 1156. 11 2. Mildred Penny; m. Jack Baldwin

V6 1157. 11 3. Winston Penny; m. Willie Jane Chaney

V6 1158. 11 4. Naomi Penny; m.1. Noel Ashinhurst (Dec.); m.2. Dan Still

V6 1159. 11 5. Ardell Penny; m. Fern Fletcher

V6 1160. 11 6. Infant Son, b.& d. 3 July 1919; bur Elm Grove Cem

V6 1161. 11 7. Reuben O'dell Penny, b. 16 March 1917, d. 21 Feb 1920; bur Elm Grove Cem

V6 1162. 11 8. Vallie Marie Penny, b. 14 April 1926, d. 22 April 1926; bur Elm Grove Cem

V6 1163. 11 9. Aurelia Penny; m. Royce Terry

V6 1164. 10 3. Reuben A. Penny, b. Apr 1896, TX, according to 1900 census; m. Emma Smith, 24 Sept 1919 in Collin Co, TX. (Bk19, p.341). His tombstone in the Blue Ridge Cem gives his birth as 8 Jan 1895 and death 29 May 1951. He was a PFC, 344 Field Artillery, 90 Division, World War I.

V6 1165. 11 1 Weyman Penny; m. Doris Malone, 29 July 1944.

V6 1166. 10 4. Otis Penny, b. TX, Jan 1898 (per 1900 census; 12 in 1910 Census)

12. REUBEN T. BRASHEARS and Elizabeth "Bettie" Harbour

[v6]**863.** [9]5. **Reuben T. Brashears**, (s/o Berry M. Brashears and Frances Pryor), b. 21 Oct 1849 in Lawrence Co, TN, d. 10 Dec 1917 of Lobar Pneumonia in Fort Worth, TX (Death Certificate). He is buried at Oldgrounds Cem, Blue Ridge, Collin Co, TX. There is no tombstone but his granddaughter, Freeda Brashears Moore, remembers when he died. She says he is buried next to his wife (her grandmother). Freeda said, "My Dad (Tom) and Uncle John went to Fort Worth and carried his body back here to bury him. The hearse that carried him to the cemetery is in an old barn over in Anna". (1989)

Reuben Brashears m.1. 16 July 1871 in Giles Co, TN, ***Elizabeth "Bettie" Harbour***, b. 1 April 1856 (tombstone), Lawrence Co, TN, d. 1 June 1895, Blue Ridge, Collin Co, TX; d/o Henry J. and Lucinda Claiborne Harbour. In the1880 census they are listed in District 6 of Gibson Co, TN, with 5 children. In 1885 or 1886, they migrated to Collin Co, TX. Reuben bought 50 acres of land "situated on the waters of Pilot Grove Creek". The land was part of Johnathan Douthitt's Survey and was "Conveyed 26 Jan 1887 by J.H. Doman and Wife" to Reuben and wife. (Land Records Collin Co, TX.) He grew cotton on his land.

The family traveled in a wagon train from Tennessee along with Reuben's brother, Henry; sisters, Dicey and Tealie; and their families. His mother, Frances Pryor Brashears, came along, and she was listed with her daughter, Tealie Penny, in the 1900 Census.

About ten years after moving to Texas, Bettie died. There is a tombstone in Oldgrounds Cem near Blue Ridge, TX, which reads,"Wife and Child of R. T. Brashears, b. April 1,1856, Died June 1, 1895." Across the bottom of the tombstone an inscription reads, "She Was a Kind and Affectionate Wife and Fond Mother and Friend to All." Above the name there is an elaborate carving of a gate with the words "gates ajar" on a scroll over the gate. A closed book with flowers on it is carved above the gate. Leaves are carved on the sides of the stone. It is a beautiful tribute to Bettie Harbour Brashears. Her children said she died with the measles.

Oldest son, John, said his father called her "Betts."

Reuben and Bettie Harbour Brashears had 11 known children:

[V6]1201. [10]1. ***John William Henry Brashears**, b. 1873, d. 1955

[V6]1202. [10]2. ***Thomas Jefferson Brashears**, b. 1875,

[V6]1203. [10]3. **R. Edward "Ed" Brashears**, b. Feb 1877 in Giles Co, TN; m. 8 Sept 1897 (Bk 10, p.493) in Collin Co, TX, ***Maggie May Caroll***, b. Oct 1881, in Kentucky. In the 1900 Census, they were living in Collin Co, TX, and his brother and sister, Berry and Sallie, were living with them. Ed and Maggie moved to Walters, OK before 1910. (7 ch; not sure of birth order):

[V6]1204. [11]1. **Kelly Brashears**, b. July 1898 in TX

[V6]1205. [11]2. **Clyde Brashears**,

[V6]1206. [11]3. **Jimmie Brashears**, *MAY NOT BE HIM* Jimmie Brashears, b. 26 March 1898, d. 18 May 1978, bur Stigler Cem, Haskell Co, OK

[V6]1207. [11]4. **Alvin Brashears**,

[V6]1208. [11]5. **Beatrice Brashears**,

[V6]1209. [11]6. **Buster Brashears**, *MAY NOT BE HIM* Buster Brashears, b. 8 Jan 1903, no death date, bur Stigler Cem, Haskell Co, OK.

[V6]1210. [11]7. **Fay Brashears**,

[V6]1211. [10]4. **Nathan T. Brashears**, b. 2 Dec 1878, Fannin, TX, d. 14 April 1961 in Fannin Co, TX; m. ***Emma White***, b. in 1878, d. in 1956. They had no children. Both are buried in the Van Alstyne cem, Grayson Co, TX. Emma had a daughter, Minta, b. 1900, when she and Nathan married. Minta used the name Brashears. In the 1910 Census, Nathan and Emma were in Collin Co, TX. The household consisted of Minta, Reuben (Nathan's father), Sherman, (Nathan's brother), and Effie (Nathan's half-sister).

[V6]1212. [10]5. ***Frances "Fanny" Brashears**, b. 1879, d. 1950
[V6]1213. [10]6. ***Berry Webb Brashears**, b. 1874, d. 1957
[V6]1214. [10]7. ***Eulalie Brashears**, b. 1886, d. 1961
[V6]1215. [10]8. ***Sarah Elizabeth "Sally" Brashears**, b. 1883, d. 1973
[V6]1216. [10]9. ***Nancy Dovie Brashears**, b. 1889, d. 1985
[V6]1217. [10]10. ***Sherman Monroe Brashears**, b. 1892, d. 1985
[V6]1218. [10]11. Infant **Brashears**, b.& d. 1894

Reuben T. Brashears m.2. in Collin Co, TX, 16 April 1896 (Bk 10, p. 160), Mrs. ***May R. "Mollie" Tilley Birdwell***, (div 26 March 1898 in Collin Co, TX; Bk N, p.278-9, No. 4712). May "Mollie" m. again in 1900 to R.W. Johnson. Reuben and Mollie had one daughter:

[V6]1219. [10]12. **Edna Brashears**, b. Oct 1896; m. 22 Sept 1913 in Westminster, TX, by Eddie Greer, Minister (Bk. 17, p. 132), ***David A. Duke***. Edna may have married (second) a Fowler later in life. Someone had written in pencil along the margin of the marriage record book ,"Edna Fowler, 517 Ton Ave, Modesto, CA." Edna and her mother were living with her grandfather, John Birdwell, in Collin Co, TX, in the 1900 Census.

On 17 Aug 1906, in the part of the Chickasaw Nation which became Pontotoc Co, OK, Reuben T. Brashears m.3. ***Dovie L. Jackson***. (in 1996, Cheryl Holder, 18034 June Forest, Humble, TX called Sybil and said she had found a marriage record for a Reuben T. Brashears, age 48, and Dovie L. Jackson, age 25. She thought the marriage took place in a village of Pontotoc, which would be south of present day Ada, in Johnson Co, OK. The marriage is recorded in Book 37, p. 1312). Reuben and his third wife had a daughter, Effie. Reuben and Effie were living with his son, Nathan, in Collin Co, TX in 1910.

[V6]1220. [10]13. **Effie Lee Brashears**, b. 4 Aug 1905, d. 22 July 1941, the victim of an accidental drowning near her home in Waurika, OK; bur Waurika Cem; m. 6 dec 1922 in Waurika, OK, ***Albert H. Howard***, b.

6 Dec 1922, Waurika, OK. They had 4 children:

[V6]1221. [11]1. O'dale Howard,

[V6]1222. [11]2. Dorothy Jean Howard,

[V6]1223. [11]3. Euel J. Howard,

[V6]1224. [11]4. Aubrey Ray Howard,

Sybil Jobe reports (1989); Information for the Reuben Brashears Family came from Census Records, marriage Records from Collin Co, TX, Death Certificates of Reuben and his son Nathan, Cem Records from Oldgrounds Cem, Reuben's marriage Record from Giles Co, TN, Records for John, Thomas, Edward, and Nathan, from Jonnie Vee (Brashears) Robertson, Records for Fanny from Clarita Ainsworth, Records for Berry from Omie Byrd, Records for Eulalie from Sybil Jobe, Records for Sally from Mary Frances Porter, Gene Naron, Zane Foster, Ella Mae Parkhill Taylor, and Odessia Parkhill, Records for Sherman from Maxine Cooper and Tommy Brashear, Records for Dovie from Clarice Spaulding, Records for Effie from Omie Byrd and Effie's Obituary.

John William Henry Brashears and Viola White

[v6]1201. [10]1. **John William Henry Brashears,** (s/o Reuben T. Brashears and Elizabeth Harbour), b. 6 Oct 1873 in Giles Co, TN, d. 23 Feb 1955 in Collin Co, TX; m. 17 Sept 1893 in McKinney, Collin Co, TX, ***Viola White***, b. 24 Aug 1877, d. 3 July 1928, Collin Co, TX. Both are buried in the Elm Grove Cem.

John was a farmer and belonged to The Methodist Church. He helped to build a Methodist Church in Westminster, Texas. The building is still standing (1989).

Jonnie Vee (Brashears) Robertson wrote of her father: "He was known as John and signed his name J.W. Brashears. For some reason, he dropped the Henry. He had very little education, but he enjoyed reading, and I guess you might say he educated himself. He read real well. He read the daily newspaper, the bible, and was interested in politics, community affairs, and church. Once he told me he attended a penmanship school, and he did have a pretty handwriting.

He grew cotton and corn on his farm. For several years he

had a syrup mill and cooked and sold syrup. He served as steward for several years in the Methodist Church in Westminster, TX. He enjoyed good gospel singing and attended singing schools in Westminster and surrounding areas. He also went to singing conventions.

Unlike some of his brothers, he was a talker. His favorite past time was fishing. He also enjoyed playing dominos and whittling. After he retired, he enjoyed going to town and visiting with his friends and trading knives. After he lost mother, he was lonely and his health began to fail. He worked hard all of his life."

John Brashears and Viola White had 10 children, all b. in Collin Co, TX.

[V6]1225. [11]1. ***Lillie Ethel Brashears**, b. 19 July 1894, Collin Co, TX, d. 17 Aug 1957, bur Seymour, TX; m. 28 Aug 1912 in Collin Co, TX, ***Ewing Tucker***. (See ch below)

[V6]1226. [11]2. **Roscoe Elbert Brashears**, b. 25 Feb 1897, Collin Co, TX, d. 3 March1959; bur Elm Grove Cem; m. ***Ona Mae Kuyhendall***, b. 1897, d. 1968; bur Blue Ridge Cem.

[V6]1227. [12]1. **Robbie Jean Brashears**; m. ***Alexander Keys,***

[V6]1228. [11]3. **Arthur E. Brashears**, b. 7 Feb 1901, Collin Co, TX. d. 17 Jan 1976, bur Lubbock, TX; m. ***Plumer White***, no ch.

[V6]1229. [11]4. **Roy C. Brashears**, b. Jan 1903, Collin Co, TX, d. Dec 1904

[V6]1230. [11]5. ***Harvey Erskin Brashears**, b. 14 March 1905, Collin Co, TX, d. 23 Oct 1969, bur Grayson, TX; m. 17 April 1926, in Anna, TX, ***Edna Sloan***, b. 1905, d. 1979, (See ch below)

[V6]1231. [11]6. **Lewis Earl Brashears**, b. 28 March 1907, Collin Co, TX, d. 30 April 1973; bur Lubbock, TX; m.1. ***Ruby Mercer***, (1 ch); m.2. c1962, in Lubbock, TX, ***Aeirial Housour***,

[V6]1232. [12]1 **Patsy Ruth Brashears**; m. ***Bennie Cryer***,

[V6]1233. [13]1. Michael Cryer,

[V6]1234. [13]2. Charley Cryer,

[V6]1235. [13]3. Debra Cryer,

[V6]1236. [11]7. **Trinver Leonard Brashears**, b. 9 Nov 1910, Collin Co, TX, d. 25 Nov 1952; bur Seymour Texas; m. ***Dorothy George***, (3 ch)

[V6]1237. [12]1. **Lonna Kay Brashears**; m. ***Raymond Motl***,

[V6]1238. [13]1. Cathy Motl,

[V6]1239. [12]2. **George Kent Brashears**; m. ______ and has 3 sons.

[V6]1240. [12]3. **Karen Brashears**; m. ______ and has a son and a daughter.

[V6]1241. [11]8. **Jonnie Vee Brashears**, b. 10 Nov 1920; m. 4 Nov 1939, ***Harlie Robertson***, b. 25 Dec 1916, d. 7 June 1986; bur Van Alstyne, TX Cem. Jonnie Vee lives in Van Alstyne, TX.

[V6]1242. [12]1. Paula Gail Robertson, b. 22 July 1945; m. Bill Blackburn.

[V6]1243. [12]2. Dennis Merle Robertson, b. 29 Sept 1952.

[V6]1244. [11]9. Infant **Brashears**; bur Elm Grove Cem

[V6]1245. [11]10. Infant **Brashears**; bur Elm Grove Cem

[v6]1225. [11]1. **Lillie Ethel Brashears**, (d/o John W. Brashears and Viola White), b. 19 July 1894, d. 17 Aug1957; bur Seymour, TX; m. 28 Aug 1912 in Collin Co, TX, ***Ewing Tucker***. They had six children:

[V6]1246. [12]1. Jennie Orene Tucker; m. W.J. Karr and lives in Seymour, TX.

[V6]1247. [13]1. Raymond Gerald Karr,

[V6]1248. [13]2. Curtis Earl Karr,

[V6]1249. [13]3. James Carrol Karr,

[V6]1250. [13]4. Ronald Jay Karr,

[V6]1251. [12]2. Jesse Floyd Tucker; m.1. Oleta Herron (1 ch, div); m.2. Ola Pearl _______ (1 ch)

[V6]1252. [13]1. Sharon May Tucker,

[V6]1253. [13]2. Susan Tucker,

[V6]1254. [12]3. Bernice Earl Tucker; m. Margaret Ball and adopted a son:

[V6]1255. [13]1. David Earl Tucker,

[V6]1256. [12]4. James Winston Tucker; m. Dottie ______

[V6]1257. [13]5. Melvin Lee Tucker; m. Orela Bates and they have a daughter and 2 sons, names unknown to me.

[V6]1258. [14]6. James Erwin Tucker; m. Virginia ______ , No children.

[V6]1230. [11]5. **Harvey Erskin Brashears**, (s/o John W. Brashears and Viola White), b. 14 March 1905, d. 23 Oct 1969; bur Van Alstyne Cem, Grayson Co, TX; m. 17 April 1926, in Anna, TX, ***Edna Sloan***, b. 1905, d. 1979. They had 3 children:

[V6]1259. [12]1. **Delton Ray "Pete" Brashears**, b. in Collin Co, TX, 29 Sept 1929; m.1. ***Joyce Ashley*** (3 ch; div); m.2. in Aug 1972, ***Theda Belle Enzensperger***, b. 15 Nov 1931 in Dallas, TX, d/o Alfred Theodore and Cecile Belle Milner Enzensperger.

[V6]1260. [12]1. **Debra Joyce Brashears**, b. 11 June 1952; m. ***Gary Hemphill***,

[V6]1261. [14]1. Ashley Lynn Hemphill, b. 9 April 1970

[V6]1262. [14]2. Colby Hemphill, b. 26 March 1976

[V6]1263. [13]2. **Patricia Sue Brashears**, b. 22 Dec1956; m.1. ***Glen*** ______ (div); m.2. ***Burt Wright***,

[V6]1264. [14]1. Candice ______ , b. 17 May 1976

[V6]1265. [14]2. Aaron Wright, b. 11 May1983

[V6]1266. [13]3. **Randall Ray Brashears**, b. 30 Sept 1960

[V6]1267. [12]2. **Imogean "Jeanne" Brashears**, b. 7 Apr 1932; m.1. ***Roy Pullen, Jr***. (div); m.2. 31 Oct 1956, ***Morris Burns***,

[V6]1268. [13]1. Bruce Pullen, b. 30 Dec 1952

[V6]1269. [13]2. Kent Burns, b. 2 Nov 1957

[V6]1270. [13]3. Keith Duane Burns, B. 20 May 1959

[V6]1271. [13]4. Kelly Wayne Burns, B. 27 Oct 1962

[V6]1272. [13]5. Barry Burns, b. 27 Oct 1965

[V6]1273. [12]3. **James Weldon Brashears**, b. 3 Feb 1936; m. 1 June 1958 in Collin Co, TX, ***Brenda Gayle Fennell*** (5 ch; div)

[V6]1274. [13]1. **Jimmie Don Brashears**,

[V6]1275. [13]2. **Kimberly Brashears**,

[V6]1276. [13]3. **Timmie Brashears**,

[V6]1277. [13]4. **Lisa Brashears**,

[V6]1278. [13]5. dau **Brashears**,

Thomas Jefferson Brashears and Lula Beck

[v6]1202. [10]2. **Thomas Jefferson Brashears**, (s/o Reuben T. Brashears and Elizabeth Harbour), b. 5 (or 9) Oct 1875 in Giles Co, TN, d. 5 Nov 1935 in Collin Co, TX; m. 2 March 1902 in Collin Co, TX (Bk 12, p.552), ***Lula Beck***, b. TN, 6 March 1887, d. 27 Oct 1980, d/o Dora Beck. Tom and Lula are buried in the Van Alstyne, TX Cem. They had 2 sons and 4 daughters:

[V6]1279. [11]1. **Stella Brashears**, b. 1904; m. ***Martin Barnett***,
[V6]1280. [12]1. Maggie Lou Barnett; m. Carl Minton (2 ch)
[V6]1281. [12]2. J.C. Barnett; m.______ (2 Ch)
[V6]1282. [12]3. Coy Wayne Barnett; m. Fay ______ (2 ch)
[V6]1283. [11]2. **Ennis C. Brashears**, b. 1906, d. 1961; m. ***Thelma Herrin***, b. 1910, d.1973; both bur Van Alstyne Cem.
[V6]1284. [12]1. **Billy Ray Brashears**,
[V6]1285. [11]3. **Freeda Brashears**, b. 1908; m.1. ***Roy Barnett***, (2 ch); m.2. ***Arthur Moore***, live in Van Alstyne, TX.
[V6]1286. [12]1 James M. Barnett; m. ______ (3 Ch)
[V6]1287. [13]1 Ronnie Barnett
[V6]1288. [13]2 Becky Barnett
[V6]1289. [13]3 Jimmie Barnett
[V6]1290. [12]2 Peggy Barnett; m. Joe Hemphill,
[V6]1291. [14]1 Cathy Hemphill
[V6]1292. [11]4. **Opal Brashears**, b. 12 Oct 1911, d. 17 Feb 1978; m. ***Jesse T. Adams***, b. 24 Sept 1911, d. 29 May 1980; both bur Van Alstyne, TX Cem.
[V6]1293. [12]1. Tommy Adams, Lives in Midland, TX.
[V6]1294. [11]5. **Odessa Brashears**; m. ***J.D. Griffin***,
[V6]1295. [12]1. Judy Griffin; m. and has 2 Sons
[V6]1296. [11]6. **Audie Lee Brashears**; m. ***Joyce*** ______, and has 2 sons and 2 grandchildren.

Frances "Fanny" Brashear and Oyd McKinney

[v6]1212. [10]5. **Frances "Fannie" Brashears**, (d/o Reuben T. Brashears and Elizabeth Harbour), b. 30 Nov 1879 in Gibson

Co, TN, d. 1 Jan 1950 at Walters, Oklahoma, bur Burk Burnett, TX. The family moved soon after her birth to Crockett Co, Tennessee. She belonged to the Methodist Church. Frances Brashears m. 1 Aug 1901 in O'Conner, OK, ***Oyd McKinney***, b. 13 Feb 1871. His mother's maiden name was Mary Shankes. Fannie and Oyd lived in Olney, OK, Hardwood, OK, and Burkburnett, TX.

Frances Brashears and Oyd McKinney had 8 children:

[V6]1297. [11]1. Georgia McKinney, b. 2 May 1902 in Hardwood, OK, d. 20 Aug 1970; bur Savana, OK; m. Cecil Harrison, b. 4 July 1890, d. 26 Aug 1949. They had 4 Children:

[V6]1298. [12]1. Geneva Harrison, b. 22 Dec 1922 in Lehigh, OK; m. 9 Sept 1943, Lewis Liedtke.

[V6]1299. [12]2. Clarence Harrison, b. 16 Oct 1926 in Lehigh, OK; m. 13 Sept 1958, Lorane Sexton

[V6]1300. [12]3. Maxine Harrison, b. 15 Sept 1932 in Lehigh, OK; m. 15 Sept 1951, Robert Ward.

[V6]1301. [12]4. Lottie Harrison, b. 16 Oct 1939 in Lehigh, OK; m. 8 March 1969, Thomas Cochran.

[V6]1302. [11]2. Leona McKinney, b. 7 Sept 1903, in Hardwood, OK, d. 1 Aug 1966 in Lawton, OK; bur Burkburnett, TX; m. Calvin Champion, d. 8 Dec 1963. They Had 8 Children:

[V6]1303. [12]1. Jack Cecil Champion, b. in Burkburnett, TX.

[V6]1304. [12]2. Jewel Champion, b. 25 March 1924 in BurkBurnett, TX.

[V6]1305. [12]3. Margreat Champion, b. 13 March 1926 at BurkBurnett, TX

[V6]1306. [12]4. Lettie Champion, b. 29 May 1928 in Lehigh, OK

[V6]1307. [12]5. Lee Roy Champion, b. 20 June 1934 in BurkBurnett, TX

[V6]1308. [12]6. Maxine Champion, b. 13 March 1936 in BurkBurnett, TX

[V6]1309. [12]7. Lester Ray Champion, b. 7 Feb 1939 in BurkBurnett, TX

[V6]1310. [12]8. Clarence Allen Champion, b. 16 Jan 1940 in Burkburnett, TX

[V6]1311. [11]3. William Marvin McKinney, b. 20 Sept 1905 in Hardwood, OK; m. 15 Aug 1926 in Wichita Falls, TX, Bonnie Dick, b. 23 Nov 1909, d. in Dallas, TX, 13 Oct 1982, d/o Henry Dick. They belonged to the Methodist Church. William was in the grocery business and Bonnie was a cashier. They lived in Wichita Falls, TX, Houston, TX, and Dallas, TX. William and Bonnie had one daughter:

[V6]1312. [12]1. Peggy Lou McKinney, b. 12 May 1927 in Wichita Falls, TX, d. in Dallas, TX, 8 Feb 1983 and is buried in Arlington, TX; m. 8 Feb 1961, Leroy Holley.

[V6]1313. [11]4. Jessie McKinney, b. 24 Feb 1907 in Hardwood, OK, d. 1920 in Hardwood, OK.

[V6]1314. [11]5. Clarita McKinney, b. 24 Aug 1910 in Hardwood, OK; m.15 June 1927, Elzy Clayton Ainsworth, b. 30 Jan 1902 in Erice, TX; s/o Christopher and Mattie Blevins Ainsworth. Clarita and Clayton are Methodists and farmers. They have lived in Burkburnett, TX, Walters, OK, and Duncan, OK. They have 3 children:

[V6]1315. [12]1. J. C. Ainsworth, b. 12 May 1930 in Hollis, OK, d. 30 May 1930.

[V6]1316. [12]2. Billie Jean Ainsworth, b. 29 July 1932 in BurkBurnett, TX; m.1. Aug 1949 in Hulen, OK, Eugene Morgan; m.2. 29 Oct 1977, Rufus R. Caldwell.

[V6]1317. [12]3. Bettie Jane Ainsworth, b. 13 May 1935 in Burkburnett, TX; m.1. Aug 1951 in Fletcher, OK, Clarence Reeder; m.2. 15 June 1963, James A. Martinez

[V6]1318. [11]6. Annie McKinney, b. 11 March 1913, d. 1915.

[V6]1319. [11]7. Evie Oleta McKinney, b. 25 Oct 1914 in Hardwood, OK; m. 25 April 1931, Grandfield, OK, Elbert Amos Sanders, d. 6 May 1981. They have 3 children:

[V6]1320. [12]1. Lottie Mae Sanders, b. 5 Sept 1932 in BurkBurnett, TX; m. Burt Fairbanks. They have 3 children and 7 grandchildren.

[V6]1321. [12]2. Mildred Joyce Sanders, b. 12 Feb 1934 in

Mangum, OK, d. 27 March 1985 in San Jose, CA; m. Earl Cox. They had 2 children and 3 grandchildren.

V6 1322. 12 3. Perry Duayne Sanders, b. 20 July 1937 in Farmersville, CA; m. Mary Rauth. They have 2 sons.

V6 1323. 11 8. Ruby McKinney, b. 13 Nov 1919, d. 1925.

Berry Webb Brashears and Ida Mae Shaw

v6 1213. 10 6. **Berry Webb Brashears**, (s/o Reuben T. Brashears and Elizabeth Harbour), b. 6 Feb 1885, Collin Co, TX, d. 20 April 1957 in Seagraves, TX and is buried in Terral, Jefferson Co, OK; m. ***Ida Mae Shaw***, b. 24 Oct 1888 in Trinity, TX, d. 1 Jan 1971 in Moore, OK; bur Terral, OK.

The 1900 Census Collin Co, TX lists him as a brother in the household of Edward Brashears. Ed gave Berry's age as 13, b. Jan 1887 in TX.

Omie (Brashears) Byrd wrote of her father: "He never stayed away from me over two weeks at a time. He told everyone that he worshiped the ground I walked on. I was always at his heels. He thought my kids were "it." They called him 'Addad'. Momma was Grannie. I went with papa to haul drift wood for the cook stove out on Red River.

Papa farmed cotton and feed corn. He loved chickens and raised them. He raised fruit trees and a garden. He loved to fish. He made us a good living.

When he was a little boy, his mother was going to whip him one day and he ran from her. He fell on a knife and cut a bad place on his stomach. He had a bad scar there.

Papa was a come easy, go easy person. He pulled tricks on anyone and teased a lot. He was a joker. He has been gone 32 years and at times it still hurts."

Berry Webb Brashear and Ida Mae Shaw had 2 daughters:

V6 1324. 11 1. **Vivian May Brashears**, b. 25 May 1910 Fleetwood, OK; m.1. 3 Nov 1928, ***Edgar Lee Vessels***, d. Feb 1971 in Terral, OK. She later m.2. ***Ben Lund***. Vivian and Edgar Had 3 Children:

[V6]1325. [12]1. Alfred Leroy Vessels, b. 26 Jan 1932 in Terral, OK, d. 10 Feb 1969.

[V6]1326. [12]2. Joyce Marie Vessels, b. 8 April 1934, d. 4 June 1934.

[V6]1327. [12]3. Rita Joy Vessels, b. 24 Nov 1938 in Ryan, OK, d. 31 Dec 1987; m. Clemency Charles Jones. They had 2 children:

[V6]1328. [13]1. Sherry Sabrena Jones Drake, b. 14 Jun 1963

[V6]1329. [13]2. Clemency Charles Jones II, b. 26 Feb 1967.

[V6]1330. [11]2. **Omie Bell Brashears**, b. 14 March 1914 in Wilson, OK; m. ***Louis Henry Locke*** and they divorced; m.2. 23 Sept 1950, ***Allen Byrd***, b. 10 Feb 1904, d. 7 Dec 1982. Omie now (1989) lives in McCloud, OK. She and Louis had 3 children:

[V6]1331. [12]1. Louis Rayford "Ray" Locke, b. 28 June 1934, Terral, OK; m. 15 Sept 1956, in Seminole, TX, Vivian Agusta Fisher, from Bartlesville, OK. They were divorced in 1981. They had six children:

[V6]1332. [13]1. Michael Ray Locke, b. 23 June 1957 In, OKlahoma City, OK, d. 9 April 1980 in Lubbock, TX. He is buried in Loop Community Cem, Loop, TX.

[V6]1333. [13]2. Anthony Eugene Locke, b. 26 Sept 1958 in Edmond, OK; m. Sue Ann Bales from Denver City, TX 28 Jun 1979 in Denver City. They Have 2 Children:

[V6]1334. [14]1. Brandon Eugene Locke, b. 18 Dec 1981.

[V6]1335. [14]2. April Dawn Locke, b. 7 Sept 1983.

[V6]1336. [13]3. Randall Allen Locke, b. 3 Oct 1961 in Seagraves, TX

[V6]1337. [13]4. Kevin Lynn Locke, b. 24 April 1964 in Brownfield, TX.

[V6]1338. [13]5. Mark Wayne Locke, b. 15 Dec 1965 In, OKlahoma City, OK.

[V6]1339. [13]6. Freda Deanna Locke, b. 2 June 1968 in Seagraves, TX; m. 14 Feb 1988 in Jones,

OK, Emery Hale, from Jones, OK.

[V6]1340. [12]2. Wanda Mae Locke, b. 31 Dec 1938 in Terral, OK; m. Jackie Don Voss in Wichita Falls, TX. He, b. 15 nov 1934. In 1972, he retired from the Air Force after 20 years of service he was from Hector, AR. They now make their home in Mcloud,, OK. They have 4 children:

[V6]1341. [13]1. Treasa Kay Voss, b. 10 May 1957 In Russellville, AR; m. Tommy Joe Dean 16 March 1979 and They Have a Daughter

[V6]1342. [14]1. Sara Marie Dean, b. 7 Feb 1986.

[V6]1343. [12]2. Beckie Ann Voss, b. 27 May 1959 in Dover, DE; m. Dennis James Harris in Mcloud,, OK. They have 1 daughter:

[V6]1344. [14]1. Shaunna Nichole Harris, b. 31 March 1986.

[V6]1345. [12]3. Mickie Lynn Voss, b. 27 May 1959 in Dover, DE; m. Ronald Charlow, and they have 2 children:

[V6]1346. [14]1. Lisa Rae Charlow, b. 17 Oct 1981

[V6]1347. [14]2. Anthony Don Charlow, b. 24mar 1984.

[V6]1348. [12]4. Gerald Don Voss, b. 10 Nov 1963 in The Phillipine Islands; m. Darla Davis in McCloud, OK 26 Sept 1986. Darla had a two year old daughter, Chrissy Davis. Darla and Gerald have one son:

[V6]1349. [13]1. Kenneth Don Voss, b. 6 Jun 1988.

[V6]1350. [12]3. Alfred Webster (Locke) Combs, b. 15 Sept 1941 in Terral, OK. Alfred was adopted by Mr. and Mrs. J. O. Combs from Dallas, TX in 1950. Alfred m.1. Doris Busbee, in 1960 and they had 2 sons; m.2. Betty Jo Shuffield Martin in 1972. Betty has 3 children by a previous marriage.

[V6]1351. [13]1. Baby Boy Died at Birth

[V6]1352. [13]2. Rickie Dean Combs, b. in Dallas Tx 2 March 1964.

Eulalie "Lou" Brashears and Dave Hicks/ Ed Barnhart/ Charles Thomas "Tom" Jobe

v6**1214.** 107. **Eulalie "Lou" Brashears**, (d/o Reuben T. Brashears and Elizabeth Harbour), b. 11 Oct 1886, Gibson Co, TN (she said), d. 25 Oct 1961, Neosho, Newton Co, MO, bur Gibson Cem, Neosho, MO. The family moved to Texas when she was six weeks old. Only her family knew her name was Eulalie. Most people called her Lou. Her grandchildren called her Granny. Notes from Sybil Jobe.

She m.1. 1 March 1900, in Collin Co, TX (Bk 11, p.538), ***Dave Hicks***, who d. c1908; they had four children; m.2 ***Ed Barnhart*** (2 ch; div); m.3. 10 April 1916, in Sulphur, OK, ***Charles Thomas "Tom" Jobe***, b. 23 March 1868, Greenup, IL, d. 24 April 1937, Neosho, MO, bur Gibson Cem.

Tom had been married before, to Nettie Jenkins, and they had 9 children. Nettie died 9 Sept 1915 near Sulphur, OK. Eulalie and Tom moved to Ada, OK where Tom worked in the glass factory. In the early 1930's, they moved to Kansas. Tom worked for a while as a carpenter and then began farming near Rome, KS. During the drought of the mid-thirties, he moved his family to Newton Co, MO, near Neosho. Two of their sons still live there. Eulalie and Tom had 4 children (see below)

Granny loved the St. Louis Cardinal baseball team. She listened to them faithfully and knew the players and what position each one played. She listened to three stories on the radio: "Ma Perkins," "Just Plain Bill," and "Stella Dallas." She sat and crocheted her rag rugs each afternoon and listened to her stories. Sometimes a baseball game might interfere.

In her younger days she liked to go fishing. She might walk for several miles to find a good fishing hole. She liked to raise turkeys and chickens. Granny did not eat much meat, not even the fish she caught. She made excellent biscuits and she enjoyed making them for her grandchildren. She was good to "nuss" the children and would sit and rub their legs gently with a piece of paper or a feather until they fell asleep.

Granny was deathly afraid of snakes and storms. When she lived in western Kansas, she spent a lot of time in the storm cellar. She talked about living through some bad storms when she was young and lived in Texas.

She could not read or write. She had problems with her vision and she said that kept her from going to school. Granny had trouble pronouncing some words. She could not say "linoleum" or "aluminum" and she called "vinegar" "big-nigger". She said "don'k" for "don't". She referred to her husband as Mr. Jobe. After he died, she lived with her children and grandchildren.

Granny would tell you that in her younger days she had a quick temper. She said that when she got mad she could "fight a circle saw." She had a keen wit and loved to tell stories about her life. She was in her 70's before she had her hair cut and curled.

Granny's life revolved around her family. She loved them dearly and they loved her. She was truly a mother, grandmother, and homemaker.

<u>Family of Eulalie "Lou" Brashears and Dave Hicks:</u>

[V6]1353. [11]1. *Velma Clara Virginia Pearl Hicks, b. 10 Feb 1901; m. Horace M. Jobe; m.2. Charles Metlock

[V6]1354. [11]2. Leroy Hicks, died young

[V6]1355. [11]3. Aaron Hicks, died young

[V6]1356. [11]4. Ethel Lee Hicks, b. 1908. She was living with her uncle, C.C. Hicks, in Waxahachi, TX in the 1910 Census. Ethel married Herbert Brown and lived in Pampa, TX. They had 5 daughters.

<u>Family of Eulalie "Lou" Brashears and Ed Barnhart:</u>

[V6]1357. [11]5. Ollie Viola Barnhart,

[V6]1358. [11]6. Floyd Earl Barnhart,

<u>Family of Eulalie "Lou" Brashears and Charles Thomas "Tom" Jobe:</u>

[V6]1359. [11]7. Lottie May Jobe, b. 1 Jan 1917, d. 27 Dec 1917 in Ada, OK; bur Rosedale Cem, Pontotoc Co, OK.

[V6]1360. [11]8. *Vernon Thomas Jobe,

[V6]1361. [11]9. *Herman T. Jobe, (twin) b. 28 Feb 1921

[V6]1362. [11]10. Raymond T. Jobe, (twin) b. 28 Feb 1921, d. 23 Aug 1921, in Ada, Pontotoc Co, OK; bur Rosedale Cem, Ada, OK.

[V6]1353. [11]1. ***Velma Clara Virginia Pearl Hicks***, (d/o Eulalie "Lou" Brashears and Dave Hicks), b. 10 Feb 1901 in Collin Co, TX; d. 17 July 1988 in, Oklahoma City, OK; bur Chapel Hill Memorial Gardens; m.1. Horace M. Jobe, b. 19 Oct 1894 in Greenup, IL, s/o Charles Thomas Jobe; d. during the flu epidemic 16 Oct 1918. Velma and Horace had one son, Jesse Ray Jobe, b. in Dec after Horace died. Velma adopted Jesse to Julius and Anna Stutzman Gingerich, of Iowa. They named him, Melvin Ray Gingerich. Velma m.2. 9 Jan 1923, in Oklahoma City, Charles Metlock Dean, b. 1 Aug 1900, Percell, OK, d. 22 Jan 1963, Oklahoma City, bur Chapel Hill Cem. Velma and Charles adopted two daughters, Mary and Betty Dean.

[V6]1363. [12]1. Melvin Ray Gingerich, (s/o Velma Clara Virginia Pearl Hicks and Horace M. Jobe; adopted by Julius and Anna (Stutzman) Gingerich) b. 14 Dec 1918 in Oklahoma City, OK; m. 7 Sep 1938 in Iowa City, IA, Dorothy Lemley, b. 6 Oct 1918 in Washington, IA, d/o Charlie Lemley and Minnie Blum Lemley.

[V6]1364. [13]1. Johnnie Ray Gingerich, b. 24 Nov 1939 in Wellman, IA; m. 28 June 1963 in Tuscon,, AZ, Mary Catherine McKulsky, b. 9 Dec 1942, d/o Francis Assisi McKulsky and Mary Margaret Morgan.

[V6]1365. [14]1. Denise Marie Gingerich, b. 13 April 1969 in Tuscon, AZ.

[V6]1366. [14]2. Christrina Susanne Gingerich, b. 16 Dec 1970 in Tuscon, AZ.

[V6]1367. [13]2. Paul Gingerich, b. 13 March 1956 in Tuscon, AZ.

[V6]1368. [12]2. Mary Helen Dean, b. 13 Jan 1945 in Oklahoma City, OK; m. Kenneth L. Stanford.

[V6]1369. [12]3. Betty Diane Dean, b. 16 Nov 1947 in Oklahoma City, OK; m. Benjamin H. Ball.

[V6]1360. [11]8. ***Vernon Thomas Jobe***, (s/o Eulalie "Lou" Brashears and Charles Thomas "Tom" Jobe), b. 6 Nov 1918 in Ada, OK; m. 12 Jun 1940 in Bentonville, AR, Eula Evelene

Garrison, b. 21 March 1923, d/o Daniel G. and Bessie Clark Garrison.

Vernon served in the US Navy during WWII. He was a machinist in the can shop of the Pet Milk Company in Neosho, MO for 43 years. Vernon and Eula belong to the Northside Baptist Church in Neosho, MO. They have four children: Jimmie Carroll Jobe; Larry Thomas Jobe; Linda Lea Jobe; and Randy Gale Jobe.

[V6]1370. [12]1. Jimmie Carroll Jobe, b. 3 Dec 1940 in Neosho, MO, d. 20 Oct 1987 in Neosho; m. Jana Kay Mapes, d/o Robert and Ella Linsley Mapes. Jimmie was a Certified Public Accountant and owned his own business in Neosho. He served in the US Air Force. They belonged to the Methodist Church. Jimmie and Jana have a son and a daughter:

[V6]1371. [13]1. Julie Kristen Jobe, b. 5 Aug 1958; m. 2 Dec 1988 in Neosho, MO, Andrew "Andy" Swift.

[V6]1372. [13]2. Jason Christopher Jobe, b. 23 Aug 1971 in Neosho, MO.

[V6]1373. [12]2. Larry Thomas Jobe, b. 9 Aug 1942 in Neosho, MO; m. Betty Lee Hogan. Larry is computer supervisor for The At&T Company. He is a graduate of Washington University in St. Louis and has a Masters Degree In Business Administration.

[V6]1374. [13]1. Bunnie Sue Jobe, b. 4 Nov 1957 (adopted); m. 24 April 1981, Harry Willson Jr.

[V6]1375. [14]1. Emily Marie Willson, b. 23 Sept 1982

[V6]1376. [14]2. Meghan Ann Willson, b. 4 May 1985

[V6]1377. [13]2. Ricky Dalton Jobe, b. 23 Feb 1960 (adopted); m. 10 June 1983 to Debra Lynn Heberer. Divorced.

[V6]1378. [14]1. Jessica Nichole Jobe, b. 27 May 1985.

[V6]1379. [13]3. Melissa Ann Jobe, b. 6 July 1968 in Stella, MO.

[V6]1380. [13]4. Larry Thomas Jobe, Jr., b. 17 July 1970 In St Louis, MO.

[V6]1381. [12]3. Linda Lea Jobe, b. 15 Feb 1946 in Neosho, MO; m. Theodore Burton Gilmore, s/o Burton and Jessie Mae Gilmore.

V6 1382. [13]1. Scott David Gilmore, b. 20 Aug 1973 In Kansas City, MO.

V6 1383. [13]2. Theodore Brett Gilmore, b. 21 Jun 1980.

V6 1384. [12]4. Randy Gale Jobe, b. 3 Nov 1954 in Neosho, MO; m.1. Rita Lynn Hilsabeck, b. 28 Sept 1954 (2 ch; div), d/o Keith and Thelma Hilsabeck; m.2. 31 Dec 1984 In Neosho, MO, Nancy Lynn Brazill, (1 ch) b. 13 Aug 1955, St. Louis, MO, d/o Hubert and Fern Robinson Brazill.

V6 1385. [13]1. Daniel Gale Jobe, b. 1 Oct 1980 in Joplin, MO.

V6 1386. [13]2. Amanda Lynn Jobe, b. 6 Feb 1983 In Joplin, MO.

V6 1387. [13]3. Jonathan Brazill Jobe, b. 29 Oct 1988 In Joplin, MO.

V6 1361. [11]9. ***Herman T. Jobe***, (s/o Eulalie "Lou" Brashears and Charles Thomas "Tom" Jobe), b. 28 Feb 1921 in Ada, OK; m. 20 July 1942, in Pineville, MO, Sybil Irene Shipley, b. 11 June 1924 in Webster Co, MO, the oldest child of David Dewey and Orpha Gertrude Crowder Shipley. Herman was a foreman and machinist in the can shop for the Pet Milk Company in Neosho, MO for 41 years, retiring in 1983. Sybil was an elementary school teacher for 29 years, retiring in 1984. Herman and Sybil have 3 sons:

V6 1388. [12]1. Jerry Lynn Jobe, b. 29 June 1943 in Neosho, MO; m. 5 June 1966 in Neosho, MO, Donna Sue Phillips, b. 1 Feb 1947, in Oklahoma City, d/o Ralph and Shirley Smith Phillips. Jerry graduated from Pittsburg Kansas State University in 1968. Jerry also has a Masters Degree from Indiana State University at Terre Haute, IN. He has been an officer in the US Army since 1968 and is a Vietnam Veteran. Jerry and Donna have two children:

V6 1389. [13]1. Amanda Corrin Jobe, b. 18 Sept 1969 in Columbia, SC; m. 2 Dec 1988 in Omaha, NE, Mark Jenkins. They are both serving in the US Air Force. They have a son, Derek Michael

Jenkins, b. 11 Nov 1990 in Omaha, NE. Amanda and Mark divorced in 1991.

[V6]1390. [13]2. Walker Phillip Jobe, b. 8 Sept 1973 in Indianapolis, IN; m. Peggy Terrell. They have a son, Brenden Terrell Jobe, b. 29 March 1996 in Fairfax Co, VA.

[V6]1391. [12]2. David Lee Jobe, b. 29 May 1945 in Carthage, MO. He is a Medical Doctor and has a practice in Joplin, MO. He also holds a Phd in Anatomy from Creighton University in Omaha, NE. David; m.1. 4 June 1966 in Joplin, MO, Linda Sue Winn (2 ch; div), b. 16 Nov 1945, d/o Roy and Velma Tolner Winn. Linda is an Elementary School Teacher. David m.2. 22 June 1981 in Reno, NV, Pearl Ann Morehead Martin, b. 1 June 1954 in Chanute, KS, d/o Thomas F. and Ruth T. Rhodes Morehead. Pearl is a Registered Nurse. She m.1. David Martin. They are divorced. They have a daughter, Leslie Ann Martin, b. 9 Sept 1976 in Joplin, MO. David and Pearl belong to the First Community Church in Joplin. They have one son.

[V6]1392. [13]1. Danen David Jobe, b. 29 May 1970 in Council Bluffs, IA; m. 2 May 1994 in Bentonville, AR, Heather James

[V6]1393. [13]2. Lori Dale Jobe, b. 2 Sept 1973 in Council Bluffs, IA; m. 19 June 1994 in Stockton, CA, Terry Niegel

[V6]1394. [13]3. Matthew Lee Jobe, b. 3 Oct 1985 in Joplin, MO.

[V6]1395. [12]3. Warren Dale Jobe, b. 7 Dec 1946 in Carthage, MO; m. 6 June 1970 in Council Bluffs, IA. Mary Ann Streff, b. 7 Jul 1945 in Alton, IA, d/o Clarence and Phyllis Krier Streff. Dale served in the US Air Force. Dale is a water and waste-water consultant and owns and operates his business in Neosho, MO. Mary Ann teaches Special Education in the Neosho Intermediate School. Dale and Mary Ann have 2 children:

[V6]1396. [13]1. Gretchen Renee Jobe, b. 4 Dec 1974 in Jacksonville, FL.

V6 1397. 13 2. Britton Dale Jobe, b. 8 Feb 1984 in Joplin, MO.

Sarah Elizabeth "Sally" Brashears and William David Parkhill

v6 1215. 10 8. **Sarah Elizabeth "Sally" Brashears**, (d/o Reuben T. Brashears and Elizabeth Harbour), b. 1 May 1883, TN, say her children. There are conflicting dates of birth and places of birth. At the time of the 1900 Collin Co, TX Census, she was living with her brother, Edward Brashears, and he gave her age as 10, b. June 1889, in Texas. Sally died 23 Jan 1973 in Dimmitt, TX and is buried in Crowell, TX.

Sybil's note: the compiler [Sybil] does not know the birth order of Berry, Eulalie, and Sally. As there were no birth records for them, we may never know. Eulalie said she had one older sister, Fanny, and two younger sisters, Sally and Dovie. She didn't mention her brothers being older or younger, except Sherman. She said he was the youngest of her mother's children.

Sally m. 27 March 1904, ***William David Parkhill***, b. 22 Oct 1872 in Lamar Co, TX, d. 4 Sept 1946 in Crowell, TX, where he is buried; s/o Bloomin Goodner Parkhill and Mary Perryman Morris Parkhill. William was married once before he married Sally, and he had one son, Elvie "L.V." Parkhill, b. 9 Aug 1900 in Dequeen, AR. Elvie m. Annie Pierce, d. 16 March 1975.

Sally's granddaughter, Gene Naron, wrote, "I loved my Grannie. She was the most important person in my life. My mom worked a lot because my dad was dead and Grannie was there to take care of us. She talked about a sister and what a beautiful skin she had and the way she cared for it. She would make fine white lye soap, lather it up and rub it into her skin and let it dry. I always thought it would probably take my skin off. I know that there were two kinds of soap— strong lye soap for the washing of clothes and fine white cold lye soap for taking a bath. After Grannie washed the clothes, she scrubbed the floors in the wash water. The rinse water went on the flower beds. It did not rain often in our part of the country and we had to save the water.

Grannie's defense against the world was her broom— cats,

dogs, kids, chickens— all got the same treatment of a good swishing with the straw end. I remember a time when Grannie's broom came into good use. I was playing in the yard in front of our house when suddenly Grannie came flying around the corner of the house waving her broom. She lifted me up with one hand and rushed back into the house. Down the road came a dog with rabies, foam coming from his mouth and snapping at the air. Old Dad Hutchins was right behind with his gun to kill it. Grannie didn't have a gun— just her trusty old broom!

Grannie had trouble pronouncing some words. I can still hear her coming around the house crying 'gentle nosses' (Moses)! On ironing day, she got tired ironing 'tacky' (khaki) pants. In her later years, she had to go to the doctor for x-rays and surgery. She said she went for 'rex-rays' and was 'rop-perated on'.

Grannie washed and ironed our dresses. She put so much starch in them, I thought that they would stand alone. She told us we might not have much, but we had better be clean, and that starch held them together long after they were faded and mended over and over.

She loved to do hand work and somehow found time to crochet. She couldn't read, so my mother read the crochet books and learned the pattern. Mother then taught it to Grannie. I learned from watching them and now when I get lonesome for them, I sit down with my old socks or scraps and make crocheted rugs like my Grannie made.

My sister taught Grannie to write her name, so she would not be embarrassed about signing her allotment checks that she got from her sons in WW II. I wrote letters for her. I would get tired of writing the long letters to her girls, so I left some of it out. She must have guessed what I was doing, for she made me read them back to her and write in what I had left out.

Roy Rogers and Gene Autry were her two favorite movie stars. She got as excited as I did in the good parts of the movies. She loved the radio, and during WW II, we saved the batteries for "Old Ma Perkins" and "Porsha Faces Life." We were never allowed to rake out scraps of food. Grannie said that was feeding the devil. If we couldn't use the food, we fed it to the dogs or birds or chickens or something besides burning it in the trash. I still don't like garbage disposals. The McNess man was always invited to stay for dinner, and she never turned a tramp away from our door without food.

Our Grampa was a stroke victim and was in bed for many years. She never tired of taking care of him. There was never a thought of finding another way. Her life was filled with hard work and helping others. She faced each day with love and a stubborn determination to do the best that she could for everyone in her household. I still miss her."

<u>Sally Brashears and William D. Parkhill had thirteen children:</u>

[V6]1398. [11]1. Baby Boy Parkhill, b. & d. 1904

[V6]1399. [11]2. Willie "Bill" Lynn Parkhill, b. 22 Feb 1905, Dequeen, AR, d. 1949; m. 8 Oct 1927, Ella Mae Athey. They had 7 children:

[V6]1400. [12]1. Hazel Mae Parkhill,

[V6]1401. [12]2. Helen Parkhill, (died as an Infant)

[V6]1402. [12]3. Venetta Lynn Parkhill; m. Wayne Whitley

[V6]1403. [12]4. Delton Parkhill; m. Mary Ann Turner

[V6]1404. [12]5. Hansel Parkhill,

[V6]1405. [12]6. Winnie Fay Parkhill,

[V6]1406. [12]7. Ray Parkhill,

[V6]1407. [11]3. Vannie Lena Parkhill, b. 11 May 1908 in Dequeen, AR; m. (1) _____ Tucker, (1 ch); m.2. 8 Oct 1927, Monroe Athey (2 ch)

[V6]1408. [12]1. Fay Tucker; m. R.L. Gamblin

[V6]1409. [12]2. Herman Monroe Athey,

[V6]1410. [12]3. Martha Athey; m. John Wiseman

[V6]1411. [11]4. Paul Thomas Parkhill, b. 24 March 1911 in Forestburg, TX, d. 8 July 1980; m. Gladys Brown

[V6]1412. [12]1. Horace Parkhill,

[V6]1413. [12]2. Douglas Parkhill,

[V6]1414. [11]5. *Zannie Lee Parkhill; m. Jodie Sidney Foster (see below)

[V6]1415. [11]6. *Linda Sue Parkhill; m.1. on 18 Oct 1930, Oliver Haskell Jones; m.2. 7 Sept 1941, Claude D. Sellers, (see below)

[V6]1416. [11]7. Odell Leon Parkhill, b. 11 May 1916 in Forestburg, TX; m. Demoin _______ , live in Morenci, AZ. Odell served in the US Army during WWII and went to Arizona to work in the mines after the war.

Demoin had 2 children by a previous marriage. Her daughter's name was Lorraine. Odell and demoin have a daughter:

[V6]1417. [12]1. Ladell Parkhill,

[V6]1418. [11]8. *Eastie Vastie Parkhill; m. Henry Dave Moore, (see below)

[V6]1419. [11]9. Sophronia "Muggie" Parkhill, b. 4 May 1919 in Texas; m. Curley Crawford and they had one son. (Name unknown to me)

[V6]1420. [11]10. Louise Parkhill, died as an infant

[V6]1421. [11]11. David William Parkhill, b. 21 Oct 1924 in Foard City, TX, d. 15 Jan 1979; m. in 1944, Orda Max Davidson,

[V6]1422. [12]1. Bobby Joe Parkhill, lives in Hurst, TX.

[V6]1423. [12]2. David Earl Parkhill, lives in Baird, TX

[V6]1424. [12]3. Lynn Parkhill,

[V6]1425. [11]12. Cecil Earl Parkhill, b. 7 May 1926 in Foard Co, TX; m. 18 Nov 1947 in Sherman, TX, Verna Odessia Foster, b. 31 March 1932 in Marshall Co, OK, d/o James Acy Foster and Sarah Elizabeth Wood Foster.

[V6]1426. [12]1. Rita Jo Parkhill, b. 16 July 1949; m.1. Mickey Job Abbott, (1 ch; div); m.2. Gary Conely,

[V6]1427. [13]1. Bryan Dana Abbott,

[V6]1428. [12]2. Clarence Decker Parkhill, b. 23 Dec 1951

[V6]1429. [11]13. Baby Girl Parkhill, b. & d. 1929

[v6]1414. [11]5. ***Zannie Lee Parkhill***, (d/o Sally Brashears and William D. Parkhill), b. 4 Sept 1912 in Montague Co, TX; m. Jodie Sidney Foster in Crowell, TX on 14 Jan 1928

[V6]1430. [12]1. Lola Christine Foster, b. 2 Nov 1928 in Crowell, TX; m. George William Petree,

[V6]1431. [13]1. Lee Ann Petree,

[V6]1432. [13]2. Lenny Ray Petree,

[V6]1433. [13]3. Sarah Roline Petree,

[V6]1434. [12]2. Edna Aline Foster, b. 21 Aug 1932 in Idalou, TX; m.1. Leonard Duncan; m.2. Bus Hardy,

[V6]1435. [13]1. Ava Dee Duncan,

[V6]1436. [13]2. Adrain Jill Duncan,

[V6]1437. [13]3. Sonny Hardy,

[V6]1438. [12]3. Joseph Wayne Foster, b. 4 Jan 1934 in Idalou, TX; m. Patsy Johnson,

[V6]1439. [13]1. Sharon Kay Foster,

[V6]1440. [13]2. Rhonda Lynn Foster,

[V6]1441. [13]3. Joseph Wayne Foster,

[V6]1442. [13]4. Calvin Foster,

[V6]1443. [12]4. Troy Gene Foster, b. 7 July 1940 in Bowie, TX; m. Jo Frances Davenport,

[V6]1444. [13]1. Carmen Foster

[V6]1445. [13]2. Zeb Foster

[V6]1446. [12]5. Sarah Jane Foster, b. 14 June 1946 in Plainview, TX; m. Gary Linden Duggan,

[V6]1447. [13]1. Darla Janell Duggan,

[V6]1448. [13]2. Lela Gay Duggan,

[V6]1449. [13]3. Linden Simms Duggan,

[v6]1415. [11]6. ***Linda Sue Parkhill***, (d/o Sally Brashears and William D. Parkhill), b. 3 June 1915 in Bowie, TX, d. 21 April 1962 in Crowell, TX; m.1. on 18 Oct 1930, Oliver Haskell Jones, s/o Robert Haskell Jones. Oliver was shot and killed, 24 Dec 1934. Linda m.2. 7 Sept 1941, Claude D. Sellers,

[V6]1450. [12]1. Mary Ruth Jones, b. 1 March 1931; m.1. 13 Sept 1950, Jessie A. Whitfield, (4 ch; div); m.2. Hiram Ostrander,

[V6]1451. [13]1. Julia Ann Whitfield; m. Geronimo Lagunas. They live in Wichita Falls, TX.

[V6]1452. [13]2. Betty Linda Whitfield, lives in Amarillo, TX

[V6]1453. [13]3. Sandra Whitfield; m. ______ Burkett,

[V6]1454. [13]4. Kathy Whitfield; m. Danny Owenby. They live in Crowell, TX.

[V6]1455. [12]2. Blanche "Gene" Genevia Jones, b. 9 Sept 1933; m. 18 Nov 1951, Jimmie Naron, b. 2 April 1929, live in Quanah, TX.

[V6]1456. [13]1. James William Naron, b. 31 Mar 1952 in Quanah, TX; m. 28 June 1974, Annabell Lee Smith, b. 16 Feb 1955

[V6]1457. [14]1. Charity Ann Naron, b. 6 Jan 1976

[V6]1458. [14]2. Jimmy Guy Naron, b. 27 Jul 1977

[V6]1459. [14]3. Lauren Linda Naron, (adopted), b. 5 June 1988

[V6]1460. [13]2. Charyl Jean Naron, b. 28 Dec 1955

[V6]1461. [12]3. Claude Dean Sellers, b. 18 Dec 1943; m. 24 June 1962, Vickie Sue Farrar (2 ch; div)

[V6]1462. [13]1. Carrie Sue Sellers, b. 2 July 1963; m. 17 May 1986 in Vernon, TX, Crit Dale Canton, b. 25 Feb 1963

[V6]1463. [14]1. Kirsten Sue Canton, b. June 1988

[V6]1464. [13]2. Mark Farrar Sellers, b.15 Oct 1966

[V6]1465. [12]4. Kenneth Roy Sellers, b. 25 Feb 1953; m. 5 June 1975 in Tyler, TX, Sharon Ann Perdue, b. 15 March 1956

[V6]1466. [13]1. Mandy Ann Sellers, b. 26 March 1977

[v6]1418. [11]8. ***Eastie Vastie Parkhill***, (d/o Sally Brashears and William D. Parkhill), b. 23 July 1918 in Forestburg, TX, d. 25 March 1957; m. on 18 Nov 1933, Henry Dave Moore,

[V6]1467. [12]1. Mary Frances Moore, b. 11 July 1934 in Crowell, TX; m. on 24 March 1955, Jesse Judson Porter,

[V6]1468. [13]1. Ramona Sue Porter, b. 4 Aug 1956

[V6]1469. [13]2. David Judd Porter, b. 12 Sept 1957, married Sharon Rogers, b. 1 April 1956.

[V6]1470. [13]3. Randall Wayne Porter, b. 19 Dec 1959; m. Lori Sturdivent and they have two daughters:

[V6]1471. [14]1. April Elizabeth Porter, b. 17 April 1978

[V6]1472. [14]2. Krissa May Porter, b. 12 May 1981

[V6]1473. [12]2. Price Dave Leon Moore, b. 18 Jan 1939, d. 23 Nov 1956 in an automobile accident.

[V6]1474. [12]3. Ella Sue Moore, b. 6 June 1943; m. Eddie Joe Herrington,

[V6]1475. [13]1. Bradley Herrington,

[V6]1476. [13]2. Brian Herrington,

Nancy Dovie Brashears
and Warner Sandy/ Seb Bird

[v6]1216. [10]9. **Nancy Dovie Brashears**, (d/o Reuben T. Brashears and Elizabeth Harbour), b. 8 Aug 1889 in Collin Co, TX; d. 18 Jan 1969; bur Sunny Lane Cem in Del City, OK; m.1. ***Warner Z. Sandy***, d. 11 Nov 1914 (3 ch); m.2. ***Seb B. Bird***, b. 14 Feb 1887, d. 4 March 1971 (7 ch).

Dovie lived with her brother, Ed, and her sister, Eulalie, after their mother died. Her daughter, Clarice, said that her mother enjoyed her 25 grandchildren and 29 great-grandchildren more than anything. Her grandchildren were always raiding her ice box, so she told her girls to feed those babies so they wouldn't be so hungry. "Mother loved to cook and have company," Clarice said.

[V6]1477. [11]1. *Elizabeth “Lizzie” Sandy, b. 1906
[V6]1478. [11]2. *Mosie S. Sandy, b. 1908
[V6]1479. [11]3. *Pearlie M. Sandy,
[V6]1480. [11]4. *Fannie Irene Bird,
[V6]1481. [11]5. *Cleo Bird,
[V6]1482. [11]6. *Clarice Bird,
[V6]1483. [11]7. Bernice Bird, b. 27 Oct 1925, d. 18 Oct 1928
[V6]1484. [11]8. Trula Mae Bird, b. 22 March 1933, d. 10 Sept 1938
[V6]1485. [11]9. *Albert J. Bird,
[V6]1486. [11]10. *Shirley Roena Bird,

[v6]1477. [11]1. ***Elizabeth “Lizzie” Sandy***, b. 29 Feb 1906; m. 10 June 1925, Orvel Jack Johnson, b. 24 Sept 1908, d. in Dec 1983. They had one daughter:

[V6]1487. [12]1. Joy Louise Johnson, b. 13 May 1926; m. Bill Joe Maddox, b. 1925. Joy Louise and Bill have 9 grandchildren.
[V6]1488. [13]1. Billie Louise Maddox,
[V6]1489. [13]2. Garland Maddox,
[V6]1490. [13]3. Janie Beth Maddox,

[V6]1478. [11]2. ***Mosie S. Sandy***, b. 12 March 1908; m. 8 June 1931, Loyce Young. They had one son:

[V6]1491. [12]1. Jimmy Lee Sandy, b. 2 May 1932, d. May 19 1978;

m. on 29 April 1952, Joyce Pearson, and they had three children:

[V6]1492. [13]1. Kathryn Loyce Sandy, b. 22 Nov 1952

[V6]1493. [13]2. Karen Lee Sandy

[V6]1494. [13]3. Jimmy Lee Sandy, b. 16 Jan 1959

[V6]1495. [12]2. Karen Lee Sandy, b. 4 Jan 1954; m. Robert Dwayne Robinson, 17 June 1972. They have two sons:

[V6]1496. [13]1. Danny Dwayne Robinson , b. 10 June 1977

[V6]1497. [13]2. Bobby Dwayne Robinson , b. 9 Nov 1980

[v6]1479. [11]3. ***Pearlie M. Sandy***, b. 11 March 1910; m. 24 Dec 1930, Rufus Kincheloe, b. 2 Nov 1911. (3 ch)

[V6]1498. [12]1. Lillie Mae Kincheloe, b. 29 Dec 1931, d. 30 June 1988; m.1. Willand Shirley, (3 ch); m.2. Mohommond Pazdel, (2 ch)

[V6]1499. [13]1. Gary Wayne Shirley, b. May 1951

[V6]1500. [13]2. Keith Brent Shirley, b. June 1952

[V6]1501. [13]3. Linda Sue Shirley, b. 11 March 1956

[V6]1502. [13]4. Daryoosh Pazdel, b. April 1961

[V6]1503. [13]5. Karieh Pazdel, b. April 1962

[V6]1504. [12]2. Franklin Dee Kincheloe, b. 7 Dec 1933; m. Barbara Womboldt, 21 Sept 1952 (3 ch)

[V6]1505. [13]1. Joanne Marie Kincheloe, b. 12 Sept 1952

[V6]1506. [13]2. Cheryl Lynn Kincheloe, b. 8 Aug 1956

[V6]1507. [13]3. Franklin Dee Kincheloe, Jr., b. 26 Aug 1957

[V6]1508. [12]3. Eugene Kincheloe, b. 7 June 1936; m. Pat ______ , (1 ch)

[V6]1509. [13]1. Debbie Kincheloe, b. May 1964

[v6]1480. [11]4. ***Fannie Irene Bird***, b. 10 Sept 1918; m. 10 Oct 1940, William Henry Baker, b. 23 Aug 1915, d. 15 Nov 1979. (5 Ch)

[V6]1510. [12]1. Katherine Delois Baker, b. 10 Feb 1939; m.1. 14 Feb 1958, George Morris Bowles, b. 1 Dec 1930 (3 ch); m.2. 24 Nov 1982, Dan Everette Seale, b. 3 Oct 1951. Dan and his first wife had two daughters: Danielle Kay Seale, b. 2 Dec 1974 and

Tiffani Dawn Seale, b. 16 Feb 1976.
V6 1511. 13 1. William Ernest Bowles, b. 19 May 1959; m. Lillie Faye Williams, 25 May 1978. (1 ch)
V6 1512. 14 1. William Brian Bowles Born 9 Oct 1980
V6 1513. 13 2. Mark Lynn Bowles, b. 16 Jun 1960
V6 1514. 13 3. India Irene Bowles, b. 21 Nov 1962; m. 19 Oct 1985, Bruce Wayne Norton, b. 23 Aug 1963
V6 1515. 12 2. William Henry Baker Jr, b. 14 Oct 1941; m. 25 Feb 1967, Sharen Lea Ball, b. 5 April 1948, (2 ch)
V6 1516. 13 1. Randall Dean Baker, b. 19 Jul 1967
V6 1517. 13 2. Jeffrey Allen Baker, b. 8 Dec 1970.
V6 1518. 12 3. Raymond Harold Baker, b. 26 Jan 1943; m.1. Janice Kroff, (3 ch; div); m.2. 30 Aug 1985, Lois McCarter.
V6 1519. 13 1. Christy Lynn Baker, b. 18 Jan 1968 and; m. Ty Balton On 20 July 1985.
V6 1520. 14 1. Karri Sheree Balton, b. 21 April 1985
V6 1521. 13 2. Russell William Baker, b. 24 Jan 1970
V6 1522. 13 3. Bradley Harold Baker, b. 22 Jan 1972
V6 1523. 12 4. Donald Leroy Baker, b. 28 Jan 1946; m.1. 15 Nov 1971, Alpha Jean Etier; m.2. Pamela Ann Kirkpatrick 1 Nov 1985. Donald adopted Alpha's daughter, Sabrina, and then they had a son; they divorced.
V6 1524. 13 1. Sabrina Sharee Baker, b. 22 Jan 1970
V6 1525. 13 2. Jason Don Baker, b. 7 Jan 1977
V6 1526. 12 5. Frances Irene Baker, b. 11 Feb 1948; m.1. July 1966, Barry Dean Harvey, (1 ch; div); m.2. in June 1973, Robert Wayne Wright, (1 ch; div); m.3. 29 Aug 1986, Joe Wayne Davis, b. 13 Oct 1931.
V6 1527. 13 1. Michelle Dawn Harvey, b. 16 Aug 1967; m. 17 Dec 1988, Charles Lee Johnson, b. 21 Oct 1966.
V6 1528. 13 2. Eric Quinn Wright, b. 21 Sept 1976

v6 1481. 11 5. ***Cleo Bird***, b. 16 Jan 1921; m. Leta Maxine Bryant, b. 12 Sept 1923. (4 ch)
V6 1529. 12 1. Gwendolyn Bird Wells, b. 19 Jul 1946. (4 ch)
V6 1530. 13 1. Tammy Leigh Whaley, b. 19 July 1965 (3 ch)

[V6]1531. [14]1. Kourtney ______, b. 26 Apr 1983

[V6]1532. [14]2. Corey ______ , b. 20 Aug 1984

[V6]1533. [14]3. Tia ______ , b. 30 Aug 1987

[V6]1534. [13]2. Leta Dannielle Sellman, b. 8 May 1970

[V6]1535. [13]3. Lori Dawn Sellman, b. 1 Feb 1972, d. 28 Sept 1978

[V6]1536. [13]4. Kristopher Dane Webb, b. 24 May 1977

[V6]1537. [12]2. Brenda Kay Bird, b. 6 Sept 1951; m. ______ Eaton. (2 ch)

[V6]1538. [13]1. Kance Prohonoff, b. 9 Aug 1969

[V6]1539. [13]2. Matthew Tobia Eaton, b. 16 Apr 1980

[V6]1540. [12]3. Danny Paul Bird, b. 25 July 1953; m. Diedre Blanche Rasco, b. 16 Sept 1960. (2 ch)

[V6]1541. [13]1. Virginia Suzann Bird, b. 27 Jul 1977

[V6]1542. [13]2. Kasey Renee Bird, b. 9 Aug 1981

[V6]1543. [12]4. Carla Jan Bird, b. 26 Oct 1954; m. ______ Heinen. (3 ch)

[V6]1544. [13]1. Alaina Christine Bird, b. 2 Apr 1977

[V6]1545. [13]2. Marcus Allen Bird, b. 28 Oct 1981

[V6]1546. [13]3. Angelita Otilia Heinen, b. 29 Dec 1983

[v6]1482. [11]6. ***Clarice Bird***, b. 22 March 1923; m. 13 April 1943, Bill Spaulding, b. 16 Mar 1924. Clarice and Bill live in Moore, OK, and have three children:

[V6]1547. [12]1. Dovie Marie Spaulding, b. 5 Aug 1946; m. 12 Oct 1962, Harold Chester Cape, b. 4 Dec 1941. (2 ch; div, 29 Nov 1988)

[V6]1548. [13]1. Chester Dwayne Cape, b. 11 May 1963

[V6]1549. [13]2. Carl Allen Cape, b. 29 Dec 1965

[V6]1550. [12]2. Nancy Pearl Spaulding, b. 11 Nov 1949; m. 5 Dec 1975, Eugene Lee Mowery, b. 27 Sept 1926, d. 25 Sept 1980. (1 ch)

[V6]1551. [13]1. William G. Mowery, b. 5 Aug 1976

[V6]1552. [12]3. George William "Willie" Spaulding, b. 20 Feb 1952; m. 17 Dec 1972, Delois Ruth Shust, b. 4 Aug 1952. (2 ch)

[V6]1553. [13]1. Jason William Spaulding, b. 8 Feb 1974

[V6]1554. [13]2. Adam Edward Spaulding, b. 5 Jan 1981

[v6]1485. [11]9. ***Albert J. Bird***, b. 8 June 1930; m. 31 May 1950, Carol Joy, b. 3 Dec 1932. (3 ch)

[V6]1555. [12]1. David Albert Bird, b. 7 Oct 1951

[V6]1556. [12]2. Susanne Carol Bird, b. 18 Aug 1953; m. 26 Nov 1976, Thomas Maywood Reynolds, b. 24 June 1952. (1 ch)

[V6]1557. [13]1. Sharon Susanne Reynolds, b. 26 June 1982

[V6]1558. [12]3. Steven Keith Bird, b. 1 April 1955; m. 8 Apr 1977, Judith Lynn Dunlap, b. 28 Jan 1959. (2 ch)

[V6]1559. [13]1. Jennifer Lee Bird, b. 1 Feb 1979

[V6]1560. [13]2. Shaun Michael Bird, b. 5 May 1982

[v6]1486. [11]10. ***Shirley Roena Bird***, b. 5 March 1937; m. 16 Sept 1955, Charles Lee Raper, b. 8 Sept 1927. (5 ch)

[V6]1561. [12]1. Elizabeth Roena Raper, b. 1 Sept 1953; m.1. 21 Jun 1969, Marvin Royston White, (1 ch; div 8 Feb 1974); m.2. 12 Jan 1976, James Douglas Denard, b. 24 Aug 1953. (1 ch)

[V6]1562. [13]1. Tonya Dannette White, b. 14 Dec 1972

[V6]1563. [13]2. Shane Douglas Denard, b. 16 Sept 1976

[V6]1564. [12]2. Charles Lee Raper, Jr., b. 26 Dec 1955; m. 2 Jul 1974, Judy Jo Plumbley, b. 21 Aug 1956. (2 ch)

[V6]1565. [13]1. Charles Lee Raper III, b. 18 Dec 1975

[V6]1566. [13]2. Doris Nicole Raper, b. 25 Apr 1977

[V6]1567. [12]3. Sherry Lynn Raper, b. 8 April 1957; m. 24 Aug 1973, Floyd Jerald Hursh, b. 29 April 1949. (2 ch)

[V6]1568. [13]1. Amanda Dawn Hursh, b. 13 March 1982

[V6]1569. [13]2. Krystina Roena Hursh, b. 7 Dec 1984

[V6]1570. [12]4. Leslie Dean Raper, b. 5 Oct 1959; m. 18 May 1985, Jana Lynn Williams, b. 13 Aug 1957. Leslie has two step-sons: B. J. Moomey, b. 6 April 1976, and Jerry Lee Moomey, b. 7 Sept 1978. Leslie and Jana have one daughter:

[V6]1571. [13]1. Leslie Raper, b. 24 May 1986

[V6]1572. [12]5. Pamela Marie Raper, b. 24 Jan 1962

Sherman Monroe Brashears and Lura Mae Cresswell

[v6]1217. [10]10. **Sherman Monroe Brashears**, (s/o Reuben T. Brashears and Elizabeth Harbour), b. 31 Oct 1892 in Collin Co, TX, d. 29 Oct 1985, bur Lockney, TX; m. c1919, ***Lura Mae Cresswell***, b. 6 June 1900, Collin Co, TX, d. 10 July 1986, d/o W.B. Cresswell. Both are buried in the Lockney, TX Cem. Sherman was a farmer and belonged to the Methodist Church. (7 ch)

[V6]1573. [11]1. **Celia Brashears**, b.& d. 1920

[V6]1574. [11]2. **Burl Weldon Brashears**, b. 19 Jan 1921, d. 15 April 1961 in Riverside, CA. He was a state school inspector in southern CA; m. ______ (2 ch)

[V6]1575. [12]1. **Bobby Brashears**,

[V6]1576. [12]2. **Patsy Brashears**,

[V6]1577. [11]3. **Floyd Brashears**, b. 29 Jan 1922 in Floyd Co, TX; m. ***Frances*** ______.

[V6]1578. [11]4. **Earl Odell Brashears**, b. 4 June 1924, d. 1 July 1941 in Glenn Rose, TX; not married.

[V6]1579. [11]5. **Sherman Monroe Brashears, Jr.**, b. 20 Jun 1932, d. 5 April 1976, bur Slaton, TX; m. ***Ikie*** ______,

[V6]1580. [11]6. **Opal Maxine Brashears**, b. 29 Aug 1934 in Lorenzo, TX; m.1. 5 Dec 1950, ***Robert Lee Daniels***, b. 29 Dec 1930 in Chillicothe, TX, s/o Vernon and Hattie Daniels (2 ch; div); m.2. ***Jack Cooper***.

[V6]1581. [12]1. Vickie Lynn Daniels, b. 12 Dec 1951 in Slaton, TX; m. 28 March 1970, Phil Green, b. 15 Jan 1948 in Floydada, TX, s/o Starks and Valarie Green. 4 ch)

[V6]1582. [13]1. Valarie Green, (twin) b.& d. 15 June 1971, bur Lockney, TX

[V6]1583. [13]2. Varonica Green, (twin) b.& d. 15 June 1971, bur Lockney, TX

[V6]1584. [13]3. Aimie Renee Green, b. 31 Jan 1973

[V6]1585. [13]4. Max Tyland Green, b. 28 Apr 1976

[V6]1586. [12]2. Tonya Renee Daniels, b. 27 Oct 1958 in Lockney, TX; m. 8 Oct 1974 in Floydada, TX, Mike Marble, s/o Fred and Carolyn Marble.

Mike was killed in 1982. Tonya and Mike had two children. Tonya m.2. 7 Oct 1983 in Hawaii, Brad Hagood, s/o Dan and Nancy Hagood of Floydada, TX. Tonya and Brad have one son.

[V6]1587. [13]1. Justin Tye Marble, b. 13 May 1976 in Lockney, TX.

[V6]1588. [13]2. Micah Lee Marble, b. 21 Oct 1980 in Lockney, TX.

[V6]1589. [13]3. Hunter Jennings Hagood, b. 4 Nov 1985 in Lubbock, TX.

[V6]1590. [11]7. **Tommy Brashears**, b. 13 July 1938 in Goodland, TX; m. 23 Dec 1955 in Seagraves, TX, ***Patricia Ann Floyd***, b. 7 Apr 1939 in Dickens, TX, d/o Doyle C. Floyd and Renee Raseberry Floyd. (3 ch)

[V6]1591. [12]1. **Kenya Dyan Brashears**, b. 9 Aug 1957 in Seagraves, TX; m. ***Scott George***, 12 Feb 1981. They have 1 son:

[V6]1592. [13]1. Scotty George, b. 18 Feb 1982.

[V6]1593. [12]2. **Gary Don Brashears**, b. 18 Aug 1958 In Spokane Wa.

[V6]1594. [12]3. **Rodney Craig Brashears**, b. 21 Sept 1961 in Seagraves, TX.

13. HENRY BRASHEARS/BRESHEARS, SR, and Eleanor Hardin

of Spartanburg SC and Lawrence TN
Probable s/o Middleton Brashears

[v6]**4.** [7]x. **Henry Breshears, Sr**, (or Brashears; the surname is spelled variously in various documents), b. SC or NC, 1769, d. 1828, Lawrence Co, TN; m. c1788, ***Eleanor _____ Hardin(?)***, b. c1768, possibly in Guilford Co, NC, d. 1837, Lawrence Co, TN, d/o Jesse Hardin and _____ Sinnet (per Southard FTW). A submission in the FHL says Henry was b. in Guilford Co, NC (no documentation given); if so, that would strengthen the probability that Henry was a son of Middleton Brashears, b. c1732-3, s/o Basil Brashears and Anne Belt, of Prince George's Co, MD, Orange/Guilford Co, NC, and Spartanburg Co, SC.

Most researchers believe this was the Henry who lived in the Spartanburg Dist, SC, in 1800.

1800 US Census : Spartanburg Co., SC -
HENRY BRESHEARS
1 male 16-26, b. 1774-1784 — Probably Henry, though the age is wrong
1 female 26-45, b. 1755-1774 — Eleanor?
3 males 0-10, b. 1790-1800 — William, John, Jesse
1 female 0-10, b. 1790-1800 — Mary "Polly"

The Breshears seem to have moved as a unit to eastern Tennessee, soon after the turn of the century, where several of them got land grants in White and Warren Counties. On 7 Feb 1815, Henry Breshears Sr got Tennessee Land Grant #11977, in Warren County, TN, 40 acres, (Book O, p.295 and Book 8, p.132; see also HSB, p. 29).

Jesse Brashears, of Lee Co, VA, and his sons, Melvry and Valdon were also in the area (Jesse died there c1813).

The Littleberry Brashears who also got a Tennessee Land Grant in Warren Co, TN, is believed to be the same as the Berry

Boshears, who lived in White Co, TN, in 1820, alongside Henry Breshears Sr's brothers, John, b. 1767, and Basil, b. c1765; Berry later moved to Lawrence Co, TN and then to AR.

Henry, however, did not stay long in Warren Co, TN. His brothers and nephews are in White Co, TN, in the 1820 Census, but Henry Breshears Sr and his sons were already early residents of Lawrence Co, TN. See tax lists below.

John Brashears, b. 1767, was also in Lawrence Co in 1819, but he seems to have gone back to White Co at the time of the 1820 census.

<u>1819 Tax Lists, Lawrence Co. TN</u>:
Henry Brashears, age c52, and wife Eleanor
William Brashears, age 30, s/o Henry & Eleanor
John Brashears, age c51, and wife Mary
Jesse Brashears, age 22-25, s/o Henry and Eleanor
Robert Brashears, s/o Isaac Brashears, of Roane Co, TN
Walter Brashears, s/o Isaac Brashears, of Roane Co, TN

<u>1819 Census of Voters of Lawrence Co, TN</u>, ordered by the court, Nov 1818.
List turned in by <u>James Farbes, Esq</u>:
Wm. Boshears; Jesse Boshears; Henry Boshears; John Boshears
(Note: Thomas Etheridge and son John lived 3 doors from these Brashears, with Archelus Hogg living 3 doors from Etheridge. Others in neighborhood: Rockleys, Lindseys, Simpsons.)
List turned in by <u>Andrew Pickens, Esq</u>:
Robert Brashears, Walker [Walter] Brashears (Note: these are sons of Isaac Brashears, of Roane Co, TN; Isaac was a s/o Robert Samuel Brashears)

<u>1820 Census, Lawrence Co. TN</u>
p.9: William Beshears, 26-45, b. 1770-1795, (son of Henry Breshears, Sr)
wife 16-26 (b. 1795-1805)
fem. 0-10
p.10: Jesse Beshears, 16-26, b. 1795-1805, (son of Henry Breshears, Sr)
wife 16-26 (b. 1795-1805)
fem. 0-10
p.10: Henry Beshears, 45+, b. bef. 1775, [Henry Breshears, Sr]
wife, 45+, b. bef. 1775
male, 45+, b. bef. 1775 [unidentified old couple; b. bef. 1775]
fem, 45+, b. bef. 1775
male, 16-26, b. 1795-1805, (Henry Breshears Jr?)
wife 16-26 (b. 1795-1805)
male, 16-26
fem., 10-16
fem., 10-16

Apparently, Henry Brashears Jr is in Henry Sr's household, along with some of the younger brothers and sisters. The other old couple? Norman Parks said it was an elderly half-brother named Isaac. The couple may have been Middleton and his wife, Elizabeth. Henry cared for this old couple until he, Henry, died, then his brother, John, took them over. See documents in John's chapter.

Families that lived between Henry Sr and his sons, William and Jesse: Thos. Etheridge, John Etheridge, Archelus Hogg, Anna Cupp, and Gibson Hogg.

Tennessee Land Grant #21592

Henry Breashears, Sr received a Tennessee Land grant for 55 acres on Knob Creek in 1824:

THE STATE OF TENNESSEE #21592

To all to whom these presents shall come, Greeting:

KNOW YE, That by virtue of warrant, N.514 dated the second day of September 1820, signed by the Secretary of State of North Carolina to the President and Trustees of the University of said State for 640 acres, on account of the military services of Joseph Bunge, Jr, dated and entered on the 18th of March 1823 by N.1261.

There is granted by the said State of Tennessee to Henry Brashears, assignee of the said President and Trustees, a certain tract or parcel of land containing Fifty-five acres by survey, bearing date the 18th day of June 1823, lying in the Seventh District in Lawrence County on Knob Creek in range six, section two and three, and bounded as follows, to wit: Beginning on an ash and beech eighteen poles north and one hundred and twenty six poles west from the northeast from said seventh range and second section, thence south one hundred thirty two and six tenth poles to a hornbeam and cucumber, thence sixty poles to the creek in all sixty six and four tenth poles to a stake, thence north one hundred thirty two and six tenth poles to a stake on a bluff, thence east thirty eight and ½ poles to the creek, in all sixty six and four tenth poles, to the Beginning

With the hereditaments and appertenances. To have and to

hold said tract or parcel of land and its appertenances to the said Henry Brashears and his heirs forever. In witness whereof, William Carroll, Governor of the State of Tennessee, hath hereunto set his hand and caused the great seal of the state to be affixed at Murfreesboro on the fifth day of March in the Year of our Lord one thousand eight hundred twenty four, and of the Independence of the United States the 48th.

By the Governor (signed) William Carroll

(signed) Daniel Graham, Secretary

Recorded 30 April 1824

Some Lawrence Co, TN, Records

After Henry Sr's death, the other heirs sold their portions of this land to the second son, John Breshears. (See deed below.)

1826 Tax Lists, Lawrence Co. TN:

#162 Bennet Brashears, probably a misreading for Robert Brashears, s/o Isaac Brashears of Roane Co, TN
#254 John Brashears, s/o Henry Sr and Eleanor
#255 Henry Brashears, s/o Henry Sr and Eleanor
#255 Jesse Brashears, s/o Henry Sr and Eleanor
#256 William Brashears, s/o Henry Sr and Eleanor
#257 Berry Brashears, b. 1790
#258 Henry Brashears Sr. He died two years later.

1830 Census of Lawrence Co, TN

p.292: Sam'l Brasher: 00001-00011 =20-30, b.1800-10
Lawrence Co, TN, Minutes Book, 1828-1834, p.225: State vs. Saml Brazier - scire facias, 7 Oct 1830. Scire Facias is an order to appear and show cause why some judgment against one should not be exercised. Samuel is a member of the Brazier/ Brasher family, s/o Allen Sterrett Brasher, of Shelby Co, AL.

p.293 Jesse Brashears 100001-22101 age 30-40, b. 1790-1800

p.294, line 10: Henry Brashen 00001-10001 age 20-30, b. 1800-10 ("Brashen" = copyist's error for Brasher)

p.294, line 11: Paul Brashen 10001-10001 age 20-30, b. 1800-10

p.294, line 12: John Brashen 120001-21001 age 30-40, b. 1790-1800

p.294, line 13: William Brashen 130001-001001 age 30-40, b. 1790-1800

p.294, line 16: Henry Brashen 21001-1000100001 age 20-30, b. 1800-10; elderly fem., age 70-80, b. 1750-60!?

p.295, line 3: John Brashears 0011000101-1100001 the old man 70-80, b. 1750-60; young man, 50-60, b. 1770-80

p.295, line 7: Nathan Brasher 110001-10001 age 30-40, b. 1790-1800
NOTE: this is Nathan Turner Breshears, b. SC 4 April 1797, d. 24 Feb 1884;

m. 26 Aug 1819, Elizabeth Catherine Keele
p.295, line 11: Middleton Brashen, 110001-110001 age 30-40, b. 1790-1800

1836 Tax Lists, Lawrence Co. TN:

District #3 (southeast corner of county, bordering Giles Co, TN and AL
Robert Brashears, 229 acres (with wife, Sarah Rankin), s/o Isaac of Roane Co, TN.
Isaac Brashears, 25 acres, 20 yr-old s/o Robert Brashears and Sarah Rankin

District #4 (directly north of Dist #3, bordering Giles Co)
Jacob Brashers, no acres mentioned (s/o John Brashears, b. 1767)

District #5 (west of Dist #4, just south of the center of the county)
Henry Brashers, 100 acres, This is Henry Brashear Jr, later of MO
Thomas Brashers, no acres mentioned, ?
John Brashers, 65 acres -- John, b. 1767, and wife Mary Berry
(Thomas Etheridge, on Knob Creek, was on corner of Districts 5 (south-central) & 6 (western; borders Wayne Co), but actually living in District 1, the southwestern-most district of the county)

District #7 (bordering Wayne Co and just north of Dist 6 and the middle of the county)
James Brashers, 12 acres, ?

Note re: these tax lists: Henry Jr was the only one of *his* clan left in Lawrence Co; all the others on the tax list were distant cousins. Henry's mother, Eleanor, was living with him. She died in 1837. In April, 1838, Henry Jr sold out and moved to Benton Co, MO. Jesse, John, Alexander, Middleton, and Nathan had moved to MO earlier. William, Henry Jr's oldest brother, is not on the Tax Lists; he may have gone to MO, but shows up by 1850 in Montgomery Co, Arkansas, where Berry Brashears, b. 1790, had gone.

Henry and Eleanor's Family

Children of Henry Breshears Sr and Eleanor Hardin:

[V6]1611. [8]1. ***William ?Arthur Breashears**, b. SC, c1790; m. in TN, ***Anna Etheridge***, d/o Thomas Etheridge. William's middle name may have been "Arthur" (per Southard FTW). William and Anna moved to Arkansas; see separate chapter.

[V6]1612. [8]2. ***John Breshears**, b. SC, 16 March 1793, d. Polk Co, MO, 25 June 1869; m. 1 March 1821, in Lawrence Co, TN, ***Naoma Ann Hogg***. John and Naoma moved to Polk Co, MO; see separate chapter.

[V6]1613. [8]3. ***Jesse Breshears**, b. SC, c1796; m.1. 2 March 1818, in Lawrence Co, TN, ***Elizabeth Bell*** (Bondsman: Nathan Turner Brashears) (*Early East Tenn Marr*, by Sistler), b. c1800-1804 (16-26 in

1820; 20-30 in 1830), d/o John Bell; m.2. ***Mrs. Mary Ellen (Franklin) Flanigan***. Jesse and Elizabeth migrated to Missiouri, about 1834. See separate chapter.

V6 1614. 8 5. **Mary "Polly" Breshears**, b. probably before 1800; m. 23 March 1825, in Lawrence Co, TN (Bondsman: Henry Breshears Sr), ***William Mays***. They are mentioned in deeds partially settling Henry's estate. They apparently remained in Lawrence Co, TN. n.f.i.

V6 1615. 8 6. ***Henry Breshears Jr**, b. SC, 23 Oct 1801, d. Wheatland, MO, 16/18 March 1860; m. c1822, in Lawrence Co, TN, ***Atsa "Atsey" Etheridge***, d/o Thomas Etheridge; Henry and Atsey moved to Benton Co, MO; see separate chapter.

V6 1616. 8 7. **Eleanor "Nellie" Breshears**, b. SC, c1804; m. 26 April 1825, in Lawrence Co, TN, ***Richard Pippin***. Richard was about 15 years older than Nellie. They are mentioned in the deeds partially settling Henry's estate. Some researchers confuse Richard with Simeon Pippin, who married Rachel Cole in Lawrence Co, TN, 12 Nov 1825. She died, and he later married Sarah Howard in Missouri in 1844. She is the Sarah Pippin of Pippin Cemetery. They were married by Alexander Breshears, JP. Roy Colbert has the following children for them, but says the line needs more research.

V6 1617. 9 1. Margaret Pippin, b. c1828, TN

V6 1618. 9 2. Mary Jane Pippin, b. c1833, TN; m. **William Marion Breshears**, b. 5 Oct 1833, (s/o Henry Breshears Jr and Atsa "Atsey" Etheridge)

V6 1619. 9 3. Henry Pippin, b. c1834, TN

V6 1620. 9 4. William Pippin, b. c1840, TN; m. 28 April 1859, Margaret Bybee,

V6 1621. 9 5. Ellen Pippin, b. c1842, in Missouri

V6 1622. 8 8. ***Margaret "Peggy" Breshears**, b. SC, 15 Feb 1811; m. ***Alexander Brashears**, b. 20 April 1807, SC.

Who this Alexander Brashears was has not been positively determined, but he was a cousin to the children of Henry Sr. He is believed to be a son of a deceased brother of Henry's, ?James Brashears, and his wife, Mary Jane Turner; that is, Alexander was a brother of Nathan Turner Brashears and Middleton Brashears the younger, and cousin to his wife, Margaret Breshears, sister of Henry Jr.

Alexander and Margaret moved c1833-35 to MO, with Nathan Turner Brashears and Middleton Brashears the younger. See Alexander's listing in "Three Brothers of Missouri" for their children.

Roy Colbert also listed a son for Henry and Eleanor: **Nathan Turner Breshears**, b. SC, 4 April 1797, d. 24 Feb 1884; m. 26 Aug 1819, ***Elizabeth Catherine Keele***, but no such person appears in any of the estate records, which are extant. He belonged to someone else. He was a brother of Alexander Brashears and Middleton Brashears the younger, but their father (the deceased ?James Brashears) has not yet been positively identified.

Etheridge Family Connections

Two of Henry Breshears Sr's sons married daughters of Thomas Etheridge, a neighbor. Thomas Etheridge received TN land grant #24627, dated the 8th of February, 1826. In time, Tom owned 1700 acres of land, but #24627 gave him only eleven acres. Thomas Etheridge, b. c1775, NC, d. 15 Oct 1855, Lawrence Co, TN (World Family Tree: Etheridge #2782, Vol 2); m. ____ ("old mother Etheridge died 6 April 1848," says a letter to Missouri, where most of their descendants moved.)

1. John Etheridge, b. 20 March 1793, d. 17 Aug 1859, Dallas Co, MO; m. 2 April 1818, Lawrence Co, TN, Sarah Wisdom, d. c1888; 7 ch: William; Lida; Matthew; Andrew; and three still born.
2. Anna Etheridge, b. c1794, NC; m. c1818, Lawrence Co, TN, ***William BRASHEARS***. William and Anna moved to Arkansas and had a large family. See separate chapter.
3. Matthew Etheridge, b. c1797-8, ?NC, d. bef 1850, Lawrence Co, TN; m. Mary Greenshaw, b. c1802, NC, d. c1875 in Point Peter, Richland Township, Searcy Co, AR; 7 ch: Rebecca; Alford (Alfred); Frank; Sarah; William H.;

Mathena; and Mariah.

4. William Etheridge, b. 2 Nov 1803, TN; m. 6 April 1829, Lucy T. Flakes, James Welch, JP, officiating in Lawrence Co, TN. 7 ch: Martha Jane; Thomas; Atsa Elizabeth; Dorcus; Lucy Tennessee; William Henry; and James C. "Dock" Etheridge.
5. City Etheridge; m. Robert M. Bailey. ?? Not in Carmen E. Collin's book, *Breshears, Jordan, and Ethridge Families of Missouri*.
6. Atsa "Atsey" Etheridge, b. 1 April 1806, TN, d. 1880, Hickory Co, MO; m. 1822, Lawrence Co, TN, ***Henry BRASHEARS Jr***. After his mother died, Henry Jr moved to Missouri, where he was a founder of Breshears Valley. See separate chapter.
7. Sarah Etheridge, b. 1807, d. after 1884; m. David Riddle, b. 1806, s/o John David Riddle. 7 ch: Henry M.; Martha E.; William M.; John M.; David F.; Sarah J.; and James M. Riddle. David and Sarah remained in Lawrence Co, TN, their whole lives.

    See suit in Lawrence Co, TN Court, 6 Sept 1856, regarding estate of Thomas Etheridge.

    David Riddle wrote Henry Breshears Jr in MO a number of times, regarding family business (according to Roy Colbert). When Jesse Brashears and Elizabeth Bell moved to MO, they sold their land to David Riddle.

Estate of Henry Breshears, Sr

Henry Breshears Sr died in Lawrence Co, TN, before 10 Oct 1828:

Lawrence Co, Tenn, Minutes Book, 1828-1834, p. 24: 10 Oct 1828. Ordered that Elender Beshears be appointed administrator of the estate of Henry Brashears, dec., who gave bond and security.

Lawrence County, Tennessee, Wills, Inventories and Settlement 1829-1847, pp. 8-9 etc., Tennessee State Library and Archives, Nashville, Tennessee: Sale of the Estate of Henry Breshears Dec'd. Recorded 10th, January 1829.

A list of property sold at the estate sale of Henry Breshears, Deceased, this 29th of Jan, 1829:

Person's name	Property sold	
Eleanor Breshears	beds and furniture	5.00
Eleanor Breshears	table shelf and pot ware	5.00
Eleanor Breshears	two wheels and sundry Articles	3.00
Eleanor Breshears	coopers ware and chairs	1.00
S. M. Cunningham	7 chairs, a tub and churn	2.56½
Alexander Breshears	1 pot	1.84½
Peter May	1 kettle	4.06½
Isaac Reeder	1 sythe	8.50
Henry Breshears Jr.	1 loom	3.00
Henry Breshears Jr.	girs	1.50
Henry Breshears Jr.	hones	.75
John Breshears	1 collar	3.37½
John Breshears	2 hides	2.37½
Wm. Breshears	1 pair stretchers	.75
Alexander Breshears	one hoe	.12
Middleton Breshears	one plow	1.12½
William Breshears	one shovel plow	.50
Eleanor Breshears	one sorrel Mare	30.00
William Breshears	one Bay Mare	12.12½
William Breshears	one sorrel horse colt	32.31½
Isaac Lindsey	one red cow and calf	8.22⅓
Alexander Breshears	one black and white heifer	3.06½
Eleanor Breshears	one calf and Bull	6.00
William Breshears Jr.	one red cow and calf	7.93
Alexander Miller	one cow and calf	7.25
William Etheridge	one speckled heifer	2.00
John Breshears	12 geese	6.00
Eli N. Cunningham	10 head hogs	12.00
Eleanor Breshears	5 head sheep and bull	3.00
Eleanor Breshears	fodder	.62⅓
Peter May	1 rifle	8.62½
Eleanor Breshears	one cats stack	1.50
Richard Pippins	one cat stack	5.00
Eleanor Breshears	one Mare saddle	1.53
Eleanor Breshears	one bedstead	.12⅛
Eleanor Breshears	two barrels	.25
John D. Riddle	1 wagon	19.00
Isaac Reeder	1 bull	.50
John Breshears	one wedge	.68¾
John Breshears	one hammer and pinchers	

James M. Wisdom, clerk.

p. 57: 6 April 1829, Eleanor Brashers, adm. of estate of Henry decd., made return of the sale.
p. 57: 6 April 1829, Committee to allot and lay off to Eleanor Brashears widow of the late Henry Brashers, dec., 1 years provisions (note variations in the spelling of the surname).

State of Tennessee— We the Commissioners appointed by the worshipful Lawrence County Court at January Term 1829 to lay off to Eleanor Breshears, Widow of Henry Breshears, deceased, one years sustainance, we in pursurence to the ad. order say that she have 35 barrels corn, 100 lbs seed cotton, 10 lbs wood, 2 prs shoes, 1 lb pepper, and of allspice, 1 lb ginger, 3 bu salt, 100 lbs flour, 1 lb steel, given under our hands this 28th, January 1829

William Wisdom (his X Mark)
Isaac Reeder
Thomas Blair

Henry Breshears Sr had received Tennessee Land Grant #21592, 55 ac. in Lawrence Co, TN, 5 May 1824 (Bk X, p.599). The heirs soon sold their shares of this land to John Breshears, second oldest of Henry Sr's sons (note again the variations in spelling of the surname within a single document):

Lawrence Co, TN Deeds F:234. Wm. Beshears and others to John Beshears, dated 4 Feb 1833, recorded 23 April 1838. Wm. Breshears, Henry Breshears, Alexander Brashears and Peggy his wife, Wm. May and Polly his wife, Richard Pippins and Nelly his wife, and Jesse Brashears of the one part to John Brashears of the 2nd part. $150. 55 ac. on Knob Creek, Dist 7, range 6, sec. 2 & 3. A stake on a bluff, crossing the creek, same land as grant #21592 to Henry Brashears. Wit: Thomas Blair, Thomas (his Mark) Etheridge. Signed by William, Henry, Jesse, Alexander, Margaret (X) Brashears, Richard (X) Pippin, Eleanor (X) Pippen, Wm May.

Lawrence Co, TN, Minutes Book, 1828-1834. p. 189: 4 Oct 1830. A deed of conveyance from Henry Brashears, Jesse Brashers, Alexander Brashers, Richard Pippen, William Brashers, and William May to John Brashers for 19 1/2 ac. was produced. Oaths of James M. Bumpass, Jesse L. Paine, Thomas J. Matthews, and Josiah S. Stockton, wits.

14. WILLIAM BREASHEARS and Anna Etheridge

v6**1611.** 81. **William (?Arthur) Breashears**, (s/o Henry Breshears Sr and Eleanor ?Hardin), b. c1790, in SC, in either Spartanburg or Greenville District, d. bef. 1860, probably near Witt Springs, Searcy County, Arkansas; m. about 1816 in Lawrence Co, TN, ***Anna Etheridge***, b. c1794, d. before 11 Aug 1884, d/o Thomas Etheridge of Lawrence Co, TN. William's middle name may have been "Arthur," (per Southard FTW).

In his early years, William and his family followed his father (see Warren and Lawrence Co, TN, documents above). After Henry Sr's death, he may have moved to MO, but did not stay long; he is on the 1849-50 Montgomery Co, AR Poll Tax list and the 1850 Census, Montgomery Co, AR.

William was in McNairy Co, TN, in 1833 when he wrote his brothers, John and Henry (Jr) Breshears. The letter shows William unsatisfied with the place he was living.

1833...State of Tennessee, McNairy Co., directed to Larnce Co [sic] TN [sic] Co Tennessee.

Dear Brother; I imbrace this opportunity to inform you that we are all well at present. Thank you. Hoping these lines will find you enjoying the like blessing. I have nother [sic] perticular to wright to you but can inform you that I am not settled here. I intend to move away from this part of the world as soon as I can. I have never had enny chance to right to you before I intend to come and see you as soon as I can. I can't tell when between now and Christmas ecept I am providentally hindered. I shall namor [sic] but remain your loving brother til deth... *WILLIAM BRESHEARS.*

Note...This letter was saved by the Henry Breshears family and taken to Missouri in 1838.

William and Anna's Family

Family of William ?Arthur Breashears and Anna Etheridge:

[V6]1623. [9]1. **Eleanor Breashears,** b. c1822, Lawrence Co, TN; m. ***Barnabus Woodard***, b. c1818. (They are in the 1850 Census of Montgomery Co, Arkansas.)

[V6]1624. [10]1. Julia Ann Woodard, b. c1840, AR

[V6]1625. [10]2. Melissa C. Woodard, b. c1842, AR

[V6]1626. [10]3. Mary I. Woodard, b. c1844, AR

[V6]1627. [10]4. James M. Woodard, b. c1850, AR

[V6]1628. [9]2. ***Matthew Breashears**, b. c1823, Lawrence Co, TN; m. ***Elizabeth Parker***. Living in 1850 and 1860 in Montgomery Co, AR.

[V6]1629. [9]3. **Henry Breashears,** b. c1825, Lawrence Co, TN; m. c1845, Searcy Co, AR, ***Mary Jane "Polly" Wood***, b. c1826, Lawrence Co, TN; they are in the 1850 Census, Montgomery Co, AR, Polk twp, with 3 ch. and the 1860 census of Marion Co, AR, with 5.

[V6]1630. [10]1. **Winney S. Brashears**, b. Searcy Co, AR c1845

[V6]1631. [10]2. **Anna Brashears**, b. Searcy Co, AR c1847

[V6]1632. [10]3. **Ellen Brashears**, b. Searcy Co, AR c1849

[V6]1633. [10]4. **Elizabeth Breashears**, b. 27 Dec 1850, Searcy Co, AR, d. 20 Aug 1923; m. c1867, in Marion Co, AR, ***William Bluford Mears***, b. 27 Sept 1843, Cannon Co, TN, d. 25 Dec 1932, Marion Co, AR (sources: 1850, 1860 census), both are buried in CowanCem, Marion Co, AR. William B. Mears was on the voters list in Marion Co, AR, in 1893. Additional data from "Vera Reeves" <velane @centurytel.net>.

[V6]1634. [11]1. Albert W. Mears, b. 15 Sept 1868, d. 5 March 1954; m. 13 Nov 1892 (Marion Co, AR, Marr), Charlotte Jane Langston, b. 18 May 1874, d. 15 Sept 1945, bur together in Cowan Cem, Marion Co, AR.

[V6]1635. [11]2. George W. Mears, b. c1870 in AR; m. 10 Nov 1892 (Marion Co, AR), Rachel Evans

[V6]1636. [11]3. Mary Anna Mears b: c1873 in AR; m. 12 July 1891, M. D. Dunlap,

[V6]1637. [11]4. Thomas J. Mears, b. 25 June 1875, d. 27 July 1881, bur Cowan Cem, Marion Co, AR

[V6]1638. [11]5. John Mears b: c1877 in AR. The Mt Echo (newspaper) reported on 13 Sept 1895, "Johney Mears, son of Bluford Mears, died on Friday."

[V6]1639. [11]6. James H. Mears, b. 24 Jul 1883, d. 7 Apr 1958, bur Cowan Cem, Marion Co, AR; m. 16 Feb 1908 (Marion Co, Marriages), Stella Hunter, b. c1887 (21 at marriage), "both of Stone County."

[V6]1640. [11]7. Benjamin F. Mears, b. 3 Sept 1886, d. 16 Feb 1970, Cowan Cem, Marion Co, AR "WW I"

[V6]1641. [10]5. **Charity Brashears**, b. 1856, Searcy Co, AR

[V6]1642. [9]4. **Jesse Breashears,** b. 1827, Lawrence Co, TN (25 in 1850, Polk Twp, Montgomery Co, AR). On 1849-50 Montgomery Co, AR Poll Tax list. No further record. married, 17 April 1849, (*Hot Springs Co, AR, marriage Records, 1825-1880*), ***Hannah J. Brashears***, b. TN, d/o John Brashears and Elizabeth Randall.

[V6]1643. [9]5. **Hardin L. Brashears,** b. 11 Aug 1830, Lawrence Co, TN, d. 10 May 1886. Served in Union Army during Civil War: enlisted in 1st Arkansas Infantry, at Fayetteville, AR; m. 7 Oct 1857, in Pope Co, AR, ***Sarah Hodges***, b. 20 Jan 1840, Lawrence Co, TN, d. 25 Oct 1921, AR. Both Hardin and Sarah are buried at Reed Cemetery, near Story, AR. Family, per *Breshears, Jordan, and Ethridge Families of Missouri*, by Carmen Elizabeth Collins, 1990, pp.71a-b, using information supplied by Arthur Stevens, of Hot Springs, AR:

[V6]1644. [10]1. **Henry Breashears**, b. 7 Oct 1858, d.14 Oct 1865.

[V6]1645. [10]2. **Grandville Kelly "Grant" Breashears**, b. 20

March 1861; m. ***Susan E.*** ____

V6 1646. 10 3. **Elizabeth Breashears**, b. 15 March 1863, d. 28 Sept 1864, bur Reed Cem, Story, AR

V6 1647. 10 4. **Mary S. Catherine Breashears**, b. 27 June 1869, d. 2 Sept 1886, bur Reed Cem, Story, AR

V6 1648. 10 5. **Tabitha Melvinia "Mellie" Breashears**, b. 5 Oct 1871; m. ***J.J.W. Chappell***

V6 1649. 10 6. **Mertie Marcelline Breashears**, b. 10 May 1874; m. ***T.M. "Mace" Scott***

V6 1650. 10 7. **Pauzety Orleans "Zettie" "Orlie" Breashears**, b. 6 April 1876, d. 1941, bur Reed Cem, Story, AR; m. ***John Elder***

V6 1651. 10 8. **Lila Elsie Breashears**, b. 3 May 1878, d. 16 April 1953, bur Reed Cem, Story, AR; m. ***Abner Luther Stevens***

V6 1652. 10 9. **Bedie W. Breashears**, b. 10 Dec 1880, bur near Clinton, AR; m. ***Tom Hooper***

V6 1653. 9 6. ***Sarah Ann Breashears,** b. c1833, Lawrence Co, TN, d. after 1880; m. 15 June 1848, in Montgomery Co, AR, ***John Humphreys***, b. 1825, TN,

V6 1654. 9 7. **Atsey Breashears,** b. c1834, Lawrence Co, TN, d. before 1884; m. ***Joseph Carter***

V6 1655. 10 1. Joseph Carter Jr

V6 1656. 10 2. Elizabeth Carter; m. ____ Robertson

15. MATTHEW BREASHEARS and Elizabeth Parker

v6 1628. 9 2. **Matthew Breashears**, (s/o William Breashears and Anna Etheridge), was born c1823 in Lawrence Co, TN and died 24 March 1865 in the Military Hospital, Little Rock, AR; bur sec. 1-428, Little Rock National Cem. On 10 June 1847, in Sulphur Springs Township, Montgomery Co, AR, he married ***Elizabeth Parker***, b. c1829, Illinois, d. 15 Nov 1874, Montgomery Co, AR., d/o William Parker and Eleanor Lanham. Matthew is in the Montgomery Co, AR, Census of 1850,

Mountain twp; on the 1849-50 Montgomery Co, AR, Poll Tax list; on 1852-55 Montgomery Co, AR, Poll Tax list; and the 1860 census, Montgomery Co, AR, where the surname is spelled "Brashers"; his children used the spelling "Breashears."

Matthew served in the Union Army during the Civil War. He enlisted 14 Jan 1864, was mustered 17 Feb 1864, at Cedar Glades, AR, and was a private in Company D, 4th Arkansas Volunteer Cavalry, under Col. Lafayette Gregg. Physically, he was described as having blue eyes, dark hair and dark complexion; six feet one inch tall. He became ill and entered the military hospital at Little Rock in November, 1864; he died there, 24 March 1865 from chronic diarrhea. (See *Arkansas' Damned Yankees--an Index to Union Soldiers in Arkansas Regiments*, p.24)

<u>Family of Matthew Breashears and Elizabeth Parker</u> (1860, 1870 Census, Mountain twp, Harold Post Office, Montgomery Co, AR. Additional ref: contribution of Gertie Stephens Owens and Carol Jo Qualls Ford to the Montgomery Co Genealogical Society publication.)

[V6]1657. [10]1. ***Louisa <u>Ellen</u> Breashears,** b. 29 Feb 1848, at Story, Montgomery Co, AR, d. there 7 Dec 1929; m. 17 June 1866, in Bucksville, Montgomery Co, AR, ***Abram Frank Lamb***, (See below)

[V6]1658. [10]2. **William F.M. Breashears,** b. c1849; m. ***Martha Lamb***, b. c1849, Sulphur Springs, Montgomery Co, AR. (Data from Deena Quick <hickorynut26@ cs.com>)

[V6]1659. [11]1. **Mary Breashears**, b. 1871, Montgomery Co, AR,

[V6]1660. [11]2. **Harmon Breashears**, b. 1873, Montgomery Co, AR,

[V6]1661. [11]3. **Eldwade Breashears**, [female] b. 1875, Montgomery Co, AR,

[V6]1662. [11]4. **Accade Breashears**, [male] b. 1877, Montgomery Co, AR,

[V6]1663. [11]5. **Decalve (or Decalb) F. Breashears**, b. 1879, Montgomery Co, AR; m. ***Onie Udora Ingram***, b. ?, d. June 1979. They are listed in 1910 US Census, Choctaw Co, Oklahoma, with mother-in-law, Paulina Ingram. Children of Decalve & Onie, born after 1913 were: (Data from Karen Ingram <Ingfam@flash.net>)

[V6]1664. [12]1. **Marie Breashears,**

[V6]1665. [12]2. **Clota Breashears,**

[V6]1666. [12]3. **Jimmie Breashears,**

[V6]1667. [12]4. **Oscar Breashears,**

[V6]1668. [12]5. **Elray Breashears,**

[V6]1669. [10]3. ***John Riley "J.R." Breashears,** b. 10 Jan 1851, Montgomery Co, AR, d. 1910-20, OK; m.1. 6 Oct 1879, in Montgomery Co, AR, ***Nancy Ann Reed***, b. c1860; m.2. 1 Sept 1889, Montgomery Co, AR, ***Mrs. Mary Jane (Bolton) Brannan***, b. Dec 1851, in GA

[V6]1670. [10]4. **Anna Melzina Breashears,** b. 26 Jan 1853, in Montgomery Co, AR, d. young; m. ***John H. Reed***, b. c1853. They had two daughters.

[V6]1671. [10]5. **Henry Wesley Breashears,** b. 26 Nov 1854, in Montgomery Co, AR,

[V6]1672. [10]6. ***Lemuel Casziel Breashears,** b. 7 Feb 1858, in Montgomery Co, AR, d. 20 June 1949; m. 25 April 1880, ***Mary Ellen Hogan***, b. c1863. His brother, Carroll, was in their HH in 1880, Yell Co, AR.

[V6]1673. [10]7. ***Carroll "Carl" Cunlee Breashears**, b. 10 Oct 1859, in Montgomery Co, AR; m. 7 Sept 1884, ***Sarah E. Hogan***, b. 1869. Carroll moved to Yell Co, AR, with his brother, Lemuel.

[V6]1674. [10]8. ***James Madison "Jim" Breashears,** b. 7 Dec 1861, in Montgomery Co, AR, d. 3 May 1937, Story, Montgomery Co, AR; m. ***Georgia A. (née Chapman) Kilby***, b. 1863, d. 1936; ?m.2. ***Omey***

[V6]1675. [10]9. **George Breashears**, b. after 1860; m. and thought to have lived in Sallisaw, OK

[V6]1676. [10]10. **Miles Monroe "Mun" Breashears**, b. c1868-69 in Cedar Glades, AR; m. ***Georgia Poe (or Pope)***, b. 1874, Ringgold (prob AR), d. young.

[V6]1677. [11]1. **Myrtle Breashears**, b. 1892, d. 1959; m. ***Fletcher Srygley Marrs***

[V6]1678. [12]1. Roxie Marrs, b. c1912, Sallisaw, OK; m.

several times; 3 ch

[V6]1679. [12]2. Edgar Cleo Marrs, d. as a toddler in OK

[V6]1680. [12]3. Herbert Marrs, b. 1915, Vian, OK, d. 1981; m. and had 3 ch

[V6]1681. [13]1. Stephen Edward Marrs, b. Sept 1945, d. Nov 1945

[V6]1682. [13]2. Marcia Elaine Marrs; m. & div twice; 5 ch

[V6]1683. [13]3. James David Marrs; n.m.

Mun was born 4 years after Matthew died. Earl Emery, a 92-year resident of Story, said his uncle told him that Elizabeth (Parker) Breashears became pregnant with Mun during the time she was helping her daughter, Louisa Ellen (Breashears) Lamb, with the birth of a child.

Figure 10: Miles Monroe Breashears. Photo from Susie Wooldridge.

In the 1870, census of Story, Montgomery Co, AR, Mun was listed as one year old, "step-son" in hh of Elizabeth Breashears (widow of Matthew Breashears).

In the 1900 and 1910 Census, Sequoyah Co, OK, he is in hh of John R. Breashears, listed as a brother. Mun is unaccounted for in 1920, but his daughter and her family are living with John R. Breashears' widow. Data from Marcia (Marrs) Moore.

Writes Marcia: "Fletcher, Myrtle, and the children moved to California, and Mun was with them for the first few years.

Family tradition has it that Mun didn't want to die so far from home and returned, but whether to Oklahoma or Arkansas I have no clue. Nor do I know anything about his wife, Georgia, save that she died young (she was born in 1874 in Ringgold, state unknown [there is a Ringgold, AR]) was supposed to be Cherokee and that her mother's name was Sally Poe or Pope. Sally was born in Cedar Glades, AR, c1853. I THINK Sally was married to Melton Monroe Hays and had a son, Martin Melton Hays (1876-1950). Sally seems to have died young too, and doesn't appear with her husband and son on the 1880 census of Blount County, Alabama. Melton Monroe Hays does show up as a landowner in Cedar Glades, Arkansas by 1890. I don't know whether he was raising Georgia Po(p)e or placed her with other relatives or what." Sources: Marcia Marrs <memarrs @email.msn.com>, Gloria Cain <Awrldtrvlr @aol.com>

Louisa Ellen Breashears and Abram Frank Lamb

[v6]1657. [10]1. **Louisa Ellen Breashears,** (d/o Matthew Breashears and Elizabeth Parker), b. 29 Feb 1848, at Story, Montgomery Co, AR, d. there 7 Dec 1929; m. 17 June 1866, in Bucksville, Montgomery Co, AR, ***Abram Frank Lamb***, b. 2 Nov 1847, Cherokee, NC, d. 12 Nov 1913, Story, Montgomery Co, AR, both bur Breshears Cem, Story, AR.

Family of Louisa Ellen Breashears and Abram Frank Lamb:

[V6]1684. [11]1. Matthew Taylor Lamb, b. 1867, Story, AR; m.1. Lydia Charlotte Qualls; m.2. Alma Margaret Stephens Willey

[V6]1685. [11]2. Reuben "Bud" Lamb, b. 1869, Story, AR; m. Elizabeth Stewart

[V6]1686. [11]3. Harrison Lamb, b. c1871, Story, AR

[V6]1687. [11]4. Henry A. Lamb, b. 1873, Story, AR

[V6]1688. [11]5. Lemuel Conway Lamb, b. 1875, Story, AR

[V6]1689. [11]6. Mary Elleber Lamb, b. 26 July 1879, Story, AR, d. 30 March 1930, bur Reed Cem; m. 9 Dec 1894, in Story, Montgomery Co, AR, Green Lee Qualls

[V6]1690. [11]7. Maude Lamb, b. 21 July 1882, Story, AR; m.

Charles Shepard

[V6]1691. [11]8. Dola Lamb, b, 1884, Story, AR; m. Sarah Louise Blakely

[V6]1692. [11]9. Charles Goodner Lamb, b. 1885, Story, AR

[V6]1693. [11]10. Abram L. Lamb, b. 1888, Story, AR; m. Annie Blair

[V6]1694. [11]11. Tinnie Mae Lamb, b. 1891, Story, AR, d. 1912, Story, AR; m. Fred Winford Southard, b. 12 May 1884, Jefferson twp, Independence, AR, d. 22 Feb 1973, Phoenix, Maricopa Co, AZ

[V6]1695. [11]1. Arlie Brison Southard, b. 19 June 1911, Story, Montgomery Co, AR, d. 22 Sept 1974, Phoenix, Maricopa Co, AZ; m. Maude Evelyn Glaze, b. 12 Dec 1912, Saltillo, Hopkins Co, TX, d. 14 Feb 1976, Phoenix, Maricopa Co, AZ, both bur Resthaven Cem, Glendale, Maricopa Co, AZ.

[V6]1696. [12]1. Eula Mae Southard; m. Norman Gettings. Ch: Norman; and Gary Gettings

[V6]1697. [12]2. Juanita Faye Southard; m. Jim Swearingen. Ch: Tracy Jo; Christy; and Stephanie Swearingen

[V6]1698. [12]3. Fred William Southard; m. Helen McGowan. Ch: Shari; Brenda; and Annie Marie Southard

[V6]1699. [12]4. Arlonzo Southard; m.1. Ruth Hauser (5 ch); m.2. Marjorie Evelyn Peterson.

[V6]1700. [13]1. Theresa Ann Southard; m.1. Joseph Burton; m.2. Chris Thompson. Ch: Joseph Alexander; and Michael Robert Burton

[V6]1701. [13]2. Carl Von Southard; m. Juanita Brown. Ch: Carl Von Southard, Jr

[V6]1702. [13]3. Susan Raye Southard; m. Thomas Dunlap. Ch: Timothy Southard; Jessica Raye; and Brandy Sue Dunlap

[V6]1703. [13]4. Carol Cathrine Southard; m. Joseph Gerardo. Ch: Joseph Alexander; Valen Arlonzo; and Alicia Nicole

Gerardo

V6 1704. [13]5. Bryson Dean Southard; m. Jennifer Tomsha. Ch: Erin Leigh; and Arlie Brison Southard, II

V6 1705. [12]5. Robert Dean Southard; m. Sostena Ramona Duran. Ch: Deanna; Rebecca; and Robert Dean Southard, Jr

V6 1706. [11]2. Chesley Southard, b. & d. 1912, Story, Montgomery Co, AR

John Riley Breashears and Nancy Ann Reed/ Mary Jane Bolton

v6 1669. [10]3. **John Riley "J.R." Breashears,** (s/o Matthew Breashears and Elizabeth Parker), b. 10 Jan 1851, Harold, Montgomery Co, AR, d. 1910-20, OK; m.1. 6 Oct 1879, Montgomery Co, AR (had been married one year in 1880), ***Nancy Ann Reed***, b. c1860 (18 at marriage; 20 in 1880, Montgomery Co, AR). In 1880, John and Nancy are living in Cedar Glades, Montgomery Co, AR, next door to his older sister, Louisa Ellen Breashears and her husband, Abram Lamb. Nancy is reported to have died as a result of childbirth (with Walter), probably after 1885.

John Riley Breashears m.2. 1 Sept 1889, Montgomery Co, AR (I.G.I. film #1985705) ***Mrs. Mary Jane (Bolton) Brannan***, b. Dec 1851, in GA (per 1900 census, they had been married 10 years; her parents b. VA; she was 69 in 1920). Mary Jane had been abandoned by her husband, who went out for a loaf of bread, never returned, and left her with two children, Sam and Sophie Brannan. She and John then had two children. Family story is that the family black-balled John for marrying an abandoned woman; so he and she moved to Oklahoma. On the way, they stopped at a country store, and there behind the counter was Mary Jane's former husband.

In 1900, John R. and wife, Mary, are in McKey twp, Sequoyah Co, Indian Territory. The 1910 census for Sequoyah County, Oklahoma, lists J.R. Breashears (age 56), his wife, Mary Breashears (also age 56) and their children, John (17) and Lizzie (15). Next door are C. Breashears (age 27), probably an older son, and his wife, Nettie (23). In J.R.'s h/h are a younger brother, Mun, and his daughter, Myrtle (age 17). In 1920, Mary is a widow, age 69; in her household are Mun Breashears, age 50, his daughter, Myrtle and her husband Fletcher Srygley Marrs.

Family of John Riley "J.R." Breashears and Nancy Reed: all born Montgomery Co, AR.

V6 1707. 11 1. **Tennessee Breashears**, b. Nov 1879,

V6 1708. 11 2. **Cornelius Breashears**, b. Aug 1881,

V6 1709. 11 3. **Levander Breashears**, b. April 1883, d. 1930s, bur Drakesland Cem; m. ***Hannah Holt***,

V6 1710. 11 4. **Walter Breashears**, b. 25 Sept 1885, Montgomery Co, AR (1886, says 1900 census), d. 15 April 1974; m. 21 Aug 1914, in Vian, Sequoyah Co, OK, ***Bessie Leora Littlejohn***, b. 21 July 1886, Paris, TX, d. 5 July 1985, Broken Arrow, Tulsa Co, OK. (Additional data from Susie Wooldridge (susieww @cox.net), who also sent pictures.)

Figure 11: Bessie Leora (Littlejohn) Breashears with children: Leo "Mutt" (younger boy), Imo (on lap), and John Breashears. Photo from Susie Wooldridge.

V6 1711. 12 1. **June Breashears**, b. June 1915, d. Sept 1915, died from Bold Hives (crib death)

V6 1712. 12 2. **Franklin James "Frank" "Son" Breashears**, b. 1917, Sallisaw, OK, d. 1958 from Leukemia; m. ***Plura Ray***,

V6 1713. 13 1. **Norma Jean Breashears**, lives in Sallisaw, OK

V6 1714. 13 2. **Jimmy Raye "Jim" Breashears**, lives in Sallisaw, OK

[V6]1715. [13]3. **Jerry Breashears**, lives in Tulsa, OK

[V6]1716. [12]3. **Gary Quentin "Doc" "Buddy" Breashears**, b. Aug 1918, d. May 1948 from Leukemia; m.1. ***Glennie Duty*** (1 ch); m.2. ***Irene Thompson*** (they never lived together); m.3. ***Dorothy Baker***,

[V6]1717. [13]1. **Emma Lynn Breashears**,

[V6]1718. [12]4. **Raymond Breashears**, b. 1920, died 3 weeks later of Bold Hives (crib death)

[V6]1719. [12]5. **Imo Breashears**, b. 30 Aug 1922, Sallisaw, Sequoiah Co, OK; m. 7 Oct 1939 in Vian, Sequoyah Co, OK, ***Marzy Autumn Johnson*** and is still living.

[V6]1720. [13]1. Shirley Ann Johnson, b. 31 Dec 1940

[V6]1721. [13]2. Jimmy Dale Johnson, b. 28 Sept 1942

[V6]1722. [13]3. Samuel Walter Johnson, b. 15 May 1945, murdered 18 June 1996

[V6]1723. [12]6. **William Phillip "Bill" Breashears**, b. 1924, d. 1929 of Creeping Paralysis (Polio)

[V6]1724. [12]7. **John Paul Edward Breashears**, b. 8 May 1930, d. 4 July 1993, of heart attack; m.1. ***Waneve Waters***, (2 daughters); m.2. ***Raylene*** ______,

[V6]1725. [13]1. **Queda Breashears**,

[V6]1726. [13]2. **Sherry Breashears**,

[V6]1727. [12]8. **Leo Russell "Mutt" Breashears**, b. 14 Sept 1935; m.1. ***Betty Sloan***; m.2. ***Ruth*** ______,

[V6]1728. [13]x. **Brenda Breashears**; m. _____ ***Sanders***,

Family of John Riley "J.R." Breashears and Mary Jane Boulton:

[V6]1729. [11]5. **John A. Breashears**, b. March 1893, Montgomery Co, AR

[V6]1730. [11]6. **Mary Elizabeth "Lizzie" Breashears**, b. April 1895, Montgomery Co, AR,

Lemuel Casziel Breashears and Mary Ellen Hogan

[v6]1672. [10]6. **Lemuel Casziel Breashears**, (s/o Matthew

Breashears and Elizabeth Parker), b. 7 Feb 1858, Harold, Montgomery Co, AR, d. 20 Jan 1949, Yell Co, AR; m. 25 April 1880 (Yell Co, AR, "by W.F. Smith, MG," Book C, p.147), ***Mary Ellen Hogan***, b. c1863 (17 in 1880), d. 1939; both bur Sunlight Cem, Plainview, Yell Co, AR. Mary Ellen was d/o John S. Hogan (1835-after 1878) and Nancy Jane Gilkey (20 April 1840-5 Aug 1918). Lem's brother Carroll was in their HH in 1880, Yell Co, AR. In 1900 Census, Lower Lafane twp, Yell Co, AR #285-287, called "Lom C." In 1910, Census, Lower Lafane twp, he's called Tom C. #343-345, probably a clerk's or copyist's error.

Family of Lemuel Casziel Breashears and Mary Ellen Hogan:

[V6]1731. [11]1. **Nancy Ellen Breashears**, b. Feb 1883

[V6]1732. [11]2. **John Smith Breashears**, b. 19 Oct 1885, d. 10 April 1948, Yell Co, AR; m. ***Ola (or Viola) Brown***, b. 17 Feb 1887, d. 15 March 1979, "w/o John S. Breashears, d/o Monroe and Lizzie (Waldon) Brown", bur together in Hunts Chapel Cem, Rover, Yell Co, AR; HH #522-525, 1910 Gilkey twp, Yell Co, w/ wife, Ola and son, Ned Brown, age 1. Family constructed from obit of son, Hays Breashears. Data sent to me by K. McGee: "Cemeteries of Yell County, Arkansas," Vol 7; interview with Lola Breashears; Yell County (Arkansas) Historical Society Publication.

[V6]1733. [12]1. **Ned Brown Breashears**, b. c1909 (1 yr old in 1910), d. bef 1999; m.1. in Yell Co, AR, ***Jewell Thomas***; m.2. ***Alyce E. Miller***

[V6]1734. [12]2. **Ted Breashears**, d. bef 1999, Rover, Yell Co, AR; m. in Yell Co, AR, ***Vera Lorene Green***,

[V6]1735. [12]3. **Lovick Hays Breashears**, b. 26 July 1912, Rover, Yell Co, AR, d. 17 Feb 1999, Russellville, AR; m.1. in Yell Co, AR, ***Velma Gladys Pelt***; m.2. ***Lola Virginia Person***,

[V6]1736. [12]4. **Minnie Sue Breashears**, b. Rover, Yell Co, AR, d. bef 1999; m.1. in Yell Co, AR, ***Erby Raymond Lewis***; m.2. _____ ***Cox***

[V6]1737. [12]5. **Robert Monroe "Bobby" Breashears**, b. 29 July 1917, Rover, Yell Co, AR, d. 30 Oct 1918, "s/o J.S. & Ola (Brown) Breashears",

Hunts Chapel Cem, Rover, Yell Co, AR

[V6]1738. [12]6. **Baxter Ewell Breashears**, b. Yell Co, AR, living in Russellville in 1999

[V6]1739. [12]7. **Mary Lou Breashears**, b. Yell Co, AR, living in Briggsville, AR, in 1999; m. ***Joseph Lee "Joe Lee" Hunt***

[V6]1740. [12]8. **Leroy Breashears**, b. Yell Co, AR, living in Russellville in 1999

[V6]1741. [12]9. **Jo Breashears**, b. c1926, Yell Co, AR, living in Little Rock, AR, in 1999; m. ***Homer Lee Lofland***, b. 24 July 1920, Yell Co, AR, d. 10 Feb 1984, Bluffton, Yell Co, AR, bur Bluffton Cem, s/o Homer Virgil Lofland and Oda P. Caviness. Jo and Homer had two children: Judy and Lena Jane Lofland. (Data from William F. "Bill" Pugh)

[V6]1742. [12]10. **Bill Breashears**, living in Dardanelle in 1999

[V6]1743. [11]3. **Edgar E. Breashears**, b. March 1886; at home in 1910

[V6]1744. [11]4. **Ola L. Breashears**, b. March 1889

[V6]1745. [11]5. **Joseph Oscar Breashears**, b. 23 Dec 1890, d. 20 Aug 1976 "Pfc, US Army, WW I" says tombstone in Salem Cem; m.1. ***Icie Gertrude*** _______, b. 19 Nov 1906, d. 16 May 1928, [1st] "wife of J.O. Breashears" in Sunlight Cem, Yell Co, AR; m.2. 24 Sept 1933, ***Beuna Lorene Grisson***, b. 12 Feb 1909, "w/o J.O. Breashears," bur with J.O. in Salem Cem, Plainview, Yell Co, AR.

[V6]1746. [11]6. **Cora Melzenia Breashears**, b. 26 Aug 1892 or 93, Plainview, Yell Co, AR, d. 10 Nov 1984, Ola, Yell Co, AR; m. 24 Sept 1916, at Plainview, Yell Co, AR, ***Robert James Lipsey***, b. 17 Nov 1891, Kingston, Yell Co, AR, d. 8 Nov 1965, Danville, Yell Co, AR, s/o Samuel B. Lipsey (1 Oct 1867-14 Jan 1945) and Ella Ann Peeler (7 Jan 1872-21 Aug 1957)

[V6]1747. [12]x. James Morgan "Jim" Lipsey, b. 1 June 1921, Ola, Yell Co, AR; m. 5 April 1942, Russellville, Pope Co, AR, Ruby Scott Spaulding, b. 16 Dec 1921, Pontotoc Co, MS, d. 1 Nov 1998,

Jefferson City, Cole Co, MO, d/o Honor Monroe Spaulding (25 May 1896-4 Oct 1973) and Virgie Richardson (20 Feb 1900-6 July 1985)

[V6]1748. [13]y. James Michael "Mike" Lipsey, b. 3 Aug 1946, Helena, Phillips Co, AR; m. 15 June 1968, Lansing, Ingham Co, MI, ________

[V6]1749. [11]7. **Mina E. Breashears**, b. Jan 1894; Minnie in 1910

[V6]1750. [11]8. **Laura J. Breashears**, b. June 1896

[V6]1751. [11]9. **Hazel Breashears**, b. Jan 1900

[V6]1752. [11]10. **Effie Breashears**, b. c1902 (8 in 1910), living in 1997; m. _____ ***Thompson***, of Danville, AR

[V6]1753. [11]11. **Virgie Adelynne Breashears**, b. 4 Sept 1904 (5 in 1910) in Plainview, Yell Co, AR, d. 6 Sept 1997, Crossett, AR ; m. ***Samuel Clifton Barry***, d. 1974 (see obit below)

[V6]1754. [12]1. Mary Jane Barry; m. _____ Gee, of Crossett, AR

[V6]1755. [12]2. Martha Rose Barry; m. _____ Dolan, of Crossett, AR

[V6]1756. [12]3. Gary Clifton Barry, of Portand, AR

[V6]1757. [12]4. Rebecca Ann Barry; m. _____ Baumgardner, of Gurdon, AR

[V6]1758. [12]5. Alice Faye Barry; m. _____ Arnold of Horatio, AR

Obit: Mr. **John Breashears** -- 10 April 1948. It is with profound regret we chronicle the death of Mr. John Smith Breashears, who passed away in a Little Rock hospital Saturday afternoon. Funeral services, conducted by Rev. George Findley, of Havana, were held at Ola Monday afternoon, burial being in the Rover Cemetery, near the former home of deceased [Error; he is actually buried in Hunt's Chapel Cem]. Pallbearers were Tom Pugh and Irby Sloan of Rover; Earl Ladd and A.L. Walden, of Danville, and Mauhon(?) Ramey and George Gleason, of Dardanelle.

John Smith Breashears was born near what is now the town of Plainview on October 19, 1884, being at the time of his death 63 years, five months and 22 days old. He had spent his entire life in Yell County, for many years being a prominent farmer and stock raiser at his farm near Rover in Fourche Valley. Three years ago he purchased and moved to a farm 4½ miles south of Dardanelle on Highway 7, where he has since resided. For many years Mr. Breashears has been a member of the Rover Baptist Church. He was a true Christian, a splendid citizen, a loyal and faithful friend, and Yell County has suffered a very real loss in his death.

He is survived by his wife, Mrs. Ola Brown Breashears; six sons, Ned of Belleville; Ted, of Upland, Calif.; Ewell, of El Paso, Tex.; Hays and Billie, of Dardanelle; and Leroy, of Russellville; three daughters, Mrs. Raymond Lewis, of Summer, Nebr.; Mrs. Joe Hunt, of Los Angeles, Calif.; and Mrs. Homer Lee Lofland, of Bluffton; seven grandchildren, his aged father, two brothers and six sisters.

[source: Mary Vinson Humphrey, Compiler (Newspaper sources; Post Dispatch, Dardanelle, Arkansas; Yell County Record, Danville, Arkansas; Courier Democrat, Russellville, Arkansas). "Yell County Arkansas Obituaries and Historical Items, Vol 1". pub; 1983 - Obituary of John Smith Breashears. pg. 34. Thanks to "Mary Fowler Leek" <maryleek@ibm.net> for the text.]

Obit: **Ola Breashears** -- 15 March 1979. Mrs. Ola Brown Breashears, 92, Dardanelle, died Thursday, March 15, at the Yell County Nursing Home. She was a native of Briggsville, widow of John S. Breashears, daughter of the late Monroe and Lizzie Waldon Brown, and was a member of the Rover Baptist Church.

Survivors include six sons, Ned Breashears, Belleville; Ted Breashears, Upton, California; Hays Breashears, Russellville; Baxter E. Breashears, London; and Bill Breashears, Ozark; a foster son, Wesley Saunders, Dardanelle; two daughters, Mary Hunt, Bluffton; and Mrs. Joe Lofland, Little Rock; two brothers, Sterlin and Crado Brown, Mansfield, Texas; 15 grandchildren; and 19 great-grandchildren.

The funeral was at 3 p.m. Saturday at the Rover Baptist Church by the Rev. Tony Berry. Burial was in Hunts Chapel Cemetery, Rover, by Humphrey Funeral Service. Pallbearers were H.M. Orsburn, Owen McDonald, D.W. Ellis, John McMillin,

Dana Merritt, James Lee Stubbs and Charles Lee Hunt. Honorary bearers were Carl Jaggers, Dr. J.O. Pennington, Virgil Thomas, Norman Ward, Gilbert Cornwell, Ed Love and Ed Taylor.

[source: Mary Vinson Humphrey, Compiler (Newspaper sources; Post Dispatch, Dardanelle, Arkansas; Yell County Record, Danville, Arkansas; Courier Democrat, Russellville, Arkansas). "Yell County Arkansas Obituaries and Historical Items, Vol 1". pub; 1983 - Obituary of Ola Brown Breashears. pg. 34. Thanks to "Mary Fowler Leek" <maryleek@ibm.net> for the text.]

Obit, **Hays Breashears**, age 86, a resident of Russellville, AR died Wednesday, February 17, 1999 at Stella Manor Nursing Home at Russellville. He was born on July 26, 1912 at Rover, AR to John and Ola Brown Breashears. He was the owner of a farm equipment business and a farmer. He was a member of the First Baptist Church of Dardanelle.

He was preceded in death by: his wife, Gladys Pelt Breashears; three brothers, Ted, Bobby and Ned Breashears and one sister, Sue Cox. He is survived by: one daughter, Patsy Burris of Pensacola, FL; three grandchildren, Robert Hays (Shannon) Burris of Little Rock, AR, Rebecca Burris and Sherry Beth (Victor) Thompson all of Pensacola, FL; two great-grandchildren, Merry Beth Josephine Thompson and Emma Leigh Victoria Thompson both of Pensacola, FL; three brothers, Bill Breashears of Dardanelle, AR, Leroy Breashears and Baxter Breashears both of Russellville, AR; two sisters, Mary Hunt of Briggsville, AR and Jo Lofland of Little Rock, AR; several nieces, nephews and cousins.

Funeral service was February 19, 1999 at the Humphrey Chapel officiated by Rev. Joe Yates and Rev. Milton Cowling. Burial was at the Rest Haven Memorial Park at Russellville, AR. Memorials may be made to the First Baptist Church of Dardanelle, AR. (Source: *Yell County Record* (weekly newspaper), Danville, Arkansas, Weds, 24 Feb 1999, v.100, No.8, p.2.)

obit: Virgie (Breashears) Barry

Mrs. Virgie Adelynne Breashears Barry, 93, of Portland, AR died Saturday 6 Sept , 1997 at the Ashley Memorial Hospital in

Crossett. She was born in Plainview, AR, Yell County, on September 4, 1904. She was the youngest of eleven children born to Lemuel Cahzeel and Mary Ellen Hogan Breashears.

She graduated from Central Baptist College in Conway in 1926 and Ouachita Baptist College (University) in Arkadelphia in 1928 with a degree in education. A devoted educator, she taught first grade in Plainview from 1928 until 1939 and third grade in Portland from 1952 until her retirement in 1969. She was a member of the Arkansas Education Association, the Ashley County Retired Teachers Association and she was a member of the Portland Baptist Church.

She was preceded in death by: her husband, Samuel Clifton Barry in 1974; a step-daughter, Nell Barnwell of Cabot and nine brothers and sisters. She is survived by her children, Mary Jane Gee and Martha Rose Dolan both of Crossett, Gary Clifton Barry of Portland, Rebecca Ann Baumgardner of Gurdon, Alice Faye Arnold of Horatio and one step-daughter, Nancy Jordan of Sheffield, AL; a sister, Effie Thompson of Danville; eight grandchildren and two great-great-grandchildren.

Funeral service was Monday at the Portland Baptist Church with Bro. Jerry Selby and Rev. Ted Grove officiating. Interment was in the Portland Cemetery. Memorials may be made to the Portland Baptist Church, P.O. Box 86, Portland, AR 71663. [source: "Yell County Record" (weekly) Newspaper, Danville, Yell Co, AR, Vol.97, No.37, 10 Sept 1997, p.2. Thanks to Joe George <jgeorge@inreach.com> for the copy. A copy was also sent to me by Mary Fowler Leek (mleek@arkwest.com).

Carroll Cunlee Breashears and Sarah E. Hogan

v6 1673. [10]7. **Carroll "Carl" Cunlee Breashears**, (s/o Matthew Breashears and Elizabeth Parker), b. 10 Oct 1859, Harold, Montgomery Co, AR, d. 26 July 1910, Plainview, Yell Co, AR; m. 7 Sept 1884 (Yell Co, AR, "by J.F. Brice, MG," Book E, p.72), ***Sarah E. Hogan***, b. 21 Oct 1869, d. 29 Aug 1910, d/o Francis P. Hogan (b. 1844) and Ledra E. _____. Carroll and Sarah are buried together in Sunlight Cem, Plainview, Yell Co, AR. #289-291 in 1900 Census, Lower Lafane twp, Yell Co, AR. #282-283, 1910 Census, Lower Lafane Twp. Their homestead was in the Fourche River bottom, Yell Co, AR, near Plainview; it is now under the waters of Lake Nimrod. Additional data from Scott Lazenby, <lazyboyroyjr @Yahoo.com>

Family of Carroll Cunlee Breashears and Sarah E. Hogan:

[V6]1759. [11]1. ***Leander (or Lee Ander) Breashears**, b. 15 July 1886, Rover, AR, d. 17 June 1956, Carlsbad, NM, bur Carlsbad Cem, Carlsbad, NM; m. 19 Dec 1909, AR, ***Emma Mae Nix***, b. 12 Sept 1892, AR

[V6]1760. [11]2. **Francis Monroe Breashears**, (male) b. 26 Sept 1888, Plainview, Yell Co, AR, d. 1962, bur Gladewater Mem Park, Upshur Co, TX; m. 18 May 1922, ***Lida Aldrich***, b. 13 Aug 1897, d. Feb 1978, Little Rock, AR

[V6]1761. [11]3. **George William Breashears**, b. 1 March 1891, Montgomery Co, AR, d. 16 Dec 1901 during an appendicitis operation, Plainview, Yell Co, AR, bur Sunlight Cem, Yell Co, AR "s/o C.C. & S.E."

[V6]1762. [11]4. **John Edmond Breashears**, b. 20 Jan 1893, Plainview, Yell Co, AR, d. 17 Feb 1972, bur Gladewater Mem Park, Upshur Co, TX. John was a Pfc, 329th Supply Co, Quartermaster Corp, in WW I.

[V6]1763. [11]5. **Harvey Breashears**, b. 26 June 1895, Plainview, Yell Co, AR; m. 3 Jan 1915, ***Etta Leach***, b. 1898

[V6]1764. [12]1. **Jimmie Breashears**,

[V6]1765. [12]2. **Bernice Breashears**,

[V6]1766. [11]6. **James Clayton Breashears**, b. 30 Jan 1898, Plainview, Yell Co, AR ("Clayton" in 1910 census)

[V6]1767. [11]7. **Elrony Mamie Breashears**, b. 10 Aug 1900, (6 in 1910), d. Nov 1989, Little Rock, AR; m. ***Joe Tillman***

[V6]1768. [11]8. **Elydia Fay Breashears**, b. c1907 (3 in 1910)

Leander Breashears and Emma Mae Nix

[v6]1759. [11]1. **Leander (or Lee Ander) Breashears**, (s/o Carroll Cunlee Breashears and Sarah E. Hogan), called "Papa Shears" by the family, b. 15 July 1886, Rover, AR (#283-284 in 1910, Yell Co, AR), d. 17 June 1956, Carlsbad, NM, bur

Carlsbad Cem, Carlsbad, NM; m. 19 Dec 1909, AR, ***Emma Mae Nix***, called "Mama Shears," b. 12 Sept 1892, AR (17 in 1910), d. 24 March 1970, Oklahoma City, OK, d/o W. Tom Nix and Cynthia ____.

Lee Ander worked in the shipyards in Alameda, CA, during WW II. He kept a Bible from which much of this data is taken. Leander and Emma split up later in life; she moved to Oklahoma City, while Leander stayed in Carlsbad, NM. She was an avid Jehovah's Witness, and Leander did not particularly care for the religion. He was an avid baseball fan. He died of cancer; she died of a heart attack. (Data from William F. "Bill" Pugh, Scott Lazenby <lazyboyroyjr@yahoo.com>, and others.)

<u>Family of Lee Ander Breashears and Emma Mae Nix:</u>

[V6]1769. [12]1. ***Elva Cloe "Memo" Breashears**, b. 16 Dec 1911, Plainview, Yell Co, AR; m. ***Carl Leon "Dado" Lazenby***, b. 15 Oct 1919,

[V6]1770. [12]2. **Olas Harland Breashears**, b. 24 Jan 1914, d. 3 March 1952, Lindsay, CO, bur Lindsay, CO; m. 23 June 1935, ***Vivian Cochran***, b. 8 Sept 1917, d. Feb 1971. Harland died in a car accident; Vivian, of cancer.

[V6]1771. [13]1. **Wayne Breashears**, b. 14 Sept 1934, AR

[V6]1772. [13]2. **Ellen Beth Breashears**, b. 27 Jan 1940, California

[V6]1773. [13]3. **Emma Jean Breashears**, b. 21 Nov 1942, CA

[V6]1774. [12]3. **Ruby Nell Breashears**, b. 28 Feb 1916, Plainview, Yell Co, AR; m.1. 13 Dec 1934, ***Carl Reed***; m.2. 1971, ***John Grayum***

[V6]1775. [13]1. Danny Reed, b. 19 July 1942, OK City; m. Pam ____. ch: David and Lisa Reed.

[V6]1776. [12]4. **Nina Louise Breashears**, b. 16 June 1919, d. 4 Nov 1971 of uremic poisoning, bur Carlsbad Cem, Carlsbad, NM; m.1. 1 July 1938, ***Will Ed Townsley***, b. 31 Jan 1920, d. ? (committee suicide); m.2. ***Kuy ____***. No ch.

[V6]1777. [12]5. **Rita Lucille Breashears**, b. 26 Jan 1922, Plainview, Yell Co, AR; m. 5 Nov 1938, OK City, ***Cleve H. White***, b. 12 Aug 1920, New Mexico

[V6]1778. [13]1. Donna Faye White, b. 9 Jan 1939, OK City;

m. ____ Bedingfield. ch: Matt and Julie Bedington, both b. Houston, TX

V6 1779. [13]2. Timothy Cleve White, b. 12 March 1947, Oakland, CA; m. 23 Feb 1973, Carlsbad, NM, Julie Kay Nunley, b. 2 July 1951, Carlsbad, NM.

V6 1780. [14]1. Sabrina White, b. 9 May 1977, Carlsbad, NM; m. ____ Davenport

V6 1781. [14]2. Lindsey White, b. 13 Juy 1979, Carlsbad, NM. Ch: Rayne White, b. Granbury, TX

V6 1782. [14]3. Garrett Taylor White, b. 14 Feb 1993, Granbury, TX

V6 1783. [13]3. Cynthia Lou White, b. 14 June 1949, Cottage Gover, OR; m. 7 June 1969, Houston, TX, Jim Martin, b. 8 July 1945, AR

V6 1784. [14]1. Wendy Martin (adopted), b. 18 April 1977, Albuquerque, NM; ch: Nicholas Martin, b. 6 Aug 1995

V6 1785. [14]2. Amy Martin (adopted), b. 17 May 1979, Albuquerque, NM; m. Feb 1998, Art Avila; ch: Brianna Avila, b. March 1999, Portsmouth, VA

V6 1786. [12]6. **Billie Lee Breashears**, b. 21 June 1925, Plainview, Yell Co, AR; m.1. ***Luanne Bradley*** (1 ch); m.2. ***Diane*** ____ (2 ch)

V6 1787. [13]1. **Lee Breashears**, m. ____ **Mansoor**

V6 1788. [13]2. **Betty Lee Breashears**, b. 27 Oct 1952, AR

V6 1789. [13]3. **Dana Lynn Breashears**, b. 3 March 1963, OK

V6 1790. [12]7. **Johnny Darrell Breashears**, b. 23 Sept 1928, Plainview, Yell Co, AR; m. 12 Aug 1948, OK, ***Vella May Abney***

V6 1791. [13]1. **Pamela Diane Breashears**, b. 8 June 1949, TX

V6 1792. [13]2. **Bill Darrell Breashears**, b. June 1952, d. ? in car accident

Elva Cloe Breashears and Leon Lazenby

v6 1769. [12]1. **Elva Cloe "Memo" Breashears**, (d/o Leander Breashear and Emma Mae Nix), b. 16 Dec 1911, Plainview, Yell Co, AR, d. 11 July 1979, Tomball, Harris Co, TX, bur Carlsbad,

NM; m. 10 Dec 1932, Plainview, Yell Co, AR, ***Carl Leon "Dado" Lazenby***, b. 15 Oct 1919, Bluffton, Yell Co, AR, d. 6 Dec 1978, Carlsbad, Eddy Co, NM, s/o Roy Lazenby and Lilly Lavina Coleman. Elva and Carl moved to New Mexico in the mid 1930s, along with her parents. Carl Lazenby worked in the potash mines around Carlsbad, NM. Elva and Carl had 3 ch:

Family of Elva Cloe Breashears and Leon Lazenby:

[V6]1793. [13]1. Bobby Leon Lazenby, b. 3 Jan 1934, Plainview, AR; m. 16 Aug 1962, Caruthersville, MO, Jane Ellen Markey, b. 24 Oct 1940, Carruthersville, MO. Bobby was a KFC manager, now retired. No ch.

[V6]1794. [13]2. Joe Ronald Lazenby, b. 30 Jan 1939, Carlsbad, NM; m. 19 Sept 1959, Erie, PA, Carole Lynn Sechrist, b. 22 Sept 1940, Erie, PA. Joe has a BS degree from Eastern New Mexico Univ; he is a retired Oil Company Manager.

[V6]1795. [14]1. Joe Carl Lazenby, b. 9 Aug 1960, Erie, PA; m.1. 3 July 1982, Clinton, MS, Angela Jane Langley; m.2. 9 April 1991, Cynthia Funk

[V6]1796. [15]1. Leigh Ann Lazenby, b. 8 May 1983

[V6]1797. [15]2. Lauren Nicole Lazenby, b. 11 Nov 1984

[V6]1798. [15]3. Anthony Carl Lazenby, b. 10 April 1987

[V6]1799. [14]2. Sherrie Lynn Lazenby, b. 14 Oct 1962, Carlsbad, NM; m. 15 Sept 1983, Clinton, MS, Martin Fox

[V6]1800. [15]1. William Chadwhick Fox, b. 8 Sept 1988

[V6]1801. [15]2. Lindsay Carole Fox, b. 14 June 1990

[V6]1802. [14]3. Laurie Ann Lazenby, b. 8 Sept 1963, Carlsbad, NM; m. 25 July 1996, Jamaica, Kenneth Johnson

[V6]1803. [15]1. Reagan Lynn Johnson, b. 29 Sept 1998, Clinton, MS

[V6]1804. [13]3. Roy Lee Lazenby, b. 21 July 1941, Carlsbad, NM; m. 17 Aug 1963, Hobbs, NM, Linda Ray Iles, b. 2 Oct 1941, McCamey, TX, d/o Ray Iles and Etta Elsie McCaffity. Roy has a B.S. from Eastern New Mexico Univ, an M.A. from Texas Tech, and a Ph.D. from East Texas State. He was president of Tomball College, 1988-1996. Linda was educated at Eastern New Mexico Univ and was secretary at Tomball High School.

V6 1805. [14]1. Kristi Lee Lazenby, b. 19 June 1965, Clovis, NM; m. 27 June 1987, Tomball, TX, James Anthony Goodman. Kristi has a Bachelor's degree from Baylor Univ and is a director of Children's Sunday School, Metro Bapt Church, Houston, TX.

V6 1806. [15]1. James Mitchel Goodman, b. 21 Oct 1991, Tomball, TX

V6 1807. [15]2. Kole Anthony Goodman, b. 28 Jan 1994, Tomball, TX

V6 1808. [15]3. Westin Lee Goodman, b. 26 Feb 1996, Tomball, TX

V6 1809. [14]2. Scott Ray Lazenby, b. 13 March 1970, San Angelo, TX; m. 13 Aug 1999, Chatham, Ontario, Holly Dorothy Grace Horton, b. 16 Dec 1975, Chatham, Ontario, Canada, d/o Samuel Nelson Horton and Doreen May Cowlan. Scott has a B.S. in Sports Management from Texas A&M University. Holly was educated at Windsor University and St. Clair College, Ontario, Canada.

Some Yell County, AR, burials that are unaccounted for:

In Salem Cem, Plainview, Yell Co, AR:

Modean Roberts Brasier, b. 10 Oct 1924, d. 8 Dec 1942

Esther Brasier Yates, b. 14 July 1904, d. 24 Sept 1969

Upper Spring Creek Cem, Yell Co, AR:

William Boyce Breashears, b. 30 Jan 1948, d. 17 Sept 1977

Lavenia (Carrol) Breashears, b. 29 Oct 1949, w/o Wm Boyce Breashears; m. 9 Aug 1969

James Madison "Jim" Breashears and Georgia Chapman

[v6]**1674.** [10]8. **James Madison "Jim" Breashears**, (s/o Matthew Breashears and Elizabeth Parker), b. 7 Dec 1861, Montgomery Co, AR, d. 10 May 1937, Story, Montgomery Co, AR, bur Breshears Cem, Story, AR; m. 6 July 1882, Montgomery Co, AR, ***Georgia A. (née Chapman) Kilby***, b. 1863, d. 1936; ?m.2. ***Omey*** ______

Family of James Madison Breashears and Georgia Chapman:

[V6]1810. [11]1. **Thomas Porter Breashears**, b. Aug 1883; m. ***Mary Vashitie Oller***

[V6]1811. [12]1. **Leslie Glen Breashears**, b. 30 Oct 1909, Story, Montgomery Co, AR, (IGI 8127305/56).

[V6]1812. [11]2. **Lillie Belle Breashears**, b. Jan 1886, m. ____ ***Stephens***

[V6]1813. [11]3. ***George Alford Breashears**, b. 1887, d. 1962; m. ***Gertrude "Getty" Agnes Southard***. They lived in Story all their lives.

[V6]1814. [11]4. **Lemuel Matthew Breashears**, b. Oct 1890

[V6]1815. [11]5. **Verdie M. Breashears** (fem), b. Oct 1895, m. ____ ***Bullard***

[V6]1816. [11]6. **Anna P. Breashears**, b. May 1898, d. 1973; m. ***Selmer Qualls***, b. 1895, d. 1976, both bur Reed Cem. Lived in Story, Montgomery Co, all their lives:

[V6]1817. [12]1. Bernice Qualls, m. Floyd Irons

[V6]1818. [12]2. Bernie Qualls, d. 1985

[V6]1819. [12]3. Bernell Qualls, m. ____ Hulsey

[V6]1820. [12]4. Bernest "Sonny" Qualls

[V6]1821. [12]5. Burvin Qualls.

George Alford Breashears and Gertrude Southard

[v6]**1813.** [11]3. **George Alford Breashears**, (s/o James Madison Breashears and Georgia A. Kilby), b. 1887, d. 1962; m. ***Gertrude "Getty" Agnes Southard***. They lived in Story all their lives.

Family of George Alford Breashears and Gertrude Southard:

[V6]1822. [12]1. **Leatrice Breashears**,

[V6]1823. [12]2. **Jim Breashears**,

[V6]1824. [12]3. **Joe Southard Breashears**, b. 18 July 1914, Story, AR, d. 24 July 1999, Malvern, AR (see obit below); m. ***Darlene*** _____

[V6]1825. [13]x. **Mary Jo Breashears**, m. _____ ***Carter***,

[V6]1826. [13]x. **Georgia Breashears**, m. _____ ***Sveda***,

[V6]1827. [13]x. **Dorene Breashears**, m. _____ ***Duncan***,

[V6]1828. [13]x. **Corene Breashears**, m. _____ ***Bragg***,

[V6]1829. [13]x. **Kitty Breashears**, m. _____ ***Buyard***,

[V6]1830. [13]x. **Jessica Breashears,** m. _____ ***Lentini***,

[V6]1831. [13]x. **Jim Breashears**,

[V6]1832. [13]x. **Curtis Breashears**,

[V6]1833. [13]x. **David Breashears**,

[V6]1834. [13]x. **Eddie Breashears**,

[V6]1835. [12]4. **Fonnie Breashears**, m. ***Eldiree Peneinger***

[V6]1836. [13]x. **Jerry Dan Breashears**, b. 1952, d. 31 March 1998 (see Obit below); m. ***Shirley Ann Burnett***

[V6]1837. [14]y. **Robert Breashears**,

[V6]1838. [14]y. **Becky Breashears**, m. _____ ***Cates***

[V6]1839. [15]z. Courtney Cates

[V6]1840. [14]y. **Tonya Breashears**,

[V6]1841. [13]x. **Joe Doyan Breashears**, of Story, AR: <breads@ipa.net>

[V6]1842. [14]1. **Samuel Mason Breashears**,

[V6]1843. [14]2. **Bridgit Marie Breashears**,

[V6]1844. [14]3. **Barry Matthew Breshears**,

[V6]1845. [15]1. **Matthew Joseph Breshears**,

[V6]1846. [13]x. **John Breashears**, of Natchez, MS

[V6]1847. [13]x. **Thomas Lee Breashears**, of Mena, AR

[V6]1848. [13]x. **Patricia Ann Breashears**, m. _____ ***Thompson***, living Tampa, FL

[V6]1849. [13]x. **Hazel Marie Breashears**, m. _____ ***Russell***, of Greenwood, AR

[V6]1850. [13]x. **Judith Elaine Breashears**, m. _____ ***Cogburn***, of Story, AR

[V6]1851. [12]5. **Ezra Breashears**,

OBIT: **Joe S. Breashears**, Malvern - Joe Southard Breashears, 85, of Malvern died Saturday, July 24, 1999, in a Hot Spring County hospital.

He was born July 18, 1914, at Story to the late George Alford and Gertrude "Getty" Agnes Southard Breashears.

Survivors include his wife, Darlene Breashears; six daughters, Mary Jo Carter, Georgia Sveda, Dorene Duncan, Corene Bragg, Kitty Buyard and Jessica Lentini; four sons, Jim Breashears, Curtis Breashears, David Breashears, and Eddie Breashears; 25 grandchildren; and 10 greatgrandchildren. Services will be 10 a.m. Tuesday at Refuge Baptist Church at Story, with Brother Ronny Noles officiating.

Burial will be in Breashears Cemetery. Arrangements are by Thornton Funeral Home, Mount Ida. (Hot Springs, AR, *The Sentinel Record*, 26 July 1999)

OBIT: **Jerry Dan Breashears**, age 46, of Belleville, AR died Tuesday, March 31, 1998 at Chambers Memorial Hospital in Danville [AR].

He was a native of Story, AR, son of the late Fonnie Breashears and Mrs. Eldiree Peneinger Breashears of Story, AR. He was a retired teacher, an Army and Air Force Veteran and a member of the Apostolic Church of Jesus Christ.

He is survived by: his wife, Shirley Ann Burnett Breashears of Belleville, AR; his mother, Mrs. Eldiree Breashears of Story, AR; a son, Robert Breashears of Fayetteville, AR; two daughters, Becky Cates and Tonya Breashears, both of Belleville, AR; three brothers, Joe Breashears of Story, AR, John Breashears of Natchez, MS and Thomas Lee Breashears of Mena, AR; three sisters, Patricia Ann Thompson of Tampa, FL, Hazel Marie Russell of Greenwood, AR and Judith Elaine Cogburn of Story, AR and one granddaughter, Courtney Cates of Belleville, AR.

Funeral service was April 4, 1998 at the Story Church of God, with Rev. Erza Minton officiating. Burial was in the Breashears Cemetery in Story. Arrangements by Cornwell Funeral Home of Danville. [source: Yell County Record (weekly) Newspaper, Danville, Arkansas, Volume 98, Number 14, page 2, Obituaries for the week of Wednesday, April 08, 1998], Thanks for copy to: Mary Fowler Leek <maryleek@attglobal.net>

16. SARAH ANN BREASHEARS and John Humphreys

[v6]1653. [9]6. **Sarah Ann Breashears,** (d/o William Breashears and Anna Etheridge), b. c1833, Lawrence Co, TN, d. after 1880; m. 15 June 1848, in Montgomery Co, AR, ***John Humphreys***, b. 1825, TN, d. before 1880, probably in Marion Co, AR. Sarah is apparently a widow in Bearden Twp, Marion Co, AR, in 1880 census (#128-128) with five children in her household (note change in surname). Data from Patricia M. Wright <ee72478@goodnet.com>.

Census: 1880, Bearden Twp, Marion Co, AR128-128

Umphrus, Sarah	40 f	frm W	TN	SC	SC
Harden	27	son	AR	TN	TN
Henry	23	son	AR	TN	TN
Nancy	20	dau	AR	TN	TN
Thomas	17	son	AR	TN	TN
Martha	9	dau	AR	TN	TN

Family of Sarah Ann Breashears and John Humphreys:

[V6]1852. [10]1. Robert Oden Umphreys, b. 3 Aug 1850, Wattsprings, Searcy Co, AR, d. 1912, Cherry Hill, Perry Co, AR; m. Melvina "Vina" Seaton, b. March 1856, Wattsprings, AR, d. 29 March 1929, St Louis, MO, both bur Cherry Hill Cem, Perry Co, AR. Ch, all b. Wattsprings, Searcy Co, AR:

[V6]1853. [11]1. Sarah Humphreys, b. 7 Nov 1876

[V6]1854. [11]2. John Nickolas Humphreys, b. 18 July 1879

[V6]1855. [11]3. S. Christopher Humphreys, b. 18 Aug 1881; m. Mollie Robinson

[V6]1856. [11]4. Martha "Mattie" Humphreys, b. 1882; m. Thomas Brooks

[V6]1857. [11]5. Arbie Humphreys, b. 1894; m. Will Norfleet

[V6]1858. [11]6. Robert Oden Humphreys, Jr

[V6]1859. [11]7. George Humphreys,

[V6]1860. [10]2. Harden L. Umphreys, b. 14 Dec 1852 (27 in 1880) (on voter list, 1893, Marion Co, AR)

[V6]1861. [10]3. Mary Ann Umphreys, b. 12 (or 28) Oct 1853; m.

_____ Seaton.

[V6]1862. [10]4. Atsey Elizabeth Umphreys, b. 22 Oct 1855, AR, d. 13 Aug 1935, bur Grove Park Cem, Broken Arrow, Tulsa, OK; m. 17 May 1874, at Witts Springs, Searcy Co, AR, William Wiley Doshier, b. 5 Jan 1854, Marion Co, AR, d. 1942, Broken Arrow, OK, bur Grove Park Cem. (Source: Family Rec. of Ernie and Willa Doshier); W.W. and Atsey are in the 1900 Census, Water Creek, AR, and the 1920 Census, Hominy, Osage Co, OK.

[V6]1863. [11]X. Daniel Franklin "Doc" Doshier; m. Lucinda Ethel Guthrie

[V6]1864. [12]Y. Alma Doshier (grandmother of Jaimie D. Wright <celticturtle@mindspring.com>)

[V6]1865. [10]5. William Henry Umphreys, b. 14 March 1857 (?; 23 in 1880); m. Edith Adams Pennington. William H. Umphreys got three homestead grants in Marion Co, AR, all in Sec 21, T17N, R15W, 5th Princ Meridian. He is on the 1893 Voters list, Marion Co, AR.

[V6]1866. [10]6. Nancy C. Umphreys, b. 30 Jan 1859 (20 in 1880)

[V6]1867. [10]7. Thomas Lafayette Umphreys, b. c1863 (17 in 1880). The county clerk has issued marriage license to the following persons this week: T.L. Umphery to Miss Louisa McGinnis. (Mt. Echo Newspaper, issue of July 16, 1886). He is on the voter list in 1893, Marion Co, AR.

[V6]1868. [10]8. Martha Ann Umphreys, b. 17 Dec 1871 (9 in 1880), d. before Oct 1905; m. 9 Dec 1888, in Marion Co, AR, James Thomas Middleton, b. 15 Oct 1867, Searcy Co, AR.

[V6]1869. [10]9. Sarah Catherine Umphreys, b. 2 Nov 1878 (per I.G.I.)

17. JOHN BRESHEARS and Naoma Ann Hogg

[V6]**1612.** [8]2. **John Breshears**, (s/o Henry Breshears Sr and Eleanor ?Hardin), b. 16 March 1795 in Spartanburg Co, South Carolina (1793 on headstone); d. 25 June 1869, at Bolivar, Polk Co, MO. On 1 March 1821 in Lawrence Co, TN, he married ***Naoma Ann Hogg***, b. 17 June 1804, Barren Run, Barren Co, KY, d. 1 Oct 1892, Bolivar, Polk Co, MO. Naoma was called variously "Oma," "Omy," "Neomi." She was the daughter of Reuben Hogg, b. NC, and Mary Wisdom, b. NC. Reuben Hogg and Mary Wisdom were married in 1799, in Grainger Co, TN.

Figure 12:John Breshears and Naoma Ann Hogg.
Photo from Cris McCarthy.

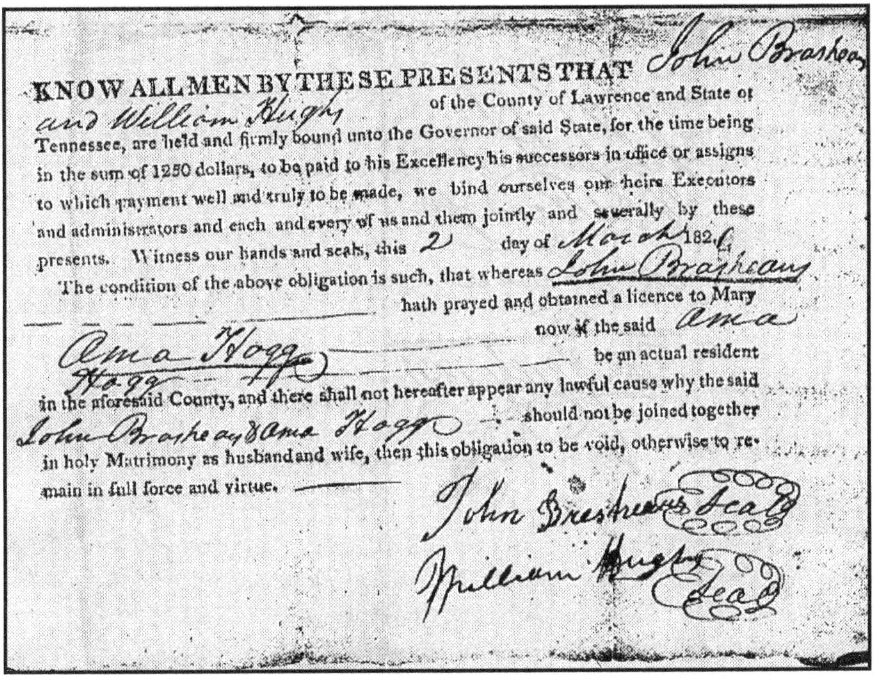
KNOW ALL MEN BY THESE PRESENTS THAT John Brashears
and William Hughs of the County of Lawrence and State of
Tennessee, are held and firmly bound unto the Governor of said State, for the time being
in the sum of 1250 dollars, to be paid to his Excellency his successors in office or assigns
to which payment well and truly to be made, we bind ourselves our heirs Executors
and administrators and each and every of us and them jointly and severally by these
presents. Witness our hands and seals, this 2 day of March 1826
The condition of the above obligation is such, that whereas John Brashears
hath prayed and obtained a licence to Mary
now if the said Ama
Ama Hogg be an actual resident
Hogg
in the aforesaid County, and there shall not hereafter appear any lawful cause why the said
John Brashears & Ama Hogg should not be joined together
in holy Matrimony as husband and wife, then this obligation to be void, otherwise to remain in full force and virtue.

John Breshears Seal

William Hughs Seal

Figure 13: John's signature may or may not be authentic.
He usually only made his mark.

As you can see in the reproduced copy above, John and Naoma's marriage bond was signed by John Breshears and William Hughs. John usually only made a mark.

John and Naoma lived in Lawrence County, Tennessee, from about 1818 till about 1838, during which time ten of their fifteen children were born. In 1838, they moved to Polk Co, MO; both are buried in the Breshears Cemetery on the Breshears homestead near Bolivar, Polk Co, MO.

Minnie (McGee) Flowler wrote the following sketch of her great great grandfather for an Eighth Grade English class assignment in 1927:

My great great grandfather lived in Tennessee many, many years ago. There were several children, they were mostly farmers. Great-Great Grandpa's name was John Breshears. His wife's name was "Oma". I don't know the names of their brothers or sisters. When Tennessee began to have many people coming from eastern states, gr-gr-grandfather and some of his brothers decided to go farther west, to Missouri, and maybe on to Texas. They had heard of the fertile land in the valleys along the streams in Missouri so they decided to go there first.

I don't know what year it was, but it was a long time before the Civil War, they loaded up their oxen drawn wagons and left for Tennessee. I don't know how the name was first spelled, but when they left Tennessee, each one changed a letter in the name. My gr-gr-grandfather came to Polk Co., Missouri and settled seven or eight miles from here. One brother settled farther north and another moved to the south. I think one went to Texas or Arkansa.

They had many hardships and when they got to the Mississippi River, it was up but going down. They had to wait for a few days before the ferry boat could cross. Two or three families moved their wagons farther north to cross. Two or three families caught up with gr-gr grandfather's wagons. At least one came here with him. One of their daughters married his son.

Gr-gr grandfather John and Oma had 15 or 16 children, some died young. Their son Jesse was my grandpa. Great grandma's name was JUMP. Her folks came about the same time as the others. There weren't many white people here when they got here. They lived in their wagons for a while, as they were building their log house.

Once a storm tore up their house. I don't know which gr-gr-grandpa's house it was. [It was John Breshear's, says Georgene Humphries.] Lots of people began to come here soon after they got here. My great grandfather GLADDEN didn't come for quite a while.

My grandmother was Mary Breshears, and my grandpa was Leslie Gladden. He died when mama was three. Grandma died a few years later. Mama lived with Uncle Dan Gladden till she got married. Daddy's grandpa and grandma came from Tennessee too but they didn't know each other. His mother came from Springfield, Illinois. Her name was Margaret ROBBINS, his was Mart McGEE. Mama told me she lived with her grandparents with her mother and little sister after her father died. She remembers when her great grandmother died.

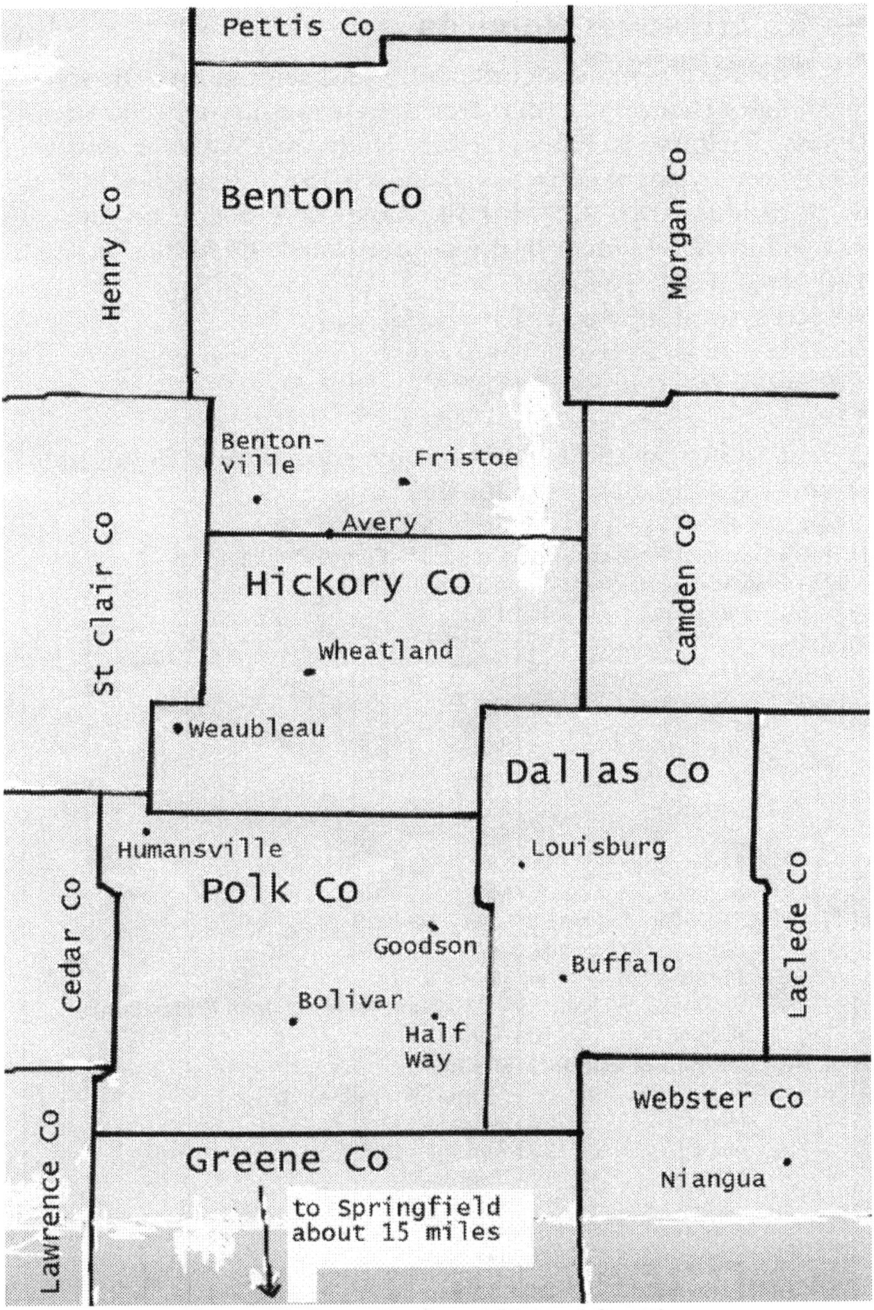

Figure 14: Some Southwest Missouri Counties and places were Breshears Families have lived.

Some Missouri Records

The 1840 census records John and Naoma Ann Breshears as living in Benton Co, MO. This area was originally counties of Dallas, Hickory, St Clair, Cedar, Dade and Webster and was accredited by act of congress 13 March 1835. John filed for land in 1840, described as "Twp 34, Range 21". When he died, he owned 520 acres, most in the section where he settled in 1840:
120 acres, lot 7, T34, R21
40 acres, lot 4, in Sec 1, T34, R21
80 acres, lot 8, in Sec 1 T34 R21
120 acres, lot 3, in Sec 2, T34 R21
12 acres lot 2, in Sec 2, T34 R21

In 1850 and 1850, John and his sons were in Polk Co, MO (Thanks to Cris McCarthy for the data):

1850 US Census: Polk County, Missouri - Film & Book form

# 806 - BREASHEARS, John		57-farmer-SC		
	Naomah	45 - Ky		
	Sarah P.	20 - Tenn		
	Jesse C.	19 - Tenn		
	Nancy G.	16 - Tenn		
	John W.	14 - Tenn		
	Margaret	13 - Tenn		
	Joseph W.	11 - Mo		
	Martin	8 - Mo		
	James K.	7 - Mo		
	Thomas B.	4 - Mo		
	Andrew J.	2 - Mo		
#811 - BRASHEARS, Reuben		26 - Tenn		
	Mary	18 - Mo.		
	Sarah A.E.	1 - Mo		
#812 - BERSHEARS, William		23 - Tenn [living w/ John Batten family]		
	Abigail	18 - Tenn		

1860 US Census: Polk County, Missouri -

#1030 - BRESHEARS, John		67 - farmer 3000-2500 - SC		
	Naoma	56 - Ky		
	Nancy	20 - Tenn		
	Margret	19 - Tenn		
	James	17 - Mo		
	Thomas	15 - Mo		
	Andrew	14 - Mo		
BASHEARS, Reuben		35 - farmer - Tenn		
	Mary	26 - Tenn		
	John	9 - Mo		
	Martha	6 - Mo	James	2- Mo

In 1870, Bolivar, Polk Co, MO, Naomi, 67, is in the household of James Breshears, age 27.
In 1880, Bolivar, Polk Co, MO, Naomia, 75, is mother in household of William A. Breashears, 52.

John's Military and Estate Records

Bounty Land Claim– Form of Declaration
for Surviving Officers or Soldiers
State of Missouri
County of Dallas

On this the 7th day of November, A.D. one thousand eight hundred and fifty, personally appeared before me, Michael Randleman, a Justice of the Peace within and for the County and State aforesaid, John Brashears, age 56 years, a resident of Polk County, in the state of Missouri, who being duly sworn according to law, declares, that he is the identical John Brashears who was a Private in the company commanded by James (?) Tate in the third regiment of footmen commanded by Steven Coplan, Col., in the War with Great Britain declared by the United States on the 18th day of June 1812, that he was drafted at Fayettville, Tennessee, on or about the 10th day of January, A.D. 1814 for the term of three months and continued in the actual service in said War, for the term of three months and 16 days and was honorably discharged at Fayettville, Tennessee, on the 26th day of April, A.D. 1814, as will appear by his original certificate of Discharge, or by the muster rolls of said Company. He makes this declaration for the purpose of obtaining bounty land to which he may be intitled under the "Act of Granting Bounty Land to certain officers and soldiers who have been engaged in the military service of the United States, passed September 28, 1850.

/s/ John Brashears

In John's file #WC-25473 in Washington, DC (reports Alta Breshears) are several unclear notations, including 120 acres, May 5/56, which seem to have been granted in Missouri.

Will of John Breshears: Polk County, Missouri:
The last Will and Testiment of John Breshears of the county of Polk and State
of Missouri-- I John Breshears considering the uncertenty of this mortal life and being of Sound mind and memory do make and publish this my last will and Testiment in maner and form following - that is to say first I give and bequeth unto my beloved wife Naoma Breshears all my personal property and real Estate during her natural life time and at her deth I give and bequeth unto my Eldest daughtor Mary Bray five dollars in money and the remainder of all my personal property and Real Estate to be Equally devided between the named heirs that is to say Henry H. Breshears, Ruben Breshears, William A. Breshears, Sariah T. Henderson, Jesse C. Breshears, Nancy G. Jones, John W. Breshears, Margaret Jump, Joseph W. Breshears, Ozias M.V. Breshears, James K.P. Breshears, Thomas H.B. Breshears and Andrew J. Breshears - and I hear by appoint William A. Breshears and Jesse C. Breshears sole Executors of this my last Will and Testiment hearby revoking all former wills by me made in witness whear of I have here unto set my hand and seal this 9th day of June AD 1869.

John (his X mark) Breshears

Filed and Probated July 17, 1869.

JOHN BRESHEARS - WAR of 1812 - FILE #WC-25473
Claim for Widows Pension for service of John Breshears in the War of 1812:
State of Missouri)
County of Dallas)
On this 12 day of May A.D. 1879, personally appeared before me a justice of the peace, the same being within and for the County and State aforesaid: Neomia Breshears aged 74 years, a resident within and of the county, in the state of Missouri who, being duly sworn according to law , declares that she is the widow of John Breshears deceased, who was the identical John Breshears, who served under the name of John Breshears as a private in the company commanded by Elijah Garam in the regiment of ______, commanded by Col. Correl in the war of 1812; that her said husband drafted at I think Sparty,

Tennessee on or about the ____ day of ______, A.D. for the term of _____ and continued in actual service in said war for the term of six months, and whose service terminated , by reason of Discharge at _______, on the ____ day of ____, AD ____. She further states that the following is a full discriptipn of her said husband at the time of his enlistment, viz. He was about 6 foot 2 in., complexion fair, hazel eyes, light hair. She further states that she was married to the said John Breshears at the town of ______, in the county of Lawerence in the state of Tennessee on the 1st day of March A.D. 1821, by Pollard Wisdom, who was a Justice of the Peace and that her name before her marriage was Neoma Hogg, and that she has not remarried since the death of the said soldier and she further states that neither herself nor her husband have been married before and that her said husband John Breshears died at his home in the state of Missouri on the 25th day of June AD 1869; and she further declares that the following have been the places of residence of herself and her husband since the date of his discharge from the Army, Viz: Lawerence Co, Tennessee and Polk County, Missouri and she further declares that she has heretofore made no application for Pension and that she is too feeble to go to the County clerk's office to be sworn and that her place of residence is _____ street, City of ____ county of Polk, state of Missouri, and that her post office address is Louisburg, Dallas Co., Missouri.

her
Neoma (X) Breshears
mark

Note that Neoma's testimony that John enlisted in Sparta, Tennessee, corroborates other data that says the family was in White Co, TN, in the 1810-1820 time frame, and that they later moved to Lawrence Co, TN, then even later to Polk Co, MO.

Family of John Breshears and Naoma Ann Hogg

(Ref: 1850, 1860, 1870 Census, Polk Co, MO; family records of Lavada Lenaghen, Minnie Eytchison, and Voyne Breshears; Polk Co, MO Cemetery records; etc. compiled by Georgene Eytchison Humphries. Sent to me by Faye Breshears; also ancestral files, FHL; major contributions from Cris Colson

McCarthy <Cris1247@aol.com>, of Boise, Idaho; Patty Warren, of Wheatland, MO; and Brenda Smith <Smithtax@todays-tech.com> of Wheatland, MO.)

[V6]1901. [9]1. ***Mary Albany Breshears**, b. 12 Jan 1822, Lawrence Co, TN, d. 26 Feb 1891, Dallas Co, MO; m.1. 29 Feb 1844, (Polk Co, MO) ***Abraham James Baker***, s/o Solomon Baker and Lucy Jones; m.2. 18 Sept 1851, ***Noah Jackson Bray***

[V6]1902. [9]2. ***Henry Hardin Breshears**, b. 2 Feb 1823, Lawrence Co, TN, d. 22 Aug 1899, Elgin, Union Co, AR; m.1. ***Catherine Baker***, b. 26 May 1826, Iowa, d/o Solomon Baker and Lucy Jones; m.2. widow ***Freeman***. Henry and Catherine are #78-78 in 1850, Dallas Co, MO, Dist 26.

[V6]1903. [9]3. ***Reuben Dobbin Breshears**, b. 1825, Lawrence Co, TN; m. 4 May 1848, at Bolivar, Polk Co, MO, ***Mary Batten***

[V6]1904. [9]4. ***William Arthur Breshears**, b. 7 Sept 1827, Lawrence Co, TN, d. 9 July 1890, Polk Co, MO; m. 19 March 1850, (Bolivar, Polk Co, MO), ***Abigail Jane Batten***, b. 30 March 1832, TN

[V6]1905. [9]5. **Sarah P. Breshears**, b. 1829, Lawrence Co, TN, d. 31 May 1873, Hickory Co, MO; m. 21 April 1859, (Polk Co, MO) ***William Henry "Wilse" Henderson***, b. 15 Feb 1828, TN, d. 23 May 1891, Hickory Co, MO, bur Henderson Cem, but moved to Avery, Hickory Co, MO. William Henderson was married, first, to **Mary Elizabeth Breshears**, d/o Alexander Brashears and Margaret Breshears. See her listing for their child.

[V6]1906. [10]1. John Thomas Henderson, b. c1861

[V6]1907. [10]2. Samuel James Henderson, b. c1863

[V6]1908. [10]x. George W. (Wright) Henderson, b. c1864, adopted

[V6]1909. [10]3. Mary Ellen Henderson, b. c1865; m. ______ Byrum

[V6]1910. [10]4. Naomi Jane Henderson, b. 11 Feb 1868, d. 24 Feb 1945, in Granger, Washington; m. Bob Norman

[V6]1911. [10]5. William Henry Henderson Jr, b. 3 Dec 1869

[V6]1912. [10]6. Sarah Frances “Fanny” Henderson; m.1. David Miller; m.2. John Pippen

[V6]1913. [9]6. ***Jesse Carroll Breshears**, b. 17 Dec 1830, Lawrence Co, TN, d. 15 Feb 1902, Polk Co, MO; m. 1 Feb 1855, in Polk Co, MO, ***Rhoda Catherine Jump***, b. 22 Dec 1838, St. Louis, MO, d. 14 May 1911, Polk Co, MO.

[V6]1914. [9]7. **Susan G. Breshears**, b. 11 March 1831, Lawrence Co, TN, d. 5 Feb 1849, Polk Co, MO; unmarried

[V6]1915. [9]8. **Nancy G. Breshears**, b. 1834, Lawrence Co, TN; m. ***James E. Jones***,

[V6]1916. [10]1. Naomi S. Jones,

[V6]1917. [10]2. Sophronia Jones,

[V6]1918. [10]3. John Jones,

[V6]1919. [10]4. Catherine Jones,

[V6]1920. [10]5. Rhoda Jones,

[V6]1921. [9]9. ***John Westley Breshears**, b. 24 Oct 1835, Lawrence Co, TN, d. 23 Dec 1913, Polk Co, MO; m.1. ***Lucy Baker***, b. 6 Sept 1839, d. 3 Sept 1888, d/o Solomon Baker and Lucy Jones; m.2. ***Caroline Bridges,***

[V6]1922. [9]10. ***Margaret Naomi Breshears**, b. 5 April 1837, Lawrence Co, TN, d. 26 Jan 1911; m. 21 Jan 1861, Polk Co, MO, ***Joseph Henry Jump***

[V6]1923. [9]11. ***Joseph W. Breshears**, the first of the children born in Missouri, b. 1839, Polk Co, MO; m.1. ***Isabell Brashears***, (d/o Jesse Brashears and Elizabeth Bell), b. 1837, Benton Co, MO, d. c1860-65 in Hickory Co, MO; m.2. ***Prudence Tipton***, d/o James Tipton and Christine Henderson

[V6]1924. [9]12. **Ozias Martin V. “Mark” Breshears**, b. 8 Nov 1842, Polk Co, MO; m. 8 July 1858, Polk Co, MO, ***Elizabeth Brown***, (data from Calstar41@aol.com)

[V6]1925. [10]1. **Sarah Breshears**, b. c1859, MO

[V6]1926. [10]2. **Reuben T. Breshears**, b. c1860, MO

[V6]1927. [10]3. **Neoma Breshears**, b. c1864, MO

[V6]1928. [10]4. **John Breshears**, b. c1867, MO

[V6]1929. [10]5. **James Breshears**, b. c1868, MO

[V6]1930. [10]6. **Loucy Breshears**, b. c1870, MO

[V6]1931. [10]7. ***Albert (or Elbert) Breshears**, b. 23 Jan 1873, Polk Co, MO, d. 12 Feb 1939, Briartown, OK; m. 10 Sept 1894, in Stigler, OK, ***Sarah Almira "Allie" Madewell***, b. 10 Nov 1878,

[V6]1932. [10]8. **George Breshears**, b. c1877, MO

[V6]1933. [9]13. ***James Knox Polk Breshears, I**, b. 18 Nov 1842, Bolivar, Polk Co, MO, d. 7 March 1927; m.1. 15 March 1866, ***Sarah Francis "Fannie" Potter***, b. 27 Oct 1847, d. 8 Sept 1868; m.2. 11 July 1869, ***Virginia P. (Byrns) Baker***, b. 10 May 1938, d. 27 April 1970, widow of George Baker, s/o Solomon Baker and Lucy Jones; m.3. 24 Dec 1871, ***Margaretta Ann Byrns***, sister of his 2nd wife.

[V6]1934. [9]14. ***Thomas Hart Benton Breshears**, b. 11 Oct 1844, Bolivar, Polk Co, MO, d. 29 Feb 1916, Eagle, Ada Co, Idaho; m. 8 Aug 1866, at Bolivar, Polk Co, MO, ***Nancy Ann Potter***, b. 8 Aug 1849, Ozark, Green Co, MO

Hickory County History

Three Breshears brothers who lived in Breshears Valley north of Wheatland. Left to right: Andrew Jackson 1845-1924, Henry Thomas 1838-1921, John Martin 1840-1922. Many descendants reside in Hickory County and elsewhere. Submitted by Helen J. Hentzl, Seattle, Wa.

V6 1935. 9 15. ***Andrew Jackson Breshears**, b. 27 June 1847, Polk Co, MO, d. 3 Jan 1921, Weister, Payette Co, ID; m. 17 March 1868, Polk Co, MO, ***Martha Melvina Hammack***, b. 6 May 1850, Dallas Co, MO

Family tradition says 16 children were born to this family; the 1830 Census of Lawrenceburg, TN, shows a possible girl child not otherwise recorded, dau of John & Naoma Ann.

Albert (Elbert) Breshears and Allie Madewell

V6 1931. 10 7. **Albert (or Elbert) Breshears**, (s/o Ozias Martin V. "Mark" Breshears and Elizabeth Brown), b. 23 Jan 1873. Polk Co, MO, d. 12 Feb 1939, Briartown, OK; m. 10 Sept 1894, in Stigler, OK, ***Sarah Almira "Allie" Madewell***, b. 10 Nov 1878, in Arkansas, d. 13 Jan 1930, Briartown, OK, d/o William Thomas Madewell and Louise Elizabeth Begley. (Grandparents of Calstar)
V6 1936. 11 1. **William Thomas Breshears**, b. 2 Sept 1898,

Figure 16: Albert Breshears and wife, Sarah Almira Madewell, with Bill Green (second husband of Sarah Isabell (Davis) Tackett, woman at far right, mother of Arthur Lee Tackett, who m. Albert's daughter Ophelia Elizabeth. The boy is Freeman Ferrill, grandson of Bill Green. Thanks for photo to Glenda South

V6 1937. [11]2. **Esther Mae Breshears**, b. 1 March 1900, Whitefield, OK, d. there, 1 July 1901,

V6 1938. [11]3. **Ophelia Elizabeth Breshears**, b. 29 Jan 1902, Ind Terr, d. 9 Jan 1990, Modesto, Stanislaus Co, CA; m. 10 March 1920, in Stigler, Haskell Co, OK, ***Arthur Lee Tackett***, b. 19 Jan 1897, Uniontown, AR, d. 13 Jan 1962, Riverbank, Stanislaus Co, CA, s/o William Samuel Tackett and Sarah Isabel Davis.

Figure 17: Children of Albert Breshears in 1918: Back: Ira Franklin, Ophelia Elizabeth; front: Jessie Clarence, Ernest Lee, Berton Calloway. Thanks for photo from Glenda South

<u>Family of Ophelia Elizabeth Breshears and Arthur Lee Tackett:</u>

V6 1939. [12]1. Charline Tackett, b. 18 July 1921, Briartown, OK, d. 30 Oct 2000, Ok City; m. 25 Sept 1939, in Riverbank, Stanislaus Co, CA, James Nathaniel Calton. (Parents of Glenda L. Calton South (cenokstar@yahoo.com), who sent data and pictures. Thanks.)

V6 1940. [12]2. Infant Tackett, still born 1922,

V6 1941. [12]3. Daisy Bell Tackett, b. 7 Aug 1923; m. 13 July 1947, in Reno, NV, Harold Weaver,

V6 1942. [12]4. Arthur Boyd Tackett, b. 14 June 1925, Briartown, OK, d. 22 Dec 1992, Modesto, Stanislaus Co, CA; m. Amelia Errglehart,

V6 1943. [12]5. Cleo Lee Tackett, b. 7 March 1931, Briartown,

OK, d. Modesto, CA; m. Roseann Bates,

V6 1944. [12]6. Leola Elizabeth Tackett, b. 9 May 1933,

V6 1945. [12]7. Terry Dean Tackett, b. 23 Sept 1941; m. 4 July 1959, in Reno, NV, John Somners,

V6 1946. [11]4. **Ira Franklin Breshears**, b. 30 Dec 1903, Briartown, Ind Terr; m. ***Bertha Hunt***,

V6 1947. [11]5. **Berton Calloway Breshears**, (twin) b. 4 Feb 1905, Briartown, Ok/ I.T., d. 28 July 1955, Modesto, Stanislaus Co, CA; m. Oct 1929, in Stigler, Haskell Co, OK, ***Lillie Treadway***,

V6 1948. [11]6. **Bertha Breshears**, (twin), b. 4 Feb 1905, Briartown, OK/IT, d. there 23 Feb 1905,

V6 1949. [11]7. **Jessie Clarence Breshears**, b. 15 April 1907, Briartown, OK, d. 6 June 1966, Modesto, Stanislaus Co, CA; m. 13 May 1927, in Stigler, Haskell Co, OK, ***Polly Bell Barnes***,

V6 1950. [11]8. **Ernest Lee Breshears**, b. 19 Jan 1912, Briartown, OK, d. 23 June 2000, Los Banos, Merced Co, CA; m. 7 July 1931, in Stigler, Haskell Co, OK, ***Sue West***,

Figure 18: Albert Breshears, crossing the Canadian River on ice in 1915. The white mare was named Goldie, the bay mare Sylvia. Thanks to Glenda South for the photo

18. MARY ALBANY BRESHEARS and Abraham James Baker/ Noah Jackson Bray

V6 1901. 9 1. **Mary Albany Breshears**, (d/o John Breshears and Naoma Ann Hogg), b. 12 Jan 1822, Lawrence Co, TN, d. 26 Feb 1891, Dallas Co, MO; m.1. 29 Feb 1844, in Polk Co, MO, ***Abraham James Baker***, b. 4 Nov 1822, Indiana, d. 7 July 1851, Dallas Co, MO, s/o Solomon Baker and Lucy Jones; m.2. 18 Sept 1851, ***Noah Jackson Bray***, b. 29 Jan 1819, Gallia Co, Ohio, d. 26 Aug 1889. Both of Mary's husbands were said to be men of means. Noah Bray held several elective offices and owned extensive stock and land.

Family of Mary Albany Breshears and Abraham J. Baker (from FHL files)

V6 1951. 10 1. James Solomon Baker, b. c1845, d. 1865, Civil War casualty.

V6 1952. 10 2. John Abraham Baker, b. 8 April 1847, d. 5 Nov 1922; m. Sarah Elizabeth Alford, b. 9 Feb 1853, Dallas Co, MO, d. 8 Dec 1898, d/o J.M. Alford and Hannah ______.

V6 1953. 11 1. Hannah Ellen Baker, b. 13 March 1877, Dallas Co, MO; m.1. Charles Anson Thornbury, b. 6 Sept 1872, Boone Co, IN

V6 1954. 11 2. James S. Baker, b. c1879, MO; m. Rosa Summit, b. c1879. James served six months in Co C, 4th MO Vol Cavalry.

V6 1955. 11 3. Susan Baker, b. c1881, MO; m. Tom Gibson, b. c1881

V6 1956. 11 4. Maud Baker, b. 7 May 1885, MO; m. William S. Thornbury, b. c1885

V6 1957. 11 5. Mary A. Baker, b. c1887, MO; m. Walter Bass, b. c1887, MO

V6 1958. 10 3. Lucy Baker, b. c1847, d. c1850

V6 1959. 10 4. Charles Abraham "Abe" Baker Sr, b. c1849; m.

Daisy Rice, b. c1849
[V6]1960. [11]1. ______ Baker,
[V6]1961. [11]2. Josephine Baker, b. 1916

Family of Mary Albany Breshears and Noah J. Bray (from FHL files)

[V6]1962. [10]5. Naomi Jane Bray, b. 12 Dec 1856, d. 2 Aug 1935; m. Nathan J. (or Matthew) Alford, b. c1844
[V6]1963. [11]1. Effie Alford, b. c1870
[V6]1964. [11]2. Alma Alford, b. Jan 1872, Buffalo, MO; m. Harry Rae, b. c1872
[V6]1965. [11]3. Melvin Alford, b. c1874; m. Dora Pendergraft, b. c1874
[V6]1966. [11]4. Luther Alford, b. 1875, d. 4 Aug 1877
[V6]1967. [11]5. Donna Alford, b. 28 Nov 1884, d. 7 Dec 1884
[V6]1968. [11]6. Noah Alford,
[V6]1969. [10]6. Noah Jackson "Jack" Bray, b. c1858, d. 1913; m. Susan Alford,
[V6]1970. [11]1. Saphona Bray, b. c1874
[V6]1971. [11]2. Naomi Della Bray, b. c1876
[V6]1972. [11]3. Hannah Bray, b. c1878
[V6]1973. [11]4. Effie Bray, b. c1880
[V6]1974. [11]5. Francis Bray, b. 18 Aug 1881,
[V6]1975. [11]6. Mollie Bray, b. c1882
[V6]1976. [11]7. Rosa Bray, b. 9 Nov 1884, Urbana, MO; m. Willie Ethridge, b. c1884
[V6]1977. [11]8. Eva Bray, b. 9 Nov 1894, MO; m. Paul Cox, b. c1894
[V6]1978. [10]7. William R. "Billie" Bray, b. c1848; m. Martha Sawyers
[V6]1979. [11]1. Nathan A. Bray,
[V6]1980. [11]2. Perlina A. Bray,
[V6]1981. [10]8. General F. Bray, b. c1852
[V6]1982. [10]9. Margaret Bray, b. c1854, MO; m. J.L. Austin,

19. HENRY HARDIN BRESHEARS and Catherine Baker

v6 1902. 9 2. **Henry Hardin Breshears**, (s/o John Breshears and Naoma Ann Hogg), b. 24 Feb 1823, Lawrence Co, TN, d. 22 Aug 1899, in Elgin, Union Co, OR; m.1. 1847, in Dallas Co, MO, ***Catherine Baker***, b. 26 May 1826, Iowa (or IN, says 1850 census), d. 14 May 1885, in Elgin, Union Co, OR, s/o Solomon Baker and Lucy James; m.2.(?) after 1885, Widow ***Freeman***

Henry was a Primitive Baptist preacher. He moved his family to Union Co, Oregon in the 1870s.

Henry H. Breshears, 26, b. TN, and Catherine, 25, b. IN, are in the 1850 census of Dallas Co, MO, Dist 26, #78-78, p.314b, with son John, 2, and dau, Lucy, 10/12. This shows that Catherine was the first wife, not the second, as some researchers have asserted. Also in hh: Joseph Baker, 22, b. IN, and Lucy Baker, 11, b. IN, probably Catherine's siblings.

Family of Henry Hardin Breshears and Catherine Baker: (family from FHL files)

V6 1983. 10 1. **John S. "Jack" Brashears**, b. 1 Nov 1847, Polk Co, MO(2 in 1850, Dallas Co, MO)

V6 1984. 10 2. **Lucy Ann Brashears**, b. 15 Aug 1849, near Bolivar, Polk Co, MO (10/12 in 1850, Dallas Co, MO), d. 2 Feb 1923, in Elgin, Union Co, OR; m. ***James Henry Cunningham***, b. c1849

V6 1985. 10 3. **Henry James Brashears**, b. 30 Jan 1854, near Bolivar, Polk Co, MO; m. ***Caroline*** ______, b. c?1854

V6 1986. 10 4. **Joseph Brent Brashears**, b. 29 July 1856, Dallas Co, MO; m. ***Mary Ellen Graham***, b. 30 May 1866, Walla Walla, WA

V6 1987. 11 1. **William Reuben Brashears**, b. 9 Feb 1883, Elgin, Union Co, OR; m.1. ***Alma Long***, b. c?1883; m.2. ***Marjorie Elizabeth Ekley***, b. 1877; m.3. ***Floe Wetzel***, b. c?1883

V6 1988. 11 2. **Jay Brashears**, b. 22 June 1889, Elgin, Union Co, OR; m. ***Clara Rysdam***, b. 26 April 1886, Elgin, Union Co, OR

V6 1989. [11]3. **Anna Mae Breshears**, b. 18 March 1892 Elgin, Union Co, OR; m. ***William Cruishank***

V6 1990. [11]4. **Effie Jo Breshears**, b. 6 Jan 1895 Elgin, Union Co, OR; m. ***Monia V. Witty,***

V6 1991. [11]5. unknown **Breshears**,

V6 1992. [10]5. **Neomah C. Breshears**, b. 2 May 1856 (something wrong with birthdate! Too near Joseph Brent Breshears), near Bolivar, Polk, MO; m. ***Sam Wickliffe***

V6 1993. [10]6 **William Reuben Breshears**, b. 1 Oct 1860, near Bolivar, Polk, MO; m.1. ***Ona Moore***; m.2. ***Madge Eckler***; m.3. ***Anna Boly***

V6 1994. [10]7. **Mary Breshears**, b. 10 Feb 1865, near Bolivar, Polk, MO; m. ***Julius Benshadler,*** b. [c1865]

20. REUBEN DOBBIN BRESHEARS and Mary H. Batten

[v6]1903. [9]3. **Reuben Dobbin Breshears**, (s/o John Breshears and Naoma Ann Hogg), b. 26 March 1824, Lawrenceburg, Lawrence Co, TN, d. 1 Dec 1881, Blaine Co, ID, bur Bellevue Cem, Blaine Co, ID; m. 4 May 1848, at Bolivar, Polk Co, MO, ***Mary H. Batten***, b. c1833, d/o James Batten and Mary Stone.

Figure 19: Reuben Dobbin Breshears. Photo from Cris McCarthy.

Figure 20: Mary H. (Batten) Breshears. Photo from Cris McCarthy.

Abigail Batten, d/o John Batten (brother to James Batten), married William Breshears, brother to Reuben. In 1880, Ava Batten, 37, sister-in-law to William Breshears, is in William and

Abigail's household, Polk Co, MO.

1860 US Census: Polk County, Missouri -

BASHEARS, Reuben		35 - farmer - Tenn
	Mary	26 - Tenn
	John	9 - Mo
	Martha	6 - Mo
	James	2 - Mo

On 1 Nov 1863, Reuben enlisted at Bolivar, Polk Co, MO, in Company L, 15th Reg't, Missouri Cavalry Volunteers, U.S. Army (Union), and was mustered 11 Aug 1864 at Humansville, MO. He was discharged at Springfield, MO, in August, 1865, and is listed as serving 20 months.

An old letter from Erma Breshears to Georgene Humphries, "Reuben was in the 15th Missouri Cavalry. I don't know much except I know my dad had his army papers in an old trunk in the wood shed. It was also on the tombstone in the Bellevue Cemetery, Bellevue, Idaho. I remember dad talking about an uncle NATE and an Aunt Sarah & Rhoda. Grandma married after grandad passed away. I can't recall the name but MOSES was his first name. Grandfather passed away before Neoma Mae and Uncle Jim went back to Missouri. Jim took Dad's share of the estate in exchange for his share of the property in Bellevue. A number of years later a POTTER (son-in-law) sued dad for a share of the Bellevue estate. It was thrown out of court, Blaine County, Idaho.

Mary's second husband was Henry C. Bobb.

Although the national archives has no record of a disability, Reuben was unable after his discharge to ever do a full day's work. Years later, he told William Stephens, a friend, that he had been thrown onto his saddle horn while in the Army. He was in considerable pain at times throughout the remainder of his life.

In 1877, at least three Breshears brothers of Missouri, Henry, Reuben, and Andrew Jackson, some of their sisters (Margaret Jump) and families, together with some of their grown children and their families, joined a wagon train bound for Idaho. They arrived at Fort Boise in August 1877 and spent the winter of 1877-78 at the fort.

W.J. Connell comments in his "Early History of Idaho,"

1913, pp.357-58: The decade including 1871 and 1880 was perhaps the most trying period in the history of Idaho Territory: up to 1870, the chief industry was placer mining, and the number of men employed in that enterprise, together with those in the towns and camps supported directly by the miners provided an excellent market for all kinds of farm product raised in the valley.

It seldom requires many years to exhaust the wealth of the average placer mining camp, and while the placer mines discovered in Idaho were no doubt more than average in extent and productiveness, yet hundreds of the best producing claims were exhausted within the first five years after the discovery; hence each succeeding year added to the melancholy of the situation, until eventually, and that too within ten years after the discovery of Boise Basin, hundreds of cabins on the hillsides and in the gulches were left tenantless and alone among the whispering pines....

Those farmers who from the first settlement of Boise and Payette Valleys, as well as those who had settled in Idaho and Nez Perce Counties, had proved the character and fertility of the soil and left nothing to conjecture as to the future possibilities of Idaho as an agricultural state. (Thanks to Cris McCarthy for the text.)

1880 U.S. Census, Territory of Idaho, Ada County

Brisheers, Rhubin	56	farmer, TN SC KY
, Mary	48	wife, TN NC TN
, James B.	22	son, MO TN TN
, William T.H.	17	son, MO TN TN
, Andrew J.	13	son, MO TN TN
, Wesley F.	13	son, MO TN TN
Potter, Martha	25	dau, MO TN TN
, Wesley	8	gr.son, MO MO MO
, James N.	6	gr.son, MO MO MO
, Rhuben E.	4	gr.son, MO MO MO
,William L.	1	gr.son, ID MO MO

Soon after the 1880 census, the Reuben Breshears family, with the exception of sons John M. and James B. moved to Bellevue, Alturas Co (area later Blaine Co??), Idaho, where Reuben died 1 Dec 1881 and was buried in the City cem there. Mary was left with several young children to support. She applied for a widow's pension and eventually got $8 per month until Jan 1897, when she remarried. She died 12 April 1899 and was buried near Reuben.

Bellevue Cem, Blaine County, *Idaho Cemetery Records,* 979.6 V22 5B, page 6:
Reuben Breshears 26 Mar 1824 - 1 Dec 1881
Mary H. Bobb age 64 died 12 Apr 1899 (Widow of Reuben Breshears and, later, wife of Henry C. Bobb)
Thomas Breshears 1863 - 1934
Martha F. Potter, wife of J.R. Potter age 33 died 9 Apr 1888
A.J. Breshears age 22 25 Oct 1866 - 26 Feb 1889
Wesley F. Breshears 25 Oct 1866 - 7 July 1922

<u>Family of Reuben Dobbin Breshears and Mary Batten</u>: (data from FHL, Cris McCarthy, and other descendants)

[V6]1995. [10]1. **Sarah A.E. Breshears**, b. 2 March 1849, Bolivar, Polk Co, MO, d. there, 1 March 1860, bur Breshears cem: "Sarah A.E., daughter of R. & M.H. Breshears"

[V6]1996. [10]2. ***John M. Breshears**, b. 23 Nov 1851, Bolivar, Polk Co, MO, d. 27 April 1919 at Star, Ada Co, Idaho; m. 11 June 1871, in Bolivar, Polk Co, MO, ***Rhoda Ann Keith***, b. 13 Dec 1852,

[V6]1997. [10]3. **Martha F. Breshears**, b. c1854, Bolivar, Polk Co, MO, 9 April 1888, Blaine Co, ID; m. ***J.R. Potter***,

[V6]1998. [10]4. ***James Batten Breshears**, b. 22 Jan 1858, Bolivar, Polk Co, MO, d. 19 Jan 1945; m. ***Harriet Luticia Bass***, b. 14 Dec 1865 Polk Co, MO

[V6]1999. [10]5. **William Thomas H. Breshears**, b. Feb 1863, Bolivar, Polk Co, MO, d. June 1929 (or 1934, per tombstone in Bellevue Cem, Blaine Co, ID); m. ***Margaret Mae "Maggie" Sharp***, b. 14 Sept 1889, Broadford, ID. Five children, among whom:

[V6]2000. [11]1. **Elijah "Lige" M. Breshears**,

[V6]2001. [11]2. **Erma Breshears**, b. 9 July 1906, Bellevue, ID; m. ***Wilburn Breshears***, b. 20 Jan 1906, Eagle, Ada Co, ID

[V6]2002. [12]1. ____ **Breshears**, b. ____ ; m. ____, b. ____

[V6]2003. [13]2. **Michael Breshears**, b. 19 Oct 1959,

Wallace, Shoshone Co, ID

V62004. 106. **Wesley Fletcher Breshears**, (twin) b. 25 Oct 1866, Bolivar, Polk Co, MO, d. 7 July 1922, Blaine Co, ID, bur Bellevue Cem; m. ***Elizabeth Davis***, b.

V62005. 111. **John Andrew Breshears**, b.

V62006. 112. **George Washington Breshears**, b.

V62007. 113. **Edna Breshears**, b.

V62008. 107. **Andrew Jackson Breshears**, (twin) b. 25 Oct 1866, Bolivar, Polk Co, MO, d. 26 Feb 1889, Blaine Co, ID, bur Bellevue Cem. "Age 22"

John M. Breshears and Rhoda Ann Keith

v61996. 102. **John M. Breshears**, (s/o Reuben Dobbin Breshears and Mary Batten), b. 23 Nov 1851, Bolivar, Polk Co, MO, d. 27 April 1909 at Star, Ada Co, Idaho; m. 11 June 1871, in Bolivar, Polk Co, MO, ***Rhoda Ann Keith***, b. 13 Dec 1852, Green Twp, Polk Co, MO, d. 23 Oct 1927, Star, Ada Co, ID, d/o James Foster Keith and Narcissa Elizabeth Howe.

After about six years of marriage in Polk Co, MO and several children, John M. Breshears and Rhoda Ann Keith joined a wagon train, along with his father and a couple of uncles. They arrived at Fort Boise, Idaho, 31 August 1877, where they spent the winter. The soon moved to Star, Ada Co, Idaho, where they made their home.

1880 US Census: Star, Ada County, Idaho (Book Form) -

BRESHEARS,	John M.	29 - farmer - Mo-Tenn-Tenn
	Roda	27 - wife - Mo-Tenn-
	Frances	8 - dau - Mo- Mo-Mo
	Cora I.	4 - dau Mo-Mo-Mo
	Albert W.	2 - son - Idaho-Mo-Mo
	Snow	7/12 - dau - Idaho-Mo-Mo

The John Breshears/Rhoda Keith farm was located near the "Home of Peace Cemetery," where some of the family is buried; it is also known as the Star cemetery.

Annie L. Bird wrote the following about Star in her "Boise, the Peace Valley," p. 245:

Star was also an early settlement. About 1869, a Christian Church was organized there and a church built about 1870. This may have been due to the fact that D.W. Fouch, a Christian

Figure 21: John and Rhoda (Keith) Breshears Family ~ ca 1888
Back row:: Rosetta, b. 1881 - Francis, b. 1872 - Snow , b. 1879
Front row:: Cora, b. 1875 - John, b. 1851 - Mae, b.1885 -
Rhoda, b. 1852 - Albert, b.1877. Photo from Cris McCarthy.

minister, was farming in the locality. In 1883, "one of them" who lived in the Star community wrote a letter to the Statesman, describing conditions. Some excerpts from that letter follow:

This place is not exactly a "burg," although to a beholder from a distance it has something of that appearance. In the radius of a mile, we have two large and comodius churches– The Christian Chapel belonging to the Christians, and the Star Chapel belonging to the Methodists– the district school house, the post office and small store, two blacksmith shops, and half a score of residences.

Our district last July enumerated seventy-five bonafide scholars. No emigrants stopping temporarily were enumerated, neither were married man and women who chance to be under 21 years old. At the October, 1882 session of the Commissioners, our district was divided for the purpose of forming a new and much needed district in the Dry Creek neighborhood, taking quite a number of scholars, but the influx into the district during the fall and winter has more than made up for the loss.

Although Star was bypassed by the branch line of the Railroad, Boise and Interurban brought her electric service for a number of years, and caused her to be a "real burg." (Thanks to Cris McCarthy for the text.)

(From Idaho Daily Statesman, April 28, 1909)

J.M. BRESHEARS DEAD.

The death of J.M. Breshears, aged 57 years, occurred early yesterday morning at his home near Star. The funeral will take place today at 2:30 o'clock at Star and interment will be in the Star Cemetery.

About 1909, also, Rhoda's mother, Narcissa (Howe) Keith moved from Bolivar, Polk Co, MO, to Idaho and spent the next eleven years with Rhoda and the grandchildren. (For more on the Howe and Keith families, contact Cris McCarthy.)

(From Idaho Statesman, Tuesday Morning, Oct 29, 1927:)

Breshears– Mrs. Rhoda Ann Breshears died Monday morning at the home of her daughter, Mrs. Etta Shaffer, two miles northwest of Star, at the age of 74 years. Mrs. Breshears came to Boise Valley August 31, 1877. She is survived by four daughters, Mrs. Cora Shaffer of Long Beach, CA; Mrs. Snow Blessingers of Star; Mrs. Etta Shaffer of Middleton; Mrs. Mae E. Beauchamp, of Nampa; and one son, Albert Breshears of Star; also one brother, Wilson Keith of Star; and one sister, Mrs. Thursa Baren of Missouri; 29 grandchildren, 13 great grandchildren. The funeral will be held Tuesday at 2:30 o'clock at the Pentecostal church at Star, and burial will be in Star Cemetery. Friends wishing to send flowers may send them to Summers and Krebs chapel Tuesday before 11 o'clock.

Family of John M. Breashears and Rhoda Ann Keith:

[V6]2009. [11]1. **Frances Elizabeth Breshears**, b. c1872, Bolivar, Polk Co, MO, d. 1904; m. 23 Oct 1892, Boise, Ada Co, ID, ***William Henry Conway***, b. 1866 (data

from Nola Conway)
[V6]2010. [12]1. Earl William Conway, b. 1894, d. 1894
[V6]2011. [12]2. Ella Mae Conway, b. 1896; m. ?? John Joplin, b. 1896
[V6]2012. [12]3. Mary Ethel Conway, b. 1898
[V6]2013. [12]4. John Bryan Conway, b. 1900, d. 1985; m.1. c1930, Jean Martin (1 ch); m.2. Edna Mae Peterson, b. 1908, d. 1997
[V6]2014. [13]1. Frances Conway, b. c1925
[V6]2015. [13]2. Vicki Sue Conway, b. 1940; m.1. Donald Mannikko; m.2. Richard O'Keefe
[V6]2016. [14]1. David Scott Mannikko, b. 1962
[V6]2017. [14]2. Daniel Dean Mannikko, b. 1965
[V6]2018. [14]3. Susan Diane Mannikko, b. 1971
[V6]2019. [13]2. Dennis Paul Conway, b. 1949; m. Nola Rae Leyde, b. 1954
[V6]2020. [14]1. Michael Dennis Conway, b. 1975
[V6]2021. [14]2. Jonathan Ramon Conway, b. 1981
[V6]2022. [14]3. Christopher Bryan Conway, b. 1986
[V6]2023. [11]2. **Cora I. Breshears**, b. 15 Sept 1875, Bolivar, Polk Co, MO, d. 27 Feb 1953; m. 1894, ***Jess Shaffer***, b. [c1875]
[V6]2024. [11]3. **Albert Winfield Breshears**, b. 3 Nov 1877, at Fort Boise, Ada Co, ID, d. 5 Dec 1940 at Portland, Multnomah Co, Oregon, bur Star Cem, Ada Co, ID; m. 11 May 1903, at

Figure 22: Wedding Picture, 1903: Albert W. and Anna (Ferrel) Breshears. Photo from Cris McCarthy.

Star, Ada Co, ID, ***Anna Ferrell***, b. 16 June 1886, Wichita, Kansas, d. 4 Jan 1967, d/o Felix Newton Ferrell and Nancy Johnson; m.2. ***Grace*** _____. (For more on Ferrell and Johnson families, contact Cris McCarthy.)

In November 1928, Albert and Anna moved to Medford, OR. In Sept 1929, Albert returned to Boise Valley, but Anna remained in Oregon. They were divorced 4 March 1930. Both remarried, and both divorced again. Albert died 5 Dec 1940 in

Figure 23: Anna (Ferrel) Breshears and three sons: from left, Oren Fay, Clifford, and Albert, Jr. Thanks to Cris McCarthy for the photo.

Portland, OR, while visiting his daughter, Mae. His body was returned to Star for burial. Anna died 4 Jan 1967 in Portland, OR, and she was buried next to Albert in Star cemetery.

Family of Albert W. Breshears and Anne Ferrel:

V6 2025. [12]1. **Anna Mae Breshears**, b. 19 May 1904, Ada Co, ID, m1. ***George A. Slane***; m.2. ***John Calliott***; m.3. ***Ben Johnson***, No children.

V6 2026. [12]2. **Oren Fay Breshears**, b. 22 June 1906, Boise, Ada Co, ID, d. 24 Sept 1980, Boise, Ada Co, ID; m.1. 28 March 1927, ***Bertha Maude Mencer***, (2 ch), d/o Edwin Mencer and May Gilbert; m.2. 22 May 1954, ***Alice Carter***,

V6 2027. [13]1. **Barbara June Breshears**, b. 1929, Ada Co, ID; m. 1947, in Eagle, Ada Co, ID, ***Calvin Colson***, b. 1928, in White City, KS, s/o William S. Colson and Edna Grace Schmidt.

V6 2028. [14]1. Bonnie Barbara Colson, b. 1950; m.1. Steve Johnson; m.2. Keith Noble; m.3. Larry Lucas. Ch:

Figure 24: The Oren Fay Breshears Family; from left: Maude (Mencer), Arnold, Barbara, and Oren. Thank to Cris McCarthy for the photo.

Shawna Michelle Noble and Wendy Maude Noble

V62029. 142. Cristy Calvean Colson, b. 1952, Boise, ID; m. Michael H. McCarthy. Ch: Tammi Ann; and Stacy Rae McCarthy. Cris McCarthy is a primary researcher in this branch of the family.

V62030. 132. **Arnold Fay Breshears,** b. 1930, Boise, Ada Co, ID; m.1. 1950,***Barbara Jean Bowers*** (2 ch); m.2.14 July 1960, ***Billie Jean Moore*** (2 ch). Arnold Fay Breshears was killed in a motorcycle accident, 15 Aug 1964.

V62031. 141. **Ronald Gene Breshears**, b. 1954, Boise, ID; m.1. ***Mary Carmen McDonald***,

V62032. 151. **Ronald Benjamin Breshears,**

V62033. 142. **Myron Fay Breshears**, b. 1957, Boise, ID; m. Kelly Kay Green,

Figure 25: The Calvin Colson Family in 1967:
from Left: Barbara (Breshears), Bonnie, Cristy, Calvin
Thanks to Cristy (Colson) McCarthy for the photo.

Figure 26: Double 5 Generation 1992 ~
Back Row: Tammi Verbarendse (dau of Cris), Wendy Wille (dau of Bonnie), Barbara (Breshears) Colson
Middle Row: Cris McCarthy, Maude Mencer-Breshears-Johnson, Bonnie Lucas
Front Row: Kylie Verbarendse and Bonnie Wille

V6 2034. 14 3. **William Thomas Breshears**, b. 1961, Boise, ID
V6 2035. 14 4. **Robert Allen Breshears**, b. 1962, Boise, ID,

V6 2036. 12 3. **Clifford Frank Breshears**, b. 2 July 1908. Ada Co, ID, d. Dec 1980, Emmett, ID; m. ***Leta Frost***,
V6 2037. 13 1. **Marletta Breshears**,
V6 2038. 12 4. **Felix John Breshears**, b. 24 July 1910, Star, Ada Co, ID, d. there, 26 July 1911
V6 2039. 12 5. **Addie Rena Breshears**, b. 8 June 1912, Star, Ada Co, ID; m. _______ ***Freeman***, No ch.
V6 2040. 12 6. **William Breshears**, b.&d. 21 Nov 1917
V6 2041. 12 7. **Albert Breshears Jr**, b. 2 Aug 1919, Star, Ada

Figure 27: 2002 - Back Row: Kylie Verbarendse, Mike & Cris McCarthy; Kneeling: Bryan Verbarendse and Conlyn McCain; Standing: Kaitlyn Verbarendse Sitting: Tammi and Dylan Verbarendse and Stacy McCarthy-McCain

Co, ID, d. 1959; m.1. ***Muriel*** ______

V6 2042. [13]1. **Anna Marie Breashears**,

V6 2043. [13]2. **Larry Lee Breshears**,

V6 2044. [13]3. **Kevin Breshears**,

V6 2045. [13]4. **Leta Breshears**,

V6 2046. [11]4. **Snow Iva Breshears**, b. Nov 1879, Star, Ada Co, ID, d. 17 Dec 1960, Ada Co, ID; m. ***Ray M. Blessinger***,

V6 2047. [11]5. **Rose Etta Breshears**, b. April 1881, Oregon, d. 20 March 1960, Ada Co, ID; m. ***Thomas Jefferson***

Shaffer,

[V6]2048. [11]6. **Charles Oliver Breshears**, b. 23 March 1883, Star, Ada Co, ID, d. there, 2 Aug 1884

[V6]2049. [11]7. **Mae T. Breshears**, b. April 1885, Star, Ada Co, ID, d. bef 1940; m. 1906, ***Belus D. Beaucp***,

James Batten Breshears and Harriet Bass

[v6]1998. [10]4. **James Batten Breshears**, (s/o Reuben Dobbin Breshears and Mary Batten), b. 22 Jan 1858, Bolivar, Polk Co, MO, d. 19 Jan 1945; m. ***Harriet Luticia Bass***, b. 14 Dec 1865 Polk Co, MO.

Family of James Batten Breshears and Harriet Bass:

[V6]2050. [11]1. **Fred Batten Breshears**, b. 9 March 1883, Star, Ada Co, ID; m. ***Flora Ethel Corrow***, b. 14 Oct 1885 Caldwell, Canyon, ID

[V6]2051. [12]1. **Warren Ervin Breshears**, b. 7 Feb 1905, Star, Ada Co, ID; m. _____, b. _____

[V6]2052. [12]2. **Cassie Juanita Breshears**, b. 14 Aug 1906, Star, Ada Co, ID; m. _____, b. _____

[V6]2053. [12]3. **Wendell Merle Breshears**, b. 4 Jan 1908, Star, Ada Co, ID; m. ***Elizabeth Pauline Shafer***, b. _____; m.2. _____, b. _____

[V6]2054. [12]4. **Virgil Roy Breshears**, b. _____; m. ***Erma Little***, b. 21 Jan 1913, Hayden, Fremont Co, ID

[V6]2055. [13]1. **Billee Jean Breshears**, b. _____ ; m. ***James Stanford Marquiss***, b. _____

[V6]2056. [13]2. **Fred Leroy Breshears**, b. 27 July 1935, Boise, Ada Co, ID; m. ***Dorothy Jean Adams***, b. _____

[V6]2057. [13]3. **Michael Joe Breshears**, b. _____; m. _____, b. _____

[V6]2058. [11]2. _____ **Breshears**, b. c1884

[V6]2059. [11]3. **Mary Ellen Breshears**, b. 28 July 1885, Star, Ada Co, ID; m. ***Alvin Salyers***,

[V6]2060. [11]4. **James Walter Breshears**, b. 30 Nov 1887, Star, Ada Co, ID; m. ***Lizzie Evert***,

[V6]2061. [11]5. **Martha Florence Breshears**, b. 22 Jan 1890, Star, Ada Co, ID; m. ***John Means***,

21. WILLIAM ARTHUR BRESHEARS and Abigail Jane Batten

[v6]1904. [9]5. **William Arthur Breshears**, (s/o John Breshears and Naoma Ann Hogg), b. 7 Sept 1827, Lawrence Co, TN, d. 9 July 1890, Polk Co, MO; m. 19 March 1850, at Bolivar, Polk Co, MO, ***Abigail Jane Batten***, b. 30 March 1832, Carroll Co, TN, d. 6 Oct 1910, Polk Co, MO, d/o John Batten and Emily King.

William Breshears, 22, b. TN, and wife, "Abagail," 18, b. TN, are in the 1850 census of Dallas Co, MO, p.314a, l.35, very near his father, John Breshears; William and Abigail had just married in March 1850, in Polk Co, MO. In 1880, they were in Polk Co, MO, and some of their children had already left home. They are both buried in the Breshears Cemetery, Polk Co, MO.

1880 US Census: Polk County, Missouri (Bolivar) -

BRESHEARS, William A.	52 - TN-SC-KY
Abigail	48 - wife - TN-NC-TN
Mary E.	26 - dau - Mo-TN-TN
Henry M.	24 - son " " "
Susan E.	22 - dau - " " "
Reuben J.	16 - son " " "
Margaret	11 - dau - " " "
Andrew J.	8 - son " " "
Eva E.	6 - dau " " "
Naomia	75 - *Mother* KY-NC-NC
BATTON, Ava	37 - sister in law TN-NC-TN

Family of William Arthur Breshears and Abigail Jane Batten: (family from FHL; data collected by Voyne Breshears and forwarded to me by Laurie Chance; Patty Warren;

[V6]2081. [10]1. ***John Morrison Link Breshears**, b. 23 Dec 1850, Polk Co, MO, d. Portales, New Mexico; m. 18 Dec 1879 in MO, ***Safrona Bathsheba Tuckness***, b. 1 Feb 1852; m.2. ***Laura Engle***,

[V6]2082. [10]2. **Mary Emily Breshears**, b. 8 Nov 1853, Polk Co,

MO, d. there 1 May 1940, bur Breshears Cem, Polk Co, MO; m. 28 Nov 1897, in Polk Co, MO, ***Marion Bridges***, b. 21 Jan 1869, Polk Co, MO, d. there 24 March 1945, bur Breshears Cem, s/o James Knox Polk Bridges and Mary E. Short,

[V6]2083. [10]3. **Henry Henibens Breshears**, b. 8 Dec 1856, Polk Co, MO, d. 1929; m. 7 Nov 1884, ***Rebecca J. Burleson***, b. 1867, d. 1941, both bur Mt Gilead cem.

[V6]2084. [11]1. **William E. Breshears**, b. c?1882 ; n;m.

[V6]2085. [11]2. **Bessie I. Breshears**, b. c?1884; m. 9 Aug 1908, ***Benton Hedlock***,

[V6]2086. [10]4. ***Susan Ellen Breshears**, b. 30 July 1857, Polk Co, MO, d. 18 March 1932, Dallas Co, MO; m. 18 Oct 1889, ***Joseph Anderson***, b. 6 April 1853,

[V6]2087. [10]5. ***Sarah M. Breshears**, b. 30 March 1860, Polk Co, MO, d. 1 Aug 1934, bur Canyon Hill Cem, Caldwell, ID; m. 10 Oct 1880, ***John Tuckness***, b. 8 April 1857. They moved to Idaho.

[V6]2088. [10]6. ***Reuben Joseph "Rube" Breshears**, b. 30 June 1864, Polk Co, MO; d. there 26 Nov 1932; m. 7 Sept 1885, in Dallas Co, MO, ***Margaret "Meg" Cena Buckles***, b. 18 April 1867, d. 28 June 1935

[V6]2089. [10]7. **Margaret Priscilla Breshears**, b. 15 July 1868, Polk Co, MO, d. 7 July 1931; m. 21 Dec 1890, ***Ira "Bud" Patison***, b. 15 Oct 1867

[V6]2090. [11]1. Squire William Patison, b. 22 Sept 1891

[V6]2091. [11]2. Mattie Belle Patison, b. 19 Feb 1894 Betholto, IL; m. John Albert Clark, b. c?1894

[V6]2092. [11]3. Ira Thomas Patison, b. 20 Jan 1896 Springfield, MO; m. _____ b. _____

[V6]2093. [11]4. _____ b. _____; m. _____ b. _____

[V6]2094. [11]5. James Donly Patison, b. 11 Nov 1900

[V6]2095. [11]6. _____ b. _____; m. William Arthur Boswell, b. 21 Sept 1895

[V6]2096. [10]8. **Andrew Jackson Breshears**, b. 5 March 1871, Polk Co, MO, d. 29 June 1947, bur Breshears Cem; m. 1891, ***Rosella Turner***, b. 23 Dec 1879

[V6]2097. [11]1. _____ b. _____; m. _____ b. _____

[V6]2098. [11]2. _____ b. _____

[V6]2099. [10]9. **Eva Ayya Breshears**, b. 27 Nov 1873, Polk Co, MO, d. 4 March 1954, bur Breshears Cem; m.1. 1894, ***Jack M. Richards***, b. 24 Aug 1868, d. 1936, bur Breshears cem; m.2. ***Joe Richards***, b. 25 Feb 1878

[V6]2100. [11]1. Walter Richards, b. c1890; m. Lena Moore, b. c?1890

John Morrison Link Breshears and Safrona Tuckness/ Laura Engle

[v6]2081. [10]1. **John Morrison Link Breshears**, (s/o William Arthur Breshears and Abigail Jane Batten), b. 23 Dec 1850, Polk Co, MO, d. 5 July 1934, Portales, New Mexico; m. 18 Dec 1879 in MO, ***Safrona Bathsheba Tuckness***, b. 1 Feb 1852, d. 1888, bur Lindley Creek cem, d/o Asbury Tuckness and Charlotte Keith; m.2. ***Laura Engle***, b. 1890, d. 1982

Family of John Morrison Link Breshears and Safrona Tuckness:

[V6]2101. [11]1. **James Henry Breshears**, b. 6 Sept 1880, MO, d. 28 July 1963, Portales, NM; m. 5 Aug 1903, ***Drucilla Ann Johnson***, b. 17 Jan 1879, d. 28 July 1963, New Mexico, d/o George Willis Johnson and Mary Elizabeth Brashears

[V6]2102. [12]1. **Lucy Breshears**,

[V6]2103. [12]2. **Mary Breshears,**

[V6]2104. [12]3. **Anna D. Breshears**, b. 17 Sept 1899; m. ______; ch: son (father of Laurie Chance); Myrtle.

[V6]2105. [12]4. **Atsy Breshears**,

[V6]2106. [12]5. **Nellie Breshears**,

[V6]2107. [12]6. **Alex "Bud" Breshears**,

[V6]2108. [12]7. **Raymond Wilbert Breshears**, b. 10 June 1904, Goodson, MO; m. 8 Sept 1920, in Eugene, OR, ***Geneva Lucretia Young***, b. 18 Aug 1903, Beaumont, TX, d/o Fred Eugene Young and Margaret Lucretia Richardson

[V6]2109. [13]1. **Wilbert Dale Breshears**, b. 25 April 1939, Eugene, OR; m. 18 Dec 1960, in

Portland, OR, ***Linda Ann Kern***, b. 29 March 1940, Idaho, d/o Robert E. Kern and Gortona Burlinggame.

V62110. [14]1. **David Dale Breshears**, b. 22 Spet 1961, Portland, OR

V62111. [14]2. **John Edward Breshears**, b. 22 Jane 1962, Corvallis, OR

V62112. [14]3. **Andrew Ray Breshears**, b. 28 Sept 1968, Los Alamos, NM

V62113. [14]4. **Heather Breshears**, b. 1 Dec 1970, Los Alamos, NM

V62114. [12]8. **Willis Link Breshears**, b. 22 April 1907, Rogers, New Mexico; m. 27 Dec 1931, in New Mexico, ***Lillian Fay Nelson***, b. 4 March 1907, Boswell City, OK, d/o W.W. Nelson, of Murfreesboro, TN, and Tina Mae Swain, of Home Grove, TX

V62115. [13]1. **Willa Fay Breshears**, b. 9 Aug 1933, Portales, NM; m.1. 24 Dec 1953, Bill Shoemaker; m.2. Roy Musgrove,

V62116. [14]1. Norma Faye Shoemaker, b. 9 Feb 1954

V62117. [14]2. Pennie Shoemaker, b. 16 June 1957

V62118. [12]9. **Roy Cecil Breshears**, b. 15 April 1913, Springfiled, MO; m. 1 Jan 1937, in Elkland, MO, ***Lura Case***, b. 23 July 1917, Olive, MO/ d/o Walter Harvey Case and Dura Este Davison, of Elkland, MO.

V62119. [13]1. **Curtis Allen Breshears**, b. 19 Dec 1938, Portales, NM; m. 30 May 1958, in Portales, NM, ***Mary Ellen Davis***, b. 23 April 1938, Winters, TX, d/o Fay Douglas Davis and Grace Margaret Jones.

V62120. [14]1. **Craig Allen Breshears**, b. 2 March 1961, Clovis, NM

V62121. [14]2. **Lance Douglas Breshears**, b. 28 June 1963, Clovis, NM

V62122. [14]3. **Kevin Lane Breshears**, b. 24 May 1968, Clovis, NM

[V6]2123. [11]2. **Charles William Breshears**, (s/o John Morrison Link Breshears and Safrona Tuckness), b. 5 March 1883, MO, d. 3 Nov 1951, Portales, NM; m. 4 Oct 1904, in MO, ***Myrtle Mae Mcfall***, b. 8 April 1886, MO, d/o Thomas Jefferson McFall and Sarah Jane Fielder, from southwest Indiana.

[V6]2124. [12]1. **Gladys Mildred Breshears**, b. 17 Dec 1905, Whittier, CA; m. 19 March 1931, Carl Wright Allison, b. 25 Sept 1898, Rushville, MO, s/o James Madison Allison and Luella Tannerhill Wright,

[V6]2125. [13]1. Charles Franklin Allison, (triplet) b. 21 Dec 1937; m. 2 Sept 1962, in Amarillo, TX, Kathy Junell,

[V6]2126. [13]2. James Frederic Allison, (triplet) b. 21 Dec 1937; m. 20 May 1961, in Plains, TX, Ivy Lee Beggs,

[V6]2127. [13]3. Frona Lou Allison, b. 21 Dec 1937 (triplet); m. 25 Sept 1958, in Clovis, NM, Leon Claix Sherburne,

[V6]2128. [12]2. **Thelma Josephine Breshears**, b. 22 Dec 1906, Moneta, CA; m. 6 June 1933, in Portales, NM, William Theodore Siefke, b. 15 Oct 1906, Walla Walla, WA, s/o William Randolph Siefke and Ann Christine ______, both from Germany.

[V6]2129. [13]1. Vivian Christine Siefke, b. 27 Feb 1934, Wetumka, OK; m. 24 July 1960, Indianapolis, IN, David Samuel McNelly, II, b. 27 Nov 1935, Ft Wayne, IN, s/o David Samuel McNelly, I, and Anna Florence Bowdus Baker,

[V6]2130. [14]1. Carla Ann McNelly, b. 22 Jan 1963, IN

[V6]2131. [14]2. Brenda Sue McNelly, b. 12 July 1964, IN

[V6]2132. [13]2. Richard William Siefke, b. 28 May 1944, Eugene, OR; m. 20 Dec 1970, in Eugene, OR, Deanna Fish,

[V6]2133. [11]3. **Francis Arthur Breshears**, (s/o John Morrison Link Breshears and Safrona Tuckness), b. 5 Nov 1885, MO, d. 24 Sept 1961, Bolivar, Polk Co, MO; m.1. 16 Oct 1907, in

MO, ***Nancy Helen Carter***, (5 ch) b. 22 Feb 1886, MO, d. 4 Jan 1929, Goodson, Polk Co, MO, d/o James Trousdale Carter and Harriet L. Arnold; m.2. ***Minnie Lea Holt***, b. c1883, of MO; m.3. ***Laura Engle***, b. c?1850

V62134. 121. **Lela Veneta Breshears**, b. 26 July 1908, Polk Co, MO; m. 6 Sept 1931, in Bolivar, MO, Jesse William House, b. 30 March 1904, Polk Co, MO, s/o Joseph Patton House and Annie Elizabeth Payne.

V62135. 131. Donald Lee House, b. 12 Feb 1933, Bolivar, MO, d. 3 June 1954, Germany

V62136. 132. Patsy Lou House, b, 8 Sept 1935, Bolivar, MO; m. 2 Aug 1958, in Aurora, MO, Harold P. Pottenger, b. 21 Nov 1932, s/o George William Pottenger and Sarah Elizabeth Ridens.

V62137. 141. Diane Elizabeth Pottenger, b. 6 Jan 1961, Moline, IL; m. David Watson. Ch: Rachel Leigh; Jessie Nichole; Hannah Kathleen; and Joseph Paul Watson.

V62138. 142. Kathleen Pottenger, b. 26 Sept 1965, Springfield, MO; m. Kenneth Ray Herman, Jr. ch: Samantha Rose; and Abigail Hope Herman.

V62139. 133. Willodean House, b. 14 Dec 1936, Bolivar, MO; m. 27 June 1959, in Bolivar, MO, Leon Estle Gullet,, b. 15 June 1930, St Clair, MO, s/o Estle Reece Gullet and Gertie Ethel Maupin,

V62140. 134. Deryll William House, b. 22 Nov 1938, Bolivar, MO, d. 13 July 1944, Springfield, MO

V62141. 122. **Voyne Leland Breshears**, b. 15 Aug 1910; m. 24 March 1940, in Bolivar, MO, ***Helen Virginia Cunnyngham***, d/o James William Cunnyngham and Mattie Chloe Johnson,

V62142. 131. **Nancy Kay Breshears**, b. 6 Sept 1946, Tulsa, OK; m. 31 Jan 1973, in Platt City, MO, ***Jay Amos***, b. 28 Dec 1946, s/o Robert Jewell Amos and Christine L. Dubois,

V62143. 141. Ronnie Amos, b. 3 Nov 1966

V62144. 142. Jason Vance Amos, b. 20 Nov 1973

V62145. [14]3. Joylyn Vinita Amos, b. 20 Nov 1973; m. Darryl Liberty. Ch: Taylor Nichole Liberty.

V62146. [13]2. **William Arthur Breshears**, b. 21 May 1949, Tulsa, OK; m. 7 July 1973, in Neosho, MO, ***Pearlene Brumfield***, b. 7 July 1953, Neosho, MO, d/o Ottis Thomas Brumfield and Bonnie Gay Hively,

V62147. [14]1. **Reggie Lee Breshears**, b. 11 March 1976; m. June 2001, ***Andrea Celeste Swearington***.

V62147a. [14]2. **Cherita Kay Breshears**, m. ***Michael Brandon Heller***.

V62148. [12]3. **Orlena Mable Breshears**, b. 30 Oct 1913, Polk Co, MO; m. 3 April 1948, in Las Vegas, NV, ***Everett Stilson Woodruff***, b. Fresno, CA, s/o Willard Frances Woodruff and Maude May Gividen

V62149. [13]1. Barbara J. Breshears, (step-dau), b. 14 Oct 1929, Fresno, CA; m. Nov 1947, in Las Vegas, NV, Herbert Clay Foster: ch: Dan Everett and Lorraine Gay Foster,

V62150. [12]4. **Kenneth Arthur "Ken" Breshears**, b. 1 Nov 1921; m. 10 Feb 1945, in Williamsville, ***Willie Faquetta "Faye" Blackwell***, b. 28 Oct 1922, Ranger, Yell Co, AR, d/o William Clarence Blackwell and Ruby Willie Gantt,

Figure 28: Ken Breshears. Photo from obituary notice, sent to me by Arledge Brashers

V62151. [13]1. **Janet Sue Breshears**, b. 7 Dec 1946, Oxnard, CA; m. 15 Jan 1971, in Dallas, TX, ***Darwin Laverne Thomas***, 19 June 1932, Robertson, Co, TN, s/o William Robbie Thomas and Modene Lula Phillips,

V62152. [12]5. **Forest Wayne Breshears**, b. 28 Nov 1927, d. 4 Dec 1927, bur Breshears cem.

Family of John Morrison Link Breshears and Laura Engle:

V6 2153. 11 4. **James Edgar Breshears**, b. 11 July 1891, MO, s/o John Morrison Link Breshears and Laura Engle, d. 19 July 1954, MO, bur Reynolds cem; m. 16 Aug 1913, ***Bessie Morris***, b. 7 July 1897, d. 5 Dec 1949, bur Reynolds Chapel, MO, d/o Ben Morris and Katie Groutmoat.

V6 2154. 12 1. **Robert W. Breshears**, b. 28 Aug 1914, Buffalo, MO; m. 3 May 1936, in Culver City, CA, ***Josephine Chamberlain***, b. 27 May 1913, Buffalo, MO, d/o Elmer Chamberlain and Dora Sherriff,

V6 2155. 13 1. **Robert Ray Breshears**, b. 26 Jan 1937, Culver City, CA; m. 4 Aug 1958, in Whittier, CA, ***Carrol Behrendt***,

V6 2156. 14 x. **Susan Breshears**, m. (Governor) ***Evan Bayh***, of Indiana, s/o former Senator, Birch Bayh, of Indiana. Susan graduated from UC-Berkeley in 1981, was Miss Southern California in 1982, Miss Pasadena and finalist for Miss California and Miss World in 1983, and earned her law degree from USC in 1984. She met Evan Bayh while she was a summer intern for U.S. Representative Pete Stark in 1981.

V6 2157. 12 2. **Otis Breshears**,

V6 2158. 11 5. **Fred Vail Breshears**, (s/o John Morrison Link Breshears and Laura Engle), b. 1 Aug 1892, Goodson, Polk Co, MO, d. 31 July 1959, MO; m. 10 March 1914, in MO, ***Emma Catherine Vincent***, b. 26 Nov 1895, Halfway, MO, d/o Thomas P. Vincent and Sarah Catherine Bridges.

V6 2159. 12 1. **Elva Lee Breshears**, b. 18 April 1915, Springfield, MO; m. 5 Sept 1936, in Marshfield, MO, ***Eva Lorraine Holloway***,

V6 2160. [12]2. **Myrtle Evelyn Breshears**, b. 13 June 1917, Halfway, MO; m. 1 Oct 1938, in Bolivar, MO, ***Clyde Faulkner***,

V6 2161. [12]3. **Eva Vale Breshears**, b. 27 July 1920, Butler Co, KS; m. 24 Dec 1938, in Bolivar, MO, ***Earl Edward Hinkle***,

V6 2162. [12]4. **Glenn Willard Breshears**, b. 13 June 1924, Halfway, MO; m. in Nebo MO, ***Laura Malinda Fulks***,

V6 2163. [12]5. **Earl Dale Breshears**, b. 30 Dec 1928, Goodson, Polk Co, MO; m. 29 Sept 1950, ***Shirley Frances Gunderson***,

Susan Ellen Breshears and Joseph Anderson

v6 2086. [10]4. **Susan Ellen Breshears**, (d/o William Arthur Breshears and Abigail Jane Batten), b. 30 July 1857, Polk Co, MO, d. 18 March 1932, Dallas Co, MO; m. 18 Oct 1889, ***Joseph Anderson***, b. 6 April 1853, d. 9 Dec 1929, both bur Upper Lindley, Dallas Co, MO.

Family of Susan Ellen Breshears and Joseph Anderson:

V6 2164. [11]1. Anna Marie Anderson, b. 9 Feb 1891, d. 26 Dec 1957, OK; m. 11 July 1909, in MO, Leonard Benjamin Almy, b. 27 May 1889, d. 26 Dec 1957,

V6 2165. [12]1. Mabel Mildred Almy, b. 9 April 1910; m. 11 Sept 1927, Armond S. Sissom,

V6 2166. [13]1. Elossie Lorene Sissom, b. 26 April 1929, d. 19 Nov 1929

V6 2167. [13]2. Dorothea Mildred Marie Sissom, b. 13 Jan 1931, d. 18 March 1931

V6 2168. [13]3. Billie Gene Sissom, b. 3 June 1933, d. 3 June 1933

V6 2169. [13]4. Vida Mary Sissom, b. 20 Dec 1936; m. 28 June 1953, James Merriaman,

V6 2170. [13]5. Walter Leonard Sissom, b. 1 June 1939; m. 3 Aug 1959, Priscilla Price,

V6 2171. [13]6. Herbert Armond Sissom, b. 31 Dec 1942;

m. 6 July 1963, Janie Saquo,

[V6]2172. [13]7. Earnest Dale Sissom, b. 9 July 1946,

[V6]2173. [13]8. Philip Wayne Sissom, b. 26 Sept 1953,

[V6]2174. [12]2. Bernice Beatrice Almy, b. 28 July 1913; m. 15 Feb 1930, Jay G. Garrison,

[V6]2175. [13]1. Wilma Irene Garrison, b. 18 Nov 1930; m. 28 July 1951, Emil Loray Chronie,

[V6]2176. [13]2. Earl Gene Garrison, b. 2 Nov 1932; m. 11 Nov 1955, Norma Lee Sulavant,

[V6]2177. [13]3. Shirley Mae Garrison, b. 3 June 1938; m. 24 Sept 1955, Howard Braden,

[V6]2178. [12]3. Frederic Joseph Almy, b. 27 Nov 1917; m. 10 Dec 1936, Gwendolyn M. Ward,

[V6]2179. [13]1. Marilyn Mae Almy, b. 11 Feb 1938; m. 23 May 1959, John Coker,

[V6]2180. [13]2. Marijo Almy, b. 6 Oct 1941; m. 27 Jan 1959, J.E. Dawson,

[V6]2181. [13]3. Peggy Gwen Almy, b. 13 Aug 1945; m. 28 June 1963, Robert Lynn Arnold,

[V6]2182. [11]2. William Andrew Anderson, b. 28 Aug 1892, b. 13 Aug 1893,

[V6]2183. [11]3. George Anderson, b. 20 Aug 1894, d. 8 Aug 1957, MO; m. 22 Feb 1920, in MO, Ida R. Kee, b. 16 Oct 1900, d/o James Madison Kee and Mary Angibell Monroe.

[V6]2184. [12]1. Fern Irene Anderson, b. 15 July 1922; m. 26 Dec 1942, Carl W. Brown,

[V6]2185. [12]2. Dorothy Marie Anderson, b. 12 Feb 1929; m. 6 Nov 1949, Herbert B. Redd,

[V6]2186. [12]3. Georgia K. Anderson, b. 30 Dec 1944,

[V6]2187. [11]4. Oscar Anderson, b. 27 Aug 1896; m. 15 Dec 1918, in Buffalo, MO, Effie Blanche Kee, b. 28 May 1896, d/o James Madison Kee and Mary Angibell Monroe,

[V6]2188. [12]1. Shirley Charlotte Anderson, b. 9 Nov 1918, d. 18 July 1921

[V6]2189. [12]2. Oscar Leland Anderson, b. 22 Nov 1921

[V6]2190. [12]3. Mary Ellen Anderson, b. 8 Oct 1923

[V6]2191. [12]4. Lawrence Eugene Anderson, b. 3 April 1929

[V6]2192. [12]5. Lyndel Lee Anderson, b. 18 June 1934

Sarah M. Breshears and John Tuckness

[V6]2087. [10]5. **Sarah M. Breshears**, (d/o William Arthur Breshears and Abigail Jane Batten), b. 30 March 1860, Polk Co, MO, d. 1 Aug 1934, bur Canyon Hill Cem, Caldwell, ID; m. 10 Oct 1880, ***John Tuckness***, b. 8 April 1857, 21 Sept 1939, s/o Asbury Tuckness and Charlotte Keith. Sarah and John moved to Idaho.

[V6]2193. [11]1. William Asbury Tuckness, b. c5 Sept 1881; m.10 March 1908, Alma Spear, b. c?1881

[V6]2194. [11]2. Bertha Ann Tuckness, b. 14 March 1883, d. 17 Sept 1925; m. 11 March 1900, Lum Richards, b. c?1883

[V6]2195. [11]3. James Ruben Tuckness, b. 30 June 1885, MO; m. 6 Nov 1907-07, in Bolivar, MO, Maud Clegg, b. c?1885

[V6]2196. [11]4. John Allison Tuckness, b. 30 March 1887, MO; m. 27 June 1917, Jordan Valley, OR, Lena Anawalt, b. c?1887

[V6]2197. [11]5. Rosa Margret Tuckness, b. 22 April 1889; m. 29 Nov 1914, Tom William Gladden, b. c?1889

[V6]2198. [11]6. Lottie Abigail Tuckness, b. 12 May 1891; m. 19 Jan 1908-10, Quincy Price Clegg,

[V6]2199. [11]7. Susan Frances Tuckness, b. 14 July 1893; m. 10 Sept 1911, Pearl Hufford, b. c?1893

[V6]2200. [11]8. Jesse Foster Tuckness, b. 11 Oct 1895; m. 15 Dec 19__, in Ekalaka, MT, Esther I. Fowler, b. c?1895

[V6]2201. [11]9. Henry Jackson Tuckness, b. 3 Oct 1897; m. 22 Sept 1920, Louise Anwalt,

[V6]2202. [11]10. Floyd Tuckness, b. 31 Oct 1901; m. ______

Reuben Joseph Breshears and Margaret Buckles

v6 2088. [10]6. **Reuben Joseph "Rube" Breshears**, (s/o William Arthur Breshears and Abigail Jane Batten), b. 30 June 1864, Polk Co, MO; d. 26 Nov 1932, Polk Co, MO; m. 7 Sept 1885, in Dallas Co, MO (Book 4, #230, "by A.A. Ramsey, JP"), ***Margaret "Meg" Cena Buckles***, b. 18 April 1867, Butler, MO, d. 28 June 1935, Jackson Co, MO, bur Breshears cem, d/o Tennessee Buckles and Margaret Pierce. Rube and Meg both bur Breshears Cem, Polk Co, MO.

Family of Reuben Joseph Breshears and Margaret Buckles:

V6 2203. [11]1. **Edward Linville Breshears**, b. 15 Jan 1887, Jackson Co, MO, bur somewhere in Oregon.

V6 2204. [11]2. ***William Jackson "Jack" Breshears**, b. 27 Aug 1889, Polk Co, MO, d. 21 July 1971, Independence, MO; m. 19 Nov 1910, in Bolivar, Polk Co, MO, ***Minnie Lois Brooks***,

V6 2205. [11]3. **Thomas Mitchell Breshears**, b. 1 Jan 1892, d. 30 Dec 1949, Ontario, Idaho

V6 2206. [11]4. **Mary Anna "Margaret" Breshears**, b. 10 Feb 1894, d. 12 July 1898, bur Breshears Cem, Polk Co, MO

V6 2207. [11]5. **Elmer Claud Breshears**, b. 9 Sept 1902, d. 13 May 1971, bur Mt. View Cem, Polk Co, MO; m.1. ***Lola Connis***; m.2. ***Edna Mabel Morris***, b. 18 July 1902, d. 30 March 1930; m.3. ***Shirley Faye Hyles***,

Family of Elmer Breshears and Lola Connis:

V6 2208. [12]1. **Lora Belle Breshears**,

V6 2209. [12]2. **Erma Lee Breshears**,

V6 2210. [12]3. **June Breshears**,

V6 2211. [12]4. **Ethel Mae Breshears**,

Family of Elmer Breshears and Edna Morris:

V6 2212. [12]5. **Claude Vernon Breshears**, b. 10 Feb 1922; d. 13 May 1987; m. ***Laurene Mae Lightfoot***, b. 12 Feb 1923, d. 23 April 1989

V6 2213. [13]1. **Claudia Sue Breshears**,

V6 2214. [13]2. **Larna Breshears**,

V6 2215. [13]3. **Norman Breshears**,

V6 2216. [13]4. **Noland Breshears**,

V6 2217. [13]5. **Nevin Breshears**,

V6 2218. [13]6. **Naman Breshears**,

V6 2219. [12]6. **Wilbur Dale Breshears**,

V6 2220. [12]7. **Evelyn Breshears**,

V6 2221. [11]6. **Homer Merritt Breshears**, b. 12 Dec 1903, d. 26 Nov 1970, bur Reed Cem, Halfway, Polk Co, MO; m. 1 Feb 1932, ***Mary Hazel Warren***, b. 25 July 1907, d/o W. Warren and Retta Shaw.

V6 2222. [12]1. **Charles Homer Breshears**, b. 1 Feb 1932; m. 28 April 1951, ***Virginia Lee Wolfe***, b. 2 Dec 1932, d/o R. Wolfe and Kathryn Rogers

V6 2223. [13]1. **Kathy Lynn Breshears**, b. 21 March1953; m. ***Robert Wagoner***,

V6 2224. [13]2. **Janet Lee Breshears**, b. 1 May 1956; m. ***Gary Drake***,

V6 2225. [13]3. **Charles Allen Breshears**, b. 27 Aug 1962; m. ***Judy Noel***,

V6 2226. [13]4. **Gail Breshears**,

V6 2227. [12]2. **Barbara Sue Breshears**, b. 19 May 1938, d. 10 Dec 1940

V6 2228. [11]7. **Reuben Alden "Buster" Breshears**, b. 10 March 1905, d. 12 July 1975, bur Mt. View Cem, Polk Co, MO; m. 5 Sept 1924, ***Velma Farmer***, b. 26 July 1904, d. 10 Dec 1999, d/o John Farmer and Susan Arminda.

V6 2229. [12]1. **Marvin Alden Breshears**, b. 3 July 1925; m. 8 Feb 1946, ***Marjorie Fay Rinck***, d/o Robert Rinck and Mary Parrott

V6 2230. [13]1. **Karen Sue Breshears**, b. 12 Nov 1946; m. ***Robert McKee***,

V6 2231. [13]2. **Kyle Max Breshears**, b. 27 May 1948; m. ***Anna Tobin***,

V6 2232. [13]3. **Lindel Dee Breshears**, b. 1 Aug 1951

William Jackson "Jack" Breshears and Minnie Lois Brooks

[v6]**2206.** [11]2. **William Jackson "Jack" Breshears**, (s/o Reuben Joseph "Rube" Breshears and Margaret Cena "Meg" Buckles), b. 27 Aug 1889, Polk Co, MO, d. 21 July 1971, Independence, MO; m. 19 Nov 1910, in Bolivar, Polk Co, MO, ***Minnie Lois Brooks***, b. 23 April 1892, Goodson, MO, d. 14 Dec 1983, Springfield, MO, d/o Theophilus Brooks and Sarah Harper. Both Jack and Minnie bur Mt. View Cem, Polk Co, MO. They named their daughters for flowers.

Figure 29: William Jackson "Jack" Breshears in 1909. Thanks to Patty Warren for the photo.

Family of William Jackson Breshears and Minnie Lois Brooks:

[V6]2233. [12]1. **Violet Eva Breshears**, b. 10 Dec 1911, Goodson, MO, d. 14 Aug 1992, Independence, MO, bur Mt. View Cem, Polk Co, MO; m.1. 12 March 1932, in Bolivar, Polk Co, MO, ***Earl Edmund Angle***, b. 25 July 1909, Halfway, MO, d. 26 Oct 1959, Mt. Vernon, MO, s/o Phillip Angle and Nora Standley; m.2. 1963, in Independence, MO, ***William Elbert Church***, b. 26 Oct 1909, d. 21 Dec 1986

[V6]2234. [13]1. Phillip Lee Angle, b. 20 Jan 1934, Limon Co, MO, d. 1 Nov 1979, Kansas City MO, bur Mt. View Cem, Polk Co, MO; m. 1 Aug 1954, in Goodson, Polk Co, MO, Martha Ann Potter, b. 19 April 1936

[V6]2235. [13]2. Kathryn Sue Angle, b. 31 July 1950, d. 30 April 1951, bur Mt. View Cem, Polk Co, MO

[V6]2236. [12]2. **Pansy Anna Jane Breshears**, b. 25 Oct 1913, d. 16 June 1990, Springfield, MO, bur Mt. View Cem,

Polk Co, MO; m. 22 Dec 1935, ***Wayne Leroy Angle***, b. 22 Oct 1913, Halfway, MO

[V6]2237. [13]1. Wilma Lois Angle, b. 22 May 1937, Polk Co, MO; m. c1958, in California, Roger Gregg,

[V6]2238. [13]2. Carol Ann Angle, b. 4 Oct 1938, California; m.1. 17 June 1944, in Strafford, MO, Paul Prosser; m.2. c1963, Don Taylor

[V6]2239. [12]3. **Nita Rose Breshears**, b. 20 Nov 1916, Goodson, MO, d. 9 May 1994, Omaha, Nebraska; m. 23 Sept 1933, in Bolivar, Polk Co, MO, ***Roy Ora Abel***, b. 10 Sept 1912, Goodson, MO, d. 17 March 1980, Popilion, Nebraska.

[V6]2240. [13]1. Ross Ray Abel, b. 23 April 1934, Colorado, d. 12 March 1985, Plattsmouth, NE; m. 15 May 1955, Virginia Lee Whally, b. 23 July 1933

[V6]2241. [13]2. Linda Lucile Abel; m. Elmer C. Jones Jr

[V6]2242. [13]3. Sandra Sue Abel; m. Thomas J. Kurt,

[V6]2243. [12]4. **Lily Margaret Breshears**, b. 1 Dec 1918, Goodson, MO; m. 22 Sept 1934, in Goodson, Polk Co, MO, ***Dwight Marshall Farmer***, b. 9 Feb 1914, Santa Paula, CA, d. 8 Nov 1994, Springfield, MO

[V6]2244. [13]1. Shirley Timothene Farmer, b. 24 April 1936; m. 17 Oct 1953, in Goodson, Polk Co, MO, Jamie George Brakebill, b. 17 Oct 1935, Santa Paula, CA

[V6]2245. [13]2. Glenda Carol Farmer, b. 22 Oct 1937, Santa Paula, CA; m. 24 Sept 1990, Walter Chapman, b. 29 Dec 1935, Kansas City, MO

[V6]2246. [12]5. **Glen D. Breshears**, b. 10 Dec 1920, Goodson, MO; m. 5 Oct 1946, in Montgomery City, MO, ***Patricia Madalene Love***, b. 16 April, Mexico, Audrian Co, MO, d/o Robert Love and Hetty Gowin

[V6]2247. [13]1. **Patricia Ann Breshears**, b. 17 June 1947, Goodson, MO; m. 28 Aug 1966, in Goodson, Polk Co, MO, ***Gary Lee Warren***, b. 24 Oct 1946, Springfield, MO. Two ch: Susie and Todd Warren.

[V6]2248. [13]2. **Randal Thomas Breshears**, b. 4 July 1948, Goodson, MO; m. 1 June 1969, at Halfway, Polk Co, MO, ***Janice Kay Short***, b. 9 Feb

1948, St. Louis, MO

V[6]2249. [13]3. **Terry Lynn Breshears**, b. 21 Oct 1953, Humansville, MO; m. 4 June 1977, in Tullahoma, TN, ***Tina Rhea Woodham***, b. 24 Sept 1957, Talladega, AL

V[6]2250. [13]4. **Kerry Glen Breshears**, b. 21 Oct 1953, Humansville, MO, d. 14 Feb 1954, Bolivar, Polk Co, MO, bur Mt. View Cem, Polk Co, MO

V[6]2251. [13]5. **Carolyn Jane Breshears**, b. 23 Nov 1959, Humansville, MO; m. 13 Aug 1972, at Halfway, Polk Co, MO, ***Frank Lewis Stoner***, b. 23 June 1947, Parkin, AR

V[6]2252. [12]6. **R.T. Breshears**, b. 2 July 1924, Goodson, Polk, Co, MO; m. 24 Nov 1951, in Independence, MO, ***Rozella Grace Stoner***, b. 13 July 1923

V[6]2253. [13]1. **Alan Louis Breshears**, b. 16 Oct 1952, Independence, MO; m. 8 May 1982, ***Sandra Lynne Lepage***, b. 9 April 1958

V[6]2254. [12]7. **Rev. Nevin Jack Breshears**, b. 2 April 1926, Goodson, Polk Co, MO; m. 21 Dec 1946, in Berryville, AR, ***Betty Josephine Lane***, b. 7 Dec 1927, Halfway, MO, d. 26 June 1994, Bolivar, Polk Co, MO, d/o William Jackson Lane and Lucy Pearl Roberts,

V[6]2255. [13]1. **Timothy Jack Breshears**, b. 26 Aug 1949, Santa Paula, CA

V[6]2256. [13]2. **Linda Marie Breshears**, b. 2 April 1952, Halfway, MO, d. 17 Oct 1952, Springfield, MO, bur Mt View Cem, Polk Co, MO

V[6]2257. [13]3. **Joseph Paul Breshears**, b. 25 Oct 1957, Humansville, MO; m. 1 May 1994, ***Margaret Sue Horton***, b. 10 March 1964

V[6]2258. [13]4. **Samuel Lee Breshears**, b. 22 Dec 1958, Humansville, MO

V[6]2259. [13]5. **Mary Ruth Breshears**, b. 17 Sept 1961, Humansville, MO; m. 20 Dec 1980, in Goodson, Polk Co, MO, ***Wayne Ethridge***, b. 10 June 1961, Bolivar, Polk Co, MO

V[6]2260. [12]8. **David Brooks Breshears**, b. 6 June 1928, Goodson, Polk Co, MO, d. 16 April 1987,

Springfield, MO, bur Mt. View Cem, Polk Co, MO; m. 14 Oct 1947, in Los Angeles, CA, ***Peggy Sue Lane***, b. 14 March 1930, Halfway, MO

[V6]2261. [13]1. **David Gary Breshears**, b. 24 March 1948, Los Angeles, CA; m. 18 Oct 1975, in Nashville, TN, ***Joanie Elaine Cantrell***, b. 7 Aug 1951

[V6]2262. [13]2. **William Kent Breshears**, b. 15 Nov 1949, Kansas City, MO; m.1. c1969, ***Gail Adams***, m.2. c1971, ***Barbara Allen***, b. 15 June 1951, m.3. c1978, ***Debbie Bethel***,

[V6]2263. [13]3. **Janice Kay Breshears**, b. 12 Dec 1951, Kansas City, MO; m. 20 Dec 1975, in Nashville, TN, ***Ted William Gaw***, b. 22 Sept 1957

[V6]2264. [13]4. **Steven Lee Breshears**, b. 28 June 1954; m. 24 March 1980, in Nashville, TN, ***Ellen Tucker Barnes***, b. 22 Sept 1957

[V6]2265. [13]5. **Kevin Lane Breshears**, b. 20 July 1961, Kansas City, MO; m. ***Tamara Pow Gleason***,

[V6]2266. [12]9. **Donald Mark Breshears**, b. 15 April 1931, Goodson, MO; m. 10 July 1953, in Aldrich, MO, ***Emma Elizabeth Payne***, b. 12 Jan 1937, Sentinel, MO, d/o James Luther Payne and Lillie Howard,

[V6]2267. [13]1. **Joan Elizabeth Breshears**, b. 26 Oct 1954, Springfield, MO; m. 1 March 1975, ***Johnnie Allen Leuty***, b. 4 May 1949

[V6]2268. [13]2. **Daniel Mark Breshears**, b. 30 Oct 1955, Springfield, MO; m. 9 April 1977, ***Sherry Jo Shadwick***, b. 12 Nov 1957

[V6]2269. [13]3. **Donna Jean Breshears**, b. 21 May 1958, Springfield, MO

[V6]2270. [13]4. **Sharon Ann Breshears**, b. 30 Oct 1962, Kansas City, MO

[V6]2271. [12]10. **Adrian Lee Breshears**, b. 25 Dec 1932, Goodson, Polk Co, MO; m. 27 June 1953, in Cliquot, MO, ***Ethel Irene Needham***, b. 25 Dec 1934

[V6]2272. [13]1. **Gwendolyn Irene Breshears**, b. 8 Feb 1954, Springfield, MO; m. 17 Aug 1973, in Blue

Springs, MO, ***Timothy Ross Cogan***, b. 11 Jan 1953

[V6]2273. [13]2. **Adrianna Gay Breshears**, b. 21 Sept 1956; m.1. 4 Sept 1977, ***Ricky Don Monks***, b. 4 Sept 1952; m.2. 10 Nov 1983, ***Gary Alan Hall***, b. 24 Sept 1950

[V6]2274. [13]3. **Melody Gail Breshears**, b. 18 July 1958, Kansas City, MO; m. 28 Aug 1978, ***Michael Ray Bromley***, b. 6 April 1952

[V6]2275. [13]4. **Al Monty Breshears**, b. 22 Oct 1959, Kansas City, MO;

[V6]2276. [13]5. **Mitzi Michelle Breshears**, b. 2 Jan 1961, Kansas City, MO; m.1. 14 March 1981, ***David Brooks Laster***, b. 26 March 1955; m.2. 11 March 1995, ***Glenn Eugene Rankin***, b. 16 June 1967

[V6]2277. [13]6. **Monica Mae Breshears**, b. 22 Feb 1962; m. 21 Aug 1990, ***Gary French***, b. 9 Nov 1961

[V6]2278. [12]11. **Jerroll Theo Breshears**, (twin), b. 18 Oct 1934, Goodson, Polk Co, MO; m.1. 31 Oct 1954, in Cliquot, MO, ***Sylvia Simmons***,; m.2. 30 March 1963, in Platt City, MO, ***Maureen Rose Stack***, b. 17 Jan 1942, Kansas City, MO

[V6]2279. [13]1. **Bruce Earl Breshears**, (s/o Sylvia Simmons), b. 2 Aug 1955, Kansas City, MO

[V6]2280. [13]2. **Michael David Breshears**, (s/o Maureen Stack), b. 15 March 1954, Kansas City, KS, m. 21 May 1988, in Bolivar, Polk Co, MO, ***Melissa Dawn Neal***,

[V6]2281. [13]3. **Karen Rose Breshears**, b. 6 Nov 1966, Kansas City, KS; m. there 18 May 1986, ***Brian Cobb***, b. there 6 Jan 1964

[V6]2282. [13]4. **Susan Kay Breshears**, b. 30 March 1970, Kansas City, KS; m. 1 Jan 1995, in Kansas City, MO, ***Gary Osten***,

[V6]2283. [12]12. **Deryll Joe Breshears**, (twin, born one day after his brother), b. 19 Oct 1934, d. 26 March 1935, Goodson, MO, bur Mt. View Cem, Polk Co, MO

22. JESSE CARROLL BRESHEARS and Rhoda Catherine Jump

v6 1913. 9 6. **Jesse Carroll Breshears**, (s/o John Breshears and Naoma Ann Hogg), b. 17 Dec 1830, Lawrence Co, TN, d. 15 Feb 1902, Polk Co, MO, bur Lindley Creek; m. 1 Feb 1855, in Polk Co, MO, ***Rhoda Catherine Jump***, b. 22 Dec 1838, St Louis, MO, d. 11 May 1911, Polk Co, MO, bur Lindley Creek Cem, d/o Rev. James Jump and Eulila Palmer.

Family of Jesse Carroll Breshears and Rhoda Catherine Jump:

V6 2341. 10 1. ***James Knox Polk Breshears, II** (named for an uncle, as well as a president), b. 15 June 1856; m. 18 Nov 1880, in Polk Co, MO, ***Rebecca J. Anderson***,

V6 2342. 10 2. ***John Henry Breshears**, b. 6 March 1858, Polk Co, MO, d. 15 Jan 1905, Polk Co, MO, bur Lindley Creek Cem; m.1. ***E.T. Gent***, b. 15 Feb 1862 (mother of the children); m.2. ***Louisa Buckles***,

V6 2343. 10 3. **Naomi Elizabeth Breshears**, b. 17 April 1860, near Bolivar, Polk Co, MO, d. 1864, age 4, bur Lindley Creek Cem.

V6 2344. 10 4. **Joseph Carroll Breshears**, b. 15 Oct 1862, MO, may have died in infancy: "Child Breshears" bur Lindley Creek Cem.

V6 2345. 10 5. **Sophronia Angeline Breshears**, b. 17 Aug 1864, Lindley Creek, Polk Co, MO, d. 8 June 1882, age 17, bur Lindley Creek Cem.

V6 2346. 10 6. ***Mary Lucinda Breshears**, b. 14 Oct 1866, Goodson, Polk Co, MO; m.1. 19 June 1885, Polk Co, MO ***Charles Leslie Gladden***; m.2. 11 Jan 1896, Dallas Co, MO, ***George W. Holt***,

V6 2347. 10 7. **George Washington Breshears**, b. 4 Dec 1868, MO, d. 1959, Bolivar, Polk Co, MO, bur Greenwood Cem, Bolivar, Polk Co, MO; m. ***Emma Patison***, b. c?1868

V62348. 111. **Jesse C. Breshears**, b. c?1894; m. ***Myrtle Farmer***,

V62349. 108. **Missouri Bell Breshears**, b. 9 March 1871, Lindley Creek, MO; d. in infancy, 6 April 1878, and bur Lindley Creek Cem, Polk Co, MO

V62350. 109. **Jesse Simon Breshears**, b. 24 Dec 1873, MO; d. in infancy, 7 Sept 1878, and bur Lindley Creek Cem, Polk Co, MO

V62351. 1010. ***Matoka Erickson Breshears**, b. 17 Oct 1876, Polk Co, MO, d. there, 29 April 1905, bur Lindley Creek Cem; m. 25 Aug 1901, ***Ida Rush***,

V62352. 1011. **Lewis Hardin Breshears**, b. 11 May 1879, MO, d. 13 Sept 1879

James Knox Polk Breshears, II and Rebecca J. Anderson

v62341. 101. **James Knox Polk Breshears, II** (s/o Jesse Carroll Breshears and Rhoda Catherine Jump; named for an uncle, as well as a president), b. 15 June 1856, near Lindley Creek, Polk Co, MO, d. 31 March 1940, Polk Co, MO, bur Greenwood Cem, Bolivar, Polk Co, MO; m. 18 Nov 1880, in Polk Co, MO, ***Rebecca J. Anderson***, b. 21 Sept 1860, d. 5 July 1915.

Family of James Knox Polk Breshears, II, and Rebecca J. Anderson:

V62353. 111. **Joseph Breshears**, b. 30 June 1884, d. 30 June 1884, Polk Co, MO, bur Lindley Creek Cem, Polk Co, MO.

V62354. 112. **Jesse Calvin Breshears**, b. 24 June 1887, d. 9 Aug 1888, bur Lindley Creek Cem, Polk Co, MO

V62355. 113. **Everett Breshears**, b. 1888, Polk Co, MO, d. 1980-90, Neosho, MO; m. 26 Nov 1911, in Bolivar, Polk Co, MO, ***Nellie Hancock***, b. c1888

V62356. 121. **Thelma Breshears**, b. 1914; m. ***Herbert Douglas***.

V62357. 131. Janice Douglas; m. Cecil Denny. Ch: Douglas; and Bradley Denny

V62358. 132. Dwight Douglas; m. Bonnie Douglas (not related). Ch: Steven Douglas

[V6]2359. [11]4. **Clara Breshears**, b. c1890, MO, d. 1985, Stanley, ID; m.1. 1910, MO, ***Oren Bernard***, b. 1886, MO; m.2. ***Jason Vaught***, b. 1888, Stanley, ID (Jason Vaught had been previously married to Clara Ethel Breshears, (#xxx) d/o James Monroe Breshears and Elizabeth Southard (see Bob Hiram Breshears entry).

John Henry Breshears and E.T. Gent

[v6]2342. [10]2. **John Henry Breshears**, (s/o Jesse Carroll Breshears and Rhoda Catherine Jump), b. 6 March 1858, Polk Co, MO, d. 15 Jan 1905, Polk Co, MO, bur Lindley Creek Cem; m.1. ***E.T. Gent***, b. 15 Feb 1862 (mother of the children); m.2. ***Louisa Buckles***, b. 1 May 1884, d. 24 March 1930, Louisburg, Dallas Co, MO, d/o William Buckles and ______.

Family of John Henry Breshears and E.T. Gent:

[V6]2360. [11]1. ***Matoke Elvira Breshears**, b. 22 Feb 1885,
[V6]2361. [11]2. ***Volina Ellen Breshears**, b. 7 Oct 1886,
[V6]2362. [11]3. ***Rhoda Catherine Breshears**, b. 29 Nov 1887,
[V6]2363. [11]4. ***Letha Louise Breshears**, b. 5 Aug 1889,
[V6]2364. [11]5. **Naomi Elizabeth "Oma" Breshears**, b. 14 Dec 1890, Polk Co, MO, d. 9 March 1979; m. ***William Thomas "Buck" Huckaby***, b. c?1891
[V6]2365. [12]1. Frances Ann Huckaby, (adopted)
[V6]2366. [11]6. **Johanna Lenora Breshears**, b. 18 Nov 1892, Polk Co, MO, d. 14 May 1973; m. ***Harrison Payne***, b. c?1893, of Polk Co, MO
[V6]2367. [12]1. Perry Alvin Payne, b. 28 May 1918, d. 3 Oct 1918
[V6]2368. [11]7. **Henry Breshears**, b. c1895, MO, d. 1980-89; m. ***Nell*** _______,
[V6]2369. [12]1. **Dale Breshears**,
[V6]2370. [11]8. **Verna M. Breshears**, b. 25 Feb 1897, d. 2 May 1941; m. ***Henry Payne***, brother of Harrison Payne, her sister's husband,
[V6]2371. [12]1. Lorene Payne, b. 8 Jan 1915; m. Bob Lake
[V6]2372. [12]2. Glen Payne, b. 2 Aug 1916; m.1. Lois _____; m.2. Bonnie ______,

[V6]2373. [12]3. Carl Payne, b. 10 Sept 1918; m. Geneva ______,

[V6]2374. [12]4. Kenneth Payne, b. 4 Feb 1921; m. Leona ______,

[V6]2375. [12]5. Lavona Payne, b. 12 April 1926, d. 21 June 1985; m. Charles R. Mishler, Sr

[v6]2360. [11]1. **Matoke Elvira Breshears**, (d/o John Henry Breshears and E.T. Gent), b. 22 Feb 1885, Polk Co, MO, d. 26 Feb 1960, Jasper Co, MO; m.10 Jan 1909, in Polk Co, MO, ***Samuel Paul Audrey***, b. 8 April 1880, d. 1 Sept 1968, Jasper Co, MO

[V6]2376. [12]1. Agnes Ruth Audrey, b. 17 June 1910; m. James Henry Breeden.

[V6]2377. [13]1. Loretta June Breeden; m. Jerry Paul Datson. Ch: Carol Ann; and Lonnie David Dotson

[V6]2378. [12]2. Edith May Audrey, b. 1912; m. ______ Steele. Ch: Larry Gene Steele

[V6]2379. [12]3. Leonard Ross Audrey, b. 1913, d. 1989; m.1. Dorothy White (3 ch: Garey Gene; Dickey; and Dale Audrey); m.2. Mary J. Stockton

[V6]2380. [12]4. Elbert Guy Audrey, b. 1915; m. _______, Ch: Carl Dean Audrey

[V6]2381. [12]5. Arthur Clyde Audrey, b. 1916; m. Mildred Virginia Smith.

[V6]2382. [13]1. Judith Lynn Audrey; m. John Leon Starchman. Ch: John Ryan; Joseph Ross; and Jewell Rene Starchman

[V6]2383. [13]2. Shirley Ann Audrey; m. Leonard O. Carnes. Ch: Christopher Douglas; and Kerry Lynn Carnes

[V6]2384. [12]6. Lois Marie Audrey, b. 1918; m. ______ Rea.

[V6]2385. [13]1. Jerry Lee Rea;

[V6]2386. [13]2. Clyde David Rea; m. Viola Gaylene Lama. Ch: David Christopher Rea

[V6]2387. [12]7. Clara Eunice Audrey, b. 1920; m. Bob Datson. Ch: Vickie Sue; Jeanie; and Linda Ann Datson

^{v6}**2361.** ^{11}2. **Volina Ellen Breshears**, (d/o John Henry Breshears and E.T. Gent), b. 7 Oct 1886, Polk Co, MO, d. 21 July 1968, Buffalo, Dallas Co, MO; m. 26 Feb 1908, in Polk Co, MO, ***George Leonidas Carter,*** b. 14 Aug 1881, d. 15 Feb 1941, Louisburg, Dallas Co, MO

^{V6}2388. ^{12}1. Wava Helen Carter, b. 24 Dec 1908 (Wava is a retired teacher)

^{V6}2389. ^{12}2. Linville George Carter, b. 3 March 1910; m. Dorothy Hawkins

^{V6}2390. ^{12}3. Tabitha Volina Carter, b. 16 April 1912, d. Sept 1990; m. Roy Grant Miller.

^{V6}2391. ^{13}1. Rosalie Miller; m.1. Sterling South; m.2. Bill Main. Ch: Sandra South; and Michael South (m. Tammy Hunt. Ch: Kayleen South)

^{V6}2392. ^{12}4. Hazel Marie Carter, b. 25 May 1914, d. 25 March 1968; m. William Arvel Barclay.

^{V6}2393. ^{13}1. Shirley Barclay; m. Joe Bass.

^{V6}2394. ^{14}1. Karen Jo Bass; m. Glenn O'Dell. Ch: Cassandra O'Dell

^{V6}2395. ^{14}2. Shirley Lou Bass,

^{V6}2396. ^{14}3. Lori Lynn Bass; m. George Crouch. Ch: Jason; and Janice Crouch

^{V6}2397. ^{14}4. Paulette Marie Bass,

^{V6}2398. ^{14}5. Rhonda Jeane Bass,

^{V6}2399. ^{13}2. Larry Barclay; m. Karen Howard. Ch: Kevin; and Aaron Barclay

^{V6}2400. ^{13}3. Gary Barclay; m. Allene Catlin. Ch: Kenneth Don Barclay

^{V6}2401. ^{13}4. Karen Ellen Barclay,

^{V6}2402. ^{12}5. Linford Leonidas Carter, b. 23 Oct 1918, d. 9 Sept 1987; m. Dorothy Pauline Pitts.

^{V6}2403. ^{13}1. Connie Carter; m. Bob Austin. Ch: Douglas Austin

^{V6}2404. ^{13}2. Janice Carter; m. Troy Fellers. Ch: Shelly; and Todd Fellers

^{V6}2405. ^{13}3. Joe Carter; m. Gloria Phillips. Ch: Kellie; Julie; and Randi Carter

^{V6}2406. ^{13}4. Carl Carter; m. Kathy ______. Ch: Kirby; Russell; Stacy; and Carl Carter, II

^{V6}2407. ^{13}5. Patsy Carter; m.1. Keith Richards; m.2.

______ Garcia. Ch: Travis Richards; and two unknown Garcia

[V6]2408. [12]6. Lloyd Reed Carter, b. 27 April 1922, d. 27 Feb 1928, age 5+

[v6]2362. [11]3. **Rhoda Catherine Breshears**, (d/o John Henry Breshears and E.T. Gent), b. 29 Nov 1887, Polk Co, MO, d. 25 July 1958, Buffalo, Dallas Co, MO; m. ***Joseph Miller***, b. c1875, Dallas Co, MO, d. 1952, Urbana, Dallas Co, MO, s/o Thomas Miller and Mary Jones.

[V6]2409. [12]1. Lionel Paul Miller, b. 3 Aug 1918, d. 8 Oct 1974; m. Maxine Eldred.

[V6]2410. [13]1. Brenda Miller;

[V6]2411. [13]2. Barbara Miller; m. ______ Boaz. Ch: David Boaz

[V6]2412. [12]2. Lela Grace Miller, b. 1921

[V6]2413. [12]3. Lawrence Allen Miller, b. 1924

[v6]2363. [11]4. **Letha Louise Breshears**, (d/o John Henry Breshears and E.T. Gent), b. 5 Aug 1889, Polk Co, MO, d. 29 Jan 1962, near Kansas City, MO; m. ***Clarence Erba Fisher***, b. 21 March 1874, d. 26 June 1952

[V6]2414. [12]1. Dean Washington Fisher, b. 27 July 1914, d. 6 March 1966; m. Lesta Fisher.

[V6]2415. [13]1. Janis Fisher; m. John Crain. Ch: Alan; and Denise Crain

[V6]2416. [13]2. Betty Fisher; m. Elvin Pettit

[V6]2417. [14]1. Randy Pettit,

[V6]2418. [14]2. Vicki Lynn Pettit; m. John Phillips. Ch: Kimberly Dawn Phillips

[V6]2419. [14]3. Terry Dean Pettit; m. Ann Hartman

[V6]2420. [14]4. Timothy Ray Pettit; m. Marie Ann Horchrick. Ch: Jeremy Ray Pettit

[V6]2421. [14]5. Cindy Pettit,

[V6]2422. [14]6. Scott Pettit,

[V6]2423. [14]7. Mark Pettit,

[V6]2424. [13]3. Lavona Fisher; m. Ivan Acock. Ch: Toni Marie; and Melissa Acock

[V6]2425. [12]2. Roy Erbie Fisher, b. 1917; m. Wilma Farmer. Ch: Twila Fisher (m. Denny Jones. Ch: Karen Sue;

and Jenefer Elaine Jones)

[V6]2426. [12]3. Ralph Thomas Fisher, b. 1919; m. Hazel Marjorie Post. Ch: Cheryl; and Marlin Fisher (m. Daion Johnson. Ch: Lance; Marla; and Brett Fisher)

[V6]2427. [12]4. Mary Lou Fisher, b. 1921; m. Dean Gladden.

[V6]2428. [13]1. Louise Gladden; m. James Williams. Ch: Kim; Deana; and Jimmy Williams

[V6]2429. [13]2. Helen Marie Gladden; m. Mike Stephens. Ch: Mary Helen; Carmine Marie; and Nancy Stephens

[V6]2430. [13]3. Wayne Gladden; m. Deborah Jane Stewart. Ch: Phillip Gladden

[V6]2431. [12]5. Jessie Van Fisher, b. 1924; m. Lillie Warner.

[V6]2432. [13]1. Dennis Fisher; m. Linda Wolfe. Ch: Richard Lee; Brenda; Roy Paul; and Robin Fisher

[V6]2433. [12]6. Herbert Lee Fisher, b. 1926

[V6]2434. [12]7. Morris T. Fisher, b. 1928; m. Kay Simpson.

[V6]2435. [13]1. Michael Fisher; m. Donna Ellington. Ch: Gerald Michael; and Matthew John Fisher

[V6]2436. [13]2. Donna Ray Fisher; m. Gary Staret. Ch: Brea Ann; and Samantha Glynn Staret

[V6]2437. [13]3. Robert A. Fisher,

[V6]2438. [12]8. Ruth Marie Fisher, b. 1929; m.1. David Clopine; m.2. Louis Ammell; m.3. Harry A. Smith

[V6]2439. [12]9. Letha Alene Fisher, b. 21 Aug 1931, d. 21 Feb 1932

Mary Lucinda Breshears and Charles Leslie Gladden/ George W. Holt

[v6]2346. [10]6. **Mary Lucinda Breshears**, (d/o Jesse Carroll Breshears and Rhoda Catherine Jump), b. 14 Oct 1866, Goodson, Polk Co, MO, d. there, 14 Oct 1907, bur Lindley Creek Cem, Polk Co, MO; m.1. 19 June 1885, Polk Co, MO ***Charles Leslie Gladden***, b. 16 April 1860, Buffalo, MO, d. 28 June 1889, Polk Co, MO; m.2. 11 Jan 1896, Dallas Co, MO, ***George W. Holt***, b. 29 May 1863, Dallas Co, MO, d. 24 Dec 1940, Polk Co, MO.

Family of Mary Lucinda Breshears and Charles Leslie Gladden:

[V6]2440. [11]1. Florence Elnora "Nora" Gladden, b. 19 April 1886, Polk Co, MO, 17 July 1970, Springfield, Greene Co, MO; m. 10 Aug 1913, in Louisburg, MO, William Kelly McGee, b. 13 March 1863, Buffalo, Dallas, MO, d. 31 July 1942

[V6]2441. [12]1. Minnie Willa McGee, b. 27 Dec 1914; m. Carl D. Fowler, b. 1921. ***Minnie (McGee) Fowler*** was a researcher in Breshears Families.

[V6]2442. [13]1. Linda Lou Fowler; m. Jack L. Crawford

[V6]2443. [14]1. Julie Lynn Crawford; m. Ray Anthony Graves. Ch: Matthew Ray; and Andrew James Graves

[V6]2444. [14]2. Jeannie Carrol Crawford; m. Pate Eugene Leach

[V6]2445. [13]2. Sandra Sue Fowler; m. Harold Don Maness. Ch: Scott Joseph; Paul Wesley; and Keith Andrew Maness

[V6]2446. [13]3. Larry Dale Fowler;

[V6]2447. [13]4. Brenda Jeanne Fowler; m. Billy Dean "Bill" Adams. Ch: Sherry Adams; (m.1. ______ Morris; m.2. ______ Amos. Ch: Cristie Morris); Danny; Billy; and Jason Adams

[V6]2448. [12]2. William Kelly McGee, Jr, b. 30 Aug 1916, Buffalo, Dallas Co, MO, d. 7 July 1969, Springfield, Greene Co, MO; m. Mary Lou Norton, b. 27 Nov 1922, d. 27 Aug 1980

[V6]2449. [12]3. Carl Lawrence McGee, b. 2 July 1918, Buffalo, Dallas Co, MO; m. Hazel Faye Ethridge.

[V6]2450. [13]1. Shirley Kay McGee,

[V6]2451. [13]2. Jimmie Ray McGee; m. Martha Tomlinson. Ch: Amy; and Ryan Kelly McGee

[V6]2452. [13]3. Janice Fay McGee; m. Gary Mitchell. Ch: Paula Lynn; Pamela Rae; and Cheryl Mitchell

[V6]2453. [11]2. Phelura Ann Gladden, b. 14 Sept 1887, Polk Co, MO, d. 27 Feb 1921, Anaheim, CA; m. 14 Nov 1906, Leo Johnson

V6 2454. [12]1. Sylvia Johnson, b. 6 Sept 1907; m. Claude O. Crain.

V6 2455. [13]1. Coney Crain; m. Aline Christian. Ch: Kelly; Jamie; Joyce (m. Scott Bullard. Ch: Jeffrey and Jason Bullard); Danny Allen; and Connie Crain

V6 2456. [13]2. Marvin Allen Crain;

V6 2457. [13]3. Genevieve Crain; m. Charles Guinn. Ch: Brad; and Jeff Guinn

V6 2458. [13]4. Ronald Arvil Crain; m. Gale Hilderbrand. Ch: Becky; and David Crain

V6 2459. [12]2. Hazel Johnson, b. 14 Jan 1909, d. 1938; m. ______ Fluetsch. Ch: John Fluetsch (m. _____. Ch: Ray; and Jay Fluetsch)

V6 2460. [12]3. Colin Lark Johnson, b. 28 July 1911, d. 10 June 1958; m. Helen Lorene Rush. Ch: Daryl (m.1. Dianne Fairchild. Ch: Hope Yvette Johnson); and Cheryl Johnson

V6 2461. [11]2. Jesse W. Holt, b. 7 Oct 1896, MO, d. 16 Aug 1897

V6 2462. [11]3. Graydon Arthur Holt, b. 30 Nov 1897, MO, d. 1 Aug 1905

V6 2463. [11]4. Zelina Catherine Holt, b. 30 Nov 1899; m. Herman Thornton

V6 2464. [12]1. Josephine Thornton, m. Leonard Flint

V6 2465. [12]2. Virginia Thornton, b. 1917, d. 1937; m. Burlu Benhem. Ch: dau Benhem

V6 2466. [11]5. Mary Elizabeth Holt, b. 12 Sept 1900, d. 31 July 1905

V6 2467. [11]6. Ruth Ann Holt, b. 13 Jan, d. 26 Sept 1902, MO

V6 2468. [11]7. Everett George Holt, b. 18 March 1903, MO, d. 1 Feb 1905

V6 2469. [11]8. Orpha Ann Holt, b. 22 June 1906, d. 21 Oct 1907

Matoka Erickson Breshears and Ida Rush

v6 2351. [10]10. **Matoka Erickson Breshears**, (s/o Jesse Carroll Breshears and Rhoda Catherine Jump), b. 17 Oct 1876, Polk Co, MO, d. there, 29 April 1905, bur Lindley Creek Cem; m. 25 Aug 1901, ***Ida Rush***, b. c?1876

Family of Matoka Erickson Breshears and Ida Rush:

V6 2470. 11 1. **Bessie Breshears**, b. 3 June 1902; m. ***Elva Meadors***,

V6 2471. 12 1. Leon Meadors, b. 25 Feb 1920; m. Imogene Richards.

V6 2472. 13 1. Sharon Meadors; m. James Jones. Ch: Jimmy Richard; Ryan; and Sharon Rochelle Jones

V6 2473. 13 2. Shirley Meadors; m. Floy Patrick. Ch: Kimberly; and Tamela Patrick

V6 2474. 12 2. Laverne Meadors, b. 6 Feb 1924; m.1. Loretta Fay Marin (2 ch); m.2. Patsy Vest

V6 2475. 13 1. Loretta Joy Meadors; m. Chuck Pope. Ch: Lauretta; and Christopher Pope

V6 2476. 13 2. Ron Laverne Meadors

V6 2477. 12 3. Kenneth Ray Meadors, b. 5 Sept 1932, Zona Varnell Abel.

V6 2478. 13 1. Olen Ray Meadors; m.1. Vicki Burns (2 ch); m.2. Cindy Van Schiver (1 ch). Ch: Denelle Ray; Janelle E.; and Junior Ray Meadors

V6 2479. 13 2. Jay Lee Meadors;

V6 2480. 13 3. Zelda L. Meadors; m. ______ Hobbs. Ch: Darci Hobbs

V6 2481. 13 4. Catalpi Meadors,

V6 2482. 12 4. Lloyd Dale Meadors, b. 18 Sept 1937; m. Carolyn Engledow.

V6 2483. 13 1. Jackie Dale Meadors;

V6 2484. 13 2. Vickie Carol Meadors; m. Roger Lee. Ch: Justin; and Jared Lee

V6 2485. 11 2. **Catherine Isabell Breshears**, b. 9 March 1904, d. 1980-89; m. ***Murl Jennings Black***,

V6 2486. 12 1. Eldridge Murl Black, b. 19 Nov 1921; m. ____.

V6 2487. 13 1. Robert Murl Black; m. ______. Ch: John Robert; and Tina Marie Black

V6 2488. 13 2. Katherine Marie Black; m. ______ Dodson. Ch: Joellen Dodson

V6 2489. 12 2. Vernice Jarrett Black, (twin) b. 13 June 1924; m. ______. Ch: Jarrett Ray; and Janet Lee Black

[V6]2490. [12]3. Bernice Fronzie Black, (twin) b. 13 June 1924; m. ______ Esther. Ch: Steven Lee Esther

[V6]2491. [12]4. George Ray Black, b. 3 Jan 1929, d. 29 Jan 1959, killed in an auto accident

[V6]2492. [12]5. Franklin D. Black, b. & d. 20 May 1936,

[V6]2493. [12]6. Donald Lee Black, b. 17 Sept 1939; m. ______. Ch: Mark Allen; and Michael Wade Black

23. JOHN WESTLEY BRESHEARS and Lucy Baker

[v6]1921. [9]9. **John Westley Breshears**, (s/o John Breshears and Naoma Ann Hogg), b. 24 Oct 1835, Lawrence Co, TN, d. 23 Dec 1913, near Bolivar, Polk Co, MO; m.1. ***Lucy Baker***, b. 6 Sept 1839, IN, d. 3 Sept 1888, near Bolivar, Polk Co, MO, d/o Solomon Baker and Lucy Jones; m.2. 19 Jan 1893, ***Caroline Ann E. (Brannon) Bridges***, b. 19 Jan 1863, d. 18 Aug 1923, widow of Thomas Bridges. John W. and Lucy bur Breshears Cem, Bolivar, Polk Co, MO.

Family of John Westley Breshears and Lucy Baker:

[V6]2541. [10]1. **Nathan J. Breshears**, b. 1858, Dallas Co, MO, d. 23 Aug 1939, OK; m. 8 Nov 1887, ***Mahalia F. Starnes***. Nancy Miller <nmm @texoma.net>, who sent data on the children: "I was told by my aunt that Mahalia and Nathan were divorced, and he married her sister. I don't know if she ever remarried."

[V6]2542. [11]1. **Nancy May Breshears**, b. May 1893, MO, d. 22 April 1958, Stockton, CA, bur Park View Cem; m.1. 10 Dec 1909, ***William Andrew Miles***, (6 ch), d. 1920; m.2. ***Luther Draper***

[V6]2543. [11]2. **Lucy Adeline Breshears**, b. 10 Dec 1897, MO (Soc Security lists her as born in 1892. On the 1900 census, she b. about 1897), d. 22 Aug 1993, bur in Henryetta, OK; m. ***Fred***

Meredith Fowler

V6 2544. 11 3. **Gladys M. Breshears**, b. 1909 in Oklahoma.

V6 2545. 11 4. **Grace Breshears** (unknown)

V6 2546. 11 5. **Nola B. Breshears**, b. 1895 in Oklahoma

V6 2547. 11 6. **Sarah G. Breshears** b. 1900, probably in Okmulgee, OK

V6 2548. 10 2. **Oma G.B. Breshears**, b. c1859, Dallas Co, MO, d. bef 1870

V6 2549. 10 3. **Naomi J. Breshears**, b. 1860; m. 2 Feb 1879, Dallas Co, MO, ***William Austin***,

V6 2550. 10 4. **Nancy Elizabeth Breshears**, b. 1861, Dallas Co, MO, d. 1944, bur Star Ridge Cem, Polk Co, MO; m. 11 June 1882, Dallas Co, MO, ***Charles Leonidas Carter***, b. 1857, Camden Co, MO, d. 1932, both bur Star Ridge cem, about 7 miles west of Louisburg. (data from Kim Callan).

V6 2551. 11 x. James Rosco Carter, b. Polk Co, MO, with Dr. J.E. Carter in attendance.

V6 2552. 11 x. Dessea Ellen Carter, b. Polk Co, MO, with Dr. J.E. Carter in attendance.

V6 2553. 10 5. **John Solomon Breshears**, b. 20 July 1864, Dallas Co, MO, d. 14 March 1936, Pharroh, Okfuskee Co, OK; m.1. ____, (4 ch); m.2. ***Myrtle*** ____, (no ch); m.3. 5 July 1903, at McIntosh, ID, ***Birdie Mae McCann***, (2 ch) b. 6 May 1906, TX, d. 23 May 1950, Oklahoma City, OK, d/o William McCann, Children by 1st wife:

V6 2554. 11 1. **Effien Breshears**, b. Dec 1884

V6 2555. 11 2. **Bertie E. Breshears**, b. Feb 1888

V6 2556. 11 3. **Wesley B. or D. Breshears**, b. March 1891, d. 7 June 1924

V6 2557. 11 4. **Ethel Breshears**,

Children by Birdie Mae McCann:

V6 2558. 11 5. ***William Henry "Buster" Breshears**, b. 11 Dec 1905, d. 11 Dec 1939, Fresno, CA; m. 19 Nov 1925, ***Ocee Opal Wells***,

V6 2559. 11 6. **Lloyd Breshears**,

V6 2560. 10 6. **Joseph M. Breshears**, b. 1866, Dallas Co, MO; m. 6 Oct 1886, Dallas Co, MO, ***Zoe B. Stearns***. Joseph and Zoe moved to Oklahoma.

[V6]2561. [11]1. **Joseph Edgar Breshears**, b. 1891, d. 1954

[V6]2562. [10]7. **William Grant Breshears**, b. 1869, Dallas Co, MO; m. 14 Feb 1880, Dallas Co, MO, ***Synthia E. Condren***, d/o Samuel Condren and Martha Southard. William and Synthia moved to Oklahoma.

[V6]2563. [10]8. **Charles Henry "Tex" Breshears**, b. 6 Sept 1871, Louisburg, Dallas Co, MO, d. 25 July 1954, Heppner, Morrow Co, OR; m. 28 Nov 1909, in Morrow Co, OR, ***Emma Cecilia Wright***, b. 25 May 1889, Kentland, Newton Co, Indiana, d. 19 Nov 1967, Heppner, Morrow Co, OR, d/o Charles Burmur Wright and Mary Willow. Thanks to Tom Breshears, <Breshtl @aol.com>, for data.

[V6]2564. [11]1. **Lucye Marie Patricia Breshears**, b. 30 Aug 1910, Lexington, Morrow Co, OR, d. 14 Oct 1999, Heppner, Morrow Co, OR; m. ***Wilbur Charles James Steagall***, b. 30 Octg 1909, Abingdon, VA, d. 6 March 1990, Heppner, Morrow Co, OR, s/o Thomas David Henry Steagall and Coral Rachel Shoun

[V6]2565. [11]2. **Helen Emma Breshears**, b. 1 Dec 1917, Lexington, Morrow Co, OR; m. 25 Dec 1941, ***Everett Laurance Crump***, b. _____, d. 9 Oct 2002, bur Willamette Natl Cem, Portland, OR

[V6]2566. [11]3. **Veronica Elizabeth Cecelia Breshears**, b. 5 Feb 1914, Lexington, Morrow Co, OR, d. 27 June 2000, Portland, OR; m.1. 7 Sept 1933, in Stevenson, WA, ***William Carl Whitlock***, b. 25 Dec 1906, Alvarado, VA, d. 16 Dec 1963, bur Brookings, OR

[V6]2567. [11]4. **Edwina Joan "Bunny" Breshears**, b. 21 May 1925, Heppner, Morrow Co, Or; m.1. 9 Aug 1942, in Heppner, Morrow Co, OR, ***Douglas Richard Gibson***; m.2. 14 July 1952, in The Dalles, OR, ***Malcom Richelderfer***,

[V6]2568. [10]9. **Thomas Benton Breshears**, b. 3 May 1874, Dallas Co, MO, d. 11 Jan 1955, Vancouver, WA, bur Park Hill Cem, Vancouver, WA; m. 1897, in Lebanon, MO, ***Nellie Jane Walker***, b. 26 March 1872, d.

June 1934, OK, bur Wewoka Cem, Seminole Co, OK, d/o Weaver Alexander Walker and Mary Ann Dawson. (Thanks to Tom Breshears <Breshtl@aol.com> for data.)

[V6]2569. [11]1. **Flora Belle Breshears**, b. 23 May 1898, Dustin, Indian Terr, d. 8 Oct 1972, Port Orchard, Kitsap Co, WA; m.1. ***John Rogers***, b. c?1898, Wewoka, OK; m.2. 12 April 1924, ***Paul Eugene Nichols***, b. 8 Sept 1898, d. 3 Feb 1941, s/o Martin Nichols and Ida Meng; m.3. ***Fred William Arndt***, b. 24 Sept 1900, d. 23 Jan 1963, bur Park Hill Cem, Vancouver, Clark Co, WA.

Figure 30: Thomas Benton Breshears, Flora Breshears Arndt, and Charles Henry "Tex" Breshears. Thanks to Tommy Breshears for the photo.

[V6]2570. [12]1. John Rogers Jr, b. c1920, Wewoka, OK

[V6]2571. [11]2. **Pearl Breshears**, b. 2 Sept 1902, d. May 1985, Vancouver, Clark Co, WA; m.1. ***Fred Ellis***, b. c1902; m.2. ***Bill Mischlich***,

[V6]2572. [11]3. **John Alexander Breshears**, b. 16 July 1905, Dustin, OK (I.T.), d. 13 May 1975, Pottsboro, Grayson Co, Texas; m. 6 Oct 1934, Wewoka, OK, ***Flora Marie Stiffler***, b. 11 Sept 1915, Wewoka, Seminole Co, OK, d. 3 May 2001, OkCity, bur Wewoka, OK, d/o William Albert Stiffler and Rosa Charlotte Boyd

[V6]2573. [10]10. **Luther M. Breshears**, b. 1879

Figure 31: John Alexander Breshears, s/o Thomas Benton Breshears, at work on his farm. Photo from Tommy Breshears.

William Henry "Buster" Breshears and Ocee Opal Wells:

[v6]2558. [11]5. **William Henry "Buster" Breshears**, (s/o John Solomon Breshears and his first, unknown wife), b. 11 Dec 1905, d. 11 Dec 1939, Fresno, CA; m. 19 Nov 1925, ***Ocee Opal Wells***, b. 6 May 1906, Kenefic, OK Terr., d/o Tommy Jack Wells and Isora Dot Campbell, (Data from Alta (Keeler) Breshears, Box 5, Sharon, OK 73857). "Buster" worked in the oil fields, and died of TB in CA, where he was buried. He was later exhumed and moved to Likowski Cem, near Pharoah, OK. Opal owned Opal's Telephone Answering Service in OK City. They were not divorced, as was reported erroneously in Buster's Obit.

[V6]2574. [12]1. **William Henry "Bill" Breshears, Jr**, b. 10 Oct 1926, Pharroh, OK; m. 10 June 1957, ***Alta Rose Keeler***, b. 1 Sept 1938, Denver, CO, d/o Elmer Lewis Keeler and Dorothy Mildred Winn. Bill served on USS Alaska in WW II, and worked for State of OK as a radio man, now retired. Alta is/was an antique dealer. They moved to Sharon, OK, in 1962. They have four children:

V62575. [13]1. **William Henry "Hank" Breshears, III**, b. 5 July 1958, Denver, Co; m. March 1963, in OK City, ***Robyn Waldrup***,

V62576. [13]2. **Lee Arthur Breshears**, b. 19 Aug 1959, Denver, CO

V62577. [13]3. **Cynthia Ann Breshears**, b. 25 Nov 1960. Denver, CO; m. ***James Poulton***, b. 23 Sept 1957, OK

V62578. [13]4. **Bruce Thomas Breshears**, b. 23 July 1961, Moorland, OK; m. ***Cynthia Young***, b. 13 March 1963

V62579. [12]2. **Virginia Lucille "Ginger" Breshears**, b. 28 Jan 1928, Pharroh, OK; m. 6 Aug 1936, ***Jerry DeWoody***, b. July 1923, OK, d. July 1988, OK City, s/o Thurman DeWoody and Lucille Rushing,

V62580. [13]1. Jerry Michael DeWoody, b. 14 March 1950. Mike had two sons by different women: Timothy Denar DeWoody and Danton DeWoody.

V62581. [13]2. Vance DeWoody, b. 6 Feb 1951; m. 20 Oct 1974, Raylyn Abbot, Vance has 3 ch, names unk to me.

V62582. [12]3. **John Thomas "Tom" Breshears**, b. 24 July 1929, Clearwater, OK; m.1. ***Katie Thompson*** (2 ch, both adopted by Katie's second husband, Edgar Webb); m.2. ***Margie Weems*** (4 ch; div.). John Thomas Breshears lived in Brewster, WA.

V62583. [13]1. **Barbara Ann Breshears**,

V62584. [13]2. **John Thomas Breshears**,

V62585. [13]3. **Linda Breshears**,

V62586. [13]4. **Anita Breshears**,

V62587. [13]5. **Buster Breshears**,

V62588. [13]6. **Timothy Breshears**,

24. MARGARET NAOMI BRESHEARS and Joseph Henry Jump

v6 1922. 9 10. **Margaret Naomi Breshears**, (d/o John Breshears and Naoma Ann Hogg), b. 5 April 1837, Lawrence Co, TN, d. 26 Jan 1911, Creston, Lincoln Co, Washington; m. 21 Jan 1861, Bolivar, Polk Co, MO, ***Joseph Henry Jump***, b. 29 May 1838, St. Louis, MO, d. 28 Feb 1897, Creston, Lincoln Co, Washington, s/o Rev. James Jump and Eulila Palmer; both are buried Sherman Cem, Lincoln Co, WA. (Family sheet by Ardis Dashiell)

On 5 Sept 1862, at age 24, Joseph Henry Jump enlisted in Co. M, 8th Regt, Missouri Cavalry Volunteers for a period of three years. On 17 Sept 1862, he was promoted to Corporal, and on 10 April 1865, to Sergeant. He was honorably discharged at Little Rock on 20 July 1865. While in the service, he was engaged in building roads and bridges through the Arkansas swamps on the White River, where he contracted a liver disease that was to plague him the rest of his life.

In 1877, in company with several Breshears brothers, Joseph and Margaret migrated to Idaho, by covered wagon, pulled by teams of oxen. They were accosted several times by Indians, but had no real trouble. The party stopped for a time in Ada Co, ID, before moving on to Cove, Oregon, in 1878. In 1883, the Jump family made its final move, to Washington Territory, where they settled on land north of Creston, WA. Their land there was described as SW¼, Sec 18, T27, R34E, WM (Washington Meridian?). Margaret's brothers returned to Ada, ID, where their Breshears descendants were numerous near the towns of Boise, Eagle, Star, and Middleton for many years.

Family of Margaret Breshears and Joseph Henry Jump:

V6 2589. 10 1. John Henry Jump, b. 28 Feb 1862, Bolivar, Polk Co, MO, d. 13 June 1946, bur Sherman Cem, Sherman, WA; m. 13 Oct 1887, Hartline, WA, Ida Ellen Crabtree, b. 30 Aug 1871, Marysville, CA, d.

21 July 1957, Crescent, WA.

V62590. 111. Elcia May Jump, b. 4 Sept 1890, d. 9 Jan 1891

V62591. 112. William Everett Jump,

V62592. 113. Lillian Cecile Jump,

V62593. 114. Etta Leonia Jump; (m. Miller),

V62594. 115. Carrie Alto Jump,

V62595. 116. Reuben Raymond Jump,

V62596. 117. Ruth Mary Jump,

V62597. 118. Mary Elizabeth Jump,

V62598. 119. Margaret Naomia Jump, (m. Anderson),

V62599. 1110. Ida May Jump; (m. Porgugue)

V62600. 1111. ??Iva Esther Jump,

V62601. 102. Mary Catherine Jump, b. 18 July 1866, Bolivar, Polk Co, MO, d. 5 Aug 1947, Opportunity, Spokane Co, WA; m.1. 30 Sept 1882, Elgin, OR, William S. Horrell; m.2. 15 July 1886, Francis M. Spencer, b. c1864, d. c1888, s/o Josiah Spencer and Jona Watkins; m.3. 5 Jan 1890, William Frank Simons;

V62602. 111. Walter William Horrell,

V62603. 112. Charles Franklin Spencer, b. 21 April 1887, Milton, OR, d. 10 Feb 1920, Creston, WA

V62604. 113. James Julian Spencer,

V62605. 114. Minnie May Simons, (m. Barhhart),

V62606. 115. Amy Belle Simons, (m. Bell),

V62607. 116. Gilbert Leroy Simons,

V62608. 117. Mary Neoma "Midge" Simons, (m. Furness),

V62609. 118. Alvah Russell Simons,

V62610. 119. Elsie Ellen Simons, (m. Furness),

V62611. 1110. Dollie Margaret Simons, (m. Hanson),

V62612. 1111. Joseph William Simons,

V62613. 1112. Veda Vera Simons, (m. Doty),

V62614. 1113. Lela Estella Simons, (m. Clark),

V62615. 1114. Frank Volney Simons.

V62616. 103. James Thomas Jump, b. 28 Sept 1867, Bolivar, Polk Co, MO, d. 10 March 1934, Creston, WA, bur Sherman Cem, Sherman, WA; m. 1902, Mary Lavina Cooper, b. England.

V62617. 111. Eleanora Myrtle Jump, b. c?1893

[V6]2618. [11]2. John Jump, b. c?1895

[V6]2619. [10]4. Rose Ellen Jump, b. 14 March 1869, Bolivar, Polk Co, MO, d. 22 July 1942, Spokane, Spokane Co, WA; m. 21 Jan 1885, George F. Snyder, b. 25 Dec 1856, Trinity Co, CA, d. 23 April 1955, Spokane, WA, s/o Daniel Snyder and Lydia J. Coman

[V6]2620. [11]1. Earnest B. Snyder, b. 18 Jan 1886

[V6]2621. [10]5. Eliza Jane Jump, b. 2 Sept 1870, Springfield, Greene Co, MO, d. 24 Dec 1951; m.1. 15 July 1886, James Franklin Spencer, b. 7 April 1860, St. Louis, MO, d. 23 April 1919, Creston WA, s/o Josiah Spencer and Jona Watkins; m.2. Frederick Hamilton, b. c1864, d. 1934

[V6]2622. [11]1. Alma Spencer

[V6]2623. [11]2. Howard Spencer

[V6]2624. [11]3. Sylvia Spencer

[V6]2625. [11]4. Rosella Spencer

[V6]2626. [11]5. Ethel Leora Spencer, b. 13 July 1893, Creston, Lincoln Co, WA; m. James William Parry, b. 11 Sept 1889, Mahoney, Schulkill Co, PA

[V6]2627. [11]6. George Spencer

[V6]2628. [11]7. Berthadine Spence, b. 1895, WA

[V6]2629. [11]8. Ruby Mae Spencer, b. May 1896, WA

[V6]2630. [10]6. William Riley Jump, b. 5 Oct 1872, Bolivar, Polk, Co, MO, d. 22 Dec 1930, Peach, Lincoln Co, WA; m. 29 Dec 1898, Etta L. Waters;

[V6]2631. [11]1. William Henry “Harry” Jump

[V6]2632. [11]2. Kathleen Henrietta “Love” Jump

[V6]2633. [11]3. Mary Grace Jump, b. 29 Dec 1912, Creston, WA, d. 31 Oct 1982, Spokane,WA, bur Holy Cross Cem

[V6]2634. [11]4. Demain Jerome “Blue” Jump.

[V6]2635. [10]7. Perry Bevly “Bev” Jump, b. 22 May 1874, Bolivar, Polk Co, MO, d. 1 Oct 1947, Spokane, Spokane Co, WA; never married.

[V6]2636. [10]8. Sarah Frances “Fannie” Jump, b. 13 March 1877, Bolivar, Polk Co, MO, d. 30 March 1907, Cedonia, Stevens Co, WA; m. 17 Nov 1894, Sprague, WA, Frederick Hamilton, b. 1864, d. 1934

V6 2637. [11]1. Mildred Loretta Hamilton,

V6 2638. [11]2. Martha Margaret "Mattie" Hamilton, b. 1 Oct 1897, Hunters, WA, d. 5 April 1907, Hunters, WA

V6 2639. [11]3. Violet Cecile Hamilton,

V6 2640. [11]4. Fred Forest "Ted" Hamilton, b. 17 Feb 1902, Hunters, WA

V6 2641. [11]5. Eunice Ellen "Tiny" Hamilton,

25. JOSEPH W. BRESHEARS and Isabell Brashears/ Prudence Tipton

v6 1923. [9]11. **Joseph W. Breshears**, (s/o John Breshears and Naoma Ann Hogg), the first of the children born in Missouri, b. 1839, Polk Co, MO, d. 19 June 1895; m.1. ***Isabell Brashears***, (d/o Jesse Brashears and Elizabeth Bell), b. 1837, Benton Co, MO, d. c1860-65 in Hickory Co, MO; m.2. ***Prudence Elizabeth Tipton***, b. ?1830, d. 2 Nov 1888, d/o James Tipton and Christine Henderson. Thanks to Susan Buce (Buce@gorge.net) for additional data and photos.

Figure 32: Joseph Breshears and Prudence Tipton. Thanks to Susan Buce for the photo.

1870 Census in Hickory County, Missouri, Page 19, 8-19,1870, lists
Breshears, Joseph age 42, b. TN,
Prudy age 40, b. KY,

Johnny age 13,	Sarah age 11,
Arcena G. age 5,	Christina S. age 5,
Omy J. age 3,	Nancy J, age 3

Family of Joseph W. Breshears and Isabell Brashears (from notes copied from family Bible and sent to me by Susan Buce). Most of these children were born around Bolivar, Polk Co, MO:

[V6]2691. [10]1. **John James Breshears**, b. 21 Apr 1857, MO, d. 15 Jan 1904, bur Lindley Creek, Polk Co, MO; m. ***Ada V. Tidwell***,

[V6]2692. [11]1. **Maudie L. Breashears**, m. & ch.

[V6]2693. [11]2. **William J. Breshears**, m. & ch.

[V6]2694. [11]3. **Claude Thomas Breshears**; m. ***Wilma Finch***, ch.

[V6]2695. [11]4. **Robert Baxter "Back" Breshears**; m. ***Maude Tadlock***, ch.

[V6]2696. [11]5. **Sara Alice Breshears**; m. ***James Arthur "Bud" Hair***

[V6]2697. [11]6. **Rose Lee Breshears**,

[V6]2698. [11]7. **James Edward Breshears**,

[V6]2699. [11]8. **Ollie Breshears**,

[V6]2700. [11]9. **Johnnie Edith Breshears**, m. ***John Flechs***. Ch.

[V6]2701. [12]x. W.D. "Dean" Flechs,

[V6]2702. [10]2. **Sara Ann Breshears**, b. 12 Aug 1859, d. 20 March 1880, age 20

[V6]2703. [10]3. **Mary Frances Breshears**, b. 18 Jan 1861, d. 15 Sep 1863, age 2½

Family of Joseph W. Breshears and Prudence Tipton:

[V6]2704. [10]4. **Arcena Grant Breshears**, b. 20 Nov 1865 (twin)

[V6]2705. [10]5. **Christina Sherman Breshears**, b. 20 Nov 1865 (twin); m. _______ ***Ross***,

[V6]2706. [11]1. Bonnie Ross,

[V6]2707. [11]2. James Ross,

[V6]2708. [11]3. Ari Coomer Ross?

[V6]2709. [10]6. **Nancy Jane Breshears**, b. 27 Mar 1867 (twin), d. 18 Feb 1871, age 3

[V6]2710. [10]7. ***Omy Jane Breshears**, b. 27 Mar 1867 (twin), d. 31 March 1902, Braggs, Muskogee Co, OK; married c1896, ***Charles Marion Buce***, b. 26 April 1863, Cherokee Co, NC, d. 20 July 1954, Ft Gibson, Muskogee Co, OK (great-granddaughter Susan Buce has a photo & list of descendants)

V62711. 108. ***Samuel Henderson Breshears**, b. 13 Jan 1872, d. 2 Dec 1952; married to ***Lillie B. Buce*** (sister of Charles).

The twins, born in 1865 and given middle names of Grant and Sherman, probably indicates the political sympathies of this family.

Bible records on Deaths:
Frances Breshears died 15 Sept. 1863
Nancy Jane Breshears died 18 Feb. 1871
Sara Lizzabeth Breshears died 20 Mar 1880
Prudence Elizabeth Breshears died 2 Nov. 1888
Joseph Breshears died 19 June 1895 (locked bowels)
Samuel H Breshears died 2 Dec. 1952

Family of Omie Jane Breshears and Charles Marrion Buce:

V62712. 111. Joseph S. Buce, b. 14 Dsec 1891, d. Feb 1964, Ft Gibson, OK

V62713. 112. Lon Buce, b. 15 Nov 1894, d. Feb 1974, Smithtown, Suffolk Co, NY; m. Anna ______, b. 19 Oct 1896, d. June 1987, Suffolk, NY. (2 ch)

V62714. 113. Jack McKinley Buce, Sr, b. 20 Jan 1897, Braggs, Muskogee Co, OK, d. 2 Nov 1944, Mosier, Wasco Co, OR, bur Mosier Cem, Mosier, OR; m. 30 Sept 1919, Birmingham, Jefferson Co, AL, Ethel Elizabeth Breining, b. 20 Sept 1901, Hamilton Co, OH, d. 2 Dec 1985, Portland,

Figure 33: Omie Jane (Breshears) Buce. Thanks to Susan Buce for the photo.

Multnomah Co, OR, d/o Jacob Rahn Breining and Elizabeth Christine "Lillie" Fels.

[V6]2715. [12]1. Jack McKinley Buce, Jr, b. 29 Aug 1920, Petit, OK, d. 18 May 1984, The Dalles, Wasco Co, OR; m. & ch.

[V6]2716. [12]2. M.J. Buce (fem), m. ______ (decd) & 6 ch.

[V6]2717. [12]3. Walter Robert "Hank" Buce, b. 3 May 1924, d. 1 March 1999, Stayton, Marion Co, OR; m. & ch.

[V6]2718. [12]4. Ruth Marie Buce, b. 22 Jan 1926, d. Aug 1982, The Dalles, Wasco Co, OR; m. & ch.

[V6]2719. [12]5. Thomas Allen Buce, b. 12 Dec 1928, d. 10 May 1997, Seattle, King Co, WA; m. & ch.

[V6]2720. [12]6. William Russel "Bill" Buce, b. 1930, d. 1992; m. & ch.

[V6]2721. [11]4. Robert "Bob" Buce, never married.

[V6]2722. [11]5. Willie Buce, died as an infant from measles

<u>Family of Samuel Henderson Breshears and Lillie B. Buce:</u>

[V6]2723. [11]1. **William "Bill" Breshears**; m. ***Nora*** ______,

[V6]2724. [12]1. **Billie Joe Breshears**,

[V6]2725. [11]2. **Charley Breshears**, b. ?, d. 15 Dec 1983; never married.

[V6]2726. [11]3. **Omie Breshears**, b. 29 Aug, d. 22 Nov 1981; m. ***Tom Lawley***,

[V6]2727. 114. **Jessie B. Breshears**, (twin), b. 9 April 1903, Braggs, Indian Terr, d. 31 Jan 1990, Sapulpa, Creek Co, OK, bur Tahlequah Cem, Tahlequah, OK; m. ***Jay Redfearn***, b. ? d. 23 Aug 1982,

[V6]2728. [12]1. Barbara Redfearn,

[V6]2729. [12]2. J.H. Redfearn,

[V6]2730. [12]3. Richard Redfearn,

[V6]2731. [11]5. **Bessie Breshears**, (twin) b. 9 April 1903, d. 22 Dec 1983; m. ***Sam Harvey***,

[V6]2732. [11]6. **Easter Breshears**, b. ?; m. ______ ***Porter***,

[V6]2733. [11]7. **John Henry Breshears**, m. at Ft Frabbs, OK, ***Odie Belle Benge*** (Osage Indian). They live in Sand Springs, OK

[V6]2734. [11]8. **Andrew Breshears**, b. 21 May 1914, d. March 1965; m. ***Minnie Fokes***,

Figure 34: The Samuel Henderson Breshears family: front row: Lillie (Buce), with John Henry on lap, the twins, Jessie and Bessie, Samuel with Easter on lap, Charley. Back row: Omie and Bill. Thanks to Susan Buce for the photo.

26. JAMES KNOX POLK BRESHEARS, I and his three wives

v6**1933.** 913. **James Knox Polk Breshears, I**, (s/o John Breshears and Naoma Ann Hogg), b. 18 Nov 1842, Bolivar, Polk Co, MO, d. 7 March 1927; m.1. 5 March 1866, ***Sarah Francis "Fannie" Potter***, b. 27 Oct 1847, d. 8 Sept 1868; m.2. 11 July 1869, ***Virginia P. Baker***, b. 10 May 1838, d. 27 April 1870 (Virginia was apparently married previously; in 1870, Polk Co, MO, there are two Baker children in James's household, Virginia and William T., as well as two Breshears children that apparently belong to his 1st wife); m.3. 24 Dec 1871, ***Margaret Ann Byrns***, d. 1927, Durant, OK.

James's mother, "Naomi," was in James's household in 1870.

1870 US Census: Bolivar, Polk County, Missouri - film & book form -

BRESHEARS, James	27 - Mo	
BAKER, Virginia	12 - Mo	
BAKER, William	6 - Mo	
BRESHEARS, Nancy	3 - Mo	
BRESHEARS, James W.	2 - Mo	
BRESHEARS, Naomi	67 -	
$5000	$795 KY	

Figure 35: James Knox Polk Breshears and Margaret Byrns. Thanks to Bill Brooks for the photo.

James K.P. Breshears and his wife, Margaret Byrns apparently moved to the neighborhood of Durant, Bryan Co, OK, where a granddaughter, Jewell Gray, died in Sept 1908, after eating a peach pit.

Family of James Knox Polk Breshears, I and Fannie Potter:

V6 2791. 10 1. **Nancy Neoma Jane Breshears**, b. 22 Dec 1866, Bolivar, Polk Co, MO, d. 9 Jan 1905; m. 5 Oct 1884, in Polk Co, MO, ***William B. Karr***

V6 2792. 10 2. **William James Breshears**, b. 3 Jan 1868, Polk Co, MO, d. 1929

Family of James Knox Polk Breshears, I and Margaret Ann Byrns:

V6 2793. 10 1. **John Thomas Breshears**, b. 17 April 1873, Bolivar, Polk Co, MO, d. 1946, Durant, OK

V6 2794. 10 2. **Riley H. Breshears**, b. 4 April 1875, Polk Co, MO, d. 1909, Durant, OK

V6 2795. 10 3. **Rita H. Breshears**, b. c1876, Polk Co, MO. Rita and Riley may have been twins.

V6 2796. 10 4. **Jesse Newton Breshears**, b. 2 June 1877, Polk Co, MO, d. 1975, Coleman, Texas

V6 2797. 10 5. ***Hattie Mae/May Breshears**, b. 30 Jan 1880, Polk Co, MO, d. 1 Jan 1948, Crowell, Foard Co, TX; m.

Figure 36: James Knox Polk Breshears and wife, Margaret Byrns, Hattie Mae (Breshears) Gray, Susan Rebecca "Lillie" (Gray) Grimes, and Edith Ethel Grimes (baby). A four generation picture, from Bill Brooks.

16 Oct 1895, at Boggy Depot, OK, ***Clarence L. "C.L." Gray***, b. 6 March 1873, Cedar Co, MO,

[V6]2798. [10]6. **Merida Frances Breshears**, b. 2 July 1882, d. 1927, OK

[V6]2799. [10]7. **Arthur Omer Breshears**, b. 7 Feb 1884, d. 1992, El Paso, TX

[V6]2800. [10]8. **Addie Ethel Breshears**, b. 9 Dec 1885, d. 1973, OK; m. _____ ***Hay***

[V6]2801. [11]1. Grace Hay; m. ______ Cook.

Hattie Mae Breshears and Clarence "C.L." Gray

[v6]2797. [10]6. **Hattie Mae/May Breshears**, (d/o James Knox Polk Breshears, I and Margaret Ann Byrns), b. 30 Jan 1880, Polk Co, MO, d. 1 Jan 1948, Crowell, Foard Co, TX; m. 16 Oct 1895, at Boggy Depot, OK, ***Clarence "C.L." Gray***, b. 6 March 1873, Cedar Co, MO, d. 13 July 1947, Crowell, Foard Co, TX, s/o Emery Clarence Gray and Susan Rebecca (or Martha) _____. (data from Bert Grimes <Grimesburg@aol.com> of Petersburg, TX, and Jeani M. Gray of Washington State: <JayGray2 @email.msn.com>

C.L. Gray and wife, Hattie Breshears, and ten of their 11 children moved by covered wagon(s) from Silo, Bryan Co, OK, to Foard Co, TX, in Dec 1914 or early 1915 (Jewel had died at the age of three before the Grays moved to Texas). The last two of their 13 children were born in Texas.

When they arrived at Crowell, Foard Co, TX, they spent the night at Johnson's wagon yard. The next day, they went to the Lewis Robertsons, where they stayed until they rented a place from Floyd Ross. Here they lived in tents while clearing the land and building their home. The children attended school in Foard City, which was located 5 miles south and 2 miles east of Crowell. There is nothing there now but a grain elevator, but in the old days Foard City had a school and stores.

In 1918, the family moved to the Steve Bell place to farm. The children went to school in Gambleville, about 3 miles east and 2 miles south of Crowell, where there was nothing but a school. In 1924, C.L. Gray bought a grocery store at Foard City and continued to farm while running the store for several years. Later, he farmed 2 miles west of Crowell and lived in a house with a wood-burning stove, which was also used for heat. They farmed about 80 acres with 4 or 5 mules. They had a barn, corral, and a rock water-well. Water was drawn from the well with a bucket and drinking water was on the back porch in a bucket with a dipper.

Figure 37: The C.L. Gray/ Hattie Breshears family about 1902. Thanks to Jeanie Gray and Bert Grimes for the Photo.

Later, C.L. Gray bought a home in Crowell by the water tower, where he lived until he passed away with yellow jaundice in 1947. Hattie died 5 or 6 months later in 1948.

Family of Hattie Mae Breshears and Clarence "C.L." Gray:

V6 2802. 11 1. James Wilson Gray, b. 22 Sept 1896, Coleman, OK, d. Feb 1978, Amarillo, TX; m.1. 2 June 1918, Rosa Lee Peeler; m.2. c1925-30, Georgann Wilson Nichols

V6 2803. 12 1. Clarence Andrew Gray, b. 28 Sept 1920

V6 2804. 12 2. Jewell Elizabeth Gray, b. 24 June 1922

V6 2805. 12 3. Rosa Lee Gray, b. 8 Oct 1923

V6 2806. 12 4. Johnnie James Gray, b. c1932

Figure 38: The C.L. Gray Family in 1922.
Thanks to Jeanie Gray and Bert Grimes for the photo.

V6 2807. 11 2. Meddie Thomas Gray, b. 26 Dec 1897, Coleman, OK, d. 25 April 1968, Lubbock, TX; m. 30 Nov 1920, Lucy May Greening, b. 31 Oct 1900, d. 5 Jan 1991, Lubbock, TX

V6 2808. 12 1. Johnnie Ray Gray, b. 24 Nov 1921

[V6]2809. [12]2. Lita Faye Gray, b. 7 Jan 1926

[V6]2810. [12]3. Eva Lois Gray, b. 17 June 1928

[V6]2811. [12]4. (baby) Gray, b. 17 Feb 1931

[V6]2812. [12]5. Hattie Bernice Gray, b. 1934, d. 1939

[V6]2813. [12]6. Roy Eugene Gray, b. 11 Aug 1937

[V6]2814. [12]7. Jerry Don Gray, b. 2 May 1940, d. 6 March 1985; m. Sarah ____

[V6]2815. [11]3. Emery Clarence Gray, b. 17 May 1899, Coleman, OK, d. May 1976, Amarillo, TX; m.1. 4 Dec 1926, Marie Johnson; m.2. 1956, Rose ______. No ch.

[V6]2816. [11]4. Susan Rebecca "Lillie" Gray, b. 16 March 1901, Coleman Co, OK, d. 19 July 1980, Lubbock, TX; m. 29 Sept 1920, in Crowell, TX, William Edwin Grimes, b. 27 Nov 1898, Moffat, Bell Co, TX, d. 12 May 1956, Floydada, TX

[V6]2817. [12]1. Edith Ethel Grimes, b. 12 Oct 1921; m.1. 20 Oct 1938, in Floydada, TX, James Roy, b. Floydada, TX, d. 1941, Italy; m.2. 21 June 1942, in Plainview, TX, Gene Paul Aylesworth, b. 28 July 1919, Plainview, TX

[V6]2818. [13]1. Paula Jean Aylesworth, b. 17 Dec 1956

[V6]2819. [13]2. Susan Carol Aylesworth, b. 1 Feb 1958

[V6]2820. [12]2. William Bert Grimes, b. 7 Nov 1934, Floyd Co, TX; m. 19 Aug 1957, in Borger, TX, Rose Marie Green, b. 13 June 1936, Borger, TX

[V6]2821. [13]1. Debra Ann Grimes, b. 30 Oct 1957, Lubbock, TX; m. 31 July 1982, in Canyon, TX, Rodney Lynn Boyer, b. 15 Aug 1958, Borger, TX

[V6]2822. [14]1. Micah Lynn Boyer, b. 12 Oct 1985

[V6]2823. [14]2. Becca Ann Boyer, b. 9 Sept 1988

[V6]2824. [14]3. Blake Lee Boyer, b. 2 Oct 1991

[V6]2825. [13]2. Amy Kay Grimes, b. 28 Dec 1962, Crosbyton, TX; m. 6 June 1987, in Petersburg, TX, Michael Wayne Adrian, b. 31 Dec 1953, Lubbock, TX

[V6]2826. [14]1. Ann Marie Adrian, b. 4 Dec 1987

[V6]2827. [14]2. Matthew Tyler Adrian, b. 15 Dec 1991

[V6]2828. [11]5. Hattie Ann Ethel "Annie" Gray, b. 17 Aug 1903,

Matoy, OK, d. 23 Aug 1999, probably in CA; m. 28 May 1927, Lester Lee Statser, b. 31 Oct 1903, Deport, TX, d. 3 May 1990, Espanola, NM.

[V6]2829. [12]1. Della Genevieve Statser, b. 24 May 1928; m. Cecil Rice

[V6]2830. [12]2. Virginia Lee Statser, b. 21 Oct 1930; m. Randall Hudson

[V6]2831. [12]3. Billie Oscar Statser, b. 7 March 1936

[V6]2832. [12]4. James Clarence Statser, b. 5 March 1941

[V6]2833. [11]6. Jewell Gertrude Gray, b. 16 July 1905, Matoy, OK, d. about Sept 1908, Durant, OK, at her grandfather's house, after she had eaten the kernel of a peach pit.

[V6]2834. [11]7. Rufus Theodore Gray, b. 5 Feb 1907, Matoy, OK, d. Nov 1983, Stamford, TX; m.1. 11 Aug 1928, Lilla Mae Hutson (no ch); m.2. 31 Aug 1933, in Hobart, OK, Alpha Omega Savage (4 ch), b. 15 Oct 1911, Blanchard, OK, d. 11 Feb 1997, Tucumcari, NM.

[V6]2835. [12]1. Rufus Wayne Gray, b. 17 Nov 1935, d. San Juan, NM

[V6]2836. [12]2. Blaine Mardell Gray, b. 18 Sept 1939

[V6]2837. [12]3. James Kenneth Gray, b. 17 Dec 1943

[V6]2838. [12]4. Perry Ray Gray, b. 6 Nov 1946

[V6]2839. [11]8. Dora Mae Gray, b. 11 May 1909, Durant, OK, d. 4 June 1989 in Dumas, TX; m. 24 Dec 1927, John Clifton Patton, b. 24 Feb 1905, d. 18 Dec 1958

[V6]2840. [12]1. Flora Mae Patton, b. 31 Dec 1929; m. Ernest Scroggins

[V6]2841. [12]2. Edwin William Patton, b. 28 Feb 19__,

[V6]2842. [12]3. Virgil Eugene Patton,

[V6]2843. [12]4. Wande Faye Patton, b. 15 Feb 1934

[V6]2844. [12]5. Edna Helen Patton, b. 7 Dec 1937

[V6]2845. [12]6. Mary Sue Patton, b. Oct 1940

[V6]2846. [12]7. Ronald Steve Patton, b. 5 Feb 1946,

[V6]2847. [12]8. J.C. Patton,

[V6]2848. [11]9. Ruby Lee Gray, b. 21 March 1911, Durant, OK (on the Jeff Jones farm), m.1. 8 Oct 1927, Ernest Phelps; m.2. 7 June 1933, Homer Adolph Martin, b. 6 Oct 1914, d. 9 July 2003, Wichita Falls, TX.

No ch.

V6 2849. [11]10. Murrell Everett "Big Doc" Gray, b. 13 Feb 1913, Durant, OK, d. 8 Feb 1963, Lubbock, TX; m. 8 Aug 1933, Ollie Lucille Spears, b. 28 Sept 1917, Crowell, TX, d. 29 Aug 2004.

V6 2850. [12]1. Martha Lois Gray, b. 22 Sept 1936

V6 2851. [12]2. Jo Ann Gray, b. 16 Oct 1940

V6 2852. [12]3. Everett Jerome Gray, b. 15 Feb 1945

V6 2853. [11]11. Freddy Earl "Little Doc" Gray, b. 3 July 1914, Silo/Durant, Bryan Co, OK, d. 30 May 2004, Tulia, TX; m. 12 Dec 1936, in Crowell, Foard Co, TX, Annie Myrtle Jones, b. 11 Nov 1919, Sulphur Springs, TX, d. 7 Sept 2002, Amarillo, TX.

V6 2854. [12]1. La Vada Annie Gray, b. 7 Aug 1939, Crowell, Foard Co, TX; m.1. 12 Dec 1958, in Happy, TX, Thomas Edwin Adkins; m.2. 3 July 1993, Douglas Glen Waters,

V6 2855. [12]2. Gaye Nell Gray, b. 23 May 1942, Crowell, Foard Co, TX; m. 15 Dec 1958, in Happy, TX, Kenneth Ray "Skeet" Bonds

V6 2856. [12]3. Thena Dolores Gray, b. 13 April 1944, m. 25 March 1966, in Amarillo, TX, Ronald Edwin Wesely

V6 2857. [12]4. Ray Vance Gray, b. 20 Feb 1952; m. 21 Oct 1972, Patricia McDaniel

V6 2858. [11]12. Rosa Lorene Gray, b. 3 Dec 1916, Foard City, Foard Co, TX, d. 10 Sept 2000; m.1. 24 Dec 1932, Cleo Spears; m.2. 1952, Bob Jones.

V6 2859. [12]1. Wanza Juanita Spears, b. 5 Oct 1933

V6 2860. [12]2. Bobbie Jean Spears, b. 2 Jan 1935

V6 2861. [12]3. Charles Elton Spears, b. 7 Feb 1937

V6 2862. [12]4. Randall Lee Jones, b. 4 Sept 1956

V6 2863. [11]13. John "Jiggs" Louis Gray, Sr, b. 17 Dec 1919, Crowell, Foard Co, TX, d. 13 Nov 1990, Arlington, Snohomish Co, WA; m. 11 May 1940, in Crowell, Foard Co, TX, Oyama Walls, b. 11 July 1921, Enterprise, Haskell Co, OK, d. 23 May 2000, Everett, Snohomish Co, WA, both bur Mountain View Cem, Auburn, WA.

V6 2864. [12]1. Brenda Annice Gray, b. 15 April 1941,

Crowell, Foard Co, TX, d. 1 Sept 1999, Seattle, King Co, WA; m. 9 Nov 1962, Tacoma, Pierce Co, WA, Donald Eugene Osborn, b. 3 July 1939, Mason City, IA

V6 2865. 13 1. Lea Ann Osborn, b. 20 July 1966, Tacoma, WA; m. 29 Dec 1989, in Tacoma, Pierce Co, WA, Jeffrey Steven Malik, b. 2 Feb 1965, Omaha, Douglas Co, NE

V6 2866. 14 1. Meghann Annece Malik, b. 17 Nov 1990

V6 2867. 14 2. Cameron Louis Malik, (fraternal twin), b. 13 Feb 1995

V6 2868. 14 3. Kyle Steven Malik, (fraternal twin), b. 13 Feb 1995

V6 2869. 13 2. Martin Eugene Osborn, b. 19 May 1968, Tacoma, WA; m. 21 Aug 1999, in Auburn, King Co, WA, Theresa "Terri" Christine Systad, b. 16 June 1968, Seattle, King Co, WA

V6 2870. 14 1. Tawnee Osborn, Theresa's dau/ adopted by Martin

V6 2871. 12 2. John Louis "Jay" Gray Jr, b. 11 April 1944, Wilmington, Los Angeles Co, CA; m. 4 April 1964, in Tacoma, Pierce Co, WA, Jean "Jeani" Marie Stanziola, b. 17 Oct 1945, Hazleton, Luzerne Co, PA, d/o James Stanziola and Bonnie Handy. Jeani M. Gray has collected and contributed much data on this branch of the family.

V6 2872. 13 1. Shaun Anyse Gray, b. 9 May 1966, Tacoma, Pierce Co, WA; m. 8 Aug 1999, in San Juan Co, WA, Jason Denison Buell, b. 1 Feb 1968, Seattle, King Co, WA

V6 2873. 13 2. Sheri Louise Gray, b. 3 July 1967, Tacoma, Pierce Co, WA; m. 7 April 1986, in Roy, Pierce Co, WA, Paul Kevin Moss, b. 13 Jan 1966, Tacoma, WA, s/o Lloyd Moss and Vada Storie

[V6]2874. [14]1. Antonia Louise Moss, b. 22 Feb 1986, Tacoma, WA

[V6]2875. [14]2. Devon Michael Moss, b. 11 May 1989, Tacoma, WA

[V6]2876. [13]3. Jaymalea "Jayme" Marie Gray, b. 8 Nov 1970, Tacoma, Pierce Co, WA; m. 27 Feb 1999, in Las Vegas, Clark Co, NV, Carlyle Jackson "Jack" Gooch III, b. 5 Feb 1970, Tacoma, WA, s/o Carlyle Gooch and Janet Zindt

[V6]2877. [14]1. Alexia Marie Gooch, b. 15 July 1999, Lakewood, Pierce Co, WA

[V6]2878. [12]3. Darrel Craig Gray, b. 22 Oct 1954, South Gate, Los Angeles Co, CA; m.1. Cori Webb; m.2. 14 Feb 1985, in King Co, WA, Joyce Marie Nickolson, b. 9 April 1958, Ballard, King Co, WA

[V6]2879. [13]1. Darrel Craig Gray Jr, b. 9 Aug 1985, Seattle, King Co, WA

[V6]2880. [13]2. Brittney Marie Gray, b. 22 Oct 1987, Seattle, King Co, WA

27.THOMAS HART BENTON BRESHEARS and Nancy Ann Potter

[v6]1934. [9]14. **Thomas Hart Benton Breshears**, (s/o John Breshears and Naoma Ann Hogg), b. 11 Oct 1844, Bolivar, Polk Co, MO, d. 29 Feb 1916, Eagle, Ada Co, Idaho; m. 21 Aug 1866, at Bolivar, Polk Co, MO, ***Nancy Ann Potter***, b. 8 Aug 1849, Ozark, Green Co, MO. In the 1870s, they moved to Idaho.

Family of Thomas Hart Benton Breshears and Nancy Potter:

[V6]2901. [10]1. **Mary Francis Breshears**, b. 12 Sept 1867, Bolivar, Polk Co, MO, d. 1868

[V6]2902. [10]2. **John Franklin Breshears**, b. 2 Sept 1869, Bolivar, Polk Co, MO, d. 1929, Eagle, Ada Co, ID

[V6]2903. [10]3. **Joseph Henderson Breshears**, b. 14 Aug 1872,

Bolivar, Polk Co, MO, d. 11 May 1931, in Eagle, Ada Co, ID; m. ***Anna Viola Saxon***, b. 9 Feb 1870, Paw Paw, MI

V6 2904. 11 1. **Lizzy Ethel Breshears**, b. 4 Jan 1894, Eagle, Ada Co, ID; m. ***Lyle R. Anderson***, b. 14 Oct 1895, Xenia, Clay Co, Illinois

V6 2905. 11 2. **Clarence Breshears**, b. 28 July 1895, Breshears Homestead, Ada Co, ID, Dry Creek; m. ***Inez Cullen***, b. c16 July 1895, Murphy, Owyhee Co, ID

V6 2906. 11 3. **Florence Cecelia Breshears**, b. 6 June 1897, Eagle, Ada Co, ID; m.1. ***Gilbert Kearns***, b. 25 Sept 1893 Eugene, Lane Co, OR; m.2. ***Gerald Moses***, b. c?1897

V6 2907. 11 4. **Archie Breshears**, b. July 1897, Eagle, Ada Co, ID

V6 2908. 11 5. ____ **Breshears**, b. ____; m. ***William Mellor***, b. 6 Feb 1907, Rock Springs, Sweetwater, Wy

V6 2909. 11 6. **Wilburn Breshears**, b. 20 Jan 1906, Eagle, Ada Co, ID; m. ***Erma Breshears***, b. 9 July 1906, Bellevue, ___ Co, ID

V6 2910. 11 7. ____ **Breshears**, b. ____; m. ____, b. ____

V6 2911. 11 8. **Floyd Breshears**, b. 4 March 1912, Eagle, Ada Co, ID; m.1. ***Lefa Irine Buffington***, b. 18 Feb 1913 Meridian, Ada Co, ID; m.2. ***Margaret Mae "Maggie" Sharp***, b. 14 Sept 1889, Broadford, __ Co, ID

V6 2912. 10 4. **Thomas Carter Breshears**, b. 26 Oct 1875, Bolivar, Polk Co, MO, d. 29 April 1947, San Pedro, California; m. 6 Man 1896, in Mnampa, ID, ***Adah Bertha Beddons***, b. 25 April 1874, KS. Nine ch, names unknown to me.

V6 2913. 10 5. **James Andrew Breshears**, b. 30 Sept 1877, Rocky Bar, Elmore Co, ID, d. 1880

V6 2914. 10 6. **Reuben Nathaniel Breshears**, b. 22 Jan 1881, Boise, Ada Co, ID, d. 1961, in Caldwell, ID; m. ***Bertie Lou Mead***, b. 11 Aug 1884, Widener, ___ Co, AR. Several ch, including:

V6 2915. 11 2. **Eva Della Breshears**, b. 21 Jan 1906, Eagle, Ada Co, ID; m. ***Willard Moore***, b. c?1906

[V6]2916. [11]6. **Louis Mead Breshears**, b. 2 July 1916, Eagle, Ada Co, ID; m. _____, b. _____

[V6]2917. [10]7. _____ **Breshears**, b. 19 Nov 1882, Boise, Ada Co, ID

[V6]2918. [10]8. **Minnie Ann Breshears**, b. 17 Jan 1886, Boise, Ada Co, ID; m. ***Ernest Lorin (or Loren Ernest) Eytchison***, b. 23 March 1877 Onega, Pottowatomie Co, KS

[V6]2919. [11]1. Walter Franklin Eytchison, b. 16 Jan 1905, Boise, Ada Co, ID; m. _____, b. _____; m. Louise Hope Laflang, b. 28 Oct 1910 Buckroe Beach, Va

[V6]2920. [11]2. Ethel Eideth Eytchison, b. 22 July 1907, Eagle, Ada Co, ID; m. George Albert Pritchard, b. 18 Sept 1908 Of, Boise Co, ID

[V6]2921. [11]3. Lester Ernest Eytchison, b. 29 Dec 1908, Eagle, Ada Co, ID; m. Myrtle Fredrica Lenaghen, b. _____

[V6]2922. [11]4. Evelyn Marie Eytchison, b. _____; m. Joseph Wilson Blair, b. 26 June 1906 Webber, Jewell, KS

[V6]2923. [10]9. _____ **Breshears**, b. 18 Nov 1887, Boise, Ada Co, ID

[V6]2924. [10]10. _____ **Breshears**, b. 14 Aug 1890, Boise, Ada Co, ID

28. ANDREW JACKSON BRESHEARS and Martha Hammack

[v6]1935. [9]15. **Andrew Jackson Breshears**, (s/o John Breshears and Naoma Ann Hogg), b. 27 June 1847, Polk Co, MO, d. 3 Jan 1921, Weister, Payette Co, ID, bur Middleton, Canyon Co, ID; m. 17 March 1868, at Bolivar, Polk Co, MO, ***Martha Melvina Hammack***, b. 6 May 1850, Dallas Co, MO, d. 15 Jan 1918, Middleton, Canyon Co, ID, d/o Andrew Hammack and Sarah McPheters. Six ch:

Family of Andrew Jackson Breshears and Martha Hammack:

[V6]2951. [10]1. **Francis Marion Breshears**, b. 16 July 1869, Bolivar, Polk Co, MO, d. May 1930, in Boise, ID; m.? 9 April 1893, ***Elizabeth Jenkins***, b. c?1869,

[V6]2952. [11]1. **Ralph Raymond Breshears**, b. 4 Dec 1894 Middleton, Canyon Co, ID; m.1. ***Mary Finegan***, b. c1894, Boise, Ada Co, ID; m.2. ***Laura Hutchison***, b. c?1894

[V6]2953. [11]2. **Arnold J. Huck Breshears**, b. 31 Jan 1897, Middleton, Canyon Co, ID; m. ***Francis Haddow***, b. c1897

[V6]2954. [11]3. **Howard Breshears**, b. 16 Feb 1899, Middleton, Canyon Co, ID; m. _____, b. _____; m. ***Mottie Esther***, b. c1896/1900 Spokane, Wa

[V6]2955. [11]4. **Sherman Breshears**, b. 24 July 1901, Middleton, Canyon Co, ID; m. ***Emily Dean Wade***, b. 7 May 1899 Vinita, Ok

[V6]2956. [10]2. **Sarah Naomi Ann Breshears**, b. 28 Aug 1871, Bolivar, Polk Co, MO, d. 25 Oct 1922, in Ada Co, ID; m. c1889, ***Samuel William Newman***, b. 1868 Fayetteville, AR

[V6]2957. [11]1. Samuel ?Edwin Newman, b. 26 June 1890, Middleton, Canyon Co, ID; m. Harriet Weir, b. c1890

[V6]2958. [11]2. Leonard Earl Newman, b. c1894, Middleton, Canyon Co, ID; m. Winnefred Ragsdale, b. c1894; m. Lydia Syms, b. c?1894

[V6]2959. [11]3. Ruby Ogle Newman, b. c28 Nov 1898, Middleton, Canyon Co, ID; m. Orville Abbott, b. c1892

[V6]2960. [11]4. Ella Newman, b. 12 March 1903, Middleton, Canyon Co, ID; m. _____, b. _____

[V6]2961. [10]3. **Ella Evalina Breshears**, b. 30 Dec 1874, Bolivar, Polk Co, MO, d. 24 Dec 1946, Gem Co, ID; m. ***James Paul Reed***, b. c?1874

[V6]2962. [11]1. Marion Reed, b. Jan 1918/1919 Emmett, Gem Co, ID

[V6]2963. [10]4. **Martha Lavada Breshears**, b. 4 Aug 1877, Bolivar, Polk Co, MO; m. ***Fredrick Henry Lenaghen***, b. 3

Sept 1865, Plattsburg, Clinton Co, NY. Lavada Lenaghen was a Breshears family researcher.

V6 2964. 11 1. Halsey Lenaghen, b. 20 Jan 1894, Middleton, Canyon Co, ID; m. Edith Mary Hawkins, b. c1894, Nelson, West Kootenai

V6 2965. 11 2. Sarah Lavada Lenaghen, b. 8 June 1895, Middleton, Canyon Co, ID; m.1. William Lorin Corbin, b. 27 March 1877, Story, KS; m.2. Orrin "Ory" Evans, b. c?1895

V6 2966. 11 3. Theresa Martha Lenaghen, b. 12 Sept 1901, Delmar, Owyhee Co, ID; m. Arthur William Bachmann, b. 16 June 1897, Knox City, Knox, MO

V6 2967. 11 4. ____, b. ____; m. Oscar Schafer, b. 8 Feb 1901, Muscada, Grant, Wi

V6 2968. 11 5. Myrtle Fredrica Lenaghen, b. ____; m. Lester Ernest Eytchison, b. 29 Dec 1908, Eagle, Ada Co, ID

V6 2969. 11 6. Delila Katherine Lenaghen, b. 24 June 1913, Middleton, Canyon Co, ID; m. Marvin Mathew Trinkle, b. 29 May 1909, Alliance, Box Butte, Colorado; m. _____, b. _____

V6 2970. 10 5. **Theresa Susan Breshears**, b. 25 July 1880, Summerville, Union Co, OR, d. c1969, OR; m. 29 June 1910, in Middleton, Canyon Co, ID, ***Austin David Harris***, b. 6 Jan 1873, Talmadge, OH, d. 27 April 1960, in Akron, Summit Co, OH, s/o Samuel W. Harris

V6 2971. 10 6. **Arthur Andrew Breshears**, b. 18 May 1885, Middleton, Canyon Co, ID, d. 26 Aug 1978, Weiser, Washington Co, ID; m. 10 Oct 1907, in Boise, Ada Co, ID, ***Eva Cornelia Hill***, b. 3 Aug 1887, Middleton, Canyon Co, ID, d. c1989-90, Weiser, Washington Co, ID, d/o Edward and Sarah Hill.

29. JESSE BRASHEARS and Elizabeth Bell/ Mary Ellen Franklin

v6 1613. 83. **Jesse Brashears**, (s/o Henry Breshears Sr and Eleanor ?Hardin), b. SC, c1796 (54 in 1850, Dallas Co, MO); m.1. 2 March 1818, Lawrence Co, TN, (*Early East Tenn Marr*, by Sistler; bond by Nathan Brashear in *LawrCo Marr Recs, 1818-1838*) ***Elizabeth Bell***, b. in Lawrence Co, TN, c1800-1805 (16-26 in 1820; 20-30 in 1830), d. after 1844, Polk Co, MO, d/o John Bell; m.2. 1849, Dallas Co, MO, ***Mrs. Mary Ellen (Franklin) Flanigan***, b. c1805 (45 in 1850), in Tennessee. Jesse seems to have kept the older spelling of the surname: Brashears.

Jesse was especially close to his cousin, Nathan Turner Brashears. Nathan was bondsman at Jesse's wedding in Lawrence Co, TN. In 1850, they lived very near each other in District 26, Dallas Co, MO; Nathan is #377-381, and Jesse and Mary are #389-393.

Jesse is listed on the 1819 Tax List of Lawrence Co, TN, and the 1819 census of voters. He is in the 1820 census, beside Henry Breshears Sr, with a wife and one dau 0-10, probably born 1819, since he had just married in 1818.

1818-1823...Lawrence Co, TN, Court Records: **David Crockett; William Brashers; John Brashers** and **Jesse Brasher** are ordered to repair the road from between Clark's place and Richard Straughns, with John Null [Hull?] as overseer. [These Brashears were sons of Henry Brashears Sr. Jesse's occupation was "Miller." John Null was reportedly married to a Brashears.]

In 1826, Jesse was on the Lawrence Co, TN, Tax list, beside Henry Jr, William, and a cluster of his brothers.

In the 1830 Census, Lawrence Co, TN, he has 5 daughters and a son (100001-22101).

In 1830 and 1833, he signed deeds in Lawrence Co, TN,

transferring his right to lands of Henry Brashear Sr to his brother, John Breshears/Brashears.

Judging from birth places of his children, Jesse migrated to Missouri, 1835-37. His first wife was still living (and gave birth to one more child in MO); so I would expect to find her grave there.

About 1849, Jesse married a second time, a Mrs. Mary Ellen (Franklin) Flanigan who (in the 1850 census, Dallas Co, MO) had several Flanigan children:

Roda Flanigan, b. c1831 (19 in 1850);
John Flanigan, b. c1833 (17 in 1850);
Lavina Flanigan, b. c1835 (15 in 1850);
Elizabeth Flanigan, b. c1837 (13 in 1850);
Thomas J. Flanigan, b. c1839 (11 in 1850).

Also in Jesse's listing in 1850: Malinda Brashears, b. c1834 (16 in 1850); Isobel Brashears, b. c1837 (13 in 1850); Jesse C. Brashears, b. c1841 (9 in 1850); Cintha E. Brashears, b. c1844 (6 in 1850). (Thanks to Cathy Hall for the info.)

Jesse and Mary Ellen apparently died between 1850 and 1860, for their daughter, Nancy, was living with her half-sister, Rhoda Flanigan in 1860. In 1870, she was living with Lavina Flanigan.

<u>Family of Jesse Brashears and Elizabeth Bell:</u> (Some researchers have H. Alexander Breshears or Alexander (Henry) Breshears in positions 3 and/or 7, but the census data does not bear them out. They must be confusing some other person with Jesse and Elizabeth's children.)

[V6]3021. [9]1. dau **Brashears**, b. c1819 (0-10 in 1820; 10-15 in 1830)

[V6]3022. [9]2. dau **Brashears**, b. c1820-25 (5-10 in 1830)

[V6]3023. [9]3. dau **Brashears**, b. c1820-25 (5-10 in 1830)

[V6]3024. [9]4. dau **Brashears**, b. c1825-30 (0-5 in 1830)

[V6]3025. [9]5. ***Robert "Bob Hiram" Brashears**, b. c1827 (0-5 in 1830), Lawrence Co, TN; m. ***Anna Breshears***, b. 24 Oct 1831, Lawrence Co, TN, d/o Henry Alexander Breshears Jr and Atsa "Atsey" Etheridge

[V6]3026. [9]6. dau **Brashears**, b. c1825-30 (0-5 in 1830).

[V6]3027. [9]7. **Malinda Brashears**, b. c1834 (16 in 1850),

Lawrence Co, TN; d. before 1870, bur Spring Branch Cem, Benton Co, MO; m. 24 Dec 1857, ***James A. Pippin***.

[V6]3028. [9]8. **Isabell Brashears**, b. c1837 (13 in 1850), Benton Co, MO, d. before 1870 in Hickory Co, MO; m. ***Joseph W. Breshears***, (s/o John Breshears and Naoma Ann Hogg), b. c1839, Polk Co, MO. See his listing for their children.

[V6]3029. [9]9. **Jesse C. Brashears**, b. c1841 (9 in 1850), Benton Co, MO

[V6]3030. [9]10. **Cynthia E. Brashears**, b. c1844 (6 in 1850), Dallas Co, MO

Family of Jesse Brashears and Mary Ellen Franklin:

[V6]3031. [9]11. ***Nancy Ellen Breshears**, b. 14 July 1850, Dallas Co, MO, d. 12 June 1908 in Dallas Co, MO, d/o Jesse Breshears and Mary Franklin; m. 15 Oct 1876 in Dallas Co, MO, (second wife of) ***George Washington "Wash" Hill***,

Robert Hiram "Bob Hiram" Breshears and Anna Breshears

[v6]3025. [9]5. **Robert Hiram "Bob Hiram" Breshears**, (s/o Jesse Brashears and Elizabeth Bell), b. c1827 (0-5 in 1830), Lawrence Co, TN, d. MO; m. 2 July 1848, in Benton Co, MO, **Elizabeth Anna Breshears**, (a first cousin, d/o Henry Breshears Jr and Atsa "Atsey" Etheridge), b. 24 Oct 1831, Lawrenceburg, Lawrence Co, TN, d. after 1877, Polk Co, MO (data from FHL, Judy Breshears, and Georgene Humphries)

[V6]3032. [10]1. **Mary Jane Breshears**, b. 26 Nov 1855, Hickory Co, MO, d. there, 1938, bur Henderson Cem, Hickory Co, MO; m. ***Owen Ruth***,

[V6]3033. [10]2. ***James Monroe Breshears**, b. 13 March 1857, Hickory Co, MO, d. 3 May 1918, Hickory Co, MO, age 61; m. ***Mary Elizabeth "Lizzie" Southard***, (d/o Moses Southard and Louisa Breshears, of the Alexander Brashears/Margaret Breshears line).

[V6]3034. [10]3. ***Hiram "Hi" Breshears**, b. c1856-58, Polk Co, MO; m. 12 Feb 1874, in Benton Co, MO, ***Mary***

Dickerson, b. c1858, Benton Co, MO.

[V6]3035. [10]4. ***Amanda "Mandy" Breshears**, b. 5 Aug 1861, AR, d. 2 Feb 1936, Hickory Co, MO, bur Jones cem, near Avery, Hickory Co, MO; m. 13 Sept 1877, in Hickory Co, MO, **Steven B. Breshears**, (s/o Madison Golman Breshears and Elizabeth Brown)

James Monroe Breshears and Mary Elizabeth Southard

[v6]3033. [10]2. **James Monroe Breshears**, (s/o Robert Hiram "Bob Hiram" Breshears and Anna Breshears), b. 13 March 1857, Hickory Co, MO, d. 3 May 1918, Hickory Co, MO, age 61; m. ***Mary Elizabeth "Lizzie" Southard***, (d/o Moses Southard and Louisa Breshears, d/o Alexander Brashears and Margaret Breshears), b. 14 Nov 1862, Benton Co, MO, d. 11 Feb 1931 in Clayton, Pushmataha Co, OK, age 68.

[V6]3036. [11]1. **Lora Ellen Breshears**, b. 23 March 1880, d. 27 Aug 1908 (per Judy Breshears; not in FHL or Georgene's lists.)

[V6]3037. [11]2. **Robert Francis Breshears**, b. 25 Jan 1884, Hickory Co, MO; m. ***M. Vanner***. Three boys:

[V6]3038. [12]1. **Jess Breshears**,

[V6]3039. [12]2. **Jim Breshears**,

[V6]3040. [12]3. **Pete Breshears**,

[V6]3041. [11]3. ***John Clarence Breshears**, b. 5 March 1887, in Kansas, d. 17 Feb 1957, Phoenix, Maricopa Co, AZ; m. 7 Sept 1910 at Russellville, Pittsburg Co, OK, ***Nettie Viola Jones***,

[V6]3042. [11]4. **Harvey Herman Breshears**, b. 26 May 1889, (or 26 March 1890) Chickasha, OK, (registered for the draft in Hutchinson, TX), d. 16 Nov 1970; m. ***Lillie May***

Figure 39: Harvey Breshears (center) and two of his army buddies. Photo from Sandra Beagles

Hamilton. They had 8 children, names unknown to me.

[V6]3043. [11]5. **Laura Breshears**, b. c1891, MO

[V6]3044. [11]6. **Grace Caroline Breshears**, b. 30 Oct 1892,Kansas, d. 27 March 1903, age 10.

[V6]3045. [11]7. **Hiram Jackson "Hi" Breshears**, b. 3 March 1894, Chickasha, Grady Co, OK, d. 5 Sept 1968, Wister, Leflore Co, OK (Registered for the draft in Hutchinson, TX); m. 23 Aug 1922, at Wister, LeFlore Co, OK, ***LaMara Mae "Marzie" Chronister***, b. 30 Jan 1901, Wister, LeFlore Co, I.T., d. 31 Dec 1992, Broken Arrow, Tulsa Co, OK, d/o Benjamin C. Chronister and Amand Elizabeth Goforth.

[V6]3046. [12]1. **Velma Elizabeth Breshears**, b. 12 Feb 1921, Howe, LeFlore Co, OK; m.1. ***Louis Scott***; m.2. _____ ***Wilson***

[V6]3047. [13]1. Lawrence A. Scott, b. 9 Oct 1946, Duncan, OK

[V6]3048. [13]2. Nancy Ann Scott, b. 30 Nov 1948, Duncan, OK

[V6]3049. [13]3. Charles Michael Scott, b. 2 Nov 1950, Duncan, OK

[V6]3050. [13]4. Tammy Scott, b. 4 Nov 1954, Duncan, OK

[V6]3051. [12]2. **John Charles Breshears**, b. 3 Nov 1928, Duncan, OK; not married.

[V6]3052. [11]8. **Myrtle Jane Breshears**, b. 21 July 1896, MO, d. after 1975; m. ***Henry Moore*** and had 2 boys, 1 girl, names unknown to me.

[V6]3053. [11]9. **Charles Westley Breshears**, b. 23 March 1899, d. ______; m. ***Gertrude Jackson*** (3 children, names unknown)

[V6]3054. [11]10. **Clara Ethel Breshears**, b. 20 Aug 1902, KS, d. 3 April 1936; m.1. ***Jason Vaught***, b. 1888, Stanley, ID (no known children); m.2. ***Oren Bernard***, b. 1886, MO; m.3. ***Alvie Hamilton*** (three children, names unknown). Jason Vaught m.2. Clara Breshears, (d/o James Knox Polk Breshears II and Rebecca Anderson. Clara and Alvie Hamilton had 3 ch, names unknown to me.

Figure 40: John Clarence and Viola (Jones) Breshears. Photo from Sandra Beagles

Figure 41: Arthur L. Breshears, Electric Company lineman in 1957. Photo from Sandra Beagles

V6 3055. 11 11. **James Lester "Jim" Breshears**, b. 11 Feb 1904; m. ***Odie Brylie*** (4 ch, names unknown to me)

V6 3041. 11 3. **John Clarence Breshears**, (s/o James Monroe Breshears and Mary Elizabeth Southard), b. 5 March 1887, in Kansas, d. 17 Feb 1957, Phoenix, Maricopa Co, AZ; m. 7 Sept 1910 at Russellville, Pittsburg Co, OK, ***Nettie Viola Jones***, b. 20 June 1892, d. 6 Feb 1957, in Phoenix, AZ (11 days between John and Viola's death; both are buried at Twin Buttes Cem, Tempe, Maricopa Co, AZ) (additional data from granddaughter, Sandra Kay Beagles <greenback95 @yahoo.com>)

V6 3056. 12 1. **Arthur Lee Breshears**, b. 22 April 1912, Quinton, Pittsburg Co, OK, d. 15 Dec 1974, Phoenix, Maricopa Co, AZ; m.1. ***Marlene Jeanie*** _____ (1 ch); m.2. 12 Sept 1933, in Antlers, OK, ***Estelle Loueller Mouse***, b. 5 July 1914, d. just after birth of the twins, 23 Aug 1944, Phoenix, AZ; the children were raised by grandfather, John Clarence Breshears.

V6 3057. 13 1. **Jeannie Darlene Breshears**, m. _____ ***Hicks***, and had one son, name unknown to me.

V6 3058. 13 2. **Rosemary Breshears**, m.1. ***Clarence*** _____; m.2. ***Danny Jennings***, by whom she had four children, names unknown to me.

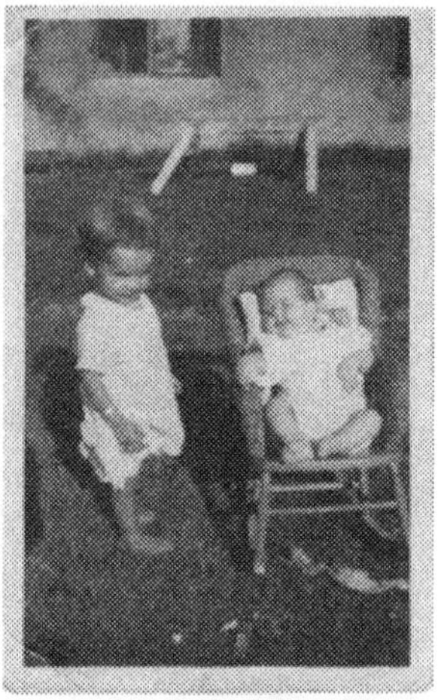

Figure 42: Rosemary and Joyce Ann Breshears (age 9 mos). Photo Sandra Beagles

V6 3059. 13 3. Girl **Breshears**, b. 1935, Clayton, OK, d. 1935-1938, bur Old Clayton Cem, Clayton, OK

V6 3060. 13 4. **Billy Breshears**, b. 1937, Clayton, OK, d. there at age 3, c1940, bur Old Clayton Cem, Clayton, OK

V6 3061. 13 5. **Joyce Ann Breshears**, b. 6 July 1940, Riverside, CA, d. in SUV roll-over 10 Aug 2003, near Gallup, NM; m.1. 15 June 1956, in Tempe, AZ, ***Johnnie Ray Beagles***, b. 10 Aug 1939, Bennington, OK, div 1974; s/o James Beagles and Helen Hammon; m.2. 1999, ***Edward Gortariz***,

V6 3062. 14 1. Sandra Kay Beagles,

V6 3063. 14 2. Kathleen Beagles,

V6 3064. 14 3. Debbie Renee Beagles,

V6 3065. 14 4. Iva Diane Beagles,

V6 3066. 14 5. David Lee Beagles, b. 2 July 1962, Phoenix, AZ, died 2 July 1962, of a collapsed lung, age 8 hours

V6 3067. 14 6. Justin Dirk Beagles,

V6 3068. 14 7. Shannon Lee Beagles,

V6 3069. 14 8. Linda Darlene Beagles,

Figure 43: Lee Breshears, s/o John Clarence and Viola Breshears. Photo Sandra Beagles

Figure 45: Floyd and Tessie Breshears with da Viola in 1938. Photo Sandra Beagles

Figure 44: Floyd Breshears in his WWII Navy uniform. Photo: Sandra Beagles

[V6]3070. [13]6. **James Arthur Breshears** (twin), b. 23 Aug 1944; m.1. Sonya ______ (1 ch, name unk); m.2. ***Phyllis Welch*** (3 ch, names unk)

[V6]3071. [13]7. **Janie Louellor Breshears** (twin), b. 23 Aug 1944; m.1. ***Jerry Maddox*** (3 ch, names unk); m.2. ______ *Hensinger*

[V6]3072. [12]2. **Floyd Eugene Breshears**, b. 4 Dec 1915, Feathersont, Pushmataha Co, OK, d. July 1975, Phoenix, AZ; m. 3 Sept 1935, at Clayton, Pushmataha Co, OK, ***Tessie N. Bishop***, b. 2 Dec 1919, Bobtown, Pushmataha Co, OK, d. Lake Havasu, AZ

[V6]3073. [13]1. **Viola Breshears**,

[V6]3074. [13]2. **Eugene Breshears**,

[V6]3075. [13]3. **Floyd Breshears Jr**,

V6 3076. [13]4. **Shirley May Breshears**,
V6 3077. [13]5. **John Thomas Breshears**,
V6 3078. [13]6. **Myron Leon Breshears**,
V6 3079. [12]3. **Lee Breshears**,
V6 3080. [12]4. **Louis Breshears**,

Hiram "Hi" Breshears and Mary Dickerson

v6 3034. [10]3. **Hiram "Hi" Breshears**, (s/o Robert Hiram "Bob Hiram" Breshears and Anna Breshears), b. c1856-58, Polk Co, MO; m. 12 Feb 1874, in Benton Co, MO, ***Mary Dickerson***, b. c1858, Benton Co, MO. After one child in MO, Hiram moved to Oklahoma and reared a second family (10 children), per Judy Breshears. Mary Dickerson (Dickson in some records) m.2. Bill Ruth.

V6 3081. [11]1. **William Robert "Bob Hi" Breshears**, b. 5 May 1875, Polk Co, MO, d. 24 Jan 1944, Weaubleau, MO; m. 3 Oct 1895, ***Eliza "Lizzie" Jane Miller***, (d/o Henry Miller and Martha Ruth), b. 27 Sept 1879, Hickory Co, MO, d. 8 Nov 1958, Hickory Co, MO. Both "Bob Hi" and Lizzie bur Gardner Cem, Hickory Co, MO.

Figure 46: William Robert "Bob Hi" Breshears and wife, Eliza Jane Miller. Photo Bill Brooks

V6 3082. [12]1. **Santford Breshears**, b. 13 July 1896, d. 9 April 1984, Weaubleau, MO; m. 23 Feb 1918, in Hermitage, Hickory Co, MO, ***Laura Gertrude Burton***, b. 17 May 1901, d. 4 Dec 1966, Hickory Co, MO, both bur Robinson Cem, St Clair Co, MO

V6 3083. [13]1. **Lewis Breshears**, m. ***Thelma Pearl***

Fields

^{V6}3084. ^{13}2. **Dimple Breshears**, m. ***Herb Buckner***

^{V6}3085. ^{12}2. **Maudie Mae Breshears**, b. 30 Dec 1897, d. 16 Nov 1974; m. 24 Jan 1915, ***Oral Rife***, b. 7 May 1893, d. 29 Jan 1955

^{V6}3086. ^{13}1. Margaret Faye Rife, b. 15 Feb 1916; m. Ira Simmons

^{V6}3087. ^{13}2. Chester Lee Rife, b. 11 June 1917, d. 13 Dec 1999; m. Maggie Ann Fields

^{V6}3088. ^{13}3. Earl Dee Rife, b. 14 Aug 1918, d. July 2000; m. Wilma Sherman

^{V6}3089. ^{13}4. Loretta B. Rife, b. 17 Oct 1919, d. 29 Jan 1976; m. Jan 1945, Donovan Scott

^{V6}3090. ^{13}5. William Orval Rife, b. 5 May 1923; m. Jan 1945, Nina Marie Majors

^{V6}3091. ^{13}6. Cleo May Rife, b. 2 March 1926; m. 21 Oct 1946, Emmitt Flotz

^{V6}3092. ^{13}7. Leo Ray Rife, b. 2 March 1926, d. 13 Oct 1958; m. March 1948, Maxine Riley

^{V6}3093. ^{13}8. Kenneth Marshall Rife, b. 7 Sept 1929; m. 5 Feb 1952, Mary Francis Fields

^{V6}3094. ^{12}3. **Eva Breshears**, b. 25 April 1902, d. 10 March 1982; m.1. _____ Davis; m.2. Tom Brown; m.3. 12 Jan 1921, Cleo Wade, b. ?, d. 24 Dec 1942

^{V6}3095. ^{13}1. Cholotte Wade; m. Nov 1953, Raymond Marrow

^{V6}3096. ^{13}2. Edward Wade; m. Wilma Phegley

^{V6}3097. ^{13}3. Juanita Wade; m. Carl Demitz

^{V6}3098. ^{13}4. William Cleo Wade,

^{V6}3099. ^{12}4. **Rena Breshears**, (twin) b. 16 July 1905; m. 8 Sept 1922, ***Mort Gumm***, b. 1891, d. 1 Nov 1979

^{V6}3100. ^{13}1. Dorothy Gumm; m. Dee Coffey

^{V6}3101. ^{13}2. Harold Gumm,

^{V6}3102. ^{13}3. Hubert Gumm; m. Maxine Baker

^{V6}3103. ^{13}4. Donald Gumm; m. Shirley Capps

^{V6}3104. ^{13}5. Tommy Gumm,

^{V6}3105. ^{12}5. **Vena Breshears**, (twin) b. 16 July 1905, d. 11 July 1993; m. 7 May 1922, ***Clarence Roy***

"Short" Masten, b. 1891, d. 1979

V63106. [13]1. Clarence Roy Masten Jr

V63107. [13]2. Katherine Masten; m. Jack Holloway

V63108. [13]3. Joe Gene Masten,

V63109. [12]6. **Gertie P. Breshears**, (twin) b. 16 Feb 1906, Wheatland, Hickory Co, MO, d. 15 March 1998; m. 6 Dec 1924, ***Romie Starkey***

V63110. [12]7. **Mertie Breshears**, (twin), b. 16 Feb 1906, Wheatland, Hickory Co, MO; m.1. 24 Feb 1925, ***John Conway***; m.2. 21 March 1931, ***Robert "Bob" Glorifield***

V63111. [13]1. Ila Mae Conway, b. 16 Oct 1926

V63112. [13]2. Robert Gene Glorifield, b. 11 May 1932

V63113. [12]8. Infant dau **Breshears**, (twin) b. 14 Dec 1916, d. 9 Jan 1917

V63114. [12]9. Infant son **Breshears**, (twin) b. 14 Dec 1916, d. 9 Jan 1917

Amanda "Mandy" Breshears and Steven B. Breshears

v63035. [10]4. **Amanda "Mandy" Breshears**, (d/o Robert Hiram "Bob Hiram" Breshears and Anna Breshears), b. 5 Aug 1861, AR, d. 2 Feb 1936, Hickory Co, MO, bur Jones cem, near Avery, Hickory Co, MO; m. 13 Sept 1877, in Hickory Co, MO, **Steven B. Breshears**, (s/o Madison Golman Breshears and Elizabeth Brown) b. 28 Feb 1853, d. 6 Nov 1943, Benton Co, MO. They and their 7 children are hh #37 in Wheatland Twp, Hickory Co, MO, in 1900 US Census. Steven's middle initial is "W" in some records; this could stand for William and the "B" for Bill. The majority of records use "B."

V63115. [11]1. **Martha Emma Breshears**, b. June 1881, Hickory Co, MO; m. ***George Thomas "Tom" Hedgepeth***, b. c?1875. Three children, including:

V63116. [12]x. Mabel Josephine Hedgepeth, b. 14 Dec 1908, Benton Co, MO, d. 13 April 1912, Benton Co, MO, bur Jones Cem, near Avery, MO

V63117. [11]2. **Horace Breshears**, b. March 1885, Hickory Co, MO, d. 1960 Sedalia, Pettis Co, MO; m. ***Elizabeth "Lizzy" Button***, b. 1883, Benton Co, MO, d.

LaMonte, MO.

V^{6}3118. ^{12}1. **Thomas Virgil Breshears**, b. ?, d. 27 Dec 1995; m. 29 Nov 1933, in Sedalie, Pettis Co, MO, Helen M. Norris, b. 21 Nov 1911, Sedalia, MO, d. 21 Nov 1996, Bothwell Regional Health Center.

V^{6}3119. ^{13}1. **Thomas D. Breshears**,

V^{6}3120. ^{13}2. **Carolyn E. Breshears**, m. ***Harold Finley***

V^{6}3121. ^{13}3. **Clara Sue Breshears**, m. ***Dale Peters***

V^{6}3122. ^{13}4. **Kathleen Breshears**, m. ***Tom Files***

V^{6}3123. ^{13}5. **David A. Breshears**, m. ***Velma*** _____

V^{6}3124. ^{13}6. **John W. Breshears**, m. ***Virginia*** _____

V^{6}3125. ^{12}2. **Gertrude Breshears**,

V^{6}3126. ^{12}3. **Janetta Breshears**,

V^{6}3127. ^{12}4. **Robert Breshears**,

V^{6}3128. ^{11}3. ***Ada Bell Breshears**, b. Dec 1889, in Indian Territory; m. ***Walter Joseph "Toad" Button***,

V^{6}3129. ^{11}4. **George Clarence Breshears**, b. Feb 1891, MO, d. c1918, near Wheatland, Hickory Co, MO, when a horse fell with him and fractured his skull; bur Jones Cem, near Avery, MO.

V^{6}3130. ^{11}5. **Della W. Breshears**, b. c1893, Benton Co, MO; m. ***Frank Proctor***, b. c?1877. Four children, names unknown to me.

V^{6}3131. ^{11}6. **Stella Mae Breshears**, b. Feb 1895, Hickory Co, MO; m. 21 Nov 1915, Benton Co, MO, ***Samuel M. Tipton***, b. c?1885. Three children, names unknown to me.

V^{6}3132. ^{11}7. **Alva Herman Breshears**, b. 19 April 1897, Hickory Co, MO, d. 13 Feb 1970, Bothwell Hosp, Sedalia, MO; m.1. 16 Dec 1916, in Avery, Benton Co, MO, ***Ada Crystal Ray***, b. 19 Feb 1896, d. 2 Sept 1964, Wheatland, Hickory Co, MO; m.2. 20 Aug 1965, ***Eula Jones***

V^{6}3133. ^{12}1. **Alma Breshears**, m. 25 Dec 1937, ***L. Ross Allen***

V^{6}3134. ^{12}2. **William Clarence Breshears**, b. 5 April 1919, Hickory Co, MO, d. there, 20 Jan 1975; m. ***Laura Lee Davis***, b. 15 July 1925

V^{6}3135. ^{12}3. **Kenneth Hayward Breshears**, b. 1 Aug 1921,

d. 30 Nov 2004; m. ***Mildred Allen***

V6 3136. [12]4. **Wayne Eugene Breshears**, m. ***Wilma Allen***

V6 3137. [12]5. **Herman Dillard Breshears**, b. 17 Nov 1927; m. 31 Oct 1949, in Avery, MO, ***Lillie Elaine Wright***, b. 17 Oct 1929, Wheatland, Hickory Co, MO, d/o Tom Wright and Anthis Bandall

V6 3138. [13]1. **Lonnie Herman Breshears**, b. 9 Dec 1950; m. ***Jo Lynn Zorn***, b. April 1953

V6 3139. [13]2. **Judy Elaine Breshears**, b. 4 May 1953; m. 26 July 1971, ***Jackie Leon Cole*** (ch: Dean Leon; and Scott Allen Cole)

V6 3140. [12]6. **Jack Lee Breshears**, m. ***Kathy*** ____

V6 3141. [12]7. **Bobby Dee Breshears**, m. ***Mary*** ____

V6 3128. [11]3. **Ada Bell Breshears**, (d/o Amanda "Mandy" Breshears and Steven B. Breshears), b. Dec 1889, in Indian Territory; m. ***Walter Joseph "Toad" Button***, b. 11 July 1886, Bentonville, Benton Co, MO, d. 18 Feb 1962

V6 3142. [12]1. Lena Florence Button, b. 7 March 1910, d. 9 Aug 1992; m. 18 Feb 1933, in Fristoe, MO, Benjamin Linn Jenkins, b. 9 April 1909, d. 27 Sept 1977

V6 3143. [13]1. Robert Lee Jenkins, b. 27 Oct 1937, Kansas City, MO; m.1. Betty E. Holcolm (2 ch: Brian R. and Brent M. Jenkins); m.2. 1954, Patricia Ann Husong (1 ch: Debora A. Jenkins)

V6 3144. [13]2. John Ronald Jenkins, b. 26 Nov 1943; m. 6 June 1964, Janice Kay Cothern. (Ch: Rhonda R. and Randall L. Jenkins

V6 3145. [12]2. Roy Horace Button, b. 8 Nov 1911, Avery, Benton Co, MO, d. 2000; m.1. Tyru Dawson; m.2. Fyrn Dawson.

V6 3146. [13]1. Cathryn Jane Button,

V6 3147. [13]2. William Carl Button,

V6 3148. [13]3. Christine Mae Button,

V6 3149. [12]3. Leta May Button, b. 31 July 1913, Avery, Benton Co, MO; m.1. 19 Dec 1929, in Fristoe, MO, John William Dawson, b. 12 April 1907, Warsaw, Benton, Co, MO, d. 19 May 1993, Sedalia, Pettis Co, MO; m.2. c1996, Shellie Bybee, d. 2000.

[V6]3150. [13]1. Betty Jo Dawson, b. 10 Jan 1931, Warsaw, Benton Co, MO; m. 9 March 1949, Benton Co, MO, Curtis Eugene Lutman, b. 14 May 1930, Ocala, FL.

[V6]3151. [14]1. Lance Eugene Lutman; m. Mary Marlene Howell.

[V6]3152. [15]1. Gregory Lance Lutman; m. Melissa Adkins

[V6]3153. [15]2. Darin Joseph Lutman; m. Alisha Ann Friar. Ch: Beau Christopher Lutman

[V6]3154. [14]2. Jan Lutman; m. Richard Dennis Adams

[V6]3155. [15]1. Richard Scott Adams; m. Dara Michelle Weller

[V6]3156. [15]2. Robert Ryan Adams; m. Sharon Elaine England. Ch: Gregory Chance; and Ashton Hope Adams

[V6]3157. [12]4. William Ralph Button, b. 3 July 1916, Fristoe, Benton Co, MO; m.1. Martha Lucille McClung, b. 6 May 1918, Waverly, Saline Co, KS, d. 12 June 1987, Sedalia, Pettis Co, MO; m.2. 26 July 1984, Susetta Marie Goodell

[V6]3158. [13]1. Edward Lamoine Button, b. 12 April 1941; m. Leila Jean Howard

[V6]3159. [13]2. Richard Mack Button, b. 20 Sept 1942; m. Annette Lynne Sules

[V6]3160. [12]5. Thomas Ray Button, b. 5 Oct 1921; m. 11 Feb 1950, Beatrice Brauer. Thomas Ray Button has written a book on Buttons.

[V6]3161. [13]1. Patricia Rae Button, b. 1 Sept 1950; m. Owen Lee Slavens (ch: John David Slavens)

[V6]3162. [13]2. David Allen Button, b. 23 Jan 1952; m. Penni Sue Wishard (ch: Brandon Rolland Button)

[V6]3163. [13]3. Margie Ann Button, b. 15 Oct 1955; m. Phillip Eugene Slavens (ch: Michael Phillip; and Lisa Marie Slavens)

[V6]3164. [13]4. Daniel Wayne Button, b. 14 Aug 1957

[V6]3165. [13]5. Malinda Button, b. 16 Dec 1960

[V6]3166. [13]6. Lucinda Dawn Button, b. 19 March 1964; m. Jurgen Mogel (ch: Lily Rae Mogel)

Nancy Ellen Breshears and George Washington Hill

^{v6}**3031.** ^{9}11. **Nancy Ellen Breshears**, (d/o Jesse Brashears and Mary Ellen Franklin), b. 14 July 1850, Dallas Co, MO, d. 12 June 1908 in Dallas Co, MO; m. 15 Oct 1876 in Dallas Co, MO, (second wife of) ***George Washington "Wash" Hill***, b, 23 Jan 1845, Dallas Co, MO, d.19 June 1918, Dallas Co, MO, s/o Alexander Hill and Lucinda Edmisson (data from descendants, Gary Swift and Kathy Sue Ann Parker; additional data from Georgene Humphries). Nancy and Wash both bur Hill Cem, Long Lane, Dallas Co, MO.

^{V6}3167. ^{10}1. Sadie Lydia Angeline Hill, b. 19 Aug 1877, Dallas Co, MO, d. 2 July 1946; m. Henry Foster Gaunt, s/o J.W. Gaunt and Ann ____

^{V6}3168. ^{10}2. Alta S. Hill, b. 28 Sept 1878, Dallas Co, MO

^{V6}3169. ^{10}3. Mary Francis Hill, b. 30 April 1881, Dallas Co, MO, d. 1 July 1954, Dallas Co, MO, bur Liberty Cem, Dallas Co, MO; m. William F. Triplett. Several children, among whom:

^{V6}3170. ^{11}x. Mary Francis Triplett, b. 1915, Dallas Co, MO; m. Ralph McGinnis, b. 17 Feb 1904, Dallas Co, MO, d. 5 June 1975, bur Oak Lawn Cem, Buffalo, MO

^{V6}3171. ^{12}1. Donald Ralph McGinnis, b. 1939, Dallas Co, MO

^{V6}3172. ^{10}4. Lavinia Clementine Hill, b. 28 May 1882, Dallas Co, MO, d. 14 May 1953

^{V6}3173. ^{10}5. Rosa Jane Hill, b. 28 Aug 1886, Dallas Co, MO, d. 23 Feb 1951

^{V6}3174. ^{10}6. Stella L. Hill, b. 9 Oct 1889, Dallas Co, MO, d. 22 Aug 1920

^{V6}3175. ^{10}7. Bessa Hill, b. 5 March 1892, Dallas Co, MO, d. 26 Dec 1951

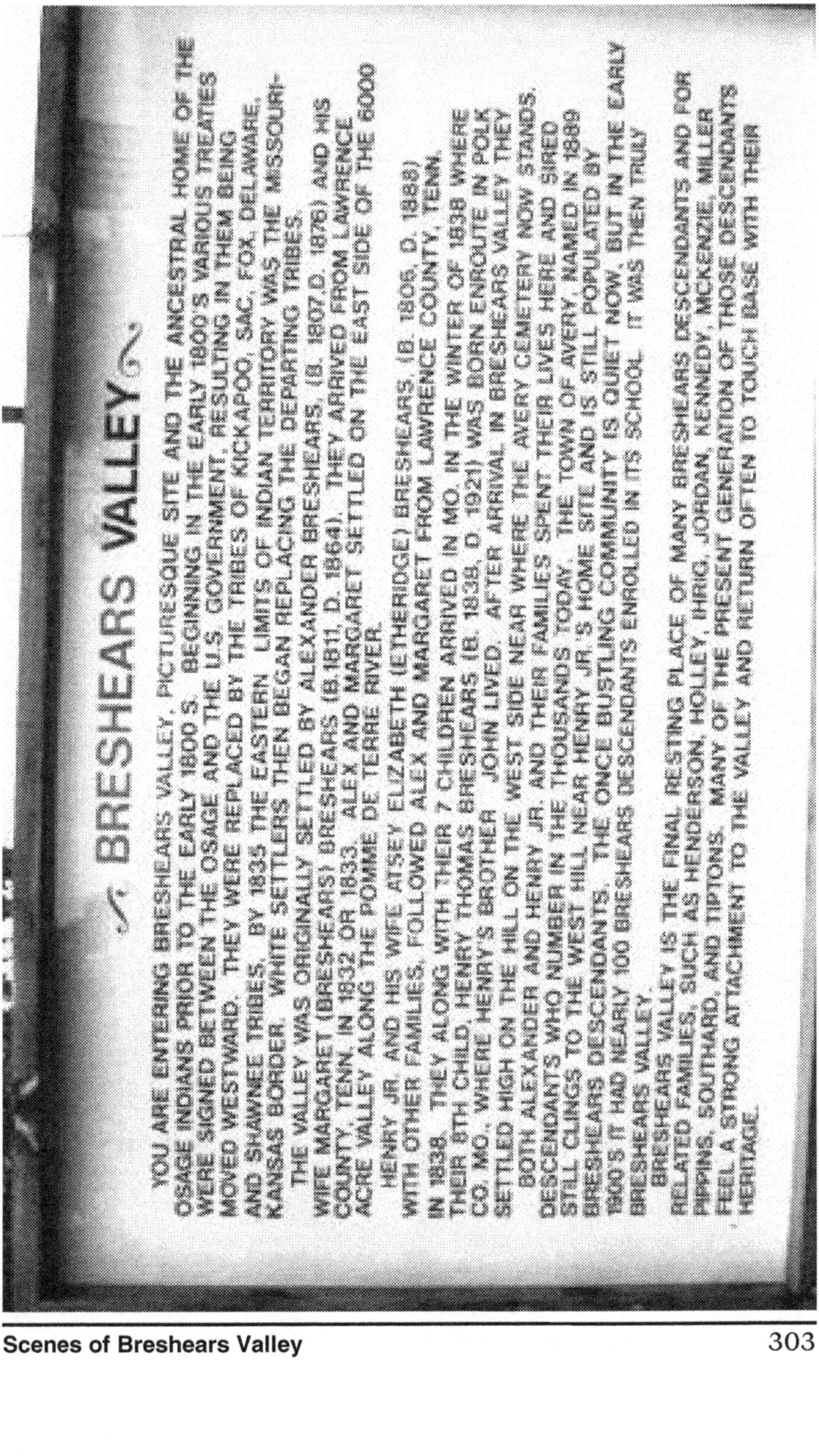
BRESHEARS VALLEY
YOU ARE ENTERING BRESHEARS VALLEY, PICTURESQUE SITE AND THE ANCESTRAL HOME OF THE OSAGE INDIANS PRIOR TO THE EARLY 1800'S. BEGINNING IN THE EARLY 1800'S VARIOUS TREATIES WERE SIGNED BETWEEN THE OSAGE AND THE U.S. GOVERNMENT, RESULTING IN THEM BEING MOVED WESTWARD. THEY WERE REPLACED BY THE TRIBES OF KICKAPOO, SAC, FOX, DELAWARE, AND SHAWNEE TRIBES. BY 1835 THE EASTERN LIMITS OF INDIAN TERRITORY WAS THE MISSOURI-KANSAS BORDER. WHITE SETTLERS THEN BEGAN REPLACING THE DEPARTING TRIBES.
THE VALLEY WAS ORIGINALLY SETTLED BY ALEXANDER BRESHEARS, (B. 1807,D. 1876) AND HIS WIFE MARGARET (BRESHEARS) BRESHEARS (B.1811, D. 1864). THEY ARRIVED FROM LAWRENCE COUNTY, TENN. IN 1832 OR 1833. ALEX AND MARGARET SETTLED ON THE EAST SIDE OF THE 6000 ACRE VALLEY ALONG THE POMME DE TERRE RIVER.
HENRY JR. AND HIS WIFE ATSEY ELIZABETH (ETHERIDGE) BRESHEARS, (B. 1806, D. 1888) WITH OTHER FAMILIES, FOLLOWED ALEX AND MARGARET FROM LAWRENCE COUNTY, TENN. IN 1838. THEY ALONG WITH THEIR 7 CHILDREN ARRIVED IN MO. IN THE WINTER OF 1838 WHERE THEIR 8TH CHILD, HENRY THOMAS BRESHEARS (B. 1838, D. 1921) WAS BORN ENROUTE IN POLK CO. MO., WHERE HENRY'S BROTHER JOHN LIVED. AFTER ARRIVAL IN BRESHEARS VALLEY THEY SETTLED HIGH ON THE HILL ON THE WEST SIDE NEAR WHERE THE AVERY CEMETERY NOW STANDS.
BOTH ALEXANDER AND HENRY JR. AND THEIR FAMILIES SPENT THEIR LIVES HERE AND SIRED DESCENDANTS WHO NUMBER IN THE THOUSANDS TODAY. THE TOWN OF AVERY, NAMED IN 1889 STILL CLINGS TO THE WEST HILL NEAR HENRY JR.'S HOME SITE AND IS STILL POPULATED BY BRESHEARS DESCENDANTS. THE ONCE BUSTLING COMMUNITY IS QUIET NOW, BUT IN THE EARLY 1900'S IT HAD NEARLY 100 BRESHEARS DESCENDANTS ENROLLED IN ITS SCHOOL. IT WAS THEN TRULY BRESHEARS VALLEY.
BRESHEARS VALLEY IS THE FINAL RESTING PLACE OF MANY BRESHEARS DESCENDANTS AND FOR RELATED FAMILIES, SUCH AS HENDERSON, HOLLEY, IHRIG, JORDAN, KENNEDY, MCKENZIE, MILLER PIPPINS, SOUTHARD, AND TIPTONS. MANY OF THE PRESENT GENERATION OF THOSE DESCENDANTS FEEL A STRONG ATTACHMENT TO THE VALLEY AND RETURN OFTEN TO TOUCH BASE WITH THEIR HERITAGE.

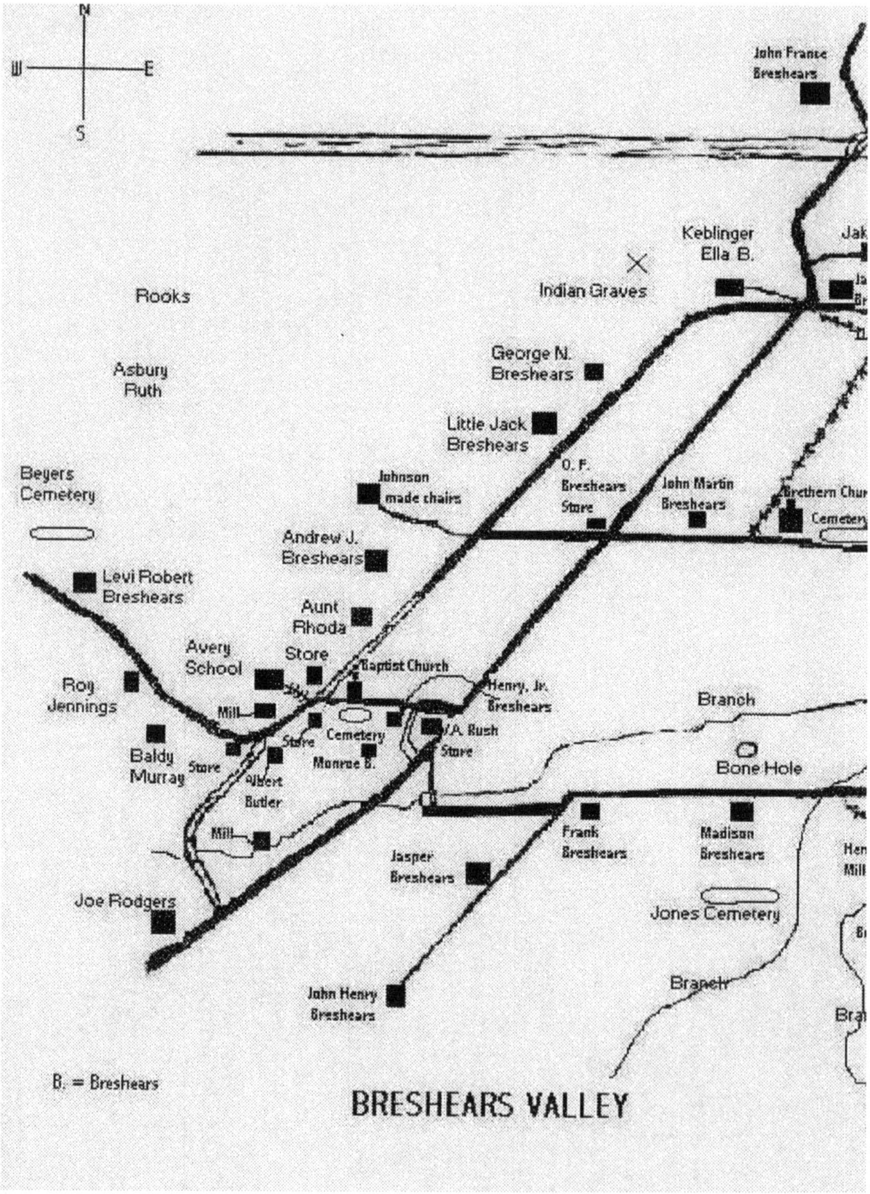

Figure 48: A map by Jim Prine, showing the location of many Breshears homes. It was said that no one lived in the valley who was not a Breshears descendant.

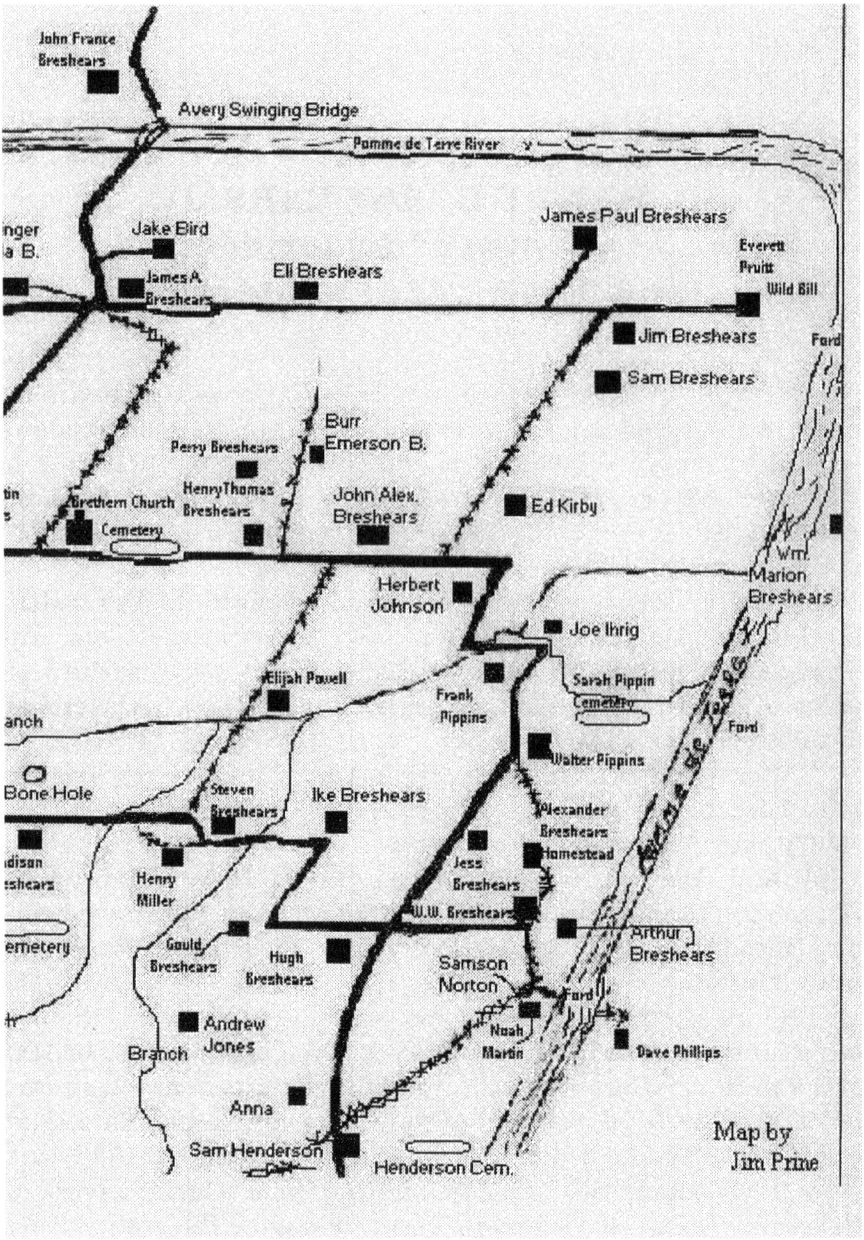

John France Breshears
Avery Swinging Bridge
Pomme de Terre River
Jake Bird
James A. Breshears
Eli Breshears
James Paul Breshears
Everett Pruitt
Wild Bill
Jim Breshears
Sam Breshears
Ford
Burr Emerson B.
Perry Breshears
HenryThomas Breshears
Brethern Church
Cemetery
John Alex. Breshears
Ed Kirby
Herbert Johnson
Wm. Marion Breshears
Joe Ihrig
Elijah Powell
Frank Pippins
Sarah Pippin Cemetery
Ford
Walter Pippins
Bone Hole
Steven Breshears
Ike Breshears
Alexander Breshears Homestead
Henry Miller
Jess Breshears
W.W. Breshears
Arthur Breshears
Gould Breshears
Hugh Breshears
Samson Norton
Ford
Andrew Jones
Branch
Noah Martin
Dave Phillips
Anna
Sam Henderson
Henderson Cem.
Map by Jim Prine

30. HENRY BRESHEARS JR, Atsa "Atsey" Etheridge, and Their Older Children

[V6]**1615.** [8]6. **Henry Breshears Jr**, (s/o Henry Breshears Sr and Eleanor ?Hardin), b. 23 Oct 1801 in NC or SC (Census data is contradictory), d. 18 March 1860, Wheatland, Hickory Co, MO, age 58; m. c1822, Lawrence Co, TN, ***Atsa "Atsey" Etheridge***, b. 1 Feb 1806, TN, d. 1888, Benton Co, MO, age 81, d/o Thomas Etheridge.

We often see Henry listed with a middle name of Alexander, but I have never seen a document with the name on it, nor any even slightly compelling evidence. Henry and Atsey lived the first years of their marriage in Lawrence County, TN, where several of their children were born.

After Henry Breshears Sr died in 1828, Henry Jr apparently took care of his mother, who died 1837. Shortly thereafter, Henry and Atsey moved to Missouri. Henry d. 16 or18 March 1860 and Atsey d. 3 Nov 1878 or 88; both were buried at Henderson Cemetery, near Wheatland, MO, but they have been moved to the Baptist Cem in Avery, MO. Their slave, Rhoda, is buried beside them.

Henry Breshears, Jr and his brother, William Breshears, got a land grant in Lawrence Co, TN. The grant #25610 of 100 acres to Henry Breshears, Jr. and William Breshears is shown below. In the brief passage of time between Henry Sr.'s land grant in 1824 and Henry, Jr.'s occupant claim in 1828, the capital of Tennessee had been moved from Murfreesboro to Nashville. Tennessee's famous governor signed the grant with a bold, "Sam Houston" rather than the formal name, "Samuel Houston."

Tennessee Land Grant #25610

To all to whom these presents shall come .... Greeting:

KNOW YE, That by virtue of certificates N 96. 97. 98. & 99. all dated the first day of March 1826 signed by the Commissioner of West Tennessee to the assignee of the Register of the Western District for 25 Acres each and entered on the 17th day of May 1826 as an occupant claim under the act of 1825 by No. 1772.

There is granted by the said State of Tennessee unto William and Henry Breshears assignee of the said Register

A certain tract or, parcel of LAND, containing one hundred acres by survey bearing date the 20th day of May 1826 lying in the Seventh District in Lawrence County on Big Shoal Creek in Range five and section two and bounded as follows, to wit: Beginning at an ash fourteen poles south from the northeast corner of entry No. 1460, thence south 55 degrees east 56 poles to said point of beginning, thence south one hundred three poles to a stake, thence north one hundred three poles to a poplar, thence west one hundred fifty-six poles to the beginning.

With the hereditaments and appertenances. To Have and to Hold, the said tract or parcel of land, with its appertenances, to the said William and Henry Breshears and their heirs forever.

In Witness Whereof, Samuel Houston, Governor of the State of Tennessee, has hereunto set his hand, and caused the great seal of the State to be affixed, at Nashville on the 24th day of March in the year of our Lord one thousand eight hundred and twenty eight, and Independence of the United States the 52nd.

BY THE GOVERNOR (signed) Sam Houston

(signed) Daniel C. Graham, Secretary

Recorded 25th March 1828

On 2 April 1838, Henry Beshears, Jr sold this 100 acres to his wife's brother-in-law, David Riddle (m. Sarah Etheridge), both of Lawrence Co, TN, for $750. Only Henry Jr signed; William was already in Arkansas. We do not know how or when William transferred his share to Henry. The land was "by Grant 25610, 7th Surveyor's Dist, Range 5, Sec 2, on Big Shoal Creek." (LawrCo, TN, Deeds, F:237) The sale was apparently in preparation for Henry and Atsey's move to Benton Co, MO.

This home was destroyed by a tornado some sixty-six years ago. The tornado carried away a special doll cradle belonging to one of twin girls in the home, but that cradle was recently located in an antique store and returned to its original owner, Hellen Parson at Wheatland. The woman on the porch in this photo is Leaner Murray Breshears, Mrs. Parson's mother.

Figure 50: Henry Breshears home in Missouri. It later blew away in a storm. Photo from Bill Brooks.

Henry's Estate in Missouri

The Will of Henry Brashears, dated 10 March 1860, Hickory Co, MO (abstract): Wife, Atsey Brashears, personal property and Land. Remainder of property to my children in equal shares. Three daus, Ann Brashears, Sally Jordan, and Attsey A. Brashears, and my two sons, John M. and Andrew Jackson. "It is understood that the heirs of each of my deceased children shall receive the one equal share of my property same as the dec'd would have received." Exrs: sons, Levi and Madison. Wit: Thomas Brashears, William Henderson, Joseph W. Brashears and William Paxton. Filed and recorded 7 April 1860 (Book W, p.50) Letters Testamentory granted unto Levi Brashears. Securities: William Henderson, Virgil S. Williams, Peter Ihrig, and Samuel Anderson (Bk B, p.150)

Family of Henry Breshears Jr and Atsa "Atsey" Etheridge

(Source: family sheets compiled in 1968 by Roy Colbert, using 1820, 1830 Censuses of Lawrence Co, TN and 1850, 1860, 1870 Censuses of Hickory Co, MO. Considerable data from *Breshears, Jordan, and Ethridge Families in Missouri*, by Carmen Elizabeth Collins, 1990.)

[V6]3221. [9]1. ***James Alexander Breshears Sr**, b. 20 April 1823, Lawrence Co, TN, d. 5 May 1857, Hickory Co, MO; m. ***Sarah Ann Jordan***.

[V6]3222. [9]2. ***Levi Robert "Lee" Breshears**, b. 13 May 1825, Lawrence Co, TN, d. 1907, MO; m. 20 May 1847, Benton Co, MO, ***Mary Anna Garner***

[V6]3223. [9]3. ***Madison Golman "Matt" Breshears**, b. 8 Nov 1827, Lawrence Co, TN, d. 3 Aug 1899, MO; m. 20 May 1848, Benton Co, MO, ***Sarah Elizabeth Brown***
See separate chapter.

[V6]3224. [9]4. ***Susanna "Sukey" Breshears**, b. 6 Jan/Feb 1829, Lawrence Co, TN; m.1. ***Shandy Jordan***, b. c?1829, d. c?1855; m.2. ***Jesse Hardin (or David) Miller***, b. c1829, MO

[V6]3225. [9]5. ***Elizabeth Anna Breshears**, b. 24 Oct 1831, Lawrence Co, TN, d. after 1877, Polk Co, MO; m. ****Robert Hiram "Bob Hiram" Breshears***, who was from the Polk Co, MO, branch of the Breshears family, s/o Jesse Brashears and Elizabeth Bell. See Bob Hiram's listing for their children.

[V6]3226. [9]6. ***William Marion Breshears**, b. 5 Oct 1833, Lawrence Co, TN, d. 1861, Camp Cole, MO; m. 9 Dec 1854, ***Mary Jane Pippin***, (d/o Eleanor Breshears and Richard Pippin), b. c1833, d. c1861-2

[V6]3227. [9]7. ***Sarah Malissa Breshears**, b. 9 March 1835, Lawrence Co, TN, d. 14 Jan 1910, Bentonville, MO; m. 17 Jan 1856, ***William Newton Jordan***

SUBSCRIPTION SCHOOL AT AVERY---About 1905. Nancy Reeder Butler, with the big bow-tie, was teacher. To her right are Edith Breshears, Ola Martin, Mora Breshears, Evie Crabtree. Second row: Iva Breshears Bird, Curtis Ihrig, Harry Breshears, Clyde Breshears, Ollie Ihrig. Bottom row: Prue Breshears, Dolly Breshears, Retta Breshears, Eathel Lopp, Stella Nation, Isadore Breshears, Elvin Breshears, Leonard Martin and Retta Breshears. Stella Nation is the only child in this picture who was not a Breshears grandchild. She was raised by Uncle Jack Breshears. Subscription schools were held after the regular school was out in the spring, parents paying, in 1905 at Avery, $2 per child in school for two months.

^{V6}3228. ^{9}8. ***Henry Thomas Breshears**, b. 22 Nov 1838, Louisburg, Dallas Co, MO, d. 1 May 1921; m. 13 Oct 1858, ***Sabrina J. Murray***

^{V6}3229. ^{9}9. ***John Martin Van Buren Breshears**, b. 19 Nov 1840, Benton Co, MO, d. 4 Feb 1922, Benton Co, MO; m. 20/30 Mary 1862, ***Susannah Ihrig***, d/o Peter Ihrig and Elizabeth Ellen "Elizzie" Tonbaugh

^{V6}3230. ^{9}10. **Matthew Calvin Breshears**, b. 12 Jan 1843, MO, d. 12 Nov 1843

^{V6}3231. ^{9}11. **Jesse Hardin Breshears**, b. 19 Sept 1845, MO, d. 25 Dec 1845

^{V6}3232. ^{9}12. ***Andrew Jackson Breshears**, b. 24 Dec 1846, Hickory Co, MO, d. 2 Nov 1924, Hickory Co, MO; m. ***Mary Jane Parsley***, b. 1850, d. after 1920

^{V6}3233. ^{9}13. ***Marcus Monroe Breshears**, b. 13 Oct 1848, Hickory Co, MO, d. 13 Nov 1909, Avery, MO; m. ***Leana Murray***

^{V6}3234. ^{9}14. ***Atsey Adaline Breshears**, b. 30 Aug 1850, Hickory Co, MO, d. 24 March 1910; m. ***Joel Ihrig***, s/o Peter Ihrig and Elizabeth Ellen "Elizzie" Tonbaugh

HICKORY COUNTY HISTORY: 1920's (Front row) Bessie Rodgers Crabtree, Edith Breshears Miller, Ida Breshears Bird; (Middle row) Stella Nation, Retha Breshears McKenzie, Ethel Breshears Myers, Hattie Breshears Hollie, Sadie Kirby McKenzie, Sadie Henderson Roberts; (Back row) Floy Davis Breshears, Mora Breshears, Virda Rodgers Blackwell, unknown. Photo submitted by Betty Cain.

V6 3235. 9 15. <u>*William Carroll Green</u> **Breshears**, b. 15 Oct 1825, VA, d. 16 Nov 1861, MO. While a wagon train was heading west, probably in 1838, a couple named Green died, leaving an orphan, William Carroll Green, who was simply taken in and raised by Henry and Atsey; he and his descendants used **Breshears** as their last name.

Peter Ihrig, father-in-law of three Breshears, possibly b. PA, is first located in Miami Co, IN, in 1850, but there are Ihrigs, including a Peter Erick, in Wayne Co, OH in 1830, when George Tonbaugh (another father-in-law) was known to have been there, having come from PA. In 1860, Peter was in Hickory Co, MO; in 1870, in Newton Co, MO; in 1880, in Washington Co, AR. He d. 21 Feb 1888, at Myrtle Point, OR. (from Roy Colbert's *Brashears/Breshears Newsletter*, No. 1, July 1974)

Peter Ihrig and Elizabeth Ellen "Elizzie" Tonbaugh had the following children:

i-1. Susannah Ihrig, b. 31 March 1842, IN; m. ***John Martin Van Buren Breshears***, (s/o Henry Breshears Jr and Atsa "Atsey" Etheridge)
i-2. John B. Ihrig; m. Mary Condley
i-3. George Nimrod Ihrig, b. c1849, Benton Co, MO; m. ***Mary Jane Breshears***, (d/o Madison Golman Breshears, s/o Henry Breshears Jr and Atsa "Atsey" Etheridge)
i-4. Clementine Ihrig (twin); m. Joseph Frederick
i-5. Valentine Ihrig (twin), d. young
i-6. Joel Ihrig, b. 8 March 1858, MO; m. ***Atsey Adaline Breshears***, (d/o Henry Breshears Jr and Atsa "Atsey" Etheridge)
i-7. Elizabeth Ellen Ihrig; m. James Franklin McCracken
i-8. Nancy J. Ihrig; m. John Allen
i-9. Mary Ihrig; m. William Eckes
i-10. Franklin B. Ihrig,

31. JAMES ALEXANDER BRESHEARS, Sr, and Sarah Ann Jordan

[v6]3221. [9]1. **James Alexander Breshears Sr**, (s/o Henry Breshears Jr and Atsa "Atsey" Etheridge), b. 20 April 1823, Lawrence Co, TN, d. 5 May 1857, Hickory Co, MO, bur Avery Cem; m. ***Sarah Ann Jordan***, b. 11 July 1832, TN, d. 22 June 1886, bur Macedonia Cem, Wheatland, Hickory Co, MO, d/o Campbell Jordan. James's estate was administered by William R. Jordan (Sarah's second husband), with securities William Y. Evans, A.F. Doak, and B. Summers, 5 March 1863 (Hickory Co, MO, Bk B, p.176).

Before James died, he and Sarah had only one child: James Alexander "Jimmy" Breshears, Jr (see below). Some researchers give James a second child: Eudona Breshears, b. c?1849, m. a cousin, Ollie Breshears, b. c1890, MO, s/o Levi Breshears and Sarah Thornton, of the Madison Golman Breshears line. But a glance at the birthdates suggests someone is scrambling the ancestral eggs. I believe they are confusing James's granddaughter Eudona with another person. Levi "Prairie Levi" Breshears did have a son named Ollie, but he married Susan Cook and went to Canada. James's second child is a confused invention.

Family of James Alexander Breshears Sr and Sarah Ann Jordan:

V6 3236. 10 1. **James Alexander "Jimmy" Breshears Jr**, b. 28 Feb 1857, Benton Co, MO, d. there, 6 April 1947, bur Macedonia Cem, Wheatland, Hickory Co, MO; m. 27 Feb 1879, ***Theodosia E. Carder***, b. 21 Dec 1860, d. 8 June 1886, Hickory Co, MO, bur Macedonia Cem; m.2. 4 Sept 1887, *Amanda Paxton*,

Family of James Alexander "Jimmie" Breshears, Jr and Theodosia Carder:

V6 3237. 11 1. **Minnie Breshears**, b. c1880, lived to be 85; m. ***Ben Cauthon***, and had 4 or 6 children, among whom: Bill Cauthon.

V6 3238. 11 2. **Arvilla A. Breshears,** b. 27 March 1882; m. ***Jesse A. Miller***, b. 7 March 1880, d. June 1956, bur Macedonia Cem. Four or five children, names unknown.

Family of James Alexander "Jimmie" Breshears, Jr and Amanda Paxton:

V6 3239. 11 3. **Nora Bell Breshears**, b. 1 July 1888; m. ***Marvin Arnold Holt***, b. 20 Feb 1885

V6 3240. 12 1. Gerald Holt, b. 22 Dec 1914; m. Jessie Marie Rife

V6 3241. 13 1. Delores Revay Holt, b. 22 Oct 1934; m.1. 26 July 1953, Francis Lee Tolivar, b. 21 Aug 1927; m.2. 18 Oct 1972, Bill Heaton

V6 3242. 14 1. Steven Lee Tolivar, b. 11 Aug 1954

V6 3243. 14 2. Michel Dee Tolivar, b. 11 Aug 1954

V6 3244. 14 3. Andrew Marvin Tolivar, b. 21 April 1956

V6 3245. 14 4. Gary Dale Tolivar, b. 31 Dec 1957

V6 3246. 13 2. Ernest Lindel Holt, b. 3 Feb 1938; m. 6 July 1956, Wilma Lee Buckner, b. 10

May 1939

V6 3247. [13]3. Anthony Reese Holt, b. 18 Dec 1952; m. 11 June 1971, Ruth Ann Weber, d/o Robert Weber

V6 3248. [12]2. Lester Breshears Holt, b. 8 Feb 1918, d. 28 March 1918

V6 3249. [11]4. ***Harriet Eudona "Dona" Breshears**, b. 15 Feb 1891, in Cross Timbers, MO, d. there, 11 Nov 1941; m. 15 Feb 1911, in Wheatland, Hickory Co, MO, a cousin, ***George William "Bill" Breshears** (s/o Levi Breshears and Sarah Thornton, of the Madison Golman Breshears line), b. 7 March 1891, Benton Co, MO, d. 12 Feb 1927, in Aztec, New Mexico. See Bill's listing for their children.

V6 3250. [11]5. **Buel Roy Breshears**, b. 19 Aug 1895, d. 8 April 1921, of pneumonia, following an operation for appendicitis; m. 24 Dec 1916, **Jessie Ruby Breshears**, (d/o Levi Breshears and Sarah Thornton, of the Madison Golman Breshears line), b. 8 Oct 1893, d. 25 Dec 1919.

V6 3251. [12]1. **Winifred C. Breshears**, b. 30 Dec 1918, Wheatland, MO; m. 2 Jan 1938, ***Wilburn Estel Pippins***, b. 5 Aug 1918, d. 18 Dec 1944, aboard destroyer U.S.S. Hull, in the Pacific; m.2. 7 May 1946, at Avery, MO, **James Everett Breshears** (s/o James Henry Breshears and Beatrice Murphy), b. 29 Jan 1914

V6 3252. [13]1. Winola Donnis Pippins, b. 17 Oct 1939; m. 21 Sept 1963, Obed D. Flandermeyer, b. 22 Nov 1939

V6 3253. [14]1. Clint Eric Flandermeyer, b. 7 Sept 1964

V6 3254. [14]2. Craig Allen Flandermeyer, b. 26 Feb 1968

V6 3255. [14]3. Clara Roe Flandermeyer,

V6 3256. [13]2. Wilma Lee Pippins, b. 10 Feb 1941, Wheatland, MO; m. 10 Feb 1961, George Vaughn, b. 26 Oct 1939

V6 3257. [14]1. Angelina Rene Vaughn, b. 13 Oct

1966

[V6]3258. [14]2. Mark Russell Vaughn, b. 22 Oct 1968

[V6]3259. [13]3. **Bertie Gail Breshears**, b. 14 Feb 1952

[V6]3260. [13]4. **James Michael Breshears**, b. 20 Dec 1956; m. ***Louisalyn Hammond***,

[V6]3261. [14]1. **Sarah Ann Breshears**,

[V6]3262. [14]2. **Michelle Lyn Breshears**,

[V6]3263. [14]3. **Stephanie Nicole Breshears**,

[V6]3264. [14]4. **James Michael Breshears, Jr**,

The widow of James Alexander Breshears, Sr, Sarah Ann Jordan, b. 11 July 1832, d. 22 June 1896; m.2. William R. Jordan, b. 16 May 1836, Warren Co, Middle TN, d. 20 Feb 1901, MO.

Their children: (Data supplied to Carmen E. Collins by Shirley Bartshe Bigler)

j-1. Nancy Jane Jordan; m.1. Lewis W. Butler; m.2. George Washington Holt

j-2. Mary Ellen Jordan; m. George Columbus Bartshe

j-3. Marshall Lafayette Jordan; d. young

j-4. Emma Mabel Jordan; m. William A. Thornton

j-5. John Wesley Jordan; m. Gussie Pitts

j-6. William Anderson Jordan; m. Lula Mae Cook Compton

j-7. Shandy Arlington Jordan; b. 28 April 1873; d. 7 March 1956; m. ***Arabella Breshears***, b. 3 Oct 1877; d. 13 May 1944

1. Floyd Jordan; b. 19 Feb 1898; d. 3 May 1967; m.1. ***Dolly Breshears*** (2 sons died in infancy); m.2. Dorothy Moore
2. S. Inez Jordan; b. 22 Nov 1900; d. 6 Oct 1991; m. George Tipton, b. 13 Dec 1900. Ch: Lavern; Edsel; William Glen Tipton

j-8. Terry Lavon Jordan; m. Norma Gardner

32. LEVI ROBERT "LEE" BRESHEARS and Mary Anna Garner

[v6]**3222.** [9]2. **Levi Robert "Lee" Breshears**, (s/o Henry Breshears Jr and Atsa "Atsey" Etheridge), b. 13 May 1825, Lawrenceburg, Lawrence Co, TN, d. 5 Dec 1907, MO; m. 20 May 1847 (MO St Hist Soc says 10 Nov 1846), Benton Co, MO, ***Mary Anna Garner***, b. 3 Nov 1825, d. 30 June 1890, both bur Byers Cem, 1¾ miles west of Avery, MO.

Levi Robert Breshears and Granddaughter, Dora Hunziker-circa 1905

Figure 53: Photo from Bill Brooks

Levi and his brother, Madison Golman Breshears, were administrators of their father's estate. Levi served in Co. I, 8th Regt Cavalry, Missouri State Militia. He lived near Fairfield, MO.

Family of Levi Robert Breshears and Mary Anna Garner:

[V6]3321. [10]?. Some researchers list, as a first child (no firm evidence), **Dora Breshears**, no birth date; m. ***John Blackwell***,

[V6]3322. [11]1. Edd Blackwell; m. Laura Southard,

[V6]3323. [11]2. Mary Blackwell; m. Johnny Bobnet

[V6]3324. [10]1. ***James Taylor Breshears**, b. 1847; m. ***Fanny Antwiler***,

[V6]3325. [10]2. **Henry T. Breshears**, b. 1849-50; m. ***S.E.*** _____

[V6]3326. [11]1. **Samuel Breshears**,

[V6]3327. [10]3. **Lucia A. "Dosia" Breshears**, b. 13 April 1852; m. ***Frank Hunziker***, b. c?1853

[V6]3328. [11]1. Dora Hunziker, b. c?1875 or Dec 1890, d. young.

V6 3329. 10 4. ***Atsey D. Breshears**, b. 11 Feb 1855, d. 1902, Hickory Co, MO; had a child out of wedlock with **Steven B. Breshears** (s/o Madison Golman Breshears), b. 28 Feb 1853, d. 6 Nov 1943, Benton Co, MO; m.1. 18 Oct 1882, ***William Joseph "Joe" Rodgers***, b. 15 Aug 1856, s/o William Rodgers and Phoebe Rough.

Figure 54: Phoebe (Rough) Rodgers and her dau/in/law Atsey (Breshears) Rodgers. Photo from Bill Brooks

V6 3330. 10 5. **William Matthew "Matt" Breshears**, b. 25 Jan 1857; m. ***Amanda Isabel Ihrig***, b. 28 July 1866, Hickory Co, MO

V6 3331. 10 6. ***Sarah Elizabeth Breshears**, b. 29 Sept 1859, Benton Co, MO, d. 6 Oct 1909, Benton Co, MO, bur Jones Cem, Avery, MO; m. 24 Nov 1878, a cousin, ***Henry Belsis Breshears** (s/o Madison Golman Breshears); see his listing for their children. Henry later married Ida Button.

James Taylor Breshears and Fanny Antwiler

v6 3324. 10 1. **James Taylor Breshears**, (s/o Levi Robert "Lee" Breshears and Mary Anna Garner), b. 1847; m. ***Fanny Antwiler***,

Family of James Taylor Breshears and Fanny Antwiler:

V6 3332. 11 1. **Henry T. Breshears**,

V6 3333. 11 2. **James Henry Breshears**, b. 29 Nov 1874, d. 13 June 1955; m. ***Beatrice Virginia Murphy***, b. 22 Sept 1879

V6 3334. 12 1. **Lucy Breshears**,

V6 3335. 12 2. **Mary Breshears**,

V6 3336. 12 3. **Atsey Breshears**,m. ______ ***Eads.***

V6 3337. 13 1. June Eads; m. Robert L. Chambers. Ch: Robert W.; Judith; Jane; Betty; and Daniel Lee Chambers

^{V6}3338. ^{12}4. **Nellie May Breshears**, b. 1899, d. 3 June 1955, Hickory Co, MO; m. ***Herbert Mezzacasa***. Ch:

^{V6}3339. ^{13}1. Herman J. Mezzacasa;

^{V6}3340. ^{13}2. Nelson Mezzacasa;

^{V6}3341. ^{13}3. Elizabeth Mezzacasa;

^{V6}3342. ^{13}4. Rev. Nadine Mezzacasa; m. _____ Scott. Ch: George; Charles; Mary Lee; Marjorie; and Stanley Scott

^{V6}3343. ^{13}5. Warren C. Mezzacasa; m. Frances Nell Covington. Ch: Tommy; Nellie Sue; and Paula Dean Mezzacasa

^{V6}3344. ^{13}6. Virginia Mezzacasa;

^{V6}3345. ^{13}7. Ottavia B. Mezzacasa; m.1. Delmar A. Freeland; m.2. ______ Jordan; m.3. Troy Barrett. Ch: S. Darlene; Joseph R.; Delmar A. Jr; and Nellie Mae Freeland; David Jordan; Sondra Barrett; Ottavia Barrett; and Carol Barrett

^{V6}3346. ^{13}8. Herman J. Mezzacasa;

^{V6}3347. ^{13}9. Joseph H. Mezzacasa; m. Mary ______. Ch: Brenda; Gerald; Keith; Jeffry; and Terry Mezzacasa

^{V6}3348. ^{12}5. **Anna Breshears**, b. 17 Sept 1899; m. ***James Harvey Chance***.

^{V6}3349. ^{13}1. Myrtle Chance; m.1. ______; m.2. ______. Ch: Jane; Joann; Marilyn; Rob; and Don ______

^{V6}3350. ^{13}2. Eugene Harvey Chance; m.1. ______; m.2. ______. Ch: Laurie Chance

^{V6}3351. ^{12}6. **James Everett Breshears**, b. 29 Jan 1914, d. 26 Feb 1991; m. 7 May 1946, in Avery, MO, ***Winifred C. Breshears***, (d/o Buel Roy Breshears and Jessie Ruby Breshears), b. 30 Dec 1918, Wheatland, Hickory Co, MO. See Winifred's listing for their children.

Atsey D. Breshears and William Joseph Rodgers

ATSY BRESHEARS AND AUNT MORA WATSON

[v6]**3329.** [10]4. **Atsey D. Breshears**, (d/o Levi Robert "Lee" Breshears and Mary Anna Garner), b. 11 Feb 1855, d. 1902, Hickory Co, MO; had a child out of wedlock with **Steven B. Breshears** (s/o Madison Golman Breshears), b. 28 Feb 1853, d. 6 Nov 1943, Benton Co, MO; m.2. 18 Oct 1882, ***William Joseph "Joe" Rodgers***, b. 15 Aug 1856, d. 12 Jan 1933, Avery, MO, s/o William Rodgers and Phoebe Rough. Steven B. Breshears m.2. Amanda "Mandy" Breshears, (d/o Anna Breshears and Bob Hiram Breshears). **Note:** Aunt Mora Watson was not an actual relative. She was born Mora Owens, on 26 Dec 1866, in Fristoe, MO; she m.1. 7 July 1889, Dr. James Logan, who d. 7 July 1891; m.2. 11 Jan 1900, Dr. James Watson, the town physician in Fristoe. She was a close acquaintance with many Breshears relatives, but not herself related. See Vol. 3 of the Benton County Books, pp. 108-9. Thanks to Glen Breshears for clearing this up.

<u>Family of Atsey D. Breshears and William Joseph Rodgers:</u>

[V6]3352. [11]1. Jim Henry (Breshears) Rodgers, b. c?1878

[V6]3353. [11]2. Lucy Ann Rodgers, b. 11 Feb 1884, d. 6 March 1962; m. Walter E. "Doc" Hunziker, b. 25 Nov 1884, d. 1986.

[V6]3354. [12]1. Celia (or Cecile) Hunziker, b. 17 Aug 1907, d. 28 Dec 19851; m. ***Paul J. "Whistle" Breshears***, (s/o James Thomas Breshears and Malinda Catherine Southard), b. 2 Aug 1904, d. 6 July 1961. See his listing for their children.

[V6]3355. [12]2. Buel E. Hunziker, b. 2 April 1909, d. 5 May 1981; m. 14 March 1934, ***Marguerite Oryene Breshears***, b. 9 May 1916, (unidentified).

[V6]3356. [13]1. Lewis Hunziker; m. Shirley ______. Ch: Arlene; and Mark Hunziker

[V6]3357. [13]2. Louise Roxanne Hunziker;

[V6]3358. [13]3. Leland Hunziker; m. Kay Fockler. Ch: Tanya Lyn; and Billy Lee Hunziker

[V6]3359. [13]4. Linda Hunziker;

[V6]3360. [13]5. Nora Nadene Hunziker; m. ***Marion Lloyd Breshears***, (s/o Lloyd Thomas Breshears and Ruth Morton). See his listing for their children.

[V6]3361. [13]6. Lois Enos Hunziker;

[V6]3362. [13]7. Lonnie Eugene Hunziker

[V6]3363. [11]3. Enoc S. Rodgers, b. 30 Dec 1886, d. 23 Aug 1909,

[V6]3364. [11]4. Myrtle Rodgers, b. 7 July 1888, Avery, MO, d. 5 July 1977, Benton Co, MO; m. 5 March 1908, Fred Baugh, b. 13 Sept 1885, d. 10 Oct 1976, Benton Co, MO

[V6]3365. [12]1. Mabel G. Baugh; m. 23 Oct 1932, Freddie Bill Glazebrook.

[V6]3366. [13]1. Shirley Glazebrook; m. John Dale Costellow. Ch: Sherry Costellow

[V6]3367. [13]2. Gloria Nell Glazebrook; m.1. Johnny Ruckman; m.2. David May. Ch: Johnna Loy Ruckman

[V6]3368. [12]2. Lela Pearl Baugh, b. 27 May 1909, d. 28 Feb 1910

[V6]3369. [12]3. Guy Roger Baugh, b. 9 Oct 1911, d. 16 Dec 1991; m. 12 March 1933, ***Sylvia Breshears***, (d/o Gouldsberry Breshears and Etta Frances Breshears), b. 24 Feb 1916, Hickory Co, MO, d. 22 May 1994, Benton Co, MO. See Sylvia's listing for their children.

[V6]3370. [11]5. Joseph Claude Rodgers, b. 19 Dec 1891, d. 10 July 1929; m. Jewel Pippins

[V6]3371. [12]1. Claude Clinton Rodgers; m. ______ Smith.

[V6]3372. [13]1. Troy Dee Rodgers; m. Alicia Gaye Sherman. Ch: Amanda; Trenton Troy; and Aliaian Laraine Rodgers

[V6]3373. [13]2. Tyson Duane Rodgers

[V6]3374. [11]6. Bessie Rodgers, b. 8 Oct 1896, Avery, MO, d. 2 Oct 1967, Windsor, MO; m. 24 Feb 1918, Ernest Manuel Crabtree, b. 24 Feb 1897, Benton Co, MO, d. 18 April 1979, Clinton, MO, s/o John Crabtree and Mary Feaster

[V6]3375. [12]1. Bondena Crabtree, b. 1920, d. 1921

[V6]3376. [12]2. Ernest Manuel Crabtree, Jr, b. 7 July 1923, Loveland, Colorado, d. 3 Dec 1981, Windsor, MO; m. Gwendolyn Kathleen Boring, b. 17 Sept 1922, d. 17 Dec 1995, d/o James and Nellie (Weaver) Boring. Gwendolyn had a child by a first marriage: Jane Kathleen Petley; m. Robert Corder. Ch: Michele Ranae; Jeffrey; and Keith Corder

Figure 56: James and Nellie (Weaver) Boring. Photo from Bill Brooks

[V6]3377. [13]1. Earnest James Crabtree; m. Renee Houghton. Ch: Elizabeth Jeanne; and Diane Kathleen Crabtree

[V6]3378. [13]2. Nancy Ann Crabtree; m.1. Carey Edwin Walden; m.2. Michael Warren Kehl. Ch: Carey Jon; Matthew Ryan; and Kristen Renee Walden; Melisa Kay; and Christopher Wayne Kehl

[V6]3379. [13]3. Mary Catherine Crabtree; m. Joseph D. Mitterer. Ch: Sarah Elizabeth; Candace Nicole; Jeremiah Franklin Mitterer

[V6]3380. [11]7. William L. Rodgers, b. Feb 1900, d. 1901.

33. MADISON GOLMAN BRESHEARS and Elizabeth M. Brown

V6 3223. 93. **Madison Golman "Matt" Breshears**, (s/o Henry Breshears Jr and Atsa "Atsey" Etheridge), b. 8 Nov 1827, Lawrenceburg, Lawrence Co, TN, d. 3 Aug 1899, Benton Co, MO, bur Jones Cem; m. 20 March 1848, Benton Co, MO ("by Burr Emerson, J.P."), ***Sarah Elizabeth Brown***, b. 18 May 1832, KY, d. 20 March 1909, Avery, Hickory Co, MO, bur Jones Cem.

Madison served in the Osage Co Home Guards at the beginning of the Civil War, but did not enlist in the State Militia. During the war, Madison and his brothers, Henry Thomas and William Marion, spent a year in Denison, TX, where son, Henry Belsis, was born.

Figure 57: Madison Golman Breshears and Elizabeth M. Brown. Photo from Bill Brooks

Family of Madison Golman Breshears and Elizabeth M. Brown:

V6 3431. 101. ***Mary Jane Breshears**, b. 18 Aug 1849, Benton Co, MO, d. 4 Feb 1915; m. 17 Dec 1867, ***George Nimrod Ihrig***,

V6 3432. 102. ***William Thomas "Wild Bill" Breshears**, b. 9 Dec 1851, Benton Co, MO, d. 28 May 1929, Antlers, OK; m.1. ***Rachel Ihrig***, b. 16 Jan 1848, Marion Co, Indiana, d. 10 Dec 1928, Antlers, OK (9 ch), d/o George Ihrig and Ruth Bell; m.(?)2. ***Anna Ihrig***,

V6 3433. 103. **Steven B. Breshears**, b. 29 Feb 1853, d. 6 Nov

1943, Benton Co, MO; m.1. **Atsey D. Breshears**, (d/o Levi Robert "Lee" Breshears), b. 11 Feb 1855, d. 1902, Hickory Co, MO (see her listing for their one child); m.2. **Amanda "Mandy" Breshears**, (d/o Anna Breshears and Bob Hiram Breshears), b. Aug 1860. Steven's middle initial is "W" in some records; this could stand for William and the "B" for Bill. The majority of records use "B." See Amanda's listing for their children and grandchildren.

[V6]3434. [10]4. ***Levi "Prairie Levi" Breshears**, b. 24 June 1856, Benton Co, MO, d. 9 Jan 1919, Hickory Co, MO; m. ***Sarah E. Thornton***,

[V6]3435. [10]5. ***Henry Belsis Breshears**, b. 17 Oct 1859, Dennison, Denton Co, TX; m.1. 24 Nov 1878, a cousin, **Sarah Elizabeth Breshears** (d/o Levi Robert "Lee" Breshears and Mary Anna Garner); m.2. ***Ida Elsie Button***,

[V6]3436. [10]6. ***John Francis "Little Frank" Breshears**, b. 14 March 1862, Benton Co, MO, d. 10 Dec 1945; m. ***Sarah M. Hodges***,

[V6]3437. [10]7. **Margaret E. Breshears**, b. 15 March 1864, MO, d. 28 March 1899; m. ***Lewis Warren Butler***, b. c1864, Benton Co, MO

[V6]3438. [11]1. Etta Butler, b. c?1890

[V6]3439. [11]2. Roma Butler, b. c?1892

[V6]3440. [11]3. Ben Butler, b. c?1894

[V6]3441. [11]4. Irma Butler, b. c?1896

[V6]3442. [11]5. May Butler, b. 1899; Margaret died when May was a baby.

[V6]3443. [10]8. **Atsey Adeline Breshears**, b. 7 Dec 1866, Benton Co, MO, d. 19 March 1908; m. ***William Elijah "Lige" Powell***, b. c1867. Lige was a very broad-shouldered man. When he died, the homemade casket wouldn't go out the door; so they had to take it apart and reassemble it outside.

[V6]3444. [11]1. Effie Powell, b. c?1893; m. **Arthur Breshears**, (s/o William (Carroll) Breshears and Victoria E. Cox), b. 1883, d. c1970. See his listing for their 8 children.

[V6]3445. [11]2. Ida Powell, b. c?1895; m. Elbert Blackwell
[V6]3446. [10]9. **George N. (or M.) Breshears**, b. 2 March 1870, Benton Co, MO, d. 22 Aug 1888
[V6]3447. [10]10. **Sarah E. "Sis" Breshears**, b. 26 Jan 1872, Benton Co, MO, d. 28 Sept 1928; m. ***John A. Jones***, b. 29 June 1870, d. 28 March 1942
[V6]3448. [11]1. Ernest Jones, b. 13 Dec 1892, d. 15 May 1914
[V6]3449. [11]2. Wilbur Jones, b. c1896; m. Nannie Campbell, b. c?1896
[V6]3450. [11]3. J. Herman Jones, b. 19 Oct 1898; m. Thelma Turret. Ch: Tony; and Margaret Jones
[V6]3451. [11]4. Grace Jones (male); m. Roma Kivett. Ch: Angelee Jones (m. Dixon Palmer)
[V6]3452. [11]5. Birdie Jones; m. Sam Robb. Ch: Shirley; Charlotte; Joyce; and Donna Robb
[V6]3453. [10]11. **Rosa Arabella Breshears**, b. 3 Oct 1877, Benton Co, MO, d. 13 May 1944; m. ***Shandy A. Jordan***, b. 28 April 1873, d. 7 March 1956
[V6]3454. [11]x. Inez Jordan, b. 22 Nov 1900, d. 6 Oct 1961; m. George Tipton, b. 13 Dec 1900
[V6]3455. [12]1. Edsel Tipton,
[V6]3456. [10]12. _(dau)___ **Breshears**, b. after 1877, d. young

Mary Jane Breshears and George Nimrod Ihrig

[v6]3431. [10]1. **Mary Jane Breshears**, (d/o Madison Golman "Matt" Breshears and Elizabeth Elizabeth Brown), b. 18 Aug 1849, Benton Co, MO, d. 4 Feb 1915; m. 17 Dec 1867, ***George Nimrod Ihrig***, b. 4 March 1845, Benton Co, MO, d. 5 Jan 1894, s/o Peter Ihrig and Elizabeth Ellen "Elizzie" Tonbaugh. Mary Jane and George are both buried in Jones Cem, near Avery, MO.

Family of Mary Jane Breshears and George Nimrod Ihrig:
[V6]3457. [11]1. George Nimrod Ihrig Jr, b. 26 Sept 1868, d. 14 Oct 1868, age 3 weeks.
[V6]3458. [11]2. Levi Benton Ihrig, b. 26 Nov 1869, MO, d. 2 Oct 1954; m. **Mary Breshears** (d/o Marcus Monroe Breshears and Leanna Murray), b. c?1869. Levi Benton Ihrig became an Elder in the Spring

Branch Church of the Brethren at Avery, MO. See Mary's listing for children.

[V6]3459. [11]3. John Peter Ihrig, b. 8 Oct 1871, d. 3 Oct 1906; m.1. Lucy Henderson (2 ch); m.2. ***Lucy Breshears***, (3 ch) (d/o Andrew Jackson Breshears and Ida Ausburn.

Children by Lucy Henderson:

[V6]3460. [12]1. Ollie Ihrig, m. ***Maggie Breshears***,

[V6]3461. [12]2. Curtis Ihrig, m. ***Athel Breshears***,

Children by Lucy Breshears:

[V6]3462. [12]3. John Peter Ihrig, Jr,

[V6]3463. [12]4. Fay Ihrig,

[V6]3464. [12]5. Tony (or Porter) Ihrig,

[V6]3465. [11]4. Cynthia Elizabeth Ihrig, b. 4 March 1874, MO, d. 6 Jan 1912; m. Delmar Lopp, b. c?1874 (s/o Lucinda Breshears and John William Lopp)

[V6]3466. [12]1. Eathel Lopp, m. Tommy Moore. Ch: Johnny; Cynthia; Zelphia; Donna Faye; and Ina Mae Moore (Ina Mae m. Bert Chaney. Ch: Sherry; and Barbara Chaney)

[V6]3467. [12]2. Sabrina Lopp,

[V6]3468. [11]5. Jacob Ihrig, b. March 1876, MO, d. 4 March 1944; m. Mary Campbell,

[V6]3469. [11]6. Norma Adeline Ihrig, b. 9 Jan 1878, MO, d. 8 Sept 1950; m. Omar Forehand

[V6]3470. [12]1. Olen Forehand,

[V6]3471. [12]2. Leland Forehand,

[V6]3472. [12]3. Myrtle Forehand,

[V6]3473. [12]4. Mary Ellen Forehand,

[V6]3474. [12]5. Buel Forehand,

[V6]3475. [11]7. Madison Ihrig, b. 5 Jan 1880, d. 17 Nov 1880

[V6]3476. [11]8. Mary Nimrod Ihrig, b. 1 Oct 1881, MO, d. 8 Sept 1967; m. John Rash,

[V6]3477. [12]1. Earl Rash,

[V6]3478. [12]2. Linnie Rash,

[V6]3479. [12]3. Ocil Rash

[V6]3480. [12]4. May Rash,

[V6]3481. [12]5. Orval Rash,

[V6]3482. [12]6. Otis Rash,

[V6]3483. [12]7. Ardys Rash,

[V6]3484. [12]8. Alfred Rash,
[V6]3485. [12]9. Edwin Rash,
[V6]3486. [12]10. John Wesley Rash,
[V6]3487. [11]9. Joseph Franklin Ihrig, b. 16 Feb 1885, MO, d. 14 Dec 1966; m.1. Stella Rodgers, (2 ch) b. c1875, MO; m.2. Emma Reno, (8 ch) b. c?1885
[V6]3488. [12]1. Nellie Ihrig, m. Otha Thompson,
[V6]3489. [12]2. Jacob Ihrig,
[V6]3490. [12]3. Hubert Ihrig, m. Minnie Blackwell
[V6]3491. [12]4. Genevieve "Jenna" Ihrig,
[V6]3492. [12]5. Lydia Ihrig, m. Alvin Eastburn
[V6]3493. [12]6. Omar Ihrig,
[V6]3494. [12]7. Earnest Ihrig, m.1. ***Yvis Breshears***, (no ch); m.2. Lennis ______. Ch: Michael; and Leanna Ihrig
[V6]3495. [12]8. Tony Ihrig, d. young
[V6]3496. [12]9. Minnie Lou Ihrig, m. Norman Rowr
[V6]3497. [11]10. Lessie Volentine Ihrig, b. 12 Dec 1890; m. Etta Fleming, b. c1790, MO
[V6]3498. [12]1. Vincil Ihrig, m. Glen Woirhaye
[V6]3499. [12]2. Lois Ihrig,
[V6]3500. [12]3. Carrie Ihrig, m. Seth Bennett
[V6]3501. [12]4. Kermett Ihrig,, b. 1918

Figure 59: Wild Bill (at left) and Rachel (Ihrig) Breshears. Photo from Bill Brooks

William Thomas "Wild Bill" Breshears and Rachel Ihrig/ Anna Ihrig

v6 3432. 10 2. **William Thomas "Wild Bill" Breshears**, (s/o Madison Golman "Matt" Breshears and Sarah Elizabeth Brown), b. 9 Dec 1851, Benton Co, MO, d. 28 May 1929, Antlers, OK; m.1. ***Rachel Ihrig***, b. 16 Jan 1848, Marion Co, Indiana, d. 10 Dec 1928, Antlers, OK (9 ch), d/o George Ihrig and Ruth Bell; he did not marry, but had children with
Rachel's sister, ***Anna Ihrig***, b. 1854, Stark Co, Indiana, d. c1900, OK (5 ch), d/o George Ihrig and Ruth Bell. Wild Bill took up freighting, first in Nebraska, then across Oklahoma to Old Mexico. He and Rachel are buried in the old family cemetery near Antlers, OK.

Family of William Thomas "Wild Bill" Breshears and Rachel Ihrig:

V6 3502. 11 1. **Ida Jane Breshears**, b. 30 Sept 1870, Pruett Place, MO, d. 30 Oct 1962, Wilson Creek, OK; bur Valley View Cem, Walla Walla, WA; m. 15 Jan 1891, ***James Henry Jordan***, (s/o Sarah Malissa Breshears and William Newton "Nute" Jordan), b.

30 Sept 1860, d. 6 Dec 1930. See his listing for their children.

V6 3503. 11 2. **Margaret Ann Breshears**, b. 6 Oct 1872, Benton Co, MO, d. 31 Dec 1969, Muskogee, OK; m. 15 Feb 1891, ***Henry Frank Miller***, b. c1872, Benton Co, MO

V6 3504. 12 1. Toye Ettie Miller, b. 20 Nov 1891, d. 13 Sept 1965, Union City, OK; m. Arty Keeley. Ch: Valentine; Lavon; Elvin; and Asil Keeley

V6 3505. 12 2. Mary Elizabeth Miller, b. 26 April 1893, d. 22 May 1966, Muskogee, OK; m. ***Roy Breshears***, (s/o George Breshears.

V6 3506. 13 1. **Velma Breshears**,

V6 3507. 13 2. **Leroy Breshears**,

V6 3508. 12 3. Ethyl Rachel Miller, b. & d. 7 April 1897,

V6 3509. 12 4. Otis Frank Miller, b. 1 Nov 1898, d. 2 March 1940

V6 3510. 12 5. Agnes Miller, b. 27 Feb 1900, d. Dec 1968; m.1. Sam Harris; m.2. Lewis ______; m.3. George Layton

V6 3511. 11 3. **Capy Breshears**, b. 19 Nov 1874, Benton Co, MO, d. 20 Aug 1876, age 20 months

V6 3512. 11 4. ***Cora Etta Breshears**, b. 8 July 1877, Hermitage, Benton Co, MO, d. 23 June 1947, OK; m. 25 Dec 1892, in El Reno, OK, ***Marion Southard***,

V6 3513. 11 5. ***Steve Franklin Breshears**, b. 17 Jan 1879, Avery, Hickory Co, MO, d. 1 May 1959, Antlers, OK; m.1. 8 Aug 1903, in Muskogee, I.T., ***Florence Elizabeth Hunter***,

V6 3514. 11 6. **Madison "Little Mattie" Breshears**, b. c1881, Benton Co, MO, drowned 3 April 1883, age 2. Wild Bill and Rachel were living at the Pruitt Place when Little Mattie fell in the water. His wool stocking caught on a snag about a quarter mile downstream. When Wild Bill found the body on May 30th, the child was badly decomposed. Rachel took off her petticoat, slipped it under the child, so they could take him home. They buried him in the yard of the Pruitt Place.

V6 3515. 11 7. ***John Wesley Breshears**, b. 1 Oct 1885, Benton

Co, MO, d. 1974; m.1. c1913, ***Dora Poston*** (mother of the children); m.2. ***Lela Rhodes***; m.3. ***Myrtle Morgan***; m.4. ***Pearl*** ____

[V6]3516. [11]8. **George Breshears**, b. 26 May 1888, Benton Co, MO, d. 17 March 1913 in a fight (went through a plate glass window); bur Muskogee, OK;

[V6]3517. [11]9. **Levi Henry Breshears**, b. 3 Jan 1889, Benton Co, MO, d. 18 May 1962; m. ***Minnie Ola Stiles***,

[V6]3518. [12]1. **Loyd Clint Breshears**, b. 2 April 1914, Antlers, OK, d. 16 Oct 1976; m.1. ***Ruby Goings*** (3 ch); m.2. ***Sue Fowler***.

[V6]3519. [13]1. **Donald Breshears**,

[V6]3520. [13]2. **Toni Jean Breshears**,

[V6]3521. [13]3. **Mike Breshears**,

[V6]3522. [12]2. **Lois Rachel Elizabeth Breshears**, b. 22 May 1916, Antlers, OK; m.1. ***Clyde Mallet***; m.2. ***Shorty Henderson***; m.3. ?***Sharon Woodcock***.

[V6]3523. [13]1. Joel Lee Mallet;

[V6]3524. [13]2. James Raymond Mallet; m. ______. Ch: Grady; Sherry; Jimmy; and Bobby Mallet

[V6]3525. [13]3. Ethel Sue Mallet; m. ______ Decker. Ch: Carrie; Christie; and Raquel Decker

[V6]3526. [13]4. Starlett Rose Mallet;

[V6]3527. [12]3. **Floyd Raymond Breshears**, b. 24 May 1918, Antlers, OK; m. ***Ruby Claycomb***,

[V6]3528. [13]1. **Floyd Raymond Breshears, Jr**, m. ______.

[V6]3529. [14]1. **Roxanne Breshears**,

[V6]3530. [14]2. **Pamela Sue Breshears**,

[V6]3531. [14]3. **Tige Raymond Breshears**,

[V6]3532. [13]2. **William Lee Breshears**, m. ______.

[V6]3533. [14]1. **Michael Breshears**,

[V6]3534. [14]2. **Tiffany Breshears**,

[V6]3535. [14]3. **Shirley Jean Breshears**,

[V6]3536. [13]3. **Tommy Wayne Breshears**, m. ______.

[V6]3537. [14]1. **Russell Breshears**,

[V6]3538. [14]2. **Amy Breshears**,

[V6]3539. [13]4. **Shirley Jean Breshears**, b. 26 Sept 1947, d. 27 Sept 1947

[V6]3540. [12]4. **Myrtle Etta Breshears**, b. 8 Oct 1923; m.1. ***Wes Brooks***; m.2. ***Buddy Ellrage***. Ch: Kenneth; and Mickie Lee Brooks; JoLeta; and unnamed Ellrage

[V6]3541. [13]2. Mickie Lee Brooks; m. ______ Renner. Ch: Jon Lee and Holly Renner

[V6]3542. [12]5. **Irene Breshears**, b. 18 Feb 1921, Antlers, OK; m.1. ***Jack Ellis***; m.2. ***Clyde Simpson***; m.3. ***Richard Osborne***. Ch: Charlene; Clyde Jr; Linda Kay; and Marsella Simpson

[V6]3543. [13]4. Marsella Simpson; m. ______ Hamilton. Ch: Zoe Linda; Rhonda Kay; and Jack Hamilton

Children of William Thomas "Wild Bill" Breshears by Anna Ihrig, Rachel's sister, and raised by Rachel:

According to Shirley Breshears Bayer <Clashb@msn.com> "Wild Bill" and Anna were never married. Anna was 4 foot 2 inches tall, weighed 120 pounds and had brown hair and eyes. She had a child, George Barnard, who went by the surname Breshears. She and "Wild Bill" then had five children. The fifth (or sixth) child died at birth and Anna buried it in the woods. She was later convicted of murder in Hickory Co, MO, and sentenced to "two years from November 19, 1890." She was discharged under the ¾ law on May 19, 1892. Wild Bill would have nothing to do with her after she got out of prison, nor would he let her sons, Marvin and Frank, go to see her. She then married (first marriage) Ed Stevens and had two children: Myrtle Stevens, b. 1893, and Ed Stevens Jr, b. 1894-95.

[V6]3544. [11]10. **Ruth Breshears**, b. 1877, d. c1900; m. 1898, ***Dan Sisk***

[V6]3545. [11]11. ***Alice Bertha Breshears**, b. 24 Feb 1880, Benton Co, MO, d. Jan 1951, in Montana; m. 12 Oct 1898, Oklahoma, ***Charlie Rogers***,

[V6]3546. [11]12. ***Marvin Breshears**, b. 27 March 1883, Hickory Co, MO, d. April 1967, in Billings, Montana; m.1. ***Martha "Mattie" Wells***, (2 ch); m.2. 15 June 1914, ***Elizabeth Millinger***, (8 ch)

[V6]3547. [11]13. ***Francis Marion "Frank" Breshears**, b. 1 Feb

1885, Hickory Co, MO, d. 13 Aug 1967 in Oklahoma; m. 23 Dec 1906, ***Sallie Wells***,

V6 3548. [11]14. **Baby Breshears**, b. c1887-90, MO, d. at birth, but Anna was convicted of murdering the baby.

Cora Etta Breshears and Marion Southard

v6 3512. [11]4. **Cora Etta Breshears**, (d/o William Thomas "Wild Bill" Breshears and Rachel Ihrig), b. 8 July 1877, Hermitage, Benton Co, MO, d. 23 June 1947, OK; m. 25 Dec 1892, in El Reno, OK, ***Marion Southard***, b. 1877, Benton Co, MO, s/o Francis Marion Southard.

Family of Cora Etta Breshears and Marion Southard:

V6 3549. [12]1. Getty Southard, b. 25 Nov 1893, Fristoe, Benton Co, MO, d. 1976; m. Ray Harriman. Ch: Christina Harriman (m. Zeke Barton. Ch: Diane; and Gail Barton)

V6 3550. [12]2. Zada Southard, b. 17 Sept 1895, d. 1896, Muskogee, OK

V6 3551. [12]3. Roscoe Charley Southard, b. 3 Jan 1897, Wagoner, OK; m. Myrtle Mullins.

V6 3552. [13]1. Arvella Southard;

V6 3553. [13]2. Verna Southard; m. Alvin York. Ch: Ellen; Vivian; and Arlene York

V6 3554. [13]3. Roscoe Southard Jr; m. Patsy Pledger. Ch: Charles; Patty; and Mary Lou Southard

V6 3555. [13]4. Oma Southard; m. H.C. Foster. Ch: Hulett; Hazel; Dawn; Juanita; and Mona Foster

V6 3556. [13]5. Juanita Southard; m. Joe Hurley. Ch: Linda; Cindy; and Steven Hurley

V6 3557. [12]4. Lora Southard, b. 23 Jan 1899, Wagoner, OK; m. Hiram Cowen.

V6 3558. [13]1. Frances Cowen; m. Leo Carlin. Ch: David; and Joyce Carlin

V6 3559. [13]2. Louise Cowen;

V6 3560. [13]3. J.C. Cowen; m. Nancy Bridges. Ch: Troy Cowen

V6 3561. [13]4. Joe Cowen; m. ______. Ch: Billy Cowen

V6 3562. [12]5. Oma Southard, b. March 1901, Union City, OK; m.

Wesley Hawkins.

[V6]3563. [13]1. Rachel Hawkins; m. Virgil McAnally. Ch: Loren; Marie; and Loma McAnally

[V6]3564. [13]2. Doris David Hawkins; m. Vinita Bennett. Ch: Diane; Max; Penny; and Donald Hawkins

[V6]3565. [13]3. J.W. Hawkins; m. Jean Thorpe. Ch: J.W, Jr; and Jayette Hawkins

[V6]3566. [13]4. Betty Jo Hawkins; m. Tom Thompson. Ch: Linda; Sue; Vera; and David Thompson

[V6]3567. [12]6. William "Bud" Southard, b. 15 March 1903, Muskogee, OK; m. Lou Ann Hawkins.

[V6]3568. [13]1. Bob Southard; m. Helen Payne. Ch: Babette; Ginny; and Steve Southard

[V6]3569. [13]2. William Paul Southard; m.1. Helen O. Guinn (ch: Bobbie Southard); m.2. Margery Tillery

[V6]3570. [13]3. Carl Wesley Southard; m. Nadine Stocton. Ch: Pam; Janice; and Randy Ray Southard

[V6]3571. [13]4. James Lee Southard; m. Betty Guthrie. Ch: Mike; and Kelly Southard

[V6]3572. [13]5. Thomas Ray Southard; m. Sue Thomas. Ch: Chris; and Marti Ann Southard

[V6]3573. [12]7. Ida Southard, b. 1 June 1905, Taft, OK; m. Andy Clagg. Ch:

[V6]3574. [13]1. Arthur Delane Clagg; m. Wanda Faye Cox. Ch: Rodney Lynn; Mickey Lee; and Calvin Delane Clagg

[V6]3575. [13]2. Ray Clagg;

[V6]3576. [13]3. Paul Andrew Clagg;

[V6]3577. [13]4. Roy Eugene Clagg; m. Ruby Short. Ch: Kenneth Eugene; Connie; and Jimmie Ray Clagg

[V6]3578. [13]5. Virginia Clagg; m. William L. Herron. Ch: Ava Carol; Deborah Kay; Nathan (twin); Nanette (twin); and Lisa Katherine Herron

[V6]3579. [13]6. Marion Francis Clagg; m. Reba Harrison. Ch: Cheryl Lynn; Karen Francis; Nella May; Jeffrey; Sarah; Sheldon Clagg

[V6]3580. [13]7. Donald Walter Clagg; m. Glenna Rose Simpson. Ch: Damon; Aaron; and Marion Clagg

[V6]3581. [12]8. Tilee Southard, b. 7 Aug 1907, Keefeton, OK; m. Matt Hawkins. Ch:

[V6]3582. [13]1. Bonnie Hawkins; m.1. Leon West; m.2. Jim Page. Ch: Paul West

[V6]3583. [13]2. Louella Hawkins; m. Coy Wright. Ch: Petty; Diane; Larry; and infant Wright

[V6]3584. [13]3. Claud Hawkins;

[V6]3585. [13]4. Dennis Hawkins;

[V6]3586. [13]5. Peggy Hawkins

[V6]3587. [12]9. Audie Bennie Southard, b. 6 Nov 1911, Okmulgee, OK; m. Ruby McWaters. Ch: Jerry; Gerald; and Sharon Southard

[V6]3588. [12]10. Eugene Southard, b. 3 March 1913, Okmulgee, OK; m1. Suzie Cowen (ch: Sue Leta Southard); m.2. Louise ______. Ch: Larry; and Sharon Southard

[V6]3589. [12]11. Bob Southard, b. 18 Oct 1918, d. 18 Oct 1918, lived 2 hours

[V6]3590. [12]12. Orville Southard, b. 17 Aug 1921; m.1. Dorothy Gamble (no ch); m.2. Kathleen _______. Ch: Ricky; Eddy; and Terry Southard

Steve Franklin Breshears and Florence Elizabeth Hunter

[v6]3513. [11]5. **Steve Franklin Breshears**, (s/o William Thomas "Wild Bill" Breshears and Rachel Ihrig), b. 17 Jan 1879, Avery, Hickory Co, MO, d. 1 May 1959, Antlers, OK; m.1. 8 Aug 1903, in Muskogee, I.T., ***Florence Elizabeth Hunter***, (mother of the children) b. 15 April 1886, Luldrow Co, AR, d. 16 Feb 1963, Antlers, OK, d/o Edward Hunter and Dona _____ (?maybe Hill or Hall; maybe 1/8 Indian); m.2. ***Minnie Couch***, b. c?1881; m.3. ***Rose Harrington (or Langford)***, b. c?1879

Family of Steve Franklin Breshears and Florence Elizabeth Hunter:

[V6]3591. [12]1. **Clem Newton Breshears**, b. 1901, Antlers, OK; m. ***Annie Duncan***,

[V6]3592. [13]1. **Duane Breshears**, b. & d. 1934

[V6]3593. [13]2. **Dolly Breshears**, b. & d. 1935

[V6]3594. [13]3. **Patricia Ann Breshears**, b. 21 Dec 1936
[V6]3595. [13]4. **Ruth Pauline Breshears**, b. 19 Oct 1938
[V6]3596. [13]5. **Neil Grady Breshears**, b. 22 Aug 1942
[V6]3597. [13]6. **Wayne Allen Breshears**, b. 3 May 1947
[V6]3598. [12]2. **Sylvia Breshears**, b. 29 March 1906, Antlers, OK; m. ***Jason Moore***,
[V6]3599. [13]1. Burl Aubrey Moore; m. Mary ______. Ch: Janet Kay; Randy; and Roy Earl Moore
[V6]3600. [13]2. Daisy Evelyn Moore; m.1. Billy Jack Hindman; m.2. Larry ______. Ch: Michael; Diane; Phyllis Jean; Larry; and infant Hindman; and infant girl _______.
[V6]3601. [13]3. Bonnie Moore; m. Bill Tupper. Ch: Billie; Jackie; Limi Lynn; Shirley Jean; and infant Tupper
[V6]3602. [13]4. Billy Jack Moore; m. ______. Ch: Sherman; Sheldon; and Sherril Moore
[V6]3603. [13]5. Dolly Viola Moore,
[V6]3604. [12]3. **Addie Breshears**, b. c1907, d. c1907
[V6]3605. [12]4. **Arlie Breshears**, b. 14 Jan 1909; m. ***Lois Harrison***, b. 15 Oct 1914
[V6]3606. [12]5. **Dona Breshears**, b. 1910, Pushmataha Co, OK; m.1. 30 Nov 1926, in Atoka Co, OK, ***William Mark Robnett***, (9 ch; div); m.2. ***Monte Barton***, (1 ch). ref: Renee Medved <medvedqueenb @cableone.net>. Ch: Addie Elizabeth; Ira; Douglas; Lily; Bobbie Ruth; Dean; Sherry Gail; Terry Dale; and Connie Robnett
[V6]3607. [12]6. **George William Breshears**, b. 22 July 1913, Antlers, OK; m ***Gladys Lorene Harrison***,
[V6]3608. [13]1. **Betty Joyce Breshears**, m. ***Homer Thomas***, ch: Ronald; girl; and boy Thomas
[V6]3609. [13]2. **Mary Faye Breshears**, m. ***Alton Scott***, ch: Allison; and John Scott
[V6]3610. [13]3. **Georgia Lorene Breshears**,
[V6]3611. [13]4. **Barbara Ann Breshears**,
[V6]3612. [13]5. **Billy Gene Breshears**, m. ***Patricia Marie Snodgrass***,
[V6]3613. [14]1. **Susan Breshears**,
[V6]3614. [14]2. **Stephen Breshears**,

V63615. [14]3. **Linda Breshears**,
V63616. [14]4. **John David Breshears**,
V63617. [14]5. **Robert Ray Breshears**; m. ***Gail*** _______.
V63618. [15]1. **Angel Breshears**,
V63619. [15]2. **Christy Breshears**,
V63620. [14]6. **Ruth Breshears**,
V63621. [12]7. **Edna May Breshears**, b. 12 July 1915; m. ***Charles Collins***,
V63622. [13]1. Perry Loyd Collins, m. Joyce Stevens
V63623. [13]2. Robert Roy Collins, m.1. Joyce_____; m.2. Martha _____
V63624. [13]3. Wanda Collins; m. ______ Stanphill. Ch: Kathy; and Monte Stanphill
V63625. [13]4. Freddie Steve Collins, b. 25 Dec 1934; m. Ruth ______. Ch: Francis; Deloris; and Steven Collins
V63626. [12]8. **Lydia Dorothy Breshears**, b. 2 Sept 1917; m. ***Louis Duncan***. Ch: David Allen; Donnie Lee; girl; Carol Jean; Benjamin "Bennie"; and Tommy Louis Duncan
V63627. [13]4. Carol Jean Duncan; m. Glen Felihkatubbe. Ch: Vicky Lou; Harold Glen; and Angela Carol Felihkatubbe
V63628. [13]5. Benjamin "Bennie" Duncan; m. Janet Murray. Ch: Robin Renee; Bobbie Jo; and Stephanie Louise Duncan
V63629. [12]9. **Walter Leroy Breshears**, b. 11 Dec 1919; m. ***Helen Rugg Overton***,
V63630. [13]1. **Margaret Sue Breshears**, m. ***J.W. Cole***. Ch: David W.; Cynthia Royce; Margaret; and Jeff Cole
V63631. [13]2. **Earl Leroy Breshears**, m. ***Louise*** ______.
V63632. [14]1. **Troy Breshears**,
V63633. [14]2. **Teresa Breshears**,
V63634. [12]10. **Loyd Breshears**, (twin) b. 3 Feb 1922, d. as a teen-ager
V63635. [12]11. **Floyd Breshears**, (twin) b. 3 Feb 1922; m. ***Patricia Ann Reed***, b. 4 Feb 1927
V63636. [13]1. **Danny Reed Breshears**, m. ***Nora Margaretha DeGroot***,

[V6]3637. [14]1. **Jeffrey Reed Breshears**,
[V6]3638. [13]2. **Floyd Don Breshears**,
[V6]3639. [13]3. **Frances Breshears**, m. ***James Brady Swafford***. Ch: James Jr; and Bobby Lynn Swafford
[V6]3640. [13]4. **Joann Breshears**, m.1. Frank Weaver; m.2. Stanley Wood. Ch: Maria Jo; and Floyd Ray (Weaver) Wood. (Stanley adopted the two children of Frank.)

John Wesley Breshears and his Four Wives

[V6]3515. [11]7. **John Wesley Breshears**, (s/o William Thomas "Wild Bill" Breshears and Rachel Ihrig), b. 1 Oct 1885, Benton Co, MO, d. 1974; m.1. c1913, ***Dora Poston*** (mother of the children); m.2. ***Lela Rhodes***; m.3. ***Myrtle Morgan***; m.4. ***Pearl*** ____

Family of John Wesley Breshears and Dora Poston:

[V6]3641. [12]1. **George Breshears**, b. 1913, Antlers, OK, d. 1913, lived 1½ days
[V6]3642. [12]2. **Rachel Breshears**, b. 24 Jan 1915, Antlers, OK; m.1. ***Clyde Johnson***; m.2. ***Troy Shiew***. Ch:
[V6]3643. [13]1. June Deloris Shiew; m. Van Bond. Ch: Van Bond Jr
[V6]3644. [13]2. Gerald David Shiew; m. June Arnold. Ch: Teresa Gail; and Sheila Lynn Shiew
[V6]3645. [13]3. Troy Marvin Shiew; m. Linda Johnson. Ch: Melinda Gail Shiew
[V6]3646. [13]4. Corinna Faye Shiew; m.1. Jim Todd; m.2. Aaron Bates. Ch: Tracy Lynn; and Karla Melissa Todd
[V6]3647. [12]3. **Dan Horace Breshears**, b. 9 March 1918, Antlers, OK, d. 4 June 1949; m. ***Lorene Sistrunk***,
[V6]3648. [13]1. **Dana Faye Breshears**,
[V6]3649. [13]2. **Terry Breshears**,
[V6]3650. [13]3. **Danny Breshears**,
[V6]3651. [12]4. **Almeda Bernice Breshears**, b. 8 Feb 1921, Antlers, OK; m.1. ***Haywood Simpson***; m.2. ***Bill Torbett***. Ch:
[V6]3652. [13]1. Janan Irene Simpson; m.1. Jerry Welch; m.2.

Joseph Patrick Clifton. Ch: Kemberley Jean Welch; and Joseph Patrick Clifton, Jr

[V6]3653. [13]2. Shirley Jean Simpson; m.1. Cleveland William White; m.2. George Lewis Bordwine; m.3. James Norman McLeod. Ch: Daniel William (White) McLeod; James Charles McLeod; and John David McLeod

[V6]3654. [13]3. Ronnie Carol Torbett; m.1. Andre Patrick Saxton; m.2. Delbert Wayne Bailey; m.3. Perry Lee Warlick; m.4. Edward Wayne Cates; m.5. John Cornelius Dowdy. Ch: Andre Patrick Saxton, Jr; Kari Ann Warlick; James Justin Dowdy

[V6]3655. [13]4. Bill Hugh Torbett; m. Cathy Sue Milner. Ch: Leslie Reshele; Julie Ann; and Haley Diane Torbett

[V6]3656. [13]5. Daniel Byron Torbett; m. Janice Marie Brown. Ch: Kiley Ann Torbett

[V6]3657. [13]6. David Steven Torbett;

[V6]3658. [13]7. Loria Ann Torbett;

Alice Bertha Breshears and Charlie Rogers

[v6]3545. [11]11. **Alice Bertha Breshears**, (d/o William Thomas "Wild Bill" Breshears and Anna Ihrig), b. 24 Feb 1880, Benton Co, MO, d. Jan 1951, in Montana; m. 12 Oct 1898, Oklahoma, ***Charlie Rogers***, b. c?1880

Family of Alice Bertha Breshears and Charlie Rogers:

[V6]3659. [12]1. Herschell Rogers, b. OK; m. Rose Lamb. Ch: Dickey; Ted; Bunky; Wanda Fay; Joe (m. ____. Ch: Steve; Kathy; and Dina Rogers); Buster; and girl Rogers

[V6]3660. [12]2. Fay Rogers, m. Harry Fink. Ch: Danny; and Shirley Fink

[V6]3661. [12]3. Rachel Wanda Rogers, b. 21 Dec 1898; m.1. Sid Ferguson; m.2. Donald E. Nickolson; m.3. Floyd Pierce.

[V6]3662. [13]1. Alice Bertha Ferguson; m. Ernest Holt. Ch: Richard; Diane; and Sherry Holt

V6 3663. 12 4. Tera Rogers, b. 11 Oct 1902; m. Glen Ferguson.
V6 3664. 13 1. Gene Ferguson;
V6 3665. 13 2. Jack Ferguson; m. Gloria Johnson. Ch: Dick; Betty Jo; Jack; Larry Gene; Annie; Sue; Lin; and Lorie Ferguson
V6 3666. 13 3. Betty Lou Ferguson;
V6 3667. 13 4. Marjorie Ferguson; m.1. Leo Johnson; m.2. Carl Swanson. Ch: Jerry; Rusty; Wade; and Tobie Johnson; Robin Swanson
V6 3668. 13 5. Peggy Ferguson; m.1. Elmer Christenson; m.2. ______ Hawkinson. Ch: Glena; and Rick Christenson
V6 3669. 12 5. Frank Rogers, b. 1909, d. 1949; m. Beulah Ferguson.
V6 3670. 13 1. Robert Kenneth Rogers; m. Edna Sample. Ch: Robert K.; Kenny; and Mary Jane Rogers
V6 3671. 13 2. William Rogers; m. Marjorie Greene. Ch: Sandy; Mistee; Suzie; Jeanie; Steve; and Tracia Rogers
V6 3672. 13 3. Mildred Rogers; m. Christopher Dragoo. Ch: Tom; Loretta; Shirley; and Cody Dragoo
V6 3673. 13 4. Bonita Rogers; m. Henry Greene. Ch: John; Henry Jr; Ronnie; Donna May; and Nancy Greene
V6 3674. 13 5. Frank Rogers, Jr; m. Jean Gilbert. Ch: Patty Jean; Donny; and Denise Rogers
V6 3675. 13 6. Janice Rogers; m. Andy Koch. Ch: Dwane; Lee; and Guy Koch
V6 3676. 13 7. Donald Leroy Rogers;
V6 3677. 13 8. Betty Rogers; m. Dick Keller. Ch: Wynette Dawn; Deveny Lynn; William Stuart; and Betty Jo Keller
V6 3678. 13 9. Jim Gerald Rogers;
V6 3679. 13 10. Jack Rogers;
V6 3680. 13 11. Judy Rogers;
V6 3681. 13 12. Beverly Ann Rogers; m. Albert Barta. Ch: Shane Travis; Cary Al; Frankie Al; and Tina Jo Barta
V6 3682. 12 6. Bonnie Rogers, b. 1911; m. Robert Ross.
V6 3683. 13 1. Dorothy Ross; m. Art Gregory. Ch: Butch

Gregory

[V6]3684. [13]2. Jim Ross; m. Betsy ______. Ch: Rod; and Ronnie Ross

[V6]3685. [13]3. Dixie Ross; m. George Haines. Ch: Vickie Haines

[V6]3686. [13]4. Patsy Ross;

[V6]3687. [13]5. Rocky Leroy Ross;

[V6]3688. [13]6. Mary Jo Ross; m. Bill Smith. Ch: Barbara; and Billy Smith

[V6]3689. [13]7. Virginia Fay Ross;

Marvin Breshears and Martha Wells/ Elizabeth Millinger

[v6]3546. [11]12. **Marvin Breshears**, (s/o William Thomas "Wild Bill" Breshears and Anna Ihrig), b. 27 March 1883, Hickory Co, MO, d. April 1967, in Billings, Montana; m.1. ***Martha "Mattie" Wells***, (2 ch) d/o John Wells and Caroline Crouch, sister to Sallie Wells, Francis Marion Breshears's wife; m.2. 15 June 1914, ***Elizabeth Millinger***, (8 ch)

Family of Marvin Breshears and Martha Wells:

[V6]3690. [12]1. **Barney "Buck" Breshears**, b. 12 June 1906, OK, d. 29 March 1993, Montana; m. 7 Nov 1941, ***Olga Melecheck***,

[V6]3691. [13]1. **Carol Lee Breshears**, m.1. ***James Michael Graves***. (3 ch) m.2. ***Douglas Lyle Graves***.

[V6]3692. [14]1. Jamie Lynn Graves; m. Larry B. Peterson. Ch: James Larry Peterson

[V6]3693. [14]2. Jodi Lee Graves;

[V6]3694. [14]3. Jennifer Anna Graves; m. Charles De Lance Ganton. Ch: Corrine Marie Ganton

[V6]3695. [12]2. **Edith Breshears**, b. April 1907, Taft, OK; m. ***Carl Schelin***. Ch: Flora; Ronald; Stanley; Malcom; and Carl Michael Schelin

Family of Marvin Breshears and Elizabeth Millinger:

[V6]3696. [12]3. **Anna May Breshears**, b. 30 May 1915; m.1. ***John Kaslelic***; m.2. ***Harold Blakeley***. Ch: Sally Ann

Kaslelic; Danielle Jean; and Alice Flora Blakely (Alice m.1. Scott Magruder; m.2. Warren C. Swanke. Ch: Barbara Ann Magruder)

[V6]3697. [12]4. **Walter Richard Breshears**, b. 12 July 1917, d. 26 Nov 1977; m. ***Theresa Hergett***.

[V6]3698. [13]1. **Rochelle Denise Breshears**, m.1. ***Gordon Stewart***; m.2. ***Frank Kriewold***.

[V6]3699. [14]1. Rocky Luther Stewart; m. ______. Ch: Holland Stewart

[V6]3700. [14]2. Gayle Denise Stewart; m. ______ Carlson. Ch: Joshua David Carlson

[V6]3701. [14]3. Kenneth Rodger Stewart;

[V6]3702. [14]4. Victoria Rose Stewart; m. ______ Johnson. Ch: Jessica Rae Johnson

[V6]3703. [13]2. **Therese Madalyn Breshears**, m. ***J. Lee Jenkins***. Ch: John J.; Tate Clifford; and Lou Michael Jenkins

[V6]3704. [13]3. **Claudie May Breshears**, (twin), m. ***Dale Dotson***. Ch: Deena Louise; Maurcena Rose; and Chris Allen Dotson

[V6]3705. [13]4. **Claudette Fay Breshears**, (twin), m. ***Larry Allen Hughes***. Ch: Clayton Allen; and Tracy Renee Hughes

[V6]3706. [12]5. **Clyde Ray Breshears**, b. 12 Aug 1919; m. 2 Sept 1939, ***Mary Louise Burnett***, b. 2 Nov 1920, d. 7 July 1999

[V6]3707. [13]1. **Alice Kay Breshears**, (adopted); m.1. John Sandlin; m.2. John Talbot. Ch: Leah Talbot

[V6]3708. [13]2. **James Clyde Breshears**, (adopted)

[V6]3709. [12]6. **Helen Rachel Breshears**, b. 25 Feb 1922, Howard, Montana; m. ***Albert Paul Fulton***.

[V6]3710. [13]1. Barbara Lee Fulton; m. Frank Osborne Patterson. Ch: Charles L.; and Kimberly Ann Patterson

[V6]3711. [13]2. Donna May Fulton; m. Keith Sand. Ch: Lynette Louise; Scott Keith; Marla; Marlene; Teri Lee; and Lewis Sand

[V6]3712. [12]7. **Stella Lorraine Breshears**, b. 24 Oct 1925, Howard, Montana; m. ***Roy Manning Whitney***.

[V6]3713. [13]1. Kathleen Ann Whitney; m. David Hutchinson.

Ch: Nichole Ann; Carrie Lynn; and Travis Manning Hutchinson

[V6]3714. [13]2. Colleen Lynn Whitney; m.1 Tom Halton; m.2. Tim McCaffery. Ch: Paul Marvin; Lee James; and Brandon Michael McCaffery

[V6]3715. [13]3. Mark Dean Whitney; m. Patty Kawaterski. Ch: Malissa Ann Whitney

[V6]3716. [12]8. **Thomas M. Breshears**, b. 1 Oct 1927, Billings, Montana; m. ***Agnes Carmichael***.

[V6]3717. [13]1. **Debra Ann Breshears**, m. ***Randolph Werholz***. Ch: Jason Richard; and Amy Christine Werholz

[V6]3718. [13]2. **Michael Gregory Breshears**, m. ***Deborah Preuninger***.

[V6]3719. [14]1. **Jennifer Lynn Breshears**,

[V6]3720. [13]3. **Rochelle Marie Breshears**,

[V6]3721. [13]4. **Patrick Thomas Breshears**,

[V6]3722. [13]5. **Mary Beth Breshears**,

[V6]3723. [13]6. **Nancy Kay Breshears**,

[V6]3724. [12]9. **Bob Breshears**, (twin) b. 17 May 1930, Billings, MT, d. 21 Jan 2000, Billings, MT; m. ***Ramona Jensen***.

[V6]3725. [13]1. **Clayton Allen Breshears**,

[V6]3726. [13]2. **Roberta Lee Breshears**,

[V6]3727. [13]3. **Brett Dwayne Breshears**,

[V6]3728. [13]4. **Jacqueline Ellen Breshears**,

[V6]3729. [12]10. **Bill Breshears**, (twin) b. 17 May 1930, Billings, MT, d. 1983, Billings, MT; m. ***Marjorie L. Henry***.

[V6]3730. [13]1. **David Breshears**,

[V6]3731. [13]2. **Stephen Breshears**,

[V6]3732. [13]3. **Robert Breshears**,

[V6]3733. [13]4. **Lori Susan Breshears**,

[V6]3734. [13]5. **Linda Marie Breshears**,

Francis Marion Breshears and Sallie Wells

[v6]3547. [11]13. **Francis Marion "Frank" Breshears**, (s/o William Thomas "Wild Bill" Breshears and Anna Ihrig), b. 1 Feb 1885, Hickory Co, MO, d. 13 Aug 1967 in Oklahoma; m. 23 Dec 1906, ***Sallie Wells***, d/o John Wells and Caroline Crouch, sister to Mattie Wells, Marvin's wife. Frank and Sallie are buried in Gibson Cem, Haskell, OK

Family of Francis Marion Breshears and Sallie Wells:

[V6]3735. [12]1. **Anna Marie Breshears**, b. 28 Dec 1907; m. ***Harry Woodard***.

[V6]3736. [13]1. Bonnie Bell Woodard; m. Junior Madewell. Ch: Don; and Janice Madewell

[V6]3737. [13]2. Bobbie Woodard;

[V6]3738. [13]3. Billie Delane Woodard; m. Naomi Smith. Ch: Terry Smith; Debra Delane; Ricky Lee; and Billy Lee Woodard

[V6]3739. [12]2. **John Elic Breshears**, b. 8 Feb 1910, Porter, OK, d. 6 June 1978, Spokane, WA; m. ***Beryl Kathryn Keeney***.

[V6]3740. [13]1. **Kenneth Carl Breshears**, m. ***Joanne Ray***.

[V6]3741. [14]1. **Kenneth Carl Breshears, Jr**,

[V6]3742. [14]2. **Bob Breshears**,

[V6]3743. [14]3. **Mark Breshears**,

[V6]3744. [13]2. **Sally Margaret Breshears**, m.1. ***John Harmon***; m.2. ***Peter D. Clark***.

[V6]3745. [14]1. Linda Harmon; m. Randy Bates. Ch: Jamie Bates

[V6]3746. [14]2. Cathy Harmon;

[V6]3747. [14]3. Mike Harmon; m. Vera ______. Ch: Kanine; and Kenneth Clayton Harmon

[V6]3748. [13]3. **Shirley Joanne Breshears**; m.1. ***Dale Meyer***; m.2. ***Clayton Bayer***. [4218 Kay Place, Las Vegas, NV 89107, in 2001; 702/878-0833; <clashb @msn.com>].

[V6]3749. [14]1. Andrea Rosalind Meyer; m. Arthur Holtz. Ch: Jeffrey Holtz

[V6]3750. [14]2. Toi Lynn Bayer;

[V6]3751. [14]3. Paula Marie Bayer

[V6]3752. [13]4. **Roy Franklin Breshears**, m. ***Carolyn Sue Mitchell***.

[V6]3753. [14]1. **Deborah Ann Breshears**,

[V6]3754. [14]2. **Tommy Breshears**,

[V6]3755. [13]5. **Coy John Breshears**, m. ***Marilyn Swanson***.

[V6]3756. [14]1. **Julie Breshears**,

[V6]3757. [14]2. **Kimberly Breshears**,

[V6]3758. [14]3. **Douglas Breshears**,

[V6]3759. [12]3. **Opal Ollie Breshears**, b. May 1912, d. 5 Dec 1913

[V6]3760. [12]4. **Velma Toleda Breshears**, b. 1914, d. 19 Aug 1916 (bitten by a mad dog)

[V6]3761. [12]5. **Earnest Wilson Breshears**, b. 2 Oct 1916, Stonebluff, OK, d. 8 Nov 1916, age 3 weeks

[V6]3762. [12]6. Boy **Breshears**, b. & d. 1917

[V6]3763. [12]7. **Thomas Carl Breshears**, b. 3 Aug 1918, Stonebluff, OK, d. 22 Feb 1978, OK; m.1. ***Marie Russell***; m.2. ***Nodain Mallicott*** (1 ch); m.3. ***Mary Acker***, (5 ch)

[V6]3764. [13]1. **Tommy Carl Breshears, Jr**, m. ***Theresa Clugston***.

[V6]3765. [14]1. **Amanda Christine Breshears**,

[V6]3766. [14]2. **Jennifer Lynn Breshears**,

[V6]3767. [13]2. **Delane Dyton Breshears**,

[V6]3768. [13]3. **Michael Todd Breshears**,

[V6]3769. [13]4. **Kelly Jo Breshears**,

[V6]3770. [13]5. **Sally Marie Breshears**,

[V6]3771. [13]6. **Steven Mark Breshears**,

[V6]3772. [12]8. **Paul Edward Breshears**, b. 11 Dec 1920, Stonebluff, OK; m. ***Glendene St. John***.

[V6]3773. [13]1. **Paul Edward Breshears, Jr**,; m. ***Doris Carpenter*** (2 ch); m.2. ***Sharon Winch Walstonon*** (1 ch).

[V6]3774. [14]1. **Paul Eugene Breshears**,

[V6]3775. [14]2. **Peggy Sue Breshears**,

[V6]3776. [14]3. **Jennifer Lynn Breshears**,

[V6]3777. [13]2. **Linda Annette Breshears**, m.1. ***Kenneth La Plante***; m.2. ***Duman "Duke" Kinney***. Ch: Curtis Dean; and Roy Glen La Plante

[V6]3778. [12]9. **Howard Breshears**, (twin) b. 19 Jan 1923,

[V6]3779. [12]10. **Harold Breshears**, (twin) b. 19 Jan 1923, d. 25 Jan 1923

[V6]3780. [12]11. **Dorothy Elizabeth Breshears**, b. 9 Oct 1924, Stonebluff, OK, d. 14 Sept 1968, Los Angeles, CA; m.1. ***Ray Scoggins***; m.2. ***Felix Garfield Day***.

[V6]3781. [13]1. Ray Eugene Scoggins; m. Deborah Sue Hunt. Ch: Monica Yvonne; Mark Eugene; and John

Wayne Scoggins

V6 3782. [13]2. Ronald Garfield Day; m. Cathy Ann Conn. Ch: Rhonda Ann; and Heather Michelle Day

V6 3783. [13]3. Dorothy Gail Day; m. Doyle McHaffie. Ch: Doyle Eugene, III; Paul; and Sandra Lynne McHaffie

V6 3784. [12]12. **Marion Franklin "Bud" Breshears**, b. 4 Dec 1928, Stonebluff, OK; m.1 Apr 1950, Van Buren, OK, ***Emma Mae Hallum***, b. 14 Jul 1932, Haskell, OK, d/o Simon Monroe Hallum (1906-1963) and Nellie Morton (1914-1969).

V6 3785. [13]1. **Marion Franklin "Buddy" Breshears, III**, b. 12 July 1951, Muskogee, OK; m. 24 Dec 1991, ***Diana Lynn Miller***.

V6 3786. [14]1. **Dawn Marie Breshears**,

V6 3787. [14]2. **Marion Franklin "B.J." Breshears, IV**,

V6 3788. [13]2. **Kathleen Jeanette Breshears**, b. 24 March 1953, La Mesa, CA; m. 21 Jan 1969, ***Harold Keith "Bud" Frost***. Ch: Keith Lee; and Buck Travis Frost

V6 3789. [13]3. **Diana Marie Breshears**, b. 21 Nov 1958, Oklahoma City, OK; m. 16 Aug 1975, ***Terry Lee Garrett***. Ch: Jeremy Lee; and Joshua Jacob Garrett

V6 3790. [13]4. **David Michael Breshears**, b. 1 Dec 1961, Manhattan, KS; m.1. 20 April 1979, ***Lawanna Stacy*** (1 ch); m.2. 4 July 1983, ***Lynora Durfey***.

V6 3791. [14]1. **Jennifer Lynn Breshears**,

Levi "Prairie Levi" Breshears and Sarah E. Thornton

v6 3434. [10]4. **Levi "Prairie Levi" Breshears**, (s/o Madison Golman "Matt" Breshears and Sarah Elizabeth Brown), b. 24 June 1856, Benton Co, MO, d. 9 Jan 1919, Hickory Co, MO; m. ***Sarah E. Thornton***, b. c?1856; both bur Jones Cem, in Breshears Valley, Benton Co, MO.

<u>Family of Levi Breshears and Sarah E. Thornton:</u>

V63792. 111. **Rosa Breshears**, b. c1878, MO; m. ____ ***Turpin***, b. c?1878

V63793. 112. ***Ollie Goldman Breshears**, b. c1885, MO, went to Canada; m. ***Susan Cosby Cook***,

V63794. 113. ***George William "Bill" Breshears**, b. 7 March 1891, Benton Co, MO, d. 12 Feb 1927, in Aztec, New Mexico; m. 15 Feb 1911, in Wheatland, Hickory Co, MO, a cousin, **Harriet Eudona "Dona" Breshears** (d/o James Alexander "Jimmie" Breshears Jr and Amanda Paxton), b. 15 Feb 1891, Cross Timbers, MO, d. there, 11 Nov 1941

V63795. 114. **Sarah Bell Breshears**, b. c?1894; m. ***Eland Blackwell***

V63796. 115. **Jessie Ruby Breshears**, b. 8 Oct 1898, d. 25 Dec 1919; m. 24 Dec 1916, a cousin, ***Buel Roy Breshears** (s/o James Alexander "Jimmie" Breshears Jr and Amanda Paxton), b. 19 Aug 1895, d. 8 April 1921. See Buel's listing for their children.

V63797. 116. **Bertha Breshears**, b. after 1898, died as a young woman

Ollie Goldman Breshears and Susan Cosby Cook

V63793. 112. **Ollie Goldman Breshears**, (s/o Levi "Prairie Levi" Breshears and Sarah E. Thornton), b. c1885, MO, went to Canada; m. ***Susan Cosby Cook***, b. 1887, VA (Data from Wendy Derennger <wderen @direct.ca>)

Family of Ollie Goldman Breshears and Susan Cook:

V63798. 121. **Rose Elizabeth Breshears**, 30 Jan 1907, MO; m. ***Harry Crandall***, b. 1944

V63799. 131. John David Crandall, b. 1945

V63800. 132. Harold Thomas Crandall, b. 1950

V63801. 122. **Loy Leonard Breshears**, b. 1911, Wheatland, MO; m. ***Elsa Bertha Schmuland***, b. 1914, Wetaskiwin, Alberta, Canada,

V63802. 131. **Judith Alma Breshears**, b. 1937,

Westaskiwin, Alberta; m.1. ***Daniel Patrick O'Malley***, b.? CA, 1965; m.2. ***Pete Steel***, b?,

V6 3803. 14 1. Anne Maureen O'Malley, b. 1966 Los Angeles, CA

V6 3804. 14 2. Kevin O'Malley, b. 1972, Los Angeles, CA

V6 3805. 13 2. **Wilma Orlis Breshears**, b. 1939, Westaskiwin, Alberta, Canada; m. ***Peter Unruh***, b. 1929, Saskatchewan, Canada

V6 3806. 14 1. Timothy Peter Unruh, b. 1963, Calgary, Alberta, Canada

V6 3807. 14 2. Kenneth Ollie Unruh, b. 1965, Calgary, Alberta, Canada

V6 3808. 14 3. Tamara Loni Unruh, b. 1968, Calgary, Alberta, Canada

V6 3809. 14 4. Jay Unruh, b. 1972, Calgary, Alberta, Canada

V6 3810. 13 3. **Wayne Loy Breshears**, b. 1941, Westaskiwin, Alberta, Canada; m.1. 1965, ***Sandy*** ____; m.2. c1974, ***Judy*** ____; m.3. c1991, ***Laurie*** ______,

V6 3811. 14 1. **Cindy Dawn Breshears**, b. 1966, Vancouver, British Columbia, Canada

V6 3812. 14 3. **Sherry Breshears**, b. ?1968, Vancouver, British Columbia, Canada

V6 3813. 13 4. **Neil Robert Breshears**, b. 1950, Westaskiwin, Alberta, Canada; m.1. 1971, ***Sheila Durand***; m.2. c.1977, ***Jeannette*** ____

V6 3814. 14 1. **Neil Breshears**, b?1978, San Diego, CA

V6 3815. 13 5. **Wendy Anne Breshears**, b. 1954, Wetaskiwin, Alberta Canada; m.1. 1976, in Mexico City, ***Timothy James Dean***, b. 1951; m.2. 1981, Smiths Falls, Ontario, Canada, ***James Ivan Muretich***, b. 1952

V6 3816. 12 3. **Sarah Audrey Breshears**, b. 1915, Wheatland, MO; m.1. 1935, ***E. Manfred Edin***; m.2. 1946, ***Thorval Erickson***, b. ?, d. 1998

V6 3817. 13 1. Alan Stanley Edin, b. 1937

V6 3818. 13 2. Lois Audrey Edin, b. 1941

V6 3819. 12 4. **Matty Aubra Breshears**, b. 1915, Wheatland, MO, d. 1919

V6 3820. [12]5. **Birdie Lucinda Breshears**, b. 1920, Wheatland, MO; m. ***John Dawson Walker***
V6 3821. [13]1. Bruce Dawson Walker, b. 1948, Wetaskiwin, Alberta, Canada; m. Jill Blythe
V6 3822. [13]2. John Brian Walker, b.1951, Wetaskiwin, Alberta, Canada; m. Joanne Doods
V6 3823. [13]3. Linda Leigh Walker, b. 1952, Wetaskiwin, Alberta, Canada
V6 3824. [13]4. Sharon Elizabeth Walker, b. 1955, Wetaskiwin, Alberta, Canada
V6 3825. [13]5. Kenneth James Walker, b. 1959, Wetaskiwin, Alberta, Canada;
V6 3826. [12]6. **Lena Oris Breshears**, b. 1922, Wheatland, MO; m. ***George Crandall***
V6 3827. [13]1. Gareth Ross Crandall, b. 1943, Wetaskiwin, Alberta, Canada; m. Bette Anderson ?
V6 3828. [13]2. Karen Lynette Crandall, b. 1945, Wetaskiwin, Alberta, Canada; m. Kenneth Nelson
V6 3829. [13]3. Leona May Crandall, b. 1949, Wetaskiwin, Alberta, Canada; m. Duane Johnson
V6 3830. [13]4. John George Crandall, b. 1951, Wetaskiwin, Alberta, Canada; m. Wendy Dodds
V6 3831. [12]7. **Wilma Jewel Breshears**, b. 1925, Wheatland, MO; m. ***Lawrence Ambler***
V6 3832. [13]1. Marilyn Ruth Ambler, b. 1947, Wetaskiwin, Alberta, Canada; m. Douglas Munro
V6 3833. [13]2. Sandra Lynn Ambler, b. 1949, Wetaskiwin, Alberta, Canada; m. Brian Lownsbury
V6 3834. [13]3. Lenora Edith Ambler, b. 1951, Wetaskiwin, Alberta, Canada; m. Conrad Johnson
V6 3835. [13]4. Grant Lawrence Ambler, b. 1952, Wetaskiwin, Alberta, Canada; m. Judy Day
V6 3836. [13]5. Susan Gail Ambler, b. 1953, Wetaskiwin, Alberta, Canada;
V6 3837. [13]6. Elaine Bertha Ambler, b. 1956, Wetaskiwin, Alberta, Canada; m. Jesse Hollar

George William "Bill" Breshears and Harriet Eudona "Dona" Breshears

v6 3794. 11 3. **George William "Bill" Breshears**, (s/o Levi "Prairie Levi" Breshears and Sarah E. Thornton), b. 7 March 1891, Benton Co, MO, d. 12 Feb 1927, in Aztec, New Mexico; m. 15 Feb 1911, in Wheatland, Hickory Co, MO, a cousin, **v6 3249. Harriet Eudona "Dona" Breshears** (d/o James Alexander "Jimmie" Breshears Jr and Amanda Paxton), b. 15 Feb 1891, Cross Timbers, MO, d. there, 11 Nov 1941

Family of George William "Bill" Breshears and Harriet Eudona Breshears:

V6 3838. 12 1. **Hubert Stanley Breshears**, b. 1 Feb 1912; m. 18 Sept 1937, ***Alice Elizabeth Hunter***, b. 31 Oct 1916
V6 3839. 13 1. **Stanley Lee Breshears**, b. 12 Oct 1938; m. ***Bonnie Lee Blume***, b. 20 Feb 1941
V6 3840. 14 1. **Cheri Lynn Breshears**, b. 30 July 1957
V6 3841. 14 2. **Yvette Alane Breshears**, b. 31 Jan 1962
V6 3842. 14 3. **Wesley Lowell Breshears**,
V6 3843. 13 2. **Lyle Leroy Breshears**, b. 26 May 1942; m. ***Beverly Becker***, no ch
V6 3844. 12 2. **Ethel Revay Breshears**, b. 2 Oct 1916, Cross Timbers, MO; m. 18 Dec 1935, ***Adam W. Mace***; m.2. ***William Virgil Palmer***, b. 15 June 1909, West Plains, MO; m.3. ***H.B. Douglas***
V6 3845. 13 1. Kenneth Gerald Mace, b. 19 Oct 1936; m. 1 July 1956, Carolyn Elizabeth Dealy
V6 3846. 14 1. Darla Louise Mace, b. 5 Sept 1957
V6 3847. 14 2. Claudia Revay Mace, b. 21 Nov 1958
V6 3848. 14 3. Curtis Dale Mace, b. 2 Feb 1961
V6 3849. 14 4. Carrie Lynn Mace, b. 20 Aug 1962
V6 3850. 13 2. Creighton Leon Palmer, b. 11 Oct 1939; m. 24 Sept 1961, Charlene Mae Rieland, b. 4 Nov 1939
V6 3851. 14 1. Jennece Renee Palmer
V6 3852. 14 2. Judith Palmer (twin)
V6 3853. 14 3. girl Palmer (twin)
V6 3854. 12 3. **Porter Dee Breshears**, b. 28 June 1919, d. 28

April 1953; m. 21 July 1941, ***Mary Ellen Nelson***, b. 30 Dec 1925

V6 3855. [13] 1. **Inez Jean Breshears**, b. 12 July 1942; m. ***Richard Lee Forman***, b. 5 April 1937. ch: Richard Forman and two girls, names unknown

V6 3856. [13] 2. **Mary Ellen Breshears**, b. 7 Dec 1946

V6 3857. [12] 4. **Eugene William Breshears**, b. 29 July 1923, d. 10 March 1924

Henry Belsis Breshears and Sarah Elizabeth Breshears/ Ida Elsie Button

Figure 61: Henry Belsis Breshears with sons Elijah (at his right) and Hoosier. Photo from Bill Brooks

V6 3435. 10 5. **Henry Belsis Breshears**, (s/o Madison Golman 'Matt" Breshears and Sarah Elizabeth Brown), b. 17 Oct 1859, Dennison, Denton Co, TX, d. 3 Oct 1948, Benton Co, MO, bur Jones Cem; m.1. 24 Nov 1878, a cousin, **Sarah Elizabeth Breshears** (d/o Levi Robert "Lee" Breshears and Mary Anna Garner), b. 30 Sept 1859, Benton Co, MO, d. 6 Nov 1909, Benton Co, MO, bur Jones Cem. After Sarah died, Henry Belsis Breshears m.2. ***Ida Elsie Button***, b. 23 Dec 1885, Bentonville, Benton Co, MO, d. 30 Nov 1975, in Kansas City, MO, and had second family.

Figure 62: Frank, Ethel, Eva (on Frank's lap), and Bill Breshears. Photo from Bill Brooks

<u>Family of Henry Belsis Breshears and Sarah Elizabeth Breshears:</u>

V6 3858. 11 1. **John Franklin "Frank" Breshears**, b. 20 Aug 1879, Benton Co, MO, d. 9 July 1956; m. 3 April 1905, ***Ethel Robinson*** (or Robertson). Frank lived in Washington and worked on farms, harvesting crops. He was nicknamed "Snuffer," because he was always sniffing his nose. When his health began failing, he wanted to go back to Missouri for a visit, but was advised against it. He said, if the died there, they could bury him there, rather than return his body to Washington. He died of a heart attack in Missouri and was buried in the Avery Cem. His children:

[V6]3859. [12]1. **William "Bill" Breshears**, b. 8 March 1906, Avery, Benton Co, MO, d. 20 March 1937

[V6]3860. [12]2. **Neva Breshears**,

[V6]3861. [12]3. **Eva Breshears**; m. ***William Fleming Jr***, (s/o William "Bill" Fleming and Fannie Adeline "Fanna" Breshears). See his listing for their children.

[V6]3862. [12]4. **John Breshears**, b. MO, d. in Omak, WA; m. _______ ***Jeffries***, John was a drinker, left his family, eventually re-married, and had another child.

[V6]3863. [13]1. **Weston Breshears**,

[V6]3864. [13]2. **Allen Breshears**,

[V6]3865. [12]5. **Ivan Breshears**, b. 4 Jan 1919, Avery, Benton Co, MO, d. 11 Jan 1978; m. _______ ***Pitts***,

[V6]3866. [12]6. **Mearl Breshears**,

[V6]3867. [11]2. ***Levi Ransom Breshears**, b. 20 Sept 1881, Benton Co, MO, d. 7 Feb 1965, Modesto, CA; m. 18 June 1903, ***Hettie Noble Button***,

Figure 63: Ezra Green and Mary Elizabeth Breshears. Photo from Bill Brooks

[V6]3868. [11]3. **William "Willie" Breshears**, b. 18 Aug 1883, d. 15 Jan 1885, bur Jones Cem, Avery, MO

[V6]3869. [11]4. **Mary Elizabeth Breshears**, b. Jan 1888; m. ***Ezra Green***,

[V6]3870. [12]1. Lillie Frances Green, b. 1 Sept 1924; m. Sherman Edgar Hart, b. 20 Aug 1913.

[V6]3871. [13]1. Mary Elizabeth Green, m. Sequoyah L.

Figure 65: Mary Elizabeth Breshears, wife of Ezra Green. Photo from Bill Brooks

Figure 64: Jacob Young, Ina Breshears, and their son, Jesse. Photo from Bill Brooks

Rogers

[V6]3872. [13]2. Sherman Edgar Hart, Jr; m.1. _____; m.2. _____. Ch: Kriston Ann Lipscomb

[V6]3873. [11]5. **Inez "Ina" Breshears**, b. 12 Dec 1891, Benton Co, MO, d. CA; m. ***William Jacob "Jake" Young***, b. before 1879 in Benton or Hickory Co, MO, d. CA, s/o Joseph Young and Harriet Strong. After moving to CA, Jake worked on the railroad in Colton, CA. After their daughter, Bessie, died, Jake and Ina took Bessie's two children to raise; they may have adopted them.

[V6]3874. [12]1. Jesse Young, b. ?, d. CA; m. ______ Afton. Jesse was killed by a street gang in CA.

[V6]3875. [13]1. Joan Young,

[V6]3876. [12]2. Bessie Young, died early, after having two children, which her parents took to raise. And, yes, says Noble King, that was their names.

[V6]3877. [13]1. Herman Dickey Young,

[V6]3878. [13]2. Dickey Herman Young,

[V6]3879. [11]6. **George T. Breshears**, b. 10 Jan 1894, d. 16 Jan 1957; m. ***Florence K. Mulkey***, b. 1893, d. 1958. George kept a store in Harper, MO, where his niece, Dona Lea Breshears, worked before moving to California.

Figure 66: George T. Breshears, as a youth. Photo from Bill Brooks

[V6]3880. [12]1. **Lloyd Thomas Breshears**, b. 16 Oct 1916, Bentonville, MO, d. 24 Oct 1992, Clinton, MO; m.1. 1934, ***Fairy Ellen Weaver***, d/o Johnny Weaver and Lula Payne; m.2. ***Vera Ruth Morton***,

[V6]3881. [13]1. **Naomi Elaine Breshears**, b. 31 Oct 1935; m.1. ______ Payne; m.2. Jerrol Briggs. Ch: Charles Payne

[V6]3882. [13]2. **Marion Lloyd Breshears**, b. 2 July 1938; m.1. _______ (1 ch); m.2. ***Nora Nadene Hunziker***, (3 ch) (d/o Buel Hunziker and Marguerite Breshears)

[V6]3883. [14]1. **Danny Loyd Breshears**, m. ***Crystal _______***.

[V6]3884. [15]1. **Allen Loyd Breshears**,

[V6]3885. [15]2. **Heather Breshears**,

[V6]3886. [14]2. **Danny Breshears**; m. ***Karen _______***

[V6]3887. [14]3. **Debbie Breshears**,

[V6]3888. [14]4. **Janice Breshears**,

[V6]3889. [11]7. **Elijah "Lige" Breshears**, b. 15 April 1896, d, 19 Oct 1924; m. ***Dollie Belle Payne***, b. 3 Aug 1895, d/o James Payne and Francis Bailey

[V6]3890. [12]1. **Edith Anna Breshears**, b. 10 Dec 1919,

Hickory Co, MO, d. 11 Jan 2000, Warrensburg, Johnson Co, MO; m. 2 April 1936, ***Troy Edward Sunderland***.

V6 3891. 13 1. Lige Norman Sunderland,

V6 3892. 13 2. Nina Michalene Sunderland, b. 1937, d. 2004; m. Lloyd M. Franklin,

V6 3893. 14 1. Terp Franklin, m. ______ Parks,

V6 3894. 14 2. Patricia Franklin, m. ______ Hankins,

V6 3895. 14 3. Gail Franklin, m. ______ Koehler,

V6 3896. 14 4. Susan Franklin, m. ______ Palomo,

V6 3897. 14 5. Sarah Franklin,

V6 3898. 14 6. Ben Franklin,

V6 3899. 14 7. Matt Franklin,

V6 3900. 14 8. Joel Franklin,

V6 3901. 14 9. Josh Franklin,

V6 3902. 13 3. Raymond G. Sunderland,

V6 3903. 12 2. **Velma Breshears**, b. 14 Dec 1921, Benton Co, MO, d. 13 Oct 1977; m. ***Gerald Cobb***. Ch: Galen; Garland; Kent; and Thelma Cobb

V6 3904. 11 8. **Hoosier Breshears**, b. 11 April 1903, in Warsaw, Kansas, d. 8 July 1956, Spokane, WA; m. ***Dorothy Avis Burns***, b. 4 March 1910, Hudson, KS, d. 24 Feb 1994. (Information from son, David C. Breshears.)

V6 3905. 12 1. **Robert Griffith Breshears**, b. 28 July 1927, d. 30 June 1973; m.1. ***Dorothy Ladell Thames***; m.2. ***Maxine Mildred***, b. 1932; m.3. ***Lillie Francis Green*** b. 1924, who had a son by a previous marriage: Edward Allen Green; he sometimes went by the name, Joe Breshears.

V6 3906. 13 1. **Nancy Ann Breshears**, m. ***John Bolt***,

V6 3907. 13 2. **Robert Bruce Breshears**, m. ***Josie ______***,

V6 3908. 13 3. **Robin Kaye Breshears**, m. ***Fred Hale***,

V6 3909. 13 4. **Brian Richard Breshears**, m. ***Caroline ______***,

V6 3910. 13 5. **Joe Breshears**, (Edward Allen Green), b. 1944; m. Shirley Kiefer. Ch: Patti Jo

Green.

[V6]3911. [12]2. **Lois Marie Breshears**, b. 21 Oct 1928, d. 19 Feb 1929, Denver, Colorado

[V6]3912. [12]3. **Howard Patrick Breshears**, b. 19 Aug 1931, Modesto, CA, d. 25 Jan 1993; m. ***Beulah Jane Breshears***,

[V6]3913. [13]1. **Clay Patrick Breshears**, m. ***Lorna*** ______,

[V6]3914. [13]2. **Guy Reuben Breshears**, m. ***Elizabeth Del Carmen Navarrete Barra***,

[V6]3915. [13]3. **Melanie Jane Breshears**; m. ***Zack Ellis***. Ch: Sydney; Zoe; and Ethan Ellis

[V6]3916. [12]4. **David Carrol Breshears**, b. 5 Sep 1932, San Bernardino, CA; m. ***Maxine Rose Voss***, b. 17 June 1935, Blunt, South Dakota

[V6]3917. [13]1. **Cynthia Lea Breshears**; m. ***Richard Duane Tobias***. Ch: Chanel Rene; and Chad Richard Tobias

[V6]3918. [13]2. **Sherri Ann Breshears**; m. ***Garry Duane Jordon***. Ch: Salena Marie; and Christian David Jordon

[V6]3919. [12]5. **Rodney Paul Breshears**, b. 27 June 1942, Omak, WA; m. ***Mary Louise Wright***,

[V6]3920. [13]1. **Paula Louise Breshears**,

[V6]3921. [13]2. **Jeffrey Martin Breshears**,

[V6]3922. [12]6. Edward Allen Green, b. 17 Sept 1944; m. Shirley Kiefer

[V6]3923. [13]1. Patti Jo Green; ch: 1 dau

Family of Henry Belsis Breshears and Ida Elsie Button:

[V6]3924. [11]9. ***Jacob "Jake" Breshears**, b. 27 July 1913, Bentonville, Benton Co, MO, d. 5 Dec 1989, Tualitin, Oregon; m. 28 July 1934, in Weaubleau, Hickory Co, MO, ***Ruby Virginia Dietz***, b. 1913, d. 2004.

[V6]3925. [11]10. **Noah Breshears**, b. 15 Sept 1916, Bentonville, Benton Co, MO, d. 22 April 2001, Port Orchard, Washington; m. ***Alta Mae Cates***, b. 28 June 1913, in Wheatland, Hickory Co, MO

[V6]3926. [12]1. **Veda Fern Breshears**, m. ***Aubery Monroe***

"Dub" Hammer. Ch: Jeffrey Monroe "Jeff"; and Joseph Jay "Joe" Hammer

V63927. 122. **Bobby Gene Breshears**, b. 1938; m.1. ***Bernetta Ann Hartford***, (2 ch), b. 1942; m.2. Patty ______.

V63928. 131. **Elissa Dee Breshears**, m. ***James Barnett***,

V63929. 132. **Larry Gene Breshears**,

V63930. 123. **Mary Maxine Breshears**, b. 1941; m. ***Delmar Marion Kenter***, b. 1938. Ch: Christene Lynn; Katrina Luann; Victor Scott; and Michael Lawrence Kenter.

V63931. 1111. **Denver Logan Breshears**, b. 20 Sept 1919, Bentonville, MO; m. 24 Sept 1940, in Warsaw, Benton Co, MO, ***Mildred Ethelene Dietz***, b. 22 June 1920, Quincy, Hickory Co, MO, d/o Robert Dietz and Effie Breshears

V63932. 121. **Harold Gene Breshears**, b. 20 May 1941, Quincy, Hickory Co, MO; m. ***Wanda Ruth Baumgarden***, b. 1945.

V63933. 131. **Ricky Gene Breshears**, m. ***Kathy Kehm Meads***.

V63934. 141. **Milinda Breshears**,

V63935. 132. **Teresa Renee Breshears**, m. ***Douglas Spackler***. Ch: Kyle Douglas; Taylor Dale; and Mason Daniel Spackler

V63936. 122. **Wilma Louise Breshears**, b. 1 May 1942, Bentonville, Benton Co, MO; m. ***James Eugene Rens***.

V63937. 131. Troy Eugene Rens; m. Jennifer Henkle. Ch: Janey Drew Rens

V63938. 132. James Timothy Rens; m. R. Snyder. Ch: Sidney Elizabeth; James Derrick; and Emily Louise Rens

V63939. 133. Tony Dale Rens; m. ______. Ch: Victoria Geraldine; and Tiffany Elaine Rens

V63940. 123. **Ronald Dee Breshears**, b. 16 Feb 1944, Bentonville, Benton Co, MO; m. ***Annabell Southers***, b. 1944.

V63941. 131. **Lore Lee Breshears**, Ch: C. David

Wendal,

[V6]3942. [13]2. **Ronna Ray Breshears**, m. ***David Howard***. Ch: Paige Marie Howard

[V6]3943. [13]3. **Waylon Dee Breshears**, m. ***Lori Bamis***.

[V6]3944. [14]1. **Traver Dale Breshears**,

[V6]3945. [14]2. **Colton Dee Breshears**,

[V6]3946. [13]4. **Donna Jo Breshears**,

[V6]3947. [12]4. **Jimmy Lee Breshears**, b. 4 May 1946, Weaubleau, Hickory Co, MO; m. ***Cathey Sue Slater***, b. 1951, d. 1994.

[V6]3948. [13]1. **Christopher Lee Breshears**,

[V6]3949. [12]5. **Donnie Ray Breshears**, b. 10 April 1952, Clinton, Henry Co, MO, d. 1971

[V6]3950. [12]6. **Lonnie Dale Breshears**, b. 26 Dec 1955, Clinton, Henry Co, MO; m. ***Donna Van Winkle Elges***, b. 1952.

[V6]3951. [13]1. Sean Elges, (step-child); m. ________. Ch: Andra Nicole; and Haley Dawn Elges

[V6]3952. [13]2. **Brandi Jo Breshears**,

[V6]3953. [11]12. **Ralph Breshears**, b. 24 June 1922, Bentonville, MO; m.1. ***Ivy Harris***, (1 ch) d. Jan 1945; m.2. ***Opal Harris***, (1 ch)

[V6]3954. [12]1. **Ray Allen Breshears**, b. 1 Dec 1942, Fairfield, Benton Co, MO, d. 27 Feb 1990, Sac Osage Hosp, Osceola, MO; m. Margaret ________

[V6]3955. [13]1. **Jason Allen Breshears**,

[V6]3956. [12]2. **Roy Allen Breshears**, b. after 1945

[V6]3957. [11]13. **Alleen Breshears**, b. 3 June 1925, Bentonville, Benton Co, MO; m. 19 May 1940, ***Woodrow Thomas Harris***, b. 26 May 1916, d. 20 May 1999, s/o Johnnie Harris and Mary Smallwood

[V6]3958. [12]1. Jackie Thomas Harris, b. 25 April 1941; m. Barbara ______. Ch: Delisa Dawn Harris, m. Kenneth Lee Jones,

Figure 67: Levi Ransom Breshears, with his father, Henry Belsis Breshears. Photos from Bill Brooks

Levi Ransom Breshears and Hettie Noble Button

[v6]**3867.** [11]2. **Levi Ransom Breshears**, (s/o Henry Belsis Breshears and Sarah Elizabeth Breshears), b. 20 Sept 1881, Benton Co, MO, d. 7 Feb 1965, Modesto, Stanislaus Co, CA; m.1. 18 June 1903, ***Hettie Noble Button***, b. 2 April 1885, Hickory Co, MO, d. 23 May 1948, Oakdale, Stanislaus Co, CA, d/o James Madison Button and Martha Emaline Rogers; m.2. ***Ella Cox***; m.3. 1952, ***Marcella Creig***, (this last marriage ended in divorce.)

Some family stories passed on to me by Bill Brooks:

Levi owned a 100-acre farm about 3/4 mile from Bentonville on the old road to Warsaw, where he and Hettie lived. They would take the kids in a wagon filled with straw and blankets to various functions and "Revivals." One such time, there was a revival at Shiloh Church, west of Bentonville.

According to daughter Lola Mae Breshears, the revival was held in the "board arbor." It began to rain very hard, and everyone decided to stay in the shelter of the board arbor that night. During the night, the boys of the church got up on the roof and kept everyone awake by "crowing" all night long.

Levi and Hettie had large family gatherings at their place on special occasions, holidays, or the arrival of out-of-town or out-of-state relatives.

About 1908, Levi and Hettie, along with Levi's older brother, Frank, and Frank's wife, Ethel, went to Oklahoma. While there, they had to guard their horses and tie them to the wagon at night, for fear they would be stolen by "indians." They soon decided Missouri was best, so they returned to their home state.

In 1914, 1915, Levi and Hettie were living in the Wheatland

Levi Ransom Breshears and Jacob (Jake)Young
At the Little Pomme de Terre Bridge

area of Hickory County, where they rented a home and farm from the dentist, Perry Scribner. Lola Mae remembers that , while living at the Scribner place, Levi and Hettie took the kids to stay overnight with Mrs. McShane. When the kids went home, they were greeted by a new sister, Inice Marie Breshears. Two years later, they went to stay overnight with Mrs. McShane again, and Lola Mae said that there would be a baby at home the next day. Sure enough, Guy Breshears was the new baby.

In the mid-to-late 1920s, Levi and his father, Henry B., co-signed a note to the hospital where his brother, Lige, was being cared for with a burst appendix. In order to satisfy his half of the debt, Levi had to sell his place. With the money that was left over, he and Hettie decided it was time to move on.

In 1928, Levi and Hettie moved to California, to the Hemet/ Colton area of Riverside County, south and east of Los Angeles. All their children, except Minnie, followed them. They worked in the orange groves. A relative named John Rash offered to get Levi a job, so they moved to Waterford, Stanislaus Co, CA, near Modesto, and eventually to Riverbank, CA. Levi did ranch work for various men (John Grohl, Clyde Booth, and others), irrigating, harvesting. He and Hettie also worked in the Riverbank Cannery, a food processing plant that produced canned peaches and tomatoes.

Bill Brooks says Levi and Hettie had a door stop in their house that was supposed to be a meteorite. It is now in the possession of their great-grandson, Greg Breshears.

Bill remembers that they also had a wind-up record player that would houses in a suitcase. The selection of records was very small in the years of WW II; they had only a couple of records— Roy Acuff singing "The Wabash Cannon Ball," and "The Great Speckled Bird," the Andrews Sisters singing "Rum and Coca Cola." As the record player unwound, the music got slower and slower. It was then time to wind up the player again.

Upon retirement, Levi and Hettie bought a 5-acre parcel of land on Patterson Road, Riverbank, CA, next to their daughter, Dona. After Hettie's death (cancer of the liver), Levi moved into the town of Riverbank and married two more times. After the death of his second wife, Ella, he married Marcella. They were later divorced. His later years were spent in Escalon, San Joaquin Co, CA, in a mobile home on the property of his daughter, Lola Mae.

In his youth, Levi had red hair, but in his older years, his hair was full and as white as snow. His physical stature was small to medium. All life long, his favorite pastime (and maybe necessity) was to always have a very large vegetable garden.

Levi died in Modesto, Stanislaus Co, CA, in 1965, almost 84 years old. He and Hettie are buried at Acacia Memorial Park, Masonic cemetery, Modesto, CA.

Family of Levi Ransom Breshears and Hettie Noble Button:

V6 3959. 12 1. ***Dona Lea Breshears**, b. 4 Dec 1904, Benton Co, MO, d. 9 Aug 1984, Modesto, CA; m.1. 26 June 1931, ***Thomas Charles "Ted" Brooks***, b. 30 Jan 1890; m.2. 6 Aug 1971, ***Merle Hobart Livingston***, b. 20 Oct 1896,

V6 3960. 12 2. **Teddy Roosevelt Breshears**, b. 26 Dec 1905, Benton Co, MO, d. 24 March 1933, MO; m. 3 Oct 1928, ***Virginia "Vergie" Elizabeth Boring***, b. 22 Nov 1906, Benton Co, MO, d. April 1967, d/o Walter Boring and Ida Sharp. As a boy of ten years, Teddy was the school janitor at L.P. Union School (aka Weaver School). Among his duties was starting fires with kerosene on cold mornings to warm up the school before the daily classes. He died early of a brain tumor. He had only one child.

Figure 70: Teddy Roosevelt Breshears in 1927. Photo from Bill Brooks

V6 3961. 13 1. (Dr.) **Darrell Breshears**, b. 8 Oct 1929, Benton Co, MO, d. 30 April 1996, Albuquerque, NM; m. 4 Sept 1949, in Nampa, Idaho, ***Helen Jean Witzel***, b. 6 Aug 1931, Alamosa, NM, d/o Gerald Witzel and Virgie

Percival. Darrell was a dentist in Albuquerque. He had three children.

V63962. [14]1. **Darro Jean Breshears**, b. 20 Nov 1951, Alamosa Co, Colorado; m.1. c1971, ***Ralph Powell***; m.2. 29 May 1980, in Albuquerque, Bernalillo Co, NM, ***Steven Kent Rowton***, b. Farmersville, CA. Ch: Brett Dree; Kyra Ann; and Hannah Suzanne Rowton

V63963. [14]2. **Gregory Scott Breshears**, b. 2 July 1958, El Paso, El Paso Co, TX; m.1. 9 Sept 1978, in Albuquerque, NM, ***Cindy Ann Lemmel*** (1 ch; div 1981); m.2. March 1985, in Albuquerque, NM, ***Linda Marie Gurrite*** (1 ch).

V63964. [15]1. **Crystal Marie Breshears**,

V63965. [15]2. **Alma Leigh Breshears**,

V63966. [14]3. **Pamela Dree Breshears**, b. 17 Dec 1964, Albuquerque, NM; m. 7 Aug 1993, in Corrales, NM, ***John David Hindi***, b. 26 Sept 1961. Ch: Shane Tristan; and Amira Dree Hindi

V63967. [12]3. **Minnie Elizabeth Breshears**, (d/o Levi Ransom Breshears and Hettie Noble Button), b. 13 Sept 1907, Benton Co, MO, d. 24 June 1996, Lowry City, St Clair Co, MO; m. 4 June 1924, ***Vessie Buel Wright***, b. 14 June 1905, St Clair, MO, d. 24 June 1980, Lowry City, MO, s/o Tatum Wright and Flora Rippetoe. Buel had lived in St. Clair County all his life. He and Minnie lived in the Wright community near Lowry City until 1944, when they moved to a farm in the Ohio Community, east of Lowry City. After Buel died in 1980, Minnie went to lived in Lowry City with her daughter, Noble (Wright) King. Minnie died suddenly in 1996. She had three children.

V63968. [13]1. Harold Lee Wright, b. 11 March 1925, St Clair Co, MO, d. 13 Aug 1983, Kansas City, MO; m. 21 Dec 1952, in Henry Co, MO, Gladys

Lorraine Cornell, b. 16 Oct 1924, Montrose, CO, d. 11 Feb 2002, Osceola, MO.

[V6]3969. [13]2. Ervin Finis Wright, b. 11 April 1929, St Clair Co, MO, d. 7 July 1999, Blue Springs, MO; m. 19 Aug 1950, in Arkansas, Alma Jean Bennett, b. 20 May 1932. Ch: Randy Ervin Wright, b. 1 Oct 1952, Butler, Bates Co, MO; and David Lee Wright, b. 2 Jan 1962, Clinton, Henry Co, MO.

[V6]3970. [13]3. Hettie Noble Wright, b. 24 Feb 1943; m. 24 Nov 1995, in Cedar Co, MO, Theron Ralph King, b. 9 July 1933, Cedar Co, MO, s/o Howard King and Eva Berry. Theron and Noble live on a 260-acre farm in rural Stockton, Cedar Co, MO, where they enjoy gardening, church, and using a pair of fine Belgian draft horses, blond geldings named Kane and Sunny, which they bought from some Amish in the neighborhood.

[V6]3971. [14]1. Douglas Shawn Newman, b. 20 June 1971 (step-child); m. 5 Aug 1995, Rhonda Angelen. Ch: Kenzie Kay; and Abigail Grace Newman.

[V6]3972. [12]4. **Lola Mae Breshears**, (d/o Levi Ransom Breshears and Hettie Noble Button), b. 28 May 1909, Bentonville, MO, d. 23 Dec 2001, Modesto, CA; m.1. ***Orval Glen "Bus" Breshears, Sr** (s/o William Jasper "Jas" Breshears of the Henry Thomas Breshears line.) Parents of Glen Breshears, of Morgan Hill, CA, who sent a great deal of data. See Orval's listing for their family story and their children. Lola Mae m.2. ***Eldon "Mack" Alsip***; m.3. ***Grimsley "Grim" Donald Reed***

[V6]3973. [12]5. **Henry Thurman Breshears**, b. 21 Dec 1910, Bentonville, MO, d. there, 19 Feb 1922

[V6]3974. [12]6. **Inice Marie Breshears**, b. 8 July 1914, Wheatland, MO; m. 20 April 1933, in Hermitage, Hickory Co, MO, ***Lowis William Breshears**, (s/o

William Wesley "Will" Breshears and Eliza Ellen Butler), b. 12 Oct 1912, Hickory Co, MO, d. 31 Oct 2002, at his home in Modesto, CA. See his listing for pictures and their children.

V6 3975. 12 7. **Guy Breshears**, b. 8 Dec 1915, Wheatland, MO, d. 23 Jan 1971, Modesto, CA; m.1. 20 April 1933, in Hermitage, Hickory Co, MO, **Oryene Florence Breshears**, (2 ch; div) (d/o William Wesley "Will" Breshears and Eliza Ellen Butler), b. 27 Feb 1913, Hickory Co, MO, d. 23 April 2002 in Fresno, CA; m.2. 24 April 1945, in Reno, Washoe Co, NV, ***Sylvene Tucker***, (1 ch), b. 21 Oct 1913, Fristoe, Benton Co, MO, d. 25 July 1997, Oakdale, Stanislaus Co, CA.

Figure 71: Guy Breshears, about 1929. Photo from Bill Brooks

After Guy and Oryene divorced, she married George Lundberg, and she and the two children moved to Millbrae, CA, with him. After many years of marriage, they retired to the mountain community of Paradise, CA (near Chico in northern California). After George died, and during the failing health of her daughter, Ann, she moved to Victorville, CA, to be with Ann and her husband, Roger Halstead. After Ann died in 1996, Oryene returned to Modesto. In 1998, she moved to Fresno, CA, to be near her son, "Bobby Guy," and his family. In the winter of 2000, Oryene was hospitalized for various chemical imbalances and spent a month in specialized care in Fresno. Afterwards, she returned to an assisted living, level 2, residence in Fresno, where she passed away in April, 2002.

Family of Guy Breshears and Oryene Florence Breshears:

V6 3976. 13 1. **Anna Gwendola Breshears**, b. 22 Jan 1934, Avery, Benton Co, MO, d. 19 Nov 1996,

Victorville, CA; m. ***Roger Wayne Halstead***,

V63977. 141. Terri Lynn Halstead; m. Stephen Ferguson. Ch: Stevie Ferguson

V63978. 142. William Wayne Halstead; m. Donna ______. Ch: Tempest Halstead

V63979. 143. Tami Renee Halstead,

V63980. 132. **Robert Guy "Bobby Guy" Breshears**, b. 6 July 1936, Waterford, Stanislaus Co, CA; m. on 17 May 1959 in San Bruno, CA, ***Alyce Park***, b. 2 Oct 1935, Dinuba, CA, d/o Ho Park and Kum Kim. Alyce was an airline stewardess when she met Bobby Guy. The lived in San Francisco the first year of marriage, then moved to Fresno, CA, where Bobby Guy attended Fresno State College and got his teaching credential. Alyce has completed two years of Junior College, and plans to return to college. Four ch:

V63981. 141. **Mychael Young Breshears**,

V63982. 142. **Jason Todd Breshears**, ***Julie Robbins***,

V63983. 151. **Jason Breshears**,

V63984. 152. **Ashley Lynn Breshears**,

V63985. 143. **Nycole Suzann Breshears**, m. ***Darl Larsen***.

V63986. 151. Kier Norbet Larsen,

V63987. 152. Emrys Mark Larsen,

V63988. 153. Brynmor Larsen,

V63989. 154. Eamonn Robert Larsen,

V63990. 155. Dathyl M. Alyce Larsen,

V63991. 156. Ransom Larsen,

V63992. 157. Cuchulainn Larsen,

V63993. 144. **Nathan George Breshears**,

V63994. 133. Anita Joy White, b. 1937; m. Chester E. Consoli, b. 1931

V63995. 141. Janet Gay Consoli,

V63996. 142. Karen Lea Consoli,

V63997. 143. Jackie Ann Consoli,

V63998. 144. Eddie Guy Consoli,

V63999. 145. Amy Lynn Consoli,

Dona Lea Breshears and "Ted" Brooks

Figure 72: Dona Lea Breshears in 1926. Photos from Bill Brooks

v6 3959. 12 1. **Dona Lea Breshears**, (d/o Levi Ransom Breshears and Hettie Noble Button), b. 4 Dec 1904, Benton Co, MO, d. 9 Aug 1984, Modesto, CA; m.1. 26 June 1931, in Reno, Nevada, ***Thomas Charles "Ted" Brooks***, b. 30 Jan 1890, Dycusburg, KY, d. 26 Feb 1967, Modesto, CA, s/o William Brooks and Delina Gratton; m.2. 6 Aug 1971, ***Merle Hobart Livingston***, b. 20 Oct 1896, d. 26 May 1979, Modesto, CA.

Family stories from son, Bill Brooks:

As the oldest child, Dona got the duty of helping take care of the younger children and helping her mother with the household chores. She loved to attend school. On numerous occasions, she was awarded a certificate for correctly spelling one hundred lessons. In her teens, she went to work in the store in Harper, MO, owned by her uncle, George Breshears. She was paid four dollars per week, and managed to save up some money. She loaned her sister, Lola Mae, and her husband, "Bus" Breshears, enough money to move to California.

Before moving to California, Dona Lea was engaged to Claude Mulkey, the brother of Florence Mulkey Breshears, the wife of George Breshears. Several years later, she marred Ted Brooks in Reno, NV.

Ted was orphaned early in Kentucky. He lived with older sisters, but was out on his own at the age of 12-14. He was once bitten on the foot by a copperhead snake, when he was a boy. The treatment was to split a live chicken open and stick the foot inside, to draw out the poisonous venom.

He was married to Beulah McAffee in Arkansas c1914. They had a son, Paul Elmer Brooks, b. 20 April 1915. Paul was last heard of living in Oregon. That first marriage ended in divorce.

When he got to California, he went to barber school in San

Francisco. He then migrated to the central valley of California and was a barber in Oakdale, Waterford, and Riverbank, all in Stanislaus County. He also loved hunting, fishing, and baseball.

He was a trader, and enjoyed buying and selling things. He traded automobiles almost yearly, and he bought and sold numerous homes in Waterford, Hickman, and Riverbank, CA. He once bought a house in Riverbank, but sold it as he was preparing to move in. In Waterford, he bought, lived in, and sold five houses within two blocks on the same street.

Ted had diabetes most of his adult life. Eventually poor circulation caused him to have both legs amputated. He used a wheelchair the last ten years or so of his life. He died 26 Feb 1967 in Modesto City Hospital, and was buried at Lakewood Memorial Park, Hughson, Stanislaus Co, CA. He was 76 years old.

After Ted died, Dona married Merle Livingston, a peach and walnut farmer of Stanislaus County. His father and mother lived on Codoni Ave in Empire, CA, on a 40-acre peach ranch. Merle and his father were partners in the operation. After the death of his parents, Merle bought the remaining part of the ranch from his siblings and continued farming this land until his full retirement in 1977.

Dona loved to cook, especially apple pies, fried chicken, green beans, mashed potatoes and gravy. "Yum," says Bill Brooks. She was a charter member of the Waterford Womens Club, a member of the Community Baptist Church in Waterford, and a member of the Grange. She loved yard work, having a good garden and tending to beautiful flowers and trees. Her greatest pride was her children and grandchildren.

Family of Dona Lea Breshears and Thomas Charles "Ted" Brooks:

V6 4000. 13 1. Jack Lee Brooks, b. 22 Jan 1932, Oakdale, Stanislaus Co, CA; m. 16 Aug 1953, in Madera, Madera Co, CA, Mary Lou Nell Weston, b. 26 Feb 1931, in Erick, OK, s/o Hobert Weston and Mahale Hess. Jack is an ordained Methodist Minister. He, Mary Lou, and their two children spent several years in Okinawa and Saipan, where Jack was the chief radio engineer for the

(Chrjistian) Far East Broadcasting Co. Upon returned to the U.S., Jack was the station manager of FEBco radio in San Mateo, CA. Jack and Mary Lou retired to the Nevada City/ Grass Valley area of CA, to be near their grandchildren and to raise llamas. Jack's favorite hobby is still radio and electronics; he can be completely absorbed in it for hours.

V6 4001. 14 1. Stephen Lee Brooks,

V6 4002. 14 2. John Michael Brooks, b. 23 Oct 1957, Hanford, Kings Co, CA; m. 24 June 1978, Patricia Ann Dooley, d/o Robert Dooley and Alleen Lemos.

V6 4003. 15 1. Brittany Michele Brooks,

V6 4004. 15 2. Brett Michael Brooks,

V6 4005. 13 2. Guy Allen Brooks, b. 21 Jan 1934, Hughson, Stanislaus Co, CA; m. 31 March 1957, in Waterford, Stanislaus Co, CA, Carmen Contreras Guerrero, b. 4 Aug 1931, in Zamaro, Mexico, d/o Miguel Guerrero and Consuelo Contreras. After a hitch in the U.S. Navy during the Korean War, Guy started college part-time. He went to work at the Stanislaus County Sheriff's office and rose to the rank of Captain. All the time, he was continuing in college: night classes at Stanislaus State College, then Hastings Law School in Stockton. After getting his law degree, he resigned from the sheriff's department and set up a private law practice in Modesto, which has been and is thriving.

V6 4006. 14 1. Patrick Thomas Brooks; m. Laurie Collins. Patrick attended Loyola Law school in southern California, then worked several years for the State Attorney General's office in Sacramento. He is now deputy City Attorney for Santa Monica, CA. Laurie grew up in the San Fernando Valley in southern California. She also has a law degree and has worked for the State of California, real estate management division.

[V6]4007. [14]2. Infant Brooks

[V6]4008. [13]3. William Charles "Bill" Brooks, Sr, b. 26 Feb 1937, Waterford, Stanislaus Co, CA (This is the Bill Brooks who sent so many photos and additional data); m. 18 Oct 1959, in Carson City, NV, Lola Fay Stroud, b. 24 June 1940, in Modesto, CA, d/o Charlie Stroud and Mary Stiles. Bill did a stint in the U.S. Navy during the Korean War, then worked for Quality Markets in Waterford, CA. He was route salesman for various bakeries, and retired from Rainbo Bakery. In 1994, he founded a small business: Brooks Construction Clean-up.

[V6]4009. [14]1. William Charles Brooks, Jr, b. 18 July 1960, Modesto, Stanislaus Co, CA. Bill Jr earned a B.A. and M.A. from Stanislaus State University, then worked for some year for K-Mart. He moved back to Modesto and Folsom to work for Blue Shield, the health care provider.

[V6]4010. [14]2. Pamela Gail Brooks, b. 9 July 1963, Modesto, Stanislaus Co, CA; m.1. 28 May 1982, in Turlock, Stanislaus Co, CA, Johnathan Dale Payne, b. 24 Nov 1962, in Indiana, s/o George Payne and Pauline ______; m.2 11 April 1992, in Lake Tahoe, Nevada, Raymond Nicholas Franco, b. 18 Jan 1952, Jersey City, New Jersey, s/o Phillip Victor Franco and Delia Georgiana Degon. Ray's parents divorced when he was young and he grew up in Los Angeles with his mother. He was first a cattle buyer, but after his first marriage to Jennie Brooks (no relation), he went into building houses, working his way up from foundations to framing to finishing. He started one house at a time, but has founded the Ray Franco Construction Co and built over 5,000 houses.

[V6]4011. [15]1. Bradley Phillip Payne,

[V6]4012. [15]2. Casey Raymond Franco,

[V6]4013. [15]3. Tiffany Brooke Franco,

Jacob "Jake" Breshears and Ruby Virginia Dietz

v6**3924.** 11 9. **Jacob "Jake" Breshears**, (s/o Henry Belsis Breshears and Ida Elsie Button), b. 27 July 1913, Bentonville, Benton Co, MO, d. 5 Dec 1989, Tualitin, Oregon; m. 28 July 1934, in Weaubleau, MO, ***Ruby Virginia Dietz***, b. 9 June 1913, Quincy, MO, d. 2004, d/o Robert Dietz and Effie Breshears.

Family of Jacob "Jake" Breshears and Ruby Virginia Dietz:

V64014. 12 1. **Kenneth Dale Breshears**, b. 27 Dec 1935, Quincy, MO; m. ***Barbra Ann Renno.***

V64015. 13 1. **Debra Lee Breshears**, m. ***Douglas John Hays.***

V64016. 14 1. **Adam Nicholas Breshears**,

V64017. 14 2. Sarah Marie Hays,

V64018. 13 2. **Ronald Dale Breshears**, m. ***Kathy Beaula.***

V64019. 14 1. Karsten Hans Bjelland, (step-child)

V64020. 14 2. Keith Lars Bjelland, (step-child)

V64021. 14 3. Katie Ann Bjelland, (step-child)

V64022. 14 4. **Rachel Lee Breshears**,

V64023. 12 2. **Allen Dean Breshears**, b. 4 Oct 1938, Quincy, MO; m.1. ***Shirley Ann Moon*** (3 ch), b. 1940, d. 1989; m.2. ***Eva Marie Harvey*** (2 ch), b. 1948,

V64024. 13 1. **Cheri Rae Breshears**, m.1. ***John William Schilling***; m.2. ***Dave Main.*** Ch: Jolene Marie Schilling; James Dean Main

V64025. 13 2. **Robert Allan Breshears**,

V64026. 13 3. **Daniel Lowell Breshears**, m.1. ***Debbie*** ______, (2 ch); m.2. ***Lisa Annette Bergman*** (1 ch)

V64027. 14 1. **Kelly Rae Breshears**, ch: Jamesa Renee Allan,

V64028. 14 2. **Robert Jake Breshears**,

V64029. 14 3. Dion Jermie Bergman,

V64030. 13 4. **Eva Lorraine (Hughes) Breshears**, (step-child); m.1. Rodney Borger; m.2. Michael Wallace Gruis. Ch: Robert Scott Borger; Charlotte Lorene Gruis; and Jacob Darrel Gruis

[V6]4031. [13]5. **Julia (Castro) Breshears** (adopted); met Richie Wilhem,

[V6]4032. [14]1. **Christopher Allan Breshears,**

[V6]4033. [12]3. **Betty Lou Breshears**, b. 24 Oct 1940, Bentonville, Benton Co, MO; m. ***William Leonard Martin***.

[V6]4034. [13]1. Wesley Leonard Martin; m. Madelyn Anna Cadena. Ch: Jessica Anna; and Jamie Lou Martin

[V6]4035. [13]2. Wayne Lee Martin; m. Debbie Blanton. Ch: Jacob Lee Martin

[V6]4036. [13]3. Tana Lynn Martin; m. Cosme Lopez. Ch: Martin Glen; and Keely Lynn Lopez

[V6]4037. [12]4. **Belvard Lee Breshears**, b. 13 Jan 1943, Warsaw, MO; m.1. ***Sherrie Mohr*** (2 ch); m.2. ***Rita Sholes***.

[V6]4038. [13]1. **Jeffery Allan Breshears,**

[V6]4039. [13]2. **Michael Lee Breshears,**

[V6]4040. [12]5. **Gary Keith Breshears**, b. 26 May 1945, Independence, MO; m. ***Eddie Marie Lyon***, b. 1949.

[V6]4041. [13]1. **Dion Jean Breshears**, m. ______ ***Segura***; m.2. ***Robert Boyd***. Ch: Alic McClain Segura; Zachery Keith Boyd

[V6]4042. [13]2. **Dary Lee Breshears**, m. ***Sandy Lynn Easton***.

[V6]4043. [14]1. **Ashleigh Kaye Breshears,**

[V6]4044. [13]3. **Cary Virginia Breshears**, m. ***John Bean***.

[V6]4045. [12]6. **Terry Gail Breshears**, b. 12 Sept 1947, Weaubleau, Hickory Co, MO; m. ***Judith June Norton***, b. 1949.

[V6]4046. [13]1. **Robert Jake Breshears**, m.1. ***Belinda*** _____; m.2. ***Kimberly Bartlett*** (3 ch)

[V6]4047. [14]1. **Jessica Dawn Breshears,**

[V6]4048. [14]2. **Elise Lindsey Breshears,**

[V6]4049. [14]3. **Karissa Mae Breshears,**

[V6]4050. [13]2. **Theresa Gail Breshears**, m. ***Jeffery Scott Will***. Ch: Mitchell Scott; and Caleb Benjamin Will

[V6]4051. [13]3. **Douglas Kieth Breshears,**

[V6]4052. [12]7. **Dewey Kent Breshears**, b. 10 Oct 1948, Wheatland, Hickory Co, MO; m. ***Norene Lillian***

Misfelt.

V6 4053. [13]1. **Brian Keith Breshears**, m. ***Michelle Foltz.***

V6 4054. [14]1. **Brianna Irene Breshears**,

V6 4055. [14]2. **Brock Jacob Breshears**,

V6 4056. [13]2. **Shawn Dale Breshears**,

V6 4057. [12]8. **John Robert Breshears**, b. 30 Aug 1951, Bend, Deschutes Co, Oregon; m.1 ***Brenda*** _____ (1 ch); m.2. ***Sheree Diane Keil***, (3 ch).

V6 4058. [13]1. Dakota Lee Self (step-child)

V6 4059. [13]2. **Michelle Sheree Breshears**,

V6 4060. [13]3. **Michael John Breshears**,

V6 4061. [13]4. **Christie Michelle Breshears**,

V6 4062. [12]9. **Judith Sue Breshears**, b. 22 July 1953, Redmond, Deschutes Co, OR; m. ***Hugh Edwes Williams, Jr.***

V6 4063. [13]1. Jennifer Alice Williams; m. David Kaulahea Ika Ali'i Oka Moku Baldwin. Ch: Eluah Kaulahea Ika Ali'i Oka Moku Baldwin

V6 4064. [13]2. Mandy Lou Williams; m. Christopher Scott Stahl. Ch: Matthew Scott; Cade William; and Cody Michael Stahl

V6 4065. [13]3. Hugh Edwes Williams, III.

V6 4066. [12]10. **Helen Jean Breshears**, b. 17 June 1955, Redmond, Deschutes Co, OR; m. ***Kelly Richard Cuddeford.*** Ch: Danita Marie Cuddeford (m. Kevin Lee Wampole: ch: Katlin Lee; and Tristan Jacob Wampole); Kelli Jean Cuddeford; and Sara Louise Cuddeford

V6 4067. [12]11. **Kary Alleen Breshears**, b. 13 Nov 1957, Redmond, Deschutes Co, OR; m. ***Raymond Louis Doubrava.*** Ch: Isaac Louis; Derke Alan; and Alicia Rae Doubrava

John Francis "Little Frank" Breshears and Sarah H. Hodges

v6 3436. [10]6. **John Francis "Little Frank" Breshears**, (s/o Madison Golman "Matt" Breshears and Sarah Elizabeth Brown), b. 14 March 1862, Benton Co, MO, d. 10 Dec 1945; m. ***Sarah M. Hodges***, b. 31 May 1864, MO, d. 30 May 1933

Family of John Francis "Little Frank" Breshears and Sarah H. Hodges:

V64068. 11 1. **Harriet Breshears**, b. 13 July 1885, MO, d. 1 June 1966; m. ***George F. Miller***, b. 5 Feb 1884, MO, d. 21 May 1959.

V64069. 12 1. Dolan Lester Miller, b. 2 June 1906; m. Ruth Flater. Ch: Jacquiline Miller

V64070. 12 2. Noble North Miller, b. 11 Oct 1909, d. 10 Feb 1952

V64071. 12 3. Nolan Kenneth Miller, b. 13 Oct 1911; m. Mary ______. Ch: Patty Miller

V64072. 11 2. **Frank Asro Breshears**, b. 25 Jan 1888, MO, d. 20 March 1964; m. 3 Nov 1909, ***Birtie Elizabeth Campbell***, b. 16 April 1888, MO, d. 2 March 1968, d/o James A. Campbell, Elder of the Fristoe Church of the Brethren. Asro was an Elder of Spring Branch Church of the Brethren at Avery, MO; he wrote the 50th Anniversary history of the church.

V64073. 12 1. **Norris Asro Breshears**, b. 3 Aug 1910, d. 24 July 1964; m. ***Ina Faye Largent***.

V64074. 13 1. **Robert Ray Breshears**,

V64075. 12 2. **Norman Breshears**, b. 23 Jan 1913, d. 28 Jan 1913, age 5 days

V64076. 12 3. **Lyle Denton Breshears**, b. 10 Nov 1914, d. 5 April 1959 (killed in an auto accident); m. 7 May 1938, ***Cleo Beatrice Wright***, b. 7 Nov 1913, d. 5 April 1959 (auto accident)

V64077. 12 4. **Galen Kirtz Breshears**, b. 7 Sept 1919; m. ***Ruth Roselle Stouffer***.

V64078. 13 1. **Gerry Everett Breshears**; m. ***Sherry Ann Veasey***.

V64079. 14 1. **Donn Glen Breshears**,

V64080. 13 2. **Ann Elizabeth Breshears**, m. ***Jack Sawyer***

V64081. 12 5. **Truman Calvin Breshears**, b. 14 Sept 1920; m. ***Ethel Bernice Fereday***.

V64082. 13 1. **Steven Truman Breshears**, m. ***Carol Louise Canaday***.

V64083. 14 1. **Lisa Annette Breshears**,

[V6]4084. [12]6. **Mary Verbalea Breshears**, b. 25 Sept 1925; m. 14 July 1944, ***Richard Frank Poulicek***, b. 1 April 1922

[V6]4085. [12]7. **Morell Morris Breshears**, b. 28 Oct 1926, d. 28 Nov 1932, (diphtheria)

34. SUSANNA "SUKEY" BRESHEARS and Shandy Jordan/ Jesse Miller

[v6]3224. [9]4. **Susanna "Sukey" Breshears**, (d/o Henry Breshears Jr and Atsa "Atsey" Etheridge), b. 6 Feb 1829, Lawrenceburg, Lawrence Co, TN, d. 15 April 1856-57, Benton Co, MO; m.1. ***Shandy Jordan***, b. c?1829, d. c?1855; m.2. ***Jesse Hardin (or David) Miller***, b. c1829, MO. After Susanna's early death, the family took over her children: Henry W. Miller was in the household of Henry Thomas Breshears in 1860; Hardin and Jackson Miller were with "Grandma" Atsey.

<u>Family of Susanna "Sukey" Breshears and Shandy Jordan:</u>

[V6]4091. [10]1. Inez Jordan, b. c?1851

[V6]4092. [10]2. Glen Jordan, b. c?1853

[V6]4093. [10]3. Floyd Jordan, b. c?1855

<u>Family of Susanna "Sukey" Breshears and Jesse Miller:</u>

[V6]4094. [10]4. William Matthew Miller, b. May 1850; m. Sarah Dickerson, b. c?1855

[V6]4095. [11]1. David Miller,

[V6]4096. [11]2. George M. Miller, b. 5 Feb 1884, MO; m. **Harriet Breshears**, (d/o John Francis "Little Frank" Breshears and Sarah M. Hodges), b. 13 July 1885, MO

[V6]4097. [11]3. Jesse H. Miller, b. c?1886

[V6]4098. [11]4. Viola Miller, b. c?1888

[V6]4099. [10]5. Henry W. Miller, b. 6 March 1852, Avery, MO, d. 26 Dec 1942, Cross Timbers, MO; m. 22 April 1870, Martha Ellen Ruth, b. 18 July 1851, Benton

Co, MO, d. 12 March 1940, Avery, MO, d/o Frank Ruth

V^{6}4100. ^{11}1. James William Miller; m. Nancy Ellen "Ellie" Ihrig, (d/o Joel Ihrig and Atsey Adeline Breshears), b. 1873. See his listing.

V^{6}4101. ^{11}2. Tom Miller, b. 26 June 1873, d. 28 Jan 1959; m. Alice Southard, b. 8 July 1874, d. 26 March 1949. Ch: Carrie (m. Reed Johnston); Claude (m. Vera ______); Frank; and Gettie Miller.

V^{6}4102. ^{11}3. Eliza Jane "Lizzie" Miller, b. 27 Sept 1879, Hickory Co, MO, d. there, 8 Nov 1958; m. **William Robert Breshears**, (s/o Hiram Breshears and Mary Dickerson). See his listing.

V^{6}4103. ^{11}4. Joe E. Miller; m. Emma J. Button, b. 10 Oct 1878, Benton Co, MO

V^{6}4104. ^{11}5. Charles W. Miller, m. Cara Harrlano

V^{6}4105. ^{11}6. Burris Emery Miller; m. **Ora A. Breshears**, (d/o William Thomas Breshears and Della Ruth). See her listing for their children.

V^{6}4106. ^{11}7. Robert Harrison Miller, b. 1889, d. 1966; m. 16 March 1910, Mona F. Button, b. 11 July 1891, Benton Co, MO, d. 26 Feb 1954, Avery, Benton Co, MO

V^{6}4107. ^{11}8. Lillie Pearl Miller, b. 27 Sept 1891, Avery, MO, d. 1 Nov 1973, Sedalia, Pettis Co, MO; m. **Delmar Roy Breshears**, (s/o William Breshears and Martha Holley), See his listing.

V^{6}4108. ^{11}9. Sam Miller, d. as young man

V^{6}4109. ^{10}6. Hardin Miller, b. 10 April 1856, d. 6 Dec 1933; m. Jude (?Judy) ______,

V^{6}4110. ^{11}1. Lizzie Miller; m. Ed Sibert,

V^{6}4111. ^{10}7. Jackson Miller, b. c1857, TX

35. WILLIAM MARION BRESHEARS and Mary Jane Pippin

v6 3226. [9]6. **William Marion Breshears**, (s/o Henry Breshears Jr and Atsa "Atsey" Etheridge), b. 5 Oct 1833, Lawrence Co, TN, d. 30 Nov 1861, of camp dysentery near Camp Cole, MO; m. 9 Dec 1854, ***Mary Jane Pippin***, (a cousin, d/o Eleanor Breshears and Richard Pippin), b. c1833, TN, d. Sept 1861, St. Clair Co, MO. (The 1850 Hickory Co, MO Census listed a Richard Pippin living down the road from Henry and Atsy. Richard had a 17 year old daughter named Mary). Data from Michelle Breon:

Information given mostly in affidavits by several individuals, including four brothers, in 1897, years after the fact: William M. Breshears enlisted on or about July 5, 1861 for the E. Osage Co. Battalion, Missouri National Guards (home guards) under a Col. Taylor. His four brother enlisted at the same time and into the same unit. He served until sometime in November or December 1861 when he went on a scouting mission with Col. Taylor and returned to catch a cold/flu. He was moved to a dutchman's house in Florence and was attended by the local physician. He reportedly died of pneumonia or back troubles sometime in December, 1861, only days before the unit was disbanded and sent home, around Christmas 1861. No headstone marks his grave.

The Civil War Pension claim by the children contains a lot of information regarding the circumstances of his short enlistment, subsequent death, his wife's death, and their children. The pension request was rejected because the information did not prove beyond any doubt of the War Department that William Breshears actually served in the war.

There was some confusion in the records between William M. and Madison Breshears. In an affidavit signed by Madison (mark only), he attempted to explain the confusion. He stated that William was indeed his brother, about 5' 9" tall, 150 lbs., with light hair, and blue eyes. He was born in Lawrence Co,

Tennessee. Madison was 6', blue eyes, light hair, and a farmer before the war. None of the brothers that signed affidavits could state by what name they were called in the muster roll, although one affidavit signed by a man who had been the clerk for the unit stated that William M. Breshears was listed in the rolls as Wm. M. Basherg.

On 23 Nov 1897, four of the five brothers were living, only William being dead. All those that could, testified in the affidavits that William had been married to a Mary Jane Pippin, though few could spell the name correctly, on December 9, 1854. In fact, the recorder for the county marriages listed her as Mary Jane Tipton. A cousin of hers, William N. Jordan, who had also married William's sister (name not mentioned; it was Sarah Malissa) spelled her name as Pippies. Some of the confusion could be attributed to illegible handwriting.

Mary had 4 children, three of whom lived. The fourth was born possibly 2 months before her death and died at most 1 month after her. The sex of the unnamed child was not mentioned. She had been having problems before the delivery and had returned to live with Atsy Breshears, where the child was born. They were making sorghum or molasses at the time of her death, which was attended by William, presumably on leave from his unit.

The birth records of the children were listed in the family Bible, though the years of the entries were written in pencil. The Bible was exhibited on October 13, 1896 to an attorney by Andrew Jackson Breshears, one of the children.

<u>Family of William Marion Breshears and Mary Jane Pippin:</u>

V6 4112. 10 1. **Rachel Jane Breshears**, b. 18 Oct 1855, Mt. Brier (or Mt. View), MO, d. 1923, Benton Co, MO; m. ***John W. Murray***, b. 1840, d. 1928, s/o Thomas and Mary Murray. Both Rachel and John Murray bur Harper Cem, Benton Co, MO.

V6 4113. 11 1. Green Murray; m. Elizabeth Gover,

V6 4114. 11 2. John Murray,

V6 4115. 11 3. ______ Murray,

V6 4116. 10 2. **Sarah Caroline "Sally" Breshears**, b. 29 March 1857, Avery, MO, d. 1936; m. ***William G. Harper***, b. 1856, d. 1926, both bur Harper Cem, Benton

Co, MO.

V64117. [11]1. Dolly Harper, m. Asa Gover

V64118. [10]3. **Andrew Jackson "Andy" Breshears**, b. 8 Aug 1859, Denton Co, TX, d. 1940; m. ***Ida May Ausburn***,

V64119. [11]1. **Willie Breshears**, m. ***Ollie Ketchum***,

V64120. [12]1. **Keith Breshears**,

V64121. [12]2. **Dean Breshears**,

V64122. [11]2. **Marvin Breshears**, (twin), d. 1918

V64123. [11]3. **Harvey Breshears**, (twin), died young.

V64124. [11]4. **Clyde Breshears**,

V64125. [11]5. **Icel Breshears**, m.1. ______ ***Butts***; m.2. ***Thomas Edwin Button***, b. 22 Jan 1897, Benton Co, MO, d. 1937, St Louis , MO, s/o John Button and Margaret Cox

V64126. [12]1. Tommy Button, ?died young; name re-used.

V64127. [12]2. Billie Button,

V64128. [12]3. Jackie Button,

V64129. [12]4. Louise Button, m. Dr. ______ Bailey

V64130. [12]5. Kenneth Allen Button, b. 22 Dec 1921

V64131. [12]6. Tommy Button,

V64132. [11]6. **Marion Breshears**, m. ***Mary E. Gaston***, b. 1888, Benton Co, MO, d. 1958, Hickory Co, MO, bur Spring Branch Cem, Avery, Hickory Co, MO.

V64133. [11]7. **Lucy Breshears**, m. ***John Peter Ihrig***, b. 8 Oct 1871, d. 3 Oct 1906, s/o George Nimrod Ihrig and ***Mary Jane Breshears***, of the Madison Golman Breshears line. See John Peter Ihrig's listing for their children.

V64134. [11]8. **Dolly Breshears**, m.1. ***Floyd Jordan***, b. 19 Feb 1898, d. 1967; m.2. ***Omer Cox***,

V64135. [10]4. child, b. July 1861, d. Oct 1861, St. Clair Co, MO

36. SARAH MALISSA BRESHEARS and William Nute Jordan

V6 3227. 9 7. **Sarah Malissa Breshears**, (d/o Henry Breshears Jr and Atsa "Atsey" Etheridge), b. 9 March 1835, Lawrenceburg, Lawrence Co, TN, d. 14 Jan 1910, Benton Co, MO; m. 17 Jan 1856, ***William Newton "Nute" Jordan***, b. 6 Dec 1833, d. 6 April 1909, both bur Dooley Bend Cem.

Family of Sarah Malissa Breshears and William Nute Jordan:

V6 4181. 10 1. Sarah Elizabeth Jordan, b. 9 Feb 1857, MO, d. 6 Jan 1892; m. Price Hollensworth (or Hollingsworth), b. 6 Dec 1834, d. 18 April 1933, both bur Dooley Bend Cem.

V6 4182. 11 1. Archie Hollensworth, b. 27 Jan 1882, d. 31 Oct 1946; m. Kate Southard, b. 15 Oct 1873, d. 17 July 1959

V6 4183. 11 2. Willie Hollensworth, b. 31 Oct 1883, d. 22 June 1936; m. Jewell Kimball, b. 23 July 1892, d. 13 Dec 1922. Ch: Theora; and Dan Hollingsworth

V6 4184. 11 3. Sigle Hollensworth, b. 4 Jan 1886; m. Doris Bastion. Ch: Midra; and Sigle Chester Hollingsworth

V6 4185. 11 4. Ora Hollensworth, b. 2 May 1888, d. 19 Sept 1974; m.1. Creth Amos, b. c1890, d. 1935, bur Antioch Cem, Pittsburg, MO; m.2. Dorothy ______,

V6 4186. 11 5. LaGettie Hollensworth, b. 19 Feb 1890, d. 2 May 1945; m. Nicholas Chasteen "Chet" Bigler, b. 1899, d. 1952. Ch: Jessy Faye; Vera Price "Helen"; Ora Carlos; Waverley Bee; J.C.; John Cecil; Oral Dee; Burnal Lee; James Eldon; and Harold Dean Bigler

V6 4187. 10 2. John Martin Jordan, b. 9 Dec 1858, d. 3 Feb 1859

V6 4188. 10 3. James Henry Jordan, b. 30 Sept 1860, d. 14 Dec

1930; m. **Ida Jane Breshears**, (d/o William Thomas "Wild Bill" Breshears and Rachel Ihrig), b. 30 Sept 1870, Pruett Place, Benton Co, MO, d. 30 Oct 1962, Wilson Creek, OK.

V64189. 111. Marshall O. Jordan, b. 11 Sept 1891, MO, d. 15 June 1921; m. Oda Godat, b. 24 Dec 1898, MO, d. 19 April 1921, s/o Jim Godat. Ch: Marshall O. Jordan, Jr, b. 18 April 1918;

V64190. 112. Myrtle Jordan, b. 26 Nov 1893, OK, d. 4 April 1968; m. George Phillip Simmons, b. 1887, d. 1947. Ch: James Phillip Delane; William Raymond; and Edna Simmons

V64191. 113. Mamie Jordan, b. 20 May 1899, d. 31 Jan 1972; m. Haskell Brown. Ch: Doria Brown (m. Robert Taylor)

V64192. 114. Raymond Newton Jordan, b. 26 Sept 1902, d. 27 Dec 1936

V64193. 104. William Eli Jordan, b. 9 Sept 1865, d. 29 Aug 1923; m.1. Theodosia Swan, b. c1865 (9 ch); m.2. Martha Bird, b. c?1865 (6 ch)

V64194. 111. Effie Jordan, b. c?1891

V64195. 112. Lizzy Jordan, b. c?1893

V64196. 113. Ethel Jordan, b. c?1895

V64197. 1110. Noah Jordan, b. c?1891

V64198. 1111. Sydney Jordan, b. c?1893

V64199. 1112. Maggie Jordan, b. c?1895

V64200. 105. Atsy Adaline Jordan, b. 7 Oct 1867, d. 3 May 1894; m. Frank Cooper, b. c?1867

V64201. 111. Vanola Cooper, b. c?1889

V64202. 112. Andy Cooper, b. c?1891

V64203. 106. Thomas Jane Jordan, b. 11 May 1870, d. 2 Dec 1943; m. Mary Ann "Molly" Mashburn, b. 4 Nov 1872

V64204. 111. Sally Jordan, b. 29 Nov 1890; m. Arbie Pierson, b. 12 Jan 1884

V64205. 112. Earl Jordan, b. 8 Oct 1893

V64206. 113. _____ Jordan; m. John Lewis Taylor, b. 1896

V64207. 107. Rosa Arvilla Jordan, b. 17 Feb 1872; m. James A. _____, b. c?1835

Figure 73: The Henry Thomas Breshears/ Sabrina Murray Family. Photo from Bill Brooks

37. HENRY THOMAS BRESHEARS and Sabrina J. Murray

[v6]3228. [9]8. **Henry Thomas Breshears**, (s/o Henry Breshears Jr and Atsa "Atsey" Etheridge), b. 22 Nov 1838, Louisburg, Dallas Co, MO, d. 12 May 1921, at Avery, Benton Co, MO; m. 14 Oct 1858, at Avery, Benton Co, MO, ***Sabrina Jane Murray***, b. 4 Feb 1842, Avery, Benton Co, MO, d. 3 Aug 1918, Avery, MO, d/o John Murray. Both Henry Thomas and Sabrina bur Brethren Spring Branch Cem.

Henry Thomas was the first of the children of Henry Breshears Jr to be born in Missouri. He donated part of his land for the Spring Branch Cemetery, and he and many of his descendants are buried there.

Henry served in Co. C, Osage County Home Guards, from June 1861 to December, and in Co. I, 8th Regt Cavalry,

Missouri State Militia, from 13 March 1862, until he was discharged for disability on 19 Nov 1963. He received a gunshot wound in the spine near Newtonia, MO, on 11 Feb 1863, having lost his horse and equipment the day before. He was described as 5 feet, 10 inches tall, fair complected, with blue eyes and light hair. A pension affidavit, signed 4 May 1898, gives the six living children, Lucinda having died. (military records in national archives)

John Henry Breshears-Effie Breshears Dietz
Henry Thomas & Sabrina Breshears
Clifford Dietz

Figure 74: A four-generations picture. Thanks to Bill Brooks for photo

Family of Henry Thomas Breshears and Sabrina Jane Murray:

[V6]4208. [10]1. **Lucinda Breshears**, b. 1 Nov 1859, Denton Co, TX, d. 1882, Avery, MO, bur Spring Branch Cem, Avery, MO; m. ***John William Lopp***, b. c1859, MO

[V6]4209. [11]1. Delmar Lopp, b. c?1874; m. Cynthia Elizabeth Ihrig, b. 4 March 1874, MO, d. 3 Oct 1906, (d/o George Ihrig and Mary Breshears)

[V6]4210. [11]2. Sabrina E. Lopp, b. 1881, d. 1882, bur Spring Branch Cem

[V6]4211. [10]2. ***John Henry Breshears**, b. 19 May 1861, Avery, Hickory Co, MO, d. 16 Jan 1941, Quency, Hickory Co, MO; m. 28 Nov 1880, ***Virginia Delilah Salisbury***,

[V6]4212. [10]3. ***William Jasper "Jas" Breshears**, b. 6 Nov 1864, Benton Co, MO; m. 16 Sept 1888, in Benton Co, MO, ***Martha Ann "Mattie" Holley***,

[V6]4213. [10]4. ***James Thomas Breshears**, b. 11 Sept 1866, d. 25 March 1936; m. 25 March 1886, ***Malinda Catherine Southard***,

[V6]4214. [10]5. ***Emma Leanna Breshears**, b. 19 Nov 1869 (or 1868), Benton Co, MO, d. 19 May 1940; m. 12

Figure 75: The Henry Thomas Breshears home.
It is probably impossible for anyone today to name all the people, but note that Henry and Sabrina are seated on a couch near the middle of the picture. Photo: Bill Brooks

June 1884, in Benton Co, MO, ***George Washington Wright***,

V64215. 106. **Perry W. Breshears**, b. 21 Dec 1871; m. ***Opal Florence "Flora" Henderson***, b. c?1871

V64216. 111. **Helen Breshears**, b. c1892; m. ***Bill Hintz***, b. c?1892

V64217. 112. **Leonard Thomas Breshears**, b. c?1894; m. ***Edna Pitts***,

V64218. 121. **Michael Thomas Breshears**, b. 6 March 1942; m. ***Olivia Garcia***,

V64219. 122. **Donna Rae Breshears**, (twin) b. 2 May 1943; m. ***Jimmie Edwards***. Ch: J.D. Edwards

V64220. 123. **Diana May Breshears**, (twin) b. 2 May 1943; m.1. ***Elvin Yoast***; m.2. ***Ronnie Smith***. Ch: Gwendolyn and Jason Yoast

V64221. 124. **Lillian Belle Breshears**, b. 15 Feb 1945;

m. ***Lonnie Shelton***. Ch: Marie and Martha Shelton

V6 4222. [12]5. Snoda Beth Breshears, b. 17 Dec 1948; m.1. ***Frank Yoast***; m.2. ***Richard Boswell***. Ch: Paula and Michelle Yoast

V6 4223. [12]6. **Gregory Breshears**, b. 4 May 1961; m. ***Glenda*** ______.

V6 4224. [13]1. **Jeremy Breshears**,

V6 4225. [13]2. **Timothy Breshears**,

V6 4226. [12]7. **Jeffrey Breshears**, b. 22 March 1963; m. ***Mary*** ______.

V6 4227. [13]1. **Jennifer Breshears**,

V6 4228. [13]2. **Christopher Breshears**,

V6 4229. [10]7. **Lillie Belle Breshears**, b. 30 May 1883, d. 30 Oct 1959; m.1. ***Ira Butterbaugh***; m.2. ***Herbert Johnson***,

V6 4230. [11]1. Lloyd Johnson, died in a motorcycle accident when young

V6 4231. [11]2. Archie Johnson, married Dorothy Williamson, Ch: Peggy; Patty; and Harold Johnson

Figure 76: The Herbert Johnson family in Clayton, OK. Photo from Sandra Kay Beagles

V6 4232. 113. Howard Johnson, m. Audra ______, ch: ______,

V6 4233. 114. Gilbert Johnson, m. Ruth ______, ch: Gilbert, Jr; and Charles Johnson

V6 4234. 115. Florence Johnson, m. Marion Williamson, Ch: Gary; Linda; and Don Williamson

John Henry Breshears and Virginia Delilah Salisbury

v6 4211. 102. **John Henry Breshears**, (s/o Henry Thomas Breshears and Sabrina Jane Murray), b. 19 May 1861, Avery, Hickory Co, MO, d. 16 Jan 1941, Quency, Hickory Co, MO; m. 28 Nov 1880, ***Virginia Delilah Salisbury***, b. 13 Jan 1863, Concord, Benton Co, MO, d. 14 March 1901, Avery, Hickory Co, MO, d/o Jefferson Salisbury and Caroline Bell. Both John Henry and Virginia are buried in Sprinch Branch Cem, Avery, MO

Family of John Henry Breshears and Virginia Delilah Salisbury:

V6 4235. 111. **Lenora Alice "Nora" Breshears**, b. 26 Sept 1881, Avery, Hickory Co, MO, d. 18 June 1982, Independence, MO; m. 28 Nov 1906, ***Charles Thomas Fleeman***, b. 27 Jan 1883, d. 20 July 1972, Independence, MO.

V6 4236. 121. John Buel Fleeman, b. 11 Nov 1907, d. 22 Dec 1929

V6 4237. 112. **Effie Bell Breshears**, b. 28 May 1884, near Avery, MO, d. 29 Sept 1963, Wheatland, Hickory Co, MO; m. 9 March 1904, in Deepwater, MO, ***Robert Alexander Dietz***, b. 10 Dec 1880, Quincy, MO, d. 21 Oct 1956, Osceola, MO.

V6 4238. 121. Cecil Nora Dietz, b. 24 Feb 1905, d. 27 Nov 1972

V6 4239. 122. Clifford Dietz, b. 28 Dec 1906; m. Lois Kennedy

V6 4240. 123. Helen Lucile Dietz, b. 11 May 1908, Wheatland, Hickory Co, MO, d. 24 Feb 2002

V6 4241. 124. Ruby Virginia Dietz, b. 9 June 1913, Quincy, Hickory Co, MO

V6 4242. 125. Mildred Ethelene Dietz, b. 22 June 1920,

Quincy, Hickory Co, MO

[V6]4243. [11]3. **Jonah Green Breshears**, b. 23 June 1887, near Avery, MO, d. 26 Dec 1965; m. 9 Jan 1910, in Clinton, MO, ***Emma Louise Munson***,

[V6]4244. [12]1. **Maxine Breshears**, (twin)

[V6]4245. [12]2. **Pauline Breshears**, (twin)

[V6]4246. [12]3. **Virginia Breshears**,

[V6]4247. [12]4. **Harold Breshears**,

[V6]4248. [11]4. **Benjamin Alonzo "Bennie" Breshears**, b. 16 Oct 1890, d. 30 March 1891, age five months

[V6]4249. [11]5. **Amos Golman "Goldie" Breshears**, b. 13 June 1893, d. of Typhoid, 7 Oct 1909, age 16.

William Jasper "Jas" Breshears and Martha Ann "Mattie" Holley

[v6]4212. [10]3. **William Jasper "Jas" Breshears**, (s/o Henry Thomas Breshears and Sabrina Jane Murray,) b. 6 Nov 1864, Benton Co, MO, d. 22 April 1948, Avery, Benton Co, MO, bur Brethren Spring Branch Cem; m. 16 Sept 1888, in Benton Co, MO, ***Martha Ann "Mattie" Holley***, b. 16 March 1870, Benton Co, MO, d. 14 Dec 1966, Benton Co, MO, bur Brethren Spring Branch Cem, d/o John William Holley and Sarafine Isabel Donnell.

Family of William Jasper Breshears and Martha Ann Holley:

[V6]4250. [11]1. **Claude Westerfield Breshears**, b. 31 Aug 1889, Avery, Benton Co, MO, d. there, 16 April 1919; m. 26 March 1916, in Benton Co, MO, ***Lucy May McKenzie*** , b. 24 Dec 1888, Bentonville, Benton Co, MO, d. 16 July 1973, Bolivar, Polk Co, MO, d/o David McKenzie and Louella Cobb. Both bur in Spring Branch Cem, Avery, MO.

[V6]4251. [12]1. **Louella Irene Breshears**, b. 22 Sept 1917, d. 18 Jan 2000, Hermitage, Hickory Co, MO; m. ***Don Herbert Edge***. Ch: David Lynn; and Janet Edge

[V6]4252. [12]2. **Leola Claudine Breshears**, b. 8 March 1919, Bentonville, Benton Co, MO; m. ***Jack Edgar Bartshe***. Ch: Dennis Neil Bartshe

[V6]4253. [11]2. **Delmar Roy Breshears**, b. 24 Dec 1891, Avery, MO, d. 21 Dec 1956, Fristoe, MO; m. 1914, in Benton Co, MO, ***Lillie Pearl Miller***, (d/o Henry Miller and Martha Ruth), b. 27 Sept 1891, Avery, MO, d. 5 Oct 2001, Sedalia, MO.

[V6]4254. [12]1. **Alberta Lillian Breshears**, b. 30 May 1915, Benton Co, MO, d. 8 Dec 1998, Cross Timbers, MO; m. ***Floy Eldert Keightley***. Ch: George Lee; Darrel Gene; and Carolyn Keightley

[V6]4255. [12]2. **Roy Allen Breshears**, b. 31 July 1917, Fristoe, Benton Co, MO, d. 16 Sept 1981, Modesto, CA; m. ***Merle Nance***.

[V6]4256. [13]1. **Gary Lynn Breshears**; m. ***Mary Faye James***.

[V6]4257. [14]1. **James Grant Breshears**,

[V6]4258. [14]2. **Kelly Jane Breshears**,

[V6]4259. [13]2. **Diane Pearl Breshears**; m.1. Jimmy Jeff Poole; m.2. John Espinola, Jr. ch: Teddi Lynn; and Toni Ann Poole

[V6]4260. [13]3. **Kay Estelle Breshears**; m. ***Michael Don Lelieur***. Ch: Michael Donald; and Matthew Roy Lelieur

[V6]4261. [12]3. **Marguerete Breshears**, b. 6 June 1919, Fristoe, Benton Co, MO; m. ***Cebert Burlin Breshears***. (s/o Eli Breshears and Lucinda Murray). See his listing for their children.

[V6]4262. [11]3. **Retta Mae Breshears**, b. 24 Nov 1894, Benton, Co, MO, d. 9 July 1992; m. ***Asa Edwin McKenzie***, b. 24 Feb 1893, d. 6 Dec 1966, s/o David McKenzie and Louella Cobb

[V6]4263. [12]1. Wilma Nadine McKenzie, b. 12 Nov 1917; m. Morris "Tuck" King. Ch" Kent; and Jim King

[V6]4264. [12]2. Betty Ruth McKenzie, b. 21 Jan 1930, d. 21 Oct 1999, Hermitage, MO; m. Dale Cain. Ch: Larry; Randy; and Patty Cain

[V6]4265. [12]3. Asa Edwin McKenzie Jr, b. 15 Oct 1933, Benton Co, MO, d. Modesto, CA; m. Joyce Baker. Ch: Twilla Coleen; Brett Edwin; and Cara Mae McKenzie

[V6]4266. [11]4. **Ethel Jane Breshears**, b. 2 Feb 1898, Benton Co, MO, d. 29 Aug 2003, Christiand Health Center, Hermitage, MO, bur Spring Branch Cem, Avery, MO; m.1. ***Thomas M. McHale***; m.2. ***Buel Forehand***,

[V6]4267. [11]5. **Zulla Belle Breshears**, b. 7 March 1901, Benton Co, MO. d. 26 Nov 1995, in Montana; m.1. May 1924, ***John "Jack" Elton***, b. 1933; m.2. 1950, ***Guy Byerly***,

[V6]4268. [12]1. Phyllis Ruth Elton, b. 5 March 1925

[V6]4269. [12]2. Doris Elaine Elton, b. June 1927

[V6]4270. [11]6. **Venora Violet Breshears**, b. 28 Oct 1903, Avery, MO, d. 21 Sept 1999, Hermitage, Hickory Co, MO; m. ***Walter Mearl Brooks***, b. 14 March 1903, Benton Co, MO, d. there, _____, s/o Thomas Brooks and Lou Edwards

[V6]4271. [12]1. Billy Gene Brooks, b. 1925; m. Doris McMinn. Ch: Garold Eugene; Dennis Wayne; and Stephen Lee Brooks

[V6]4272. [12]2. Donald Dean Brooks, b. 24 Feb 1931, Windsor, MO; m. Joann Kahle. Ch: Lisa Renee; and Linda Christine Brooks

[V6]4273. [12]3. Ronald Glenn Brooks, b. 10 Feb 1938; m. Lavonne Williams. Ch: David Glenn; Karen Denise; and Cheryl Brooks

[V6]4274. [11]8. **Oleta Eunice Breshears**, b. 3 May 1916, Avery, MO; m.1. 10 May 1942, ***Frank Dorman***, b. 21 Oct 1912, Hermitage, Hickory Co, MO, d. Feb 2000, Dallas, TX; m.2.28 Aug 1948, ***George Maurer***, b. 17 May 1919, Watertown, NY, d. Feb 1999, Warrensburg, MO

[V6]4275. [11]7. **Orval Glen "Bus" Breshears**, b. 7 Dec 1907, Avery, Benton Co, MO; m. 7 July 1926, in Warsaw, MO, **Lola Mae Breshears** (d/o Levi Ransom Breshears and Hettie Noble Button),

Orval Glen "Bus" Breshears and Lola Mae Breshears

v6 4275. 117. **Orval Glen "Bus" Breshears**, (s/o William Jasper "Jas" Breshears and Martha Ann Holley), b. 7 Dec 1907, Avery, Benton Co, MO, d. 23 Nov 1966, Escalon, San Joaquin Co, CA, bur Wood Cem; m. 7 July 1926, in Warsaw, MO, **Lola Mae Breshears** (d/o Levi Ransom Breshears and Hettie Noble Button), b. 28 May 1909, Bentonville, MO, d. 23 Dec 2001.

"Bus" hated his given name, so he always insisted on being called "Bus," short for "Buster." When he and Lola Mae were courting, he would ride his horse, "Prince," from Avery to Bentonville to see Lola Mae. They were married in Warsaw, MO in 1926. The newly-weds lived in the "weaning house" on the hill above Henry B's house for about three or four years.

When Bus and Lola Mae moved to California in 1936, Bus took a job milking on a farm in the Milnes area of Stanislaus County in Central California, near Modesto. After a year of that, he went to work in the canneries, and also did a variety of other jobs— irrigating, being a laborer, etc.

After 1942, Bus was a carpenter the rest of his life, and lived on a small, 20-acre ranch on Mahon Road, in Escalon, San Joaquin Co, CA. He took pride in building well: when he built something, it was built to last. He and Lola Mae turned a small, two-room house into a large modern two-story home. Lola Mae did the texturing, painting, and some of the carpentry herself.

Bus died of cancer 23 Nov 1966, in Escalon, San Joaquin Co, CA, and was buried in Burwood Cemetery, Escalon, CA. He was 59 years old.

Lola Mae had always been a hard worker and took care of herself. One story is told of her being victimized by a cousin, Jake Breshears in Missouri. He would tease her and throw rocks at her. She finally had had enough and chased Jake up on the porch of her father's house (Levi Ransom Breshears), caught Jake, got him down, straddled him, and "beat the socks off him." This pommeling went on until Aunt Ida, Jake's mother, came out and pulled Lola Mae off. Needless to say, Jake never threw rocks at Lola Mae again.

Lola Mae related that her father, Levi Ransom Breshears, liked to tell spooky stories at night. Every time the stories got spookiest, younger brother Guy would have to go to the bathroom. Older sister Lola had the duty of taking Guy out behind the chicken house (they had no outhouse at the time), so he could "do his duty." When they got back to the house, Lola said she would open the door and jump way inside the room, because of the fright.

Her uncle, Lige Breshears, was also quite a joker. The barn on Henry B's place was large and scary to the little kids, because they feared that blacks might be hiding in it. One time, Lige put soot on his face to make himself look black. Someone told him to put grease on with it, to make it more real. So Lige put on the "make-up" and started chasing the little kids, cheered on by his brother, Hoosier. But the funniest part was when Lige had such a terrible time trying to get the soot off. The grease had made it almost indelible.

When Lola Mae and Bus moved to California in 1936, they lived at first in a place that had no electricity. They had a wind charger for lights, when the wind blew, and an ice-box to keep their perishables fresh. An ice man made regular deliveries to the area. After a year of being a milker on the Milnes farm, they moved and Bus went to work in the canneries.

During World War II, Lola Mae was a genuine "Rosie the Riveter." She worked as a "tack welder" in the shipyards at Stockton. She would tack pieces of the ships together, so that the machine welders could do their job of securing the pieces permanently. She and the family were/are proud of her war effort. She also donated over two gallons of blood during the war and received a citation.

Lola Mae had to help run the 20-acre ranch near Escalon and raise a family in trying times. After Bus died, she operated the farm by herself for some years, then moved to Modesto and lived in the same house on Snead Drive for over thirty years. She was always active in church and family affairs.

She married twice more. On 4 Jan 1948, she married Eldon "Mack" Alsip, who died about 1972 in Texas. On 29 Dec 1975, she married in Modesto, CA, Grimsley "Grim" Donald Reed, b. 16 May 1911, in Boydsville, AR, d. 10 Nov 1998, in Modesto, CA.

In 1999, Lola Mae celebrated her 90th birthday. Her sons, Glen, JayDee, and Maurice put on an elaborate party in her honor, held in her church's hall. Close to a hundred friends and relatives for all over and out of state attended to honor her.

In her last few years, Lola Mae was in and out of the hospital with Non-Hodgkins Lymphoma, Chemo-therapy, weakness, shingles, two cases of pneumonia, loss of hearing because of fluid build-up, and finally a fractured right hip. At 11:44 p.m., Dec 23, 2001, she passed away in Hylond Convalescent Hospital in Modesto. Son, Glen, was at her bedside. She had been a Missionary Baptist from an early age and firmly believed in God. She said she was not afraid of death and was prepared to go. She was 92 years, 6 month, and 25 days old.

Family of Orval Glen "Bus" Breshears and Lola Mae Breshears:

V6 4276. 12 1. **Jay Dwight Breshears**, b. 23 July 1927, Avery, Benton Co, MO; m.1. in 1950, ***Ruby Kathryn Gann*** (3 ch), b. 22 Dec 1934, d/o Edgar Gann and Esther ______; he met, but never married ***Carmen Loyd Stover***; m.2. in 1962, ***Loyce Riggs***, b. 1925; m.3. on 10 Jan 1968, ***Norma Jean Marshall***, b. 12 Aug 1937.

V6 4277. 13 1. **Martha Ann Breshears**, b. 2 Sept 1950, Redwood City, CA; m.1. c1971, ***Thomas Bauer***, b. 26 April 1951; m.2. c1983, ***Peter Ecklund***, b. 19 July 1955, Juneau, Alaska. Martha worked many years for the State of Alaska; later, she was Executive Director of a convalescent hospital in Juneau, AK.

V6 4278. 14 1. James Mathew Bauer,

V6 4279. 14 2. Sandy Lee Bauer,

V6 4280. 14 3. Kelly Ecklund,

V6 4281. 13 2. **Jerry Dwight Breshears**, b. 27 Feb 1952, d. 1952

V6 4282. 13 3. **Larry Jay Breshears**, b. 14 Jan 1955; m. 1978, ***Naomi Wythe***.

V6 4283. 14 1. **Jessie Jay Breshears**; met. ***Crystine Dutra***.

V6 4284. 15 1. **Kylie Alicia Breshears**,

V6 4285. 14 2. **Heather Breshears**, m. ______

V6 4286. 15 1. **Cassandra Breshears**,

V6 4287. 14 3. **Katrena Breshears**, m. ______

[V6]4288. [15]1. **Samantha Breshears**,

[V6]4289. [13]4. Johnathan Bart Stover, b. 24 Feb 1959. Johnathan is a teacher in Kennewick, WA. He has two children: Michelle; and Brandon Stover.

[V6]4290. [12]2. **Glen Junior Breshears**, b. 5 Jan 1930, Windsor, MO, lives Morgan Hill, CA; m. 4 Nov 1961, at Reno, NV, ***Velda Mae Medcalf***, b. 16 April 1941, Rawlins, WY, d/o Roscoe Frank Medcalf and Hanna Louisa Poppa. Glen and Velda divorced in 1984.

[V6]4291. [13]1. **Gregory Glen Breshears**, b. 14 July 1962, Sacramento, CA

[V6]4292. [13]2. **Victoria Lynn Breshears**, b. 13 Oct 1965, Carmichael, CA; m.1. July 1985, in Carmel, CA, ***Dean Yates***, b. 1963, Ozark, MO (div); m.2. 28 Oct 1990, ***George James Disses***, b. 1 June 1957, San Francisco, CA, s/o Chris Disses and Elizabeth Calimeris.

[V6]4293. [14]1. Leah Mellisa Yates, b. 9 April 1986, San Jose, CA

[V6]4294. [14]2. Jamie Lynn Disses, b. 4 May 1992, San Jose, CA

[V6]4295. [12]3. **Claude Maurice Breshears**, b. 27 Aug 1932, Avery, Benton, Co, MO; m. 18 Aug 1956, in Escalon, San Joaquin Co, CA, ***Bertsie Mae Sobrero***, b. 26 Jan 1937, in Molalla, Oregon, d/o James Sobrero and Bertsie Kretz. After a hitch in the U.S. Nave, Maurice worked at a Chevron gas station in Manteca, San Joaquin Co, CA. He later became manager, then owner of the station until he retired.

[V6]4296. [13]1. **James Maurice Breshears**, b. 5 March 1958, d. 18 March 1958, bur Lathrop Cem, Manteca, San Joaquin Co, CA.

[V6]4297. [13]2. **Ronald Glen Breshears**, b. 6 Oct 1959, Manteca, CA; m. 17 Dec 1977, ***Glenda Marie (Houston) Triglia***, b. 5 May 1959, d/o Glen Houston and Marie Schneider.

[V6]4298. [14]1. **Jennifer Lea Breshears**,

V6 4299. [14]2. **Diana Lynn Breshears**,
V6 4300. [14]3. **Tina Michelle Breshears**,
V6 4301. [13]3. **Terri Lynn Breshears**, b. 13 June 1962, Manteca, CA; m. 14 Feb 1981, in Manteca, San Joaquin C, CA, ***Ron Gomes***, b. c1959.
V6 4302. [14]1. Jason Michael Gomes,
V6 4303. [14]2. Kenneth Paul Gomes,
V6 4304. [13]4. **Julie Ann Breshears**, b. 17 Dec 1970, Manteca, CA; met.1. ***Shawn Edward Davis***, b. 26 July 1972; m.2. c1994, ***Ronald William Tanner***, b. 15 Feb 1973.
V6 4305. [14]1. Crystal Terese Davis/Tanner
V6 4306. [14]2. Timothy James Douglas Tanner
V6 4307. [14]3. Kevin Austin Tanner,

James Thomas Breshears and Malinda Catherine Southard

v6 4213. [10]4. **James Thomas Breshears**, (s/o Henry Thomas Breshears and Sabrina Jane Murray), b. 11 Sept 1866, d. 25 March 1936; m. 25 March 1886, ***Malinda Catherine Southard***, b. 11 Feb 1869, d. 22 Feb 1929, d/o Frank and Caroline Southard.

Family of James Thomas Breshears and Malinda Southard:
V6 4308. [11]1. **Lillie Alice Breshears**, b. 2 March 1887, MO, d. 27 July 1964; m. ***Johnnie Tipton***, b. c?1887. Ch: Raymond; and Ralph Tipton
V6 4309. [11]2. **Hattie Jane Breshears**, b. 3 Feb 1889; m. ***Joe Holler***, b. c?1889
V6 4310. [11]3. **Nancy Sabrina Breshears**, b. 10 April 1891, d. 3 Nov 1968, bur Hickory Co, MO; m. 20 March 1913, ***William M. "Willie" Henderson***, b. 29 April 1889, d. 24 Jan 1969. Ch: Lucille; Imogene; Goldena; Catherine; William J.; and James A. Henderson
V6 4311. [11]4. **Eva Dorcus Breshears**, b. 8 Sept 1893; m. ***James Peter Crabtree***, b. c1893. Ch: Gene Crabtree
V6 4312. [11]5. **Iva May Breshears**, b. 2 Nov 1896, d. 1988; m. ***Jacob R. "Jake" Bird***, b. c1896. Ch: Denton;

Quenton; and Emanuel Bird

[V6]4313. [11]6. **Rella Prue Breshears**, b. 27 Aug 1899, d. 7 Dec 1961; m.1. ***William Crabtree***; m.2. ***George Friedrich***. Ch: Evelyn; and James Crabtree; Peggy Friedrich

[V6]4314. [11]7. **Bernie Belmont Breshears**, b. 12 May 1902, d. 17 Oct 1945, bur Washington State; m. ***Clara Friedrich***,

[V6]4315. [12]1. Frieda Friedrich, m. David Grajeda

[V6]4316. [12]2. Linda Lee Friedrich,

[V6]4317. [11]8. **Paul J. "Whistle" Breshears**, b. 2 Aug 1904, d. 6 July 1961; m. ***Celia (or Cecile) Hunziker***, b. 17 Aug 1907, d. 28 Dec 1965, d/o Walter Hunziker and Lucy Rodgers

[V6]4318. [12]1. **Eloise Breshears**, b. 29 Dec 1927; m. ***Bob Donnahue***. Ch: Tonyah Donnahue

[V6]4319. [12]2. **Rodney Breshears**, b. 24 May 1934; m. ***Dorotha Antwiler***.

[V6]4320. [13]1. **Robert Allen Breshears**; m. ***Christine Rodriguez***

[V6]4321. [11]9. **Hazel Nadine Breshears**, b. 30 Jan 1912, d. 27 Feb 2002, Bothwell Regional Hosp, Sedalia, MO; m. 1933, ***Pertie Williams***,

[V6]4322. [12]1. Sue Williams, b. 11 Aug 1934

[V6]4323. [12]2. Pertie Williams, Jr, b. 29 March1941

Emma Leanna Breshears and George Washington Wright

[v6]4214. [10]5. **Emma Leanna Breshears**, (d/o Henry Thomas Breshears and Sabrina Jane Murray), b. 19 Nov 1869 (or 1868), Benton Co, MO, d. 19 May 1940; m. 12 June 1884, in Benton Co, MO, ***George Washington Wright***, b. 27 July 1864, d. 12 July 1939, s/o William Wright and Nancy Henderson.

<u>Family of Emma Leanna Breshears and George W. Wright:</u>

[V6]4324. [11]?. Mable F. Wright, b. 10 April 1885 (error; see Lawrence's birth), d. 28 June 1956

[V6]4325. [11]1. Lawrence Westerfield Wright, b. 15 May 1885, d. 4 July 1941, Springfield, MO; m. Dora M. Cox, b. 10

April 1885, d. 28 June 1956

[V6]4326. [12]1. Roy Desmond Wright, b. 1910, d. 1914

[V6]4327. [12]2. Wanda Lydia Wright, b. 28 March 1912, d. 29 Nov 1938

[V6]4328. [12]3. Cleo Beatrice Wright, b. 7 Nov 1913, d. 5 April 1959 in a car accident; m. 5 May 1938, **Lyle Denton Breshears**, b. 14 Nov 1917, d. 5 April 1959 in a car accident.

[V6]4329. [12]4. William Keith Wright, b. 10 Aug 1917, d. 1959; m. Fontalla Powell

[V6]4330. [12]5. Geraldine Wright, b. 10 Jan 1919

[V6]4331. [11]2. Charles William Wright, b. 11 Oct 1886, d. 28 March 1963, VA Hosp, Kansas City; m. 18 Sept 1921, Winnie Vernal Wilson, b. 25 March 1895, d. 25 Oct 1968

[V6]4332. [12]1. Wilson Eldridge Wright, b. 2 Jan 1923

[V6]4333. [12]2. Charles Irvin Wright, b. 18 Aug 1926

[V6]4334. [12]3. Reuben Sidney Wright, b. 7 Aug 1929

[V6]4335. [12]4. Conrad Maurice Wright, b. 29 Sept 1931

[V6]4336. [11]3. Lucinda Alice Wright, b. 14 Sept 1888, d. 8 Oct 1961; m. 7 March 1921, in Hickory Co, MO, Elmer A. Walker, b. 8 Feb 1878, d. 8 Oct 1961

[V6]4337. [12]1. Beatrice Walker, b. 13 April 1923

[V6]4338. [12]2. Wilma Walker, b. 24 Jan 1925

[V6]4339. [12]3. Kenneth Walker, b. 18 July 1926

[V6]4340. [11]4. Richard Wright, b. 29 Nov 1890, d. 23 Aug 1892

[V6]4341. [11]5. Vernon Wright, b. 4 April 1893, d. 23 Sept 1977; m. Clara Margaret Berneking, b. 22 Jan 1898

[V6]4342. [12]1. George Vernon Wright, b. 11 Oct 1925

[V6]4343. [12]2. Ann Emelyn Wright, b. 7 Feb 1927

[V6]4344. [12]3. Donald Henry Wright, b. 27 Feb 1929

[V6]4345. [12]4. Richard Dale Wright, b. 11 Nov 1933

[V6]4346. [11]6. Thomas Wright, b. 28 Jan 1895, d. 25 Nov 1965, Wheatland, MO; m. 9 March 1924, in Hermitage, MO, Anthus Mabel Bandel, b. 26 Dec 1897, Hickory Co, MO

[V6]4347. [12]1. Howard Bandel Wright, b. 9 Jan 1926

[V6]4348. [12]2. John William Wright, b. 12 Dec 1927

[V6]4349. [12]3. Lillie Elaine Wright, b. 17 Oct 1929

[V6]4350. [12]4. Mary Lou Wright, b. 30 Sep 1930

[V6]4351. [12]5. James Thomas Wright, b. 20 Nov 1932, d. 10 April 1992

[V6]4352. [11]7. James Lewis Wright, b. 27 Dec 1896, MO, d. 16 Nov 1982, MO; m. 25 Sept 1921, **Lena Helen Breshears**, (d/o Jesse Breshears and Pricie Murray), b. 7 Oct 1903, Hickory Co, MO, d. 21 Dec 1994, Bolivar, Polk Co, MO

[V6]4353. [12]1. Hamilton Dale Wright, b. 30 July 1922, Redlands, CA, d. 9 July 2002, Springfield, Greene Co, MO

[V6]4354. [12]2. Helen Gale Wright, b. 25 Feb 1924

[V6]4355. [12]3. Gwen Lee Wright, b. 14 Dec 1932, Wheatland, Hickory Co, MO

[V6]4356. [11]8. Jessie H. Wright, b. 26 Dec 1898, d. 16 Oct 1949; m. Dec 1924, Mabel Copp,

[V6]4357. [12]1. Anita Wright, b. 4 July 1926

[V6]4358. [12]2. Dorothy Wright, b. 15 Jan 1928

[V6]4359. [12]3. Kenneth Wright, b. 26 April 1931

[V6]4360. [12]4. James Keel Wright, b. 24 June 1933, d. Oct 1954

[V6]4361. [11]9. Beatrice Loretta Wright, b. 6 Aug 1903; m. Dec 1923, Bennie H. Walker, b. 13 June 1893, d. 22 Jan 1966

[V6]4362. [12]1. Inez Louie Walker, b. 2 July 1926

[V6]4363. [12]2. Sidney Walker, b. 20 July 1928

[V6]4364. [12]3. Billy Walker, b. 31 July 1930

[V6]4365. [11]10. Sydney Wright, b. 15 March 1907, d. 1 April 1964; m. 26 Dec 1931, Edna Mae Myers, b. 17 Feb 1909,

38. JOHN MARTIN VAN BUREN BRESHEARS and Susannah Ihrig

V6 3229. 9 9. **John Martin Van Buren Breshears**, (s/o Henry Breshears Jr and Atsa "Atsey" Etheridge), b. 19 Nov 1840, Fairfield, Benton Co, MO, d. 4 Feb 1922, in Kansas Old Soldier's Home, bur Avery Cem, Benton Co, MO; m. 20 March 1862, Wheatland, Hickory Co, MO, ***Susannah Ihrig***, b. 31 March 1842, IN, d. 3 Oct 1909, Avery, MO, d/o Peter Ihrig and Elizabeth Ellen "Elizzie" Tonbaugh.

John and Susannah settled in Breshears Valley, near Avery, in Alexander Township of Benton Co, MO (later in Hickory Co), and they lived there until Susannah died in 1909. John stayed on the place for a few years, and then stayed with one of the boys until about 1920, when he went to live at the Kansas Old Soldier's Home, where he died. He is buried at Spring Branch Cem, near his old home.

Family of John Martin Van Buren Breshears and Susannah Ihrig:

V6 4411. 10 1. **Mary Clementine Breshears** b. 27 Nov 1863, MO, d. in infancy.

V6 4412. 10 2. ***George N. Breshears**, b. 28 Feb 1865, KS or MO, d. 28 April 1938, Benton Co, MO; m. 25 Nov 1886, in Benton Co, MO, ***Rebecca Jane Butler***,

V6 4413. 10 3. ***William Marion Breshears**, b. 27 Dec 1866, near Avery, Benton Co, MO, d. 24 Aug 1931, Warsaw, Benton Co, MO; m. 5 April 1888, in Benton Co, MO, ***Sarah Francis Southard***, (d/o Richard Alexander Southard and Mary Annetta Cooper),

V6 4414. 10 4. ***Elizabeth Ellen "Lizzie" Breshears**, b. 15 Sept 1869, Benton Co, MO, d. 12 Dec 1941, Tonasket, WA; m. 28 Sept 1890, ***Henry Mason (or Methuselah) Colbert***,

[V6]4415. [10]5. **Fanny Adeline "Fanna" Breshears**, b. 8 March 1871, Benton Co, MO, d. 31 Oct 1933; m. ***William "Bill" Fleming***, b. c?1762

[V6]4416. [11]1. William Fleming Jr, m. **Eva Breshears**, (d/o John Franklin "Frank" Breshears and Ethel Robinson)

[V6]4417. [12]1. Ronald Fleming,

[V6]4418. [12]2. Donald Fleming,

[V6]4419. [10]6. ***Burr Emerson Breshears**, b. 20 May 1873, Benton Co, MO, d. 3 Dec 1940, (heart attack) Omak, Okanagan Co, WA; m. 10 July 1898, at Avery, Hickory Co, MO, ***Mary Rebecca "Becky" Rash***,

[V6]4420. [10]7. **Ezra Benton Breshears**, b. 22 Jan 1881, near Avery, Benton Co, MO, d. 20 Feb 1964, Tonasket, Okanagan Co, WA; m. 1913, at Conconully, WA, ***Lillie Rhoda Chedzoy***, b. c?1881. Children, per Roy Colbert's *Brashears/Breshears Newsletter* in July 1974.

[V6]4421. [11]1. **Lennie Ethel Breshears**,; m. ***J. Wallace "Wally" Jones***,

[V6]4422. [11]2. **Edith Minnie Breshears**,; m. ***William E. Burrell***,

[V6]4423. [11]3. **Benton Breshears**, d. in infancy

[V6]4424. [11]4. **Nora Emily Breshears**, b. 1917, d. 1976; m. ***Royal Neil Thornton***,

[V6]4425. [11]4. **Grace Adeline Breshears**, (twin); m. ***Henry Otto Rhode***,

[V6]4426. [11]5. **Archie Martin Breshears**, (twin); m. ***Dorothy Jones***,

[V6]4427. [11]6. **Helen Roberta Breshears**, (twin); m. ***Keane Francis Gau***

[V6]4428. [11]7. **Henry Robert Breshears**, (twin),

[V6]4429. [11]8. **Marion Michael "Skip" Breshears**; m. ***Shirley Shaughnessy***

[V6]4430. [10]8. **Alice Jane "Allie" Breshears**, b. 27 March 1882, Benton Co, MO; m. ***Edward Kirby***, b. c1882

[V6]4431. [11]1. Marie Kirby, b. Benton Co, MO, d. California; m. **Lloyd Breshears**, (s/o Hugh Walter Breshears and Burnettie A. Maxwell), b. 16

Figure 77: In the center of the picture: 9. John Martin Van Buren Breshears and his wife, 14. Susannah Ihrig; to John Martin's right, 5. Rebecca Jane (Butler) Breshears (wife of George N.), with 6. Mora Susan Breshears on her lap; to Susannah's left: 19. Elizabeth "Lizzie" (Breshears) Colbert, with 20. Leona May Colbert on her lap and 21. Elmer Colbert at her feet.
Back zig-zag row: 1. George N. Breshears; 2. Ezra Benton Breshears (boy slightly in front of George N.; 3. (beside George N.) Burr Emerson Breshears; 4. (boy in front of Burr) John Clay Breshears; 8. Fannie A. (Breshears) Fleming; 12. Henry Colbert (man behind the others); 13. Alice Jane Breshears (girl behind Susannah; 16. William Marion Breshears (tall man behind Alice); 18. Sarah Francis "Fannie" (Southard) Breshears (wife of William Marion), holding17. Rona Francis Breshears;
Front row: 7. Cora Adaline Breshears; 10. Bonnie E. Breshears; 11. Luther Valentine Breshears; 15. Riley Harrison Breshears. Thanks to Bill Brooks for the photo.

Sept 1901, Benton Co, MO, d. c1995, CA. See his listing for their children.

[V6]4432. [11]2. Audrey Kirby,

George N. Breshears
and Rebecca Jane Butler

v6 4412. 10 2. **George N. Breshears**, (s/o John Martin Van Buren Breshears and Susannah Ihrig), b. 28 Feb 1865, KS or MO, d. 28 April 1938, Benton Co, MO; m. 25 Nov 1886, in Benton Co, MO, ***Rebecca Jane Butler***, b. c1860, Hickory Co, MO, d. after 1938, Benton Co, MO, d/o Henry Butler and Martha Skinner. Both George and Rebecca are buried in Spring Branch Cem, Avery, MO.

Family of George N. Breshears and Rebecca Jane Butler:

V6 4433. 11 1. **John Clay Breshears**, b. c1887, Benton Co, MO, d. Montana; m. ***Fannie Barrett***, b. c1887

V6 4434. 12 1. **Clemuel Breshears**,

V6 4435. 11 2. **Bonnie E. Breshears**, b. 20 Sept 1888, d. 23 June 1907; m. ***Herman Weaver***

V6 4436. 11 3. **Cora Adaline Breshears**, b. 10 Sept 1890, Benton Co, MO, d. 7 Jan 1971, Prineville, Washington; m. ***Patrick N. Chancellor***, b. 9 June 1886, d. 14 July 1988, Hickory Co, MO. Ch: Floy; George; and Ora Faye Chancellor

V6 4437. 11 4. **Mora Susan Breshears**, b. 25 Oct 1894, Benton Co, MO, d. there, 10 March 1967; m. **Arthur Donald Breshears**, (s/o Robert E. Lee Breshears and Mary Frances "Fannie" Holley), b. 14 Jan 1895, Benton Co, MO, d. there, 2 July 1985. See his listing for their child.

V6 4438. 11 5. **Harry Breshears**, b. 2 (or 8) Feb 1897, Benton Co, MO, d. 25 Dec 1964, Hickory Co, MO; m. ***Hettie Bird***, b. 19 April 1901, Benton Co, MO, d. 25 Feb 1973, Hickory Co, MO

V6 4439. 12 1. **Ralph Eugene Breshears**, b. 12 April 1921, d. 18 Feb 1923, bur Spring Branch Cem, Avery, MO

V6 4440. 12 2. **Roy Lee Breshears**, b. 10 Sept 1922; m. ***Fern Kendrick***.

V6 4441. 13 1. **Carl Lee Breshears**; m. ***Sue Reno***.

V6 4442. 14 1. **Troy Allen Breshears**,

V6 4443. 13 2. **Edsel Neal Breshears**; m. ***Ellen Lurten***.

V64444. [14]1. **Michelle Diane Breshears**,

V64445. [13]3. **Gary Dean Breshears**,

V64446. [13]4. **Isaac Lynn Breshears**,

V64447. [13]5. **Cathy Fern Breshears**; m. ***Willard Palmer***. Ch: Brittany Chantell; and Megan Catherine Palmer.

V64448. [12]3. **Alvin Ray Breshears**, b. 8 Nov 1924; m. ***Floy Dendrick***.

V64449. [13]1. **Sue Breshears**,

V64450. [12]4. **Harrel Gene Breshears**, b. 25 April 1928

V64451. [12]5. **Ila Marie Breshears**, b. 7 Nov 1930; m. ***Lawrence Martin***,

V64452. [12]6. **Ina Faye Breshears**, b. 31 Dec 1931; m. ***Leonard Payne***,

V64453. [11]6. **Ira Breshears**, b. Jan 1899, Benton Co, MO, d. 21 Nov 1980, Santa Maria, CA; m. ***Nora Fay Lowery***, b. 24 July 1900, Benton Co, MO, d. 30 Dec 1994, Santa Maria, CA.

V64454. [12]1. **Merdith I. "Merd" Breshears**, b. 7 July 1923, Benton Co, MO, d. 7 Aug 1994, Santa Maria, CA; m. ***Willorene*** _____,

V64455. [13]1. **Gary M. Breshears**, of Santa Maria, CA

V64456. [13]2. **Sheri Breshears**, m. _____ ***Keller***, of Blue Springs, MO

V64457. [12]2. **Malvern Breshears**, of Kansas City, MO

Obit: Fay Breshears, 2 Jan 1995: A graveside service will be held at 2 p.m. Thursday at the Santa Maria Cemetery for Mrs. Fay Breshears, 94, of Santa Maria. She died Dec 30, 1994 at a local convalescent center.

Mrs. Breshears was born July 24, 1900, in Benton County, MO. She had been a Santa Maria resident since 1953 and had lived in Warrensburg, MO, area most of her life. Prior to World War II, she was a school teacher for the Benton County School District. During World War II, she worked for Pratt-Whitney Co, building aircraft parts. After moving to Santa Maria, she worked for her son at Mal's Western Shop on East Church Street. She later worked as a bookkeeper for Wilson's Western Wear.

Survivors include her son, Mal Breshears, Kansas City, MO; two grandchildren, Sherie Keller of Blue Springs, MO, and Gary

M. Breshears, Santa Maria; three great-grandchildren and numerous nieces and nephews. She was preceded in death by her husband, Ira Breshears, who died Nov 21, 1980, and by her son, Merd Breshears, who died Aug 7, 1994. Pastor Bruce McLain of Pine Grove Baptist Church will officiate her service.

Obit: Merdith Breshears, 9 Aug 1994: Graveside service will be held at 2 p.m. Thursday in the Santa Maria Cemetery with the Rev. Bruce McLain of the Pine Grove Baptist Church officiating for Merdith I. "Merd" Breshears, 71, of Santa Maria. He died Aug 7, 1994, at his residence of a lengthy illness.

Merdith Breshears was born July 7, 1923, in Benton County, MO. He was a resident of Santa Maria since 1953, moving here from Missouri. He was employed with Vandenberg Air Force Base for 16 years as a data analyst. Following his retirement, he became very involved with his wife's business, Willie's Insurance Services. He was a veteran of World War II, serving in the U.S. Army Signal Corps in the Pacific Theater. He was a member of the American Legion Post 534, Orcutt; VFW McGinley Bros Post 2521, Santa Maria, and National Rifle Association. His hobbies were photography and rebuilding automobiles.

Survivors include his wife of 48 years, Willorene Breshears of Santa Maria; son, Gary Breshears of Santa Maria; daughter Sheri Keller of Blue Springs, MO; mother, Nora Fay Breshears of Santa Maria; brother Mal Breshears of Kansas City, MO; three grandchildren. Visitation will be held from 2 to 7 p.m. Wednesday at the Dudley-Hoffman Mortuary. Memorial contributions may be made to the National Rifle Association, 1600 Rhode Island Ave, N.W., Washington, DC 20036.

William Marion Breshears and Sarah Francis Southard

v6 4413. 10 3. **William Marion Breshears**, (s/o John Martin Van Buren Breshears and Susannah Ihrig), b. 27 Dec 1866, near Avery, Benton Co, MO, d. 24 Aug 1931, Warsaw, Benton Co, MO; m. 5 April 1888, in Benton Co, MO, ***Sarah Francis Southard***, (d/o Richard Alexander Southard and Mary Annetta

Figure 78: Luther Valentine Breshears, his wife, Mary Catherine Bird, Frank Bird, and Edith Breshears. Photo from Bill Brooks.

Cooper), b. 11 April 1871, d. 26 June 1948. Both William and Sarah are buried in Spring Branch Cem, Avery, MO.

Family of William Marion Breshears and Sarah F. Southard:

V6 4458. 11 1. **Luther Valentine Breshears**, b. 19 May 1889, Benton Co, MO, d. there, 27 Dec 1963; m. ***Mary Catherine Bird***, b. 6 March 1892, Benton Co, MO, d. there, 4 Jan 1980. Both are buried in Spring Branch Cem, Avery, MO.

V6 4459. 12 1. **Lillian Frances Breshears**, b. 6 Oct 1915

V6 4460. 12 2. **Lila Odetta Breshears**, b. 24 Sept 1916; m. ***Gil Zimmerman***

V6 4461. 11 2. **Riley Harrison Breshears**, b. 24 July 1891, Avery, Benton Co, MO, d. 6 April 1966, Fristoe, Benton Co, MO; m. 16 April 1916, in Avery, Benton Co, MO, ***Nellie Irene Crabtree***, b. 2

Figure 79: Willie (?brother) and Nellie Irene Crabtree in 1912. She was 12 years old. Photo from Bill Brooks

Jan 1900, Fairfield, Benton Co, MO, d. 16 Nov 1964, Fristoe, MO, d/o Thomas Crabtree and Mary Nowell. Riley and Nellie are buried in Spring Branch Cem, Avery, MO.

[V6]4462. [12]1. **William Donald Breshears**, b. 24 Jan 1918, Avery, Benton Co, MO, d. 6 Jan 1920, bur Spring Branch Cem, Avery, MO.

[V6]4463. [12]2. **Helen Eunice Breshears**, b. 10 Nov 1920, Avery, Benton Co, MO; m. ***William Arnold Hockman***, b. 8 July 1920

[V6]4464. [13]1. Marietta Marlene Hockman, b. 8 Dec 1940; m. 22 Jan 1960, John B. Singleton, b. 16 Aug 1939

[V6]4465. [14]1. Kimberly Diane Singleton, b. 9 Aug 1962; m. 6 June 1981, William Cleon Raymond, b. 29 Nov 1958

[V6]4466. [15]1. William Dustin Raymond, b. 22 June 1984

[V6]4467. [14]2. Kellie Sue Singleton, b. 5 May 1968; m. 24 May 1986, David Stephenson, b. 25 March 1961

[V6]4468. [15]1. Joseph Daniel Stephenson, b. 22 June 1988

[V6]4469. [15]2. Keith Stephenson,

[V6]4470. [15]3. Linc Stephenson,

[V6]4471. [15]4. Wyatt Stephenson,

[V6]4472. [13]2. Brenda Mae Hockman, b. 9 March 1947; m.1. 14 Feb 1964, Darrel Gene Keithley (s/o Floy Keithley and Alberta Breshears); m.2. 24 Aug 1985, Ray Eugene Smith

[V6]4473. [14]1. Darla Jean Keithley, b. 4 March 1966; m. Jerry Lacy

[V6]4474. [15]1. Tiffany Diane Lacy, b. 9 Aug 1986

[V6]4475. [14]2. Dana Lynn Keithley, b. 9 Feb 1968

[V6]4476. [14]3. Jason Smith, m. Kelli Rousher. Ch: Davin Ray Smith

[V6]4477. [14]4. Jeff Smith,

[V6]4478. [12]3. **Florence Pauline Breshears**, b. 12 May 1923, Avery, Benton Co, MO; m. ***Thomas***

Francis Kirby, b. 30 Jan 1916

V6 4479. [13]1. Janet Nell Kirby, b. 27 May 1940; m.1. 24 Oct 1967, Larry Eugene Box; m.2. Larry Turner

V6 4480. [14]1. Tommy Eugene Box, b. 31 May 1968

V6 4481. [13]2. Carol Ann Kirby, b. 30 Oct 1943

V6 4482. [13]3. Sarah Beth Kirby, b. 24 March 1948, d. 24 March 1948

V6 4483. [12]4. **Betty Faye Breshears**, b. 24 Oct 1925, Avery, Benton Co, MO; m. ***Raymond W. Redman***

V6 4484. [13]1. Steven Dane Redman, b. 5 May 1951; m. Ann Marie Squires. Ch: Ryan Dane Redman

V6 4485. [13]2. Joel Ray Redman, b. 26 Feb 1954; m. Judy Brawley Bronkowske. Ch: Riley Joen Ray; and Stephen Joshua Charles Redman

V6 4486. [12]5. **William Thomas Breshears**, b. 29 Sept 1932, Fristoe, Benton Co, MO; m. ***Joyce*** _____

V6 4487. [13]1. **Jan Breshears**,

V6 4488. [13]2. **Darlene Breshears**,

V6 4489. [13]3. **Larry Breshears**,

V6 4490. [13]4. **Lorie Nell Breshears**,

V6 4491. [13]5. **Angela Kay Breshears**,

V6 4492. [11]3. **Rona Francis Breshears**, b. 30 Sept 1893, Benton Co, MO, d. there, 24 Jan 1969; m. ***Floy Davis***, (d/o Ed Davis and Sarah Ihrig), b. c?1873, Benton Co, MO, d. 3 May 1964,

V6 4493. [12]1. **Avis Davis Breshears**, m. **Ernest Ihrig**

V6 4494. [13]1. Darlene Ihrig; m. Steven Coffman: ch. Hilary and Amber Coffman

V6 4495. [13]2. Jane Ihrig; m. Gene Roth. ch: Darrell Roth

V6 4496. [13]3. Barbara Ihrig; m. Nick Faulkner. ch: Wendy; Lynnette; Barbie; Nicky; and John Faulkner

V6 4497. [13]4. Gale Sue Ihrig; m. Mike McMillan

Elizabeth Ellen "Lizzie" Breshears and Henry M. Colbert

v6 4414. [10]4. **Elizabeth Ellen "Lizzie" Breshears**, (d/o John Martin Van Buren Breshears and Susannah Ihrig), b. 15 Sept 1869, Benton Co, MO, d. 12 Dec 1941, Tonasket, WA; m. 28 Sept 1890, ***Henry Mason (or Methuselah) Colbert***, b. c1869, WA, d. Molson, WA, s/o John T. Colbert and Permillia Jane Shelton; m.2. "late in life", ***August Peterson***. Oma (Colbert) Smith wrote the article on her parents' family in Roy Colbert's *Brashears/Breshears Newsletter*, in July 1974.

Family of Elizabeth Ellen Breshears and Henry M. Colbert:

V6 4498. [11]1. Elmer Leroy "Roy" Colbert, b. 1891, d. 1971; m. Carlyn Umscheid

V6 4499. [12]1. Roy Colbert, b. 1919; m. Barie

V6 4500. [11]2. Leona May (or Nellie) Colbert, b. 1894, d. 1957; m. Ollie Arthur "Babe" Cook

V6 4501. [11]3. Neomi Jane "Oma" Colbert; m.1. John Sherman Cook; m.2. Chester Phillip Smith

V6 4502. [11]4. Minnie Ellen Colbert, b. 20 Oct 1899, d. 21 Nov 1899, age 1 month.

V6 4503. [11]5. John Henry Colbert, b. Molson, WA; m. Ester Owens

Burr Emerson Breshears and Mary Rebecca "Becky" Rash

v6 4419. [10]6. **Burr Emerson Breshears**, (s/o John Martin Van Buren Breshears and Susannah Ihrig), b. 20 May 1873, Benton Co, MO, d. 3 Dec 1940, (heart attack) Omak, Okanagan Co, WA; m. 10 July 1898, at Avery, Hickory Co, MO, ***Mary Rebecca "Becky" Rash***, b. 10 June 1879, IN, d. 16 Sept 1954, of cancer, d/o Richard R. Rash. Becky's brother, William Rash, also moved to the Okanagan Valley, WA. Daughter Barbara (Breshears) Wood contributed the article on her parents' family to Roy Colbert's *Brashears/Breshears Newsletter* in July 1974.

Family of Burr Emerson Breshears and Mary Rebecca Rash:

V6 4504. [11]1. infant Breshears, d. at birth (premature)

V64505. 11 2. **Reuben Saylor Breshears**, b. 5 Jan 1900, MO, d. Aug 1955, WA (stroke); m. ***Florence Mohler***

V64506. 11 3. **Ralph Emerson Breshears**, b. 12 May 1902, Chesaw, Okanagan Co, WA, d. 23 May 1973 (killed in an orchard accident), Omak, Okanagan Co, WA; m. ***Betty*** ____,

V64507. 11 4. **Florence Maybelle Breshears**, b. 22 Sept 1903, Kipling, Okanagan Co, WA, d. 6 March 1964, Lexington, KY; m. ***Earl Leland Swallom***,

V64508. 11 5. **Clara Bernice Breshears,** b. 29 July 1905, Kipling, Okanagan Co, WA; m. ***Raymond Henry Downey***,

V64509. 11 6. **Esther Breshears**, (twin), b. 16 Dec 1906, Kipling, Okanagan Co, WA, d. 20 Dec 1906, age 4 days.

V64510. 11 7. **Lester Breshears**, (twin), b. 16 Dec 1906, Kipling, Okanagan Co, WA, d. cJan 1907, age 1 month.

V64511. 11 8. **Richard Raymond Breshears**, b. 16 March 1909, Kipling, Okanagan Co, WA; m.1. ***Iona Shaw***; m.2. ***Geraldine Howell***

V64512. 11 9. **Lois Evelyn Breshears**, b. 14 Aug 1912, Omak, Okanagan Co, WA;

V64513. 11 10. **Hilda Rebecca Breshears**, b. 5 Jan 1915, Omak, Okanagan Co, WA; m. ***Wilbur Gerald Freese***,

V64514. 11 11. **Roger Harvey Breshears**, b. 9 Oct 1921, Omak, Okanagan Co, WA; m. ***Lilla Lavine Corum***

V64515. 11 12. **Barbara Jean Breshears**, b. 28 Nov 1922, Omak, Okanagan Co, WA; m. ***Roy Lee Wood***, b. c?1822.

39. ANDREW JACKSON BRESHEARS and Mary Jane Parsley

v63232. 9 12. **Andrew Jackson Breshears**, (s/o Henry Breshears Jr and Atsa "Atsey" Etheridge), b. 24 Dec 1846, Hickory Co, MO, d. 2 Nov 1924, Avery, Hickory Co, MO; m. 1867, ***Mary Jane "Jennie" Parsley***, b. 8 Feb 1850, MO, d. 27 March 1940. Andrew served 60 days in the Union Army at the end of the Civil War. He is buried at Spring Branch Cem. Andy kept a store at Avery. See photo, next page.

Figure 80: In front of Andy Breshears Store in Avery, about 1910. From left: Joel C. Owen, Molly (Owen) Logan, Mary Ann Owen, Andrew Jackson Breshears Sr, Mary Jane (Parsley) Breshears, Sam Breshears, Andrew Jackson Breshears, Jr (with hands on son, Murrell Breshears, Etta (Owens) Breshears, Todd and Nellie Button. Photo: Bill Brooks

Family of Andrew Jackson Breshears and Mary Jane Parsley:

V6 4561. 10 1. **Andrew Jackson "Andy" Breshears Jr**, b. 20 Jan 1872, MO, d. 17 June 1952; m. 16 Jan 1901, ***Etta Owens,*** b. Sept 1876.

V6 4562. 11 1. **Murrell Breshears**, d. Oct 1970, California; m. ***Ethel Starke***,

V6 4563. 12 1. **Twilla Lou Breshears**, m. ***Jim Barnett***,

V6 4564. 12 2. **Mary Sue Breshears**, m. ***Tony Marles***,

V6 4565. 12 3. **Barbara Sue Breshears**, m. ***Gary Coley***,

V6 4566. 11 1. **Mervin Clell Breshears**, 28 Sept 1911, Avery, Benton Co, MO, d. 5 Oct 1995, Wyoming; m.1. 27 May 1939, ***Beatrice Boe***, (1 ch); m.2. 24 Dec 1983, ***Margie Sundberg***,

V6 4567. 12 1. **Diana Breshears**; m. ***Leo Morrell***. Ch: Leanna and Andrew Morrell

V6 4568. 10 2. ***Goulsberry "Gulie" Breshears**, b. 3 April 1874,

Benton Co, MO, d. 14 Sept 1946, Hickory Co, MO; m. **Etta Frances Breshears**, (d/o Isaac David "Ike" Breshears and Elva Jane Breshears),

[V6]4569. [10]3. **Berdet Breshears**, b. 9 Nov 1875, d. 24 Jan 1876. Berdet's name and dates were entered in Andrew Jackson Breshears's family bible.

[V6]4570. [10]4. ***Eli Breshears**, b. 20 July 1877, Benton Co, MO, d. 18 Jan 1958, Wheatland, Hickory Co, MO; m. 29 March 1903, MO, ***Lucinda Jane Murray***,

[V6]4571. [10]5. ***Samuel Breshears**, b. 7 Nov (or Dec) 1879, d. 9 April 1930; m. 1903, ***Ettie Baugh***,

[V6]4572. [10]6. **Homer Noland Breshears**, b. 1 April 1881, d. 9 Oct 1964; m. 17 April 1907, ***Daisy Ethel Bailey***,

[V6]4573. [11]1. **Hubert Noland Breshears**, b. 16 March 1911, d. 14 Dec 1959; m. ***Imogene*** ______,

[V6]4574. [10]7. **Atsey Jane Breshears**, b. 20 Feb 1884, d. 6 Aug 1972; m. 22 Sept 1901, ***Roy William Jennings***, b. 25 March 1882, d. 2 April 1958

[V6]4575. [11]1. Tracy Warden Jennings, b. 25 Oct 1902, Avery, Benton Co, MO, d. 9 Jan 1977, Clinton, MO; m. Lee Moore, b. 13 May 1908, Mintone CA, d. 4 Aug 1995, Clinton, MO

[V6]4576. [11]2. Lloyd Durward Jennings, b. 9 Dec 1904, d. 21 March 1930

[V6]4577. [11]3. Ethel Jennings, b. 1912, d. 25 Nov 1989; m. Gerald Baird. Ch: Natalie; Gerald Jr; and Patricia Ann Baird.

[V6]4578. [11]4. Arnold Jackson Jennings, b. 13 Nov 1920, d. 6 March 1944; m. Ursa May Garrison. Ch: Arnola Ann; and Janice Jennings.

[V6]4579. [11]5. Infant Jennings, b. & d. during WW II

[V6]4580. [10]8. **Della Breshears**, (twin) b. 26 Nov 1886, MO, d. 3 March 1972, Lowry, St. Clair Co, MO; m. 1907, Benton Co, MO, ***John William Murray Jr***, b. Aug 1885, MO, d. 14 June 1967, Lowrey City, St. Clair Co, MO, s/o John William Murray and Rebecca Jane Rodgers.

[V6]4581. [11]1. Ned Murray, b. 31 Aug 1909, Benton, Co MO, d. Sept 1980, Lowrey City, St. Clair Co, MO; m. Opal Baxter, b. 1909, d. 1993.

V64582. 121. Ruby Glea Murray. B. Feb 1926, m. William Edwin Breon (for more, contact Michelle Breon, 3136 Wellington Rd, Alexandria, VA 22302);

V64583. 122. Bille Dee Murray, b. 28 Jan 1930, d. 31 Jan 1992; m. Mary Parry;

V64584. 123. Zella Lou Murray, (twin) b. 13 Nov 1933; m.1. John T. Hartman, m.2. Billie Jo Knight;

V64585. 124. Donnie Dale Murray, (twin) b. 13 Nov 1919; m. Sharon Kay Stephan,

V64586. 112. infant son, died at birth

V64587. 113. Anna Lee Murray, b. 26 Jan 1917, MO, d. 6 July 1990, killed in a farm accident at home, Lowery City, St. Clair Co, MO; m. 14 Feb 1938, John Blackwell, b.?, d. 1982. Ch: Jackie William Blackwell.

V64588. 109. **Ella Breshears**, (twin), b. 26 Nov 1886, d. 15 Dec 1923; m. ***Lum L. Weaver***, b. 21 Feb 1883, Benton Co, MO, d. 17 Aug 1957

V64589. 111. Infant Weaver, b. & d. 10 March 1907

V64590. 112. Mabel Helen Weaver, b. 13 Dec 1912 (twin), near Bentonville, Benton Co, MO, d. 3 Oct 1981; m. Don E. Copp, b. 1 Jan 1914, Benton Co, MO, d. 22 March 1997. Ch: Donna Jean; and Greta Copp.

V64591. 113. Infant Weaver, b. & d. 13 Dec 1912 (twin)

V64592. 114. Pearl Imogene Weaver, b. 5 Nov 1919, near Bentonville, Benton Co, MO, d. 19 Aug 1998, Osceola, MO; m. Loren Woodrow Murray, b. 21 May 1918, d. 15 June 1995. Ch: Carol Sue; and Danny Lee Murray.

Goulsberry "Gulie" Breshears and Etta Frances Breshears

v64568. 102. **Goulsberry "Gulie" Breshears**, (s/o Andrew Jackson Breshears and Mary Jane Parsley), b. 3 April 1874, Benton Co, MO, d. 14 Sept 1946, Hickory Co, MO; m. **Etta Frances Breshears**, (d/o Isaac David "Ike" Breshears and Elva

Jane Breshears), b. Oct 1879, Benton Co, MO, d. 16 Oct 1956, Hickory Co, MO. Both are buried in Avery Cem, north of Wheatland, Hickory Co, MO.

Family of Goulsberry Breshears and Etta Frances Breshears:

^{V6}4593. ^{11}1. **Roscoe D. Breshears**, b. 29 March 1900, d. 26 March 1978; m.1. ***Grace Lowery***, (2 ch); m.2. ***Mabel A.*** ______, (1 ch), b. 7 April 1898, d. 1977

^{V6}4594. ^{12}1. __dau___ **Breshears**, m. ______ ***Shorts***

^{V6}4595. ^{12}2. **Neva Breshears**, m. ***Kenneth Lyons***

^{V6}4596. ^{12}3. **Paul Alexander Breshears**,

^{V6}4597. ^{11}2. **Carl C. Breshears**, b. 5 April 1905, Hickory Co, MO, d. there, 22 April 1920, age 15, bur Spring Branch Cem, Avery, MO.

^{V6}4598. ^{11}3. **Sylvia Breshears**, b. 4 Feb 1916, Hickory Co, MO, d. 22 May 1994, Benton Co, MO; m. 12 March 1933, ***Guy Roger Baugh***, (s/o Fred Baugh and Myrtle Rodgers), b. 9 Oct 1911, Benton Co, MO, d. there, 16 Dec 1991,

^{V6}4599. ^{12}1. Barbara Lou Baugh, m. Vernon Gemes. Ch: Connie; Lyndell; Larry; and Stanley Gemes

^{V6}4600. ^{12}2. Roger Alan Baugh, b. 22 March 1939; m. Betty Louise Downs

^{V6}4601. ^{12}3. Dennis Lee Baugh, b. 29 Oct 1953, d. 18 Oct 1973; m. Sandra Jane ______,

^{V6}4602. ^{11}4. **Ruby Evelyn Breshears**, b. 1925, Hickory Co, MO, d. 13 Jan 1981; m. 12 Aug 1942, ***Leland Gist***, b. 9 Dec 1914, d. March 1980. Ch: Vickie Lynn; and Ronnie Gist.

^{V6}4603. ^{11}5. **Adella Breshears**, b. Benton Co, MO, d. Hood River, OR; m. ***Denver Harper***, b. Benton Co, d. Hood River, OR. Ch: Billy; Neva; and Ruth Harper.

^{V6}4604. ^{11}6. **Edgar Breshears**, b. Hickory Co, MO, d. Hood River, OR; m. ***Inice Faye Roberts***,

^{V6}4605. ^{11}7. **Arley Breshears**, b. Hickory Co, MO, d. Los Angeles, CA; m. ***Geraldine Stewart***,

^{V6}4606. ^{11}8. **Leta Mae Breshears**, b. Hickory Co, MO, d. 6 Oct 1990; m. 31 Aug 1940, ***Harry Stover***. Ch: Sandra; Gary; and William Richard Stover.

^{V6}4607. ^{11}9. **Olaf Breshears**, b. ____

Eli Breshears
and Lucinda Jane Murray

v6 4570. [10]4. **Eli Breshears**, (s/o Andrew Jackson Breshears and Mary Jane Parsley), b. 20 July 1877, Benton Co, MO, d. 18 Jan 1958, Wheatland, Hickory Co, MO; m. 29 March 1903, MO, ***Lucinda Jane Murray***, b. 29 Sept 1883, Hickory Co, MO, d. 29 Sept 1948, MO

Family of Eli Breshears and Lucinda Jane Murray:

V6 4608. [11]1. **Elsie Breshears**, b. 12 Dec 1904, Avery, Benton Co, MO, d. 15 Jly 1988, North Kansas City, MO; m. 12 Nov 1924, **Floyd Earl Breshears**, b. 10 Feb 1904, d. 30 June 1954; m.2. 20 April 1961, ***Ollie H. Ihrig***, b. 13 Nov 1892, d. 12 Nov 1976, Clinton, MO

V6 4609. [12]1. **Wanda Lee Breshears**, m. ***James H. Brooks, Sr***,

V6 4610. [13]1. James H. Brooks, Jr; m. Linda Faye Kitchen. Ch: Jason Joshua; James H. III; and Timothy Jordan Brooks

V6 4611. [13]2. Rebecca Brooks; m. David Silas. Ch: David Adam Silas

V6 4612. [13]3. Lisa Pearl Brooks; m. Gregg Smith. Ch: Jared Brooks Smith

V6 4613. [12]2. **William Francis Breshears**, m. ***Ruth West***,

V6 4614. [13]1. **Victoria Diane Breshears**; m. ***Dan Enloe***. Ch: Andrew Kyle; Kara Kylene; and Melissa Elaine Enloe

V6 4615. [13]2. **Scott Alan Breshears**; m. ***Cindy*** ______.

V6 4616. [14]1. **Molly Sue Breshears**,

V6 4617. [14]2. **Mallory Ann Breshears**,

V6 4618. [14]3. **Matthew Scott Breshears**,

V6 4619. [13]3. **Samuel Francis Breshears**; m. ***Janice Phillips***.

V6 4620. [14]1. **Brian Breshears**,

V6 4621. [14]2. **Richard Michael Breshears**,

V6 4622. [13]4. **Russell Wayne Breshears**; m. ***Regina*** ______.

V6 4623. [14]1. **Kaylee Dawn Breshears**,

V6 4624. [14]2. **Kassie Collene Breshears**,

V6 4625. [11]2. **Letha Laverne Breshears**, b. 15 June 1905, Avery, Benton Co, MO, d. 11 Oct 1995, Sedalia, Pettis Co, MO; m. 15 June 1934, ***Lowell Earnest Cobb***, b. 9 May 1904, d. 14 July 1965. Ch: Shirley Joann; Billy Joe; and Lowell Earnest Cobb, Jr.

V6 4626. [11]3. **Ray Breshears**, b. 14 April 1910, Avery, Benton Co, MO, d. 5 Oct 1998, Springfield, Greene Co, MO; m. 21 Feb 1932, ***Fratie Ellen Henderson***, b. 8 March 1910, d/o George Henderson and Malissa Breshears.

V6 4627. [12]1. **Alfred Neil Breshears**, b. 1934; m. ***Lucille Elaine Bybee***,

V6 4628. [13]1. **Judy Gail Breshears**, m. ***Richard McWhitney***.

V6 4629. [13]2. **Jeffry Dennis Breshears**; m. ***Sally Lane Shaw***.

V6 4630. [14]1. **Brett Matthew Breshears**,

V6 4631. [14]2. **Jack Christopher Breshears**,

V6 4632. [13]3. **Joyce Elyce Breshears**; m. ***Steven Wayne Branstetter***; m.2. ***Samuel Verl Henderson, Jr***. ch: Heather Nichole; and Steven Wayne Branstetter, Jr

V6 4633. [12]2. **Wilma Jean Breshears**, b. 15 Feb 1936; m. ***Hervie Beck***,

V6 4634. [11]4. **Cebert Burlin Breshears**, b. 18 April 1918, Avery, Benton Co, MO; m. ***Marguerete Breshears***, b. 6 June 1919, Fristoe, Benton Co, MO, d/o Delmar Breshears and Pearl Miller

V6 4635. [12]1. **Vearl Joyce Breshears**, b. 5 Dec 1939, Fristoe, Benton Co, MO; m. ***Arne Buchave Bidstrup***, ch: Dane Marvin; and Craig Marvin Bidstrup

V6 4636. [12]2. **Burlin Dale Breshears**, b. 2 Nov 1954, Sedalia, Pettis Co, MO; m. ***Carolyn Dickey***

V6 4637. [11]5. **Doris Jean Breshears**, b. 29 Jan 1925, Benton Co, MO; m. 5 May 1943, ***Asa Bill Staten***, b. 10 May 1922, Wheatland, Hickory Co, MO, d. 13 Aug 1951, Springfield, Greene Co, MO.

V64638. 121. Deena Sue Staten; m. Walter Quick. Ch: Tanny LaJean; and Suzanne Gale Quick

Samuel Breshears and Ettie Baugh

v64571. 105. **Samuel Breshears**, (s/o Andrew Jackson Breshears and Mary Jane Parsley), b. 7 Nov (or Dec) 1879, d. 9 April 1930; m. 1903, ***Ettie Baugh***, b. 18 April 1884, MO, d. 19 Aug 1962.

Family of Samuel Breshears and Ettie Baugh:

V64639. 111. **Virgil Glenn Breshears**, b. 1904; m.1. ***Jean Nance***, (1 ch); m.2. ***Jewel Balke-Cumpton***, (1 ch)

V64640. 121. **Elaine Breshears**,

V64641. 122. **Judy Kay Breshears**; m. ***Gerry L. Terry***. Ch: Eugene Arnett Terry

V64642. 112. **Lawrence Ivan Breshears**, b. 20 Sept 1907, near Avery, MO, d. 21 Dec 1981, Osceola, MO; m. 25 Aug 1927, ***Zelma Marie Bird***, b. 28 April 1911, Fairfield, Benton Co, MO, d. 2 Oct 1980, Clinton MO.

V64643. 121. **Bernice L. Breshears**, b. 18 Oct 1928; m. ***Lewis Wheeler***, Ch: Jeffrey L.; and James E. Wheeler

V64644. 122. **Willis D. Breshears**, b. 30 Sept 1930; m. ***Carol Bockelman***,

V64645. 131. **Cheryl Breshears**,

V64646. 132. **Ronny Breshears**,

V64647. 133. **Randy Breshears**,

V64648. 134. **Rick Breshears**,

V64649. 123. **Mary Maxine Breshears**, b. 8 Jan 1933; m. ***John Dehart***,

V64650. 131. Donald Dean Dehart, m. Lee Ann _______.

V64651. 132. Frank Dehart, m. Leta Stewart,

V64652. 133. Robert Dehart, m. Louise Herd,

V64653. 134. Steve Dehart, m. Mary Maxine _______.

V64654. 124. **Valentine Joleen Breshears**, b. 14 Feb 1935, d. 21 Oct 1994; m. ***Jack Logan***, Ch: Timothy Lee Logan

V6 4655. [12]5. **Willard E. Breshears**, b. 11 July 1937, d. 21 Jan 1983; m. ***Catherine Chancellor***,

V6 4656. [13]1. **Theresa Jean Breshears**,

V6 4657. [13]2. **Jerry Gail Breshears**; m.1. ***Cindy J. Carey***; m.2. ***Judy Mae Creasey***.

V6 4658. [14]1. **Joshua Tate Breshears**,

V6 4659. [14]2. **Alex Joseph Breshears**,

V6 4660. [14]3. **Aaron Justin Breshears**,

V6 4661. [12]6. **Wilford G. Breshears**, b. 9 Nov 1939; m. ***Betty Osborne***,

V6 4662. [13]1. **Cynthia Breshears**, m. ***George W. Jarman***,

V6 4663. [13]2. **Angela Marie Breshears**; m. ***Jackie Dale Hammond***. Ch: Jake; Caleb; Shane; and Seth Jackson Hammond

V6 4664. [13]3. **Carey Glen Breshears**; m. ***Dena Kaye Adams***.

V6 4665. [14]1. **Andrew Glen Breshears**,

V6 4666. [14]2. **Anthony Justin Breshears**,

V6 4667. [12]7. **Linda Kay Breshears**, b. 7 Dec 1950; m.1. ***Virgil Wombles***; m.2. ***Gene Dougherty***,

V6 4668. [13]1. David E. Wombles,

V6 4669. [13]2. Kenny Wombles,

V6 4670. [13]3. Clint Wombles; m. Lori Crow, ch: Jeremy Lee; and Allen Ray Wombles

V6 4671. [13]4. Shanna Dougherty.

V6 4672. [11]3. **Louella Breshears**, m.1. ***Mal Youngblood***; m.2 ***O.E. Underwood***,. Ch: Charmaine; Malton Bart; and Deidra Cheryl Youngblood.

V6 4673. [11]4. **Pearline Breshears**, m. ***Ervin Frisk***, Ch: Dwaine; Gloria; Marlene; Steve; and Stan Frisk

V6 4674. [11]5. **Perna Breshears**, (twin) b. 30 Nov 1915, d. 7 April 1987; m. ***Audrey McCowan***.

V6 4675. [12]1. **Jackie Allen Breshears**; m. ***Ann Drake***.

V6 4676. [13]1. **Katheryn Sue Breshears**, m. ***Gary Dean Martinez***.

V6 4677. [13]2. **Jackie Ann Breshears**; m. ***Harley _______***.

V6 4678. [12]2. **Robert Breshears**; m. ***Frances Conrad***.

V6 4679. [13]1. **Patrick Neal Breshears**; m. ***Lori Ann***

Wolfe.

V6 4680. [14]1. **Blake Orra Breshears**,

V6 4681. [14]2. **Haille Breshears**,

V6 4682. [13]2. **Robert David Breshears**; m. ***Marcine Lovell Noland***..

V6 4683. [14]1. **Joshua Robert Breshears**,

V6 4684. [14]2. **Lacey Jo Breshears**,

V6 4685. [12]3. **Dawn Etta Breshears**; m.1. ***Brian Martin***; m.2. ______ ***Wise***. Ch: Katie Rachel and Andrew D. Martin

V6 4686. [11]6. **Verna Breshears**, (twin), b. 30 Nov 1915, m. ***Ira Noel Woihayer***. Ch: Carol; and Ronald Woihayer

V6 4687. [11]7. **Noble Breshears**, b. 8 June 1927; m.1. ***LeEtta*** ______, (2 ch); m.2. ***Sheila Vereker***, (2 ch)

V6 4688. [12]1. **Debbie Breshears**,

V6 4689. [12]2. **Karl Breshears**,

V6 4690. [12]3. **Marla Breshears**,

V6 4691. [12]4. **Tim Breshears**,

40. MARCUS MONROE BRESHEARS and Leanna Murray

V6 3233. [9]13. **Marcus Monroe Breshears**, (s/o Henry Breshears Jr and Atsa "Atsey" Etheridge), b. 13 Oct 1848, Hickory Co, MO, d. 13 Nov 1909; m. ***Leanna Murray***, b. 1 July 1853, d. 12 Dec 1924, of Lagrippe, Avery, MO; both bur Avery Cem.

Family of Marcus Monroe Breshears and Leanna Murray:

V6 4692. [10]1. **Mary Breshears**, b. 1872; m. ***Levi Benton Ihrig***, (s/o Mary Jane Breshears and George Nimrod Ihrig), b. 26 Nov 1869, MO

V6 4693. [11]1. Infant Ihrig, b. c?1895, died young

V6 4694. [11]2. Ogden Ihrig, b. _____, d. as young man

V6 4695. [11]3. Otis Ihrig, b. _____, drowned _____

V6 4696. [11]4. Prudence Ihrig, m. Loren Sibley. Ch: Gary

Ogden Sibley.

[V6]4697. [11]5. Ray Ihrig, b. _____, d. young

[V6]4698. [11]6. Wealthy Ihrig, m. Avery Flemming. Ch: Pauline; and Royce E. Flemming.

[V6]4699. [10]2. **Maude Breshears**, b. 1874, d. young

[V6]4700. [10]3. **Samuel Breshears**, b. 16 June 1877, d. young

[V6]4701. [10]4. **Arvilla Breshears**, (twin) b. 25 May 1880; m. ***Robert Marvin Henderson***, b. 20 Sept 1881

[V6]4702. [11]1. Guy Henderson, b. _____; m. **Wilma Fern Breshears**, (d/o Robert E. Lee Breshears and Mary Frances "Fannie" Holley)b. 13 Oct 1904, Benton Co, MO, d. Nov 1984

[V6]4703. [12]1. Robert Milford "Bob" Henderson, b. 17 Sept 1927; d. 1 Dec 1995; m. Edna _____. Ch: _____ Henderson

[V6]4704. [11]2. Retta Henderson, m. Guy Henderson. Ch: Clyde; Fern; and Bessie Henderson.

[V6]4705. [11]3. Eula Faye Henderson, b. 16 March 1909, Avery, MO, d. 4 Aug 1999, Savoy, Illinois

[V6]4706. [11]4. Bessie Henderson, b. _____

[V6]4707. [10]5. **Elbert Breshears**, (twin) b. 25 May 1880; m. ***Mollie Forehand***,

[V6]4708. [11]1. **Emil Breshears**,

[V6]4709. [11]2. **Bert Breshears**,

[V6]4710. [10]6. **Archie Breshears**, b. 19 Jan 1884

[V6]4711. [10]7. **Minnie Breshears**, b. Jan 1888; m. ***William Ketchum***

[V6]4712. [10]8. **Bertchie Breshears**, b. Aug 1890; m. ***Louise Miller***,

[V6]4713. [11]1. **Zelma Breshears**, m. c1934, ***Morris Holley***, b. 1909

[V6]4714. [11]2. **Mabel Breshears**, m. ***Monroe Smith***,

[V6]4715. [11]3. **Ellen Breshears**, (twin to Helen); m. ***Everett Thompson***,

[V6]4716. [11]4. **Helen Breshears**, (twin to Ellen); m. ***Victor Parsons***,

41. ATSEY ADALINE BRESHEARS and Joel Ihrig

v6 3234. 9 14. **Atsey Adaline Breshears**, (d/o Henry Breshears Jr and Atsa "Atsey" Etheridge), b. 20 Aug 1850 (or 54), Hickory Co, MO, d. 24 May 1910, Benton Co, MO; m. Jan 1870, ***Joel Ihrig***, (s/o Peter Ihrig and Elizabeth Ellen "Elizzie" Tonbaugh), b. 8 March 1858, MO, d. 2 Jan 1891, Benton Co, MO. Both Atsey and Joel bur Jones Dem, near Avery, Benton Co, MO.

Family of Atsey Alaline Breshears and Joel Ihrig:

V6 4717. 10 1. C.E. Ihrig, b. 1871

V6 4718. 10 2. Safrona Ihrig, b. c1872; m.1. Sam Blackwell, m.2. Silvester Hess (or Tess, or Gess) Rogers

V6 4719. 11 1. Adam Blackwell,

V6 4720. 11 2. Noah Rogers, drowned when he was 15 years old

V6 4721. 10 2. Nancy Ellen "Ellie" Ihrig, b. c1873; m. James William Miller, (s/o Henry W. Miller and Martha Ellen Ruth)

V6 4722. 11 1. Carrie Miller, d. young; m. ______ Day

V6 4723. 11 2. Silvia Miller

V6 4724. 11 3. Atsy Miller; m. Walter Bailey

V6 4725. 10 3. Sarah Catherine Ihrig, b. c1875; m. Ed J. Davis, brother of John Davis, husband of her sister, Nora.

V6 4726. 11 1. Floy Davis, b. Benton Co, MO, d. 3 May 1964; m. ***Rona Francis Breshears**, (s/o Riley Harrison Breshears and Nellie Irene Crabtree). See his listing.

V6 4727. 11 2. Rolla Davis, m. Stella Nation

V6 4728. 11 3. Leo Davis, d. c1966; m. Edna Davis,

V6 4729. 11 4. Celia Davis, m. Jim H. Paine. Ch: Eleanor Paine.

[V6]4730. [11]5. Thelma Davis, m. Dillon Tipton
[V6]4731. [11]6. Vivian Davis, d. c1952
[V6]4732. [11]7. Bob Huston Davis; m.1. ______, m.2. ______,
[V6]4733. [11]8. Lynn Davis, m.1. ______, m.2. ______,
[V6]4734. [11]9. Edna Davis, m. Wilbur Nation. Ch: Bernard Nation.
[V6]4735. [10]4. Nora Arabella "Dory" Ihrig, b. c1877; m. John Davis, brother of Ed J. Davis, husband of her sister, Sarah.
[V6]4736. [11]1. Edith Davis,
[V6]4737. [11]2. Relda Davis, m. Howard C. Burns
[V6]4738. [11]3. Ira Davis,
[V6]4739. [11]4. Harry Davis,
[V6]4740. [11]5. Gladys Davis, m. ______,
[V6]4741. [10]5. Laura V. Ihrig, b. c1880, d. young
[V6]4742. [10]6. Harry Eathen Ihrig, b. April 1883, d. 1961; m. Hettie Murray,
[V6]4743. [11]1. Dorothy Ihrig,
[V6]4744. [11]2. Hazel Ihrig,
[V6]4745. [11]3. Kent Ihrig,
[V6]4746. [11]4. Cotton Ihrig,
[V6]4747. [10]7. Carl Valentine Ihrig, b. c?1889, d. young
[V6]4748. [10]8. Joel Oliver "Ollie" Ihrig, b. 11 May 1891, d. 28 Dec 1915; m. Anna Roth, b. 27 Jan 1894
[V6]4749. [11]1. Marian L. Ihrig, m. Ernest M. Thacker. Ch: Joel Ernest; Alice Lorelie; and Elizabeth Thacker.
[V6]4750. [11]2. Clinton Joel Ihrig, m. Mae Marie Farris. Ch: David Clinton; and Gail Ann Ihrig.
[V6]4751. [11]3. Olive LeVeda Ihrig, b. 19 July 1928

42. WILLIAM CARROLL (GREEN) BRESHEARS and Mary Orleana Rice

[v6]3235. [9]15. William Carroll Green, b. 15 Oct 1825, VA, d. 16 Nov 1861, MO. While a wagon train was heading west, probably in 1838, a couple named Green died, leaving an orphan, William Carroll Green. Henry and Atsey simply took him in and raised him; he used Breshears as his last name.

William Carroll (Green) Breshears, m. 1 March 1843, in Benton Co, MO, ***Mary Orleana Rice***, b. 6 Aug 1825, d. 18 Jan 1911. He died of camp dysentery while serving in the Civil War. Descendants from widow's pension records.

Family of William Carroll Breshears and Mary Orleana Rice:

[V6]4801. [10]1. **Martha Jane Breshears**, b. 28 Sept 1845

[V6]4802. [10]2. **Susanna Breshears**, b. 27 Feb 1847

[V6]4803. [10]3. **Margaret "Peggy" Breshears**, b. 2 Aug 1849; d. 18 Nov 1873; m. ***Daniel R. Southard***

[V6]4804. [10]4. **John Franklin Breshears**, b. 29 Feb 1852, d. young

[V6]4805. [10]5. ***Isaac David "Ike" Breshears**, b. Benton Co, MO, 29 Aug 1854; m. 15 Sept 1878, in Benton Co, MO, ***Elva Jane Breshears***, (d/o James Breshears and Sarah Henderson),

[V6]4806. [10]6. ***William Carroll Breshears** Jr, b. 17 Oct 1857, d. 27 Aug 1919; m. ***Victoria E. Cox***,

[V6]4807. [10]7. **Francis Marion Breshears**, b. 13 June 1860; m.1. ***Mary Gaston***, (d/o Silas Gaston and Nancy Ellen Breshears, of the Alexander Brashears and Mary Jane Harper line), d. at age 17 in childbirth; m.2. ***Margaret*** _____. Some of the birthdates in the following list are too close together; errors, but where?

[V6]4808. [11]1. **William Breshears**, b. 8 May 1881

[V6]4809. [11]2. **Bessie V. Breshears**, b. July 1881

[V6]4810. [11]3. **Gracie I. Breshears**, b. Dec 1882

[V6]4811. [11]4. **Rellia Breshears**, b. March 1883

[V6]4812. [11]5. **Marion Breshears**, b. May 1884

[V6]4813. [11]6. **Martha Breshears**, b. Nov 1885

[V6]4814. [11]7. **John Breshears**, b. June 1887

[V6]4815. [11]8. **Charles Breshears**, b. Feb 1894

[V6]4816. [11]9. **Major Breshears**, b. March 1896

[V6]4817. [11]10. **Margaret Breshears**, b. Oct 1897

[V6]4818. [11]11. **Lulia M. Breshears**, b. Sept 1898

Isaac David "Ike" Breshears and Elva Jane Breshears

v6 4805. [10]5. **Isaac David "Ike" Breshears**, (s/o William Carroll Green Breshears and Mary Orleana Rice), b. Benton Co, MO, 29 Aug 1854, says Pension application and family Bible (cem stone shows I.D. Breshears, b. 28 Aug 1853), d. 25 June 1937, Hickory Co, MO, bur Spring Branch Cem, Avery, MO; m. 15 Sept 1878, in Benton Co, MO, ***Elva Jane Breshears***, (d/o James Breshears and Sarah Henderson), b. 26 Jan 1862, Benton Co, MO, d. there, 20 March 1915.

Family of Isaac David Breshears and Elva Jane Breshears:

V6 4819. [11]1. **Etta Frances Breshears**, b. 29 Oct 1879, Benton Co, MO, d. 16 Oct 1956, Hickory Co, MO; m. ***Gouldsberry Breshears**, (s/o Andrew Jackson Breshear and Mary Jane Parsley). See his listing for their children.

V6 4820. [11]2. **Emma V. Breshears**, b. 30 Aug 1881, Hickory Co, MO, d. 15 Sept 1881, Benton Co, MO, bur Pippin Cem, but moved to Spring Branch Cem, Avery, MO

V6 4821. [11]3. **John Harrison Breshears**, b. 1884, Benton Co, MO, d. there, 1961; m.1. ***Emma Demitz***; m.2. ***Sarah Hooper***; m.3. ***Myrtle Button***, b..25 Dec 1880, Benton Co, MO, d. 13 April 1911, MO, d/o John Button and Margaret Cox

Family of John Harrison Breshears and Emma Demitz:

V6 4822. [12]1. **Olan Breshears**, b. 16 May 1910, MO, d. 24 April 1937, MO

V6 4823. [12]2. **John Howard Breshears**, b. 10 Dec 1912, MO, d. 20 July 1944, in Europe, WW II casualty

V6 4824. [12]3. **Ruben Breshears**, b. 19 June 1915, MO, d. _____ MO; m. ***Elma Gaston***, b. 14 Jan 1917, Benton Co, MO

V6 4825. [12]4. **Rosalie Breshears**, b. & d. 29 Jan 1918

V6 4826. [12]5. **Opal Breshears**, b. MO; m. ***Herbert R. Page***, b. 20 Oct 1890, d. 29 June 1971, Hickory Co,

MO

[V6]4827. [12]6. **Seth Breshears**, m. ***Blanche Walker***,

[V6]4828. [12]7. **Phena Breshears**, m. 1939, ***Everett Turpin***, b. 1910, d. 19 Oct 2000, Cox Med Center, Springfield, MO. Ch: Larry; Lavonne; and Deborah Turpin

Family of John Harrison Breshears and Sarah Hooper:

[V6]4829. [12]8. **Duane Breshears**,

[V6]4830. [11]4. **Ottie Daniel Breshears**, b. 9 July 1891, Benton Co, MO, d. 1961, MO; m. ***Jessie Thomas Brown***, b. 29 June 1895, Benton Co, MO, d. after 1970, Hickory Co, MO, both bur Spring Branch Cem, Avery, MO

[V6]4831. [12]1. **Lillie Frances Breshears**, b. 20 Dec 1914, d. 17 Dec 1934

[V6]4832. [12]2. **Harold Eugene Breshears**, b. 3 July 1918, Benton Co, MO, d. there, 14 April 1949; m. 4 March 1939, ***Daisy Marie Hood***, b. 31 Oct 1920, d. 10 April 1974, Hickory Co, MO

[V6]4833. [12]3. **Warren G. Breshears**, b. 4 Nov 1920, d. 1970s, Hickory Co, MO, bur Breshears Cem, Avery, Hickory Co, MO; m.1. ______ (1 ch); m.2. ***Ruth Ann Gaston***, (7 ch) (Thanks to Elaine Breshears <ebresh@aol.com> for additional data.

[V6]4834. [13]1. **James Kelly Breshears**, believed living in Oskaloosa, LA

[V6]4835. [13]2. **Warren Kelly Breshears**,

[V6]4836. [13]3. **Frankie Leon Breshears**,

[V6]4837. [13]4. **Lily Carol Breshears**, m. ______ ***Beals,***

[V6]4838. [13]5. **Neal Boyce Breshears**,

[V6]4839. [13]6. **Elaine Breshears**,

[V6]4840. [13]7. **Anita Ruth Breshears**, m. ______ ***Gunn,***

[V6]4841. [13]8. **Norman Lee Breshears**, lives 2004 at Halfmoon Bay, CA

[V6]4842. [12]4. **Blondia Belle Breshears**, m. ***Wilbur Robinett***,

[V6]4843. [12]5. **Elva Jane "Bobby" Breshears**, m. ***Eugene Shields***,

V64844. 126. **Mary Lou Breshears**, m. ***Lloyd Wesver***,
V64845. 127. **Norvel James Breshears**, b. 21 Feb 1916, Benton Co, MO; m.1. ***Lucie Ellen Paxton***, (mother of the child), b. 29 Nov 1915, Hickory Co, MO; m.2. 12 April 1936, in Wheatland, Hickory Co, MO, ***Vivial Tuck***,
V64846. 131. **Orene Breshears**; m. ***Larry Paul Wood***. S/o George Wood and Helen Dietz. Ch: Travis Morgan; Ginger Lee; and James Lewis Wood
V64847. 115. **Leerhoi? Breshears**, b. 15 Aug 1894, d. 25 Aug 1894, age 10 days

William Carroll Breshears Jr and Victoria E. Cox

v64806. 106. **William Carroll Breshears Jr**, (s/o William Carroll Green Breshears and Mary Orleana Rice), b. 17 Oct 1857, d. 27 Aug 1919; m. ***Victoria E. Cox***, b. 25 June 1859, d. 8 Nov 1939. While Wm Carroll Breshears was married to Victoria, he carried on a long love affair that lasted over ten years with Martha Belle Button, b. 2 May 1861, Sedalia, MO, d. 1898, Fairfield, MO, d/o Hezekiah Button and Mary Bybee. They would meet in the woods; Wm and Martha had two children: Ida Button and Floyd Button.

Family of William Carroll Breshears Jr and Victoria E. Cox:
V64848. 11X?. **Julius "Bud" Breshears**,
V64849. 11Y?. **Melissa Emmeline Breshears**, probably b. c1880-82; m. 5 Aug 1897, ***George Washington Henderson***,. They had children: Leslie; Raymond; Mamie; Julius; Otis; Roy; Oral; George Orvis; Oris; and Fratie Ellen Henderson (m. ****Ray Breshears***, s/o Eli Breshears and Lucinda Murray. See his listing.)
V64850. 111. **Arthur Breshears**, b. 1883, d. c1970; m. ***Effie Powell***, d/o William Powell and Atsey Breshears.
V64851. 121. **Eva Breshears**,
V64852. 122. **Billie Breshears**,
V64853. 123. **Ellis Breshears**,

V6 4854. [12]4. **Ila Breshears**,

V6 4855. [12]5. **Leona Breshears**,

V6 4856. [12]6. **Elvin Breshears**,

V6 4857. [12]7. **Irene Breshears**,

V6 4858. [12]8. **Louis Breshears**,

V6 4859. [11]2. **Ollie Breshears**, b. 22 Feb 1885, d. infancy, 1885

Figure 81: Bart Shinn's planting, 1913. Photo from Bill Brooks

V6 4860. [11]3. **Bertha E. Breshears**, b. April 1887, d. 19 May 1913; m. ***A.B. "Bart" Shinn***, b. 1883, d. c1957. They had ch: Retha; Lena; and Julia Shinn. When Bertha died in 1913, the whole clan showed up to do Bart's planting.

V6 4861. [11]4. **Edith L. Breshears**, b. Nov 1889, d. 1985; m. ***Walter Shinn***, b. 1888, d. 1967. They had ch: Basil; Boyd; Geneva; Gladys; Howard; and Hubert Shinn.

V6 4862. [11]5. **Delmer Harvey Breshears**, b. Feb 1891; m. ***Lizzie Foster***, in son Rolla's Obituary, father is called Harvey D. Breshears.

V6 4863. [12]1. **Rolla Ervin Breshears**, b. 27 July 1920, Benton Co, MO, (79 in 2000), d. 16 April 2000(see obit below); m. 10 July 1957, ***June Voyles***, b.?, d. 2 May 1992

[V6]4864. [13]1. **Rolla Wayne Breshears**, of Macks Creek, MO

[V6]4865. [13]2. **Larry Breshears**, of Wichita, KS

[V6]4866. [13]3. **Karla Breshears**, m. ______ ***Tennison***, of Clinton, MO

[V6]4867. [12]2. **Russell Breshears**, d. before April, 2000

[V6]4868. [12]3. **Leland Breshears**, of Weaubleau, MO

[V6]4869. [12]4. **Elmer Neal Breshears**, d. before April, 2000

[V6]4870. [12]5. **Richard Breshears**, of Collins, MO

[V6]4871. [11]6. **Andrew C. Breshears**, b. Feb 1893, d. c1950; m. ***Florence Tuck***, b. c1980

[V6]4872. [12]1. **Virgil Breshears**,

[V6]4873. [12]2. **Velma Breshears**,

[V6]4874. [12]3. **W.A. Breshears**,

[V6]4875. [12]4. ??**Virgie Breshears**,

[V6]4876. [11]7. **Elsie A. Breshears**, b. May 1895; m. ***Wilbur Tipton***,. Ch: Noel; Kenneth; and Idella Tipton.

Obituary: **Rolla Ervin Breshears**, 79, Wichita, Kan., formerly of Weaubleau, died Sunday, April 16, 2000, in Medicalodge Healthcare of Wichita. The son of Harvey D. and Lizzie Foster Breshears, he was born in Benton County near Iconium July 27, 1920. He married June Voyles on July 10, 1957, and she preceded him in death May 2, 1992. A resident of Wichita, Kan., for the past 10 years, he was a lifelong resident of the Weaubleau area. He was a retired farmer. He was also preceded in death by two brothers, Elmer Neal Breshears and Russell Breshears. Survivors include three children, Rolla Wayne Breshears of Macks Creek, Larry Breshears of Wichita, Kan., and Karla Tennison of Clinton; two brothers, Richard Breshears of Collins and Leland Breshears of Weaubleau; four grandchildren and two great-grandchildren. Services were Tuesday, April 18, in Murray Chapel, Humansville, with the Rev. Mike Brixey officiating. Pallbearers were Larry Breshears, Jim Tennison, Dewayne Tennison, Jeff Sutton, Mark Fox and Leland Breshears Jr. Interment was in Humansville Cemetery. Memorial contributions may be made to the National Kidney Foundation. (Thanks to Diana Cooper, (diana536074 @yahoo.com)

43. JAMES BRASHEARS and THREE BROTHERS of Missouri:

Some researchers (and a family tradition among descendants of Middleton Brashears (the Younger) and Nathan Turner Brashears) have asserted that Middleton Brashears (the Younger), Nathan Turner Brashears, and Alexander Brashears were brothers, possibly sons of ?James Brashears, who was probably s/o Middleton Brashears (the Elder), b. c1732, MD, s/o Basil Brashears, b. 1714, and Anne Belt. They lived near each other, usually near John Brashears, b. 1767, and Thomas Brashers, b. c1771, who were said to be brothers of ?James Brashears. Middleton (the Younger) named sons John and Nathan. Nathan has grandsons named Middleton and Alexander. I tend to accept that they were siblings, probably sons of ?James Brashears. I think (no firm documentation) they are descendants of Basil Brashears and Anne Belt.

The spelling of the surname in this branch of the family is rather more erratic than in most branches. About half the records dealing with Basil Brashear(s) give his surname with an "s"; the other half do not. Middleton (the Elder)'s surname is fairly consistently spelled with the "s." The family in Missouri is Brashears, Breshears, Beshears, and occasionally something else.

James Turney Bushiers and Thomas C. Bushiers were on a July 1791 list of people who owed the estate of Edwin Hickman money for ferriages and store accounts (Davidson Co, Territory of the U.S. South of the Ohio River, Will Bk 1, pp.223-228). These could be (no proof) ?James Brashears and his brother, Thomas, who lived in 1820 with/near Basil, John, Berry, and Middleton (the Younger), in White Co, TN.

[V6]**6.** [7]x. ?**James ?Turney Brashears**, (probably a s/o Middleton Brashears, the Elder, and apparently a brother of Basil Brashear Sr, b. c1765, John Breshears Sr, b. c1767, and Henry Breshears Sr, b. c1769); m. ***Mary Jane Turner***.

The story in one branch of the family is that the father, James Brashears, died when Nathan Turner Brashears was a teen-ager (c1815-20, possibly shot in Maury Co, TN), the mother re-married before the 1820 census, but Nathan could not get along with the step-father; so he left home at a very early age.

James's Family

James Brashears and Mary Jane Turner were probably the parents of:

[V6]4931. [8]1. ***Middleton Brashears (the Younger)**, b. SC, 1794-5 (56 in 1850); m. ***Jane*** ____, b. 1792-94. (1820 White Co, TN; 1830 Lawrence Co, TN, p.295, line 11: 110001-110001); they moved c1833-34 to Benton Co, Missouri. Many of their descendants spell the surname "Beshears."

[V6]4932. [8]2. ***Nathan Turner Breshears**, b. 4 April 1797, SC or GA, d. 24 Feb 1884, Dallas Co, MO; m.1. 26 Aug 1819, in Lawrence Co, TN, ***Elizabeth Catherine Keele***, b. 21 Nov 1800, Bedford Co, TN, d. 10 Aug 1858; m.2. ***Matilda Decker***, m.3. 21 March 1872, in Dallas Co, MO, ***Charity Lamar***. Nathan is in the census 1830 Lawrence Co, TN, p. 295, line 7: 110001-10001); he moved in 1833/34 with Middleton (the Younger) and Alexander to Benton Co, Missouri.

[V6]4933. [8]3. **James Brashears [Jr]**, b. [1805]; included in a FHL chart; no documentation offered.

The documents we do have: James Brashers has 12 acres on the 1836 Tax Lists, Lawrence Co, TN, District #7 (bordering Wayne Co and just north of Dist 6 and the middle of the west boundary of Lawrence County);

James Brashears m. ***Delila Vincent***; Lawrence Co, TN, marriage License issued 25 July 1837 by Charles Hicks, Clerk. Endorsed:

"Solemnized July the 24th day A.D. 1837, by S. Carrell, J.P."

James G. Bashiears, age 30-40 is in the 1840 census, Lawrence Co, TN, p.128.

No further information.

V6 4934. 84. ***Alexander Brashears**, b. 20 April 1807, SC, m. ***Margaret "Peggy" Breshears***, b. 15 Feb 1811, SC, d/o Henry Brashears/Breshears Sr and Eleanor (Harden?). Alex and Margaret moved to MO, c1833/34. They were first cousins, which would mean that Alexander's father was a brother to Henry Breshears Sr. Roy Colbert maintained that Alexander was a cousin of Henry Breshears Jr, Margaret's brother, near whom they lived in Benton Co, MO.

V6 4935. 85. **Rebecca Brashears**, b. TN, c1814 (46 in 1860, Pulaski Co, AR); m. 17 Aug 1831, ****Andrew "Drury" "Drew" Boshears***, b. c1813, TN (47 in 1860, Pulaski Co, AR, Owen twp, family #155), s/o Berry Brashears/ Boshears Sr and wife Anna. Lawrence Co, TN marriage Bond, 5 Aug 1831; bondsmen: Drury (X) Brashers and /signed/Alf (or Alx) Besher (See the reproduction in Chapter 2). Not surprisingly, Rebecca and Drew named a son Alexander. See their listing in "Berry Boshears of Arkansas."

V6 4912. 86. **Susannah Brashears**, b. c1805, SC; m. 14 Feb 1828, Lawrence Co, TN, ***William Scags*** (Alexander Beshers signed the marriage bond, spelled Brashers by the clerk; this marriage record was found recently among loose papers in Lawrence Co, TN); m.2. **Preston Green**. Susannah is without a spouse in 1840, then with Preston Green in 1850. In 1870 and 1880 the Green family is in Benton Co, AR. (Data from Katherine Carruthers <sharkay@swbell.net>)

V6 4913. 91. James M. (?Middleton?) Scags, step-son to Preston Green in 1850, Lawrence Co, TN; n.f.i.

V6 4914. 92. Sarah A. Scags, m. Coss or Cop or Cox Davis,

(per daughter Caroline's death certificate; very difficult to decipher letters of first name)

[V6]4915. [10]1. Caroline Davis, b. 1855, Carter Co, MO; m. Philander Rose.

[V6]4916. [9]3. Elvira Scags, (youngest dau), b. 1872, d. 20 July 1922, AR; m. Cincinnatus Berry Crook, b. 28 Nov 1814, TN, d. after 1880, AR, s/o David Crook and Rebecca Adkins. The C.B. Crook family moved c1860 to Benton Co, in NW Arkansas. Data from Linda Brown <elldabee@prodigy.net> of Antioch, CA.

[V6]4917. [10]1. Martha J. Crook, b. 6 May 1849 in TN, d. 13 May 1926; m. William W. Kuykendall, b. 06 Jan 1851 in TX, d. 24 May 1922

[V6]4918. [10]2. Joshua Crook, b. c1855 in MO, d. c1916 in prison?

[V6]4919. [10]3. Thomas Jefferson Crook, b. 13 May 1856 in MO, d. 23 Dec 1944 in Los Angeles, Los Angeles Co, CA; m. c1872, Lula B.______ ,

[V6]4920. [10]4. Susan Rebecca Crook, b. 9 Dec 1860 in Bentonville, Benton Co, AR, d. 16 Feb 1951 in Fairland, Ottawa Co, OK; m. William Franklin Blythe, b. 19 Feb 1858 in AR, d. 18 Aug 1922 in Washington Co, AR

[V6]4921. [10]5. Mary Ellen Crook, b. 20 May 1863 in Washington Co, AR, d. 30 July 1922; m. 23 April 1879 in Sebastian Co, AR, Lemuel Moses Blythe/Holland, b. 11 Jan 1860 in Scott Co, AR, d. 27 July 1926 in AR

[V6]4922. [10]6. Francis Americus Crook, b. 1872 in Van Buren, AR; m. 5 May 1892 in Washington Co, AR, Mark Anderson

[V6]4923. [8]7. **Nancy Brashears**, b. c1812; m. 15 Feb 1831, in Lawrence Co, TN, ***William Davis*** (Alexander Beshers signed the marriage bond, spelled Brashers by the Clerk; record found recently among loose papers in Lawrence Co, TN). William

Davis (without a wife) is in the 1850 Census, Ripley Co, MO. (Data from Katherine Carruthers <sharkay@swbell.net>)

V64924. 91. Sarah Davis, (oldest dau)

V64925. 9x. Margaret Davis, (youngest dau)

44. MIDDLETON BRASHEARS (the Younger), and Jane _____

v67. 81. **Middleton Brashears** (the Younger), (possibly (unproven) s/o ?James Brashears and Mary Jane Turner), b. SC, c1794 (56 in 1850), d. MO, 1850-60; m. ***Jane*** ______, b. c1792-94, TN, d. after 1860, probably in MO.

We know very little about Middleton Brashears (the Younger). Born in SC, he followed the clan to White Co, TN, then to Lawrence Co, TN, then moved with his brothers to Missouri about 1833/34, where he is found in some censuses.

1820 Census of White County, TN (all p.369):
Middleton Bashers, age 16-25, b. 1795-1804,
wife, 16-25,
fem., 0-10.

His neighbors in White Co, TN (enumerated on same page) included Basil Brashears Sr, b. c1765, John Brashears Sr, b. c1767, Thomas Brashears, b. c1771, and Berry Brashears, b. 1790. Shortly after 1820, all of these men and their families moved to Lawrence Co, TN, where Henry Breshears Sr, b. c1769, already lived.

1829. Middleton Brashears has a note outstanding in the estate of Henry Brashears Sr, Lawrence Co, TN.

1830 Census of Lawrence Co, TN, p.295, line 11: (near Nathan and John)
Middleton Brashen 110001-110001 age 30-40, b. 1790-1800

Judging from places and birthdates of children, Middleton and Jane migrated to Benton Co, MO in c1834 (along with Alexander Brashears), then in the 1840s moved to Stoddard Co, MO.

Family of Middleton Brashears, (the Younger), and Jane (   ):
(ref: censuses, marriage records, data from the late Nellie Bly (Crain) Williams, gggd/o Middleton)

V6 4951. [9]1. **Catherine Brashears**, b. TN, c1820, indicated by 1820 Census, White Co, TN, d. ? (one report, unsubstantiated, says she d. 1851, IL, possibly at birth of her sixth child); m. 14 April 1844, Benton Co, MO, ***Henry T. Hayes***, b. 1817, TN, d. c1883, Ash Hill, Butler Co, MO.

For some reason, their children are in the household of Catherine's brother, Nathan Beshears, in 1860 (see below). Henry T. "Hayse," m.2. 8 March 1870, Butler Co, MO (Book B, p.101), ***Emily J. Beshears***, age 17, b. MO–apparently a different Emily Brashears from the wife of John Brashears, Catherine's brother.

V6 4952. [10]1. William Hayes, b. 1844, MO; m. 14 Feb 1864, Cape Girardeau, MO, Martha J. Pharris

V6 4953. [10]2. Elizabeth Hayes, b. 1845, MO; m. _____ Foster

V6 4954. [10]3. Mary Jane Hayes, b. Dec 1844, d. 13 Jan 1924, Bernie, Stoddard Co, MO; m. 2 July 1868, Union Co, IL, Franklin Farrell

V6 4955. [10]4. Rebecca Hayes, b. 1840, Stoddard Co, MO; m. John Andrew Jackson Ham

V6 4956. [10]5. Jacob Hayes, b. 1850; m. 2 Sept 1870, Butler Co, MO, Melissa Mires

V6 4957. [10]6. John Henry Hayes, b. 9 Aug 1851, Bernie, Stoddard Co, MO, d. 14 Sept 1924, Maldin, Dunklin Co, MO, bur Bernie, Stoddard Co, MO; m.1. 13 Nov 1874, Stoddard Co, MO, Margaret Bell Ham, d/o John Andrew Jackson Ham, m.2. 28 April 1890, Parthena Blades

V6 4958. [11]x. Sarah Elizabeth Hayes, b. 7 Oct 1880, Malden, Dunklin Co, MO, d. 4 June 1971, Lonoke, AR; m. 11 April 1909, (Stoddard Co, MO) Samuel Marshall Crain, b. 25 March 1851, Ewing, IL, d. 27 April 1936, Bernie, Stoddard Co, MO, bur Gregory Cem, s/o James Crain and

Lucinda Drummond

V64959. 12x. Nellie Bly Crain, b. 22 Nov 1912, Stoddard Co, MO; m.1. 11 July 1932, (Edwardsville, Madison Co, IL) Joseph Henry Davis; m.2. Ralph Kimball Livsey; m.3. Fred Williams.

V64960. 92. **Eliza Bashiers**, b. 1823, TN (indicated by 1830 Census, Lawrence Co, TN; in Middleton's hh in 1850)

V64961. 101. **Middleton Brashears, III**, b. MO, Sept 1850, (1/12 in 1850 in hh of Middleton and Jane Brashears, both of whom were 56 years old; probably a grandson? possibly [no documentation] s/o Eliza). N.f.i.

V64962. 93. ***John Beshears**, b. c1825, TN (indicated by 1830 Census, Lawrence Co, TN; 45 in 1870, Stoddard Co, MO; 74 in 1900 census, Stoddard Co, MO); m. 27 May 1849, Alexander Co, IL, ***Emily J. Skidmore***, b. TN, c1835 (35 in 1870), d. 1870-1880.

V64963. 94. **Jane Brashears**, b. 1828 (indicated by 1830 Census, Lawrence Co, TN), prob d. bef 1860; m. _____ ***Wall***. There are two Wall children in h/h of Nathan Brashears, in 1860, Stoddard Co, MO.

V64964. 101. Middleton Wall, b. MO, c1850 (10 in 1860, hh of Nathan Beshears, Jane's brother)

V64965. 102. Jane Wall, b. MO, c1853 (7 in 1860, hh of Nathan Beshears)

V64966. 95. (male), b. 1825-30 (indicated by 1830 Census, Lawrence Co, TN)

V64967. 96. **Nathan Beshears**, b. c1834, TN (per 1850 Census). Nathan was listed as "lame" and unmarried in 1860; yet he seems to be the care-giver of the family.

V64968. 97. **Sarah Beshears**, b. 1835, MO; m.1. ***John Gibson***, b. c1831, TN (young couple next door to Middleton's hh in 1850 Census); m.2. 1 Nov 1868, Randolph Co, AR, ***Thomas Jefferson Brashers***, b. c1817, TN, s/o Jacob Beshears Sr, s/o John Brashears Sr, b. 1767. Sarah apparently had two

Gibson children, who are listed as step-sons in Thomas J. Brasher's hh in 1870.

V[6]4969. [10]1. Martin J. Gibson, b. c1857, TN (13 in 1870)

V[6]4970. [10]2. William Gibson, b. c1863, AR (7 in 1870)

V[6]4971. [10]3. **Martha Beshears**, b. c1870, AR (3/12 in 1870)

V[6]4972. [9]8. **Mary Beshears**, b. 1837, MO (13 in 1850 Census)

<u>1850 US Census, Stoddard Co, MO, Liberty Twp</u>, 19 Oct, #535:

Middleton Bashiers,	56, b. SC c1794
Jane Bashiers,	56, b. TN
Nathen Bashiers,	17, b. TN c1833
Mary Bashiers,	13, b. MO c1837
Middleton Bashiers,	1/12, b. MO, Sept 1850
Eliza Bashiers,	27, b. TN c1823 (H/H #536); d/o Middleton and Jane
John Gibson,	19, b. TN c1831; hus/o Sarah (Brashears) Gibson, next entry
Sarah Gibson,	15, b. MO c1835; d/o Middleton and Jane, wife of John Gibson

<u>1860 US Census, Stoddard Co, MO, Liberty Twp</u>, #75:

Nathen Beshears	26, b. TN c1834 (lame)
William Hays,	18, b. MO c1842 -- Hayes = ch of Nathan' sister, Catherine Hayes
Elizabeth Hays,	16, b. MO c1844
Mary J. Hays,	14, b. MO c1846
Rebecca Hays,	11, b. MO c1849
Jacob Hays,	9, b. MO c1851
John Henry Hays,	8, b. MO c1852
Middleton Wall,	10, b. MO c1850 -- Wall = ch of Nathan's sister, Jane Wall
Jane Wall,	7, b. MO c1853
Jane Beshears,	68, b. TN c1792 (apparently widow of Middleton)

<u>1870 US Census, Randolph Co, AR</u>, #245, Current River Twp:

Thomas Beshears,	56, b. TN
Sarah	46, wife, should be 36, if same as 1850 Stoddard MO
Martin J. Gibson,	13, "step-son", b. TN
Wm. Gibson	7, "step-son", b. AR
Jane P. Law	103, (no relationship given; but probably mother of Thomas's 1st wife), b. TN c1767
Martha Beshears	3/12, "dau", b. AR

H/H #246: Thomas J. Gibson, 21, b. TN, and Mary Gibson, 27, b. TN

John Breshears
and Emily J. Skidmore

V6 4962. 93. **John Beshears**, (s/o Middleton and Jane Brashears), b. c1825, TN (45 in 1870, Stoddard Co, MO, #166-166; 74 in 1900 Stoddard); m. 27 May 1849, (Alexander Co, IL, "by Stephen James, acting J.P.") ***Emily J. Skidmore***, b. c1833, TN (35 in 1870, Stoddard), d. 1870-1880.

John Breshears was said to be a "Barge" man who worked on the Mississippi; that would explain how he met his wife in Illinois and had his first child there. This John Beshears may be the John T. Besheres who enlisted 31 Jan 1863 at West Plains, MO, in the Union Army.

There is considerable confusion about his wife. Emily is listed as wife of John Breshears in the 1870 US Census, Stoddard Co, MO (#166-166, Liberty Twp, Athens post office). On 8 March 1870, she or another Emley J. Beshears, age c17, m. Henry T. Hayes, age 50, in Butler Co, MO (Book B, p.101), but that Emily, b. MO, is only 17 years old in the 1870 census of Ash Hill, Poplar Bluff P.O., Butler Co, MO (p.3, census taken 3 Aug 1870).

In the 1880 US Census, John Beshares, 55, widower, laborer, b. TN, parents b. TN, is in Washington twp, Van Buren Co, p.452c, with daughter Manda, 12, b. MO.

John Breshears, 74, is father-in-law in hh of Cline Wilson and Catharine Beshears in 1900 US Census, Stoddard Co, MO.

Family of John Breshears and Emily J. Skidmore: based on data from Nellie Bly (Crain) Williams; 1830 Lawrence Co, TN US Census; 1840 Benton Co, MO; 1850, 1860 Stoddard Co, MO (#63, Liberty Twp; also in John's H/H in 1860: Louisa Hardin, 15, b. AR c1845); 1870 Stoddard Co, MO (#166-166, Liberty twp); 1900 Stoddard Co, MO; Marr. recds. Butler Co, MO:

V6 4973. 101. **Mary C. Beshears**, b. c1850, IL

V6 4974. 102. **Catherine Beshears**, b. Sept 1853, MO (17 in 1870, Stoddard); m.1. 2 Jan 1876, (Butler Co, MO), ***Charley Roberson***, b. Feb 1860, AR; m.2. ***Cline Wilson***. In Cline and Catherine Wilson's hh in 1900, are fa-in-law, John Beshears, 74; Hannah Roberson, b. Oct 1881, AR, step-dau;

William H. Roberson, b. Oct 1884, MO, step-son; Maranda Beshears, b. March 1887, MO, niece; and James H. Beshears, b. Sept 1884, MO, nephew, these last two probably children of Catherine's brother, Nathan Beshears, and Nancy Taylor.

V6 4975. 11 1. Hannah Roberson, b. Oct 1881, AR

V6 4976. 11 2. William H. Roberson, b. Oct 1884, MO

V6 4977. 10 3. **Nathan Beshears**, b. c1856, MO (12 in 1870, Stoddard), d. c1890-1900; m. 16 July 1876, (Butler Co, MO), ***Nancy E. Taylor***. Undocumented children: (nephew and niece in hh of Nathan's sister, Catherine Wilson, in 1900 US Census)

V6 4978. 11 1. **James H. Beshears,** b. Sept 1884, MO

V6 4979. 11 2. **Maranda Beshears,** b. March 1887, MO

V6 4980. 10 4. **(?James) Ahab Beshears**, b. c1860, AR (4/12 in 1860 Stoddard; not in 1870 US Census)

V6 4981. 10 5. **Amanda B. Beshears**, b. Aug 1869, Stoddard Co, MO, (2 in 1870, Stoddard; 12 in 1880); m.1. 14 June 1883 (at Bernie, Stoddard Co, MO), ***R. Winfield Scott Moody***, b. 22 May 1861, Dunklin, MO, d. 16 April 1889, bur Bernie, Stoddard Co, MO, "27 yrs, 10 mo, 25 da," s/o Jasper Moody and Rosetta ____; m.2. 9 April 1890, (Butler Co, MO) ***George W. Harper***, b. Dec 1867, s/o Don Harper and Lucinda ____.

V6 4982. 11 1. John Isaac Moody, b. 15 Aug 1884, Stoddard Co, MO

V6 4983. 11 2. Genetta Brown, b. Jan 1897 (adopted)

45. NATHAN TURNER BRESHEARS and Elizabeth Catherine Keele

[v6]**8.** [8]2. **Nathan Turner Breshears**, (probably s/o ?James Brashears and Mary Jane Turner), b. 4 April 1797, SC, d. 24 Feb 1884, Dallas Co, MO, bur Wollard Cem there and has a stone; m.1. 26 Aug 1819, in Lawrence Co, TN, ***Elizabeth Catherine Keele***, b. 21 Nov 1800, Bedford Co, TN, d. 10 Aug 1858, bur Wollard Cem, Dallas Co, MO, beside her husband. They had seven children.

Nathan Turner Breshears m.2. c1859/60, ***Matilda Kelly Decker***, b. 1811, KY, d. 4 Oct 1871; m.3. 21 March 1872, "at home of J. Breshears," Dallas Co, MO, ***Charity Lamar***, b. 1814, NC. Nathan had no children by his second and third wives, and no burial data for them has been discovered.

Some family researchers have listed Nathan Turner Breshears as a son of Henry Brashears/Breshears Sr, b. 1769, North Carolina, d. 1828, Lawrence Co, TN, but no such person appears in any of the estate records of Henry Breshears, which are extant. He belonged to someone else.

A family tradition among his descendants says he was a nephew of Henry Brashears/Breshears Sr. They say he was a son of a brother of Henry who d. young; the mother re-married, and Nathan Turner couldn't get along with the step-father, so left as an early teen-ager.

Living so near John and Middleton Brashears in 1830, and moving to Missouri at the same time as Alexander and Middleton would suggest close ties with them, rather than the Henry Breshears Sr family. Some ancestral files in FHL, Salt Lake City, list him without documentation as a son of James Breshears and Jane Turner. His middle name would make sense of that.

The first record I have of Nathan Turner Brashears/ Breshears is the

1830 US Census of Lawrence Co, TN (Brashen = copyist's error for Brasher)
p.292: Sam'l Brasher: 00001-00011 =20-30, b.1800-10; Lawrence Co, TN,

Minutes Book, 1828-1834, p.225: State vs. Saml Brazier - scire facias, 7 Oct 1830. Scire Facias is an order to appear and show cause why some judgment against one should not be exercised. This Samuel Brasher was s/o Allen Sterrett Brasher, of Shelby Co, AL

p.293 Jesse Brashears 100001-22101 age 30-40, b. 1790-1800
p.294, #10 Henry Brashen 00001-10001 age 20-30, b. 1800-10
p.294, #11 Paul Brashen 10001-10001 age 20-30, b. 1800-10
p.294, #12 John Brashen 120001-21001 age 30-40, b. 1790-1800
p.294, #13 William Brashen 130001-001001 age 30-40, b. 1790-1800
p.294, #16 Henry Brashen 21001-1000100001 age 20-30, b. 1800-10; elderly fem., age 70-80, b. 1750-60!?
p.295, #3 John Brashears 0011000101-1100001 the old man 70-80, b. 1750-60; young man, 50-60, b. 1770-80
p.295, #7 Nathan Brasher 110001-10001 age 30-40, b. 1790-1800; (Nathan Turner Breshears, b. SC, 4 April 1797, d. 24 Feb 1884, m. 26 Aug 1819, Elizabeth Catherine Keele,)
p.295, #11 Middleton Brashen 110001-110001 age 30-40, b. 1790-1800

Nathan Turner Brashears is <u>not</u> in either the 1826 nor 1836 tax lists of Lawrence Co, TN; he was a bit young for the first (no property), had moved away before the second. Nathan moved to Benton Co, MO, 1833/34 and was in the 1840 US Census there.

In July 1849, Nathan Turner Breshears purchased land on the Niangua River, about 8 miles south of Buffalo, Dallas Co, MO, and moved there, according to Leni Howe; this land stayed in the family until 1952, when James Henry Howe, son-in-law of Nathaniel John Breshears, sold it and moved to Buffalo. See also article in *Dallas Co, MO, History*, which says that Nathan and Elizabeth had a no name infant, b. before 1820.

<u>Family of Nathan Turner Breshears and Elizabeth Catherine Keele</u>: (Sources: Rhonda S. Hunt, 5527 J.J. Hwy, Walnut Grove, MO 65770; Walter Paul Breshears, Box 769, Alturas, CA 96101; Mrs. Leni E. Howe, HC 85, Box 291-B6, Buffalo, MO 65622)

V6 5031. 9 1. no name **Breshears**, b. & d. bef 1820

V6 5032. 9 2. **Sidney Elizabeth Breshears**, b. 6 March or 23 May 1822, Lawrence Co, TN, d. c1897, Dallas Co, MO; m. c1838-39, ***Aaron D. McDaniel***, b. 1817, OH (partial source: FHL). Aaron and Sidney McDaniel and an infant daughter are living in Nathan Turner Breshears' household in 1840, Benton Co,

MO. Sidney may have m.2. ***William Calvin Greene***.

V6 5033. 10 1. Nancy Elizabeth McDaniel, b. 1839; m. Joseph McDonald,

V6 5034. 10 2. Benjamin McDaniel, b. 1845

V6 5035. 10 3. Nathan Betson McDaniel, b. 1849; m.1. Permelia Gann, m.2. Mary Francis Silkey,

V6 5036. 10 4. Rachel Ann McDaniel, b. 1850; m. William N. Haston,

V6 5037. 10 5. Aaron Frank McDaniel, b. 8 April 1851, d. 10 Sept 1905; m.1. Lucy Self, m.2. Missouri Routh,

V6 5038. 10 6. Sydney E. McDaniel, b. 1857; m. Jeremiah Haston Jr,

V6 5039. 10 7. Margaret McDaniel, b. 1859; m.1. George Mathis, m.2. ______ Greene,

V6 5040. 9 3. ***John K. Robert Breshears**, b. 1 March 1825, Lawrence Co, TN, d. 10 Jan 1905, bur Wollard Cem, Dallas Co, MO; m.1. 21 Oct 1846, in Benton Co, MO, ***Lucretia Wright***, b. 1830, NC, d. c1857 (3 ch); m.2. ***Mrs. Comfort Trayser***, d. 1868 (1 ch); m.3. ***Mary Delila Barclay***, b. 22 March 1839, MO, d. 24 Feb 1915 (7 ch), d/o Derret H. Barclay and Lucretia Davidson.

V6 5041. 9 4. ***James Keele Breshears**, b. 23 June 1829, Lawrence Co, TN (20 in 1850, Dallas Co, MO), d. 17 Jan 1887; m. 8 June 1851, ***Mary Ann "Molly" McDonald***, b. 13 June 1837, Bedford Co, TN, d. 15 Dec 1918, d/o Zadock W. McDonald and Manerva Cavin.

V6 5042. 9 5. **Andrew Jackson Breshears**, b. 19 Aug 1833, Lawrence Co, TN (17 in 1850, Dallas Co, MO), d. 3 Aug 1856, bur Wollard Cem, Dallas Co, MO.

V6 5043. 9 6. ***Calvin Breshears**, b. 22 May 1835, Benton Co, MO (15 in 1850, Dallas Co, MO), d. 23 June 1909, Dallas Co, MO, bur Wollard Cem; m.1. ***Missouri Jane Davison***, b. 1 April 1843, d. 25 July 1873; m.2. 22 Jan 1874, in Dallas Co, MO, ***Malissa Catherine Silkey***,

V6 5044. 9 7. **William Madison Breshears**, b. 17 March 1839,

Benton Co, MO (11 in 1850, Dallas Co, MO), d. 8 Aug 1856, Dallas Co, MO, bur Wollard Cem. Note that two of the brothers died within 5 days of each other in Aug 1856; there was an epidemic of typhoid fever.

John K. Robert Breshears and his Three Wives

[v6]5040. [9]3. ***John K. Robert Breshears**, (s/o Nathan Turner Brashears and Elizabeth Catherine Keele), b. 1 March 1825, Lawrence Co, TN, d. 10 Jan 1905, bur Wollard Cem, Dallas Co, MO; m.1. 21 Oct 1846, in Benton Co, MO, ***Lucretia Wright***, b. 1830, NC, d. c1857 (3 ch); m.2. apparently in TN, Mrs. ***Comfort Trayser***, d. 1868, according to John's military records (1 ch); m.3. bef 1870, in MO, ***Mary Delila Barclay***, b. 22 March 1839, MO, d. 24 Feb 1915 (7 ch), d/o Derret H. Barclay and Lucretia Davidson. John returned to Tennessee and lived there from 1852 to 1868, then moved again to Missouri.

Figure 82: John K. Robert Breshears and Mary Delila Barclay. Photo from Bill Brooks

In the 1850 US Census, Dallas Co, MO, p.336a, l.40, (very close to Nathan Turner Breshears) is John R. Breshears, wife "Lucetta," b. NC, and a dau, Elizabeth.

Family of John K. Robert Breshears and Lucretia Wright:

[V6]5045. [10]1. **Elizabeth Breshears**, b. 1849-50 (1/12 in 1850)
[V6]5046. [10]2. **Samuel (or Sampson) Breshears**, b. 1853
[V6]5047. [10]3. **Mary F. Breshears**, b. 1856; m. 26 Dec 1875, in Dallas Co, MO, ***William A.H. Owens***

Family of John K. Robert Breshears and Comfort Trayser:

[V6]5048. [10]4. **Matilda Breshears**, b. 1864; m. 1885, William F. Patterson.

Family of John K. Robert Breshears and Mary Barclay:

Figure 83: George C. Breshears, who died in the Spanish American War. Photo from Bill Brooks

[V6]5049. [10]5. ***Robert D. Breshears**, b. 11 Feb 1870, d. 30 Aug 1937, bur Mt Olive Cem, Dallas Co, MO; m.1. 1896, ***Elizabeth A. Barnett***, b. 12 May 1875, d. 13 July 1906 (4 ch); m.2. 1907, ***Mrs. Lizzie Ann Weeks/Smith/Patterson***, b. 1870 (1 ch).

[V6]5050. [10]6. **George C. Breshears**, b. 1872, d. Sept 1901 at Manila, Phillipine Islands, bur Wollard Cem, Dallas Co, MO. Veteran of Spanish-American War, Co. A, 1st U.S. Inf, killed later in Phillipines, per *History of Dallas Co, MO.*

[V6]5051. [10]7. **James Nathan Turner Breshears**, b. 6 Sept 1873, MO, d. 17 March 1962; m. 1900. ***Laura Francis Powell***, b. 22 Aug 1873, d. 4 Jan 1950, d/o M.R. Powell and Mary E. Carter

[V6]5052. [11]1. **Delphia Breshears**, b. 1902, d. 1979; m. ***Henry Shipman***, b. 1896

[V6]5053. [11]2. **Georgia Elvira Breshears**, b. 1904; m. ***Herbert Silvey***

[V6]5054. [11]3. **Gilbert Minard Breshears**, b. 1913, d. 1989; m. ***Velma Hylton***

[V6]5055. [12]1. **Doyle Breshears**,

[V6]5056. [12]2. **Jack Breshears**,

[V6]5057. [12]3. **Karen**

Figure 84: Children of Gilbert and Velma Breshears: Back: Doyle, Jack, Karen; Seated: Joe, Ron, Bill. Photo from Bill Brooks

Breshears,

^{V6}5058. [12]4. **Joe Breshears,**

^{V6}5059. [12]5. **Ron Breshears,**

^{V6}5060. [12]6. **Bill Breshears,**

^{V6}5061. [10]8. **Sidney E. Breshears**, b. 1875

^{V6}5062. [10]9. **Charity L. Breshears**, b. c1877

^{V6}5063. [10]10. ***John Carroll Breshears**, b. 4 Nov 1879, d. 11 June 1959; m. Oct 1907, ***Clora Ann McKee***, b. 1886, d. 1954

^{V6}5064. [10]11. **Noah S. Breshears**, b. Feb 1885; m. ***Ruby Ruth***

Robert D. Breshears and his Two Wives

^{v6}5049. [10]5. **Robert D. Breshears**, (s/o John K. Robert Breshears and Mary Barclay), b. 11 Feb 1870, d. 30 Aug 1937, bur Mt Olive Cem, Dallas Co, MO; m.1. 1896, ***Elizabeth A. Barnett***, b. 12 May 1875, d. 13 July 1906 (4 ch); m.2. 1907, ***Mrs. Lizzie Ann Weeks/Smith/Patterson***, b. 1870 (1 ch).

Family of Robert D. Breshears and Elizabeth A. Barnett:

^{V6}5065. [11]1. **Bertha M. Breshears**, b. 12 Aug 1893, d. 9 April 1906

^{V6}5066. [11]2. **Nancy Breshears**, b. 1897, d. 1973; m. ***Caleb E. McCurry***

^{V6}5067. [11]3. **Gertrude Breshears**, b. 1900, d. 1991; m. ***Samuel N. Jackson***, b. 1888

^{V6}5068. [11]4. **Mary Francis Breshears**, b. 1903; m. ***Arbra Mayabb***

^{V6}5069. [11]5. **Carrol Breshears**, b. 1906

Family of Robert D. Breshears and Lizzie Ann Weeks:

^{V6}5070. [11]6. **William Everett Breshears**, b. 1908, d. 1975; m. ***Merle Owens***

Figure 85: James Nathan Turner Breshears. Photo from Bill Brooks

Figure 87: Laura (Powell) Breshears. Photo from Bil Brooks

Figure 88: Henry and Delphia (Breshears) Shipman. Photo from Bill Brooks

Figure 86: Georgia E. (Breshears) Silvey, Gilbert M. Breshears, and Velma (Hylton) Breshears. Thanks for photo to Bill Brooks.

John Carroll Breshears and Clora Ann McKee

V6 5063. 10 10. **John Carroll Breshears**, (s/o John K. Robert Breshears and Mary Barclay), b. 4 Nov 1879, d. 11 June 1959; m. Oct 1907, ***Clora Ann McKee***, b. 1886, d. 1954

Figure 89: John Carroll Breshears and Clora Ann McKee. Photo from Bill Brooks

Family of John Carroll Breshears and Clora Ann McKee:

V6 5071. 11 1. **Raymond Robert Breshears**, b. 1904, d. 1990; m. ***Ressie Clark***, living 1988 in Oregon,

V6 5072. 11 2. **Hobart Jefferson Breshears**, b. 1906, d. 1989; m. ***Viola*** ____; living 1988 in Oregon,

V6 5073. 11 3. **John Lester Breshears**, b. 1908, d. 1970; m. ***June*** ____

V6 5074. 11 4. **Harley Sylvester Breshears**, b. 1911, living 1988 Norborne, MO; m. ***Norma Newton***, (partial family from obit of Kay Breshears Carper)

V6 5075. 12 x. **Virgil E. Breshears Sr**, m. ***Eileen Harmon***, d/o Clarence Harmon of Richmond, MO

V6 5076. 13 x. **Kay Breshears**, b. 25 April 1965, Independence, MO, d. 1 Feb 1988, Aurora, CO; m. 6 June 1985, ***Ronald D. Carper Jr***, of West Virginia.

V6 5077. 14 y. Michael Carper, b. 1986

V6 5078. 13 x. **Virgil E. Breshears Jr**, m. 1991 at Richmond, MO, ***Genia M. Oliphant***.

V6 5079. 13 x. **Mary Ellen Breshears**, living Colo Springs, Colo, in 1988

[V6]5080. [11]5. **Harvey Levi Breshears**, b. 27 Sept 1913, Buffalo, MO, d. 24 Feb 1994, Rogers, AR; m.1. ***Bernice Berdell Reynolds***, b. c1921, d. 17 May 1985 (mother of the children); m.2. ***Frances Ragland***, (see Harvey's and Berniece's obits, below)

[V6]5081. [12]1. **Sandra Breshears**, m. _____ ***Clayborn***,

[V6]5082. [12]2. **Mary Breshears**, m. _____ ***Byrd***, living Clarksville, AR

[V6]5083. [12]3. **Donna Breshears**, m. _____ ***Cantrell***, living Hunt, AR

[V6]5084. [12]4. **Jimmie Dale Breshears**, of Russellville, AR

[V6]5085. [11]6. **Lola Gertrude Breshears**, b. 1916, d. 1961; m. ***Clarence McComer***

[V6]5086. [11]7. **Elmer Marvin Breshears**, b. 1918; m. ***Martha Moore***; living 1988 Stover, MO,

[V6]5087. [11]8. **Clara Opal Breshears**, b. 30 Jan 1919, Buffalo, MO, d. 13 Nov 1988, Marshall, MO; m. 30 June 1934, in Marshall, MO, ***Elmer N. Newton***, d. 9 Dec 1966,

[V6]5088. [12]y. Peggy Newton, m. Ronald McKown, of Independence, MO

[V6]5089. [12]y. Helen Newton, m. Bobby Ford, of Marhsall, MO

[V6]5090. [12]y. Jane Newton, m. Robert Gerit, of Stover, MO

[V6]5091. [12]y. son

[V6]5092. [12]y. daughter

[V6]5093. [11]9. **Florence Genevieve Breshears**, b. 1920; m. ***Paul England***, of Gilliam, MO; living Marshall, MO, 1993

[V6]5094. [11]10. **Erna (or Ernie) Ralph Breshears**, b. Aug 1921; m. 1939 ***Etha Dooley***, living 1988 Marshall, MO

[V6]5095. [11]11. **Alfred Clifton Breshears**, b. 1923; m. ***Ina Sapp***, living 1988 Marshall, MO

[V6]5096. [11]12. **Jesse Harlan Breshears**, b. 1924, d. 1993; m. ***Wilma Shaffer***, living 1988 Waverly, MO

[V6]5097. [11]13. **Jewell Mae Breshears**, b. 1927, d. 1991; m. ***Earl Waters***, of Arkansas

[V6]5098. [11]14. **Dorsey Gene Breshears**, b. 1933, d. 1983; m. ***Carol*** _____

Obit, **Kay (Breshears) Carper**, Richmond, MO, *News*, 3 Feb 1988:

Mrs. Kay (Breshears) Carper, 22, of Lafayette, Colo, formerly of Richmond, died Monday, Feb 1, 1988, at Fitzsimmons Medical Center, Aurora, CO, following a lengthy illness. ... Mrs. Carper was born April 25, 1965 in Independence to Virgil Breshear Sr and Eileen Harmon.

While both were in the Army in Germany, she met and later was married to Ronald C. Carper Jr, of West Virginia on June 6, 1985. He remains with the Army and survives of the home. Also surviving are a son, Michael Carper, 2, of the home; her parents of Lafayette; a sister, Mary Ellen Breshears of Colorado Springs; the maternal grandparents, Mrs. and Mrs. Clarence Harmon of Richmond; and the paternal grandparents, Mr. and Mrs. Harley Breshears of Norborne.

The (Richmond, MO) *Daily News*, 1 May 1991

Nancy Morris of Independence announces the forthcoming marriage of her daughter Genia M. Oliphant, to Virgil E. Breashears Jr, s/o Virgil E. and Eilene Breshears Sr, of Hardin. ...

(photo caption) Patrol officer Virgil E. Breshears Jr of Richmond Police Department, judges entries in the *Daily News* Christmas Poster Contest.....

Obit, **Harvey Levi Breshears,** 80, (*The Spectator*, Ozark, AR, 3 March 1994, p.19) b. 27 Sept 1913, in Buffalo, MO, d. 24 Feb 1994, in Rogers, AR; resident of Pea Ridge, formerly of Clarksville, native of Ohio; hus/o Frances Ragland Breshears, s/o late John Carroll Breshears and Cora Ann McKee, bur Liberty Hill Cem near Hartman, AR.

Survivors include his wife, Frances Ragland Breshears; two daughters, Mary Byrd of Clarksville and Donna Cantrell of Hunt; one step-daughter, Margaret Jannette Breshears of Russellville; one son, Jimmie Dale Breshears of Russellville; one stepson, Jimmie Dwayne Garrison of Fort Smith; one sister, Genevieve England of Marshall, MO; three brothers, Ralph and Clinton Breshears, both of Marshall, MO, and Harley Breshears of Norborne, MO; 21 Grandchildren and 38 great-grandchildren.

Obit, **Mrs. Berniece Berdell Breshears**, 64 (b. c1921), of Clarksville, d. Fri, May 17 (Pope Co, AR *Citizen Democrat*, 20 May 1985). Survivors: husband, Harvey Breshears; son Jim Breshears of Clarksville; 3 daughters, Sandra Clayborn of Ozark; Mary Byrd of Clarksville; Donna Cantrell of Russellville; 2 brothers, Orla Reynolds of Kansas City, KS; Verl Reynolds of Kansas City, MO; 5 sisters, Erma Jones and Mae Coots of Kansas City, KS; Vida Richards of Los Angeles, CA; Anna Knight of Tulsa, OK; Velda Hopkins of Slater, MO; 15 grandchildren, 13 great-grandchildren.

Obit **Claria Breshears Newton**, Marshall, MO, *Democrat-News*, Tues, 15 Nov 1988: Claria Breshear Newton, 78, of Marshall, died Sunday, Nov 13, 1988, at John Fitzgibbon Memorial Hospital. Graveside services will be held at 10:30 a.m., Wednesday, Nov 16, in the Ridge Park Cemetery. Rev. Randy Mahurin will officiate. Visitation will be from 7 to 8:30 p.m. Tuesday at the Sweeney-Reser-Wills Funeral Home.

Born Jan 30, 1919, in Buffalo, MO, she was the daughter of the late John and Cloria McKee Breshears. On June 30, 1934, in Marshall, she married Elmer N. Newton, who preceded her in death Dec 9, 1966. She was a resident of Marshall most of her life and was employed by Banquet Foods for 17 years.

Survivors include three daughters, Mrs. Ronald (Peggy) McKown of Independence, MO; Mrs. Bobby (Helen) Ford of Marhsall; Mrs. Robert (Jane) Gerit of Stover; 13 grandchildren and 10 great-grandchildren; eight brothers: Raymond Breshears and Hubert Breshears of Oregon, Harley Breshears of Norborne, MO, Harvey Breshears of Arkansas, Elmer Breshears of Stover, MO, Ernie Breshears and Alford Breshears, both of Marshall, and Jessie Breshears of Waverly, MO; two sister, Jewell May Waters of Arkansas and Florence Geneive England of Gilliam, MO; several neices and nephews. She was preceded by one son, one daughter, two brothers, and one sister.

James Keele Breshears and Mary Ann McDonald

v6 5041. 9 4. **James Keele Breshears**, (s/o Nathan Turner Breshears and Elizabeth Keele), b. 23 June 1829, Lawrence Co, TN, d. 17 Jan 1887 of pneumonia; "Co. I, MO Cavalry, formerly of Dallas Co, d. at his home in N. Springfield on the 17th, of lung fever... was buried at Wollard graveyard in Washington twp [Dallas Co, MO] on Wed of last week"; m. 8 June 1851, ***Mary Ann "Molly" McDonald***, b. 13 June 1837, Bedford Co, TN, d. 15 Dec 1918, d/o Zadock W. McDonald and Manerva Cavin.

Family of James Keele Breshears and Molly McDonald, all b. Dallas Co, MO:

V6 5099. 10 1. **Minerva Beulah "Lou" "Lula" Breshears**, b. 20 June 1853, d. 15 June 1909; m.1. 23 March 1869, in Dallas Co, MO, ***Napoleon Louis Edwards***; m.2. 30 June 1879, Mt Vernonm, Lawrence Co, MO, ***Milton Smith***

V6 5100. 11 1. James Matthew Edwards, b. [1875]; m. Lutie ______ . Ch: James Edwards.

V6 5101. 11 2. Nettie Jane Smith, b. 28 July 1875, d. 7 May 1951, bur Greenlawn Cem, Springfield, MO; m. Walter McMasters, and had 4 ch.

V6 5102. 10 2. **Middleton Edward Breshears**, b. 13 Feb 1855, d. 15 Feb 1855

V6 5103. 10 3. **Eliza Jane Breshears**, b. 29 Feb 1856, d. 15 April 1930; m. ***Kenneth Lewis Burdette***,

V6 5104. 11 1. Joseph Hampton Burdette; m. Minnie ______. Ch: Nathan; and William Burdette.

V6 5105. 11 2. Noah William Burdette; m. Della ______ . No ch.

V6 5106. 11 3. Lola Burdette; m. Charlie Alexander. Ch, but name unk.

V6 5107. 10 4. **Nancy Delilah "Lila" Breshears**, b. 9 Dec 1858, d. 8 March 1908; m.1. ***John Wilkerson***, m.2. ***William J. Burdette***, b. [1855]

V6 5108. 11 1. Nettie Wilkerson, m. ______ Ch: Hiacent; Milbern; and Irwin ______ .

V6 5109. 11 2. John Wilkerson,

[V6]5110. [10]5. **Olivia Ann "Livy Ann" Breshears**, b. 18 Feb 1861, d. 9 Sept 1928; m.1. 1878, ***John Russell***, m.2. 1888, ***James W. Montgomery***, b. 1862, d. 1932

[V6]5111. [11]1. Stella May Russell, b. 7 May 1882, d. 1968; m. Arvil (Orvil) Kesterson, b. 1879, d. 1930. Ch: Lorene; and Homer Kesterson

[V6]5112. [11]2. Lula May Russell, b. 7 May 1885, d. 7 June 1907; m. John Cheffey,

[V6]5113. [11]3. Vernie Montgomery, b. 27 Dec 1888, d. Jan 1889

[V6]5114. [11]4. Joseph Zadock Montgomery, b. 1 Jan 1891, d. 8 Nov 1966; m.1. Lorena L. ______ (1 ch); m.2. Nina ______

[V6]5115. [12]1. Ferne Montgomery; m. ______ Aldridge

[V6]5116. [11]5. Myrtle Montgomery, b. 1897,

[V6]5117. [11]6. Paul Montgomery [twin], b. 25 Jan 1899, d. 16 June 1986; m. Amanda Burns, b. 6 June 1898, d. 21 Feb 1980.

[V6]5118. [12]1. Martha Montgomery; m. ______ Cates,

[V6]5119. [12]2. Helen Montgomery; m. ______ Putnam,

[V6]5120. [12]3. Olivia Montgomery; m. ______ Wade,

[V6]5121. [11]7. Pearl Montgomery [twin], b. 25 March 1899, d. 16 Feb 1929; m. Romie Caldwell, ch: Jimmie Caldwell.

[V6]5122. [11]8. Cristeen Montgomery, b. 24 July 1902

[V6]5123. [10]7. ***Nathan Joseph Breshears**, b. 15 June 1863, d. 11 Dec 1936, m. 14 Aug 1884, ***Martha Elizabeth Montgomery***,

[V6]5124. [10]8. ***Zadock Calvin "Zade" Breshears**, b. 8 Aug 1865, d. 9 Aug 1954, Greene Co, MO, bur Bellview Cem; m. 1903, ***Susan Livonia Stratton***,

[V6]5125. [10]9. **William Thomas "W.T." Breshears**, b. 24 Nov 1867, d. 23 April 1945, Dallas Co, MO, bur Bellview Cem; m. 1895, ***Lucinda Francis "Cindy" Webster***, b. 20 July 1877, Sweetwater, TN, d. 1959, bur Bellview cem.

[V6]5126. [11]1. **Clarence O'Bryan Breshears**, b. & d. 27 Dec 1895

[V6]5127. [11]2. **William Ralph Breshears**, b. 6 March 1897,

d. 8 Jan 1974; m. 1918, ***Elsie Pierce***, b.?, d. 2 Sept 1971.

[V6]5128. [12]1. _dau__ Breshears, m. ***John Burgland***,

[V6]5129. [11]3. **Anna Buetta Breshears**, b. 20 Feb 1900, d. 1977; never married.

[V6]5130. [11]4. **James A. Breshears**, b. 11 Dec 1901, d. 17 Oct 1976, bur Liberty cem, northeast of Springfield, MO; m.1. ***Maurine Parkhurst***; m.2. ***Ola Dooley***.

[V6]5131. [12]1. **Gordon Breshears**,

[V6]5132. [12]2. **Barbara Breshears**, m. ______ ***Probst***,

[V6]5133. [11]5. **Essie May Breshears**, b. 1905, d. 1906

[V6]5134. [11]6. **Nettie Marie Breshears**, b. 1908, d. 1911. A Marie Breshears Gregg was a teacher at old Charity Grade School, after 1949, per *History of Dallas Co, MO*; obviously not this person.

[V6]5135. [11]7. **Raymond F. Breshears**, b. 30 Oct 1909; m. ***Jessie Morgan***,

[V6]5136. [11]8. **Zadock Clifford Breshears**, b. 24 Dec 1911; m. ***Velma Powell***,

[V6]5137. [11]9. **Mary Doris (or Darris) Breshears**, b. 1915, d. 30 Dec 1993; m. ***Clell Powell***, 7 ch, names unknown.

[V6]5138. [10]10. **Sarah Rebecca "Sadie" Breshears**, b. 8 April 1871, d. 3 Feb 1936; m. ***John L. Roper***, b. 25 Sept 1863, d. 5 Jan 1925, both bur Bellview cem.

[V6]5139. [11]1. Asa William Roper, b. 1 Dec 1890, d. 28 June 1901, age 10½.

[V6]5140. [11]2. Roy Roper; m. Bessie ______ ch: Fay; Billie; and two others, Roper

[V6]5141. [11]3. Harry Roper; m. Nola ______ No ch.

[V6]5142. [11]4. Omar Martin "Pat" Roper, b. 7 May 1897, d. 1 July 1986; m. Alma ______ , b. 12 March 1899, d. 30 Dec 1989, both bur Hazelwood cem.

[V6]5143. [11]5. Dee Roper; m. Perna ______ ch: J.D.; Donald Roper

[V6]5144. [11]6. Sadie Mae Roper, b. 25 July 1904, d. 5 Aug 1908, bur Bellview cem.

[V6]5145. [11]7. Inez Maxine Roper, b. 30 June 1912, d. 6

April 1913, bur Bellview cem.

V6 5146. [10]11. **John Samuel Breshears**, b.&d.26 Jan 1872

V6 5147. [10]12. **Della Louisa Breshears**, b. 6 Nov 1876, d. 18 June 1965; m. 1904, ***Benjamin F. Scott***, b. 22 April 1873, d. 12 May 1962, both bur Bellview cem.

V6 5148. [11]1. Donna Beulah Scott, b. 26 April 1912, d. 13 June 1928, bur Bellview cem

V6 5149. [11]2. Linda Irene Scott, b. 26 Dec 1917, [may have died the same day], bur Bellview Cem

V6 5150. [11]3. Mary Olivia Scott; m. Jay Simpson. 4 ch; unk

1880 US Census, Greene Co, MO, N. Springfield twp: #22-p.24

Jas K. Beeshears,	51, b. 1829, TN, NC, TN
Mary Ann	42, TN, TN, TN
Eliza J. Beeshears,	24, MO, TN, TN
Nathan J. Beeshears,	16, MO, TN, TN
J. C. Beeshears,	14, MO, TN, TN
Wm. Thos. Beeshears,	12, MO, TN, TN
Sarah Beeshears,	9, MO, TN, TN
Della Beeshears,	3, MO, TN, TN

Nathan Joseph Breshears and Martha Elizabeth Montgomery

v6 5123. [10]7. **Nathan Joseph Breshears**, (s/o James Keele Breshears and Mary Ann McDonald), b. 15 June 1863, Dallas Co, MO, d. 11 Dec 1936, at Springfield, Greene Co, MO, bur. Greenlawn Cem; m. 14 Aug 1884, ***Martha Elizabeth Montgomery***, b. 28 March 1866, d. 19 July 1953, d/o John H. Montgomery and Mary Ann Rice.

Family of Nathan Joseph Breshears and Martha Montgomery:

V6 5151. [11]1. **Walter E. Breshears**, (twin), b. 23 May 1885, d. 31 Jan 1959; m. ***Amy Lee*** ____, b. 10 Nov 1884, d. 5 May 1945, both bur Greenlawn Cem; lived in Springfield, MO. Walter worked for Sloan & Breshears.

V6 5152. [12]1. **Irma Breshears**, m. ***Paul Bowman***,

V6 5153. [12]2. **Edna Breshears**, m. ***Henry Hedley***,

V6 5154. [11]2. **Berty Evert Breshears**, (twin), b. 23 May 1885, d.

30 April 1886, Greene Co, MO, of hepatitis, complicated by erysipilas, Dr. A. Mc F. Brown.

V65155. 113. **Ida E. Breshears**, b. 3 May 1888, d. 1962, Greene Co, MO, bur Greenlawn Cem; m. ***Frank C. Delo***, b. 1884, d. 1954

V65156. 121. Earl Delo; m. Mary ______

V65157. 122. Everett Delo; m. Holly ______

V65158. 114. ***James Harley Breshears**, b. 2 Oct 1890, Webb City, MO

V65159. 115. **Ethel Silvia Breshears**, b. 15 May 1893, Webb City, MO, d. 1981, Springfield, Greene Co, MO, bur Bellview Cem; m. ***Joseph Leslie (or Lester) Hunt***, b. 1889, d. 1964

V65160. 121. Betty Hunt, m. Jack Harmon,

V65161. 122. Gordon Leslie Hunt, d. 1963; m. Mary Jacqueline McBride, b. 5 April 1929

V65162. 131. Michael Lee Hunt, m. Virginia Vanderbilt and had children Lori Michelle and Amber Hunt

V65163. 132. James Leslie Hunt, b. 10 Oct 1950; m. Rhonda Sue Ball, b. 7 Jan 1952

V65164. 141. Jason Leslie Hunt, b. 21 Feb 1973

V65165. 142. James Eric Hunt, b. 8 April 1976

V65166. 143. Shaun Leslie Hunt, b. 3 May 1978

V65167. 123. James Lawrence Hunt, b. 5 Dec 1915, d. 25 March 1916

V65168. 124. William "Billie" Hunt, b. 15 Aug 1918, d. 25 Oct 1918

V65169. 116. **Edith T. Breshears**, b. 13 Jan 1896, d. 1980, Greene Co, MO, bur Greenlawn Cem; m.1. ***John Montgomery***; m.2. ***John T. Hoffman***, b. 1892, d. 1967. No ch.

V65170. 117. **Joseph Eldon Breshears**, b. 11 Feb 1899,

V65171. 118. **William Calvin Breshears**, b. 31 Dec 1901, d. July 1956; m. ***Lillie McCallum***, b. 1903. William was a truck driver for Loose-Wiles, in Springfield.

V65172. 119. **Lenora E. Breshears**, b. 22 Dec 1904, d. June 1959, Greene Co, MO, bur Greenlawn Cem; m. ***William Lamen Martin***, b. 1908, d. 1975

V65173. 121. Betty Ann Martin, m. Carl Scott, ch: Karen;

Eddy; and Paul Scott.

V65174. [12]2. Max Martin,

V65175. [12]3. Lamen Martin, Jr.

V65176. [11]10. **Edgar E. Breshears**, b. 3 Feb 1908, d. 22 April 1989; m. 21 Feb 1931, ***Lucille Chandler***, b. 23 June 1910,

V65177. [12]1. **Robert Joseph Breshears**, b. 25 May 1935

V65178. [12]2. **Janice Marie Breshears**, b. 28 Juen 1941

V65179. [12]3. **Jon Chandler Breshears**, b. 29 Dec 1945

V65180. [12]4. **Donald Jeffrey Breshears**, b. 2 July 1949

James Harley Breshears and Jessie Maude Stafford

v65158. [11]4. **James Harley Breshears**, (s/o Nathan Joseph Breshears and Martha Elizabeth Montgomery), b. 2 Oct 1890, Webb City, MO, d. 29 Aug 1958, Vallejo, CA; m.1. ***Jessie Maude Stafford***, b. 2 April 1890, Dallas Co, MO, d. 1945, Alameda, Alameda Co, CA, d/o Nathaniel Byrd and Nancy Drucilla (Hill) Stafford; m.2. ***Jeanette ?Eshfield***, m.3. ***Theodosia Marle (Noland) Parker***. Jessie (Stafford) Breshears m.2. U.S. Hardison. James was a driver for Springfield Tractor Co, and lived in Springfield, MO.

Children of James Harley Breshears and Jessie Maude Stafford, all, b. Springfield, Greene Co, MO:

V65181. [12]1. **Gladys Helen Breshears**, b. 16 Sept 1918, d. 10 Dec 1927

V65182. [12]2. **James Doyle Breshears**, b. 23 Sept 1922, d. 4 July 1979; m. ***Masel Mason***,

V65183. [12]3. **Gene N. Breshears**, b. 28 Feb 1924, d. 9 April 1986; m. 31 Oct 1958, ***Winifred D. Wilson***,

V65184. [12]4. **Walter Paul Breshears**, b. 11 March 1928, living 1993 in Alturas, CA; m. 3 April 1948, ***Barbara Noland***,

Zadock Calvin "Zade" Breshears and Susan Livonia Stratton

V6 5124. 10 8. **Zadock Calvin "Zade" Breshears**, (s/o James Keele Breshears and Molly McDonald), b. 8 Aug 1865, d. 9 Aug 1954, Greene Co, MO, bur Bellview Cem; m. 1903, ***Susan Livonia Stratton***, b. 5 April 1877, d. 26 May 1964, d/o William Anderson Stratton, and Harriett Saphrona Brown.

Zadock was a carpenter for Frisco Railroad. Before her marriage, Susan taught school in Greene Co rural schools.

Data from JoAnn (Breshears) Ashlock. When JoAnn was a senior in high school, her parents moved to Florida, but she stayed in Springfield, MO, so she could finish high school. Grandpa "Zade" was almost deaf from a railroad accident, but she would pull her chair up "close to his and talk loud into his best ear (not very good) and he fed me much information on the family. Thankfully, I wrote most of it down."

Family of Zadock Calvin "Zade" Breshears and Susan Livonia Stratton:

V6 5185. 11 1. **William Joseph "Joe" Breshears**, b. 11 May 1906, Springfield, MO, d. 22 Jan 1983, Independence, MO; m.1. 17 Sept 1927, in Springfield, MO, ***Frances Evelyn Curtis***, b. 20 July 1905, rural Greene Co, MO, d. 28 Jan 1969, Butler Co, MO, d/o Lewis Addison Curtis and Clara Lucindy Smith; m.2. 27 Sept 1969, in Kansas City, KS, ***Frances Choun Knowles*** (this ceremony was performed by the groom's son, Donald Lee Breshears).

V6 5186. 12 1. **JoAnn Breshears**, b. 24 Oct 1929, Springfield, MO; m. 30 Aug 1953, in Phenix City, AL, ***Richard Allen Ashlock***, b. 9 Jan 1926, Hagaman, Macoupin Co, IL, s/o Jesse Roscoe Ashlock and Genevieve Elton Wahl. JoAnn Ashlock supplied a great deal of data on descendants of John Keele Breshears, for which many thanks.

V6 5187. 13 1. Mary Elizabeth Ashlock, b. 28 Sept 1954, Salzburg, Austria (while Richard was in

U.S. Army); m.1. 25 Aug 1973, Denison, TX, Michael Alan Coldiron, (div 1981); m.2. 12 Aug 1983, in Ft Worth, TX, Alvin Orice "Sonny" Corbell, Jr, b. 21 July 1940, Ft Worth, TX, s/o Alvin Orice Corbell and Myrtle Ivy Boyd.

V6 5188. 14 1. Chloe Ivy Corbell, b. 22 Jan 1986, Ft Worth, TX

V6 5189. 14 2. Crystal Laura Evelyn Corbell, b. 18 July 1989, Bedford, TX

V6 5190. 14 3. Alvin Aiden Richard Corbell, b. 20 Aug 1993, Ft Worth, TX

V6 5191. 13 2. Steven Joseph Ashlock, b. 28 Jan 1956, Ft. Carson, CO; m. 17 May 1980, in Dallas, TX, Berta Ruth Farr, b. 9 June 1954, Dallas, TX,

V6 5192. 14 1. Natalie Joy Ashlock, b. 6 Dec 1980, Dallas TX

V6 5193. 14 2. Douglas Alexander Ashlock, b. 14 Jan 1988, Dallas, TX

V6 5194. 12 2. **Donald Lee Breshears**, b. 18 May 1934, Springfield, Mo; m. 11 June 1961, Cedar Falls, IA, ***Barbara Garver Smith***, b. 13 Feb 1935, IA.

V6 5195. 13 1. **Anne Evelyn Breshears**, b. 26 March 1962; m. ***Jeffrey Chapman***, a school teacher.

V6 5196. 14 1. Ryan Austin Jeffrey Chapman, b. 6 Sep 1990, WA

V6 5197. 14 2. Kyle Anson Collin Chapman, b. 13 May 1993, WA

V6 5198. 13 2. **Joseph Raymond Breshears**, b. 27 Nov 1964; m. 28 May 1988, Lamoni, IA, ***Julie Holz***, b. 6 April 1964, Greene Co, IA.

V6 5199. 14 1. **Deborah Mikal Sisna Breshears**, b. 3 May 1989, Lamoni, IA.

V6 5200. 14 2. **Shanee Breshears**, b. 18 Oct 1991, Lamoni, IA.

V6 5201. 14 3. **Neshamah Breshears**, b. 10 Jan

1994, Lamoni, IA.

[V6]5202. [13]3. **Kathryn Ruth Breshears**, b. 26 Jan 1967

[V6]5203. [12]3. **Robert Lewis Breshears**, b. 29 June 1937, Springfield, MO; m. 1 July 1961, in Independence, MO, ***Mary Jo Tipton***, b. 11 Jan 1938, FL

[V6]5204. [13]1. **Lisa Kae Breshears**, b. 5 Oct 1963; m. 27 Dec 1986, Independence, MO, ***Duane Claire Smith***, b. 29 Sept 1964,

[V6]5205. [14]1. Adam Christopher Smith, b. 1 June 1993, Independence, MO,

[V6]5206. [13]2. **William Joseph "Jody" Breshears, II**, b. 6 Dec 1966, Albuquerque, NM; m. 28 Dec 1991, in St Louis, MO, ***Pamela Jean Petcu***,

[V6]5207. [14]1. **Nathan Daniel Breshears**, b. 23 Oct 1993, Iowa City, IA.

[V6]5208. [14]2. **Lauren Elizabeth Breshears**, b. 9 July 1996, Iowa City, IA.

[V6]5209. [13]3. **Suzanne Tipton Breshears**, b. 25 May 1969; m. ***Jared Suddaby***,

[V6]5210. [11]2. **Albert James Breshears**, b. 1 March 1908, Springfield, MO, d. 6 Feb 1995, Anaheim, CA (see obit below), m. 11 July 1942, ***Eunice Rachel Day***, b. 8 Oct 1912, Clarksville, Johnson Co, AR, d. 24 March 1991, Anaheim, CA, a great-great-granddaughter of Jesse Brashears of Johnson Co, AR. Jesse was s/o Isaac Brashears of Roane and Perry/Decatur Co, TN.

[V6]5211. [12]1. **Susan Day Breshears**, b. 5 Oct 1948, Independence, Jackson Co, MO; m. 8 Jan 1970, Overland Park, Johnson Co, KS, ***Forrest J. Aull, Jr***, b. 23 Jan 1948,

[V6]5212. [13]1. Jennifer Suzanne Aull, b. 27 Oct 1973, Overland Park, KS.

[V6]5213. [13]2. Melanie Kathleen Aull, b. 9 Sept 1973, Overland Park, KS.

Albert James Breshears, (**obituary** in *The Johnson County Graphic*, Clarksville, AR, 8 Feb 1995), b. c1908-9, Springfield, MO, d. 6 Feb 1995, at his home in Anaheim Hills, CA, age 86.

He was a former resident of Kansas City, MO, where he was a member of Bethany Baptist Church, an Army veteran, graduate of the University of Texas, native of Springfield, MO, and retired claim agent for Francisco Railroad Company. He was a son of the late Zadoc and Susan Stratton Breshears, and was preceded in death by his wife, Eunice Day Breshears.

He is survived by one daughter, Mrs. Forrest J. (Susan) Aull of Yorba Linda, Calif; two granddaughters, Jennifer Aull of San Francisco, and Melanie Aull of Yorba Linda; two nephews; and one niece.

Funeral will be at 2 p.m. Saturday, Feb 11, at Roller-Cox Funeral Home Chapel with Burley King Officiating. Burial will be in Bethelehem Cemetery.

Pallbearers will be John Ray, Carl Day, Lynn Day, Harley Williams, Bob Breshears, Don Breshears, and Dr. H. Thomas McSwain. Visitation will be from 7-9 p.m. Friday, Feb 10, at Roller-Cox Funeral Home Chapel.

From Jewel Philips, 11 Feb 1995: "This man married my first cousin (Eunice Day Brashears). She was a descendant of Jesse Brashears, s/o Isaac Brashears of Roane and Perry Co, TN. In fact, Jesse was her g.g.grandfather, as he was mine. ... My cousin died several years back. I had met this man from time to time at family reunions, funerals. He was a very nice man. I would always tease them about marrying kinfolks, but never got down to discussing genealogy.

Figure 90: Calvin Breshears' birthday celebration in May, 1907.
Back row: 1. Ben Breshears; 2. Walter Breshears; 3. Riley Breshears; 4. John Breshears; 5. George Breshears; 6. Halleck Breshears; 7. Charley Breshears; 8. Jake Breshears; 9. Arch Breshears;
Next row: 10. Bailey Green; 11. Willis Breshears; 12. Vernie Green; 13. Bertha Gaunt Pitts; 14. Nel Selsor Breshears; 15. Blanche Breshears; 16. Rosa Breshears Asbury; 17. Bessie Gaunt Mallard; 18. Mary Breshears; 19 Ola Breshears Howe; 20. Decia Breshears Neiman; 21. Virgil Breshears;
Next row: 22. Ora Green; 23. Albert Breshears; 24. Ethel Breshears Anglen; 25. Elsie Breshears; 26. Ines Green; 27. Ancil Breshears Terrill; 28. Anna Green Cheek; 29. Lewis Breshears; 30. Jesse Breshears; 31. Fred Breshears;
Next row: 32. Millie Ray Breshears; 33. Mary Gaunt Breshears; 35. James Price Breshears; 35. Calvin (Cal) Breshears; 36. Genia Breshears Green; 37. Jane Hoover Breshears; 38 Maida Breshears; 39. Bertha Rogers Breshears;
Front row: 40. Lester Ray Breshears; 41. Ezra Breshears; 42. Cleo Breshears; 43. Lonnie Breshears; 44. Zetta Breshears; 45. Phena Green; 46. Claude Breshears (on box by dog in front); 47. Helen Breshears; 48. Marvin Breshears.

Calvin Breshears and Missouri Jane Davidson/ Malissa Catherine Silkey

[v6]5043. [9]6. **Calvin Breshears**, (s/o Nathan Turner Breshears and Elizabeth Catherine Keele), b. 22 May 1835, Benton Co, MO, d. 23 June 1909, Dallas Co, MO, bur Wollard Cem; m.1. 1859, ***Missouri Jane Davidson***, b. 1 April 1843, TN,

Figure 91: Calvin Breshears, in May 1907

d. 25 July 1873, Dallas Co, MO, bur O'Bannon/ Bennett Cem, Dallas Co, MO, d/o John Davidson and Hester Wilson; m.2. 22 Jan 1874, ***Malissa Catherine Silkey***, b. 26 April 1851, Ky, d. 20 Oct 1906, Dallas Co, MO, d/o Joseph Silkey and Mary Mills.

Calvin served in Co. A, 24th Regt of Missouri Infantry, U.S. Army, from 20 Aug 1861 to 14 Oct 1864, and was honorably discharged at St. Louis by Capt. Jno A. Thompson. His discharge notes that he was 25 when he enlisted, was six feet, six inches tall, had dark complexion, blue eyes, and auburn hair. His surname is spelled "Brashears" on the discharge.

Family of Calvin Breshears and Missouri Jane Davidson:

V6 5251. 10 1. **Eugenia Ann Breshears**, b. 9 Aug 1861, d. 11 June 1926, Yell Co, AR; m.1. 20 Aug 1876, in Dallas Co, MO, ***Baily Green***, b. c1856, MO, d. 1916; m.2. 1919, ***Benjamin Murrow***

V6 5252. 11 1. William Calvin Green, b. c1877, MO, d. 1956; m. 1896, Amanda Ruth Gaunt, b. c1875, MO

V6 5253. 11 2. Millie J. Green, b. c1879, MO, d. 1929; m. 1897, Thomas I. Lakey

V6 5254. 11 3. Thomas J. Green, b. 1882, MO, d. 1958; m. Pearl Evans

V6 5255. 11 4. Martha C. Green, b. 1885, MO, d. 1956; m.1. 1900, John H. Evans; m.2. Robert Miles

V6 5256. 11 5. Lula May Green, b. 1887, MO, d. 1963; m.1. 1907, Frank Thompson (g/pa of Lois Faulconer); m.2. Grover Smith

^{V6}5257. ^{11}6. Vernie Green, b. c1890, MO, m. Sarah Dame

^{V6}5258. ^{11}7. Dona Inez Green, b. 1892, MO, m. 1912, Charles R. Lakey

^{V6}5259. ^{11}8. Ora J. Green, b. c1895, MO, d. 1974; m. 1917, Homer Jones

^{V6}5260. ^{11}9. Anna Bell Green, b. c1897, MO, d. 1966; m.1. Allen F. Cheek; m.2. ____; m.3. Westley F. Anglin, b. 1891

^{V6}5261. ^{11}10. Phenia Green, b. 1901,

^{V6}5262. ^{10}2. ***Nathaniel John Breshears**, b. 29 March 1864, Washington, Dallas Co, MO, d. 24 July 1935, Lindsay, Tulare Co, CA; m.1. 1884, ***Martha Lou Silkey***, b. 15 Nov 1861, d. 17 April 1885; m.2. 13 Nov 1887, ***Sarah Jane Hoover***, b. 14 April 1868, d. 23 June 1949

^{V6}5263. ^{10}3. **Sarah Delilah Breshears**, b. 7 May 1866, d. 17 Sept 1867, bur O'Bannon/Bennett Cem, Dallas Co, MO

^{V6}5264. ^{10}4. **Matilda Caledonia Breshears**, b. 17 Oct 1867, d. 28 Feb 1898, Dallas Co, MO, bur Wollard Cem; m. 6 Sept 1888, ***Thomas Bean Gaunt***, b. 18 March 1866, d. 29 June 1930

^{V6}5265. ^{11}1. Haden Delmar Gaunt, b. 23 July 1889, MO, d. 1978; m.1. 1920, Martha Ethel Beckner, b. c1889; m.2. 1938, Clara Cuddington

^{V6}5266. ^{11}2. Bertha Exona Jane Gaunt, b. 15 Jan 1891, MO, d. 1970; m. 1915, Hugh M. Pitts, b. c1893, MO

^{V6}5267. ^{11}3. Bessie Ellen Gaunt, b. 28 Nov 1894, MO, d. 1950; m. 1912, George Edgar Mallard, b. c1894, MO

^{V6}5268. ^{10}5. **Chitty Victoria Breshears**, b. Nov 1869, d. Aug 1870, bur O'Bannon Cem, Dallas Co, MO.

^{V6}5269. ^{10}6. ***James Price Breshears**, b. 25 Jan 1871, d. 27 July 1930, Dallas Co, MO; m. 3 Nov 1889, ***Mary Ellen Gaunt***, b. 20 Jan 1871, d. 15 Nov 1942

Family of Calvin Breshears and Malissa Catherine Silkey:

V6 5270. 10 7. **Joseph Hallic Breshears**, b. 15 Dec 1874, d. 25 Dec 1956, bur Oak Lawn Cem, Buffalo, Dallas Co, MO; m. 4 Nov 1894, ***Molly Jane Ray***, b. 12 Dec 1871, KS, d. 21 Nov 1951, d/o Thos B. Ray and Sarah A. Moberly

V6 5271. 11 1. **Ancil Lee Breshears**, b. 1897, MO, d. 1985; m. 1917, ***Emery Terrill***

V6 5272. 11 2. **Lester Ray Breshears**, b. 1899, MO, d. 1907, bur Wollard Cem

V6 5273. 11 3. **Blanche Breshears**, b. 1904, MO, d. 1943, bur Oak Lawn Cem, Buffalo, MO

V6 5274. 11 4. **Lova Alice Breshears**, b. 1911, d. 1996; m. 1936, ***Earl Palmer***

V6 5275. 10 8. **George William Breshears**, b. 22 Aug 1877, Dallas Co, MO, d. 26 June 1944, Springfield, Greene Co, MO; m. 28 April 1899, ***Albertha "Bertha" Rogers***, b. 28 May 1879, Dallas Co, MO, d. 20 Feb 1973, Springfield, Greene Co, MO, d/o Henry J. Rogers and Jersey A. Friend.

V6 5276. 11 1. **Mata Breshears**, b. 20 May 1900, d. 8 March 1996; m.1. ***Louis Frank Isley***, m.2. ***Charles R. Powell***

V6 5277. 12 1. Thelma Jean Isley, b. 2 March 1930, Springfield, Greene Co, MO

V6 5278. 12 3. Louis Franklin Isley, b. 12 Oct 1934, Springfield, MO

V6 5279. 11 2. **Marvin Blake Breshears**, b. 12 Jan 1907, Dallas Co, MO, d. 23 Aug 1991, Springfield, MO; m.1. ***D. Smalley***; m.2. 25 April 1940, ***Edna Pauline Boehm***, b. 14 March 1916, Talmage, ME.

V6 5280. 12 x. **Jo Ann "Jody" Breshears**, b. 20 Nov 1941, Springfield, MO; m. 17 June 1961, Harrison, Boone Co, AR, ***John Clifton***, b. 29 March 1937, Springfield, MO. addr (1997) 2503 E. Grand, Springfield, MO 65804)

V6 5281. 13 1. Paula Lynn Clifton, b. 26 Feb 1966, Springfield, MO; m. 7 June 1991,

John Edward Schnoebelen Jr, b. 28 Feb 1962, St. Louis, MO

[V6]5282. [10]9. **Permelia Breshears**, b. & d. 18 Nov 1878, bur Seaton Cem

[V6]5283. [10]10. **Margaret Breshears**, b. & d. 28 Aug 1879, bur Seaton Cem

[V6]5284. [10]11. **Arch Wakefield Breshears**, b. 16 Oct 1881, d. 24 Jan 1936, bur Wollard Cem

[V6]5285. [10]12. **Charley Oliver Breshears**, b. 26 Dec 1882, d. 19 Sept 1942; m. 1904, ***Nell Selsor***, m.2. 1913, ***Bertha Killion***, b. 25 June 1894, d. 6 Jan 1952; Charley and Bertha bur Charles Charity Community cem, Dallas Co, MO.

[V6]5286. [11]1. **Willie Verlin Breshears**, b. 6 Oct 1916, d. 1980; m. ***Agnes Nixon***,

[V6]5287. [10]13. **Levi Jacob Isaac Breshears**, b. 16 March 1885; m. 1912, ***Norma Brasier***,

[V6]5288. [10]14. **William Riley Breshears**, b. 1 April 1887, d. 24 Oct 1946, bur Wollard Cem

[V6]5289. [10]15. **Mary Lou Ella Breshears**, b. 24 March 1889, d. 30 Nov 1952, CA; m. ***Manford Tackett***, b. 8 Feb 1882, d. 20 Sept 1935

[V6]5290. [11]1. Harley Eugene Tackett, b. 1916, d. unm.

[V6]5291. [11]2. Cecil Tackett, b. 1917; m. Frances _____

[V6]5292. [11]3. James Tackett, b. 1919; m. Maxine J. George

[V6]5293. [11]4. Anna Irene Tackett, b. 1922; m. James Durward Harlow

[V6]5294. [11]5. Mary Catherine Tackett, b. 1927, d. 1987, bur Lindsey, CA

[V6]5295. [11]6. Ralph Manford Tackett, b. 1924, d. ?1962

[V6]5296. [10]16. **Benjamin Thomas Breshears**, b. 17 March 1891, d. 18 Aug 1922; m. 28 Dec 1910, ***Mary Elizabeth "Lizzie" Gann***, b. 1892, d/o John T. Gann and Nancy Jane Anglin

[V6]5297. [11]1. **Howard Breshears**, b. & d. 3 Sept 1913, bur Gann Cem

[V6]5298. [11]2. **Pearl Breshears**, b. 1915; m.1. ***F. Keller***; m.2. ***Limon Lacey***

[V6]5299. [11]3. **Evelyn Breshears**, b. 1922; m. 1944, ***Dale Andreason***

[V6]5300. [10]17. **Hanna Elza Breshears**, b. 5 Sept 1893, d. 22 April 1972; m. 23 Oct 1910, ***Noah Jones***, b. 22 Feb 1886, d. 10 Nov 1972

[V6]5301. [11]1. Jewell Jones, b. 1911; m. Charles R. Mack

[V6]5302. [11]2. Beulah Juanita Jones, b. 1914; m. Chester E. Hobbs

[V6]5303. [11]3. Opal Jones, b. 1916, d. 1951; m. Donald Shaw

[V6]5304. [11]4. Paul Jacob Jones, b. 1920, d. 1982; m. June Flood

[V6]5305. [11]5. Joe Jones, b. 1922; m.1. Mary ____; m.2. Lillian Adams

[V6]5306. [11]6. Barbara Jones, b. 1930; m.1. Beryl Shinn; m.2. Bolo McCorkle

[V6]5307. [11]7. Earl Jones, b. ?; m. Donna ____

Nathaniel John Breshears and Martha Lou Silkey/ Sarah Jane Hoover

[v6]5262. [10]2. **Nathaniel John Breshears**, (s/o Calvin Breshears and Missouri Jane Davidson), b. 29 March 1864, Washington, Dallas Co, MO, d. 24 July 1935, Lindsay, Tulare Co, CA, ?bur Seaton Cem, Dallas Co, MO; m.1. 1884, ***Martha Lou Silkey***, b. 15 Nov 1861, d. 17 April 1885, nine days after birth of her only child, bur Seaton Cem, Dallas Co, MO, d/o Joseph Silkey and Mary Mills; m.2. 13 Nov 1887, ***Sarah Jane Hoover***, b. 14 April 1868, Dallas Co, MO, d. 23 June 1949, Lindsay, Tulare Co, CA, d/o James Willoughby Hoover and Nancy Caroline Robinson. On 29 June 1906, Rev. N.J. Breshears helped organize Cedar Ridge Free Will Baptist Church in Dallas Co, MO, and he was elected Pastor. He also Pastored Benton Branch, Freewill Baptist Church, 1908-1911, 1913-1914, 1920-1921. He was pastor of Good Hope Southern Baptist Church, Webster Co, MO, in 1926.

Child of Nathaniel John Breshears and Martha Lou Silkey:

[V6]5308. [11]1. **Lewis Albert Breshears**, b. 8 April 1885, d. 8 July 1885, bur Seaton Cem, Dallas Co, MO.

<u>Family of Nathaniel John Breshears and Sarah Jane Hoover</u>:

[V6]5309. [11]2. **Nancy Viola Breshears**, b. 14 Oct 1888, d. 13 May 1968; m. 19 July 1908, ***James Henry Howe***, b. 22 Nov 1882, d. Nov 1961

[V6]5310. [12]1. Howard Hurble Howe, b. 1909, SD, d. 1980, CA; m. Rose Bower

[V6]5311. [12]2. Ethel Marie Howe, b. 1911; m. 1932, Forest P. Triplett

[V6]5312. [12]3. Myrtle Irene Howe, b. 1913, d. 1995; m. 1938, Arch L. Erickson

[V6]5313. [12]4. Clara Delores Howe, b. 1915; m. 1957, Erling Markussen

[V6]5314. [12]5. Edward Virgil Howe, b. 1919; m. 1941, at Buffalo, MO, Leni Elizabeth Creasser, b. 1922, Colorado Springs, CO

[V6]5315. [12]6. John Wilburn Howe, b. 1921, d. 1934, bur Wollard Cem, Dallas Co, MO

[V6]5316. [12]7. Billie Wayne Howe, b. 1924, d. 1991; m. 1948, B. Maxine Lemons

[V6]5317. [11]3. **Rosa May Breshears**, b. 11 Dec 1889, Dallas Co, MO, d. 13 June 1931, Buttonwillow, Tulare Co, CA; m. 5 Feb 1911, ***Arch Asbury***, b. 1886, d. 1970

[V6]5318. [12]1. Faye L. Asbury, b. 1911; m. 1937, Everett W. Moyer

[V6]5319. [12]2. May E. Asbury, b. 1914; m. 1941, John H. Watjen

[V6]5320. [12]3. Phebe L. Asbury, b. 1916, d. 1996; m. 1937, Norman C. Moyer

[V6]5321. [12]4. Ruth L. Asbury, b. 1918; m. 1942, Joseph H. McKinney

[V6]5322. [12]5. Pearl E. Asbury, b. 1920; m. 1940, Stanford H. Brown

[V6]5323. [12]6. Opal C.J. Asbury, b. 1922, d. 1994; m. 1943, Arthur J. Bushman

[V6]5324. [12]7. Dorcas V. Asbury, b. 1925; m. 1949, Adam P. Milechi, II

[V6]5325. [12]8. Arch Paul Asbury, b. 1928; m. 1948, Luvenny Towery

[V6]5326. [11]4. **Walter Alexander Breshears**, b. 18 Sept 1891, d. 30 July 1946, CA; m. 8 Dec 1920, Kings City, CA, ***Hazel Prine***, b. 1901, d. 1973, d/o Louis G. Prine

[V6]5327. [12]1. **Loretta May Breshears**, b. 1922, d. 1991; m.1. ***Charles Smith***; m.2. ***Jack Tallant***

[V6]5328. [12]2. **Edward Virgil Breshears**, b. 1924, d. 1968; m. ***Pallie E. Hensley***

[V6]5329. [12]3. **Helen Pearl Breshears**, b. 1928; m.1. ***Stacy Hunt***; m.2. ***George W. White Jr***

[V6]5330. [12]4. **Nathan John Breshears**, b. 1930; m. ***Sandra D. Miller***

[V6]5331. [12]5. **Theodore P. Breshears**, b. 1934, m. ***Charlene A. King***

[V6]5332. [12]6. **Herbert E. Breshears**, b. 1937; m. ***Bonnie M. Honey***

[V6]5333. [11]5. **Virgil Martin Breshears**, b. 2 Sept 1893, d. 30 March 1919, U.S. Army WWI

[V6]5334. [11]6. **Dosha Esther Breshears**, b. 13 Sept 1895, d. 20 Sept 1978, Springfield, OR; m. 28 Feb 1916, ***John Neiman***,

[V6]5335. [11]7. **Jesse Herbert Breshears**, b. 9 Oct 1897, d. 10 Dec 1976, Cayucas, Santa Barbara Co, CA; m. 25 Nov 1919, ***Ruth P. Gann***,

[V6]5336. [12]1. **Youlanda Breshears**, b. 2 June 1924, d. 11 June 1924

[V6]5337. [11]8. **Fred Calvin Breshears**, b. 1 Jan 1899, d. 29 March 1969, Powhattan, AR; m.1. ***Lora Terrill***; m.2. ***Francine Cooper***

[V6]5338. [11]9. **Zetta Florence Breshears**, b. 20 Sept 1901, d. 2 Jan 1978, Riverside, Riverside Co, CA; m. 25 Dec 1920, ***Robert Vern Wingo***, b. 1897

[V6]5339. [11]10. **Claude Hershel Breshears**, b. 31 July 1903, d. 19 Sept 1979, Malibu, CA; m.1. ***Mary Gann***; m.2. ***O. Bell***; m.2. ***Lily*** _____

[V6]5340. [11]11. **Birdie Helen Breshears**, b. 15 Feb 1906, Dalla Co, MO, d. 30 Dec 1992, Lindsay, Tulare Co, CA; m. 14 July 1923, Lindsay, Tulare Co, CA, ***Ray Elster Fultz***, b. 6 Nov 1902, d. 24 Dec 1968, Lindsay, Tulare Co, CA, s/o Levi Martin Fultz and Susan Parthen Brundridge

V6 5341. [12]1. Donald Wilbur Fultz, b. 13 July 1925, Hemet, Riverside Co, CA; m. 20 May 1948, Las Vegas, NV, Jacquelyn Funkhouser, b. 18 June 1929, Pomona, Los Angeles Co, CA, d/o Clair Willard Funkhouser and Frieda Margaret Tableman

V6 5342. [13]1. (baby girl) Fultz, b.& d. 26 Aug 1949, Riverside, CA

V6 5343. [13]2. Linda Susan Fultz, b. 10 April 1952, Lindsay, Tulare Co, CA; m. 9 Oct 1977, Elk Grove, Sacramento Co, CA, Danny L. Sharpes; ?m.2. ____ Gravelle

V6 5344. [13]3. Nancy Ann Fultz, b. 2 Jan 1954, Lindsay, Tulare Co, CA; m. 6 March 1976, Fair Oaks, Sacramento Co, CA, Mark Melenchek

V6 5345. [12]2. Larry Wayne Fultz, b. 16 Oct 1937, Lindsay, Tulare Co, CA; m. 9 Oct 1941, Las Vegas, NV,

______

V6 5346. [11]12. **Ruby Evelyn Breshears**, b. 1 Feb 1911, Long Land, Dallas Co, MO, d. 19 Jan 1971, Bakersfield, Kern Co, CA; m. 1928, ***Kenneth M. Dunbar***,

James Price Breshears and Mary Ellen Gaunt

v6 5269. [10]6. **James Price Breshears**, (s/o Calvin Breshears and Missouri Jane Davidson), b. 25 Jan 1871, d. 27 July 1930, Dallas Co, MO; m. 3 Nov 1889, ***Mary Ellen Gaunt***, b. 20 Jan 1871, d. 15 Nov 1942, d/o John William Gaunt and Exonia A. Gerhart. J.P. Breshears was a farmer.

Family of James Price Breshears and Mary Ellen Gaunt:

V6 5347. [11]1. **William M. Breshears**, b. Feb 1891, Dallas Co, MO

V6 5348. [11]2. **Albert Foster Breshears**, b. 1893, d. 1959; m. 1914 ***Delilah Pinkley***,

V6 5349. [12]x. **Orville Breshears**, b. 1917

V6 5350. [13]x. **Harold Gene Breshears**, b. 1942

V6 5351. [14]x. **Christie Lou Breshears**, b. 1970

V6 5352. [11]3. **Sylvia Ethel Breshears**, b. 21 Dec 1894, Dallas

Co, MO, d. 1956; m. 1913, ***Westley F. Anglin***, b. 1891, Dallas Co, MO

V[6]5353. [11]4. **Lewis Calvin Breshears**, b. 1897, Dallas Co, MO, d. 1972; m. 1914, ***A. Omega M. Baker***

V[6]5354. [12]x. **Leonard Franklin Breshears**,

V[6]5355. [13]x. **Janis Breshears**, Jan Penly-Donley <josie2@centurytel. net>

V[6]5356. [11]4. & [11]5. twin daughters, b. & d. 25 July 1900, bur Seaton Cem, Dallas Co, MO

V[6]5357. [11]6. & [11]7. twin daughters: **Ada** and **Vada Breshears**, b. 4 Jan 1901, d. as infants

V[6]5358. [11]8. **Ernest Cleo Breshears**, (twin), b. 4 Jan 1903, Dallas Co, MO, d. 1979; m. 1922, ***Nona Cheek***

V[6]5359. [11]9. **Lonnie Leo Breshears**, (twin), b. 4 Jan 1903, d. 11 Nov 1919, bur Seaton Cem, Dallas Co, MO

V[6]5360. [11]10. **Ezra Paul Breshears**, b. c1906, Dallas Co, MO, d. 1988, CA; m. 1926, ***Ora Evans***

V[6]5361. [11]11. **Matilda Jane Breshears**, b. 1908, d. 1994; m. 1926, ***William F. Anglin***

V[6]5362. [11]12. **Belva Retta Eugenia Bertha Breshears**, b. 1911, d. 1994; m. 1928, ***Charlie Wise***

46. ALEXANDER BRASHEARS and MARGARET BRESHEARS

[v6]**10.** [8]4. **Alexander Brashears**, (probably (no documents) s/o ?James Brashears and Mary Jane Turner), b. 20 April 1807, SC; m.1. c1827, in Lawrence Co, TN, ***Margaret "Peggy" Breshears***, b. 15 Feb 1811, SC, d. 30 April 1864, Benton Co, MO, d/o Henry Brashears/Breshears Sr and Eleanor (Harden?); m.2. Mrs. ***Mary Jane (Harper) Murray***, b. 1828, MO; died 9 April 1880 in Benton Co, MO, widow of Thomas Murray and d/o of John M. and Nancy Harper. Mary Jane had two children by her first marriage: Thomas Riley Murray and John Murray; and two children by Alexander Brashears: George Harper Brashears and Nancy Ellen Brashears. (See "Brashears/Breshears Newsletter," July 1974, announcing the Omak Picnic, by Roy Colbert.) A "History of Hickory Co, MO" has Alexander's birthplace as Warren Co, TN.

Alexander Brashears is not listed in the 1830 US Census of Lawrence Co, TN; yet it is clear that he and Margaret lived in the county.

The names of Alexander Breshears and his wife, Margaret, appear in the estate documents of her father, Henry Breshears Sr, who d. 1828 in Lawrence Co, TN.

Lawrence Co TN Minutes Book, 1828-1834, p.188: 5 July 1830, records three transfers of a plat and certificate in the name of Erasmus Tippitt for 25 acres: first, from said Tippett to Berry Brashers, was produced and proven by the oath of Franklin Buchanan, witness; second, ?? by 2/3 by ?? [can anyone ungarble the reading?] from said Brashers to Elisha Franklin and [third,] from said Franklin to Alexander Brashers, was produced and proven by oaths of Nathan McClen? and Augusten W. Bumpass, witnesses.

Lawrence Co TN Minutes Book, 1828-1834, p.481: 1 April 1833, "Alexander and William C. Brashers, orphan children, are bound apprentices to Alexander Brashers, whereupon an indenture was entered into accordingly." The Younger Alexander and William C. Brashers, orphans, have not been identified, but were possibly nephews.

On 25 Dec 1833, Alexander Brashears bought 23 acres from William Wisdom, 7th Dist, Range 5, Sec 3, on Knob Creek, $175, Grant #19458, dated 16 April 1831. Witnesses: John Wisdom, Daniel Lindsey. (LawrCo, TN, Deeds, D:289). Soon afterward, Alexander and Margaret moved to Benton Co, MO. Birthplaces and dates of their children would indicate that they moved to Missouri, 1833-35.

In a book *Breshears, Jordan, and Ethridge Families of Missouri*, by Carmen Elizabeth Collins, she states that in 1833 Alexander sold his own land and his wife Margaret's (Peggy's) share of Henry Sr's land, and he, Nathan Turner, and Middleton Breshears (the Younger) went on to settle the Breshears Valley in Benton Co, MO. Margaret (Peggy) was a sister to Henry Breshears Jr. (Additional data from Cathey Pauley-Toliver <ctoliver @socket.net>)

Alexander was known as "Squire" Breshears. His cattle brand, registered in Benton Co, MO, in 1842 was one of the first three brands in the county. Alexander was one of the first residents of Breshears Valley.

"Located in Missouri, astride the Hickory-Benton County line, bounded on the east and north by the Pomme de Terre River, and on the west by high hills, lies six thousand fertile acres that have come to be known as *Breshears Valley*. Well-watered by several springs and covered with wild grass and hay, the valley was, once, abundant in deer, wild turkey, and other game." (Roy Colbert's description.) "Between 1865 and 1900, the Valley was, surely, the *Breshears Nation*, as it was said that no one owned land in the Valley who was not named Breshears, or whose wife was not a Breshears girl."

Roy Colbert's text about Alexander Brashears: "In 1835, with the Indians removed and the land opened to the white man, Alexander Brashears/ Breshears, wife Margaret, and family left their home and friends in Lawrence County, Tennessee, to settle on land only recently vacated by a tribe of Kickapoo Indians. Three years later, in 1838, Alex's cousin, Henry Brashears/ Breshears, who was also his brother-in-law, brought his family to the Valley. Alex built his home at the eastern side of the valley, near the river, while Henry settled down to raise his family on the western side.

"There are indications that the two men were not close friends, though they were related by blood and marriage--but they helped each other as neighbors on the frontier had to do through necessity. Alex was a gregarious person, who was a leader and a councilor to the other settlers of the Valley and surrounding country. He became a Justice of the Peace and performed many marriages. In Tennessee, his ancestors were horse traders and the trait seems to be handed down even to his descendants of today.

"Henry seems to have been the quiet farmer, who wished only to be left alone to till his land and raise his family. This farmer and part-time blacksmith built a comfortable home, raised a large family, and was an honest, law-abiding and unassuming man."

1850 US Census, Benton Co, MO: #214:		
Alexander Brashears,	43, b. SC, c1807	
Robert Brashears	32, b. TN, c1818	[? a young couple?]
Elizabeth Brashears,	28, b. TN c1822	
Margarete Brashears,	43, b. SC, c1807, wife of Alexander	
Mary E. Brashears,	16, b. TN, c1834	
John A. Brashears,	14, b. MO, c1836	
James H. Brashears,	11, b. MO, c1839	
N.J. Brashears, (f)	7, b. MO, c1843	
1850 US Census, Benton Co, MO, #215:		
Alexander Brashears,	27, b. TN c1823	This is probably the orphan.
Louisa Brashears,	23, b. TN c1827	[née Blackstone]
William C. Brashears,	4, b. MO c1846	
James T. Brashears,	2, b. MO c1848	

In 1870, Alexander Brashears was in Hickory Co, MO, where he probably died.

The Robert and Elizabeth Brashears in Alexander's household in 1850 are surely a young couple; they're far too old to be children of Alexander and Margaret, as one FHL chart asserts. The younger Alexander next door is surely the orphan whom Alexander and Margaret were bound to take care of in Lawrence Co, TN, in 1833.

Family of Alexander Brashears and Margaret "Peggy" Breshears: (Some of their family went back to spelling the surname "Brashears." Data on descendants from censuses, marriage records, notes of Huetta Breshears, of Wheatland, MO.)

[V6]5401. [9]1. ***Louisa Breshears**, b. c1831, Lawrence Co, TN, d. 1870, TX or AR; m. ***Moses Southard***, b. c1821, Lawrence Co, TN.

[V6]5402. [9]2. **Mary Elizabeth Brashears**, b. 5 June 1833, Lawrence Co, TN, d. probably in childbirth, 27 May 1855, Benton Co, MO, bur Henderson Cem, moved by U.S.Corps of Engineers to Avery Cem; m. c1853. ***William Henry "Wilse" Henderson***, b. 15 Feb 1828, TN, d. 23 May 1891, Hickory Co, MO. After Mary died, Wilse m.2. ***Sarah P. Breshears***, (d/o John Breshears and Naoma Ann Hogg).

[V6]5403. [10]1. Minnie Henderson, b. c1855; m. ______ Parsley

[V6]5404. [9]3. ***John Alexander Brashears**, b. 18 Aug 1835, Benton Co, MO, d. 19 March 1901; m. ***Nancy Jane Tipton***,

[V6]5405. [9]4. ***James H. Breshears**, b. 14 Sept 1838, Benton Co, MO, d. 18 March 1879, Benton Co, MO; m. ***Sarah Lizabeth Henderson***,

[V6]5406. [9]5. **N.J. Brashears**, (fem) b. c1843, MO (7 in 1850) [Some records have this individual as Andrew Jackson Breshears, b. 1843, d. bef 1860]

Family of Alexander Brashears and Mary Jane Harper: (per Roy Colbert)

[V6]5407. [9]6. **George Harper Brashears**, b. 14 Oct 1865, Benton Co, MO, d. OK; m. 25 Nov 1884, in OK, ***Polly North***. They had 5 children; names unknown to me.

[V6]5408. [9]7. **Nancy Ellen Brashears**, b. 1865, d. 27 July 1888, bur Harper Cem; m. c1887, ***Silas Gaston***,

[V6]5409. [10]1. Mary Gaston, b. 1888, d. 1905, age 17; m. **Francis Marion Breshears,** (s/o William Carroll Green Breshears and Mary Orleana Rice) See his listing.

Families of two of the orphans whom Alexander and Margaret raised:

V65410. 9x. **Robert Brashears,** b. c1818 (32 in 1850); m. ***Elizabeth _______,***

V65411. 9y. **Alexander Brashears**, b. c1823 (27 in 1850); m. ***Louisa Blackstone,***

V65412. 101. **William C. Brashears**, b. c1846, MO (4 in 1850)

V65413. 102. **James T. Brashears**, b. c1848, MO (2 in 1850)

Louisa Breshears and Moses Southard

v65401. 91. **Louisa Breshears**, (d/o Alexander Brashears and Margaret "Peggy" Breshears), b. c1831, Lawrence Co, TN, d. c1870, TX or AR; m. ***Moses Southard***, b. c1821, Lawrence Co, TN, d. after 1865, AR or TX. Moses Southard was said to be a southern sympathizer, who took the family to Texas during the Civil War. The children apparently made their way back to MO after the war, alone.

Family of Louisa Breshears and Moses Southard:

V65414. 101. Daniel Scott Southard Sr, b. 1 Sept 1847, Benton Co, MO, d. 1920, near Cross Timbers, MO; m. c1881, Elvie J. _____, b. April 1854, d. 1924, MO. While Moses was in the south,Daniel lived with his uncle, James H. Breshears.

V65415. 111. Daniel Scott Southard Jr, b. c1882

V65416. 112. John M. Southard, b. c1884; m. Carrie Harlan

V65417. 113. Martha Southard, b. Feb 1886, d. 1963, MO; m. George C. Chasteen, b. 1881

V65418. 114. Richard W. Southard, b. Sept 1887

V65419. 115. Walter Franklin Southard, b. 24 Nov 1890, d. 19 March 1918, Hickory Co, MO, bur New Home Cem; m. Mealie Mae Mullins, d/o George Mullins and Maude Barber. After Walter Southard died, Mealie Mae m.2. ***Everett Robert Breshears***, (s/o William

Thomas Breshears and Della Beth), (see below)

V65420. 121. Faye Ida Mae Southard, b. 28 Nov 1913; m. Orville Admire

V65421. 122. Chloeia Franklin Southard, b. 31 July 1918; m. c1938, Earl Stevens, s/o Abe Stevens and Fredonia ____.

V65422. 131. Dianna Kay Stevens, b. c1939; m.2. Harold McCoy; m.2. Charles McCormack

V65423. 116. Arminta Southard, b. ___, d. May 1916, MO, m. ______ Dobson

V65424. 102. George M. Southard, b. 30 Dec 1849, Benton Co, MO, d. there, 22 June 1915; m. Mary P. ______, b. 17 July 1845, d. 5 April 1915, Benton Co, MO, both bur Concord Cem, Benton Co, MO.

V65425. 103. Richard Alexander Southard, b. c1852, Benton Co, MO; m. Mary Annetta Cooper,

V65426. 111. Sarah Francis Southard, b. 11 April 1871, d. 26 June 1948; m. 5 April 1888, in Benton Co, MO, **William Marion Breshears**, (s/o John Breshears and Susannah Ihrig), b. 27 Dec 1866, near Avery, Benton Co, MO, d. 24 Aug 1931, Warsaw, Benton Co, MO. See his listing for children.

V65427. 104. Margaret A. Southard, b. c1854, Benton Co, MO

V65428. 105. Elizabeth Allie Southard, b. c1856, Benton Co, MO

V65429. 106. Mary Elizabeth Southard, b. 14 Nov 1862, Benton Co, MO, d. 11 Feb 1931, Clayton, Pushmataha Co, OK; m. **James Monroe Breshears**, (s/o Robert Hiram Breshears and Anna Breshears) b. 13 March 1857, Hickory Co, MO, d. 3 May 1918, Hickory Co, MO. See James Monroe Breshears's listing for their children.

Figure 92: The John Alexander Breshears family in 1897
Back Row: William Breshears, Noah Martin, Hugh Breshears, Jess Breshears, Edd Breashears;
Next row down: Lee Breshears, Joe Breshears, holding his daughter Ethel (later, Myers), Venus (Cates) Breshears, Charley Breshears, Mary Margaret Breshears, who was blind, and Dora (Breshears) Pippin,
Front row: Fannie (Holley) Breshears, holding A.D. Breshears with Lottie (Martin) Breshears by her side, Eliza (Butler) Breshears, holding Edith (Breshears) Miller, Phebia (Breshears) Martin, holding Ola, John A. Breshears, Nancy Jane (Tipton) Breshears, Annie (Dickey) Breshears, holding Dina. Next to John A. is Beulah (Breshears) Byrum, and next to Nancy is Sadie Breshears.

John Alexander Brashears and Nancy Jane Tipton

v6 5403. 93. **John Alexander Brashears**, (s/o Alexander Brashears and Margaret "Peggy" Breshears), b. 18 Aug 1835, Benton Co, MO, d. there, 19 March 1901; m. 3 April 1857, (ceremony performed by her father) in Benton Co, MO, ***Nancy Jane Tipton***, b. 22 May 1940, Illinois, d. 28 April 1933, Benton Co, MO, d/o Rev. James A. Tipton Jr and Mary J. Henderson. John Alexander Breshears was a strong member of the Dunkard Church. He was for a time postmaster at Avery, Hickory Co, MO.

Both John A. and Nancy are buried at Spring Branch cem, Avery, Hickory Co, MO.

Family of John Alexander Brashears and Nancy Jane Tipton:

V6 5430. 10 1. **James Henry Breshears**, b. 28 Aug 1858, d. 8 Aug 1871, almost 13 years old, bur Sarah Pippin cem.

V6 5431. 10 2. **Mary Margaret Breshears**, b. 28 May 1860, Benton Co, MO, d. 18 March 1929, unmarried. Mary Margaret was blind throughout her life; yet was able to live alone, function well, and do her own housework, according to family members. She owned one of the first radios in Breshears valley.

V6 5432. 10 3. **Thomas B. Breshears**, b. 29 March 1862, d. 7 Aug 1866, Benton Co, MO, bur Sarah Pippin Cem.

V6 5433. 10 4. **John H. Breshears**, b. 6 Sept 1863, Benton Co, MO, d. 22 Aug 1867, Benton Co, MO, bur Sarah Pippin Cem.

V6 5434. 10 5. ***Edward Franklin Breshears**, b. 9 Dec 1865, Benton Co, MO, d. there, 21 March 1915; m.19 July 1887, in Benton Co, MO, ***Annie M. Dickey***, (mother of the children), b. 13 Sept 1869, Benton Co, MO, d. there, 17 Jan 1911; m.2. c1912, in Benton Co, MO, ***Sadie Hamilton***,

V6 5435. 10 6. ***Robert E. Lee Brashears**, b. 12 March 1868, Benton Co, MO, d. there, 7 Jan 1944; m. 14 March 1890, ***Mary Frances "Fannie" Holley***

V6 5436. 10 7. ***William Wesley "Will" Breshears**, b. 1 Sept 1869, Avery, Hickory Co, MO, d. there, 30 April 1949; m. 23 Nov 1893, in Benton Co, MO, ***Eliza Ellen Butler***,

V6 5437. 10 8. **Phoebe Jane Breshears**, b. 22 Aug 1871, Benton Co, MO, d. there, 15 Dec 1909; m. 13 Dec 1891, in Benton Co, MO, ***Noah E. Martin***, b. 16 Aug 1866, Benton Co, MO, d. 1 Feb 1951, Wheatland, Hickory Co, MO. Both are buried in Spring Branch Cem, Avery, MO.

V6 5438. 11 1. Homer D. Martin, b. 26 Jan 1893, Hickory Co, MO, d. 1893, age 10 months

V65439. 112. Ola Martin, b. c1894, Hickory Co, MO, d. ____ in Kansas

V65440. 113. Leonard V. Martin, b. 28 April 1896, d. 13 May 1924, bur Spring Branch Cem, Avery, MO

V65441. 114. Myrtle Martin, b. c1898, Hickory Co, MO, d. 1992, Minnesota

V65442. 115. Willard Martin, b. 14 Nov 1900, Hickory Co, MO, d. c1978, Pierre, SD; m. Ann ______,

V65443. 116. Alva E. Martin, b. 8 July 1904, d. 15 Dec 1904, 5mos, bur Spring Branch Cem, Avery, MO

V65444. 117. Edna Martin, b. 1905, Hickory Co, MO; m. ______ Nelson, b. IA, d. Inwood, Iowa

V65445. 118. Una Martin, b. 1907, Hickory Co, MO, d. 15 July 1996, Rapid City, SD; m. _____ Nierson

V65446. 119. Twin infant sons Martin, b.&d. 9 Sept 1909

V65447. 109. **Joseph Delmer "Dell" Breshears**, b. 10 July 1873, Benton Co, MO, d. 13 Sept 1955, Wheatland, Hickory Co, MO; m. c1895, in Hickory Co, MO, ***Eva L. Crates***, b. 6 Jan 1878, Hickory Co, MO, d. there, 1 March 1972. Both are buried in Sumner Cem, Hickory Co, MO.

V65448. 111. **Ida Ethel Breshears**, b. 4 Jan 1896, Hickory Co, MO, d. there, 15 July 1984; m. 2 April 1916, in Hickory Co, MO, ***Cyrus C. Myers***, b. 5 Dec 1893, Hickory Co, MO, d. there, 1 Dec 1984

V65449. 121. Doris Eugene Myers, b. 18 July 1921

V65450. 112. **Berchie Edgar Breshears**, b. 11 Feb 1898, Hickory Co, MO, d. 1 March 1971, Benton Co, MO; m.1. ***Cora Lula Blackwell***, b. 19 April 1900, d. 18 Sept 1962, Benton Co, MO; m.2. 3 April 1963, in Benton Co, MO, ***Myrtle C. Williams***, b. 1904, d. 1991,

V65451. 121. **Quentin Breshears**,

V65452. 113. **Alma M. Breshears**, b. 17 March 1911, Hickory Co, MO, d. there, 19 Aug 1986; m. 19 April 1930, in Hickory Co, MO, ***Clifford H. Crates***, b. 7 Aug 1905, Hickory Co, MO, d.

there, 10 March 1982

V6 5453. [12]1. Robert Gerald Crates, b. 11 July 1931, d. 24 May 1980; m. Jane ______. Ch: James Edward; Robert Gerald Jr; Robin; and Shirley Crates

V6 5454. [12]2. John Joseph Crates,

V6 5455. [12]3. Beverly Crates,

V6 5456. [10]10. ***Hugh Walter Brashears**, b. 17 Feb 1875, Benton Co, MO, d. 29 Feb 1952, Benton Co, MO; m. 24 June 1897, in Benton Co, MO, ***Bernetta A. Maxwell***,

V6 5457. [10]11. **Jesse Green Breshears**, b. 23 Oct 1876, Avery, MO, d. 2 Feb 1957, Wheatland, Hickory Co, MO, age 80y, 2m, 9d, bur Spring Branch Cem; m. 28 Dec 1902, ***Price Murray***, b. 11 June 1882, Hickory Co, MO, d. there, 8 Jan 1969, d/o John Murray and Rebecca Rogers. Both are buried in Spring Branch Cem, Avery, MO. Jesse was a farmer and livestock trader; lived his whole life near Avery, Hickory Co, MO.

V6 5458. [11]1. **Lena Helen Breshears**, b. 7 Oct 1903, Hickory Co, MO, d. 21 Dec 1994, Bolivar, Benton Co, MO; m. 25 Sept 1921, ***James Lewis Wright***, b. 27 Dec 1896, MO, d. 16 Nov 1982, MO, (s/o George Wright and Emma Breshears). James Wright was a farmer, book-keeper, teacher, preacher, and served 7 years in the MO legislature. Both he and Lena are buried in Spring Branch Cem, Avery, MO.

V6 5459. [12]1. Dale Wright, b. 1905, Redlands, CA

V6 5460. [12]2. Helen Wright, b. 1907; m. _____ Davis

V6 5461. [12]3. Gwen Wright, b. 1909; m. _____ Mills

V6 5462. [11]2. **Elif Breshears**, b. c1905, d. c1910, age 5yrs, bur Spring Branch Cem, Avery, MO.

V6 5463. [11]3. **Nina Faye Breshears**, b. 20 Dec 1912, Hickory Co, MO, d. 10 June 1977, Springfield, MO; m.1. ***Woodrow Stark***; m.2. ***Judson W. Lee***

V6 5464. [12]1. Sandra Sue Stark,

V6 5465. [12]2. Lowell Richard Lee,

V6 5466. [10]12. **Dora Belle Breshears**, b. 2 Dec 1878, Avery, MO, d. 30 Jan 1958, Benton Co, MO; m. 21 Sept 1910, in Benton Co, MO, ***Charles Walter Pippins***, b. 17 May 1881, Benton Co, MO, d. there, 3 Sept 1966, s/o W. Pippins and Sarah Henderson (or Breshears). Dora and Charles both buried Spring Branch Cem, Avery, MO.

V6 5467. [11]1. Archie A. Pippins, b. 25 Feb 1916, Benton Co, MO, d. 7 Oct 1971, Hickory Co, MO, bur New Home Cem; m. 5 Oct 1935, Marie Downs, b. 7 Jan 1920, Benton Co, MO, d. 11 Jan 2001, Hermitage Care Center, Hermitage, MO, d/o Samuel Downs and Mega Clark.

V6 5468. [12]1. Wilma Darlene Pippins, b. 9 Oct 1936, d. 11 July 1939, 2y, 9m

V6 5469. [12]2. Willa Mae Pippins, b. c1938; m. Larry Ingles. Ch: Maria; and Becky Ingles

V6 5470. [11]2. Merlin Pippins, b. 9 July 1917, Benton Co, MO, d. 23 March 1998, St John Regional Hosp, Springfield, MO; m.1. Jewell Brown, b. 23 July 1919, Benton Co, MO, d. there, 28 July 1964; m.2. c1964, Jewel Harmon, b. 25 April 1906

V6 5471. [12]1. Mary Ann Pippins, b. c1938; m. Carl DeFreese,

V6 5472. [11]3. Orville Franklin Pippins, b. 16 March 1914, Benton Co, MO, d. there, 30 July 1915, bur Spring Branch Cem, Avery, MO.

V6 5473. [10]13. **Charles J. Breshears**, b. 17 May 1881, d. 1 May 1902, age 21, bur Spring Branch Cem, Avery, MO

V6 5474. [10]14. **Henry Clark Breshears**, b. 18 April 1883, d. 4 Sept 1884, bur Sarah Pippin Cem,

Edward Franklin Breshears and Annie M. Dickey

V6 5434. 10 5. **Edward Franklin Breshears**, (s/o John Alexander Breshears and Nancy Jane Tipton), b. 9 Dec 1865, Benton Co, MO, d. there, 21 March 1915; m.19 July 1887, in Benton Co, MO, ***Annie M. Dickey***, (mother of the children), b. 13 Sept 1869, Benton Co, MO, d. there, 17 Jan 1911; m.2. c1912, in Benton Co, MO, ***Sadie Hamilton***,

Family of Edward Franklin Breshears and Annie M. Dickey:

V6 5475. 11 1. **Orlando F. Breshears**, b. 3 March 1889, Hickory Co, MO, d. 5 May 1891, age 2

V6 5476. 11 2. **Sadie C. Breshears**, b. 11 Nov 1890, Hickory Co, MO, d. 17 Oct 1910, Benton Co, MO; m. ***Lloyd Cardwell*** , Sadie died of a gunshot wound in the heart; thought to have been killed by her husband.

V6 5477. 11 3. **Dena Breshears**, b. c1895, Benton Co, MO, d. _____, Philadelphia, PA; m. ***William Brennan***,

V6 5478. 11 4. **Larry Lee Breshears**, b. c1898, Benton Co, MO, d. 13 Jan 1981, Benton Co, MO; m. ***Ada Bell Kidwell***,

V6 5479. 12 1. **James Russell "Jim" Breshears**, b. 29 April 1928, Fristoe, Benton Co, MO; m. ***Jean Lee Ohlhausen***.

V6 5480. 13 1. **David Lee Breshears**; m. ***Amie Lynn Bell***.

V6 5481. 13 2. **Karin Lynn Breshears**; m. ***Scott Eckert***. Ch: Sarah Elizabeth Eckert

V6 5482. 13 3. **Kristin Joy Breshears**,

V6 5483. 11 5. **Grace Breshears**, b. c1900, Benton Co, MO, d. _____, Kansas City, MO; m. ***Lawrence Jackman***,

V6 5484. 11 6. **Karma Breshears**, b. c1902, Benton Co, MO, d. Chicago, IL; m.1. (after death of her sister, Dora Mae) ***Everett Flodin***, m.2. _______ ***Applewhite***,

V6 5485. 11 7. **Dora Mae Breshears**, b. 17 May 1904, Benton Co, MO, d. there, 26 Sept 1943; m. ***Everett Flodin***,

V6 5486. 11 8. **John A. Breshears**, b. 17 Dec 1906, Benton Co, MO, d. there, 12 April 1908,

Robert E. Lee Brashears and Mary Frances "Fannie" Holley

v6 5435. 10 4. **Robert E. Lee Brashears**, (s/o John Alexander Brashears and Nancy Jane Tipton), b. 12 March 1868, in Breshears Valley, on the Benton-Hickory County line, d. 7 Jan 1944; m. 14 March 1890, ***Mary Frances "Fannie" Holley***, b. 13 April 1873, Benton Co, MO, d. there, 31 March 1963, d/o John Holley and Isabel Donnell. Both are buried in Concord Cem, Fristoe, Benton Co, MO.

Family of Robert E. Lee Brashears and Mary Frances Holley:

V6 5487. 11 1. **Beulah Belle Breshears**, b. 1 Jan 1891, Benton Co, MO, d. 30 Aug 1992, over 100 years old, bur Fristoe Cem; m. 7 May 1913, ***Arlie D. Byrum***, b. 22 Nov 1887, Benton Co, MO, d. 19 Jan 1953, Fristoe, Benton Co, MO.

V6 5488. 12 1. Thelma Chloe Byrum, b. 15 Jan 1914, d. 6 May 1994; m. 27 April 1935, Hubert Durham.

V6 5489. 13 1. Clinton Leroy Durham; m. _____. ch: Mary Jean, Larry, Debra, and John Durham

V6 5490. 12 2. Samuel Noral Byrum, b. 3 Dec 1915; m. Irene Estes.

V6 5491. 13 1. Wanda Arlene Byrum; m. _____ Peterson. ch: Betty Peel and Eric Peterson

V6 5492. 12 3. William Oral "Rass" "Joe" Byrum, b. 29 March 1917, d. 12 June 1994, bur Fristoe Cem; m. 8 Oct 1955, Pauline Vinson. no ch.

V6 5493. 12 4. Robert Loren "Jack" Byrum, b. 20 Feb 1919, d. 24 June 1994, bur Fristoe Cem; m. 10 Nov 1949, Daisy L. Marmaduke. ch: Nancy, Kathy, Amy, and Tammy Byrum

V6 5494. 12 5. Kenneth Leland "Pete" Byrum, b. 9 May 1921; n.m.

V6 5495. 12 6. Mary Ruth Byrum, b. 10 May 1923, d. 15 Feb 1936

V6 5496. 12 7. Carroll Dale "Shorty" Byrum, b. 30 Dec 1925; m. 18 April 1953, Mary Jane Boring. no ch.

V6 5497. 12 8. Calvin Joe Byrum, b. 20 Nov 1927

[V6]5498. [12]9. infant Byrum, b.&d. 5 Nov 1929

[V6]5499. [12]10. Verna Mae Byrum, b. 30 March 1932; m. 10 March 1951, Roy E. Stull. no ch.

[V6]5500. [11]2. **Lottie Mae Breshears**, b. 11 Dec 1892, Benton Co, MO, d. 27 June 1996, Asbury, MO, age 103, she had been a member of the Asbury Baptist church for 75 years; m.5 July 1916, in Warsaw, Benton Co, MO, ***Floyd E. Martin***, b. _____, d. 13 Jan 1968, Asbury, MO

[V6]5501. [12]1. John Lee Martin, b. c1919

[V6]5502. [12]2. Frances Martin, b. c1927

[V6]5503. [11]3. **Arthur Donald Breshears**, b. 14 Jan 1895, Benton Co, MO, d. there, 2 July 1895; m. ***Mora Susan Breshears***, (d/o George N. Breshears and Rebecca Jane Butler), b. 25 Oct 1894, Benton Co, MO, d. there, 10 March 1967. Both are buried in Concord Cem, Benton Co, MO.

[V6]5504. [12]1. **Alma Roberta Breshears**, b. 15 Aug 1918, Benton Co, MO, d. 20 July 2002; m. ***Harold Ralph "Buss" Aery***, b. 23 Feb 1916, d. 24 May 1978, Benton Co, MO

[V6]5505. [11]4. **Lemuel Breshears**, b. 7 Sept 1897, Benton Co, MO, d. there, 21 Oct 1900

[V6]5506. [11]5. Son **Breshears**, b. 20 Sept 1900, Benton Co, MO, d. 26 Oct 1900

[V6]5507. [11]6. **Nancy Marie Breshears**, b. 7 Oct 1901, Benton Co, MO, d. 30 Jan 1979; m.1. ***Elzia Lusk***; m.2. ***James "Jim" Montgomery***, d. when his son was about 3 months old; m.3. ***Ray J. Ecton***, b. 23 Aug 1893, d. _____,

[V6]5508. [12]1. Mary Lee Lusk; m. William J. Henderson

[V6]5509. [12]2. Patricia Lusk; m. _____ Waggoner

[V6]5510. [12]3. Doyle Montgomery

[V6]5511. [11]7. **Wilma Fern Breshears**, b. 13 Oct 1904, Benton Co, MO, d. 13 Nov 1984; m.1. ***Guy Henderson***, (s/o Robert Marvin Henderson and Arvilla Breshears); m.2. ***Sherman Bybee***, s/o Bluford Bybee and Elizabeth _______. See Guy's listing for their child.

[V6]5512. [11]8. **Lucille Breshears**, b. 10 March 1907, Benton Co,

MO, d. 26 June 1992, Kennewick, WA; m. ***Garnet W. "Mutt" Fleishman***, Ch: Susan or Kent Fleishman.

V6 5513. 11 9. **Eldon Breshears**, b. 11 Jan 1910, Benton Co, MO, living in Port Hadlock, WA in July 1996; m. ***Wilma Jenkins***

V6 5514. 12 1. **Nancy (or Susan) Breshears**, (adopted)

V6 5515. 11 10. Girl **Breshears**, b. & d. 3 Nov 1915, Benton Co, MO,

William Wesley "Will" Breshears and Eliza Ellen Butler

v6 5436. 10 7. **William Wesley "Will" Breshears**, (s/o John Alexander Breshears and Nancy Jane Tipton), b. 1 Sept 1869, Avery, Hickory Co, MO, d. there, 30 April 1949; m. 23 Nov 1893, in Benton Co, MO, ***Eliza Ellen Butler***, b. 28 June 1871, White Cloud, MO, d. 25 Dec 1947, Avery, MO, d/o Henry Butler and Martha Skinner. Both Will and Eliza are buried in Avery Cem, Avery, MO.

Family of William Wesley Breshears and Eliza Ellen Butler:

V6 5516. 11 1. **Edith Eldora Breshears**, b. 20 April 1895, Hickory Co, MO, d. 1981, CA; m. 23 March 1918, in Hickory Co, MO, ***Forest Houston Miller***, b. 1886, Benton Co, MO, d. 18 April 1978, Stanislaus Co, CA, s/o John Miller and Nannie Ingram.

V6 5517. 12 1. Forest Wayland Miller, b. 11 June 1918, Benton Co, MO, d. c1960, Sonoma, CA; m.1. Genevieve ______; m.2. Bea Stanbaugh

V6 5518. 12 2. Winifred Oryene Miller, b. 15 May 1920, Benton Co, MO; m. "Bud" Budke

V6 5519. 11 2. **Sylvia Jane Breshears**, b. 20 June 1897, Hickory Co, MO, d. there, 22 Sept 1898, bur Jones Cem, Avery, MO

V6 5520. 11 3. **Eva Mae Breshears**, b. 9 July 1899, Hickory Co, MO, d. 18 March 1993, Independence, MO; m. 9 June 1922, Wheatland, Hickory Co, MO, ***Farrell Edgar Breshears***, (s/o Samuel Breshears and Ettie Baugh), b. 6 Oct 1903, Benton Co, MO, d.

there, 19 Oct 1980. Both are buried in Riverside Cem, Warsaw, MO.

V6 5521. [12]1. **Edwin Burrell Breshears**, b. 11 Dec 1925, Benton Co, MO, d. 16 March 1972, Columbia, MO; m. 30 Oct 1943, in Benton Co, MO, ***Helen Hazel Hosmann***, b. 3 March 1934, Benton Co, MO,

V6 5522. [13]1. **Joe Breshears**,

V6 5523. [13]2. **Lois Breshears**, m. ***Mike Miller***. Ch: Julie Ann; and Jason Miller

V6 5524. [13]3. **Dean Breshears**,

V6 5525. [12]2. **Betty Jane Breshears**, b. 25 Aug 1933, Benton Co, MO; m. ***Kenneth Witte***. Ch: Sally; and Steve Witte

V6 5526. [12]3. **Judith Ann Breshears**, b. 1 March 1937, Benton Co, MO; m. ***Joe Howard Murphy***, b. 27 March 1930, Smithville, MO, d. 28 Feb 1994, Independence, MO. ch: Debby; and Jimmy Murphy

V6 5527. [11]4. **Nelly Irene Breshears**, b. 4 Nov 1901, Avery, MO, d. 28 July 1996, Morre-Few Nursing Home, Nevada, MO; m. 23 Aug 1930, in Kansas City, MO, ***James Eddie "Edd" Prine***, b. 30 Dec 1895, Hickory Co, MO, d. 11 Sept 1975, Nevada, Vernon Co, MO

V6 5528. [12]1. James Eddie Prine, Jr, b. 6 May 1927; m. Mary Wanda Springer.

V6 5529. [13]1. Mary Elaine Prine,

V6 5530. [13]2. James Duane Prine; m.1. Linda Kay Thomas (1 ch); m.2. Angela Drake (2 ch); m.3. Johnette Davidson (1 ch). Ch: Jennifer; James Lee; Jessica Dawn; and Jamie Lee Prine.

V6 5531. [11]5. **Charles Noel Breshears**, b. 20 Oct 1903, Hickory Co, MO, d. there, 16 Oct 1907, bur Jones Cem, Avery, MO

V6 5532. [11]6. **Ora Franklin Breshears**, b. 28 April 1908, Hickory Co, MO, d. June 1979, CA; m. ***Wilma Frances Holley***, b. 7 July 1907, Benton Co, MO, d/o John Holley and Mettie Mitchener

V[6]5533. [12]1. **William Holley Breshears**, b. 18 June 1936, Avery, Hickory Co, MO; m. ***Betty Agee***, d/o William Agee and Beatrise Sweet

V[6]5534. [13]1. **Holley Ann Breshears**; m. ***Tim Copetti***.

V[6]5535. [13]2. **Don Keith Breshears,**

V[6]5536. [12]2. **Barbara Sue Breshears**, (twin) b. 27 July 1937, Avery, Benton Co, MO; m. ***Donald Franklin Ferriera***, s/o Lewis Ferriera and Exa Jacobson

V[6]5537. [13]1. Jana Lynne Ferriera; m. Jeffrey D. Mitchell.

V[6]5538. [13]2. Julie Renne Ferriera; m. James R. Meyers.

V[6]5539. [13]3. Jill Denise Ferriera; m. Dennis M. Silva.

V[6]5540. [12]3. **Beverly Rue Breshears**, (twin), b. 27 July 1937, Avery, Benton Co, MO; m. ***Harold Dean McCoy***, b. 10 Jan 1933, Holdenville, Hughes Co, OK, s/o John McCoy

V[6]5541. [13]1. Sharon Kay McCoy (step-child); m. Dale Lamb,

V[6]5542. [13]2. Delisa Dinette McCoy (step-child); m. Robert Walls

V[6]5543. [13]3. Brett Alan McCoy, b. Modesto, CA

V[6]5544. [12]4. **Richard Kent "Dick" Breshears**, b. 17 Dec 1946, Modesto, Stanislaus Co, California; m. ***Suzanne Cecille Carrere***, b. 5 Nov 1946, Oakdale, Stanislaus Co, CA, d/o Francis Carrera and Frances Compton

V[6]5545. [13]1. **Jocelyn Marie Breshears,**

V[6]5546. [13]2. **David Michael Breshears,**

V[6]5547. [11]7. Infant **Breshears**, b. & d. 21 July 1908, bur Jones Cem, Avery, MO

V[6]5548. [11]8. **Loie Pearl Breshears**, b. 23 Aug 1909, Hickory Co, MO, d. 19 Aug 1990, Oakdale, CA; m. 26 Dec 1935, ***Joe Tom Pearson***, b. 1917, d. 10 July 1978, Oakdale, CA, s/o William Pearson and Sarah Jordan.

V[6]5549. [12]1. Linda Sue Pearson, b. 20 Nov 1938; m. Warren Green, b. 28 Sept 1934

V[6]5550. [11]9. ***Lowis William Breshears**, b. 12 Oct 1912,

Hickory Co, MO; m. 20 April 1933, ***Inice Marie Breshears***, (d/o Levi Ransom Breshears and Hettie Noble Button), b. 8 July 1914,

V6 5551. 11 10. **Oryene Florence Breshears**, b. 27 Feb 1913, Hickory Co, MO, d. 23 April 2002 in Fresno, CA; m. 20 April 1933, in Hermitage, Hickory Co, MO, ***Guy Breshears***, (s/o Levi Ransom Breshears and Hettie Noble Button), b. 8 Dec 1915, Wheatland, Hickory Co, MO, d. 23 Jan 1971, Modesto, CA; m.2. May 1948, in Reno, NV, ***George Lundburg***, d. 1993, Paradise, CA. See Guy Breshears' listing for children.

Lowis William Breshears and Inice Marie Breshears

v6 5550. 11 9. **Lowis William Breshears**, (s/o William Wesley Breshears and Eliza Ellen Butler), b. 12 Oct 1912, Hickory Co, MO, d. 31 Oct 2001, at his home in Modesto, Stanislaus Co, CA; m. 20 April 1933, in Hermitage, Hickory Co, MO, by Judge Courch, ***Inice Marie Breshears***, (d/o Levi Ransom Breshears and Hettie Noble Button), b. 8 July 1914, Wheatland, Hickory Co, MO.

As a young man, Lowis loved to smoke a good cigar and play cards. He and his brother, Ora Franklin Breshears, would often walk about three miles to Lowell and Gladys Breshears' place to play card. They played "Pitch" and "Pinocle," which was Lowis's favorite game.

When Inice Marie was 17, she told Lowis that when she had a boy, she would name him Chad, and when she had a girl, she would name her Cheryl. A few years later, they married, and she named their son Chad and their daughter Cheryl. She had picked out these names from some books she had read.

In 1935, Lowis and Inice moved to Stanislaus Co, CA, where Lowis went to work for the George Sawyer ranch in Oakdale. His job was mainly to feed sheep in the holding barns located on the ranch. He would use a dog to control and move the sheep. Sometimes, he was called upon to ride a horse and herd cattle, but most of the time he fed sheep.

A co-worker had a brother who worked for the Southern

Figure 94: Lowis Breshears, c1913. Photo from Bill Brooks

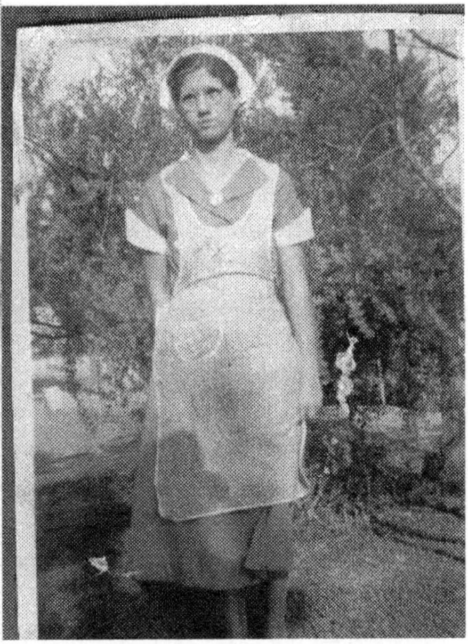

Figure 93: Inice Marie Breshears, c1929. Photo Bill Brooks

Pacific Railroad. Lowis drove to Tracy, CA, and put in an application. In just a few days, he was called to report to the Sacramento Division of Southern Pacific in Roseville, CA.

At first, Lowis worked as a "fireman." His main job was to refill the water tanks on the locomotive on the run from Roseville to Sparks, Nevada. The tanks held 22,500 gallons. The first water-stop was at Colfax, CA, only 35 miles from Roseville. The second stop was at Emigrant Gap near the summit of the Sierra Nevada. Each time they stopped, the tank would be down to about 2000 gallons. From Emigrant Gap to Sparks, NV, was 65 miles, mostly downhill, and they made it on the water from Emigrant Gap. He figured out that the train got about 30-35 miles for each 20,000 gallons of water. He couldn't recall how much fuel oil the train used, but it didn't compare with the amount of water required.

Lowis said that the locomotives rarely shut down completely. Instead, they would turn the fuel oil down to a trickle to keep the firebox hot. If one did go out, Lowis said he would take rags soaked in kerosene and throw them into the firebox, then throw in a match. That would create a draft and the pistons of the locomotive would make a vacuum, pulling air into the firebox, making a blowtorch effect to start the engine.

Lowis and Inice resided in Roseville, CA, and Fair Oaks, CA, during the time Lowis was an engineer for Southern Pacific Railroad, Sacramento Division. Most of his work took him from Roseville to Sparks, Nevada, and back, but occasionally to other places, sometimes to Fresno, CA.

Lowis was in a train accident when another train ran a signal in the railyard and collided with the train he was engineering. He was scaled by steam over 20% of his body and suffered a dislocated shoulder and a broken leg. He spent about a month in the Southern Pacific Hospital in San Francisco, recovering from his wounds.

Lowis once pulled an experimental train of 200 cars from Sparks, Nevada, to Roseville, CA. He engineered the first of five engines in the front, while another engineer controlled three engines about 25 cars from the rear. The train was so long that, on some of the turns, the front and rear of the train were going in opposite directions.

One his most memorable trips was in the 1950's when his train was sent to dig out the snowbound passengers in "The City of San Francisco," which was marooned in the Sierra Nevada. Unfortunately, Lowis's snow plow also got mired in the snow and another train had to be called to free the others.

Lowis said he killed only one person with a train, a vagrant who fell from about five cars behind the engine, down under the wheels of the train. Another close call was in Reno, Nevada, which has a 20-mile an hour speed limit for trains. Lowis saw a man come out of a casino, comb his hair, straighten his hat, and then walk out onto the tracks as if saying "go ahead, hit me." The locomotive bumped him off the track. It took about 150 yards to get the train stopped. When Lowis had walked back, the medical people were working on him and he was alive.

After his retirement, Lowis, Inice, and daughter Cheryl Ann moved to Modesto, Stanislaus Co, CA. In 1989, Lowis underwent a quintuple heart bypass surgery and, a few months later, surgery to remove a brain tumor. In Dec 2000, Lowis suffered a mild heart attack and had to have a pacemaker installed. On 22

March 2001, he suffered a massive heart attack, but survived. He died 31 Oct 2001, at his home in Modesto, CA.

Family of Lowis William Breshears and Inice Marie Breshears:

V6 5552. [12]1. **Chad Lowis Breshears**, b. 11 Dec 1934, Waterford, Stanislaus Co, CA, d. 1 Nov 1995, Stanford Medical Center, Palo Alto, CA; m. ***Patricia Ann McKinley***, b. 22 June 1935, St Louis, MO; d/o Leroy McKinley and Melva Thomas

V6 5553. [13]1. **Christine Lori Breshears**, b. 28 Dec 1959, Fair Oaks, CA; m.1. 7 July 1978, ***Timothy Carl Routh***; m.2. 1979, in AZ, ***James S. Davis***.

V6 5554. [14]1. Charles Scott Davis,

V6 5555. [14]2. Christine Davis,

V6 5556. [13]2. **Lisa Joyce Breshears** b. 2 March 1961, in Fair Oaks, CA; m.2. ***Mark Fossum***,

V6 5557. [14]1. **Lauren Breshears**,

V6 5558. [13]3. **Eric Chad Breshears**, b. 11 Oct 1964 in Fair Oaks, CA; m. ______ . Chad is a Lieutenant in the Oakland, CA, Police Department.

V6 5559. [14]1. **Alexander Breshears**,

V6 5560. [14]2. **Scott Breshears**,

V6 5561. [12]2. **Cheryl Ann Breshears**, b. 3 Aug 1943. Cheryl had Downs Syndrome. She loved to collect dolls and salt and pepper shakers. She enjoyed gardening and yard work.

Hugh Walter Brashears and Bernetta A. Maxwell

v6 5456. [10]10. **Hugh Walter Brashears**, (s/o James Alexander Brashears and Mary Jane Tipton), b. 17 Feb 1875, Benton Co, MO, d. 29 Feb 1952, Benton Co, MO; m. 24 June 1897, in Benton Co, MO, ***Bernetta A. Maxwell***, b. 5 June 1880, Benton Co, MO, d. there, 19 March 1962, d/o John Maxwell and Nancy Daniel. Hugh and Bernetta both buried in South New Home Ce, Cross Timbers, MO.

Family of Hugh Walter Brashears and Bernetta A. Maxwell:

[V6]5562. [11]1. **Isadore Breshears**, b. 4 April 1898, Benton Co, MO, d. there, 19 Aug 1985; m.1. ***Invin Smith***; m.2. ______ ***Hess***,

[V6]5563. [11]2. **Lloyd Brashears**, b. 16 Sept 1901, Benton Co, MO, d. c1995 in California; m. ***Marie Kirby***, (d/o Edward Kirby and Alice Jane "Allie" Breshears, d/o John Martin Van Buren Breshears), b. Benton Co, MO, d. CA,

[V6]5564. [12]1. **Geraldine Breshears**,

[V6]5565. [12]2. **Kermit Breshears**,

[V6]5566. [11]3. **Ramah "Ramie" Breshears**, b. 26 Feb 1903, Benton Co, MO, d. 8 May 1996, St Johns, Springfield, MO; m.1. 12 Nov 1921, ***Homer Henderson***, b. 28 June 1895, Fristoe, Benton Co, MO, d. 26 Feb 1980, Liberty, Hickory Co, MO (div); m.2. 12 July 1983, ***Ira Fahnestock***, b. ____, d. 26 Oct 1992

[V6]5567. [12]1. Homer Durl Henderson,

[V6]5568. [12]2. Yvonne Henderson; m. Charles Edward Shinn.

[V6]5569. [13]1. Kelly Shinn; m. Mark Beyer

[V6]5570. [13]2. Karen Shinn; m. Jeff Shrable. Ch: Jacqueline Shrable

[V6]5571. [12]3. Barbara Henderson; m.1. Don Drennon; m.2. Paul Garrett. Ch: Pamela; and Sue Drennon

[V6]5572. [12]4. Dean Henderson; m.1. Leta Mae Darby; m.2. Nedra ______. Ch: Michael Dean; and Michelle Henderson

[V6]5573. [12]5. Ivan Murl Henderson; m. Lucille ______,

[V6]5574. [12]6. Samuel Verl Henderson; m. Louise Cunningham

[V6]5575. [13]1. Johnny Henderson,

[V6]5576. [13]2. (Rev.) Mike Henderson; m. Debbie ______. Ch: Mike Jr; Matthew; and Ramie Henderson

[V6]5577. [13]3. Samuel Verl Henderson, Jr; m.1. Joann _____; m.2. Joyce Elyse Breshears, d/o Alfred Breshears and Lucille Bybee. Ch: Crystal; Victoria; and Josiah Henderson

[V6]5578. [13]4. Steven Henderson; m. Anita ______. Ch: Cori; Stephanie; and Jamie Henderson

[V6]5579. [11]4. **Lowell Breshears**, b. c1907, Benton Co, MO; m. 20 May 1931, in J.E. Jackson Home, Buffalo, Polk Co, MO, ***Gladys Bybee***. Lowell was a school teacher who taught more than 30 years, more than 20 of them at Warsaw, MO

[V6]5580. [12]2. **Neal Breshears**, b. c1931; m. ***Barbara ______.***

[V6]5581. [13]1. **Sherri Renee Breshears**; m. ***Brian Jett***. Ch: Steven; and Ashley Jett

[V6]5582. [13]2. **Lisa Diane Breshears**; m. ***Ron Harland Everly***,

[V6]5583. [13]3. **Sheila Ann Breshears**; m. ***Mark Kersey***. Ch: Matthew Clayton Kersey

[V6]5584. [12]2. **Ronald Gene Breshears**; m. ***Lonnis Gilford***.

[V6]5585. [13]1. **Chad Breshears**,

[V6]5586. [13]2. **Meredith Ann Breshears**,

[V6]5587. [13]3. **Adam Stroemmer Breshears**,

[V6]5588. [13]4. **Paige Elizabeth Breshears**,

[V6]5589. [12]3. **Voyn Breshears**; m. ***Ann*** ______.

[V6]5590. [13]1. **Terry Lane Breshears**; m. ***Susan Gail Young***,

[V6]5591. [14]1. **Jason Breshears**,

[V6]5592. [14]2. **Jaci Breshears**,

[V6]5593. [11]5. Infant **Breshears**, b. & d. 15 March 1908, Benton Co, MO

[V6]5594. [11]6. **Ina Breshears**, b. 15 July 1913, Benton Co, MO; m. 9 Aug 1931, ***Lloyd Jerry Tucker***, b. 5 April 1904, Benton Co, MO, d. 24 Aug 1979, Cross Timbers, Benton Co, MO

[V6]5595. [12]1. Ester Tucker; m. John D. Shinn.

[V6]5596. [13]1. Jonna Shinn; m. Kenny Moulder. Ch: Casey; and Baylee Moulder

[V6]5597. [13]2. Chris Shinn; m. Christine Bray

[V6]5598. [13]3. Jennifer Shinn,

[V6]5599. [13]4. Robert Shinn; m. Sherry Winfield. Ch: Adrienne Leah Shinn

[V6]5600. [12]2. Evalene Tucker; m. Richard Shinn

[V6]5601. [13]1. Debbie Shinn; m. Ray Nance. Ch: Jessi

Nance

V65602. [13]2. Donna Shinn; m. Bill Hart. Ch: Craig; and Amanda Hart

V65603. [11]7. **Elvin Breshears**, b. 21 Oct 1899, Avery, Benton Co, MO, d. 21 Dec 1991, Columbia Regional Hosp, Columbia, MO; m. ***Myrtle Tipton***, b. 1898, Benton Co, MO, d. 29 Dec 1984, Convalescent Home, Brunswick, MO, d/o James Tipton and Mary Suiter. Elvin and Myrtle both buried in Ridgepark Cem, Marshall, MO.

V65604. [12]1. **Earl E. Breshears**, b. _____

V65605. [12]2. **Harold Dean Breshears**, b. 1935; m. _____

V65606. [13]1. **Larry Dean Breshears**, b. 24 Feb 1958

James H. Breshears and Sarah Lizabeth Henderson

v65405. [9]4. **James H. Breshears**, (s/o Alexander Brashears and Margaret "Peggy" Breshears), b. 14 Sept 1838, Benton Co, MO, d. 18 March 1879, Benton Co, MO; m. c1859 in Benton Co, MO, ***Sarah Lizabeth Henderson***, b. 1840-42, IL, d. 1921-25, Avery, Hickory Co, MO. Both were buried at the Pippin cemetery, but were later moved to the Spring Branch Cem at Avery. (Additional data from Tom Crow <murder1 @mmind.net>)

Family of James H. Breshears and Sarah Lizabeth Henderson:

V65607. [10]1. **Samuel A. Breshears**, b. 9 May 1860, Benton Co, MO, d. 13 Nov 1873, age 13, Benton Co, MO, bur Pippin Cem, but moved to Spring Branch Cem.

V65608. [10]2. **Elva Jane Breshears**, b. 22 Jan 1862, Benton Co, MO, d. there, 20 March 1915, bur Spring Branch cem; m. 15 Sept 1878, in Benton Co, MO, **Isaac David "Ike" Breshears**, (s/o William Carroll (Green) Breshears and Orleana Rice), b. Benton Co, MO, 29 Aug 1854, says Pension application and family Bible (cem stone shows I.D. Breshears, b. 28 Aug 1853), d. 25 June 1937, Hickory Co, MO, bur Spring Branch Cem, Avery, MO. See his listing for their family.

[V6]5609. [10]3. **James Robert Breshears**, b. 1864-65, Benton Co, MO; m. 8 Dec 1887, in Hickory Co, MO, ***Evalina North***

[V6]5610. [10]4. ***William Thomas Breshears**, b. 8 Feb 1867, Benton Co, MO, d. c1948, near Fristoe, MO; m.1. ***Louisa C. Owens*** (1 ch); m.2. ***Della M. Ruth***, b. 1883, Benton Co, MO, d. there, 1918 (2 ch); m.3. ***Esta Rickson***, b. 1894, d. 1974, Fristoe, Benton Co, MO (3 ch)

[V6]5611. [10]5. **George Washington Breshears**, b. 1869, Benton Co, MO, d. after 1900, near Chelsea, OK; m. 15 Dec 1887, in Benton Co, MO, ***Emma J. Burton***, b. 19 Nov 1868, Hickory Co, MO, d. 11 Aug 1899, Benton Co, MO, d/o Ab Burton and Cynthia Daniel

[V6]5612. [11]1. **Dorothea Adeler Breshears**, b. 1891; m. ______ ***Dellar***,

[V6]5613. [11]2. **Fletcher Goldman Breshears**, b. 1893, Benton Co, MO, d. Claremore, OK; m. ***Dorothy*** ______,

[V6]5614. [11]3. **James Breshears**, b. 1895

[V6]5615. [11]4. **Floyd Breshears**, b. 1897

[V6]5616. [11]5. **Thomas Clinton Breshears**, b. 1899

[V6]5617. [10]6. **Joseph Newton Breshears**, b. 18 Feb 1876, Benton Co, MO, d. 15 Jan 1962, near Vinita, OK, bur Rider Cemetery near Adair, OK; m. ***Hester Louduski Chance***, b. 20 Sept 1887, d. 14 Oct 1952

[V6]5618. [11]x. **Sarah Elmeda Breshears**, b. 16 Sept 1910, Avery, MO, d. 25 Jan 2004, Chouteau, OK; m. 1 July 1929 in Pryor, OK, ***Rola Walter Crow***, b. 25 June 1910, d. 3 Oct 1998 (Grandparents of Tom Crow, of Tulsa, OK)

[V6]5619. [10]7. **Sarah Elizabeth "Lizzy" Breshears**, b. 27 April 1878, Benton Co, MO, d. 1 July 1946, Hickory Co, MO; m. ***John Henry Miller***,

[V6]5620. [11]1. Ethel Miller,

[V6]5621. [11]2. Grace Miller,

[V6]5622. [11]3. Berchie Miller,

[V6]5623. [11]4. Roy Miller,

William Thomas Breshears and His Three Wives

V6 5610. 10 3. **William Thomas Breshears**, (s/o James H. Breshears and Sarah Lizabeth Henderson), b. 8 Feb 1867, Benton Co, MO, d. c1948, near Fristoe, MO; m.1. ***Louisa C. Owens*** (1 ch); m.2. ***Della M. Ruth***, b. 1883, Benton Co, MO, d. there, 1918 (2 ch); m.3. ***Esta Rickson***, b. 1894, d. 1974, Fristoe, Benton Co, MO (3 ch). Thanks to Huetta Laverne (Newell) Breshears for data.)

Family of William Thomas Breshears and Louisa Owens:

V6 5624. 11 1. **William W. Breshears**, b. ____, d. March 1979, Arcata, Humboldt Co, CA. He had lived several years in state of Washington, returned to CA. Had a son who was killed in an accident, name unknown.

Family of William Thomas Breshears and Della Ruth:

V6 5625. 11 2. **Ora A. Breshears**, b. 1890, Benton Co, MO, d. 1938, bur Fristoe Cem; m. ***Burris Emery Miller***, (s/o Henry W. Miller and Martha Ellen Ruth)

V6 5626. 12 1. Vedora Miller, b. c1918; m. Robert McFarland, s/o Charley McFarland. Ch: Louise McFarland

V6 5627. 12 2. Reuben T. Miller, b. 10 Jan 1918, d. 7 Aug 1980, bur Fristoe Cem; m. 8 March 1942, Juanita B. Brooks. ch: dau, Jim, and John Miller

V6 5628. 12 3. Laurie Miller, b. c1920; m. ____ Neese

V6 5629. 12 4. Roy Kenneth Miller, b. 9 Dec 1925, d. 7 Jan 1974

V6 5630. 11 3. **Everett Robert Breshears**, b. 21 June 1892, Benton Co, MO, d. 13 Oct 1958, Independence, MO; m.1. c1912, ***Lola Mullins*** (3 ch), b. 30 July 1895, MO, d. 16 Dec 1918, MO, d/o George Mullins and Maude Barber; m.2. c1922, ***Mealie Mae (Mullins) Southard***, (1 ch?), b. 1891, MO, d.

1958, MO, d/o George Mullins and Maude Barber and widow of Walter F. Southard

[V6]5631. [12]1. **Zelma Breshears**, b. c1913; m.1. c1931, ***Stanley Davidson***; m.2. c1940, ***Jasper Lombardo***; m.3. c1950, ***Raymond Thomas***

[V6]5632. [13]1. Robert Winston Davidson, b. 2 March 1934; m. Mary Anderson. Ch: Robert and Deborah Davidson

[V6]5633. [13]2. Larry Leroy Davidson, b. c1936; m.1. ***Thelma Breshears*** (8 ch); m.2. ____ Rhea

[V6]5634. [12]2. **Odie Robert Breshears**, b. 10 Feb 1915, Benton Co, MO, d. 20 Jan 1987 Hickory Co, MO, bur Cross Timbers Cem; Odie served in the US Army in WW II, as a Tech 5.

[V6]5635. [12]3. **Alma Breshears**, b. c1917, d. 1919

[V6]5636. [12]4. ***Everett Dean Breshears**, b. 26 Sept 1923, Warsaw, Benton Co, MO; d. 30 June 1998, Wheatland, MO; m. 4 May 1946, ***Huetta Laverne Newell***, see below.

[V6]5637. [12]x.?. **Chloe Breshears**, (possible daughter of Everett Robert Breshears and Mealie Mae Mullins), m. ***Irl M. Stevens***, b. 25 Oct 1909, Cross Timbers, MO, d. 23 Oct 1997, Hermitage, Hickory Co, MO,

Family of William Thomas Breshears and Esta Rickson:

[V6]5638. [11]4. **Lowell Breshears**, (fem), b. c1921; m. ***William Kirby***

[V6]5639. [12]1. Veryl Kirby, b. c1941; m. Clifford Neil Crain. ch: son and dau Crain

[V6]5640. [12]2. Meryl Kirby, b. c1942; m. ____ Charles. ch: son and dau Charles

[V6]5641. [11]5. **Oma Breshears**, b. c1922; m. ***Harold Brooks***

[V6]5642. [11]6. **Sidney Breshears**, b. c1924; m. ***Virginia Copenhaven***

[V6]5643. [12]1. **Linda Breshears**, b. c1946

[V6]5644. [12]2. **Carol Breshears**, b. c1948

Everett Dean Breshears
and Huetta Laverne Newell

[v6]5636. [12]4. **Everett Dean Breshears**, (s/o Everett Robert Breshear and Mealie Mae Mullins), b. 26 Sept 1923, Warsaw, Benton Co, MO; d. 30 June 1998, Wheatland, MO; m. 4 May 1946, ***Huetta Laverne Newell***, d/o Hugh Newell and Goldie Armbruster.

Family of Everett Dean Breshears and Huetta Laverne Newell:

[V6]5645. [13]1. **Harry Lee Breshears**, (twin) b. 15 Sept 1947, d. 17 Sept 1947, Cross Timbers, Hickory Co, MO, bur New Home Cem

[V6]5646. [13]2. **Larry Dean Breshears**, (twin), b.&d. 15 Sept 1947, Cross Timbers, Hickory Co, MO, bur New Home Cem

[V6]5647. [13]3. **Betty Ann Breshears**, b. 23 June 1950, Independence, Jackson Co, MO; m.1. 1970, in Independence, MO, ***Danny Edmund Oakes***; m.2. 4 July 1980, in Pomme de Terre, Hermitage Co, MO, ***Clarence Wilbur Jackson***, s/o Carl Jackson and Trilla Bastion

[V6]5648. [14]1. Carl Brandon Breshears Oakes, b. 2 Feb 1968, Independence, Jackson Co, MO; m. 20 Sept 1989, in Hickory Co, MO, Lisa Ann Mullins, d/o Dennis Mullins and Susie Peters.

[V6]5649. [15]1. Sarah Marie Irene Oakes, b. 2 July 1997, Osage Beach, MO

[V6]5650. [15]2. William Dean Oakes, b. 23 Oct 1995, Lake Ozark Gen Hosp, Osage Beach, MO

[V6]5651. [13]4. **Lonnie Dean Breshears**, b. 9 June 1957, Independence, MO; m.1. 21 May 1979, in Hickory Co, MO, ***Mary Newton*** (noch); m.2. 25 April 1985, in Hickory Co, MO, ***Paula Buttry*** (1 ch)

[V6]5652. [14]1. **Alex Breshears**, b. 2 June 1987, Cox Med Center, Springfield, MO

[V6]5653. [13]5. **Carolyn Sue Breshears**, b. 5 Jan 1959, Independence, MO; m.1. 8 April 1977, Independence, MO, ***Daniel Conrad Smith Jr***;

m.1. 1979, ***Eddie Hayes***; m.3. 1982, ***Norval "Pete" Rife***; m.4. 1989, ***Karl Morris***; m.5. 1995, ***James Herrick***

V6 5654. 14 1. Daniel Nathan Smith, b. 31 March 1978, Osceola, MO

V6 5655. 14 2. James Daniel Herrick, b. 21 Oct 1996

V6 5656. 14 3. Marshall Wayne Herrick, b. 10 June 1998

V6 5657. 13 6. **Donna Lynn Breshears**, b. 21 May 1960, Independence, MO

47. BERRY BRASHEARS (BOSHEARS) and Anna ______, of Arkansas

We don't really have any documentation of who Berry Boshears parents were. Some of the family in Arkansas thought that his father was named Absalom, which would harmonize with this Brashears family— it's not a common name, but it ***is*** used in the Kentucky branch, the Tennessee branch, and the North Carolina branch.

In addition, circumstances, residences, and naming patterns make me want to add a brother to Basil, b. c1765, John, b. c1767, and Henry, b. c1769: "The Phantom Absalom Brashears," so let's hypothesize that there really was a man named Absalom.

[v6]12. [7]x. **Absalom Brashears** (unknown, undocumented, hypothetical son of Middleton Brashears): who would be the father of at least the following children, who seem to be siblings:

[v6]13. [8]1. ***Berry Brashears/Boshears**, b. 1790, SC; m. ***Anna*** _____, they lived in White Co, TN, Lawrence Co, TN, McNairy Co, TN, Tishomingo Co, MS, White Co, AR, Montgomery Co, AR, and Pulaski Co, AR.

[V6]14. [8]2. **Nancy Elizabeth Brashear**, b. 1793; m. 20 Oct 1823, Lawrence Co, AL, ***Andrew Wilson***

[v6]15. [9]1. *Robert Brashear Wilson, b. Lawrence Co, AL, 1827 (See data with John Brashear and Elizabeth "Betsy" Randall.)

[v6]16. [8]3. **Robert H. Brasher**, m. 16 April 1819, in Lawrence Co, AL, ***Sally L. Rhea***. I don't have any evidence for adding Robert; just a hunch based on the place and time of his marriage. Sally Rhea was d/o John Rhea Sr: Loose Records of Madison Co, AL, by Ganrud, vol 4, p.84: Estate of John Rhea paid sums to Phillip B. Mason, in right of wife,

Nancy; Joseph Nail, in right of wife, Esther; Robert Brashears [in right of wife Sally]; William Rhea's heirs; Margaret Wright's heirs; and John Rhea Jr, all heirs of John Rhea Sr. John Rhea Jr made bond in Giles Co, TN, 13 Dec 1834.

Be careful not to confuse this Robert H. Brashear with the Robert B. Brashears in Lawrence Co, TN, s/o Isaac Brashears. The Lawrence Co Robert married a woman named Sarah "Sally" Hankins, whose surname has been erroneously reported (including by me) to be Rhea.

v6 17. 84. ***John Brashear**, b. 1796, d. c1861, Hot Springs Co, AR; m.1. in Lawrence Co, AL, ***Elizabeth "Betsy" Randall***, b. 1800; m.2. a widow, ***Elizabeth (Baugh) Chambers***, b. 1794, SC,

V6 13. 81. **Berry Brashears,** (also Breshears, Beshears, Boshears, etc) b. Pendleton Dist, SC, c1790 (age 60 in 1850 Census, Montgomery Co, AR); m. ***Anna*** _______, b. SC, c1795. Anna (Boshears) Locke, now deceased, a descendant in Arkansas, spent many years in immensely arduous research, which is essential to this chapter.

In addition to Anna (Boshears) Locke, who spent nearly 40 years and a great deal of money (some for professional researchers) on the family of Berry Boshears, and Dorothy Elliott, who exchanged volumes of data with whomever would respond--both ladies regrettably now deceased--those who have sent significant data to me include the following:

Charles Scott Breshears, 11 Deerfield Drive, Sherwood, AR 72120

Lois Cooper, 1218 Seven Drive, Hobbs, NM 88240.

Gerry Rylant, 759 Palm, Lodi, CA 95240

Betty Howard, 1227 Hazel Ave, Pinole CA 94564

Several circumstances (the pronunciation of the surname; the names that run in the family; places of residence) lead me to believe that Berry is from the Benois Brasseur branch of the Brashear family and, more specifically, from Basil Brashears and Anne Belt, of the North Carolina Brashears colony.

One of the reasons I think Berry was from this branch of the family is the apparent pronunciation of the name. The Greenville, SC, colony of Brasher families accented the first syllable and made the vowel long, BRAY-sher, and, when Census people or county clerks goofed, they goofed with the second, unaccented syllable: Brassure, Brasier, Brayshur, Brasher, etc.

The Brashears colony of Guilford Co, NC, which included Basil, Middleton, Robert C., Robert Samuel, Jesse, etc. pronounced their name with the accent on the second syllable and a more or less indeterminant vowel in the first syllable, Bra-SHEAR, and often Br'-SHEAR and B'SHEAR, with and without the "s". The Census and court people get the second syllable right, but mess up the first, unaccented syllable: Breshear(s), Broshear(s), Bershear(s), Brasher(s), Basher(e(s), Beshear(s), Boshear(s), etc. These are the (mis)spellings of Berry's name in Tennessee and Arkansas.

When Anna (Boshears) Locke asked her grandfather, Henry Clay Boshears, about the spelling of the name, he said it had originally been "Brashears," but he had changed it to "Boshears" for simplicity's sake.

Two or three branches of Berry's descendants in Arkansas thought that Berry's father's name was Absalom. That is a name that runs in the North Carolina branches of the family, and in no other that I know of. Jesse is another name more or less unique to these branches.

Berry seems to be a son of a deceased brother of Basil Sr, 1765, John Sr, 1767, and Henry Sr, 1769, who seem to be (no solid proof) sons of Middleton Brashear. Without compelling proof, let's say that Berry's father (the phantom, deceased brother) was "Phantom-Absalom," a son of Middleton Brashears, s/o Basil Brashears and Anne Belt. If these speculations are correct, that would put Berry in the 8th generation of Brashears families in America, and I am going to start numbering his generations accordingly. If anyone comes up with any documents to either prove or disprove this theory, please send them to me.

Berry's Paper Trail

WARREN CO, TN, LAND GRANTS: 4 Feb 1815: Tennessee Land Grant, 2 acres, to Littleberry Brashears. (HSB, p.29; not now listed in card index in Nashville)

In White and Lawrence Counties, Tennessee, Berry hangs around with Basil Brashears Sr, b. c1765; John Breshears Sr, b. 1767; his brother, Henry Brashears Sr, b. 1769; and Thomas Brashears, b. c1771. I think (cannot yet prove) that these are sons of Middleton Brashears, b. c1732-33, s/o Basil Brashears, b. 1714, and Anne Belt.

1820 census, White Co, TN

p.369: **Berry Bashere**, (210010-31010) age 26-45, b. 1775-1794, (he was 30, b. 1790)
wife, 26-45, b. 1775-1794 = wife: same age-bracket as Berry
male, 10-15, b. 1805-10
fem, 10-15, b. 1805-10; possibly Drucilla
male, 0-10, b. 1810-20; possibly James Monteville, b. 1810
male, 0-10, b. 1810-20 = Andrew "Drew", age 7, b. 1813
fem. 0-10, b. 1810-20
fem. 0-10, b. 1810-20
fem. 0-10, b. 1810-20

In Lawrence Co, TN, Berry lived right in the middle of the Henry Breshears Sr clan:

Tax List of Lawrence Co, Tn, 1826:

#253	Henry Brashears	25-yr-old s/o Henry Sr and Eleanor Brashears
#254	John Brashears	33-yr-old s/o Henry Sr and Eleanor Brashears
#255	Jesse Brashears	34-yr-old s/o Henry Sr and Eleanor Brashears
#256	William Brashears	36-yr-old s/o Henry Sr and Eleanor Brashears
#257	Berry Brashears	36-yr-old s/o ?Phantom- Absalom?
#258	Henry Brashears	57-yr-old Henry Brashears Sr, wife Eleanor

On 9 Feb 1828, Berry Brashears was bondsman for Lucinda Brashears, in her marriage to George Cerat (should be Suratt) (*Lawrence Co, TN, marriages*). She was probably his daughter.

He apparently sold out and left soon afterward. Note that the surname was still spelled "Brashears."

Lawrence Co, TN Minutes Book, 1828-1834, p.188: 5 July 1830, records three transfers of a plat and certificate in the name of Erasmus Tippitt for 25 acres: first, from said Tippett to Berry Brashers, was produced and proven by the oath of Franklin Buchanan, witness; second, ?? by 2/3 by ?? [can anyone ungarble the reading?] from said Brashers to Elisha Franklin and [third,] from said Franklin to Alexander Brashers, was produced and proven by oaths of Nathan McClen? and Augusten W. Bumpass, witnesses.

This has to be the Berry, b. 1790; John's (b. 1767) son, Berry, b. 1814, is only 16 years old, and Berry Jr is not yet born. By 1830, Berry had left the county: he is in the 1830 Census, McNairy Co, TN. Descendants differ on where Berry Jr was born in 1832; some say in Tennessee, some say in Tishomingo Co, Mississippi.

The younger Berry Brashears, b. 1814, remained in Lawrence Co, TN, where his father, John Brashears Sr, b. 1767, died in 1852:

Heirs of John Brashears, dec'd, to Wm. E. Newton, 6 March 1856. Two tracts: Grant #18755 for 273 ac. and #27968 for 50 ac. in Lawrence Co, TN. ... Heirs: Berry Brashears, Elizabeth Franklin ... "Each heir owning 1/6 said tract, being on the water of Bluewater in range 4 & 5, Sec. 2."

signed: Berry Brashears,
Prien Masterly [X] Paier,
Mary Brashears

(Lawrence Co, TN Deeds, Book M, p.593. Apparently, only two of the heirs are selling their undivided share; Mary is their mother, widow of John Brashears Sr, who would have a 1/3 dower of the estate during her lifetime. She would have to sign (relinquish her dower) for any of the children to sell their shares of the estate. But we either have a terribly sloppy, inattentive, inaccurate clerk writing the deed, or our copyists are dingy. Looking again at the original to see what it says didn't help me to clear this up.)

Another report on this transfer has Martha Matilda Prier signing. Martha Martela Brashears married William Pryor, 20

Oct 1846. Elizabeth (?Mrs. Brion) Franklin has not been found anywhere else in the records.

However, these two transfers, along with the younger Berry inheriting a share of TN Grants #18755 and #27968, look to me like pretty positive evidence that Berry Brashears, b. 1814, was a son of John Brashears Sr, b. 1767, and that Berry Brashears, b. 1790 was not.

1830 Census, McNairy Co, TN:
Berry Beshears, (0011001-002101) b. 1780-90; [Why no children 0-10? There are lots of children aged 10-20, ten years later.]
wife, age 30-40, b. 1790-1800.
dau, b. 1810-15, age 15-20 in 1830
son, b. 1810-15, age 15-20 in 1830
dau, b. 1815-20, age 10-15 in 1830
dau, b. 1815-20, age 10-15 in 1830
son, b. 1815-20, age 10-15 in 1830

1840 Census of Tishomingo County, MS: p. 232 (reel #M704, roll 219)
Berry Brashears, (31100001-0021101) b. 1780-90

Wife age 40-50, b. 1790-1800	
fem. 20-30, b. 1810-20	
fem. 15-20, b. 1820-25	
male, 10-15, b. 1825-30	
fem. 10-15, b. 1825-30	
fem. 10-15, b. 1825-30	Nancy, b. 1830
male, 5-10, b. 1830-35	Little Berry, b. 1832
male, 0-5, b. 1835-40	Henry, b. 1835-6
male, 0-5, b. 1835-40	Larkin, b. 1837
male, 0-5, b. 1835-40	"unknown", b. 1835-40, not in 1850

Also on p.232, 1840 Census, Tishomingo Co, MS
Drury Beshears, (11001-01001), age 20-30, b. 1810-1820
Basil Beshears, (011001-111001), age 30-40, b. 1800-1810
Charles McCue, (2000101-1111001) b. 1790-1800

On p.231: **George Beshear**, (00010-0001000001) age 15-20, b. 1820-25; wife, same age; ?grandmother, 70-80, b. 1860-70. [Apparently, this is a son of Isaac, s/o John, b. 1767; this George later shows up in Randolph Co, AR; his brother Isaac Jr is in Pulaski Co, AR, with Berry's sons, ?then in Randolph Co, AR.]

Nearby: Wm. H. Simpson (10001-20001)
Thomas Simpson (000000001-000200001), age 60-70, b. 1870-80
James McGue [McHughes?] (00001-10001)

The 1845 State Census of Tishomingo Co, MS, lists 7 Brashears families:

p.21, col.2,	Drura Boshears	4 males	2 females
p.21, col.2,	Berry Boshears	7 males	4 females
p.21, col.2,	Henry Boshears	2 males	2 females
p.21, col.2,	Jacob Boshears	3 males	7 females
p.21, col.2,	Peter Boshears	3 males	3 females
p.21, col.2,	Isaac Boshears	2 males	1 female
p.1, col.2,	Thomas Boshears	2 males	4 females

The Clan in Arkansas

Some branches of the family in Arkansas had the information that Berry had a son, James, b. 1810, who lived in Arkansas and later moved to Texas. This is James M. Brashears, of Angelina Co, TX:

James married 1830-32, in TN or AL, ***Mary Elizabeth "Lizzie" Maribe Jones***, b. 26 March 1813, TN, d. after 1880, TX, d/o Martin William "Gobbler" Jones and Rhoda Hodges. James and "Lizzie" moved with the Jones family to White Co, AR about 1832.

In 1837, James Beshares was taxed in White Co, Arkansas for 1 horse valued at $50 and 3 head of cattle, 3 yrs old. In 1838, he was taxed for 30 cattle and 3 horses, $960. Isaac Boocher was taxed there in 1837 for 1 horse and 10 cattle.

From 1839 to 1846 (except 1842: no records), James Beshears was on the White Co, AR, Tax Lists, variously as James Beshears, James Bersharars, James Beshares, James Bershears, and James Breshear; in each case, he paid one poll tax. "Jas. Beshears" is listed in the 1840 census index for White Co, AR, but I don't have the number, age-brackets, and sexes of children in his household. Does anyone? Texas census records of birth places of children would suggest that this James moved from Arkansas to Texas in 1846-47. See "Brashears Families of Angelina Co, Texas."

In 1838, William Bashears (s/o Henry Breshears Sr, b. 1769) was taxed for 320 acres in White Co, AR (NW 1/2, S32, T10N, R7W; value $960), which Anna Locke described as located on "Hiway 157 Sunnydale north of Searcy 17 miles east." In 1847, William Beshears was taxed for 320 acres--160 acres in SW 1/4, Sec 20, T6N, R8W, and 160 acres in SE 1/4, Sec 20, T6n, R8W, White Co, AR.

The 1848/49 Poll Tax list for White Co, Arkansas, includes Wm. Beshares, Berry Beshares, Jacob Beshares, A. Beshares, and Brazelle Beshares.

Many of this clan moved to Montgomery Co, Arkansas. The 1849/50 Poll Tax records of Montgomery Co, AR include William Beshears, Andrew Beshears, Isaac Beshears, Berry Beshears, Matthew Beshears, Jesse Beshears, and Henry Beshears.

The 1852-55 Poll Tax lists of Montgomery Co, AR include Drury Brashears, Isaac Brashears, Berry Brashears, Berry Brashears, Matthew Brashears, and Simpson Burks (m. Nancy, d/o Berry).

William Breshears, b. c1790, in the following census list is s/o Henry Breshears Sr, b. c1769; Matthew and Henry are his sons. Basil is s/o Basil Brashears Sr, b. c1765; and Drury is s/o Berry Breshears, b. 1790.

1850 Census, Montgomery Co, AR, Mountain twp:
#D-38: **Basil Breshears**, 42, farmer, b. TN, c1808; s/o Basil Brashear Sr, b. c1765
  Eliza Ann Breshears, 23, b. TN, c1827; nee Elizabeth Ann Simpson
  Peter Breshears, 15, b. TN c1835
  Elizabeth Breshears, 13, b. MS, c1837
  Thomas R. Breshears, 2, b. MS, c1848
  Sally Breshears, 1, b. MS, c1849
#D-39: **Berry Breshears**, 60 farmer, b. SC, c1790: "old man Berry"
  Anna Breshears, 45, b. SC, c1805 [age 45 is a mistake for 55; b. 1795]
  Berry Breshears [Jr], 18, b. TN c1838
  Henry Breshears, 15, b. TN, c1835
  Larkin Breshears, 13, b. TN c1837
  Gilbert Smith, 29, farmer, b. TN c1831
#D-55: **Matthew Breshears**, 26, b. TN c1824, farmer, s/o William, b. 1790
  Elizabeth Breshears, 20, b. IL c1830
  Louisa E. Breshears, 2, b. AR c1848
  William F.M. Breshears, 1, b. AR c1849
1850 Census, Montgomery Co, AR, Polk twp:
#D-22: **Henry Brashears**, 24, farmer, b. TN c1826; s/o William, b. 1790
  Polly Jane Brashears,24, b. TN c1826
  Winney Brashears, 5, b. AR, c1845
  Anna Brashears, 3, b. AR c1847
  Ellen Brashears, 1, b. AR c1849
#D-22: **William Breshears**,60, b. SC c1790; s/o Henry Sr, b. 1769
  Anna Breshears, 44, b. NC c1806
  Jesse Breshears, 25, b. TN c1825
  Harding Breshears, 20, b. TN c1830
  Asta Breshears, 16f, b. TN c1834

#D-32: **Drury Breshears**, 40, farmer, b. TN c1810; s/o Berry, b. 1790
Rebecca Breshears, 35, b. TN c1815
Alfred Breshears, 13, b. TN c1837
William Breshears, 10, b. TN c1840
Alexander Breshears, 10, b. TN c1840
Sis (Narcissa) Breshears, 5, b. TN c1845
Infant (unnamed) 6/12, b. AR 1850

<u>1860 census, Pulaski Co, AR, Owen twp</u>, 8 July 1860, p.21:
#152-185: **Robert Beshears**, 39, b. TN, 1821, farmer, $1000, $410; s/o Berry
Rebecca E. Beshears,36, b. TN, c1824
Sarah Jane Beshears, 9, b. AR, c1851
Emery C. Beshears, 6, b. AR, c1854
Emily M.C. Beshears, 5, b. AR, c1855
Nancy H.E. Beshears, 2, b. AR, c1858
Dona Leana Beshears, 6/12, b. AR, cJan 1860
Robert H. McCue, 21, b. MS, c1839, laborer
#153-136: **Brazil Beshears**, 50, b. TN, c1810, farmer, s/o Basil, b. c1765
Eliza A. Beshears, 36, b. MS, c1824
Peter Beshears, 23, b. MS, c1837: by 1st wife
Robert Beshears, 14, b. MS, c1846: Robert Thomas Simpson,
William A. Beshears, 10, b. MS, c1850
Isaac E. Beshears, 6, b. AR, c1854
Michael Beshears, 9/12, b. AR, cOct 1859
William Simpson, 19, b. TN, c1841
#154-137: **Isaac Beshears**, 39, b. TN, c1821, farmer, #200, $600; s/o Isaac Brashears, b. c1795, gs/o John Brashears Sr, b. 1767
Siony Beshears, 33, b. TN, c1827, Sidney, d/o Lewis Owl, Indian
William Beshears, 15, b. MS, c1845
George Beshears, 13, b. MS, c1847
Nancy Beshears, 10, b. MS, c1850
Martha Beshears, 9, b. AR, c1851
Jacob Beshears, 7, b. AR, c1853
Clerinda Beshears, 5, b. AR, c1855
Sallie Beshears, 2, b. AR, c1858
#155-138: **Andrew Beshears**, 47, b. TN, c1813; s/o Berry, b. 1790
Rebecca Beshears, 46, b. TN, c1814
Alfred Beshears, 23, b. MS, c1837
William Beshears, 18, b. MS, c1842
Alexander Beshears, 18, b. MS, c1842
Narcissa Beshears, 15, b. MS, c1845
Elizabeth Beshears, 11, b. AR, c1849
Robert Beshears, 7, b. AR, c1853
Francis Beshears (m) 4, b. AR, c1856
#156-139: Ellen McCue, 45, b. TN, 2 Jan 1816; Berry's dau
Robert McCue, 21, b. MS, c1839, farmer
Elizabeth McCue, 15, b. MS, c1845
Amaziah McCue, (m) 12, b. AR, c1848
Henry McCue, 8, b. AR, c1852

1860 Census, Saline Co, AR, Union twp, Brazil P.O., p.87:
#565-565: **Berry Bashears**, 70, farmer, b. SC, "Old man Berry"

Anna Bashears,	65, b. NC	
Nancy Bashears,	30, b. TN	Berry's dau; m.1. Burks; m.2. Brazil
Monteville Bashears,	6, b. AR	s/o Berry Bashears Jr
Henry Brashears,	4, b. AR	s/o Berry Bashears Jr
Mary Bashears,	3, b. AR	d/o Berry Bashears Jr
Jasper Bashears,	6/12, b. AR	s/o Berry Bashears Jr
Anna Bashears,	10, b. AR	[surname Burks; Nancy's dau]
Mary Bashears,	8, b. AR	[surname Burks; Nancy's dau]
Matilda Bashears,	2, b. AR	[surname Brazil; Nancy's dau]
Fillmore Bashears,	6/12, b. AR	[Tillman Brazil; Nancy's son]

In Berry's 1860 census listing, Monteville, Henry, Mary, and Jasper Bashears are the orphans of Berry Bashears Jr. In 1870 Pulaski Co, AR, these children are in h/h of James and Mary Andrews (widow re-married), both age 33, b. TN and GA.

Nancy, age 30, is Berry and Anna's daughter; she m.1. Simpson Burks, m.2. Richard Isom Brazil. Anna, 10, and Mary, 8, are her children by her first marriage; Matilda, 2, and Tillman, 6/12, are her children by her second marriage.

Some other stray data:

Mary Bashear, b. c1851 (age 25 in 1876), m. 18 Nov 1876, Pulaski Co, AR, William Otrace, b. c1854 (age 32 in 1876).

J.J. Breshears, b. c1854 (23 in 1877); m. 11 Feb 1877, Pulaski Co, AR, Atholine Cochran, b. c1857 (20 in 1877).

Berry Boshears' Family

Anna Locke was told that Berry ("Old Man Berry") had 16 children by two wives, including sons, Basil and Drury, and a daughter, Ellen McCuen. [Documents now make it look like she was wrong on Basil.] Anna also said Basil was the oldest of Berry's children by the first wife, then Andrew, some girls, Alfred, and Robert, the youngest. His second wife was Anna ______. She said the family lived in the vicinity of Lexington, KY, before moving to Arkansas. [But none of the children seem to be born in KY, and Basil's Civil War service record gives his name Basil Brashears Jr.]

It looks like Berry Breshears was married only once. His wife, as Charles S. Breshears, of Sherwood, Arkansas, points out, is listed in all the censuses but one as b. c1795; the 1850 census (which says she was 45, i.e. b. c1805) is probably in error.

<u>Children of Berry Brashears/Boshears</u>: (Data from 1820 Census of White Co, TN, 1830 Census of McNairy Co, TN, 1840 Census of Tishomingo Co, MS, 1850 Census of Montgomery Co, AR; Tax Lists, cemeteries; notes by Anna Locke, Charles S. Breshears, and others.)

[V6]5701. [9]1. female **Brashears**, b. c1810 (10-15 in 1820; 15-20 in 1830); probably **Lucinda Brashears**, who m. 9 Feb 1828, Lawrence Co, TN, ***George Suratt***, (with Berry Brashears as bondsman. George Suratt's name is often misspelled in records as "Cerat," He signed the marriage bond as George C. Rat.) He was born 23 Jan 1803, and died 10 Sept 1857. (Data from Christine <CGenie1@aol.com>). They had children: Jacob, Margaret (Christine's line), Malinda (Matilda), Nancy, Tabethe, Clarie, Mary, Lucie, Angeline (Rebecca), John, and William P. Suratt.

[V6]5702. [9]2. ***James M. (Monteville?) Brashears**, b. TN, 1810, who lived in White Co, AR, 1832-1846, then migrated to TX. See "Brashears Families of Angelina Co, TX."

[V6]5703. [9]3. ***Andrew "Drew" "Drury" Boshears**, b. 1813, TN (40 in 1850 Montgomery Co, AR; 47 in 1860 Pulaski Co, AR, Owen twp.), m. 17 Aug 1831 in Lawrence Co, TN, ***Rebecca Brashears***, b. TN, c1814 (46 in 1860, Pulaski Co, AR), sister of Alexander Brashears, who signed the marriage bond. At the time of this marriage, Berry, the father, was living in McNairy Co, TN; so 18-year-old Drew apparently went back to Lawrence Co to marry a 17-year-old cousin.

[V6]5704. [9]4. ***Ellen Brashears**, b. 2 Jan 1816, TN (45 and head of household in 1860 Pulaski Co, AR), d. 28 April 1899, bur Spring Valley Cem at Ferndale, Pulaski Co, AR; m. ***Samuel McCue or McHughes***.

[V6]5705. [9]5. female **Brashears**, b. 1815-1820, possibly

Elizabeth H. Brashears**, m. 2 Nov 1841, in Green Co, AR (Co seat: Paragould), ***John Harmon Wyatt,

or possibly **Elizabeth "Lizzie" "Betsy Ann" Boshears**, m. ______ ***Phillips***, and had a dau, Molly Phillips, who m. William Beard.

[V6]5706. [9]6. ***Robert Henry "Uncle Bob" Boshears**, b. 1820, TN: in 1860, 70, & 80 Census, Pulaski Co, AR, Owen twp.

[V6]5707. [9]7. female **Brashears**, b. 1820-1825, possibly **Martha Jane Boshears**, m. ***George Britt***, and had dau, Martha Britt,

[V6]5708. [9]8. male **Brashears**, b. 1825-30,

[V6]5709. [9]9. female **Brashears**, b. 1825-30 (per census), probably **Arenia Breshears**, b. 9 June 1826, TN, d. 28 Sept 1872, Alcorn Co, MS; m. ***Monteville Nichols***, b. 14 Jan 1819, TN, d. 18 May 1872, Alcorn Co, MS, both bur Tuscumbia Baptist Church Cem, Alcorn Co, MS. Data from Nan Roose <nanarnpops@aol.com> The 1860 Tishomingo Co, MS census lists Monterville Nichols, 40; Arenia, 34; A. (Anna), 13; William, 11; Tabitha, 9; Lavina, 7; Berry, 6; Martha, 4; and Lenora, 1, all born in MS.

Tippah Co MS Land and Deed Abstracts (Bk J, p.464) records that Berry & Amy (Anny?) Breshears (Beshears) of Tishomingo Co, conveyed land to Mountaville Nichols on 12 Oct 1848. We think Berry Breshears is Arenia's father.

Nan continues: "The younger son, Abram Berry Nichols, b. 6 May 1855, d. 25 Jan 1912, bur Tuscumbia cemetery; m. Nancy Easley, b. 13 Dec. 1858; d. 25 July 1930, dau of W.M. Easley & Charlotty [maybe Smith]. Berry & Nan (for whom I was named) had 4 children, among them my grandfather Mattie Bruce Nichols."

[V6]5710. [9]10. ***Nancy H. Brashears**, b. 28 Sept 1830, Lawrence Co, TN (30 in 1860 Saline Co, AR, in H/H of Berry Sr; 48 in 1880 Garland Co, AR; 64 in 1894); m.1. 15 March 1849, ***Simpson Burks***, who d. 2 April

1854 on Sumter Farm, near Searcy, White Co, AR; m.2. 7 May 1856, ***Richard Isom Brazil***. See Nancy's 1894 application for Civil War Widow's Pension, below.

V6 5711. 9 11. ***Berry Brashears Jr**, "Little Berry", b. 1832, TN or MS, (18 in 1850 Montgomery Co, AR), on 1852-55 Montgomery Co, AR, Poll Tax list; d. 1859, Saline Co, AR; m. 1853, ***Mary Jane Smith***,

V6 5712. 9 12. ***Henry Clay Brashears**, I, b. 3 Dec 1835, TN, d. 13 Nov 1894, Garland Co, AR; m. 29 Sept 1859, Montgomery Co, AR, ***Martha M. Godwin***, b. Aug c1844, MS, d. 14 Nov 1904, Garland Co, AR,

V6 5713. 9 13. **Larkin R. Brashears**, b. 1837, McNairy Co, TN, (13 in 1850 Montgomery Co, AR; Larkin gave age 20, b. c1844, McNairy Co, TN, when he enlisted in Co D, 4th AR Cav, U.S. Army on 28 Feb 1864). His service records say he "died Aug 13, 1864, at his brother's." (see *Arkansas' Damned Yankees--an Index to Union Soldiers in Arkansas Regiments*, p.24)

V6 5714. 9 14. unknown male **Brashears**, b. 1835-1840 (indicated by 1840 census; not in 1850)

ANDREW "DRURY" "DREW" BOSHEARS and REBECCA BRASHEARS

v6 5703. 9 3. **Andrew "Drury" "Drew" Boshears** , (s/o Berry Boshears Sr and wife Anna), b. 1813, TN (40 in 1850 Montgomery Co, AR; 47 in 1860 Pulaski Co, AR, Owen twp. family #155); m. ***Rebecca Brashears***, b. TN, 1814 (46 in 1860 Pulaski Co, AR), sister of Alexander Brashears of Lawrence Co, TN and Benton Co, MO. Alexander Brashears was a Justice of the Peace and the care-giver in this branch of the family.

Drury [X] Brashers m. Rebecca Brashers; Lawrence Co, Tn marriage Bond, 5 Aug 1831; bondsmen: Drury (X) Brashers and /signed/Alf (or Alx) Besher (his name is clearly Alexander Brashers in the Clerk's handwriting; see copy below). Endorsed: "I solumnised the within on the 17th 1831, Jeremiah G. ?Deredy." Alexander Brashears had married a cousin, Margaret

Breshears, d/o Henry Breshears Sr, in LawrCo, TN. About 1833-34, Alexander and Margaret moved to Benton Co, MO. Drew is on 1849-50 and 52-55 Montgomery Co, AR, Poll Tax list.

Children of Andrew Boshears and Rebecca Breshears:

[V6]5715. [10]1. **Alfred Boshears**, b. MS, c1837 (age 23 in 1860 Pulaski Co, AR)

[V6]5716. [10]2. **William Boshears**, (twin) b. MS, c1842 (age 18 in 1860 Pulaski Co, AR; 28 in H/H of widow, "E. Boshaws," age 39, in 1870 Pulaski, Owen Twp)

[V6]5717. [10]3. **Alexander Boshears**, (twin) b. MS, c1842 (age 18 in 1860 Pulaski Co, AR)

[V6]5718. [10]4. **Narcissa Beshears**, b. MS, c1845 (age 15 in 1860 Pulaski Co, AR)

[V6]5719. [10]5. **Elizabeth Beshears**, b. AR, c1849 (age 11 in 1860 Pulaski Co, AR)

[V6]5720. [10]6. **Robert Beshears**, b. AR, c1853 (age 7 in 1860 Pulaski Co, AR)

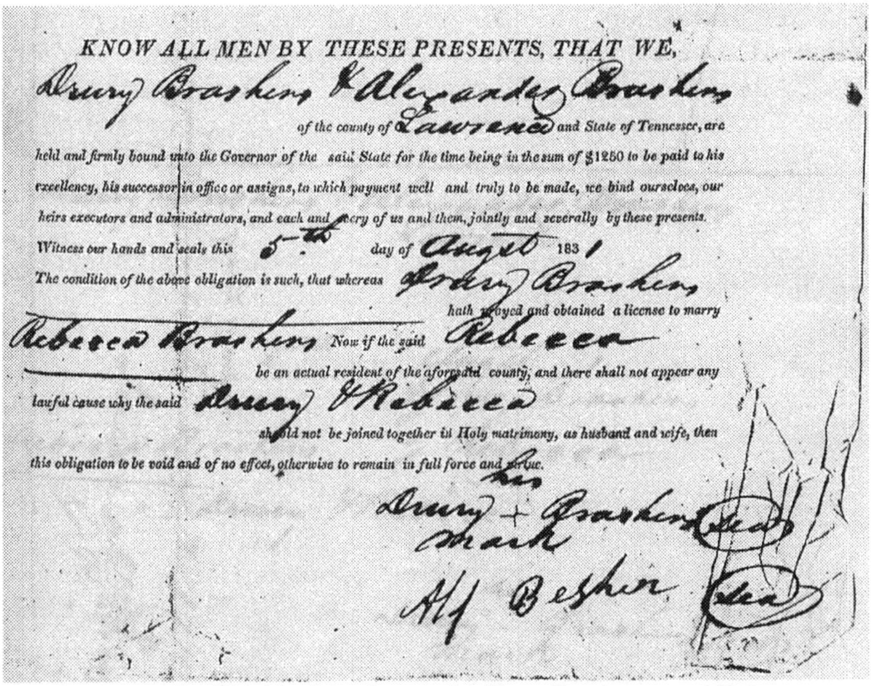
KNOW ALL MEN BY THESE PRESENTS, THAT WE, Drury Brashears & Alexander Brashears of the county of Lawrence and State of Tennessee, are held and firmly bound unto the Governor of the said State for the time being in the sum of $1250 to be paid to his excellency, his successor in office or assigns, to which payment well and truly to be made, we bind ourselves, our heirs executors and administrators, and each and every of us and them, jointly and severally by these presents. Witness our hands and seals this 5th day of August 1831

The condition of the above obligation is such, that whereas Drury Brashears hath prayed and obtained a license to marry Rebecca Brashears Now if the said Rebecca be an actual resident of the aforesaid county, and there shall not appear any lawful cause why the said Drury & Rebecca should not be joined together in Holy matrimony, as husband and wife, then this obligation to be void and of no effect, otherwise to remain in full force and virtue.

Drury his + mark Brashears (Seal)

Alx Besher (Seal)

Lawrence Co, TN, Marriage license for Drury Brashears and Rebecca Brashears, signed by Alx Besher (Alexander Brashears).

V6 5721. 10 7. **Francis Beshears**, (m) b. AR, c1856 (age 4 in 1860 Pulaski Co, AR)

ELLEN BRASHEARS and Samuel McHughes

v6 5704. 9 4. **Ellen Brashears** , (d/o Berry Boshears Sr and wife Anna), b. 2 Jan 1816, TN (45 and head of household in 1860 Pulaski Co, AR), d. 28 April 1899, bur Spring Valley Cem at Ferndale, Pulaski Co, AR; m. ***Samuel McCue or McHughes*** (data from g-gr/son, Ivan McHughes Bauknight).

We had thought for a while that Ellen belonged to Basil Brashear Jr, because she lives near him a great deal. But Nancy H. Brashears swore in her Civil War Widow's pension application that Ellen's son, Amiziah McHughes, was her nephew. That would make Ellen a sister of Nancy and a daughter of Berry.

Ellen moved with her parents to Tishomingo Co, MS, where she apparently married and had two children. About 1849, Samuel and Ellen McCue joined others in a wagon train destined for Arkansas. Samuel died enroute and was reportedly buried "beside the trail" in Tennessee. Ellen continued to Bebee, White Co, AR, where a number of Boshears/Brashears families lived in 1850; there her third child was born. At some time later, she moved on to Owen Twp, on the western edge of Pulaski Co, AR, where her cousin, Basil, lived.

Ellen McCue is Fam #156 in 1860 US Census, Pulaski Co, AR. In 1870, she is in hh of William McHughs, age 21, a son.

Family of Ellen Brashears and Samuel McHughes:

V6 5722. 10 1. Robert McCue (or McHughes), b. Mississippi, c1839, d. 1868, bur Spring Valley Cem at Ferndale, Pulaski Co, AR

V6 5723. 10 2. Elizabeth McHughes, b. Mississippi, c1845; m. Rev. Hugh H. Brady, b. 1831, OH

V6 5724. 10 3. William Amaziah McHughes, b. Bebee, White Co, AR, 14 June 1849 (21 in 1870), d. 26 Oct 1931, Little Rock, AR, bur Spring Valley Cem at Ferndale, Pulaski Co, AR; m. 13 Dec 1877, Susan Lavena Stewart, b. 1 Feb 1859, Natural Steps, AR,

d. 31 Jan 1936, Little Rock, d/o James Stewart and Rosa Ann Tucker.

V6 5725. [11]x Mary Ruhama McHughes, b. 21 May 1894, Ferndale, AR; m. 22 Dec 1919, Little Rock, AR, William Emory Bauknight, b. 4 Sept 1891, Lexington Co, SC, d. 20 Jan 1961, Florence, SC, s/o George Lucius Bauknight, and Mary Alice Bickley.

V6 5726. [12]x. Ivan McHughes Bauknight, b. 23 Feb 1928, Florence, SC, m. 17 Feb 1951, Columbia, SC, ____. Ivan is a family researcher; lives (1997) 8815 SW 160th St, Miami FL 33157-3522.

V6 5727. [10]4. Henry McHughes, b. 1852, AR, out of wedlock, said to be son of a traveling salesman, bur Spring Valley Cem at Ferndale, Pulaski Co, AR; m. Evaline ____.

ELIZABETH H. BRASHEARS and John Harmon Wyatt

Some researchers claim this Elizabeth H. Brashears, who married John Harmon Wyatt in Greene Co, AR, in 1841, as a daughter of Berry Boshears. Greene Co, AR, is in the northeastern corner of the state, plausibly on the route from TN or Tishomingo Co, MS, to White Co, AR, and Elizabeth could have married John Harmon Wyatt during a rest stop. Others of Berry's family were involved slightly with other families of Greene Co, AR.

I'm not convinced, but I'll enter the data here and let the alligators devour me for my mistakes.

John Harmon Wyatt was from Perry/Decatur Co, TN, where Wyatts and Brashears intermarried a number of times (see vol 3). Some of the Wyatt family moved early to Arkansas and then to Texas. From *History of Texas, supplemented with Biographical Mention of Many Families of the State*, Vol. 1, Central Texas (Chicago: Lewis Publ Co, 1896), p.85 (biographical sketch of Simpson Loyd; thanks to Dennis Ward for a Xerox copy):

"Abraham Wyatt was born in South Carolina and served in the Continental Army, which he entered at the age of thirteen, in the year 1775. Lavina Masengale [Massingale] became his wife and they had the following children:

John Wyatt, who married Mary Murphy
Susan Wyatt, who became the wife of George Martin
Daniel Wyatt, who married Mary Johnson
Solomon Wyatt, who married a Miss Plunckett
Samuel Wyatt, who married Mary Johnson
Abraham Wyatt [Jr], who married Sarah McCormack
Nancy Wyatt, who became the wife of Amos Collier
Elizabeth Wyatt, who married Isaac Beshears
Sarah Wyatt, who became Mrs. Daniel Murphy
Isham Wyatt, who married Mary Murphy
Absalom Wyatt, who married Sarah Henley
Martha Wyatt, who became the wife of Moses Collier
William Wyatt, who married Mary Beshears
Reuben Wyatt,"

This sketch of the Wyatts disagrees somewhat with the census data, some deeds, and the traditions passed down by their descendants in western Tennessee. Perhaps the grandson who moved to Arkansas and Texas at a very early age got some of his Wyatt ancestry mixed up a bit. Note that, in his list, above, Mary Murphy is wife of two sons of Abraham Wyatt, and so is Mary Johnson.

Documents in Decatur Co, TN show that ***Isham Wyatt***, b. 27 June 1799, SC, d. 1878, Decatur Co, TN, m. 23 Aug 1827, in Perry Co, TN, **Mary Brashear** (not Murphy), b. 19 Oct 1806, d. bef. 1847, though we have been unable to identify Mary. ***William Wyatt*** married **Elizabeth Brashears**, d/o John Brashears and Charity Bradley, not the unidentified Mary Brashears (see the deeds in v.3). In vol. 3, I hypothsized that this Elizabeth H. Brashears was somehow connected with John Brashears and Charity Bradley, but I had no idea how.

V6**5705. Elizabeth H. Brashears**, (possibly d/o Berry Boshears), m. 2 Nov 1841, in Greene Co, AR (Co seat: Paragould), ***John Harmon Wyatt***, b. c1825, d. c1865, s/o John and Mary (Murphy) Wyatt, gs/o Abraham and Lavinia (Massingale) Wyatt.

Elizabeth H. Brashears and John Harmon Wyatt, had ten children, the first 9 born in Greene Co, AR.

V6 5728. 1. Sarah E. Wyatt, b. 15 Apr 1842
V6 5729. 2. Martha A. Wyatt, b. 4 Sep 1844
V6 5730. 3. John Wyatt, b. 2 Nov 1847
V6 5731. 4. William Wyatt, b. 11 Feb 1849
V6 5732. 5. Nancy M. Wyatt, b. 29 Jan 1851
V6 5733. 6. Mary Jane Wyatt, b. 9 Apr 1853
V6 5734. 7. Tennessee C. Wyatt, b. 8 Aug 1855
V6 5735. 8. Sarah M. Wyatt, b. 6 Jan 1857
V6 5736. 9. Virginia C. Wyatt, b. 13 May 1861
V6 5737. 10. Caroline Wyatt, b. 21 Jan 1872, Washington Co, AR. ??John Harmon Wyatt was supposed to have died about 1865.

ROBERT HENRY "UNCLE BOB" BOSHEARS and Rebecca E. _____/ Mary Ellis

v6 5706. 9 6. **Robert Henry "Uncle Bob" Boshears**, (s/o Berry Boshears Sr and wife Anna), b. 1820, TN (39 in 1860; 50 in 1870; 58 in 1880 Owen twp, Pulaski Co, AR. Listed as "Boshaws" in 1870 Pulaski. "Uncle Bob" married first, ***Rebecca E.*** ________, b. TN, c1824 (36 in 1860 Pulaski Co, AR); m.2. 25 Nov 1879, Pulaski Co, AR, ***Mary Ellis***, b. c1844 (35 in 1879). In several of the censuses, Robert Boshears is listed as "Boshaws."

Family of Robert Henry "Uncle Bob" Boshears and Rebecca:

V6 5738. 10 1. **Sarah Jane Beshears**, b. AR, c1853, (7 in 1860 Pulaski, AR; 17 in 1870); m. 25 Feb 1877, Pulaski Co, AR, ****Thomas Robert Simpson***, (s/o Eliza Ann Simpson and Basil Brashears Jr). Thomas and Sarah Jane are fam #140-141 in 1880 Census, Holland twp, Saline Co, AR, with first two children. See Thomas's listing under Basil Brashears Jr for their children.

V6 5739. 10 2. **Emery C. Beshears**, b. AR, c1854, (6 in 1860 Pulaski)

V6 5740. 10 3. **Emily Melisa C. Beshears**, b. AR. c1855-6 (5 in 1860 Pulaski; 14 in 1870); m. 1879, Saline Co,

AR, ***Thomas Young Craig***, b.c1843 (36 in 1879)

V6 5741. [11]1. Elleanor Craig, b. 1869

V6 5742. [11]2. Nora Criag, b. 1873

V6 5743. [11]3. Zilpher Criag, b. 1875

V6 5744. [11]4. Cora Craig, b. 3 Feb 1878, d. 30 Dec 1929; m. J.R. Tackett,

V6 5745. [11]5. Stena Craig, b. 1880

V6 5746. [11]6. Ola Craig, b. Jan 1882

V6 5747. [11]7. Effie Craig, b. April 1886

V6 5748. [11]8. Thomas Craig, b. Jan 1889

V6 5749. [11]9. Lola Craig, b. Jan 1894

V6 5750. [10]4. ***Nancy Henrietta E. Beshears**, b. AR, 31 Dec 1857, AR (2 in 1860 Pulaski; 12 in 1870; 22 in 1880), d. 15 March 1928 in Saline Co, AR; m. 20 Nov 1883, Pulaski Co, AR, ***John Lewis Kirkpatrick***, b. 14 Nov 1855, White Co, AR. For more on Kirkpatricks, see below.

V6 5751. [10]5. **Donna Lenora Beshears**, b. AR, Jan 1860 (6/12 in 1860 Pulaski; not in 1870)

V6 5752. [10]6. **Robert Beshears**, b. c1861, AR (9 in 1870 Pulaski)

In the 1880 Census of Owen Twp, Pulaski Co, AR, William A. Breshears (s/o Basil Brashears Jr), his wife Sarah, and their first two children are in Uncle Bob's household. Note that Thomas R. Simpson, s/o Basil Brashears Jr and Eliza Ann Simpson, m. Uncle Bob's daughter, Sarah Jane Breshears.

Robert Boshears	58, TN SC SC
Mary	25, AL TN TN (second wife)
Nancy (dau)	22, AR TN SC
Willie	28, AR TN SC (s/o Basil Brashears Jr)
Sarah (wife of Willie)	24, AR GA
Leander (son of Willie)	3, AR AR AR
Rhody (dau of Willie)	1, AR AR AR

1870 Census, Pulaski Co, AR, Owen Twp, p.370: And who?? are these?:

#78-79: E. Boshaws,	39f, Keeping house, b. TN c1831
Eliza Boshaws,	14f, b. MS c1856
Thomas Boshaws,	9m, b. AR c1861
William Boshaws,	28m, farmer, b. MS c1842 s/o Andrew and Rebecca Brashears

Kirkpatrick and Brashears Connections

Lewis Kirkpatrick, (father of James Howard Kirkpatrick), b. 20 Sept 1807 in Big Bottom, Jackson Co, TN, d. 10 Sept 1843 in White Co, AR; m. c1825 in Jackson Co, TN, Pressia Ford, b. c1809, SC, d. c1880, White Co, AR, d/o Levi Ford and Sarah Walker. Data from descendant Michael Barton (jmichaelbarton @hotmail.com).

Lewis Kirkpatrick and Pressia Ford had children:

1. Sarah Kirkpatrick, b. 1826, TN, d. before 1860 in White Co, AR; m. c1843, in White Co, AR, James Hartley, b. c1826, Coshocton Co, OH. They are in the 1850 census of Royal twp, White Co, AR, with children: Alford, 6; and John, 2. In 1860, Montgomery Co, AR, James Hartley is alone with the same children.
2. Unknown Kirkpatrick, b. c1828, AR
3. *James Howard Kirkpatrick, b. 1829; m. 12 May 1852, in White Co, AR, ***Louisa Brashears***, (unidentified) see below for children.
4. Sira Kirkpatrick, b. 1833, White Co, AR, d. before 1873;
5. Alfred T. Kirkpatrick, b. 1835, White Co, AR, d. 9 Nov 1862, St. Louis, MO, bur Jefferson Barracks National Cem, St Louis Co, MO;
6. Crawford Walker Kirkpatrick, b. 1838, White Co, AR, d. 10 Oct 1862, in St. Louis, St Louis Co, MO; m. 31 Jan 1860, in Montgomery Co, AR, Delphina M. Lamb, b. 15 March 1845, GA, d. 1915 Beebe, White Co, AR, d/o Reuben Lamb and Mary Fox.
7. John H. Kirkpatrick, b. July 1843, White Co, AR, d. 1907, El Paso, White Co, AR; m. 15 Aug 1871, in White Co, AR, Sarah Sandford, b. Aug 1850, Shelby Co, TN, d. 1908, White Co, AR.

After Lewis Kirkpatrick's death, Pressia (Ford) Kirkpatrick m.2. 10 June 1846, in White Co, AR, **William Beshers**, (unidentified), who d. 10 Dec 1849 in White Co, AR. They had a son: **Taylor Besherse**, b. c1846 (age 3 in 1850, White Co, AR).

The "Layton," b. 1846, in Pressia's 1860 census listing is probably a mistaken reading for Taylor Breshears. The widow,

P. Besherse/Breshears, is in the 1850 and 1860 censuses of Royal twp, White Co, AR, with her Kirkpatrick children and Taylor Bersherse. In 1870, she was living with a (?grand) daughter, Mary Heddleson.

James Howard Kirkpatrick, b. c1829, AR (s/o Lewis Kirkpatrick and Pressia Ford), m. 12 May 1852, (White Co, AR, Bk A, p.33), ***Louisa Brashears/Breshears***, (unidentified, but possibly a d/o Berry Brashears, or Basil Brashears, which would put her in the ninth generation, b. c1829 in TN. Data from Michael Barton (jmichaelbarton @hotmail.com).

They are in the 1860 census, Montgomery Co, AR, and the 1870 census, White Co, AR, with three children.

Family of Louisa Brashears and James Howard Kirkpatrick:

V6 5753. 10 1. Pressley Kirkpatrick, b. March 1853, White Co, AR, d. 1914; m. 1873, Mary Jane Brown, b. August 1855, AR, d. 1912. Censuses: 1880, 1900, 1910 White Co, Royal twp. Ch:

V6 5754. 11 1. Eliza Kirkpatrick;

V6 5755. 11 2. Frances Kirkpatrick;

V6 5756. 11 3. Cordelia Kirkpatrick,

V6 5757. 11 4. Walter Kirkpatrick;

V6 5758. 11 5. Louisa Kirkpatrick;

V6 5759. 11 6. Presley C. Kirkpatrick.

V6 5760. 10 2. *John Lewis Kirkpatrick, b. 14 Nov 1855, White Co, AR, d. 6 June 1925, Ferndale, Pulaski Co, AR; met (1) Kate Duckworth; m.2. 20 Nov 1883, in Pulaski Co, AR, ***Nancy Henrietta E. Beshears***, b. 31 Dec 1857, AR, d. 15 March 1928, Saline Co, AR, d/o Robert Henry "Uncle Bob" Boshears and his first, unknown, wife. For family, see below.

V6 5761. 10 3. Amos M. Kirkpatrick, b. 12 Jan 1860, Montgomery Co, AR, d. 22 April 1934, White Co, AR; m. 24 Aug 1881, in White Co, AR, Belle Price, b. Aug 1867, White Co, AR, d. 5 April 1947, Pulaski Co, AR. They are in the 1900 Census, Royal twp, White Co, AR; 1910 Butler twp, Lonoke Co, AR; 1920, City of Beebe, White Co, AR. Ch:

V6 5762. 11 1. Marie Kirkpatrick;

[V6]5763. [11]2. Clara Kirkpatrick;
[V6]5764. [11]3. Vernie E. Kirkpatrick;
[V6]5765. [11]4. Cassie Kirkpatrick;
[V6]5766. [11]5. Otis Kirkpatrick.

Nancy Henrietta E. Beshears and John Lewis Kirkpatrick

[v6]5750. [10]4. **Nancy Henrietta E. Beshears**, (d/o Robert Henry "Uncle Bob" Boshears and [probably] his first, unknown, wife), b. 31 Dec 1857, AR (2 in 1860 Pulaski; 12 in 1870; 22 in 1880), d. 15 March 1928 in Saline Co, AR; m. 20 Nov 1883, Pulaski Co, AR, ***John Lewis Kirkpatrick***, b. 14 Nov 1855, White Co, AR (28 in 1883), d. 6 June 1925, Ferndale, Pulaski Co, AR, s/o James Howard Kirkpatrick and **Louisa Breshears**. The following birthdates are calculated from the 1900 census, Holland Twp, Saline Co, AR, and the 1910 and 1920 census of Owen and Ferndale twps, Pulaski Co, AR:

Family of Nancy Henrietta E. Beshears and John Lewis Kirkpatrick:

[V6]5767. [11]1. Oscar W. Kirkpatrick, b. March 1884
[V6]5768. [11]2. Donald "Donnie" D. Kirkpatrick, (female), b. Nov 1886
[V6]5769. [11]3. Robert A. Kirkpatrick, b. Dec 1888
[V6]5770. [11]4. James L. Kirkpatrick, b. Feb 1894
[V6]5771. [11]5. Rebecca E. Kirkpatrick, b. March 1891
[V6]5772. [11]6. Luther Kirkpatrick, b. c1894 (listed as a son, 16, in 1910 Pulaski; does not appear in any other census)
[V6]5773. [11]7. Sarah R. Kirkpatrick, b. c1895 (listed as a daughter, 25, in 1920 Pulaski; does not appear in any other census)
[V6]5774. [11]8. Franklin W. Kirkpatrick, b. June 1896

Contact descendant Michael Barton (jmichaelbarton @hotmail.com) for more on Kirkpatricks.

NANCY H. BRASHEARS and Simpson Burks/ Richard Isom Brazil

V6 5710. [9]10. **Nancy H. Brashears**, (d/o Berry Boshears Sr and wife Anna), b. 28 Sept 1830, Lawrence Co, TN (30 in 1860 Saline Co, AR, in H/H of Berry Sr; 48 in 1880 Garland Co, AR), d. after 1894, when she applied for a Civil War Widow's Pension; m.1. 15 March 1849, ***Simpson Burks***, who d. 2 April 1854 on Sumter Farm, near Searcy, White Co, AR; m.2. 7 May 1856, ***Richard Isom Brazil***.

Figure 96: Mr. Brazil (believed to be Richard Isom Brazil), Clarkie Clay Boshears (1902-1917), and Henry Clay Boshears, nephew of Nancy H. Brashears. Thanks for photo from Jenny Henry.

Nancy's oldest daughter, Anna, m.1. Andrew J. Riley, s/o Thomas Jefferson Riley and his first wife, Mary Lynch. After Mary (Lynch) Riley died, Thomas Jefferson Riley, m.2.c1849, MS, Nancy Caroline Brady. This Nancy (Brady) Riley is in the 1880 census with several Riley children: Frances R. Riley, (23 in 1880); Samantha E. Riley, (19); James C. Riley, (17); Margarette L. Riley, (12); Thomas D. Riley, (6); George D. Riley, (3). Some of us have confused this Nancy (Brady) Riley with Nancy H. (Brashears) Burks/Brazil.

<u>Nancy H. Brashears had two children by each of her husbands:</u>

V6 5775. [10]1. Anna Burks, b. 1 Jan 1850; m.1. Andrew J. Riley, d. c1888, s/o Thomas Jefferson Riley and his first wife, Mary Lynch; m.2. c1890, James Blackburn; m.3. John M. Riley, a half-brother to Andrew J. Riley.

V6 5776. [10]2. Mary Burks, b. c1852 (8 in 1860); m.1. Frederick Meredith; m.2. ______ McClure,

V6 5777. [11]x. Nancy Arminda "Mindy" Meredith, b. Nov 1871, d. 1939, bur Avant Cem; m. 11 or 14 Jan 1890, at Mt. Tabor Church, "by Elder

W.S. Gamble," Montgomery Co, AR, **DeKalb "Cab" Brashears**, (s/o Henry Clay Brashears and Martha M. Godwin), b. 6 April 1868, Cedar Glades, Garland Co, AR, d. 8 March 1919, Buckville, Garland Co, AR, bur Avant Cem

V6 5778. 11 x. Frederick A. Meredith, b. 3 July 1876, Cedar Glades, AR, d. 7 Jan 1957, Hot Springs, Ar, bur Greenwood Cem; m. 11 Nov 1900, **Mary Elizabeth Brashears**, (d/o Henry Clay Brashears and Martha M. Godwin), b. 12 Nov 1883, Cedar Glades, AR, d. 19 Dec 1956, Hot Springs, AR.

V6 5779. 10 3. Amanda Matilda Brazil, b. c1857-58 (2 in 1860), d. 7 March 1865

V6 5780. 10 4. Tillman W. Brazil, b. Jan 1860 (6/12 in July 1860), d. 7 May 1865

Deposition of Nancy H. (Brashears) Burks/Brazil, Oct 1894, in support of her application for a Civil War Widow's pension. Her first application was denied on the grounds that she couldn't prove that Richard Brazil was dead. She appealed and was given an extended hearing. This deposition is from the second application.

"I was 64 years old the 28th day of last month...He (Richard) enlisted Sept. 8, 1864 & was discharged with the Regt, I reckon, yet I don't know that to be a fact, for I never saw him after he went off...My maiden name was **Nancy H. Brashears**. I was born in Lawrence Co., Tenn and was raised in Tishamingo Co, Miss. When I was in my 20th year, I moved to Arkansas. The furst year we lived near Searcy, White Co, Ark. While there, I was married to a ***Simpson Burks***. We were married March 15, 1849, I think. Squire Combs married us. I had 2 children by Burks viz: Anna & Mary...Mr. Burks died down here on the Sumpter farm on Saturday the 2nd day of April, 1854, I reckon it was...I remained a widow 2 yrs. I think. I was then married to ***Richard Isom Brazil***. We were (illegible) river. We all moved i.e. my parents, down into Saline Co., Ark. just before Christmas & Mr. Brazil and I were married the 7th of May following--1856, I think. Marcus Miller, a Justice of the Peace married us. We were married at my father's house...

"We did not live peaceably together. Brazil was a very disagreeable man, and we didn't get along good at all. We had fusses along & along. I had 2 children by him viz: Amanda Matilda and Tillman W. They both died in time of the war, one the 7th of March & 'tother the 7 of May 1865, I reckon. Mr. Brazil and I had separated twice before he went into the army, and we lived apart one time about 6 mos. The other time not so long. In the spring of 1864, about April, Mr. Brazil and I had a fuss. We were just living in the woods and had some planks set up against a pole, and me and my daughter were chopping wood for our living and Brazil was getting the money for it. I wanted him to build a house, and he wouldn't do it. And he got mad over it, and I got mad too and then the fuss was on. We didn't come to blows. He packed his duds and lit out, and I did not... hear from him directly until...

"I heard through some of my neighbors that he was at Little Rock in the Army & I went to see him. I think that was in the Summer of 1865, about July, I think. I was in there with him about an hour...He had federal uniform on. We met at a neighbor's house that time & we never spoke to each other...He wouldn't speak to me, & I wouldn't speak to him. I thought he ought to speak first. That is the last time I ever saw Richard Brazil or heard from him...I have written to find him. I have written to his own people at Brazil P.O., Saline Co, Ark. I wrote to Wylie Fowler & Amiziah McHughes. Wylie Fowler's wife is Brazil's cousin. McHughes is my nephew."

"Brazil was about 30 yrs. old, when he went off--medium height, slim spare built man, complexion fair, dark hair & blue eyes...He had been married before he married me. His first wife was Elizabeth Talton. I never saw her. He brought her to Arkansas with him. He had one child by her, named William [Brazil]. William lived with his Uncle Washington Brazil near Brazil P.O., Ark. until Richard & I were married, and then William was brought home, & he lived with us, until after his father & I separated in the Spring of 1864; that summer William left me and went to his father, & he got him a place with a widow named Fielder...we were then living about 1½ miles from Little Rock, Ark. The (battle) lines were close, and we had to go nearer into town. We lived that close together, & we had nothing to do with each other & never saw each other, only the one time above mentioned. The boy Willie died in time of the war, so I heard... I heard that the Fielder woman had an heir by Richard Brazil. He staid there & got her to do his washing..."

"Richard's first wife died, so they said. He had some woman's clothes that he brought to me when we were married...He had not been a widower but a very short time before he & I married. He come to Saline Co to his brother's with one child, Willie, afterwards..."

"I have no means of support. I have one cow & 2 yearlings. No real estate..."

"I heard Brazil speak of a man named Maynard E. Maynard who lived in the Arkansas river bottoms on Big Maumell, right at the Pinnacle. I heard his (Brazil's) wife died down there... I heard his brother Washington Brazil went up about St. Louis, MO. I don't know his whereabouts... If Patsie Fowler of Brazil, Saline Co., Ark. can't give you the whereabouts of the Brazil family, I don't know who could."

Deposition of Anna (Burks) Blackburn, Cedar Glades, Ark, 10 OCT 1894:

"I am 44 yrs. old. I was born Jany. 1, 1850; occupation: day laborer. The claimant in this case is my mother. I am a child of her first husband---Burks. My first husband was A. J. Riley. He died 6 yrs. ago in Nov. I was a widow 2 yrs. and then married James Blackburn. He & I couldn't 'gee hosses' & we separated..."

"I remember ***Richard Brazil***. I was only a little girl, 5 or 6 yrs. old when mother married him...He & mother did not live peaceably together. Sometimes they got along very well and sometimes they had right smart little rackets. Yes, I have seen them fight...when he and mother separated the last time...we were living in camps and mother had some planks set up on end against a pole in two forks, and my little sister Matilda was sick and about to die. That was about 1½ miles from Little Rock. Mother & Brazil had a fuss and he left."

Deposition of Mary (Burks) McClure, Nancy's other daughter, Taken at Cedar Glades, Ark, 10 OCT 1894:

"I recollect that Richard Brazil was my step father...I

remember that he & mother did not get along well together. I have seen them fight. He never whipped her but he tried..."

In a later "General Affidavit," Mary states: "Richard I. Brazil...enlisted and left home, because he was afraid of his neighbors who were Rebels..."

Nancy H. Brashear's Widow's Pension application was rejected permanently, on the grounds that Richard had abandoned his family prior to enlistment.

"LITTLE BERRY" BRASHEARS and Mary Jane Smith

V6**5711.** 911. **Berry Brashears (Boshears), Jr "Little Berry"**, (s/o Berry Boshears Sr and wife Anna), b. c1832, TN, says his 1850 census listing in Montgomery Co, AR; (Anna Locke, a granddaughter said he was born 1832 at Black Hawk, Holmes Co, Mississippi-- Henry Clay Boshears told his daughter, Zula Mabry, the same thing), d. c1859, Saline Co, AR; m. 1853, ***Mary Jane Smith***, b. 17 Jan 1838, Holly Springs, Marshall Co, Miss, d. 2 June 1919, Maumelle, Pulaski Co, AR, d/o Joseph G. Smith, b. c1794, SC, and his wife Elvira ______ b. c1798, SC. (See 1850 US Census, Marshall Co, MS, #170-170.)

One family story is that Berry had been sick with measles. He and Mary Jane walked down to the garden to check on the corn that was just coming up. They got caught in a rain shower. Berry took sick with a high fever and, within three days, he was dead.

Children of (Little) Berry Brashears/Boshears and Mary Jane Smith, In 1860 US Census, Pulaski Co, AR (Brazil twp, p.87, #565-565), Little Berry and Mary Jane's children are in the household of his parents, Berry and Anna Bashears:

V65781. 101. **Monteville Boshears (Brashears),** b. 13 July 1854, Paron, Saline Co, AR, d. 28 Jan 1935; m. 13 Feb 1881, ***Velonine "Nona" Key***, b. 2 Oct 1866, IA, d. 11 March 1918. (in 1900 census, Maumelle Twp, Perry Co, AR, as "Montie Borchears" with four children; they had been married 18 years and had 5 children, 4 of them still living:

V65782. [11]1. **Henderson Boshears**, b. Dec 1886, AR (per 1900 census); m. ***Lottie Smith***,

V65783. [11]2. **Everett Boshears**, b. Oct 1889, AR (per 1900 census); m. ***Fannie Boshears***,

V65784. [11]3. **Eunice Boshears**, b. July 1892, AR (per 1900 census); m. ***Charley Thompson***,

V65785. [11]4. **Grace Boshears**, (dau), b. Sept 1897, AR (per 1900 census); m. ***Walter Green***, b. 14 March 18??, d. May 1968, Pulaski Co, AR.

V65786. [11]5. **Iona Boshears**, m. ______ ***Garrett***

V65787. [11]6. **Arkie Boshears**,

V65788. [10]2. ***Henry Clay Boshears (Brashears),** b. 20 Nov 1856, Paron, Saline Co, AR, d. 9 April 1928, Maumelle, Pulaski Co, AR, buried Martindale Cem, Maumelle. Had 17 children by three women; see below.

V65789. [10]3. **Mary J. "Mollie" Boshears (Brashears),** b. 10 Oct 1858, Paron, Saline Co, AR, d. 17 March 1879, m. 3 Sept 1876, in Pulaski Co, AR, ***John Long***, b. ?, d. 1878; both bur Martindale Cem, Pulaski Co, AR. No record of children.

V65790. [10]4. **Jasper H. (or W.) Boshears (Brashears),** b. 25 Dec 1859, Paron, Saline Co, AR; m. c1889 (married 11 yrs in 1900), ***Arizona "Zonie" Brazil***, b. 8 Dec 1866, AR (per 1900 census, Maumelle twp, Perry Co, AR), d. 28 Feb 1934. Mother, Polly Anderson, was in Jasper's household in 1910, US Census, Perry Co, AR, Maumelle Twp, fam 19-19. In the 1900 US Census, Maumelle Twp, Perry Co, AR, **George Boshears**, b. Feb 1880, AR, is listed as a brother in Jasper's household. Perhaps he is really George Anderson, and got listed with the wrong surname in 1900?

V65791. [11]1. **Effie Boshears**, (dau), b. May 1890, AR (per 1900 census)

V65792. [11]2. **Myrtle Boshears**, b. Sept 1895, AR ("Martha" per 1900 census; 14 in 1910)

V65793. [11]3. **Odessa V. Boshears**, b. c1902 (son; 8 in

1910)

V6 5794. 11 4. **Harvey Boshears**, b. 6 April 1903 (son; 7 in 1910), d. Nov 1980, Pulaski Co, AR; m. ______

V6 5795. 11 5. **Elijah H. Boshears**, b. c1908 (son; 2 in 1910)

After Berry Jr's death, the children went to live with grandpa Berry (1860 census). Mary Jane (Smith) Brashears m.2. James "Jim" Anderson (or Andrews?) and had children:

- "Sug" Anderson, m. Bert Wilson;
- Mollie (Myry) Anderson, m. Jack MacDonald;
- "Zone" Anderson, m. John Joyce;
- William B. "Bud" Anderson, b. Oct 1878; m. ____.

James and Mary Andress (Anderson) are in the 1870 census, Pulaski Co, AR, p.357, fam #9-9, with two Anderson children and her four Boshears children. In 1910, Perry Co, AR, (dist 165, sh 10b, Maumelle twp, #179-179) Mary J. is mother in household of William B. Anderson, b. Oct 1878; she is also in the 1910 US Census in household of her son, Jasper W. Boshears, in Perry Co, AR, Maumelle twp, fam #19-19. She had borne ten children seven of them living in 1910. She died in 1919, and is buried in Martindale Cem as Mary Jane Anderson.

HENRY CLAY BRASHEARS, and his Seventeen Children

v6 5712. 10 2. **Henry Clay Boshears (Brashears),** (s/o Berry Boshears Jr and Mary Jane Smith), b. 20 Nov 1856, Paron, Saline Co, AR; d. of Bright's Disease, 9 April 1928, Maumelle, Pulaski Co, AR; buried Martindale Cem, Maumelle, for which Henry had donated the land.

Henry was a farmer in the Martindale community. He grew cotton and vegetables, and raised cows. He owned his own cotton gin, which he and his family ran. He also ginned cotton for the rest of the community. Daughter Ellon Catherine Boshears remembered tying the bundles of ginned cotton, getting them ready to be shipped. The cotton was then hauled by buckboard to the dock at Ledwedge on the Arkansas River.

Later, Henry Clay Boshears built a new log house from logs

he cut on his own farm. Coyn Whitfield Smith remember it being built in the "dog trot" style— two bedrooms on one side and two on the other, with a long, open hall in the middle. Across the back were the kitchen and dining area. Out back was a well, where the family kept their milk.

Henry had 17 children by three women:

Henry Clay Boshears, did not marry ***Mary Ann C. Merritt***, b. c1857, Calhoun Co, AR, d/o John Merritt, b. 1814, NC, and his wife Sarah, b. 1826, SC or Alabama. When Mary discovered she was pregnant, she gave HCB an ultimatum: "Marry me before it shows, or forget it altogether." HCB was poor, had a very ill mother, and just couldn't afford it. So the child was born out of wedlock, and HCB and Mary never married. Mary later married a man named Pillow or Pillas and had three children: Ed, Emma, Gussie.

Henry is said to have recognized Vonnie Boshears as a daughter; she visited sometimes with her Boshears siblings, who found her a sweet, gentle person. She reported that Old Man Pillow beat her mother, and finally simply abandoned the family.

<u>Child of Henry Clay Boshears and Mary Ann C. Merritt:</u>

V6 5796. 11 1. **Mary Lavonia "Vonnie" Boshears,** b. 5 March 1877, Maumelle, AR, d. 4 Sept 1945, Roland, AR; m. 12 Feb 1891 (Pulaski Co, AR, Bk 16, p.70) ***Joe Lee Harding***, b. 1864, Oklahoma Indian Territory, d. 27 Aug 1936, Roland, AR; son of _____ half Cherokee or Choctaw mother, who is buried near Lonoke, OK.

V6 5797. 12 1. *Pearl Mae Harding, b. 7 June 1894, Oklahoma Territory, d. 22 March 1957, Klammath Falls, OR; m.1. Joe Calvin Thomas, (see below)

V6 5798. 12 2. Fred Harding, b. 1895, Oklahoma Territory, d. infant, 1895

V6 5799. 12 3. Charles Marion Harding, b. 189_, AR, d. 1963, Tulare, CA; m. Dorothy Holtsman. 4 ch: Raymond; Curtis John; Charles; and Cathy Harding

[V6]5800. [12]4. Ruben Curtis Clay Harding, b. 9 Jan 1907, Bigelow, AR; d. May 1979, Roland, AR; m. Esther Vivian Clifton, b. 18 April 1909, Maumelle, AR, d. Roland, AR. 10 ch: Margarete; John Lee; Curtis Wilburn; Dorothy Melvine; Maurene; Everett Fay; Wilmer Ray; Billy Wilburn; Evelyn Patricia; and Ailene Harding.

[V6]5801. [12]5. Cecil Pete Harding, b. 1908, Roland, AR, d. there 1927; not married

[V6]5802. [12]6. Everett Conway Harding, b. 1908, Roland, AR, d. 1991; m. Bertha Leona Davidson

[V6]5803. [12]7. Faye Jessie Harding, b. 1911, England, AR, d. 1968, Marysville, CA; m. ______ Donald.

[V6]5797. [12]1. **Pearl Mae Harding**, (d/o Mary Lavonia Boshears and Joe Lee Harding), b. 7 June 1894, Oklahoma Territory, d. 22 March 1957, Klammath Falls, OR; m.1. Joe Calvin Thomas, b. Dec 1882, Alexander, Saline Co, AR, d. March 1931, England, AR; son of Joseph Thomas, b. c1849, SC, d. ca 1900, AR, and his wife, Susan _____ b. c1840, SC; m.2. Henry Tabor; m.3. Floyd Thomas

[V6]5804. [13]1. Vernon Lee Thomas, b. 10 Jan 1912/13, d. 21 Dec 1981, Turner, Oregon; m.1. Arlenia _______; m.2. Jewel Lucille _______

[V6]5805. [13]2. Theo Thelma Thomas, b. 3 Sept 1915, Grant Co, AR; m. Wesley Benjamin Howard, b. 4 Oct 1913, Tuscumbia, Ala, d. WW II, 16 April 1945, Germany, buried in Little Rock, AR; son of William Henry Howard, b. 16 April 1862, Ala, d. 19 Oct 1942, Lonoke, AR, and his wife Laura Sylvester Davis, b. 30 Oct 1879, AL, d. 9 June 1937, Scott, England, AR.

[V6]5806. [14]1. Joe Wesley Howard, b. 25 Sept 1937, Little Rock, Pulaski Co, AR; m. Betty Joanne Vargas, b. 31 March 1936, Richmond, CA

[V6]5807. [15]1. Denise Lynelle Howard, b. 8 June 1956, Oakland, CA; m. William Kientzler Whitehead, b. 23 June 1955, Spokane, WA

V65808. [16]1. Estella May Whitehead, b. 7 Oct 1977, Bremerton, WA

V65809. [16]2. William Brandon Whitehead, b. 26 April 1981, Honolulu, HI

V65810. [15]2. Joseph William Howard, b. 11 Feb 1959, Oakland, CA; m. Carmen Able; children: Sherry Able, Mike Able

V65811. [15]3. Jeanette Renee Howard, b. 31 July 1962, Richmond, CA; m.1. Joel Land Juchniewicz; m.2. Jeffrey Jay Johnson

V65812. [16]1. Brian Anthony Juchniewicz, b. 13 March 1981, Berkeley, CA

V65813. [16]2. Dustin Michael Johnson (Jeff's child, b. 19 Sept 1981, Iowa City, IA

V65814. [13]3. Wilmer Calvin "Buddy" Thomas, b. 20 Dec 1925, d. 25 Aug 1987, Pinole, CA; m.1. Juanita Cole; m.2. Carleen Dobler

V65815. [13]4. Infant Thomas, twin of Wilmer, died at birth, 20 Dec 1925

V65816. [13]5. Ernest Clayton Thomas, b. 24 Dec 1927, AR; m.1. Virginia _____; m.2. Helen ______

Henry Clay Boshears, m.1. 25 Feb 1877 (Pulaski Co, Marr Bk 2, p.220, "by L.M. Harris, J.P."), ***Mary Catherine Martindale***, b. 18 Nov 1856, Maumelle or Nevada Co, AR, d. 29 March 1888, Maumelle, Pulaski Co, AR, bur Martindale Cem, Maumelle; d/o George W. Martindale Sr and his wife Nancy C. Lewis.

Henry Clay Boshears and George W. Martindale were good friends and hunting partners. George Martindale was one-half Cherokee Indian. Mollie Boshears remembered him plaiting his hair. He owned a grist mill and was an outstanding citizen in the community. It was said he could sing songs all night, and never sing the same song twice. He was an avid bear hunter and had two bear dogs, one named "Ring."

George W. Martindale was born c1830 in Alabama, and died c1888 in Arkansas. Nancy C. Lewis was born c1834 in Tennessee and died c1879 in Arkansas. They were married 12 Oct 1851, in Hempstead Co, AR, by Hugh White, J.P. Their children included:

John D. Martindale;
George W. Martindale, Jr;
Mary Catherine Martindale;
Elizabeth C. Martindale;
Susan A. Martindale;
William L. Martindale.

(See 1870 US Census, McCool twp, Perry Co, AR, p.1, #6-6.)

Family of Henry Clay Boshears and Mary Catherine Martindale:

[V6]5817. [11]2. **Nancy Ann "Nania" Boshears,** b. 14 Jan 1878, Maumelle, Pulaski Co, AR, d. 21 Jan 1883, bur. Martindale Cem. Maumelle, Pulaski Co, AR

[V6]5818. [11]3. **George Henry Boshears,** b. 21 Feb 1880, Maumelle, AR; d. 12 Aug 1962, Little Rock, AR, bur. Pinecrest cem, Little Rock, AR; m. 29 Nov 1902, ***Mollie Williams***, b. 31 Aug 1885, Pulaski Co, AR, d. 9 June 1977, AR, bur Pinecrest cem; d/o Abraham L. Williams and Sophronia Hutto. See 1920 US Census, Roland, Pulaski Co, AR, fam #72-73.

[V6]5819. [12]1. **Anna Boshears**, b. 5 Nov 1903; m. 11 Aug 1932, ***Lloyd Everett Locke***, d. 22 July 1974; no children. Anna Locke was a tireless researcher in this branch of the family.

[V6]5820. [12]2. **Clyde Abraham Boshears**, b. 12 Dec 1905, d. 26 March 1906

[V6]5821. [12]3. **Odie Euretta Boshears**, b. 24 March 1907; d. 2 Jan 1989, lived: Little Rock, AR; m. 16 Dec 1928, ***Charles Richard Blackburn***,

[V6]5822. [13]1. Sharon Lynn Blackburn; m. Cecil Burks. Ch: Tammy; Kathy; and Bonnie Burks

[V6]5823. [13]2. Carryl Ann Blackburn,

[V6]5824. [12]4. **Herman Clinton Boshears**, b. 26 March 1909, d. 16 Feb 1966; m. Aug 1932, ***Rosalyn Moore***, d/o John Wesley Moore (1878–1939) and Maude Irene Henderson (1888–1972)

[V6]5825. [13]1. **Clinton Boshears**; m. ***Cynthia Oglesby***,

[V6]5826. [14]1. **Bowden Boshears**; m. ***Shannon Boshears***,

[V6]5827. [13]2. **Gaylon Boshears**; m. ***Carolyn Boyd***,

V6 5828. [14]1. **Gaylon Boshears, Jr**,

V6 5829. [14]2. **Boyd Boshears**,

V6 5830. [14]3. **Tara Boshears**,

V6 5831. [13]3. **Barron Belmont Boshears**; m. ***Jenny Ann Storthz***,

V6 5832. [14]1. Catherine Elizabeth Newell

V6 5833. [12]5. **Hazel May Boshears**, b. 23 April 1911, d. 29 Sept 1922

V6 5834. [12]6. **Edith Elizabeth Boshears**, b. 11 June 1918, AR; d. 6 Jan 2001, last residence: Little Rock, AR; m. 3 Sept 1940, at Lonoke, AR, ***Andrew Jesse Latta***,

V6 5835. [13]1. Robert Latta, m.1. Loretta Warner (ch: Courtney and Heather Latta); m.2. Carol Lameerau,

V6 5836. [13]2. Linda Latta; m. Jackie Dale McCarrah. Ch: Matthew Clay McCarrah

V6 5837. [12]7. **Raymond Henry Boshears**, b. 22 Dec 1922, d. Jan 1987, last residence: Little Rock, AR; m. ***Frankie Lee Manasco***,

V6 5838. [13]1. **Ronald Clay Boshears**; m. ***Millie Fowler***,

V6 5839. [14]1. **Christopher Boshears**,

V6 5840. [11]4. **Dora Minnie Lee Boshears,** b. 4 July 1882, Maumelle, d. in infancy, 7 Aug 1882, bur. Martindale Cem, Maumelle, Pulaski Co, AR

V6 5841. [11]5. **Dee Forest Boshears,** b. 4 Aug 1883, Maumelle, Pulaski Co, AR; d. 29 Oct 1969, AR, last residence: Roland, AR; m. 4 Jan 1910, ***Ava J. Clifton***, b. 1 Aug 1891, AR, d. 19 July 1969, AR; both bur Rainey Cem, Roland, Pulaski Co, AR.

See 1920 US Census, Maumelle, Pulaski Co, AR, fam #80-80.

[V6]5842. [12]1. **Percy Boshears**, b. 14 Nov 1911, AR; d. 17 Nov 1915, AR; bur Rainey Cem, Roland, AR

[V6]5843. [12]2. **Rutha Mae Boshears**, b. 27 Sept 1913, Pulaski Co, AR; d. 20 Dec 1944, bur Rainey Cem; m. ***James Morden***.

[V6]5844. [13]1. Ruth Ann Morden; m. ______ Smith,

[V6]5845. [12]3. **Delbert C. Boshears**, b. 22 Dec 1916, Pulaski Co, AR, d. 14 Sept 1979, AR; m. ***Shirley L. Short***, b. 22 Aug 1919, d. 12 July 1997, both bur Rainey Cem. One child from Shirley's previous marriage: Bobby Ray Hemphill

[V6]5846. [11]6. **Gypsy Mae Boshears,** b. 1 May 1886, Maumelle, d. 23 Aug 1946, Roland, Pulaski Co, AR; m. 21 April 1901, Pulaski Co, AR, ***Joel Richard Williams***, b. c1878 (he was a boarder in Henry's household in 1900), s/o Allen Williams and Narcissa Brown. Eight ch, all b. Pulaski Co, AR.

[V6]5847. [12]1. Henry Allen Williams, b. 27 Jan 1901, d. 9 July 1991, Pulaski Co, AR; m. 14 Feb 1923, Roland, Pulaski Co, AR, Eva Chaney, both bur Kennerly Cem, Roland, Pulaski Co, AR. ch: Sonny and Lucille Williams. Henry and Eva are grandparents of Lou Alice Hoyle, who m. Jerry Lynn Smith.

[V6]5848. [12]2. Lola Mae Williams, b. 1 Dec 1906, d. 8 Aug 1989, AR; m. 9 Sept 1922, AR, William M. "Bill" McDonald, b. 12 Dec 1903, d. 3 Feb 1989. Ch: Harold and Dorothy (m. Johnny Daniels) McDonald

[V6]5849. [12]3. Cassie Lena Williams, b. 14 July 1909, d. 18 April 1978, Little Rock, AR; m. in Roland, Pulaski Co, AR, Virgil Price Whitt, b. 19 Aug 1904, d. 19 Jan 1983; s/o Henry Clayton Whitt and Ellen Moore. Twelve ch, 1st seven, b. Roland, Pulaski Co, AR (data from Richard W. Whitt):

[V6]5850. [13]1. Aubrey Clatyon Whitt, b. 12 Nov 1924; m. Minnie (McGhee) Chinault

[V6]5851. [13]2. Infant Whitt, b. 16 July 1926, d. July 1926, Roland, AR

[V6]5852. [13]3. Oma Louise Whitt, b. 16 July 1926; m. Odell Quinn, b. 24 Nov 1923, d. Oct 1981, s/o Mack Quinn

[V6]5853. [13]4. Phyllis Treva Whitt, b. 26 Aug 1928; m. Jewel Burton Ryles,

[V6]5854. [13]5. Virginia Lee Whitt, b. 16 Jan 1931; m.1. Eugene Bentley; m.2. Estel Cruse

[V6]5855. [13]6. Virgil Price Whitt Jr, b. 24 Nov 1934, d. 25 Dec 1995, Little Rock, AR; m. Estelita Romero Rey, b. Cajidiocan, Romblon, The Philippines.

[V6]5856. [13]7. Richard Wayne Whitt, b. 25 May 1940; m. in Desha Co, AR, Betty Sue Freeman, d/o Willie Clarence Freeman and Mary Jewell Higgins

[V6]5857. [13]8. Joyce Kay Whitt, b. 9 May 1943, Little Rock, AR; d. 4 July 1997, Frostproof, Florida; m.1. Jerry Sellers; m.2. Bill Grice

[V6]5858. [13]9. William Ray Whitt, b. 9 May 1943, Little Rock, AR; d. 9 Feb 1944, Little Rock, AR

[V6]5859. [13]10. Larry Odell Whitt, b. 19 Oct 1944, Roland, AR; m. in Little Rock, AR, Marilyn J. Beard

[V6]5860. [13]11. Russel Curtis Whitt, b. 8 Oct 1946, Roland, AR; m. Helen Lawanda O'Neal, d/o Ed O'Neal

[V6]5861. [13]12. Lynda Darlene Whitt, b. 10 April 1949, Roland, AR; m. Kenneth Paul Mackey

[V6]5862. [12]4. Bertha Lee Williams, b. 3 Jan 1912, d. 7 Aug 1929, Pulaski Co, AR, age 17, ruptured appendix.

[V6]5863. [12]5. Marvin Forrest Williams, b. 20 Nov 1914, d. 18 Dec 1979, Little Rock, AR; m.1. 11 Sept 1946, Velma Clark (2 ch); m.2. 24 Jan 1972, Jean Scott

[V6]5864. [13]1. Judy Williams,

[V6]5865. [13]2. Ronald Forrest Williams,

V6 5866. [12]6. William Hilbert Williams, b. 10 Oct 1919, d. 13 Feb 1972, Bakersfield, CA; m. 2 Nov 1946, Marian Marshall. Ch: Richard Marshall Williams, b. c1951

V6 5867. [12]7. Inez Pauline Williams, b. 13 Feb 1922, d. 12 Aug 1986; m. 2 Dec 1942, AR, Moyer Liles Kryer, b. 22 Dec 1921, d. 2 Oct 1988. Ch: Sandra Marie (b. 1945) and Buddy Kryer (b. 1949)

V6 5868. [12]8. Katherine Williams, b. 23 Jan 1924; m.1. Edward Christian; m.2. Hershal Moreland. Ch: Gary Hershal Moreland.

Henry Clay Boshears, m.2. ***Ella Jane (Hambrick) Martindale***, b. 4 March 1867, Griffin, GA, d. 4 May 1934, bur Martindale Cem, Maumelle; widow of George W. Martindale Jr. Henry had lost his first wife, and Ella had lost her first husband (who were brother and sister); so they married to take care of the children. Ella had one child by her first marriage: Jesse Ray Martindale, b. 26 Sept 1886, d. 7 Sept 1910. Henry Clay Boshears and Ella had ten children: (Source: Family Bible of Henry Clay Boshears, in possession of Zula May Mabry of Roland, AR, and 1900 census, Maumelle Twp, Pulaski Co, AR.)

Ella Jane Hambrick's parents were William Jefferson Hambrick, b. 1835, Pike Co, GA, d. 1883, and Lucinda Harper, b. 1834, d. 1913. They were married 15 May 1856, in Newton, GA. William Jefferson Hambrick was son of Hiram J. Hambrick, b. 1805, GA, d. 1859; and Nancy Green, b. 1810, GA. William and Lucinda Hambrick had moved from Atlanta, GA, to Pine Bluff, AR, where William was killed. He is buried in Mt Zion Cem, Pine Bluff, AR. Lucinda then moved to Maumelle to live with daughter, Ella Jane. Ella Jane's siblings were: Nancy; Sarah E.; William Hiram; Alfred; Mollie; Zulla; and Carrie Hambrick.

Ella Jane died from complications after gall bladder surgery, which was done in Little Rock. Ella had come home to recover at Zula May Mabry's house, developed an infection, and died.

Coy (Whitfield) Smith remembers going to the woods with her Granny to look for roots, berries, and bark to make dyes to

Figure 98: The Henry Clay Boshears/ Ella Hambrick Family, about 1900. From left to right: Jessie Martindale (Ella's son by first marriage); Joel Richard Williams (boarder; later Gypsie's husband); Richard A. Boshears (in Ella's arms); Ella Hambrick Martindale Boshears; Robert Berry Boshears; William G. Boshears; Henry Clay Boshears; Dee Boshears; George Boshears; Gypsie Boshears; Ellen Boshears; and Hattie Boshears (sort of smudged at far right). Thanks to Richard Whitt for the photo.

color her quilt material. They would also look for greens to cook. A peddler named Mr. Wheeler would come around in the Maumelle community now and then; Granny bought her needles and sewing thread from him. She also remembers that Granny dipped snuff. She would go to the woods, get a twig off a certain tree; chew the end until it was bristled out, then dip in into the snuff and put it in her cheek.

Family of Henry Clay Boshears and Ella Jane (Hambrick) Martindale

V6 5901. 11 7. **Ellon Catherine Boshears,** b. 8 July 1889, Maumelle, AR, d. 1 July 1987; m. 4 Dec 1904, Pulaski Co, AR ("by A. McNeely, J.P."), ***William Henry Whitfield***, b. 15 March 1885, AR, d. 21 Jan 1946; both bur Martindale Cem. People would come from miles around for Henry to sharpen their knives and/or cut their hair. He was a frail man with dark brown hair and blue eyes. Ellon was of medium build with long black hair and blue eyes. She wore her hair curled in a bun at the back of her head. In later years, she wore a 22½ dress and always wore a flannel shirt and a apron. She only took the apron off to go to church. They had ten children and ?hundreds of granchildren, many of whom are still living. Family members should get in touch with Jenny Henry, 655 Weldon Church Road, Bernice, LA 71222.

Figure 99: Ellon Boshears and Henry Whitfield, in a carnival mood. Thanks for photos from Jenny Henry.

[V6]5902. [12]1. Girl Whitfield, (twin) bur Martindale Cem, Pulaski Co, AR

[V6]5903. [12]2. Boy Whitfield, (twin) bur Martindale Cem, Pulaski Co, AR

[V6]5904. [12]3. Gladys Jane Whitfield, b. 18 Feb 1909, d. 6 May 1993, age 84; m. Monroe Smith, b. 24 May 1905, d. 23 March 1970. Ch: Gladys Evelyn; Monroe, Jr; Kenneth Eugene; Barbara Sue; Betty Lou; Gaye Louise; Martha Rae; and William Edwin Smith

[V6]5905. [12]4. Flossie Edna Whitfield, b. 15 June 1911; m. Ebenezer Frank Bivins, b. 11 May 1899, d. 12 Nov 1976, s/o Ebenezer Franklin Bivins and Mary Elizabeth Edwards. Ch: William Eugene; Edna Carolyn; Mary Ann; Franklin Gail; Alma Rose; Donal Ray; Janis Kay; and Freda Kathryn Bivins

[V6]5906. [12]5. Lois Evelyn Whitfield, b. 17 Ocvt 1914; m.1. Fate McGhee, b. 1908, d. 1936; m.2. Harold Lane Barnes, b. 31 Dec 1916, CA, d. 27

Standing: Gertrude Bost Boshears
William Henry Whitfield holding Gladys Jane,
Ellon CatherineBoshears Whitfield
holding Flossie Edna

March 1952, CA; m.3. ______ Plank; m.4. ______ . Ch: Harold Ray Barnes

V6 5907. 12 6. Herschel Ray Whitfield, b. 26 June 1917, d.

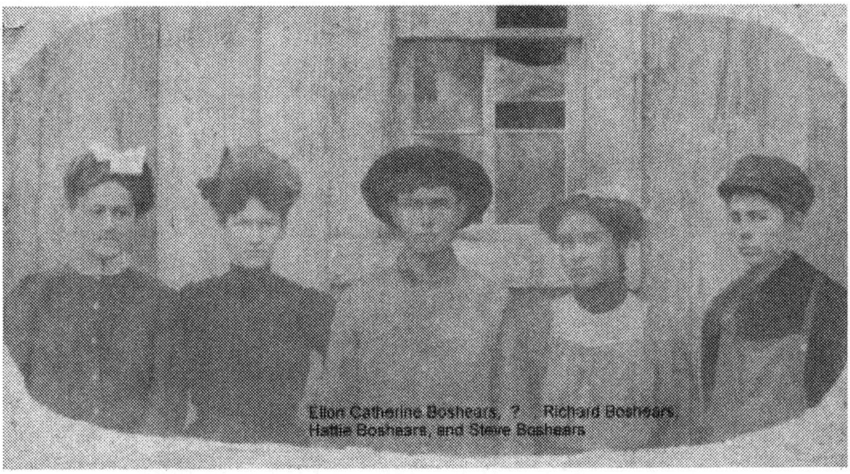

Ellon Catherine Boshears, ? Richard Boshears, Hattie Boshears, and Steve Boshears

31 March 2001; m.1. Gladys E. Adair, b. 9 Oct 1903, d. 17 May 1974; m.2. 3 Sept 1946, Willma Lucille Phillips, b. 25 Sept 1925. Ch: Margie Lynn; June Rae; Herschel Eugene "Buddy"; and Wilma Janet Whitfield

[V6]5908. [12]7. Clarence Eugene Whitfield, b. 24 Nov 1919, d. 31 March 1998, Corvallis, OR; m. Eddie Lorane Stracener, b. 4 Feb 1924, d. 1996, OR. Ch: Eugene (d. at birth, name re-used); Michael Eugene; William Ray; and Ronda Whitfield

[V6]5909. [12]8. Coy Blanche Whitfield, b. 19 Sept 1921; m. Calvin Noah Smith, b. 31 Aug 1913, d. 29 Jan 2000. Ch: Margaret Diann; Linda Sue; Judith Elaine; Jerry Lynn; Margie Dean; Jenny Lavonne; Pamela; and Terry Wayne Smith

[V6]5910. [12]9. Murriel Nadean Whitfield, b. 28 April 1925; m. 31 Aug 1946, Woodrow Wilson White, b. 8 Jan 1918, d. 15 May 1988, CA. Ch: Woodrow Wilson Jr; and Donald Eugene White

[V6]5911. [12]10. Shirley Margarite Whitfield, b. 26 March 1932; m.1. Hugh Engram Moss, b. 20 Nov 1925, d. 29 April 1968; m.2. John Kenneth Lambros, b. 7 Jan 1891, Greece, d. 16 April

1961, AR; m.3. Otha Eugene Pedigo. Ch: Wallace Engram; Freddie Joe; and Jeannie Sue Moss; and Timothy Eugene; and Jeffery Carl Pedigo

[V6]5912. [11]8. **Hattie Lee Boshears,** b. 8 Feb 1891, Maumelle, d. 14 Oct 1972, Maricopa, CA, bur Bakersfield, CA; m. ***Joe Hansen***,

[V6]5913. [12]1. Ernest Hanson; m. Mary Watson

[V6]5914. [11]9. **Robert Berry Boshears,** b. 24 Jan 1893, Maumelle, d. 3 Dec 1929, CA, bur Martindale Cem, Pulaski Co, AR; m. ***Gertie Best***, b. 14 March 1914, d. 4 Aug 1975, AR (1 ch); m.2. ***Betty*** ______ ***Lopez***, who had three children from a previous marriage: Robert; Geri; and Don Lopez

[V6]5915. [12]1. **Vernon Hershall Boshears**, b. 31 Dec 1912, AR, d. 20 Sept 1984, Kern Co, CA; m.1. ***Gussie Parks***; m.2. ______ .

[V6]5916. [13]1. **Barbara Ann Boshears**, m. ***Thomas Meisch***. Ch: Thomas Jr; and Timothy Meisch

[V6]5917. [12]2. **Viva Boshears**, m. ***Matthew Burnett***,

[V6]5918. [12]3. **Chester C. Boshears**, b. 6 Oct 1917, d. 7 March 1995, Pulaski Co, AR; m. ***Beulah Pyle***, b. c1922, d. 28 Jan 2000, d/o Jesse Pyle

[V6]5919. [13]1. **Robert Boshears**, m. Jean ______ , live in Conway, AR

[V6]5920. [14]1. **Wendy Boshears**, m. ______ ***Romaine***. Ch: Amanda Romaine

[V6]5921. [13]2. **Juanita Boshears**, m. ***Ray McNeely***,

[V6]5922. [13]3. **Jacqueline Boshears**, m. ***Billy Satterfield***,

[V6]5923. [11]10. **William Jefferson Boshears,** b. 2 March 1895, Maumelle, d. 28 Sept 1895 or 1905; not married.

[V6]5924. [11]11. **Joseph Henderson Boshears**, b. 28 Jan 1898, d. 17 March 1898; not married.

[V6]5925. [11]12. **Richard Addison Boshears,** b. 26 Aug 1899, Maumelle, d. 15 Oct 1977, Little Rock AR; m. 19 June 1926, ***Lorene Pritchard Hasty***, b. 5 Jan 1906, d. 1 Dec 1977, d/o Martin Andrew Pritchard and Adelaide Stiles.

[V6]5926. [12]1. **Wanda Odell Boshears**, m. Dick Munson. Ch: Kay Munson

[V6]5927. [11]13. **Clark Clay Boshears,** b. 21 Feb 1902, Maumelle, d. 9 June 1917, age 15

[V6]5928. [11]14. **Stephen Clifford "Steve" Boshears,** b. 13 Jan 1905, Maumelle, d. 1 July 1975, Kern Co, CA; m. ***Elsie Alexander***,

[V6]5929. [12]1. **Wilma Boshears**; m.1. ***Robert Roach***; m.2. ______ ***Garland***. Ch: Wilma Roach

[V6]5930. [12]2. **Bonnie Boshears**, m. ***Randy Coats***,

[V6]5931. [12]3. **Robert Boshears**, m. ***Raula Pocarena***,

[V6]5932. [11]15. **Zula May Boshears,** b. 7 May 1907, Maumelle, d. 25 Aug 1990, Roland, AR; m.1. ***Coburn Simpson***, b. 10 Jan 1904, d. 26 Aug 1972; m.2. ***Burl Mabry***, b. 21 March 1904, d. 20 Aug 1971, s/o William Thomas Mabry. Ch: Virginia Lee Simpson; Patricia Ann; William Henry "Hank"; and Bobby McArthur Mabry

[V6]5933. [11]16. **Rubye Sadie Boshears,** b. 1 March 1910, Maumelle, d. 19 Nov 1929, from complication after a mastoid operation in Little Rock, AR

[V6]5934. [11]17. **Roy Truman Boshears,** b. 5 April 1913, Pulaski Co, AR, d. 4 Nov 1998, bur Union Cem, Bakersfield, CA; m. ***Ruth Elizabeth Cheever***.

[V6]5935. [12]1. **Jeranne Ruth Boshears**, m.1. Herbert Wayne Englen; m.2. James William Lanier. Ch: Andrea Key; and Alicia Ruth Englen; and Herbert William Lanier

[V6]5936. [12]2. **Charles Gregory Boshears**, m.1. Carolyn Lee

Harris (1ch); m.2. Susan Campbell (2 ch)

V6 5937. [13]1. **Daniel Keith Boshears,**

V6 5938. [13]2. **Carrie Lynn Boshears,**

V6 5939. [13]3. **Leslie Elizabeth Boshears,**

HENRY BRASHEARS
and Martha Godwin

V6 5712. 9 12. **Henry Brashears**, (s/o "Old man Berry" and Anna Brashears), b. 3 Dec 1835, TN (15 in 1850 Montgomery Co, AR), d. 13 Nov 1894, Baxter twp, Garland Co, AR; m. 29 Sept 1859, Montgomery Co, AR, ***Martha M. Godwin***, b. Aug c1844, MS (age 16, in 1860 Montgomery Co, AR), d. 14 Nov 1904, Garland Co, AR, d/o Josiah Godwin, b. IL, 1813, and Louisa Jane Blocker, b. MO, 1821.

Henry enlisted 28 Feb 1864 as a private in Co. H. 4th Regiment, Arkansas Cavalry, U.S. Army, under Captain John F. Landers, to serve three years. He was discharged 30 June 1865, at Little Rock. At the time of discharge, he was age 28, b. c1836, Tishomingo Co, MS. Gerry Rylant has a copy of his discharge and pension application; (see also *Arkansas' Damned Yankees--an Index to Union Soldiers in Arkansas Regiments*, p.23).

On 15 Dec 1890, Henry applied for a pension, while living in Cedar Glades, Montgomey Co, AR: "My lunges being the trouble with me now and am criple in both hands by cattar be stiff fingers." On 7 May 1895, while living at Cedar Glades, Montgomery Co, AR, Martha applied for a widow's pension. She had two children under 16 at home.

(Data from 1880 Census, Garland Co, AR; Bible of Moses T. Brashears Jr; Military Records; marriage records, etc. collected by Gerry Rylant, Lois Cooper, and others). In the 1900 census, Martha stated that she had bourne 13 children, 8 of them living.

Family of Henry Brashears, and Martha Godwin:

V6 5940. 10 1. **Amanda Brashears**, b. 18 April 1860 (1/12 in 1860 Montgomery AR), d. 7 June 1865

V6 5941. 10 2. **Anna Brashears**, b. 13 Sept 1861, d. 13 Oct 1861, bur Avant Cem, Garland Co, AR

V6 5942. 10 3. **Calvin Brashears**, b. 20 Feb 186?, d. 6 March 1865, bur Avant Cem, Garland Co, AR

V6 5943. 10 4. **Marion Brashears**, b. 29 Dec 186?, d. 5 Oct

1875??

[V6]5944. [10]5. ***DeKalb "Cab" Brashears**, b. 6 April 1868, Cedar Glades, Garland Co, AR, d. 8 March 1919, Buckville, Garland Co, AR; m. 14 Jan 1890, at Mt. Tabor Church, Montgomery Co, AR, ***Nancy Arminda "Mindy" Meredith***,

[V6]5945. [10]6. **Nancy Josephine Brashears**, b. 24 Jan 1869, Cedar Glades, AR; m. lic. 9 June 1887, (Montgomery Co, AR, marriage Book), ***Thomas Shelton Ratliff***, b. c1868 (19 in 1887; no further info)

[V6]5946. [10]7. ***Moses Taylor Breshears Sr**, b. 13 March 1870, Cedar Glades, AR, d. 26 Sept 1942, Hot Springs, AR; m. 9 March 1890, Montgomery Co, AR, ***Rose Lee Noles***, b. 10 Jan 1874

[V6]5947. [10]8. **William Henry Brashears**, b. 8 June 1872, Cedar Glades, AR, d. 27 Dec 1937; never married. He was blinded as a boy by exploding gunpowder said to be a souvenir of the Civil War. All the family remembered him as a kind and fun-loving man. When the children held on to his cane to go visiting neighbors, he would tease them by telling them to watch out for the holes. He knew where all the holes were and, if a child went near one, it was he who would tell the child not to step into it. "Uncle Bill" is remembered as the best broom-maker in Avant.

[V6]5948. [10]9. **Louisa "Lige" Brashears**, b. Feb 1875, d. 16 Oct 1921. Lige never married, but had a son, who it is said was a Bailey.

[V6]5949. [11]1. **Marion Breshears**, b. 1899; m. 16 Oct 1921, Garland Co, AR, ***Mayflower Meeks***, b. 1893, d/o William Henry Meeks and Emma Green.

[V6]5950. [12]1. **Freeman Breshears**,

[V6]5951. [10]10. ***Robert Monroe "Bob" Brashears**, b. 20 Oct 1878, Cedar Glades, AR, d. 9 Feb 1950, bur Avant Cem, Garland Co, AR; m. ***Almedia Bates***,

[V6]5952. [10]11. ***Mary Elizabeth Brashears**, b. 12 Nov 1883, Cedar Glades, AR, d. 19 Dec 1956, Hot Springs, AR; m. 11 Nov 1900, ***Frederick A. Meredith***, (s/o

Frederick Meredith and Mary Burks), b. 3 July 1876, Cedar Glades, AR, d. 7 Jan 1957, Hot Springs, Ar, bur Greenwood Cem.

V6 5953. 10 12. ***Alice Lou Brashears**, b. 15 May 1887, d. 18 July 1936, bur Avant Cem, Buckville, Garland Co, AR; m. 18 March 1905, Garland Co, AR, ***Will Cass***, b. 26 June 1887, s/o John Cass and Shneth Revis.

DeKalb Brashears and Nancy Arminda Meredith

v6 5944. 10 5. **DeKalb "Cab" Brashears**, (s/o Henry Brashears and Martha M. Godwin), b. 6 April 1868, Cedar Glades, Garland Co, AR, d. 8 March 1919, Buckville, Garland Co, AR, bur Avant Cem; m. 11 Jan 1890, at Mt. Tabor Church, "by Elder W.S. Gamble," Montgomery Co, AR, ***Nancy Arminda "Mindy" Meredith***, b. Nov 1871, Cedar Glades, AR, d. 1939, bur Avant Cem, d/o Frederick Meredith and Mary Burks. (Mary Burks was a d/o Nancy H. Brashears, d/o Berry Brashears/Boshears.)

"Cab" and "Mindy" had 8 children; after "Cab" died, Arminda m.2. on 5 Aug 1920, Thomas Benson (no ch). Effie (Breshears) Godwin said she had a half-brother: DeKalb had an illegitimate son with Ann Taylor: Dunk (probably Duncan) Taylor.

Effie, "Cab" and "Mindy's" youngest daughter, in a letter to Gerry Rylant: Mother "told me about my Dad. This was when they was first married. My Dad worked for 5 days for a hen aday, and she set them when they started to set and she raised a pretty bunch of chickens." And again: "she told me about going to Oklahoma in an ox-driven covered wagon one winter, and at that time they just had the oldest boy. My mom fixed a bed in the back of the wagon and kept them covered up. She said it was so cold till the spokes of the wagon froze solid."

"Mom also made her own soap to wash with. Never owned a washing machine. Rubbed her clothes with her hands, and she said like overalls and quilts, they had a big block and a big flat oar like you paddle a boat with. She wet and soaped them and lay them on that block and beat them. They called it a

Figure 104: The DeKalb Breshears Family, about 1912-13.
Front row: William H. Breshears (with banjo), DeKalb Breshears, holding Bessie Breshears, Arminda (Meredith) Breshears, holding Effie Breshears (tiny baby), and Pearl Breshears (just behind Arminda's shoulder);
Back row: Will Qualls, Neal Breshears, Mattie Breshears, Delila (Breshears) Qualls, holding Nora Qualls, and Marion Breshears.
The photo is a scan of a bad Xerox copy of a photo that once belonged to the now-defunct Arkansas Bank and Trust Co. I could not locate a good copy.

bathing block."

DeKalb is listed in the censuses as a farmer who owned his own farm, but there were people living 1982 (Dret Hill, age 87; daughter Effie) who remembered him as a blacksmith. Dret remembered DeKalb making a new wagon in his shop. Effie remembered that he made brooms, but that he shoed horses a lot. Effie was in the blacksmith shop when he had the stroke that resulted in his death: "Me and some of the kids was playing around in the shop. He was always teasing the kids, and we all thought he was playing."

Effie: "Yes, Mom did make all our clothes. She bought the cloth with the chicken and eggs. Cloth cost 5 cents a yard. I heard her tell about taking a basket of eggs and bought all the girls dresses." She also remembered Tom Benson, whose children from a previous marriage, "separated Mom and him."

Family of Dekalb Brashears and Nancy Arminda Meredith:

[V6]5954. [11]1. ***William Henry Breshears**, b. 11 Feb 1891, Cedar Glades, AR; m. 4 Oct 1915, Montgomery Co, AR, ***Cynthia Jane Robbins***,

[V6]5955. [11]2. **Arthur Cornelius "Neal" Breshears**, b. May 1893, Cedar Glades, AR, d. from ruptured appendix, c1913, bur avant Cem.

[V6]5956. [11]3. **Delila E. "Lila" Breshears**, b. Sept 1895, Cedar Glades, d. c1926, bur Avant Cem; m.1. ***Will Qualls***, (3 ch); m.2. ***Ira Linderman***, (1 ch)

[V6]5957. [12]1. Nora Qualls, b. c1909; m. August Avant,

[V6]5958. [12]2. Geneva Qualls, m. Damon Scott,

[V6]5959. [12]3. Alene Qualls, m. Frank Robertson,

[V6]5960. [12]4. Ruby Linderman,

[V6]5961. [11]4. ***Martha "Mattie" Breshears**, b. 6 July 1897, Cedar Glades, AR; m. 11 Nov 1916, Avant, AR, ***Hugh Gaston Anderson***,

[V6]5962. [11]5. **Jesse James Breshears**, b. Jan 1900, d. of diptheria at about six months of age, bur two graves west of DeKalb Breshears in unmarked grave.

[V6]5963. [11]6. **Pearl Breshears**, b. 1904, d. ?, her grave was moved to the New Cedar Glades Cem when Lake Quachita was filled; m.1. 24 Dec 1922, ***Henry Murders***, s/o John Murders and Tempie Wright (2 ch); m.2. ***Houston (Newkirk) Richardson***, (3 ch)

[V6]5964. [12]1. Mildred Murders, b. 6 Nov 1923; m. 10 Nov 1940, Odell Blake, s/o John Blake and Nancy Godwin

[V6]5965. [13]1. Lewis Blake, b. 25 July 1942

[V6]5966. [13]2. Larry Blake, b. 19 Aug 1944

[V6]5967. [13]2. Linda Blake, b. 19 Feb 1953

[V6]5968. [12]2. Marvin Murders, m. Bonnie Meeks, s/o Luther Meeks and Sally Pate

V6 5969. [13]1. Michael Murders, b. 19 Aug 1952
V6 5970. [12]3. Bessie Richardson, d. inf.
V6 5971. [12]4. Juanita Richardson, m. Elmo Miller,
V6 5972. [12]5. Jessie Richardson,
V6 5973. [11]7. **Bessie Marie Breshears**, b. 26 July 1907, Cedar Glades, AR, d. 1939, Avant, AR, bur Avant cem; m.1. 25 Jan 1925, Garland Co, AR, ***Lonnie Godwin***, s/o George Godwin and Flora Minton (1 ch); m.2. Greeley Abbott,
V6 5974. [12]1. Leola Godwin,
V6 5975. [11]8. **Effie Breshears**, b. 9 Sept 1912, Cedar Glades, AR; m. 12 Sept 1925, Montgomery Co, AR, ***Robert Godwin***, s/o George Godwin and Flora Minton.
V6 5976. [12]1. Waymon Godwin,
V6 5977. [12]2. Norma Dean Godwin, m. Harold Lillard,
V6 5978. [12]3. Mozella Godwin,
V6 5979. [12]4. James Godwin,
V6 5980. [12]5. Glen Godwin,

William Henry Breshears and Cynthia Jane Robbins

v6 5954. [11]1. **William Henry Breshears**, (s/o Dekalb Brashears and Nancy Arminda Meredith), b. 11 Feb 1891, Cedar Glades, AR, d. 31 Oct 1957 from injuries received when he was hit by a truck when crossing the street in front of Meredith's Grocery on Spring St, Hot Springs, AR, bur Avant Cem, Buckville, Garland Co, AR; m. 4 Oct 1915, Montgomery Co, AR, ***Cynthia Jane Robbins***, b. 16 Nov 1897, Cedar Glades, AR, d. 30 March 1947, bur Avant cem, d/o Samuel Robbins and Rosa Lee Robinson.

Family of William Henry Breshears and Cynthia Jane Robbins:
V6 5981. [12]1. **Bertha Breshears**, b. 28 July 1916, Avant, AR; m. ***Charlie Robertson***,
V6 5982. [13]1. Maggie Bell Robertson,
V6 5983. [13]2. Leonard Robertson,
V6 5984. [13]3. Bonnie Marie Robertson,
V6 5985. [13]4. Charlene Robertson,
V6 5986. [12]2. **Cora Leola Breshears**, b. 31 May 1921, Avant, AR, d. 6 July 1967, Hot Springs, AR, bur Avant Cem;

m. 23 May 1937, ***Hudson Roebuck Abbott***, b. 7 Sept 1913, s/o Burley Simpson Abbott and Rachel Carolina Godwin,

V6 5987. 12 3. **Rosie Breshears**, b. 14 July 1921 (Gerry: How was she b. 2 months after her sister???); m. 5 March 1941, ***John Austin Jones***, b. 2 Feb 1913, s/o Robert P. Jones and Alice Gamble. Austin Jones was a widower with three children: Charlene, Elton, and Erma Dean Jones. He and Rosie had 5 children.

V6 5988. 13 1. Earl D. Jones, b. 23 March 1943, Hot Springs, AR, d. April 1944, bur Rock Spring Cem, Garland Co, AR

V6 5989. 13 2. Marilyn Jones, b. 24 March 1946, Hot Springs, AR, m. James DeHart, (div)

V6 5990. 14 1. Brian Todd DeHart,

V6 5991. 13 3. Linda Sue Jones, b. 11 April 1948, Hot Springs, AR

V6 5992. 13 4. Alice Janie Jones, b. 11 April 1955, Hot Springs, AR

V6 5993. 13 5. John Everet Jones, b. 22 Sept 1957, Hot Springs, AR; m. Jacqueline Slater, b. 2 Nov 1957, Harbor City, CA, d/o Roy F. Slater Sr and Francis Webb,

V6 5994. 14 1. Kristy Lynn Jones, b. 30 April 1975, Hot Springs, AR

V6 5995. 14 2. John Evert Jones Jr, b. 13 Jan 1978, Hot Springs, AR

Martha Breshears and Hugh Gaston Anderson

v6 5961. 11 4. **Martha "Mattie" Breshears**, (d/o Dekalb Brashears and Nancy Arminda Meredith), b. 6 July 1897, Cedar Glades, AR, d. 10 July 1964, bur Cherokee Memorial Park, Lodi, CA; m. 11 Nov 1916, Avant, AR, ***Hugh Gaston Anderson***, b. 23 July 1897, Cedar Glades, AR, d. 25 July 1930, Ola, Yell Co, AR, bur New Bethany Cem, Ola, AR, s/o Robinson Caruso Anderson and Ester Caldonia Meeks.

Family of Martha Breshears and Hugh Gaston Anderson:

^{V6}5996. ^{12}1. Delma Anderson, (twin) b. 18 Nov 1917, d. 29 Oct 1957, Lodi, San Joaquin Co, CA, bur Cherokee Mem Park, Lodi, CA; m. 24 Jul, Casa, AR, Mazie Faulkner, d/o Ethie Faulkner and Ethel Gaydon,

^{V6}5997. ^{13}1. Joyce Nell Anderson, b. 9 Feb 1939; m. David Delmain Barr,

^{V6}5998. ^{14}1. Pamela Lynn Barr, b. 20 Aug 1957

^{V6}5999. ^{14}2. Debra Lynette Barr, b. 27 Feb 1959; m. Elbert Lee Rayburn,

^{V6}6000. ^{15}1. Shelly Ann Rayburn, b. 3 Jan 1976

^{V6}6001. ^{14}3. Steven Eugene Barr, b. 1 Nov 1960

^{V6}6002. ^{13}2. Patsy Evelyn Anderson, b. 5 Dec 1940, d. 1945, bur Cherokee Mem Park, Lodi, CA

^{V6}6003. ^{13}3. Ronald Steven Anderson, b. 10 May 1956; m. Patricia Ann Bishop,

^{V6}6004. ^{14}1. Ronda Renee Anderson, b. 28 Oct 1965

^{V6}6005. ^{14}2. Brandy Lynn Anderson, b. 3 June 1971

^{V6}6006. ^{14}3. Yancy Jason Anderson, b. 29 July 1971

^{V6}6007. ^{13}4. Stanley Keith Anderson, b. 7 Dec 1954

^{V6}6008. ^{12}2. Velma Anderson, (twin) b. 18 Nov 1917; m. Herman Ocsar "Jim" George, b. 8 Oct 1911, d. 9 March 1978, Sacramento, CA, bur East Lawn Sierra Hills Mem Park, s/o Robert “Bob” George and Ella Stepson Meeks. Robert George was b. 1847, Yell Co, AR, was a Yankee, and married three times, the third time in 1911 to Ella; he had 21 children.

^{V6}6009. ^{13}1. Joe Wayne George, b. 14 March 1938; m. Karen Ross,

^{V6}6010. ^{14}1. Joe Wayne George Jr, b. 15 June 1964

^{V6}6011. ^{14}2. Evonne Michelle George, b. 4 May 1965; m. Gregory Ralph Conner,

^{V6}6012. ^{15}1. Andrew Thomas Conner, b. 27 July 1995

^{V6}6013. ^{14}3. Crystal George, b. 13 Feb 1969

^{V6}6014. ^{13}2. Harman Oscar George Jr, b. 14 March 1940

^{V6}6015. ^{13}3. Marilyn Louise George, b. 22 Oct 1941; m. Anthony DeMeio; no ch

^{V6}6016. ^{13}4. Barbara Ann George, b. Sept 1942; m. Ronald

C. Sexton,

[V6]6017. [14]1. Jeanne Marie Sexton, b. 7 Aug 1963

[V6]6018. [14]2. Constance Lee Sexton, b. 4 June 1966

[V6]6019. [12]3. Helen Grace Anderson, b. 28 Nov 1919, AR, m. 21 Nov 1937, Woodbridge, CA, William H. "Bill" Johnson, s/o Harrison A. Johnson and Clara Gasperson,

[V6]6020. [13]1. Evert Glen Johnson, b. 1 Oct 1938; m. Luella Mae Richard, no ch

[V6]6021. [12]4. Roy Anderson, b. 29 Oct 1923, AR; m. 17 May 1942, Reno, NV, Allen Daniels, d/o Rhymon Peter Daniles and Mary Emma Bordeaux,

[V6]6022. [13]1. David LeRoy Anderson, b. 5 Oct 1944; m. Debra Kopping,

[V6]6023. [14]1. John David Anderson, b. 21 Nov 1971

[V6]6024. [14]2. Derrick Anderson, b. 28 April 1973

[V6]6025. [14]3. Gloria Sue Anderson, b. 7 Dec 1947; m. Edward Pechan,

[V6]6026. [14]1. Stephanie Pechan, b. 21 March 1965

[V6]6027. [14]2. Michelle Pechan, b. 25 July 1967

[V6]6028. [14]3. Denise Pechan, b. 2 Aug 1969

[V6]6029. [13]3. John Randall Anderson, b. 10 Oct 1950

[V6]6030. [13]4. Michael Alan Anderson, b. 8 Oct 1953

[V6]6031. [12]5. Mildred Geraldine "Gerry" Anderson, b. 18 Nov 1927, Ola, Yell Co, AR; m.1. 17 Feb 1946, Reno, NV, Clyde Henry Rylant, b. 21 Dec 1919, Hitchock, Blaine Co, OK, d. 11 Oct 1974, Lodi, CA, bur Cherokee Mem Park, Lodi, CA, s/o Henry David Rylant and Susie Elenor Coffield; m.2. 1 Jan 1981, Las Vegas, NV, Arbie Forrest Church,

[V6]6032. [13]1. Sandra Kay Rylant, b. 29 Dec 1953; m. Michael Allen Bauer, s/o Elmer Bauer and Mary Harper.

[V6]6033. [14]1. Amanda Merideth Bauer, b. 1 Aug 1975

[V6]6034. [13]2. Larry Keith Rylant, b. 21 Feb 1956

Moses Taylor Breshears Sr and Rose Lee Noles

v6 5946. 10 7. **Moses Taylor Breshears Sr**, (s/o Henry Brashears and Martha M. Godwin), b. 13 March 1870, Cedar Glades, AR, d. 26 Sept 1942, Hot Springs, AR; m. 9 March 1890, Montgomery Co, AR, ***Rose Lee Noles***, b. 10 Jan 1874, Birmingham, AL, d. 19 Jan 1948, Hot Springs, AR, d/o John Noles, b. 1840, GA, and Rebecca Eliza Conway, b. c1840, GA.

Family of Moses Taylor Breshears Sr and Rose Lee Noles:

V6 6035. 11 1. **James Monroe Breshears**, b. 3 Feb 1891, Cedar Glades, AR, d. 29 Dec 1962, Story, Montgomery Co, AR, bur Reed Cem, Montgomery Co, AR; m.1. 1 March 1909, ***Nellie Blake***, m.2. ***Myrtle Wilson***,

V6 6036. 12 x. **Doyle Dayton Breshears**; m. ***Henryetta*** _____.

V6 6037. 11 2. **George W. Breshears**, b. 9 Oct 1893, Cedar Glades, AR; m. 20 April 1913, Garland Co, AR, ***Edna Halsell***, b. Aug 1896, d/o Reason Halsell and Nancy V. Wheeler,

V6 6038. 12 1. **Marvin D. Breshears**,

V6 6039. 12 2. **Ras F. Breshears**, m. ***Effie Phillips***,

V6 6040. 12 3. **Laura Breshears**, m. ***Arthur Cline***,

V6 6041. 12 4. **Jesse W. Breshears**, m. ***Mildred Aldridge***,

V6 6042. 12 5. **Joe T. Breshears**, m. ***Eliza Ellis***,

V6 6043. 12 6. **George J. Breshears**, m. ***Iva Cochran***,

V6 6044. 12 7. **Paul Breshears**, m. ***Margie*** ______,

V6 6045. 11 3. **Leona E. Breshears**, b. 31 March 1895, Cedar Glades, AR; m. ***Harley Rowland***,

V6 6046. 11 4. **Alice L. Breshears**, b. 4 Sept 1897-8, Cedar Glades, AR, d. 23 Dec 1918, bur Reed Cem, Story, Montgomery Co, AR; m. ***Thomas Henry Rowland***, who m.2. Alice's sister, Nettie.

V6 6047. 11 5. **Ivy Marinda Breshears**, b. 6 Sept 1899; m. ***Gib Johnson***,

V6 6048. 12 1. Ova Johnson, m. Grover Abbott,

V6 6049. 12 2. Gracie Johnson, m. Bert Abbott,

V6 6050. 12 3. William Johnson,

V6 6051. 12 4. Ruby Johnson, d. inf.

Figure 105: The Moses Taylor Breshears Family, about 1908.
Front row: Moses Taylor Breshears, holding Henry J. Breshears, Nettie Mae Breshears, Maudie E. Breshears, Rose Lee (Noles) Breshears, holding tiny baby Anna Mae Breshears, and Ivy Marinda Breshears (behind Rose's shoulder).
Back row: Alice L. Breshears, Leona Breshears, James Monroe Breshears, and George W. Breshears.
The picture is a scan of a bad Xerox of a photo that belonged to the now-defunct Arkansas Bank and Trust Co; I could not locate a good copy of the picture.

V6 6052. 11 6. **Nettie Mae Bell Breshears**, b. 8 Nov 1903, Montgomery Co, AR, d. 7 Oct 1963, Oklahoma City, bur Rest Haven Cem, OK city; m. 5 May 1919, Garland Co, AR, ***Thomas Henry Rowland***, b. 20 Feb 1892, Little Rock, AR, s/o George Washington Rowland and Isabell McClenden.

12 1. Lonnie Thomas Rowland, b. 13 April 1920
12 2. Donie Mae Rowland, b. 13 Jan 1921
12 3. Earl Loyd Rowland, b. 15 Nov 1922
12 4. Glen Dale Rowland,
12 5. Harold Nathan Rowland,
12 6. Gracie Bernice Rowland, b. 13 Jan 1924
12 7. Ella Marie Rowland,

[12]8. Mildred Doris Rowland,

[12]9. Ruby Lee Rowland, b. 9 Aug 1927, Prague, OK

[V6]6053. [11]7. **Maudie E. Breshears**, b. 19 Nov 1904, Cedar Glades, AR; m.1. ***Alfred Anderson***, m.2. 19 Nov 1928, Garland Co, AR, ***John Kindred***,

[V6]6054. [11]8. **Henry J. Breshears**, b. 10 March 1906, Cedar Glades, AR; m.1. 1927, Garland Co, AR, ***Addie Mae Emerson***, m.2. ***Imogene Wilson***,

[V6]6055. [11]9. **Anna Mae Breshears**, b. 2 May 1908; m. 22 Aug 1924, Garland Co, AR, ***Carl Francis***,

[V6]6056. [11]10. **Samuel Franklin Breshears**, b. 22 Oct 1910, d. 27 March 1966, Visalia, CA, bur Exeter, CA; m. 22 Oct 1929, ***Hester Rowland***,

[V6]6057. [11]11. **Margaret Parthina Breshears**, b. 29 Aug 1912; m. 21 Dec 1931, Garland Co, AR, ***G. Lark Bradford***,

[V6]6058. [11]12. **Nora Ethel Breshears**, b. 2 Jan 1915, d. 30 Dec 1980, Dallas, TX; m.1. ***G. Lark Bradford***,

[V6]6059. [11]13. **Moses Taylor Breshears Jr**, b. 10 April 1917, Cedar Glades, Montgomery Co, AR; m.lic. 20 Dec 1935, Garland Co, AR, m. 21 Dec 1935, Montgomery Co, AR, ***Ester Victoria Abbott***, b. 8 June 1920, Buckville, Garland Co, AR, d/o James Monroe Abbott, b. 18 Jan 1894, Cedar Glades, AR, and Lillie Mae Cass, b. 1894, Cedar Glades, AR

[V6]6060. [12]x. **Lois Wanda Jean Breshears**, b. 1 Dec 1936, Fannie, Montgomery Co, AR; m. 31 May 1955, Visalia, CA, ***Joseph Elmo Cooper***, b. 13 June 1935, OK.

Robert Monroe Brashears and Almedia Bates

[v6]5951. [10]10. **Robert Monroe "Bob" Brashears**, (s/o Henry Brashears and Martha M. Godwin), b. 20 Oct 1878, Cedar Glades, AR, d. 9 Feb 1950, bur Avant Cem, Garland Co, AR; m. ***Almedia Bates***, b. 17 Dec 1880, d. 12 July 1962, bur Avant Cem, d/o James Bates and Francis Riley.

Family of Robert Monroe Brashears and Almedia Bates:

[V6]6061. [11]1. **Vestle Robert Breshears**, b. 13 Oct 1901, residing 1980 Mt. Pine, AR

[V6]6062. [11]2. **Nevadie Breshears**, b. 11 Aug 1904, Avant, AR, residing 1980, Avant, AR; m. 20 Feb 1925, Garland Co, AR, ***Marion Godwin***, b. 1901, s/o George Godwin and Florence Minton.

[V6]6063. [12]1. Ernest Godwin,

[V6]6064. [12]2. Orvil Godwin,

[V6]6065. [12]3. Thurman Godwin,

[V6]6066. [12]4. Arrie May Godwin,

[V6]6067. [12]5. Olonso Godwin,

[V6]6068. [12]6. Nathan Godwin,

[V6]6069. [12]7. George Godwin,

[V6]6070. [12]8. Lillie Lavern Godwin,

[V6]6071. [12]9. Bobby Gene Godwin,

[V6]6072. [12]10. Darrell Godwin,

[V6]6073. [12]11. infant,

[V6]6074. [11]3. **Estle Kalb Breshears**, b. 22 March 1908, d. 28 July 194?, bur Avant Cem

[V6]6075. [11]4. ***Avie Artimas Breshears**, b. 28 Feb 1910; m. 12 Oct 1928, in Joplin, Montgomery Co, AR, ***John Floyd Covey***,

[V6]6076. [11]5. ***Sadie Breshears**, b. 19 April 1911, Avant, AR, residing 1980 Boonville, CA; m. in Cedar Glades, AR, ***Virgil Edward Housley***,

[V6]6077. [11]6. ***Lola Ethel Breshears**, b. 31 March 1914, Avant, AR, residing 1980, Hot Springs, AR; m. 9 Sept 1929, in Joplin, Montgomery Co, AR, ***Jim Covey***,

[V6]6078. [11]7. **William Oscar Breshears**, b. 1 Aug 1915, Avant, AR, d. 4 May 1974, bur Langley Cem, Pike Co, AR; m. ***Hazel York***, no ch.

[V6]6079. [11]8. **Ollie Breshears**, b. 6 Jan 1917, Avant, AR, residing 1980 Mt. Pine, AR

[V6]6080. [11]9. **Bethel Argus Breshears**, b. 4 Feb 1919, Avant, AR

[V6]6081. [11]10. **Brook Breshears**, b. 24 Sept 1923; m.1. ***Eva Beard***, (4 ch); m.2. ***Karen Foust***, (1 ch)

[V6]6082. [12]1. **Steven Breshears**,

[V6]6083. [12]2. **Winfred Breshears**,

[V6]6084. [12]3. **Jackie Breshears**,

V6 6085. 124. **Howard Breshears**,
V6 6086. 125. **Brook Breshears Jr**, b. 25 Dec 1973
V6 6087. 1111. **Valley Breshears**, b. 27 Oct 1927, residing 1980 Mt. Pine, AR

Avie Artimus Breshears and John F. Covey

v6 6075. 114. **Avie Artimas Breshears**, (d/o Robert Monroe Brashears and Almedia Bates), b. 28 Feb 1910, residing 1980 Hot Springs, AR; m. 12 Oct 1928, in Joplin, Montgomery Co, AR, ***John Floyd Covey***, b. 12 Aug 1905, Porum, Muskogee Co, OK, s/o John L. Covey and Lucy Underwood.

Family of Avie Artimus Breshears and John F. Covey:

V6 6088. 121. Infant Covey, b. & d. 12 May 1930, bur Joplin Cem, Joplin, AR
V6 6089. 122. Della Mae Covery, b. 24 Sept 1931, Crystal Springs, Garland Co, AR; m. 24 May 1952, Mt. Ida, Montgomery Co, AR, Carl J. Rogers, b. 12 May 1931, Sparkman, Callas Co, AR, s/o Carl McDavie Covey and Junie Mae Hutson.
V6 6090. 131. David Ray Rogers, b. 8 Dec 1963
V6 6091. 132. Debbie Sue Covey, b. 6 Dec 1967
V6 6092. 133. Carl Dean Covey, b. 21 Jan 1969
V6 6093. 123. Louie Covey, b. 25 Dec 1933, Spriro, LeFlore Co, OK; m. 4 May 1956, Garland Co, AR, Mary Elizabeth Pasley, b. 19 Nov 1937, d/o James and Lydia Pasley. Four ch, all b. Hot Springs, AR:
V6 6094. 131. Lydia Christine Pasley, b. 18 Feb 1957; m.1. Gene Moulden, (1 ch); m.2. Johnny Harmon, (1 ch)
V6 6095. 141. Grady Louis Moulden, b. 30 Jan 1973
V6 6096. 142. Delta Michelle Harmon, b. 8 April 1976
V6 6097. 132. Sheila Diane Covey, b. 13 Aug 1958; m. Edward Ray Downen,
V6 6098. 141. Tracy Shawn Downen, b. 4 Oct 1974
V6 6099. 142. Shannon Ray Downen, b. 2 Sept 1975
V6 6100. 133. Jennie Louise Covey, b. 2 Aug 1960
V6 6101. 134. Mary Kay Covey, b. 12 Aug 1955,
V6 6102. 124. Grady Covey, b. 24 Jan 1936, Omaha, Bowie Co,

TX; m. 21 May 1956, Garland Co, AR, Deloris Warner, b. 11 Oct 1939, d/o G.W. and Clarice Warner,

V6 6103. [13]1. Grady Monroe Covey, b. 27 Dec 1956, d. at birth, bur Greenwood Cem, Hot Springs, AR

V6 6104. [12]5. Johnny Monroe Covey, b. 20 Oct 1940, Brady Grove, Garland Co, AR; m.1. 12 Aug 1965, Garland Co, AR, Charlene Victoria Stephens, b. 19 Dec 1947, s/o Charlie and Dorothy Stephens (2 ch); m.2. 21 June 1972, Linda Marie Eslinger (1 ch).

V6 6105. [13]1. Vicki Jo Covey, b. 21 March 1966, Hot Springs, AR

V6 6106. [13]2. Stefannie Ann Covey, b. 17 June 1967, Little Rock, AR, d. 4 June 1973, bur Pleasant Hill Cem, Garland Co, AR

V6 6107. [13]3. Johnny Monroe Covey Jr, b. 1 Aug 1973

V6 6108. [12]6. Brady Covey, b. 17 Sept 1943, Brady Grove, Garland Co, AR; m. 8 March 1968, Rita Jean McComas, b. 22 June 1950, d/o Toby and Lettie McComas.

V6 6109. [13]1. Susan Michelle Covey, b. 8 April 1970, d. 20 April 1970, bur Avant Cem

V6 6110. [13]2. Brady Michiel Covey, b. 18 Dec 1972, Hot Springs, AR

Sadie Breshears and Virgil Edward Housley

v6 6076. [11]5. **Sadie Breshears**, (d/o Robert Monroe Brashears and Almedia Bates), b. 19 April 1911, Avant, AR, residing 1980 Boonville, CA; m. in Cedar Glades, AR, ***Virgil Edward Housley***, b. Cedar Glades, AR, d. 26 Aug 1973, CA, s/o William Robert Housley and Josephine Hall.

Family of Sadie Breshears and Virgil Edward Housley:

V6 6111. [12]1. Lucille Elsie Housley, b. 7 June 1911, Cedar Glades, AR; m. 7Dec 1948, Claude Blake, s/o John Blake and Nancy Godwin.

V6 6112. [13]1. Ronald Blake, m. Marilyn ______,

V6 6113. [14]1. Michael Dean Blake,

^{V6}6114. ^{14}2. Nicholas Eugene Blake,
^{V6}6115. ^{13}2. Donald Blake,
^{V6}6116. ^{13}3. Lonnie Blake, m. Crystal ______
^{V6}6117. ^{14}1. Michelle Renee Blake,
^{V6}6118. ^{13}4. Johnny Blake, m. Sherri ______,
^{V6}6119. ^{14}1. John Blake,
^{V6}6120. ^{13}5. Tommy Blake,
^{V6}6121. ^{12}2. Virgil Robert Housley, b. 12 Feb 1932, n.m.
^{V6}6122. ^{12}3. Delsa Christine Housley, b. 18 Sept 1938, Cedar Glades, AR, m. 9 Nov 1954, Orville Dean,
^{V6}6123. ^{13}1. Debbie Dean, m. Harlye Jaide,
^{V6}6124. ^{14}1. Shawn Jaide,
^{V6}6125. ^{12}4. Wanda Loraine Housley, b. 6 Oct 1940, Cedar Glades, AR; m. Bill Owens,
^{V6}6126. ^{13}1. Billy Michael Owens,
^{V6}6127. ^{13}2. Bobby Allen Owens,
^{V6}6128. ^{13}3. Richy Layne Owens,
^{V6}6129. ^{12}5. Josie Arine Housley, b. 29 Nov 1944; m. 8 March 1973, William F. Lee,
^{V6}6130. ^{13}1. Tommy Lee,
^{V6}6131. ^{13}2. William Keith Lee,
^{V6}6132. ^{12}6. Billy Edward Housley, b. 4 Jan 1948, Mt. Pine, AR; m.1. Sylvia Mills, (2 ch); m.2. Deborah ___, (2 ch)
^{V6}6133. ^{13}1. William Ray Housley,
^{V6}6134. ^{13}2. Tonya Louise Housley,
^{V6}6135. ^{13}3. Dustin James Housley,
^{V6}6136. ^{13}4. John Robert Housley,
^{V6}6137. ^{12}7. Betty Sue Housley, b. 11 March 1953, Indio, CA; m.1. Henry Huron, (2 ch); m.2. Richard Shinski, m.3. Ishmael Cervantes,
^{V6}6138. ^{13}1. Troy Allen Huron,
^{V6}6139. ^{13}2. Kristie Michelle Huron,

Lola Ethel Breshears and Jim Covey

^{v6}6077. ^{11}6. **Lola Ethel Breshears**, (d/o Robert Monroe Brashears and Almedia Bates), b. 31 March 1914, Avant, AR, residing 1980, Hot Springs, AR; m. 9 Sept 1929, in Joplin, Montgomery Co, AR, ***Jim Covey***, b. 20 Aug 1910, Muskogee Co, OK, s/o John L. Covey and Lucy Underwood.

Family of Lola Ethel Breshears and Jim Covey:

[V6]6140. [12]1. Jesse Raymond Covey, b. 28 Nov 1930, Crystal Springs, Garland Co, AR; m.1. Dovie Lou Magby, (2 ch); m.2. Carolyn (Duke) Kelly,

[V6]6141. [13]1. Gary Gene Covey, b. 8 Oct 1957, Hot Springs, AR

[V6]6142. [13]2. David Raymond Covey, b. 16 March 1960, Hot Springs, AR

[V6]6143. [12]2. Floyd Alvin Covey, b. 28 Nov 1932, Crystal Springs, AR; m. 20 Dec 1957, Garland Co, AR, Patricia Ann Robbins, b. 20 Sept 1940,

[V6]6144. [13]1. Patty Ann Covey, b. 12 Nov 1958; m. 14 Oct 1960, William Allen Ramsey,

[V6]6145. [13]2. Penny Lou Covey, b. 24 Jan 1960,

[V6]6146. [13]3. Timothy Alvin Covey, b. 29 April 1962

[V6]6147. [13]4. Tommy Floyd Covey, b. 8 June 1966

[V6]6148. [12]3. Daniel Roy Covey, (twin) b. 8 March 1934, Crystal Springs, AR; m. 7 April 1961, Wilma Sue Cosard, b. 13 Sept 1942

[V6]6149. [13]1. Cynthia Sue Covey, b. 29 Nov 1961, d. Aug 1963, bur Oakwood Cem, Montgomery Co, AR

[V6]6150. [13]2. Robert Covey, b. 23 Sept 1963

[V6]6151. [13]3. Mark Covey, b. 29 May 1968

[V6]6152. [13]4. Diana Michelle Covey, b. 20 Nov 1973

[V6]6153. [12]4. David Troy, (twin) b. 8 March 1934, d. inf, bur maddox Cem, Garland Co, AR

[V6]6154. [12]5. Clayton Monroe Covey, b. 9 Feb 1937, Crystal Springs, AR; m. 31 Une 1961, Nancy Ann Cruchfield, b. 17 May 1943

[V6]6155. [13]1. Lodene Ann Covey, b. 11 March 1963

[V6]6156. [13]2. Ramona Gail Covey, b. 28 March 1967

[V6]6157. [13]3. Clayton Monroe Covey Jr, b. 20 April 1972

[V6]6158. [12]6. Lola Ethel Covey, b. 26 May 1941, Hot Springs, AR; m. 26 May 1961, Garland Co, AR, W.D. Barnes,

[V6]6159. [13]1. William David Barnes, b. 2 Feb 1967

[V6]6160. [13]2. Lori Susann Barnes, b. 20 Oct 1968

[V6]6161. [13]3. Jimmy Clyde Barnes, b. 18 Feb 1968

[V6]6162. [12]7. Dorothy Mae Covey, b. 10 July 1943, Avant, AR;

m. 6 Jan 1961, Eugene Cockrell, b. 21 Oct 1935
V66163. [13]1. Richy Eugene Cockrell, b. 17 Aug 1961
V66164. [13]2. Eugenia Lynn Cockrell, b. 24 Nov 1962
V66165. [12]8. Shirley Ann Covey, b. 16 Feb 1945, Hot Springs, AR; m.1. Charles Watson, (1 ch); m.2. Billy Don Tabor, b. 27 Nov 1942
V66166. [13]1. Charles Watson Jr, b. 9 July 1963
V66167. [12]9. Jimmy Loyd Covey, b. 22 July 1948; m.1. Mary Wright, (2 ch); m.2. Debbie ______,
V66168. [13]1. Shelly Ruth Covey, b. 14 Nov 1973
V66169. [13]2. Gregory Lee Covey, b. 22 June 1977

Mary Elizabeth Brashears and Frederick A. Meredith

v65952. [10]11. **Mary Elizabeth Brashears**, (d/o Henry Brashears and Martha M. Godwin), b. 12 Nov 1883, Cedar Glades, Montgomery Co, AR, d. 19 Dec 1956, Hot Springs, AR, bur Greenwood Cem; m. 11 Nov 1900, a cousin, ***Frederick A. Meredith***, s/o Frederick Meredith and Mary Burks, (d/o Nancy H. Brashears, d/o Berry Brashears/Boshears), b. 3 July 1876, Cedar Glades, AR, d. 7 Jan 1957, Hot Springs, AR, bur Greenwood Cem.

Family of Mary Elizabeth Brashears and Frederick A. Meredith:
V66170. [11]1. William Herbert Meredith, b. 14 Oct 1902; m. Lydia Gladden,
V66171. [12]1. Essie Meredith,
V66172. [12]2. James Meredith,
V66173. [11]2. Arthur Meredith, b. 21 Aug 1904; m. Lena Sharpe, b. 30 Sept 1905, d/o George Washington Sharpe and Mary Elizabeth Speers.
V66174. [12]1. Opal Meredith, b. 27 March 1927; m. Wayne Irons,
V66175. [13]1. Larry Irons,
V66176. [13]2. Tim Irons,
V66177. [12]2. Mary Elizabeth "Toppie" Meredith, b. 9Aug 1929; m. Virgil "Buddy" Teague,
V66178. [13]1. Marty Teague,

[V6]6179. [12]3. Billy Dean "Brownie" Meredith, b. 1 Jan 1932; m. Juanita Hamilton,
[V6]6180. [13]1. Jolena Meredith,
[V6]6181. [13]2. Dennis Meredith,
[V6]6182. [13]3. Diana Meredith,
[V6]6183. [13]4. Amy Meredith,
[V6]6184. [12]4. Branalou Meredith, b. 21 June 1933; m. A.D. Stroope,
[V6]6185. [13]1. Beverly Ann Stroope,
[V6]6186. [13]2. Donald Ray Stroope,
[V6]6187. [12]5. LaVell Meredith, b. 13 Nov 1935; m. William Efrid,
[V6]6188. [13]1. Glen Efrid,
[V6]6189. [13]2. Benjamin Efrid,
[V6]6190. [12]6. Jack Meredith, b. 31 May 1937; m. Donnie Emerson,
[V6]6191. [13]1. Jack Douglas Meredith,
[V6]6192. [13]2. Melanie Denise Meredith,
[V6]6193. [12]7. Ida Fern Meredith, b. 19 June 1939; m. Jackie Robinson,
[V6]6194. [12]8. A.J. Meredith, b. 10 March 1941; m. Mary Lou Burgess,
[V6]6195. [13]1. Tod Meredith,
[V6]6196. [13]2. Tonya Meredith,
[V6]6197. [12]9. Linda Meredith, b. 3 March 1943; m. Billy Heaton,
[V6]6198. [13]1. Kelly Heaton,
[V6]6199. [11]3. Jessie Meredith, b. 29 June 1906; m.1. Lennie Burrough, m.2. Evelyn Smith,
[V6]6200. [11]4. Nettie Mary Ann Meredith, b. 10 Nov 1908, d. 4 Aug 1978;
[V6]6201. [11]5. Robert Roy Meredith, b. 10 Nov 1908; m.2. Mildred (Lynch) Bain,
[V6]6202. [11]6. Harley Meredith, b. 3 Jun1914; m. Lois Loden,
[V6]6203. [11]7. Herman Meredith, b. 3 March 1916; m. Pauline Alberts,

Alice Lou Brashears and Will Cass

v6 5953. [10]12. **Alice Lou Brashears**, (d/o Henry Brashears and Martha M. Godwin), b. 15 May 1887, d. 18 July 1936, bur Avant Cem, Buckville, Garland Co, AR; m. 18 March 1905, Garland Co, AR, ***Will Cass***, b. 26 June 1887, s/o John Cass and Shneth Revis.

Family of Alice Lou Brashears and Will Cass:

V6 6204. [11]1. John Henry Cass, b. 10 Dec 1905; m. Nancy Phillips,
V6 6205. [11]2. Dora Bernice Cass, b. 29 Oct 1907; m. Ted Phillips,
V6 6206. [11]3. Anna May Cass, b. 13 June 1910; m. Epp Leonard Hill,
V6 6207. [12]1. Clyde Eugene Hill, b. 25 Aug 1928
V6 6208. [12]2. Arvil Vernice Hill, b. 22 July 1930
V6 6209. [12]3. Rosie Alene Hill, b. 14 Sept 1932
V6 6210. [12]4. Willie Perry Hill, b. 10 July 1935
V6 6211. [12]5. Alice Arletha Hill, b. 7 Sept 1937
V6 6212. [12]6. Freeman Leonard Hill, b. 5 March 1940
V6 6213. [11]4. Lessie Elizabeth Cass, b. 29 Aug 1911; m. Paul Fisher,
V6 6214. [11]5. James Monroe Cass, b. c1912, bur Avant Cem
V6 6215. [11]6. Lizzie Cass, b. 5 Aug 1919; m. Harry Mayberry,
V6 6216. [11]7. Ethel Cass, b. 11 July 1921; m.1. Louie Kenner, m.2. John Burks,
V6 6217. [11]8. Molly May Cass, b. 13 July 1924; m. Dale Ennis,

48. JOHN BRASHEAR (Berry's Brother?) and Betsy Randall/ Elizabeth Chambers

^{v6}**17.** ^{8}4. **John Brashear**, (hypothetical s/o The Phantom Absalom Brashear), b. 1796, d. c1861, Hot Springs Co, AR; m.1. in Lawrence Co, AL, ***Elizabeth "Betsy" Randall***, b. 1800, and had eight children; m.2. a widow, ***Elizabeth (Baugh) Chambers***, b. 1794, SC, and had one more child, Wm Gouldsberry Brashears. John was living in Lawrence County, Alabama, in 1827 when his oldest son was born; then lived about ten years in Tennessee; then migrated c1838-43 (per birthplaces of children) to Hot Springs County, Arkansas. He is in the 1850 census there. He died intestate and his estate was probated in 1861 in Hot Springs Co.

<u>Children of John Brashears and Elizabeth Randall</u> (family records of Josephine Collie, of Malvern, AR, and division of estate in 1861):

^{V6}6301. ^{8}1. ***Philip Randall Brashears**, b. 1827, Lawrence Co, Alabama; m. 16 Sept 1849 (Hot Springs Co, AR) ***Mary Elizabeth Brown***, b. 1829 in GA.

^{V6}6302. ^{8}2. **William Brashears**, b. TN (This person is often confused with his nephew, William Franklin Brashears, who m. Evelyn Freedonia Deere.)

^{V6}6303. ^{8}3. **Martin Brashears**, b. TN

^{V6}6304. ^{8}4. **Bruce Brashears**, b. TN

^{V6}6305. ^{8}5. **Hannah J. Brashears**, b. c?1830, TN; m. 17 April 1849 (Hot Springs Co, AR, marriage Records, 1825-1880), ***Jesse Brashears***, (s/o William Breashears and Anna Etheridge)

^{V6}6306. ^{8}6. **Sarah M. Brashears**, b. 1835, TN; m. 7 Aug 1853 (Hot Springs Co, AR, marriage Records, 1825-1880), ***Robert Baw***

^{V6}6307. ^{8}7. **Malcolm G. Brashears**, b. 1838, TN; m. 30 Sept

1858 (Hot Springs Co, AR, marriage Records, 1825-1880), ***Susan Grant***

V6 6308. 8 8. **Thomas J. Brashears**, b. 1843, AR

V6 6309. 8 9. **Susan Ann Brashears**, b. 1845, AR; m. 14 Jan 1880 (Hot Springs Co, AR, marriage Records, 1825-1880), ***Ezekiel Fitzhugh***, age 54 in 1880.

Child of John Brashears and Elizabeth (née Baugh) Chambers:

V6 6310. 8 10. **William Gouldsberry Brashears**, b. 24 Aug 1848 (or 58), Hot Springs Co, Arkansas, d. there 18 Dec 1906, bur. Rockport Cem; m. 28 Dec 1886, ***Ellen Cass (Fitzhugh) Phillips***, a widow.

V6 6311. 9 1. **Pearl Brashears**, b. 17 Nov 1887, Hot Spring Co, AR

V6 6312. 9 2. **Lelia Ann Brashears**, b. 15 Oct 1889, Hot Springs Co, AR, d/o W. Goulds Berry Brashears, says IGI 7822105/50

Philip Randal Brashears and Mary Elizabeth Brown

v6 6301. 8 1. **Philip Randall Brashears**, (s/o John Brashears and Elizabeth Randall), b. 1827, Lawrence Co, Alabama, d. 1869, Grant Co, AR; m. 16 Sept 1849 (Hot Springs Co, AR, marriage Records, 1825-1880), ***Mary Elizabeth Brown***, b. 1829 in GA. Philip and Mary are in the 1850 Census of Hot Springs Co, AR, Polk Twp. Philip was a Cpl in C.S.A. during the Civil War. Phillip m.2. c1887, ***Artimissa "Missie" Dial***, who had been married previously to Wesley Toler. And they [?the Tolers?] had children Clara, Huel B., Thomas, according to Dobie (obie01@aol.com)

Family of Philip Randall Brashears and Mary Elizabeth Brown: (re: HSB, p.87 and info from R.F. Walker)

V6 6313. 9 1. **Emma Evelyn Brashears**, m. ***Homer Toler***,

V6 6314. 9 2. ***William Franklin Brashears**, b. 10 Oct 1853, Leola, Grant Co, AR, d. 13 Oct 1929, Brush Creek, Grant Co, AR; m. ***Evelyn Freedonia Deere***, b. 12 Nov 1862, Grant Co, AR, d. 12 July 1948

[V6]6315. [9]3. ***Orlando Brashears**, b. April 1857, Leola, Grant Co, AR, d. 31 March 1885; m. 22 April 1877, ***Fannie Bladgett***, b. 18 Aug 1858,
[V6]6316. [9]4. **Phillip Martin Brashears**, b. 1864, d. 1954
[V6]6317. [9]5. **Benjamin Bruce Brashears**, b. 1866

William Franklin Brashear and Evelyn Fredonia Deere

[v6]6314. [9]2. **William Franklin Brashears**, (s/o Phillip Randall Brashears and Mary Elizabeth Brown), b. 10 Oct 1853, Leola, Grant Co, AR, d. 13 Oct 1929, Brush Creek, Grant Co, AR; m. ***Evelyn Freedonia Deere***, b. 12 Nov 1862, Grant Co, AR, d. 12 July 1948.

Family of William Franklin Brashears and Evelyn F. Deere:

[V6]6318. [10]1. **Felix Brashears**, b. 2 Oct 1879, d. 1954; m. ***Callie Page***
[V6]6319. [11]1. **Clinton Brashears**,
[V6]6320. [10]2. **Mary E. Brashears**, b. 8 May 1881, d. 1883
[V6]6321. [10]3. **Ebenezer Brashears**, b. 14 Sept 1883 at Leola, Grant Co, AR; m. 17 Jan 1912, ***Mary Edith Bludworth***, b. 4 Nov 1888, Pilot Grove, TX. Ebenezer was a merchant in Roxton, TX, in 1929, and submitted his family history to Henry Sinclair Brashear; see HSB, p.87.
[V6]6322. [11]1. **William Bludworth Brashears**, b. 19 Jan 1917
[V6]6323. [10]4. **Cleveland Brashears**, b. 20 May 1885, d. 1924; m. ____
[V6]6324. [10]5. **Hattie Brashears**, b. 31 Jan 1887, d. 1963; m. ***Samuel Riggan***. Ch: Armon Riggan, Elton Riggan, Imogene Riggan Murry, Willine Riggan Vaden, Hershel Riggan.
[V6]6325. [10]6. **Herman Dale Brashears**, b. 19 June 1889, d. 1890
[V6]6326. [10]7. **Ethel May Brashears**, b. 6 June 1891, d. 1918; m. ***Thomas Addison "Tom Add" Riggan***,
[V6]6327. [11]x. _____ Riggan
[V6]6328. [12]y. Tommy Riggan; m. Pat _____, of Brush

Creek, Grant Co, AR. Pat Riggan <rigganp@ezclick.net>

V66329. 108. ***Maynard Earl Brashears**, b. 16 Sept 1892, d. 20 Feb 1961; m. 7 Dec 1916, ***Dorothea Evola Crow***, b. 21 June 1900, Paron, AR,

V66330. 109. **Irene Rae Brashears**, b. 6 Dec 1893, d. 1971; m. ***Clifton J.C. Williams***,

V66331. 1010. **Lillian Brashears**, b. 5 Feb 1895, d. 1979; m. ***Henry Ross***

V66332. 1011. **Cora Brashears**, b. 11 Feb 1897, d. 1965; m. ***S.E. Connell***

V66333. 1012. **Oscar Dewey Brashears**, b. 9 Jan 1899, d. 1902

V66334. 1013. **Arlin Clifton Brashears**, b. 24 Sept 1900, d. 1977; m. ***Esther Bailey***

V66335. 111. **Troy Brashears**,

V66336. 112. **June Brashears**, m. ____ ***Baker***

V66337. 1014. **Frances Katie Floy Brashears**, b. 12 May 1904, d. 1931; m. ***Marnice D. Heard***

v66329. 108. **Maynard Earl Brashears**, (s/o William Franklin Brashears and Evelyn Freedonia Deere), b. 16 Sept 1892, Brush Creek, Grant Co, AR, d. 20 Feb 1961, Little Rock, AR, bur Brush Creek, Grant Co, AR; m. 7 Dec 1916, ***Dorothea Evola Crow***, b. 21 June 1900, Paron, AR, d. 4 Sept 1984, Malvern, AR, bur Brush Creek Cem, Grant Co, AR, d/o Matthew H. Crow (b. 2 May 1865, d. 15 March 1905, age 39) and Ella Jackson Weaver (b. 22 Dec 1874, Jacksonville, AR, d. 9 June 1909, Paron, AR, age 35). (Thanks to descendant Robert Franklin Walker, (deafpony@aol.com) for data.)

Family of Maynard Earl Brashears and Dorothea E. Crow:

V66338. 111. **Donald Matthew Brashears**, b. 26 Oct 1917, d. 20 Feb 1919

V66339. 112. **Sudie Evelyn Brashears**, b. 16 July 1918; m. ***Leland D. Lamb***, b. Leola, AR, d. there 4 April 1994

V66340. 121. Leland Dwight Lamb, b. 22 April 1937, Leola, AR, d. 10 Jan 1994; m. Kathryn Bird

V66341. 131. Casey D. Lamb, b. 6 Oct 1971, Little Rock, AR

[V6]6342. [13]2. Scottie D. Lamb. B. 14 Aug 1972, Little Rock, AR

[V6]6343. [13]3. Kelly Delinda Lamb, b. 26 Feb 1976, Little Rock, AR

[V6]6344. [12]2. David Earl Lamb, b. 31 Dec 1951, Leola, AR; m. Jean _____

[V6]6345. [13]1. Renee Lamb, b. 22 Oct 1980

[V6]6346. [13]2. Heather Lamb, b. 3 March1983

[V6]6347. [11]3. **Marjorie Marie Brashears**, b. 30 May 1922; m. ***Willie Aaron Jones***,

[V6]6348. [12]1. Garry Don Jones, b. June 1945; m.1. Gail _____ (1 ch: Ashley Jones); m.2. Patricia _____ (2 ch: Sarah and W. Aaron Jones).

[V6]6349. [12]2. Michael Jan Jones, b. 4 June 1946; m.1. Janelle _____ (1 ch: Aliza Jones); m.2. Nancy Crary (no ch)

[V6]6350. [12]3. Beverly Kay Jones, b. 10 Aug 1955; m. 18 June 1976, Terrence Steed.

[V6]6351. [13]1. Stacy Marie Steed, b. 9 Aug 1977;

[V6]6352. [13]2. Shelley Steed, b. 11 June 1980;

[V6]6353. [13]3. Stephanie Steed, b. 25 Oct 1988

[V6]6354. [11]4. **Rosalie Brashears**, b. 15 March 1926; m. ***Hewie Franklin Walker***, b. 6 Aug 1921, d. 6 April 1993, s/o Jesse Edward Walker (b. 23 Aug 1888, d. 1944) and Sara Ellen Burrow, d/o Milton Burrow

[V6]6355. [12]1. Reita Ann Walker, b. 12 Aug 1946, Springhill, LA; m. Robert William Miller, s/o Carl H. Miller Sr and Frances Cameron

[V6]6356. [13]1. Amy Allyson Miller, b. 11 Oct 1969, Little Rock, AR; m. Judge Edward Reinhold, b. 1957, VA, s/o E. Reinhold and Regina _____

[V6]6357. [13]2. Maria Kathleen Miller, b. 23 Sept 1977, Little Rock, AR; m. Andrew Preston, b. 23 July 1967, London, England

[V6]6358. [12]2. Robert Franklin Walker, b. 20 Nov 1958, Pine Bluff, AR; no ch. <deafpony@aol.com>

Orlando Brashears and Fannie Bladgett

v6 6315. 9 3. **Orlando Brashears**, (s/o Philip Randall Brashears and Mary Elizabeth Brown), b. 28 April 1857, Leola, Grant Co, AR, d. 31 March 1885; m. 22 April 1877 (*Hot Springs Co, AR, Marriage Records, 1825-1880*), ***Fannie Bladgett***, b. 18 Aug 1858, ?Dallas County, AR (Data on Orlando and his descendants from ARCfiles, FHL. Not verified.)

Family of Orlando Brashears and Fannie Bladgett:

V6 6359. 10 1. **Philip Randale Brashears**, b. 11 June 1878, Grant Co, AR. He was described as an old bachelor who loved to fish.

V6 6360. 10 2. **Annie Elizabeth Brashears**, b. 26 Nov 1879, Sandy Springs, Grant Co, AR; m. ***John Henry Rankin***, b. 15 Jan 1876, near Middelton, Hardeman Co, TN

V6 6361. 11 1. ?dau Rankin; m. Joseph Henry Meux, b. 15 March 1885 Hot Springs, Garland County, AR

V6 6362. 12 x. Esther Blanche Meux; m. Donald Charles Hoffman,

V6 6363. 11 x. Ethel Rankin, b. 27 Dec 1903, Leola, Grant Co, AR

V6 6364. 11 x. (twins) Rankin, b. 27 July 1910, Leola, Grant Co, AR

V6 6365. 10 3. **Edna Pearl Brashears**, b. 15 April 1881, Grant Co, AR; m. ***Thel Heard***,

Hot Springs Co, AR, Marriage Records, 1825-1880

Orlando Brashears, 19, of Grant Co, to Fannie Bladgett, 18, of Dallas Co: 22 Apr 1877

Elijah C. Linycomb, 20, to Cynthia E. Brashears, 18, Clear Creek Twp; 31 Mar 1878

Benjamin Fitzhugh, 57, to Elizabeth B.C. Brashers, 31, at residence of Elizabeth B.C. Brashears: 12 Feb 1862

49. Nancy Elizabeth Brashear and Andrew Wilson

Berry and John apparently had a sister named Nancy Elizabeth Brashear, who married Andrew Wilson and lived in the same places as John and Berry, including Greene Co, AR.

[V6]14. [8]2. **Nancy Elizabeth Brashear**, b. 1793; m. 20 Oct 1823, Lawrence Co, AL, ***Andrew Wilson***. They named their only son, Robert Brashear Wilson.

Lawrence Co, Alabama, marriages:
Robert H. Brasher to Sally L. Rhea, 16 April 1819
Robert Wilson to Anne Hartgrove, 19 Dec 1822
Andrew Wilson to Elizabeth Brashear, 20 Oct 1823

[V6]15. [9]1. Robert ***Brashear*** Wilson, (s/o Andrew Wilson and **Nancy Elizabeth Brashear**), b. 3 May 1827, Lawrence Co, AL, d. Kendall Co, TX, 1898; m. 16 Nov 1845, in Greene Co, AR, *Lavinia Wyatt*, b. 21 Feb 1829, TN, d. 1908, Kendall Co, TX.

Robert Brashear Wilson knew and corresponded with his cousin, William Gouldsberry Brashears, s/o John Brashear and Elizabeth (Baugh) Chambers.

Lavinia Wyatt Wilson was a sister of the John Harmon Wyatt (m. Elizabeth H. Brashears, [v6]5705-- unidentified, but probably a d/o Berry Boshears) who lived in Greene Co, AR at the time of the 1850 census. Lavinia and Robert Brashear Wilson also lived in Greene Co, AR, 1839—1845-6, according to a great granddaughter, Lucille Wilson Tilton, now deceased. Robert Brashear Wilson's parents, Andrew and Elizabeth (Brashears) Wilson also lived in Greene Co. In fact, the two families, father and son, lived in the same house or next door to each other for the rest of the father's life.

Lavinia and Robert Brashear Wilson lived in Hot Springs Co, AR, from 1845-6 until 1860. They then lived a year or two in Colorado Co, TX and moved to Kendall Co, TX where they both died.

Robert Brashear Wilson and Lavinia Wyatt had 11 ch:

^{V6}6366. ^{10}1. John Coffey Wilson, b. 1846, Hot Springs Co, AR; m.1. Martha Jane Raines; m.2. Ida Marquart,

^{V6}6367. ^{10}2. Andrew Jackson Wilson, b. 1848, Hot Springs Co, AR ; m. Margaret R. Pettitt,

^{V6}6368. ^{10}3. Elizabeth Dane Wilson, b. 1850, Hot Springs Co, AR; m. Henry Bierschwale,

^{V6}6369. ^{10}4. Margaret Ann Catherine Wilson, b. 1852, Hot Springs Co, AR; m. Jesse J. Rose,

^{V6}6370. ^{10}5. Robert Harmon Perry Franklin Wilson, b. 1854, Hot Springs Co, AR; m. Sarah Hogue,

^{V6}6371. ^{10}6. Phillip Dowell Wilson, b. 1856, Hot Springs Co, AR; m. Lydia Holland,

^{V6}6372. ^{10}7. Leonidas Wilson, b. 1858 Hot Springs Co, AR; m. Finette Wilson,

^{V6}6373. ^{10}8. James Washington Wilson, b. 1860, Hot Springs Co, AR; m. Sarah C. Gass. They had 9 children, all b. Kendall Co, TX.

^{V6}6374. ^{11}1. Lonie Elizabeth Wilson, b. 1879; m. Frank Rose,

^{V6}6375. ^{11}2. James Monroe Wilson, b. 1882; m. Rosa Shirley,

^{V6}6376. ^{12}1. Reuben Monroe Wilson, b. 1912, Kerr Co, TX; m. in St. David, AZ, Margaret Tilton,

^{V6}6377. ^{12}2. Lucille M. Wilson, b. 1918, Kerr Co, TX; m. Dick Wesley Tilton. Lucille Tilton was for many years an active research in Brashears genealogy. She lived and died in St. David, AZ.

^{V6}6378. ^{12}3. Winona Elizabeth Wilson, b. 1922, St. David, AZ; m. Herman Self,

^{V6}6379. ^{11}3. Leonard Wilson, b. 1884; m. Hattie Tucker,

^{V6}6380. ^{11}4. Myles Wilson, b. 1885; m. Annie Larrimore,

^{V6}6381. ^{11}5. Alfred Hillington Wilson, b. 1889; m. Doretta Bierschwale,

^{V6}6382. ^{11}6. Jack David Wilson, b. 1891; m. Hulda Fischer,

^{V6}6383. ^{11}7. Pearl Wilson, b. 1893; m. Grover Cleveland James,

^{V6}6384. ^{11}8. Albert Wilson, b. 1897; m. Opal Toalson,

[V6]6385. [11]9. Mattie Wilson, b. 1899; never married.

[V6]6386. [10]9. Lavinia Caroline Wilson, b. 1862, Kendall Co, TX; m.1. Jacob Pyburn; m.2. William Remling,

[V6]6387. [10]10. Martah Ellen Wilson, b. 1867, Kendall Co, TX; d. there 1867

[V6]6388. [10]11. Mylous Wilson, b. 1869, Kendall Co, TX; n.f.i.

Letters written from Comfort, TX, in 1895 by Robert Brashear Wilson, son of Andrew and Nancy Elizabeth (Brashear) Wilson, to Wm. Gouldsberry Brashears, youngest son of this John, were signed "your cousin," and thus indicate that John Brashears and Nancy Elizabeth (Brashears) Wilson were brother and sister. They also had a brother, Robert H. Brashears. The letters were owned by a great-granddaughter of John, Josephine Collie, of Malvern, Arkansas, and are now among her estate papers in the Historical Society of Malvern. Malvern is the county seat of Hot Springs Co, AR.

50. BRASHEARS FAMILIES OF ANGELINA CO, TEXAS

Co-author: Larry Pleasants

JAMES M. "JIM" BRASHEARS and Mary Elizabeth Maribe Jones

[v6]**5702.** [9]2. **James M. (?Monteville) "Jim" Brashears**, (s/o Berry Brashears and Anna ______), b. 25 May 1810, possibly White Co, TN, d. after 1871, in Freestone Co, TX, where he was on the tax list in 1871; m. 1830-32, in TN or AL, ***Mary Elizabeth "Lizzie" Maribe Jones***, b. 26 March 1813, TN, d. after 1880, d/o Martin William "Gobbler" Jones and Rhoda Hodges. In the 1880 Census, Freestone Co, TX, Rebey ______ is "mother-in-law" of Richard Harding, the second husband of Davilla Ann (Brashears) Rose-Harding. We believe "Rebey" was a nickname/shortening (last two syllables) of Maribe.

Some of the following information is from the *History of Angelina Co*, 1992, and was sent me by Larry Pleasants <lcp47@aol.com>. Larry used Census records, family letters, and histories of White Co, AR; Polk Co, TX; Angelina Co, TX; Leon Co, TX; Freestone Co, TX; family bibles, and earlier genealogies.

The 1820 census of White Co, TN, and the 1830 census of McNairy Co, TN, indicate that Berry Brashears had a son, b. 1810-1815, but we have been unable to identify him, as we have others of his children (Drew, Robert, Ellen) born in the same period. In 1840, Tishomingo Co, MS, Berry's son, Drew, and daughter, Ellen McHughes, are living near him, but the other son is absent, he was already in Arkansas (see below).

The names that run in the families of Berry's children and grandchildren include Henry, Robert, Larkin, Basil, William, Andrew, Doyle, Ellen, Rebecca, Elizabeth, Rhoda, Maude, Narcissa. Similar names among the Brashears families of

Angelina Co, TX, make me feel that they descend from a son of Berry, named James Monteville Brashears, b. 1810.

James Brashears in Arkansas

James Brashears and Maribe Jones married soon after the 1830 census, and James probably went to live with his father-in-law's family. Martin William "Gobbler" Jones had lived in Jefferson Co, TN; Jackson Co, TN (1830 census); and Lawrence Co, AL (just across the state line from Lawrence Co, TN). About 1830-32, Martin Jones moved his whole family to Arkansas and settled on the headwaters of Bull Creek, near present-day El Paso, AR. James and Maribe Brashears went with them, accompanied by eight other families. Martin Jones founded "Old Royal Colony" in White County, southwest of present-day Searcy, Arkansas.

After the formation of White Co, in 1835, James Beshears and Martin Jones are shown on a petition voting to locate the county seat at Searcy. James Beshears is also shown in White County Poll Tax Lists from 1836-1846.

In 1837, James Beshares was taxed in White Co, Arkansas for 1 horse worth $50 and 3 head of cattle, 3 yrs old. In 1838, he was taxed for 30 cattle and 3 horses, $960. From 1839 to 1846 (except 1842: no records), he appears variously as James Beshears, James Bersharars, James Beshares, James Bershears, and James Breshear; in each case, he paid one poll tax.

In the 1840 Census of White County, Arkansas (p. 246), Jas. Beshears is shown as the head of household of six. Looking ahead at the 1850 Census we can make an educated guess for each household member in the 1840 Census:

one male 20-30 (James M., father);
one female 20-30 (Maribe, mother);
one female 5-10 (Malinda, daughter, born about 1833).
one male 5-10 (John, son, born about 1834);
one male under 5 (Walker, son, born about 1836);
one female under 5 (Lucinda, daughter, born about 1838);

Shortly after 1840, Berry Brashears and most of his family moved also to White Co, AR. The 1848/49 Poll Tax list for White Co, Arkansas, includes Wm. Beshares, Berry Beshares, Jacob Beshares, A. Beshares, and Brazelle Beshares.

The Move to Texas

About 1846, James Brashears moved (along with the Martin Jones family and other families in a group of fifteen wagons) from the "Old Royal Colony" to Angelina Co, TX. The group stopped to rest for several weeks in Leon County, TX, then at Jones Prairie in Polk Co, TX, where many of the Jones group liked the rich black loam so much that they stayed there permanently. Martin Jones, after a rest, went on and founded Jonesville in present-day Angelina Co, TX.

J. Beshears, 39, b. c1810, and Mary M. Beshears, 37, b. c1812-13, are in the 1850 census of Angelina Co, TX (#139), with children

Malinda Beshears,	17, b. AR
John Beshears,	15, b. AR
Walker Beshears,	13, b. AR
Lucinda Beshears,	12, b. AR
Bery Beshears,	10, b. AR
Rhoda Beshears,	8, b. AR
Fetna Beshears,	4, b. AR
Robert Beshears,	3, b. TX
Elvira Nash,	17, b. AR (This is Talitha Elvira (Jones) Nash. She is the daughter of Jesse R. Jones and Messaline Burks; therefore Jim and Maribe's niece)

Take special notice that only four sons, John, Walker, Berry and Robert, are shown in this census. Judging by birthplaces and dates of children, James would have moved from Arkansas to Texas in 1846-47.

Voting records in Angelina County mention James several times. In 1850, he is shown in Beat #3 voting as James Beshers. In 1851, he votes in the town of Marion as James Bresheares. Then in 1853, Beat #3, James Brashears votes with J. M. Brashears and father-in-law M. W. Jones. Again in 1855 in Beat #2, James Beshears votes with John M. Beshears and Martin Jones.

Jim was a farmer and stockman and later a Sheriff (according to the Leon County History). He had a survey of land just south of Jonesville. The largest land grants were 640 acres, but most were much smaller. Texas Land Abstract Titles show that James Brashear was granted a land patent (Patent # 595) for 320 acres on April 28, 1859. His brand was "10", the year of his birth 1810. It was registered in Angelina County on June 15, 1855. The brand "10" was transferred to his wife, Maribe, January 15, 1856.

James Brassiers, 60 (incorrect; should be 50) and Lizzie M., 50, are hh #339, in 1860 Census, Angelina Co, TX, with children, Berry M., 19; Fanny, 14; Robert, 12; and "Deville" (Davilla Ann), 6. Clustered around them are several of their children:

#236: Jesse Brassiers
#340: Jackson Brassiers
#341: Walker J. Brassiers
#345: James B. Moore (m. Rhoda E. Brashears)

Martin William "Gobbler" Jones had served in the Arkansas legislature, where, it is said, if he opposed a speaker, he would gobble like a turkey. Gobbler Jones moved to Angelina Co, TX, in 1845 and settled briefly on Jones Prairie. He donated the land for the Jones Cemetery at Jonesville, a few miles south of Huntington.

James Brashear and Martin Jones were instrumental in having the Angelina County seat relocated in 1854 from Marion Ferry to Jonesville. The Court House stood near Martin Jones's home from 1854-1858.

They and other family members, especially the Joneses, were intensely involved in a political feud with locals around 1858 over the issue of the county seat being moved from Jonesville to Homer. The feud became violent. Martin Jones moved to Leon County around 1860. James and Maribe Brashears stayed in Angelina County, along with his daughter Lucinda Brashear Neyland's family. During the Civil War, the feud died down, but after the war the feud flared up again, with even more violence.

On March 30, 1867, John Lewis Neyland, a close political ally and in-law of James Brashear, was killed. This prompted some of the Brashears, Neylands and others to move to Freestone County and the Redland Community in Leon County.

James "Jim" Brashear moved to the Redland Community in Leon County, TX, twice, according to Dr. Doyle Brashears of

Lufkin. The first time was before the Civil War, when he was involved in the feud about relocating the county seat of Angelina County from Jonesville to Homer. He is said to have returned to Angelina County after his sons went off to the Civil War and the feud had died down somewhat. The other time was after the Civil War, when he and his two "youngest children" (per a Freestone County history), Robert C., 22, and Davilla Ann, 16, moved to Freestone Co, TX, in 1870.

The 1870 Census of Freestone County, Texas, shows James Brashies (HH#339), age 54, born in Tennessee, with son R. C., age 21, and daughter Devilla, age 16, both children born in Texas. James's age is incorrect again; he should be about 60. His daughter, Lucinda Neyland, and family are shown in the same household. His wife, Maribe, is not listed, but she was in the 1880 census in the household of her youngest daughter, Davilla Ann and her husband, Richard Harding.

The last time James Brashear's name appears in the records is on the Freestone County, Texas tax list in 1871. James is possibly buried at Jonesville, Angelina Co, TX, but may be in Oakwood Cem, Freestone Co, TX. Family legend suggests he and Lizzie are buried at Centerville Cem, Leon Co, TX.

James and Maribe's Sons

Three of James's sons served in the Civil War: Berry Simpson Brashears, Jesse Marion Walter Brashear, and John M. Brashears. Walt was a fiddler and played for the locals as the soldiers left from Marion Ferry, which had been the county seat until Gobbler Jones and others had it moved to Jonesville.

However, as Larry C. Pleasants points out, there is much confusion and contradiction in genealogy records, Angelina County history books, and family records, about the sons born to James M. Brashears and Mary Elizabeth Maribe Jones prior to the birth of their son Berry S. Brashears, born in 1841. Larry reports:

In the 1860 Angelina Census, three other Brashears besides James Brassiers are shown; their names are also spelled Brassiers.

Immediately below the household of James Brassiers (HH339) in the census is Jackson Brassiers (HH340), age 32, with wife Julie, age 22 and son John C., age 4. He owns 300 acres of land. Jackson is shown to be born circa 1828 in Arkansas, but his parents did not go to Arkansas until after 1830.

Immediately below Jackson is Walker J. Brassiers (HH341), age 28, with wife Pauline, age 23 and daughter Kate, age 5. He is shown to own 200 acres of land.

Another Brashear, Jessie W. Brassiers or Brassius, age 24 (HH230), born in Arkansas, is shown with wife Elizabeth (Forrest), age 21, born in Mississippi, and daughter Mary A., age 1. Angelina County Marriage records confirm that on September 8, 1858, M. W. Brashears married Elizabeth Forrest. The same census taker recorded all four Brassiers families.

The Brashear son shown in the 1850 census by the name of John, who would be age 25 in 1860, is the not shown in the 1860 Angelina County Census with wife Nancy Clementine, age 18 and son, John C., 9 months old. Nor can John M. and Nancy be found elsewhere in the 1860 Texas Census or any other census record.

If this Jackson Brashear, age 32, and the Walker Brashear, age 28, shown in the 1860 Angelina County Census, are the sons of James and Maribe, then in the 1840 Census, Jackson would have been 12 years old and Walker 8 years old. In the 1840 Census, no Brashear male is shown age 10-15 and only one is shown age 5-10. Additionally, there is no Jackson, age 22; nor is there a Walker, age 18 shown in the same household as James M. in the 1850 census, although both could have been out of the house at this time.

This Jackson Brashears and Walker Brashears are not listed elsewhere in the 1850 Census records, nor are their marriages shown in Angelina County Marriage Records from 1846-1897.

In fact, these two Brashear families just show up in 1860 and disappear after 1860. Some of the Brashears moved from Angelina County to other counties such as Freestone, Polk and Leon, but this Jackson and Walker Brashears are not listed in the census records for those counties either in 1870 or 1880. Nor does a Brashear child named Kate, Katie or Kathie Brashears, age 15, appear in the 1870 Texas Census anywhere.

The mystery is why is there is not a John M. Brashear

married to a Nancy Clementine shown in the 1860 Angelina County Census? And why is there both a Walker J. and a Jesse W. Brashear shown in the same census?

There are some similarities between Jackson shown in the 1860 census and John M. Brashears. Both had a son named John C., who would have been almost a year old when the census was taken in 1860. In the Land Title Abstract Indices of Original Land Owners of Angelina County Texas, J. M. Brashears was awarded 320 acres which is the same amount of land that Jackson is shown to own in the 1860 census.

Evidence shows that John M. Brashears and Nancy Clementine Treadwell were together before the 1860 census. According to Angelina County Marriage records and their marriage license, J. M. Brashears married N. C. Treadwell on October 7, 1858. Nancy (age 8) is shown with the Stephen Treadwell family in the Leake County, Mississippi Census in 1850, but she is no longer in the Stephen Treadwell household shown in the 1860 Angelina County Census. Nancy C. Brashear's obituary in 1891 from the Lufkin newspaper confirms her marriage to J. M. Brashear.

In all of the records of J. M. Brashear, he is referred to either as John, Jack or J. M. In the 1880 Angelina County Census, he is listed as "Jas M.", which is a standard abbreviation for James, but "Jas" was more likely the census taker's abbreviation for "Jackson". A review of the census records shows that the census taker spelled out the name "James" elsewhere in many places. Also, the census taker had room to spell out "James M.", but not enough room to spell out "Jackson M.". (Note: The middle initial, M., could be for Martin, Marion or Monteville, because James and Maribe used names from both the Brashear and Jones families in their children's names.)

Other records around this time also show the Brashears. In the Land Title Abstract Indices of Original Land Owners of Angelina County Texas, James Brashears, J. M. Brashears and J. W. Brashears are all shown as recipients of Land Awards. A map at the Temple Archives in Diboll, Texas shows separate land parcels near Huntington belonging to only three Brashears— James Brashear, J. W. Brashear and J. M. Brashear, all located adjacent to one another. (This supports the fact that in the 1860 Census that James Brashears had two sons living next door to him.)

Angelina County Commissioner Court minutes from 1846-1855 mention the Brashears several times. On Feb. 19, 1850 a Brashears is mentioned regarding roadwork at Odell Creek, which was just north of the present Huntington, Texas.

On Feb. 19, 1851 a James and Jack Brashears are mentioned related to roadwork on the mail route.

Then on Feb. 19, 1852 a paragraph on roadwork on Berry Road mentions James Brashears and son.

Meeting in Marion, Texas on Feb. 21, 1853, the court again mentions James Brashears and son working with some of the Joneses on Shawnee Road from Dunigans to Shawnee Creek.

In *The History of Angelina County*, Civil War Records and various other lists of Civil War soldiers, three Brashears are shown serving together in Company D of the Seventh Texas Cavalry in 1861: Berry S. Brashears, Walker "Walk" Brashears and John M. Brashears (some Angelina County records of Company D Muster Rolls list John as Jack). The Lufkin News reported in its May 17, 1972 issue that "J. M. Brashears, 28 years old, was commissioned a corporal on March 10,1862." Civil War records also show that Jesse made corporal.

In the Angelina County Civil War records listing dependents of the service men, records show: Clementine Bras(s)iers (wife of John/Jack), Elizabeth Brassiers (wife of Jesse W. (Walker)) and F. S. Brashears (wife of Berry). There are no dependent listings for a Julia or Pauline Brassiers, the wives of Jackson and Walker J. shown in the 1860 Census.

Some genealogy researchers suggest that the 1860 Census's Jackson Brassiers (32) married to Julia (22) with son John C. (4) is the same person as John M. Brashear. If true, why is the wife shown as Julia instead of Nancy Clementine. John married Nancy Clementine in the fall of 1858 and their son John C. was born in 1859. For these to be the same Brashear male son of James and Maribe Brashears, the census taker would have had to make numerous errors. It seems unlikely that four mistakes could have been made in one household record. In comparison: wrong age for Jackson, age 32 instead of age 26; wrong name and age for his wife, Julia, age 22, instead of Nancy Clementine, age 18; and wrong age for John C., age 4 instead of 10 months.

The same genealogy researchers also suggest that the 1860 Census's Walker J. Brassiers married to Pauline is the same person as J. W. Brashears married to Elizabeth. If true, then the census taker listed the same person twice, in different households, with two different families in the 1860 census. This mistake is (almost) impossible.

John Clisby Brashears's mother was Nancy Clementine, not Julia. (It is important to note that in this line of the Brashear family there were numerous sons named John C. or Robert C. - the initial "C" was for Clisby, Calvin or Calloway.)

In a letter written by N. C. Brashears in 1888, she addresses John Clisby Brashears, (born September 1859) "Mr. J. C. Brashears, Dear Son." In the letter she calls him "Johney." The letter is signed, "from your affectionate mother, N. C. Brashears." Other family records also support the idea that John Clisby is Nancy Clementine Brashear's son. [The original letter is at the Temple Archives in Diboll, Texas in a collection of archives from John Clisby Brashears. Larry Pleasants has a digital copy.]

In an 1886 letter to N. C. Brashears, her cousin writes this to Nancy: "How is John doing? Emma remembers how fond her mother was of Jack". This seems to refer to Nancy's husband as John and Jack, unless John refers to son John Clisby. [The original letter is at the Temple Archives in Diboll, Texas. Larry Pleasants has a digital copy.]

On the surface there seems to be too many contradictions for the 1860 Census's Jackson Brassiers (32) married to Julia (22) with son John C. (4) to be the same Brashears as John M. Brashear and family. It seems even more unlikely that Walker J. Brashears and Jesse W. Brashears the same Brashears male person. But why would James and Maribe have named two sons Walker and two sons Jackson?

After three years of extensive research, I [Larry Pleasants] believe that the census taker(s) in 1860 made some serious errors or some unusual circumstances created the errors. Except for the 1860 census, all records— marriage, Civil War, court, census, letters, etc.— indicate that James and Maribe Brashears only had four sons: John, Walter, Berry and Robert.

I therefore believe that the following persons from the

census of 1860 simply did not exist, but are complicated confusions with better data:

V6 6421. 10x. **Jackson M. Brashears**, b. c1828, AR (32 in 1860, Angelina Co, TX, hh #340, next door to James and Lizzie); m. ***Julia Jones***, b. c1838, AL (22 in 1860)

V6 6422. 11 1. **John C. Brashears**, b. c1856, Jonesville, Angelina Co, TX (4 in 1860)

V6 6423. 10y. **Walker Jesse Brashears**, b. c1832, Old Royal Colony, White Co, AR (28 in 1860, Angelina Co, TX, hh #341); m. ***Pauline*** _______, b. c1837, AL (23 in 1860).

V6 6424. 11 1. **Kate Brashears**, b. c1855, Jonesville, Angelina Co, TX (5 in 1860)

<u>Family of James M. "Jim" Brashears and Mary Elizabeth "Lizzie" Maribe Jones</u>:

V6 6425. 10 1. **Malinda Brashears**, b. c1833, Old Royal Colony, White Co, AR (17 in 1850), d. 1860-61, Tyler Co, TX; m.1. license issued 5 April 1849, Polk Co, TX, ***Bradford Baker***, m.2. license issued 18 Aug 1849, Tyler Co, TX, ***Bentley Barnett***, b. c1815-18, GA. They are in the 1850 and 1860 census of Tyler Co, TX, with 5 children. After Malinda died, Bentley m.2. Rebecca Hensarling, on 14 Aug 1861; they named their first child Malinda.

V6 6426. 11 1. John F. Bentley, b. c1850

V6 6427. 11 2. David C. Bentley, b. c1852

V6 6428. 11 3. Mary B. Bentley, b. c1855

V6 6429. 11 4. Nancy C. Bentley, b. c1856

V6 6430. 11 5. Thomas U. Bentley, b. c1859

V6 6431. 10 2. ***John M. "Jack," "Jackson" Brashears**, b. 25 Jan 1834, Old Royal Colony, White Co, AR (15 in 1850), d. 1896; m. 7 Oct 1858, in Angelina Co, TX, ***Nancy <u>Clementine</u> Treadwell***, b. 20 Sept 1842, Alabama, d. 17 Feb 1891, near Lufkin, TX. They are hh 167/38 in 1870 Census, Angelina Co, TX, Pennington P.O. (3 doors from "Walter"). John served in Co D, 22nd Texas Infantry, C.S.A.

V6 6432. 10 3. ***Jesse Marion Walter "Walt" Brashears**, b. 26 Feb

1836, Old Royal Colony, White Co, AR (13 and "Walker" in 1850, d. 30 Nov 1885, Jonesville, Angelina Co, TX; 24 in 1860, Angelina Co, TX, hh #236), d. 30 Nov 1885; m. 8 Sept 1858, in Angelina Co, TX, ***Frances Elizabeth "Lizzie" Forest***, b. 21 Feb 1836, Alabama. They are hh #167-41 in 1870 Census, Angelina Co, TX, Pennington P.O. (3 doors from John). Jesse Walter served in Co D, 22nd Texas Infantry, in the Civil War, and Elizabeth F. Brashears received a Confederate widow's pension in Angelina Co, TX.

V6 6433. 10 4. ***Lucinda Marie Brashears**, b. 15 Feb 1838, Old Royal Colony, White Co, AR (12 in 1850), d. 16 Jan 1918, Redland Community, Leon Co, TX; m. 31 May 1858, in Angelina Co, TX, ***James Smiley Neyland***, b. 2 Oct 1838, Amite Co, MS,

V6 6434. 10 5. **Berry Simpson Brashears**, b. 7 Jan 1841, Old Royal Colony, White Co, AR (10 in 1850; "Berry M." 19 in 1860), d. 4 March 1889, Leon Co, TX; m. 12 Aug 1860, in Angelina Co, TX, ***Frances Susanna Everett***, b. 21 Jan 1843, (births, marriage, and three children recorded in Jesse Walter Brashears Bible, in possession of Doyle H. Brashear, as of July 2004). Berry and Frances moved to Freestone Co, TX, in 1865. Berry served in Co D, 22nd Texas Infantry, the Confederate States Army, 7th Texas Cavalry, 1861-1865, and Frances S. Brashears received a widow's pension in Freestone Co, TX.

V6 6435. 11 1. **J. (or S.) Franklin Brashairs**, b. 23 June 1861

V6 6436. 11 2. **Martha "Mattie" Eugenia Brashear**, b. 27 Oct 1864, Freestone Co, TX; m. 1884, Freestone Co, TX, ***Armond Lafiest Bacon***, b. 14 Jan 1853, Anderson Co, TX, d. 10 Jan 1903, Freestone Co, TX, bur Oakwood Cem; they raised 8 children: Lon, Anna, Lena, Mattie May, Tissie, Joseph C., Reuben, and Doodie Bacon. "Obviously," says the Freestone County History from which this is taken, "some of these are nick-names."

V6 6437. [11]3. **Caldonia "Catey Sonia" Brashears**, b. 2 Feb 1867, Angelina Co, TX

V6 6438. [11]4. **John Brashears**, b. 1870

V6 6439. [11]5. **Robert Brashears**, b. 1878

V6 6440. [10]6. **Rhoda E. Brashears**, b. c1843, Old Royal Colony, White Co, AR (8 in 1850; 17 in 1860, Angelina Co, TX, hh #345, wife of James B. Moore); m. 6 Oct 1859, ***James Berry Moore***, b. c1832, IL (per 1860 census), d. c1862, El Paso, TX. James B. Moore served in the 7th Texas Cavalry, with his four brothers-in-law.

V6 6441. [10]7. **Fetna "Fannie" Brashears**, b. c1845, Old Royal Colony, White Co, AR, (4 in 1850; 14 in 1860); m. 11 Feb 1862, in Angelina Co, TX, ***William R. Selman***, b. c1843, TX. William Sellman served in Co D, 22nd Texas Infantry, in the Civil War.

V6 6442. [10]8. **Robert Calvin Brashears**, b. c1847, Jonesville, Angelina Co, TX (3 in 1850; 12 in 1860, Census, Angelina Co, TX); m. 23 Sept 1872, in Cherokee Co, TX, ***Amanda Lockett Tackitt***, (2 ch), b. 1855, LA, d/o Nathan Van Buren Tackitt and Elizabeth Potter. *A History of Freestone Co, TX*, says Robert C. Brashears had lived in Freestone Co since 1865; he was on a list of voters there, November 1869. He was apparently back in Angelina County during the 1890s.

V6 6443. [11]1. **Eugene Brashears**, b. 1874, Cherokee Co, TX

V6 6444. [11]2. **Marion Brashears**, b. 1878, Cherokee Co, TX

V6 6445. [10]9. **Davilla Ann Brashears**, b. 5 Jan 1854, Angelina Co, TX (6 in 1860), d. 8 Dec 1912, Freestone Co, TX; bur Oakwood Cem, Freestone Co, TX; m.1. 11 Sept 1872, in Freestone Co, TX, ***Grantham "Grant" Rose***, b. 1847, AL, d. 1875, Freestone Co, TX, s/o Thomas Rose, b. 1808, GA; m.2. 13 Jan 1876, in Freestone Co, TX, ***Richard D. Harding***, a stonemason, b. c1848 in England, d. c1905 in Freestone, Co, TX. Davilla and Richard Harding "raised a large family" in Freestone Co, but the article by Mrs. Llewellyn Rose in the local history from which this comes did not name them. In 1880, mother-in-law Maribe "Robey" Breashears was in their household, as were three children.

V66446. [11]1. Robert Jefferson "Jeff" Rose, b. 13 Sept 1873 in Freestone Co, TX, d. there 12 Juen 1946; m. 1896, in Freestone Co, TX, Sallie Llewellen, in Freestone Co, TX. About 1912, Jeff and Sallie moved to Oakwood, where their house was on the Freestone/Leon County line: they slept in Leon County, but took their meals in Freestone County. (Re: *A History of Freestone Co, TX,* 1978)

V66447. [12]1. Llewellyn Rose, lived Austin, TX

V66448. [12]2. Myrtis Rose, m. ______ Dodson, lived Woodland Hills, CA

V66449. [12]3. Travis Earl Rose, lived in Texarkana

V66450. [11]2. Walter W. Harding, b. c1877

V66451. [11]3. Ada E. Harding, b. c1879

[NOTE: The Bible of Jesse Walter Brashears, which the Warren grandchildren of Jesse Walter "Walt" Brashears gave to Dr. Doyle H. Brashears of Lufkin, TX, contains the entry: "Berry Simpson Brashear and F.S. Brashear were married, Aug 12, 1860." Berry was listed in 1860 census as Berry M. Brashear. Berry might have been a mumbler and the census-taker understood his muttered "Simpson" as "M", and Susanna may have used only her middle name.

In the Jesse Walter Brashear Bible, before the children of Jesse, the family of his brother, Berry Simpson Brashears, is listed:

***B.S. Brashairs**, b. 7 Jan 1841*

***F.S. Brashairs**, b. 21 Jan 1843*

Berry Simpson Brashears and F.S. Brashears married August 12, 1860

***J. (or S.) Franklin Brashairs**, b. 23 June 1861*

***Martha E. Jenia Brashear**, b. 27 Oct 1864; d. 1885*

***Catey S(onia?) Brashears**, b. 2 Feb 1867*

R.W. Conley (or Corley), b. 16 Sept 1866, Freestone Co, TX

I'd almost be willing to bet R.W. Conley is Catey's husband;

which would suggest that these entries were made long after the actual births, deaths, marriages, etc. Then follows Jesse's children, beginning with M.A. Brashear (Mary Annie), oldest child of Jesse.

Also in the bible:

S.(?) Sterns, b. 28 May 1832
M.J. (or F.) Sterns, b. 16 Sept 1833
Mabel Sterns, d. 15 Oct 1869
James T. Maroney, b. 27 Jan 1886
A.(?) C.(?) Brashears, d. 23 Sept 1885

JOHN M. "JACKSON" BRASHEARS and Nancy Clementine Treadwell

v6 6431. 10 2. **John M. "Jack" "Jackson" Brashears**, (s/o James M. Brashears and Mary Elizabeth "Lizzie" Maribe Jones), b. 25 Jan 1834, Old Royal Colony, White Co, AR, parents b. TN, d. Angelina Co, TX, 1898; m. 7 Oct 1858, in Angelina Co, TX, ***Nancy Clementine Treadwell***, ("N.C. Treadwell" in marriage book; marriage performed by "G.H. Martin, J.P."; #189 in Marr recs of Angelina Co), b. 20 Sept 1842, in Alabama, d. 1891, near Lufkin, Angelina Co, TX, d/o Stephen Treadwell, b. GA, and Faith Jordan, b. SC.

John and Clementine Brashears are hh #167/38 in 1870 census, Angelina Co, TX, with children John, Jane, Maria, Josiah, Calloway, and Katie. Jas. M. (hard to read; may be John) and "Clematine" Brashears were in 1880 Census of Angelina Co, TX. John M. Brashears was a Lieutenant in Co D, 7th Texas Cavalry, along with brothers Jesse, and Berry. His cattle brand was "34," the year of his birth.

Family of John M. Brashears and Nancy Clementine Treadwell:

V6 6452. 11 1. ***John Clisby Brashears**, b. 5 Sept 1859, Angelina Co, TX (10 in 1870; 20 and "John K" in 1880), d. 3 April 1936, Angelina Co, TX, bur Prairie Grove Cem, Angelina Co, TX; John stated in 1920 that his father was born in Arkansas and his mother in Alabama.

V6 6453. 11 2. **Rhoda Jane Brashears**, b. 3 June 1861, Angelina Co, TX ("Jane," 8 in 1870, Angelina), d. 1895; m.

29 March 1885, Angelina Co, TX, ***John M. Graham***, b. c1860, Angelina Co, TX.

^{V6}6454. ^{12}1. Butler Graham, b. c1886

^{V6}6455. ^{12}2. Beulah Graham, b. c1887

^{V6}6456. ^{12}3. Bertha Graham, b. d1889; m. Grover C. Carrell Sr, b. c1887, Texas

^{V6}6457. ^{13}1. Milton Carrell, m. Daphna Beshannon.

^{V6}6458. ^{14}1. Shirley Ann Carrell, m. Don Hudnall, ch: Donna Hudnall

^{V6}6459. ^{14}2. Milton Carrell, m. Deidra Breazeale. Ch: Leanna Carrell

^{V6}6460. ^{13}2. Wilburn Carrell, m. Catherine Russell. Ch: Kay Carrell, m.1. John Agan, m.2. George Bill Perry

^{V6}6461. ^{13}3. Lucille Carrell, m. Finis Gibbs

^{V6}6462. ^{13}4. Grover C. Carrell Jr, b. 28 Feb 1924, Huntington, Angelina Co, TX, d. 2 April 1988; m.1. Vada Hopson (4 ch); m.2. Dorothy ______ (1 ch). Ch: Karen; Sharon; Keith; Kenneth; Grover C. III Carrell

^{V6}6463. ^{13}5. Bertie Lee Carrell, m. _____ Tipton

^{V6}6464. ^{11}3. **Maria Maude Brashears**, b. 9 June 1864, Angelina Co, TX (6 in 1870), d. 1896; m. 21 Jan 1894, in Angelina Co, TX, ***Alfred Carpenter***,

^{V6}6465. ^{11}4. **Josiah M. "Buck" Brashears**, b. 12 May 1866, Angelina Co, TX (4 in 1870). Possibly the **James H. Brashear**, b. c1867, age 43 in 1910 Census, Anderson Co, TX, with wife ***Bertie*** _____, age 28 (b. c1882) and two sons:

^{V6}6466. ^{12}1. **Bruce Brashears**, age 4 (b. c1906)

^{V6}6467. ^{12}2. **Carlton Brashears**, age 1 10/12 (b. c1908).

^{V6}6468. ^{11}5. ***Robert Calloway "Cal" Brashears**, b. 30 Nov 1867, Angelina Co, TX; m. 30 Oct 1892, in Angelina Co, TX, ***Maggie Elizabeth Lott***,

^{V6}6469. ^{11}6. **Kate "Faithie" C. Brashear**, b. 5 Jan 1870 (5/12 in 1870), d. c1895; m. 23 July 1891, in Angelina Co, TX, ***J.L. "Tom" Spencer***, b. c1868. They lived in Crockett, Houston Co, TX.

^{V6}6470. ^{11}7. **Theodocia "Docie" Brashears**, b. 14 April 1871,

d. 1895; m. 23 Sept 1893, in Angelina Co, TX, ***D.A. "Lonnie" McCarthy***,

v6 6471. 11 8. **Stephen L. Brashears**, b. 12 May 1873 or 74, TX (per 1900 census; in hh #326, unmarried, with brother, Tom), d. 1901

v6 6472. 11 9. ***Carlton Dole Brashears**, b. 23 Jan 1876, Angelina Co, TX; m. 5 Nov 1900, in Angelina Co, TX, ***Malissie Claudine Sims***,

v6 6473. 11 10. **Thomas G. Brashears**, b. 25 Sept 1872, Angelina Co, TX (per 1900 census, in hh #326, unmarried, with brother, Steve). Thomas later lived in Louisiana.

v6 6474. 11 11. ***Artilla Mable "Cricket" Brashear**, b. 21 July 1880, Angelina Co, TX, d. 6 Sept 1966, Lufkin, Angelina Co, TX; m. c1899, in Trinity Co, TX, ***Ellie Jeptha Douglass***,

v6 6475. 11 12. **Needum Clyde Brashear**, b. 3 Oct 1883, Angelina Co, TX, d. 2 Jan 1958, Conroe, TX, bur Jonesville Cem, Huntington, Angelina Co, TX; m. ***Daisy*** _____

John Clisby Brashears and Rosa Louella McClendon

v6 6542. 11 1. **John Clisby Brashears**, (s/o John M. Brashears and Nancy Clementine Treadwell), b. 5 Sept 1859, TX, Angelina Co, TX, d. 3 April 1936, bur Prairie Grove Cem, Angelina Co (John K. in hh of "Jas" M. Brashears, in 1880 Census of Angelina Co). John Clisby Brashears m.1. 27 Jan 1889, in Angelina Co, TX, ***Mary E. Clayton***, b. c1864, Angelina Co, TX, d. bef 1893 (no ch), bur Treadwell Cem, Angelina Co, TX, d/o William Austin Clayton and Mary Ann Lucretia Ellis; m.2. 29 Oct 1893, in Angelina Co, TX, ***Rosa Louella McClendon***, b. 30 Dec 1870, prob. Angelina Co, TX, d. Dec 1960 (tombstone in Prairie Grove Cem has no date, as of 1966), d/o William Montgomery McClendon and Francis Virginia Ellis. John C. and Rosie Brashear are hh #112 in 1900 Census, Angelina Co, TX, with first two children. John's middle name was after his great uncle, Clisby Riggs "Tib" Jones, b. 18 Feb 1808, Jefferson Co, TN, older brother of Mary Elizabeth Maribe Jones.

Family of John Clisby Brashears and Rosa Louella McClendon:

Figure 106: John Clisby Brashears. Thanks for photo to Ron McClendon

^{V6}6476. ^{12}1. **Virginia Clementine "Virgie" Brashears**, b. 4 Oct 1894, TX (per 1900 census), d. 1984, Lufkin, Angelina Co, TX; m. ***Lee Roy Stewart***, b. 12 Dec 1891, Louisiana, d. 19 Sept 1959, Lufkin, Angelina Co, TX, bur Fairview Cem, Angelina Co, TX.

^{V6}6477. ^{13}1. Carmen Stewart, b. c1915, TX

^{V6}6478. ^{13}2. Carlton Stewart, b. c 1917, TX

^{V6}6479. ^{13}3. Benice Guy Stewart, b. after Jan 1920, TX

^{V6}6480. ^{12}2. ***Richard Filmore Brashears**, b. Dec 1897, Lufkin, Angelina Co, TX, d. 17 May 1967; m. 28 Oct 1922, Angelina Co, TX, ***Esther Cordelia Havard***,

^{V6}6481. ^{12}3. **John Marion "Johnny M." Brashears**, b. 1900, TX, d. 1954, bur Prairie Grove Cem, Angelina Co, TX; m. 25 May 1926, Angelina Co, TX, ***Wilmoth Ollie Warner***, b. 1904, d. 1848, bur Prairie Grove Cem.

^{V6}6482. ^{13}1. **Robert Brashears**, (twin) b. 1926, d. 1926

^{V6}6483. ^{13}2. Baby **Brashears**, (twin) b. 1926, d. 1926

^{V6}6484. ^{13}3. **Enoch Harold Brashears**, b. 22 Nov 1928; m. 17 Nov 1948, ***Charlene Turner***,

^{V6}6485. ^{14}1. **Thomas Wayne Brashears**,

^{V6}6486. ^{14}2. **Belinda Jo Brashears**, m. ______ ***Bleskowski***,

^{V6}6487. ^{14}3. **Doyle Brashears**,

[V6]6488. [14]4. **Teresa Brashears**,

[V6]6489. [14]5. **Brian Brashears**,

[V6]6490. [13]4. **Gordon Glenn "Tip" Brashears**, b. 18 Aug 1929, Angelina Co, TX; m. 2 Nov 1951, ***Sally Louise Griggs***,

[V6]6491. [14]1. **Glenda Louise Brashears**,

[V6]6492. [14]2. **Randall Keith Brashears**,

[V6]6493. [14]3. **Martin Kendal Brashears**,

[V6]6494. [14]4. **Robert Murph Brashears**,

[V6]6495. [14]5. **Michael Kevin Brashears**,

[V6]6496. [14]6. **Kelly La Mae Brashears**,

[V6]6497. [13]5. **Lewis Boyce "Snoopy" Brashears**, b. 1 Dec 1932; m. ***Betty Joy McDuffie***,

[V6]6498. [14]1. **Johnny Brashears**,

[V6]6499. [14]2. **Brenda Brashears**,

[V6]6500. [13]6. **Bennie Carroll Brashears**, b. c1932

[V6]6501. [12]4. **Mollie Maude Brashears**, b. 9 June 1903, Burke, Angelina Co, TX, d. 23 April 1993, Lufkin, Angelina Co, TX, bur Fairview Cem, Angelina Co, TX; m. 23 Dec 1923, Angelina Co, TX, ***Charles "Charlie" Monroe Foster***, b. 2 Dec 1890, DeRidder, Beauregard Parish, LA, d. 20 Jan 1970, Lufkin, TX, bur Fairview Cem, s/o Lucious Leonard Foster and Nancy Margaret Davis,

[V6]6502. [13]1. Charles Monroe Foster Jr, b. 15 Oct 1924, Burke, Angelina Co, TX, d. after 1993; m. 7 Feb 1948, Lufkin, Angelina Co, TX, Patsy Ruth Woodward, b. 17 Dec 1931, Denver, CO, d. 23 May 1949, Lufkin, Angelina Co, TX (ch: Elon M. Foster); m.2. Audrey Mae Hopson, (5 ch: Stuart Wayne, Virginia Kay, Pamela Ann, Candace Marie, and Connie Lynn Foster)

[V6]6503. [13]2. Mary Lois Foster, b. 8 Nov 1926, Burke, Angelina Co, TX; m.1. Tommy Eaves, m.2. Tommy Wayne Hill, b. Angelina Co, TX (ch: Larry Douglas and Sharon Denise Hill, m. Clyde "Jack" Anderson, ch: Carl Tracye; Nathan Douglas; and Aaron Daniel Anderson),

V6 6504. 13 3. John Gareth Foster, b. 25 March 1941, Burke, Angelina Co, TX; m. 1959 in GA, June Angela Sneed, b. 27 Feb 1941, VA (ch: Kelly Layne, Chris Cory, and Dana Theresa Foster)

Richard Filmore Brashears and Esther Havard

v6 6480. 12 2. **Richard Filmore Brashears**, (s/o John Clisby Brashears and Rosa Louella McClendon), b. Dec 1897, Lufkin, Angelina Co,TX (per 1900 Census), d. 17 May 1967, bur Fielders Cem, Angelina Co, TX; m. 28 Oct 1922, Angelina Co, TX, ***Esther Cordelia Havard***, b. 1 Jan 1899, TX, d. 28 Oct 1922, Angelina Co, TX; d/o John Thomas Havard and Ella Jane Squyres,

V6 6505. 13 1. **Richard Filmore "Cotton" Brashears Jr**, b. 1 Nov 1923, Angelina Co, TX; m. 3 Nov 1945, at Memphis, TN, ***Mary Gladys Hall***, b. June 1925, MS, d. 1984, Angelina Co, TX

V6 6506. 13 2. **Ruby Leona Brashears**, b. 26 July 1925, Angelina Co, TX; m. 30 Aug 1941 in Angelina Co, TX, Wiley J.C. Flurry, b. 8 March 1920, Angelina Co, TX. Six ch, all b. Angelina Co, TX:

V6 6507. 14 1. Patsy Ruth Flurry, b. 13 March 1941, m. Kelly Glaze. Ch: Michael Glaze

V6 6508. 14 2. Reginald Eugene Flurry, b. 23 Sept 1942, m. Velma Colbert. Ch: Stewart; Phyliss; and Melissa Jane Flurry

V6 6509. 14 3. Catherine Ann Flurry, b. 9 May 1949, m. Kenneth Marshall. Ch: Kenny Lynn; Deborah Kay; and Kimberly Marshall

V6 6510. 14 4. Geraldine Flurry, b. 6 Oct 1949, Lufkin, m. Dave Paterson. Ch: Suzanne; Roxanne; and Sean Paterson.

V6 6511. 14 5. Connie Lou Flurry, b. 22 June 1955, Lufkin, m. Keith Sims. Ch: Ryan Keith Sims

V6 6512. 14 6. Judy Lanell Flurry, b. 23 Nov 1959, Lufkin, m. Ray Modisette. Ch: Cara Leray; Rayla Gabriel; and Chesni Kay Modisette

V6 6513. 13 3. **Daphne Cudelya Brashears**, b. 19 March 1927, Angelina Co, TX; m. c1943, in Angelina Co, TX, Luther Clovis Whitehead, b. 9 Feb 1925

V6 6514. 14 1. Doris Jean Whithead, m. Floyd Calhoun. Ch:

Kayce Charyse; and Corey Beamon Calhoun

V6 6515. [14]2. Eddie Wayne Whitehead, m.1. Carolyn Steel. Ch: Luther Wayne; and Michael Paul Whitehead. Eddie m.2. Mary Foxworthy; m.3. Dora Huizar.

V6 6516. [14]3. Audrey Beth Whitehead, m.1. Bobby Hall. Ch: Melissa Beth; and Lancy Lee Hall; Audrey m.2. Steven Ray Versland.

V6 6517. [14]4. Linwood Clovis Whitehead, m.1. Janis Fisher. Ch: Tonya Lin; and Aundria Kay Whithead. Linwood m.2. Jennetta Alsobrooke Taylor

V6 6518. [13]4. **Kenneth Ray Brashear**, b. 24 Jan 1929, Angelina Co, TX; m. 18 June 1960 in Angelina Co, TX, ***Sarah Jane Reynolds***, b. 6 Jan 1940, Angelina Co, TX

V6 6519. [14]1. **Kenneth Charles Brashear**, b. 30 Aug 1961, Angelina Co, TX; m. 28 Dec 1985, in Lufkin, Angelina Co, TX, ***Keri Kimberly Dennis***, b. 6 May 1963, Lufkin, TX

V6 6520. [14]2. **John P. Brashear**, b. 17 Feb 1965, Angelina Co, TX; m. 14 Aug 1987 in Lufkin, Angelina co, TX, ***Helen Bernice Norton***, b. 7 Dec 1966

V6 6521. [15]1. **Brittany Elizabeth Brashear**, b. 12 Feb 1990

V6 6522. [15]2. **John Dexter Brashear**, b. 23 Sept 1991

V6 6523. [13]5. **Doyle Edwin Brashears**, b. 23 Sept 1932, Angelina Co, TX, d. 30 Oct 1936, bur Fielders Cem, Angelina Co, TX

V6 6524. [13]6. **James Hollis "Cotton" Brashear**, b. 17 May 1936, Angelina Co, TX; m. 31 Dec 1959 in Angelina Co, TX, ***Frances June Wise***, b. 7 May 1937, San Augustine Co, TX. Three ch, all b. Angelina Co, TX

V6 6525. [14]1. **Tamesha De Ann Brashear**, b. 24 Jan 1963, m.1. 1 Jan 1985, in Angelina Co, TX, ***Peter Paul Fernandez***, b. 16 March 1961 in Switzerland; m.2. Jan 1998, in Nacodoches, Nacodoches Co, TX, ***Michael Will***.

V6 6526. [15]1. Ian Paul Fernandez,

V6 6527. [15]2. Amanda Justine Fernandez,

[V6]6528. [14]2. **Linwood Keith Brashear**, b. 18 April 1965, m. ***Trace Lynn Holcomb***, b. 15 March 1967, in Angelina Co, TX

[V6]6529. [15]1. **Racheal Rebekka Brashear**, b. 19 April 1999, Nacogdoches, TX

[V6]6530. [14]3. **Alysa Annette Brashear**, b. 21 April 1966, m. 3 Jan 1987, in Angelina Co, TX, ***Vertis Bass***, b. 4 May 1963,

[V6]6531. [15]1. James Keith Bass, b. 7 Feb 1995, Nacogdoches, TX

[V6]6532. [15]2. Megan Elizabeth Bass, b. 13 May 1997, Nacogdoches, TX

[V6]6533. [13]7. baby **Brashear**, b.&d. 30 Oct 1936, Angelina Co, TX

[V6]6534. [13]8. **Joyce Brashear**, b.&d. 3 Oct 1938, Angelina Co, TX

[V6]6535. [13]9. **Barbara Ann Brashear**, b. 9 Dec 1941, Angelina Co, TX, d. 28 July 1942.

Robert Calloway "Cal" Brashears and Maggie Elizabeth Lott

[v6]6468. [11]5. **Robert Calloway "Cal" Brashears**, (s/o John M. Brashears and Nancy Clementine Treadwell), b. 30 Nov 1867, Huntington, Angelina Co, TX (3 in 1870; 12 in 1880), d. 1912, Angelina Co, TX; m. 30 Oct 1892, in Angelina Co, TX, ***Margaret "Maggie" Elizabeth Lott***, b. 1 April 1872, Crawford Co, AR (age 7 in 1880, Crawford Co, AR), d. 13 Oct 1941, Houston, Harris Co, TX, d/o Joshua "Jack" Lott, b. 1834, GA, and Nancy ______.

On the marriage license, Maggie's surname is listed as Hill. She may have been married previously, but no documentation has been found. In 1900, father-in-law, Jack Lott, and brother-in-law, Edgar Lott, b. 1877, are in Cal's household. Cal was a druggist and ran general merchandise stores in Zavalla, San Augustine Co, TX. Joshua Lott operated a saloon in Zavalla; in 1906, R.C. "Cal" Brashears is listed as a saloon keeper, so he must have taken over Josh's saloon.

Family members report that Cal had appendicitis and was on his way to Houston to be operated on. He died on the train of a burst appendix. He is probably buried in Zavalla. The Robert C. Brashears and the R.C. Brashears in Old Center Cem, Angelina Co, TX, are NOT Robert "Cal" Brashears.

In 1920, Mrs. M.E. Brashears is head of household in the census of Angelina Co, TX (ED 5, Sheet 11). Three daughters and one son are still at home. In 1930, Maggie is age 59, with son, Denver, 19.

<u>Family of Robert Calloway "Cal" Brashears and Maggie Elizabeth Lott;</u>

[V6]6536. [12]1. **Roy Calvin Brashear**, b. 13 March 1895, Angelina Co, TX; d. 6 Sept 1980,Liberty Co, TX, bur Sec 12, Forest Park Lawndale, Houston, Harris Co, TX; m. ***Minnie Avis Stacy***,

[V6]6537. [13]1. **Evelyn Jean Brashear**, b. 25 Aug 1927, Harris Co, TX

[V6]6538. [13]2. **Roy Calvin "Sonny Boy" Brashear, Jr**, b. 1924, Harris Co, TX, d. 1939

[V6]6539. [12]2. ***James Jackson "Jack" Brashear**, b. 7 Dec 1897, Lufkin, Angelina Co, TX, d. 18 Dec 1970, Pasadena, Harris Co, TX; m. 24 April 1920, in Lufkin, Angelina Co, TX, ***Nora Elizabeth Parrott***,

[V6]6540. [12]3. **Edgar E. Brashear**, b. 18 July 1899, Angelina Co, TX, d. 28 June 1970, Houston, Harris Co, TX

[V6]6541. [12]4. **Nany Pearl Brashear**, b. 1901; m. ***Theodore B."Teddy" Johnson***, b. 24 Nov 1885, d. Nov 1973, Dayton, Liberty Co, TX. In the 1950s, Pearl and Teddy Johnson bought some property from Pearl's brother, Jack Brashear, in Tarkington Prairie, TX (between Cleveland and Dayton). They lived next door to Jack and Nora Brashear, and Pearl and Jack's sister, Fay, lived across the street.

[V6]6542. [12]5. **Kattie Fay Brashear**, b. 1904, Angelina Co, TX, d. 18 Nov 1973, Liberty Co, TX. Never married. She lived across the street from her siblings, Pearl and Jack.

[V6]6543. [12]6. **Bessie Mae Brashear**, b. 19 Nov 1906, Angelina Co, TX, d. 23 May 1993, Anderson Co, TX; m. ***Warner Christian Lund***,

V6 6544. [13]1. Warner Christian Lund, Jr, b. 10 Dec 1919

V6 6545. [12]7. **Geneva Brashear**, b. 19 Nov 1909, Angelina Co, TX, d. 15 Aug 1983, Liberty Co, TX; m. ***Warren "Andy" Anderson***

V6 6546. [12]8. **Denver Brashear**, b. 24 May 1911, Lufkin, Angelina Co, TX, d. 10 Dec 1991, Houston, Harris Co, TX; m.1. ***Mildred Dietz***; m.2. ***Mary Lorene Stacey***; m.3. ***Jewell Truhitte***.

V6 6547. [13]x. **Shirley Ann Brashear**, b. 6 Sept 1937, d/o Denver Brashear and Mary Lorene Stacey, per info in Texas Births.

James Jackson Brashear and Nora Elizabeth Parrott

v6 6539. [12]2. **James Jackson "Jack" Brashear**, (s/o Robert Calloway "Cal" Brashears and Maggie Elizabeth Lott), b. 7 Dec 1897, Lufkin, Angelina Co, TX, d. 18 Dec 1970, Pasadena, Harris Co, TX; m. 24 April 1920, in Lufkin, Angelina Co, TX, ***Nora Elizabeth Parrott*** , b. 2 Jan 1901, Nacogdoches, TX, d. 10 Aug 1993, Houston, Harris Co, TX, d/o Pryor Parrott and Eliza Ann Eddings

Jack worked at many trades: logging in San Augustine Co, TX; painter; rackman; pumper in the oil field; in the 1920s, he owned a store with his father-in-law in Broaddus, TX. His brother-in-law, Ollie Parrott, operated a restaurant in back of the store. During the Depression, Jack extended credit to people so they could have food, shelter, and clothing. Many of these people failed to make payment, and the store went bankrupt. Jack and his family moved to Deer Park, Harris Co, TX, about 1928. Jack retired from Shell Oil in 1953 after 24½ years of service. Both Jack and Nora are buried in Grandview Cem, Deer Park, Harris Co, TX. Jack served in both WWI and WWII; his gravestone reads Pvt 48 Co 165 Depot Brig WWII.

After retirement Jack and Nora bought a hundred acre tract in Tarkington Prairie, Texas where they built a two car garage that they lived in temporarily until they built their house. Jack and Nora lived on their farm for several years. Although Jack was sick often with stomach and other health problems, he still managed to raise a few cows and hogs and farm a small garden. Nora canned vegetables, raised chickens and cooked really good country meals. Quite often their children and grandchildren would all come to visit together. The entire family would have a great time with the boys and men playing baseball or football while the women chatted.

Jack and Nora moved to Lynchberg Crossing across the ship channel from the San Jacinto Monument around 1963 on property adjacent to their daughter Jeanette's family home. In his last few years, Nora could not care for Jack, so Jack was in a nursing home in Baytown and then in Pasadena.

<u>Family of James Jackson Brashear and Nora Elizabeth Parrott:</u>

[V6]6548. [13]1. **Vernon Everett Brashear**, b. 28 Nov 1921, Lufkin, Angelina Co, TX, d. 4 Sept 1993, Wimberley, TX; m. ***Tessie Lucille Thompson***, b. 15 Sept 1922, d. 4 Feb 1993, Wimberly, TX

[V6]6549. [14]1. **Linda Ruth Brashear**, b. 23 Sept 1942

[V6]6550. [14]2. **Byron Everett Brashear**, b. 18 Dec 1950

[V6]6551. [14]3. **Sherry Brashear**, b. 10 Nov 1955

[V6]6552. [13]2. **Doyle Jackson Brashear**, b. 25 June 1925, Broaddus, San Augustine Co, TX; m. 7 Feb 1947, in Houston, Harris Co, TX, ***Mary Elizabeth Hicks***,

[V6]6553. [14]1. **Tyrena Brashear**, b. 11 Feb 1947

[V6]6554. [14]2. **Ric Lanier Brashear**, b. 31 May 1949, Houston, Harris Co, TX, d. 10 March 2001, Houston, TX

[V6]6555. [14]3. **Barry Lee Brashear**, b. 17 Sept 1950

[V6]6556. [13]3. **Garvis Nell Brashear**, b. 27 Sept 1927, Broaddus, San Augustine Co, TX, d. 3 June 1999 at Autumn Hills Nursing Home, Friendswood, TX; m.1. 19 Jan 1946, in Houston, Harris Co, TX, ***Walter Clement Pleasants***; b. 31 Oct 1925, Tarboro, Edgecomb Co, NC, d. 26 June 1998, in Belcamp, MD, s/o James Pleasants and Arete Nelms; m.2. ***Fred Leon Harper***;

Walter served in World War II as a First Class Gunner's Mate. Based on information Walter wrote in a Family Bible (owned by Gay Atkinson, Walter's second wife), he entered the U.S. Navy on March 27, 1943 at the age of 17. After gunnery school, Walter sailed on four ships that went to

Panama, Honduras, Chili, New Guniea, Australia, Italy and Sicily. On March 2, 1946 he received an honorable discharge.

Towards the end of his Navy service, Walter became ill with toncilitis and was sent to a hospital in Galveston, Texas. While there he met and started seeing his first wife, Garvis Nell Brashear.

He was an Operating Engineer. Walter started out in the excavation and construction business, working around the U.S. In 1952 he worked on the Alaskan Highway.

<u>Family of Garvis Nell Brashear and Walter Clement Pleasants:</u>

^{V6}6557. ^{14}1. Jerold Pleasants,

^{V6}6558. ^{14}2. Larry Clement Pleasants, b. 30 Oct 1947, Houston, Harris Co, TX. <LCP1947@aol.com> who sent information; m.1. 8 Sept 1968, in Houston, Harris Co, TX, Lois Adwina Wood (3 ch; div); m.2. 4 March 1988, in Redstone, CO, Catherine Marie Pool, b. 20 Aug 1955, Fort Sill, Lawton, OK (1 ch), d/o Robert Pool and Mary Love

^{V6}6559. ^{15}1. James Leon Pleasants, b. 19 July 1970

^{V6}6560. ^{15}2. Deborah Joy Pleasants, b. 13 March 1973

^{V6}6561. ^{15}3. Kurtis Lane Pleasants, b. 5 Feb 1978, Houston, Harris Co, TX; m. 4 June 1996 in Friendswood, TX, Stephanie Ann Mertz, b. 14 Jan 1978, Bryan, TX

^{V6}6562. ^{16}1. Leslie Ann Pleasants, b. 16 May 1996, Houston, TX

^{V6}6563. ^{16}2. Tyler James Pleasants, b. 7 Dec 1998, Winter Harbor, ME

^{V6}6564. ^{16}3. Trey Owen Pleasants, b. 9 June 2004, Waldorf, MD

^{V6}6565. ^{15}4. Robert Laurence Pleasants, b. 23 Dec 1989, Denver, CO

^{V6}6566. ^{14}3. Lonnie Dale Pleasants, b. 8 Aug 1949, Houston, Harris Co, TX

[V6]6567. [13]4. **Jeanette Brashear**, b. 8 May 1930, Houston, TX; m. 12 Sept 1947, ***Sam Matney***, b. 22 Jan 1925, s/o A. Matney and Nana ______

[V6]6568. [14]1. Michael Matney, b. 12 July 1949, Houston, TX

[V6]6569. [14]2. Mark Matney, b. 19 Nov 1960,

Carlton Dole Brashears and Malissie C. Sims

[v6]6472. [11]9. **Carlton Dole Brashears**, (s/o John M. Brashears and Nancy Clementine Treadwell), b. 23 Jan 1876, Angelina Co, TX (5 in 1880), d. 19 April 1914, in Bold Springs, Polk Co, TX, of pneumonia; m. 5 Nov 1900, in Angelina Co, TX, ***Malissie Claudine Sims***, b. 14 Nov 1879, d. 3 May 1973, Angelina Co, TX, d/o William Sims and Josephine Berry. Carlton moved his family to Bold Springs, TX in 1908, along with one of his wife's brothers and his family. They worked in a sawmill. After Carlton died, Malissie moved the family back to Lufkin, Angelina Co, TX.

Family of Carlton Dole Brashears and Malissie C. Sims:

[V6]6570. [12]1. **Esther Jackson Brashear**, b. 10 Aug 1901, d. 2 June 1983; m. 1923, ***Jessie "Fiddler" George***

[V6]6571. [13]1. Joyce Lanell George, b. 1927, d. 1996; m. Joe Lediker.

[V6]6572. [14]1. Joe Lediker, Jr, b. 1950

[V6]6573. [14]2. Kenneth Lediker, b. 1955

[V6]6574. [13]2. Nila Fay George, b. 1930, d. 1994; m. Jack Case

[V6]6575. [14]1. Jacquelyn Case, b. 1953

[V6]6576. [14]2. Mark Case, b. 1955

[V6]6577. [12]2. **Ollie Faye Brashear**, b. 20 March 1906, d. 9 Aug 1984; m.1. ***Percy Lalumandier***; m.2. 1946, ***Melton Campbell***

[V6]6578. [13]1. Claudia Lanell Lalumandier, b. 1940; m. 1960 Major Greene

[V6]6579. [14]1. Deidre Greene,

[V6]6580. [14]2. Taylor Greene,

[V6]6581. [12]3. **Carlton Dole Brashear Jr**, b. 21 Aug 1908, Bold Springs, Polk Co, TX, d. 10 March 1977, Angelina

Co, TX; m. 4 Sept 1938, in Lufkin, Angelina Co, TX, ***Pauline Durham***, b. 29 Sept 1911 in Angelina Co, TX, d/o George Durham and Erma Trammell.

V66582. [13]1. **Carla Kay Brashear**, b. 6 Jan 1951, Lufkin, Angelina Co, TX; m. 20 Oct 1973, in Lufkin, Angelina Co, TX, ***Danny Roth***, b. 11 Oct 1951, Panama City, Panama

V66583. [14]1. Jeffrey Todd Roth, b. 22 Aug 1975, Lufkin, TX

V66584. [14]2. Emily Rose Roth, b, 27 May 1979, Lufkin, TX

V66585. [14]3. Erin Elise Roth, b. 25 April 1982, Lufkin, TX

V66586. [14]4. Kayla Danielle Roth, b. 26 March 1986, Lufkin, TX

Artilla Mable Brashear and Ellie Jeptha Douglass

v66474. [11]11. **Artilla Mable "Cricket" Brashear**, (d/o John M. Brashears and Nancy Clementine Treadwell), b. 21 July 1880, Angelina Co, TX, d. 6 Sept 1966, Lufkin, Angelina Co, TX; m. c1899, in Trinity Co, TX, ***Ellie Jeptha Douglass***, b. 11 June 1854, MS, d. 11 Aug 1936, Lufkin, Angelina Co, TX, both bur Jonesville Cem, Huntington, Angelina Co, TX.

Family of Artilla M. Brashear and Ellie Jeptha Douglass:

V66587. [12]1. Atilla Mable Douglass, b. 31 Oct 1901, Corrigan, TX, d. 3 March 1992; m.1. Ollie Lee Parrott, b. 5 Jan 1897, Nacogdoches, TX, d. 28 Aug 1982, Diboll, TX, s/o Pryor Parrott and Eliza Eddings. Atilla and Ollie are buried at Garden of Memories, Lukfin, Angelina Co, TX.

V66588. [13]1. Eunice Irene Parrott, b. 6 Feb 1924, San Augustine, TX

V66589. [13]2. Delbert Willis Parrott, b. 18 April 1926, Broaddus, San Augustine Co, TX

V66590. [13]3. Edward Jackson Parrott, b. 10 June 1928, Broaddus, TX

V66591. [13]4. Buford Lee Parrott, b. 25 May 1930, Zavalla,

San Augustine Co, TX

^{V6}6592. ^{13}5. Grover Winfred Parrott, b. 7 July 1931, Zavalla, TX

^{V6}6593. ^{13}6. James Carl Parrott, b. 26 March 1934, Zavalla, TX

^{V6}6594. ^{12}2. Ellie Jeanette Douglass, b. 27 April 1911, Browndell, Jasper Co, TX, d. April 1987; m. William Riley Haygood

^{V6}6595. ^{13}1. Ben Thomas Haygood, m. 25 Aug 1967, in Mt Pleasant, Titus Co, TX, Nancy "Nan" Brown, d/o Joe Brown and Esther Johnson

^{V6}6596. ^{14}1. Paul Thomas Haygood,

^{V6}6597. ^{14}2. Ben David Haygood,

^{V6}6598. ^{13}2. Karen Dawn Haygood,

^{V6}6599. ^{13}3. Susan Jeanette Haygood,

^{V6}6600. ^{12}3. Stephen Presley "Doug" Douglass, b. 1 Jan 1913; m.1. Bonnie Barrington (1 ch; div); m.2. Dorothy ______

^{V6}6601. ^{13}1. Sharron Douglass,

JESSE MARION WALTER BRASHEAR and Frances Elizabeth Forest

^{v6}6432. ^{10}3. **Jesse Marion Walter "Walt" Brashear**, (s/o James M. Brashear and Mary Elizabeth "Lizzie" Maribe Jones), b. 26 Feb 1836, d. 30 Nov 1885, (says granddaughter, Buena; 1835-1896 says stone) bur Treadwell Cem, Huntington, TX; m. 8 Sept 1858, ***Frances Elizabeth "Lizzie" Forest***, b. April 1839 (per 1900 census), d. 27 April 1917 (1837-1917 says stone) bur Treadwell Cem, d/o Anthony H. Forest, b. 1820, SC, d. 26 Dec 1881, and Julia Ann Bozeman, b. 1817, d. 1879, m. 19 Oct 1833.

Jesse W. and Elizabeth Brassiers, 24 & 21, are hh #236, in 1860 Census, Angelina Co, TX, with Mary A. Brasher, age 1, and James Welch, 40, b. SC, in the household. Walter (sometimes copied as "Nathan") and Lizzie Brashears are hh #167/41 in 1870 Census, Angelina Co, TX, with children Annie, Lizzie, Samuel, and Marthie. They are hh 246/269 in the 1880 Census, Angelina Co, TX, with children Lizzie through Cubie.

Jesse served in Co. D, 7th Regiment, Texas Mounted Cavalry, Confederate States Army, and the 3rd Regiment (Sibley's Brigade). He enrolled for service 12 Nov 1861 and was mustered into service, 2 Dec 1861 at San Antonio, TX. He was first in the 22nd Texas Infantry, but transferred to the cavalry, 1 Jan 1863. He was captured 14 April 1863 at Bayou Teche, Louisiana, and was a prisoner of war for one year. He rose to the rank of Corporal.

On 21 Sept 1899, Elizabeth F. Brashears received a Confederate Widows pension; she was living at Homer, Angelina Co, Texas. The papers give her marriage date to Jesse, his death date, etc. She died 27 April 1917, in the home of her son, R.C. Brashears.

<u>Family of Jesse Marion Walter Brashear and Frances Elizabeth Forest</u>:

[V6]6602. [11]1. **Mary Annie Brashear**, b. 4 June 1859, Jonesville, Angelina Co, TX, d. 28 Dec 1900, Huntington, Angelina Co, TX; m.1. ***Bennie Shofner***; m.2. 3 Sept 1876, in Jonesville, Angelina Co, TX, ***James A. "Jacob" Spidle***, b. c1857; m.3. 11 March 1881, ***Steve D. Stevens***, b. Jan 1838, Alabama.

[V6]6603. [12]1. A. Spidle, b. 1877; m. Agee ______ . Ch: Dewitt and Agee Spidle.

[V6]6604. [12]2. W.A. “Cap” Spidle,

[V6]6605. [12]3. Dewitt Spidle,

[V6]6606. [12]4. Jesse Stevens, b. July 1882

[V6]6607. [12]5. Villus V. Stevens, b. Dec 1884

[V6]6608. [12]6. Payton Stevens, b. Jan 1888

[V6]6609. [12]7. Douglas Stevens, b. July 1890

[V6]6610. [12]8. Hester Stevens, b. 1892; m. ______ Chism

[V6]6611. [12]9. Hal Stevens, b. April 1895

[V6]6612. [12]10. Clidia Belle Stevens, b. Nov 1898

[V6]6613. [12]11. Mae Stevens, (not in some researchers’ lists)

[V6]6614. [11]2. **Elizabeth W. "Lizzie" Brashear**, b. 3 Nov 1862, Jonesville, Angelina Co, TX, d. before 1900; m. 24 Sept 1881, in Angelina Co, TX, ***James Alford "Jim" Sowell***, b. c1860

[V6]6615. [12]1. James Blackburn Sowell,

[V6]6616. [12]2. Walter Evans Sowell, killed, World War II

^{V6}6617. ^{12}3. George Monroe Sowell,

^{V6}6618. ^{11}3. **Samuel M. Brashear**, b. 23 June 1867 (per 1900 census), Jonesville, Angelina Co, TX; m. ***Martha Williams***, b. Jan 1869, TX (per 1900 Census). They are hh #252 in 1900 Angelina Co, TX, with four children.

^{V6}6619. ^{12}1. **George Custer Brashear**, b. Aug 1891, TX

^{V6}6620. ^{12}2. **Elizabeth Brashear**, b. March 1894, TX

^{V6}6621. ^{12}3. **Bryan Brashear**, b. Sept 1897, TX (lived at Humble, TX, in 1935-6)

^{V6}6622. ^{12}4. **Alma Norma Brashear**, b. Sept 1899; m. ***Walter Diehl***

^{V6}6623. ^{11}4. **Martha Jane "Mattie" Brashear**, b. 30 May 1869, Jonesville, Angelina Co, TX, d. 1886 at age 16, bur Treadwell Cem, Huntington, Angelina Co, TX

^{V6}6624. ^{11}5. ***Robert Calvin "R.C." Brashear, II**, b. 6 Nov 1871, Jonesville, Angelina Co, TX, d. 4 March 1948, bur Old Center Cem, Lufkin, TX; m.1. ***Jennie Elizabeth McMullen***, b. Feb 1878, TX (3 ch), d. 1906; m.2. ***Pearl Eliza Wade*** (6 ch), d/o _____ Wade and Mary Adelia Mollie Crow, b. 12 Nov 1851, San Augustine Co, TX, d/o James M. Crow, b. 1 Jan 1818, TN, d. San Augustine Co, Texas; see below.

^{V6}6625. ^{11}6. **Georgia A. Brashear**, b. 18 Feb 1874 ("George W." "son" in 1880), Jonesville, Angelina Co, TX, d. 1973, Woodsboro, Refugio Co, TX; m. 22 Jan 1890, in Angelina Co, TX, ***Robert L. Warren***, b. c1859, d. 1929

^{V6}6626. ^{12}1. Gordon L. Warren, b. 1893, d. 1992

^{V6}6627. ^{12}2. Chester Warren, b. 1895, d. 1964

^{V6}6628. ^{12}3. Doris Warren, b. 1909, d. 1993. Doris lived in San Antonio, TX

^{V6}6629. ^{11}7. ***William Anthony "Gus" Brashear**, b. 23 Jan 1877, Homer, Angelina Co, TX, d. 28 April 1941,Beaumont, Jefferson Co, TX; bur Ingleside, TX; m. ***Georgia Augusta Scarborough***, b. 24 April 1888

^{V6}6630. ^{11}8. **Cuba F. Brashear**, b. 11 Dec 1880, Homer, Angelina Co, TX, d. Kenton, Cimmaron Co, OK;

m.1. c1903, ***Will Wasson***, m.2. after 1904, ***Henry Hood***,

V66631. [12]1. Ben Hood, b. 13 April 1911
V66632. [12]2. Ellen Hood, b. 1915, d. 4 Aug 1915

Robert Calvin Brashear, II, and Jennie McMullen/ Pearl Wade

v66624. [11]5. **Robert Calvin "R.C." Brashear, II**, (named after an uncle; s/o Jesse Marion Walter Brashears and Frances Elizabeth Forest), b. 11 Nov 1871, in Jonesville, Angelina Co, TX, d. 4 March 1948, bur Old Center Cem, Lufkin, Angelina Co, TX; m.1. 17 Jan 1895, in Angelina Co, TX, ***Jennie Elizabeth McMullen***, b. Feb 1878, TX (3 ch), d. 1906, bur Old Center Cem, Lufkin, TX, d/o William Thomas McMullen and Josephine Mathews; m.2. after 1906, in Angelina Co, TX, ***Pearl Eliza Wade*** (6 ch), R.C. and Jennie are hh #257 in 1900 census, Angelina Co, TX, with daughter, "Buna." Also in hh, Elizabeth Brashear, b. April 1838, AL, apparently his mother.

Family of R.C. Brashear II and Jennie Elizabeth McMullen:

V66633. [12]1. **Buena Vesta Brashear**, b. 27 March 1898, TX (per 1900 Census), d. 19 June 1985, TX; m. ______ ***Thorpe***,
V66634. [13]1. June Thorpe,
V66635. [12]2. **Eula Brashears**, b. 4 March 1900, TX, d. 22 Feb 1901
V66636. [12]3. ***Robert Calvin Brashear Jr (III)**, b. 13 June 1902, Angelina Co, TX, d. 12 Dec 1956, Lufkin, Angelina Co, TX, bur Old Center Cem, Lufkin, TX; m. ***Mississippi Millenium "Missie" Hubbard***, b. 2 Oct 1900,
V66637. [12]4. **Ruby Gordon Brashear**, b. 11 April 1906, TX, d. 29 Aug 1985, TX (raised by her grandmother McMullen); m. ______ ***Emanuel***,
V66638. [13]1. Maxine Emanuel,
V66639. [13]2. Travis Reece Emanuel,

Children of R.C. Brashear II and Pearl Eliza Wade:

V66640. 125. **Memory Caulie Brashear**, b. 3 June 1908, d. 4 Sept 1995, Angelina Co, TX; m. ***Clemmie H. Hubbard***, bur Rocky Spring Cem, Angelina Co, TX

V66641. 126. **Cue B. Brashear**, b. 7 Sept 1912, Angelina Co, TX, d. 20 Sept 1979, Angelina Co, TX, bur Rocky Springs Cem, Angelina Co, TX

V66642. 127. **Minnie Lee Brashear**, b. 3 Dec 1914, Angelina Co, TX, d. 2 Nov 1988, Crockett, Houston Co, TX; m.1. ______ ***Roberts***; m.2. ______ ***Clark***.

V66643. 131. Patsy Roberts,

V66644. 128. **John Curtis Brashear**, b. 1920, d. 1976, Angelina Co, TX; was a Private First Class in World War II

V66645. 129. **Weldon Elizabeth Brashear**, m. ***Kyle Alexander***,

V66646. 1210. **Andrew Boyce Brashear**, b. 29 June 1926, d. 20 Oct 2000

V66647. 13x. **Linda Brashear**, b. _____ 1956; m. ______ ***Matteauer***,

Robert Calvin Brashear, III, and Mississippi Hubbard

v66636. 123. **Robert Calvin Brashear Jr (III)**, (s/o Robert Calvin Brashear, II, and Jennie Elizabeth McMullen), b. 13 June 1902, Angelina Co, TX, d. 12 Dec 1956, Lufkin, Angelina Co, TX, bur Old Center Cem, Lufkin, TX; m. ***Mississippi Millenium "Missie" Hubbard***, b. 2 Oct 1900, in Mississippi, d. 21 Dec 1977 in Lufkin, Angelina Co, TX, d/o William Hubbard, and Anna Kirkpatrick.

Family of Robert Calvin Brashear, III, and Mississippi Hubbard:

V66648. 131. **Dr. Doyle Hubbard Brashear**, b. 13 June 1924; m. ***Agnes Barbara Tuinistra***,

V66649. 141. **Barbara Anne Brashear**, b. 2 April 1947; m. ***Jack Davis***,

V66650. 151. Jason Todd Davis, b. 24 Aug 1971

V66651. 152. Erin Elizabeth Davis, b. 4 Aug 1975

V66652. 142. **Richard Dale Brashear**, b. 26 Dec 1949; m. ***Elke Johnson***,

V66653. 151. **Katherine Marie Brashear**, b. 10 June 1978

V66654. 143. **Michael Jay Brashear**, b. 31 Aug 1951; m.

Karen Eidson,

^{V6}6655. ^{15}1. **John Austin Brashear**, b. 25 June 1982

^{V6}6656. ^{15}2. **Ryon Clark Brashear**, b. 10 Aug 1987

^{V6}6657. ^{14}4. **Steven Paul Brashear**, b. 17 June 1973

^{V6}6658. ^{14}5. **Daniel Keith Brashear**, b. 8 Aug 1956; m. ***Nancy Bolze***,

^{V6}6659. ^{15}1. **Kaitlyn Amber Brashear**, b. 18 March 1995

^{V6}6660. ^{13}2. **Jennie Nell Brashear**, b. 14 Oct 1926; m. ***Patrick Caton***, no children.

^{V6}6661. ^{13}3. **Claudette Marie Brashear**, b. 1 Sept 1936, m. ***Byron Lynn Beaird***, b. 14 June 1936, Doucett, TX.

^{V6}6662. ^{14}1. Jennifer Beaird, (twin) b. 7 Aug 1961; m. Brian Kempton,

^{V6}6663. ^{15}1. Matthew Brian Kempton, b. 13 Aug 1983

^{V6}6664. ^{15}2. Lindsey Marie Kempton, b. 23 Sept 1984

^{V6}6665. ^{15}3. Jake Beaird Kempton, b. 20 May 1986

^{V6}6666. ^{15}4. David Andrew Kempton, b. 7 March 1989

^{V6}6667. ^{15}5. Hillary Ann Kempton, b. 9 Sept 1991

^{V6}6668. ^{14}2. Jeanette Beaird, (twin) b. 7 Aug 1961; m. John Taylor,

^{V6}6669. ^{15}1. Ashley Marie Taylor, b. 18 Sept 1990

^{V6}6670. ^{15}2. Briana Lee Taylor, b. 22 Feb 1992

^{V6}6671. ^{15}3. Rachel Lynn Taylor, b. 15 March 1994

^{V6}6672. ^{14}3. Randall Carter Beaird, b. 2 Jan 1963; m. Angie Sullivan,

^{V6}6673. ^{14}4. Melanie Beaird, b. 1 Feb 1964; m. Ken Ellsworth,

^{V6}6674. ^{15}1. Paige Ellsworth, b. 9 Sept 1986

^{V6}6675. ^{15}2. Audrey Ellsworth, b. 22 Sept 1988

^{V6}6676. ^{15}3. Brenn Ellsworth, b. 9 May 1991

^{V6}6677. ^{15}4. Shelby Ellsworth, b. 28 March 1994

^{V6}6678. ^{14}5. Melissa Beaird, b. 22 Jan 1965

^{V6}6679. ^{14}6. Jason Douglas Beaird, b. 6 Oct 1968; m. Jordan Peterson,

^{V6}6680. ^{13}4. **Dorris Jean Brashear**, b. 14 March 1938; m. ***Richard Arnold Collmorgen Sr***,

^{V6}6681. ^{14}1. Richard Arnold Collmorgen Jr, b. 2 Feb 1964; m. Leslie Moore.

V6 6682. [14]2. David Ross Collmorgen, b. 2 March 1966; m. Angie McClendon,

V6 6683. [15]1. Clayton Ross Collmorgen, b. 27 May 1994

V6 6684. [14]3. Joseph Todd Collmorgen, b. 28 Feb 1967; m. Robin Goodwin,

William Anthony Brashear and Georgia Scarborough

v6 6629. [11]7. **William Anthony Brashear**, (s/o Jesse Marion Walter Brashears and Frances Elizabeth Forest), b. 23 Jan 1877 at Huntington, Angelina Co, TX, d. 28 April 1946, in Beaumont, Jefferson Co, TX, bur. Ingleside, San Patricio Co, TX (near Corpus Christi); m. 10 April 1904, in Angelina Co, TX, ***Georgia Augusta Scarborough***, b. 24 April 1888, in Huntington, Angelina Co, TX, d. 19 March 1968 in Palestine, Anderson Co, TX, bur. Palestine, Anderson Co, TX, d/o William Bascom Scarborough and Lucretia Collins.

Family of William Anthony Brashear and Georgia Augusta Scarborough (data from Steve Riddle (sriddle@inx.net) to Larry Pleasants):

V6 6685. [12]1. **Robert Doyle Brashear**, b. 15 Nov 1905 at Atoka, Coleman Co, TX, d. 9 May 1978, Ingleside, TX, bur Prairie View Cem, Aransas Pass, San Patricio Co, TX; m.1. ***Evelyn Payne***, d. 29 July 1950 (no children); m.2. ***Jimmie Crenshaw***, b. 6 Dec 1926, d/o William Jackson Crenshaw, b. 19 June 1889, d. 21 Oct 1980, and Etha Bert Wood, b. 31 Oct 1895, d. 5 Sept 1967. Jimmie (Crenshaw) Brashear m.2. Damon Brickley; they lived at Ingleside, TX.

V6 6686. [13]1. **Susan Leigh Brashear**, b. 12 July 1952 at Corpus Christi, Nueces Co, TX; m. 14 Sept 1980, ***Will Marchetti***, b. 11 Nov 1933, San Francisco, CA, s/o Guilermo Marchetti and Renatta Carzella

V6 6687. [14]1. Robert Mario Marchetti, b. 18 July 1981

V6 6688. 12 2. **Bonnie Elizabeth Brashear**, b. 15 Sept 1907, d. 29 Nov 1974, m. ***Harry Death***,
V6 6689. 12 3. **Lelia Nell Brashears**, b. 29 Nov 1915, d. 27 Nov 1987, m. ***John Anderson***,
V6 6690. 13 1. Gladys Ann Anderson, b. 1953; m. ______ Fox, lives Tyler, TX
V6 6691. 12 4. **William "Bill" Walker Brashear**, b. 24 Sept 1923; m. ***Marjorie "Marge" Massey***,
V6 6692. 13 1. **Robert "Bob" Brashear**, b. 28 Aug 1958; m. Kim ______ ,
V6 6693. 14 1. **Christopher Weston Brashears**, b. 22 March 2000
V6 6694. 13 3. **Rebecca "Becky" Brashear**, b. 29 March 1962
V6 6695. 12 5. **Mayme Elaine Brashear**, b. 9 Oct 1925; m.1. ***Joe French***, m.2. ***Charles Fister***,
V6 6696. 13 1. William Brashear French, b. 22 May 1953
V6 6697. 12 6. **Harold Eugene Brashear**, b. 29 May 1927, d. 1992

LUCINDA MARIE BRASHEARS and James S. Neyland

v6 6433. 10 4. **Lucinda Marie Brashears**, (d/o James M. "Jim" Brashears and Mary Elizabeth Maribe Jones), b. 15 Feb 1838, Old Royal Colony, White Co, AR (12 in 1850), d. 16 Jan 1918, Redland Community, Leon Co, TX; m. 31 May 1858, in Angelina Co, TX, ***James Smiley Neyland***, b. 2 Oct 1838, Amite Co, MS, d. 1 Sept 1921, Centerville, Leon Co, TX, s/o John Neyland and Elizabeth Owens. They lived in Freestone Co, TX, at least 1870-1874 (census and tax lists); by 1880, they had moved to Leon Co, TX, and are buried in Centerville. James S. Neyland was a preacher. Four children in 1870 census, Freestone Co, TX; one had died, others were born later:

Family of Lucinda Marie Brashears and James S. Neyland:

V6 6698. 11 1. James Lewis Neyland, b. 10 May 1859, Jonesville, Angelina Co, TX, d. 19 Jan 1948, Bowling, Leon Co, TX; m. Frances Eldora Winn, b. 30 Oct 1864,

d. 1 Feb 1949, Bowling, Leon Co, TX.

^{V6}6699. ^{12}1. Eva Agnes Neyland, m. George Washington Wilkerson. 9 ch:

^{V6}6700. ^{13}1. Reba Wilkerson, m. ______ Broussard;

^{V6}6701. ^{13}2. Dovie Wilkerson, m. ______ Hathorn;

^{V6}6702. ^{13}3. Winnie Wilkerson, m. ______ Livingston;

^{V6}6703. ^{13}4. Lewis Wilkerson;

^{V6}6704. ^{13}5. R.L. Wilkerson;

^{V6}6705. ^{13}6. Dewitt Wilkerson;

^{V6}6706. ^{13}7. R.V. Wilkerson, m. Jackie ______

^{V6}6707. ^{14}1. Burlon Wilkerson, m. Jan ______ (ch: Trey; Krista; and Melanie Wilkerson)

^{V6}6708. ^{14}2. Lanny Wilkerson,

^{V6}6709. ^{14}3. Reidel Wilkerson,

^{V6}6710. ^{13}9. C.L. Wilkerson;

^{V6}6711. ^{13}10. "Van" Wilkerson.

^{V6}6712. ^{12}2. Ina Neyland, b.?, d. Winters, TX; m. Will Robinson,

^{V6}6713. ^{12}3. Robert Ennis Neyland, m. Mattie Burney. 6 ch:

^{V6}6714. ^{13}1. Vela Ozelle Neyland, m. Audrey Neal Todd

^{V6}6715. ^{14}1. Jackie Ann Todd, m. Marion Maness. (Ch: Jeri Lynne; Derek Thomas; and Kenric Neil Maness)

^{V6}6716. ^{13}2. Roger Ennis Neyland, m. Mattie Jo Cundriff;

^{V6}6717. ^{13}3. Thelma Lee Neyland, m. Cecil Beeler;

^{V6}6718. ^{13}4. FannieLou Neyland, m. Reece Price;

^{V6}6719. ^{13}5. Mattie Margaritte Neyland, m. Cleatus Embray;

^{V6}6720. ^{13}6. Robbie Jo Neyland, m. William Lowell Gregg

^{V6}6721. ^{12}4. Leonard Vivian Neyland, m. Minnie Powell. 4 ch:

^{V6}6722. ^{13}1. Lou Ila Neyland, m. Mullard Klute;

^{V6}6723. ^{13}2. Lela Mae Neyland; m. Frank T. Cook;

^{V6}6724. ^{13}3. Gladys Vivian Neyland;

^{V6}6725. ^{13}4. Gertrude Neyland, m. James Whitacre

(ch: Jimmie Lea Whitacre, m. Plemon Nerron)

^{V6}6726. ^{12}5. Erma Dewitt Neyland, m. Reba Faison. 2 ch: Curtis and James Lewis, III,

^{V6}6727. ^{12}6. Cuvier Curtis Neyland,

^{V6}6728. ^{12}7. Nettie Bertha Neyland, b. 19 Dec 1887, d. 1 Jan 1976; m.1. Allan McCormick; m.2. Lee Wall; m.3. Will Sheve; m.4. Watson Comer

^{V6}6729. ^{12}8. Winnie Ida Neyland, b. 3 March 1896, m. Claude Payne. 6 ch:

^{V6}6730. ^{13}1. J.C. Payne, m. Mary Lauchlan;

^{V6}6731. ^{13}2.Frances Victoria Payne; m. Alvin Duncan;

^{V6}6732. ^{13}3. Nettie Kathleen Payne, m. Ray Wadsworth;

^{V6}6733. ^{13}4. Mary Evelyn Payne, m. Henry Hoke;

^{V6}6734. ^{13}5. Joy Laquita Payne, m. Herman Smith;

^{V6}6735. ^{13}6. Donald Keith Payne, m. Rita Joy Turner.

^{V6}6736. ^{11}2. Julia M. Neyland, b. May 1859 (probably twin to James Lewis), d. 29 July 1863, Angelina Co, TX

^{V6}6737. ^{11}3. Robert Lee Neyland, b. 26 May 1866, Jonesville, Angelina Co, TX, d. 5 Nov 1954, Leon Co, TX; m.1. Nettie Caroline Reed, (8 ch) b. 1871, Leon Co, TX, d. 1908, d/o William Reed and Nettie ______ ; m.2. Mary Susie Porter Price (4 ch)

^{V6}6738. ^{12}1. Alva Reed Neyland (twin)

^{V6}6739. ^{12}2. ______ Neyland,

^{V6}6740. ^{12}3. Robert Thaddeus Neyland, b. 21 Dec 1889; m. Amana Holliman. 3 ch:

^{13}1. Nettie Elizabeth Neyland, m. Jesse Posey;

^{13}2. Robbie Azeoll Neyland, m. Maple Pollard;

^{13}3. William Howell Neyland, m. Tina Perez

^{V6}6741. ^{12}4. Lola Esther Neyland, b. 3 June 1892, Leon Co, TX; m. Leonard Clyde Wall. 5 ch:

^{V6}6742. ^{13}1. Valda Opal Wall, m. Carl Hardee;

^{V6}6743. ^{13}2. Henry Lois Wall, m. Morris Hayrie;

^{V6}6744. ^{13}3. Wyman Ben Wall, m. Ruby Gertrude Bryant Davis;

^{V6}6745. ^{13}4. Margie Lee Wall, m.1. Harvey Walker, m.2. Ben J. Ellison;

[V6]6746. [13]5. Leonard Clyde Wall Jr, m. Grace Reynolds

[V6]6747. [12]5. Lucy Annie Neyland, b. 14 Nov 1894; m. B.J. Simpson. 3 ch:

[V6]6748. [13]1.Elsie Ray Simpson, m. Jack Shuffler; ch:

[V6]6749. [14]1. Dorothy Nell Shuffler; m.1. Monte Backwell, m.2. Conner Schillin;

[V6]6750. [14]2. Waldo Shuffler, m.1. Judy ______; m.2. Mary ______ ; m.3. Virginia Knight;

[V6]6751. [14]3. Benny Kenneth Shuffler, m.1. Judy ______, m.2. Eva ______ , m.3. Barbara ______ ;

[V6]6752. [14]4. Janice Larue Shuffler, m.1. Carleton ______ , m.2. John Anderson

[V6]6753. [13]2. Willie Merle Simpson, m.1. Warren Shuffler, m.2. George T. Wilkerson;

[V6]6754. [13]3. Joe B. Simpson, m. Doris Shive

[V6]6755. [12]6. Bessie Neyland, bur Centerville Cem, Leon Co, TX

[V6]6756. [12]7. Willie Ella Neyland, b. 8 June 1897, d. 8 Aug 1979, Palestine, TX; m. Herman Wallace Wilkerson, b. 19 March 1895, d. 1979. 4 ch:

[V6]6757. [13]1. Robert Cameron Wilkerson, m. Lou Evedyne Andrews;

[V6]6758. [14]1. Luann Wilkerson, m. Roger Valentine

[V6]6759. [13]2. Mary Jo Wilkerson, m. Weyman Earl Martin, (ch: Mary Joyce; Rebecca Sue; Weyman Earl, Jr);

[V6]6760. [13]3. Alice Joyce Wilkerson. m. Claude Marcus Kolb, (ch: Claudia Jean; Linda Joyce; Nancy Marie; and Joseph Wallace Kolb);

[V6]6761. [13]4. Wallace Reed Wilkerson, m. June Marshall. Ch: Marshall Reed Wilkerson; Amy Wilkerson

[V6]6762. [12]8. Jewell Hester Neyland, b. 21 July 1901; m. Jeff Davis Posey. 4 ch:

[V6]6763. [13]1. Ellen Louise Posey, m. B.W. Ratliff; ch: Vicky Bryonette Ratliff; Gary Wayne

Ratliff

[V6]6764. [13]2. Arnold Davis Posey, m. Rachel Harp; ch: Frank Anthony; Monte Lewis; Debra Ann; Cynthia Kay; Sheila; and Patsy Diane Posey.

[V6]6765. [13]3. Jeffie Nell Posey, m. Glenn Smith; ch: Gregory Tyson; and Randall Troy Smith

[V6]6766. [13]4. Patricia Ann Posey m.1. Robert E. Pendleton, Jr, m.2. Tommy Sandell. Ch: Robert E. Pendleton, III; and Jennifer Paige Pendleton; Tommy Chad Sandell; and James Courtney Sandell

[V6]6767. [12]9. Ruby Ella Neyland,

[V6]6768. [12]10. Eula Mae Neyland, m. Austin Lawrence Jenkins. 1 ch:

[V6]6769. [13]1. Betty Jean Jenkins, m. L.A. Watson; ch: Larry Thomas Watson; Billy Lynn Watson; Sandra Gail Watson; Kenneth Wayne Watson; and Donnie Gene Watson

[V6]6770. [12]11. James Rarden Neyland; m.1. Mary McFachern (no ch); m.2. Velma Olene Hodges (3 ch):

[V6]6771. [13]1. Charles Wayne Neyland, m. Betty Belle Barker; ch: Brett Wayne Neyland

[V6]6772. [13]2. James Elwyn Neyland, m. Elien Jane Raphael; ch: Douglas Bryan Neyland; and Laura Meredith Neyland

[V6]6773. [13]3. Robert Stephen Neyland, m. Holly Jean Scholles. Ch: Genevieve Marie Neyland

[V6]6774. [12]12. John Lewis Neyland, II, (named for an uncle); m.1. Frances Cundiff (no ch); m.2. Audrey Faye Hardin (no ch); m.3. Margaret Kerbo Hardin, 4 ch:

[V6]6775. [13]1. Janet Louise Neyland, m. James Lawrence Walker;

[V6]6776. [13]2. Lynda Kay Neyland, m. David Wayne Martin; ch: Kimberly Kay Martin

[V6]6777. [13]3. Marcy Sue Neyland, m. Robert Langham Conner;

V6 6778. 13 4. John Lewis Neyland, III.
V6 6779. 11 4. Cora C. Neyland, b. 23 Sept 1868, d. 11 Feb 1947, Leon Co, TX; m. William Evans, both bur Centerville Cem, Leon Co, TX
V6 6780. 12 1. Willard T. Evans, m. Necie Ethridge. 3 ch: Esther; Dewie; Irene
V6 6781. 12 2. Herman T. Evans, m. Eula Etheridge. Ch: Travis
V6 6782. 12 3. Herbert Evans, m. Gonima Ansley. Ch: Roger
V6 6783. 12 4. Bernard Evans,
V6 6784. 12 5. Mamie Rebecca Evans, m. Pleas Ethridge. 2 ch: Alford; Eloise
V6 6785. 12 6. Lydia Josephine Evans, m. Will Hullam. Ch: J.B. Hullam
V6 6786. 11 5. Laura M. Neyland, b. 5 June 1870, TX, d. 17 June 1946; m. 21 Nov 1899 Flournoy Montgomery Simms,
V6 6787. 12 1. Maime Gertrude Simms, m. Gerald Reed,
V6 6788. 12 2. Ethel Simms, m. Thomas C. Ellis,
V6 6789. 12 3. Myrtle Simms, m. Russell C. Ellis,
V6 6790. 12 4. ______ Simms, d. at birth
V6 6791. 12 5. James Lee Simms, m. Eunice Dezelle,
V6 6792. 12 6. Albert Neyland Simms, m. Estelle Dezelle,
V6 6793. 12 7. William Thomas Simms, m.1. Letha Elizabeth Thomas; m.2. Lorene Artilla Craddock,
V6 6794. 11 6. Elizabeth Neyland, b. 7 Nov 1873, d. 8 Nov 1873
V6 6795. 11 7. Ina Neyland, b. 6 Oct 1875, TX, d. 8 Nov 1975, TX
V6 6796. 11 8. Fannie Eugenia Neyland, b. 9 July 1881, TX, d. 30 Aug 1960, Harris Co, TX; m. 3 Dec 1899, in Leon Co, TX, Ira Luke Dickey,
V6 6797. 12 1. Oma Dickey, m.1. Leslie Dean; m.2. ______ Burnett,
V6 6798. 12 2. Grace Dickey, m. ______ Tarpley,
V6 6799. 12 3. Clive Dickey, m. ______ Satterwhite,
V6 6800. 12 4. Ernest Dickey, m. ______ . 5 ch: Card Watson; Clive; Bonna, m. Rex Ellis; Marti Watson; and Michelle Dickey

Contacts: Ronald R. McClendon, 5712 Sweetwater, N.W., Albuquerque, NM 87120

Jimmie Brashear, P.O.Drawer M, Ingleside, TX 78362
Pat Welch, 131 Roderick Drive, St. Louis, MO 63137; 314/867-1536
Dr. Doyle H. Brashear, 1226 Ellis, Lufkin, TX 75901; 409/634-5344
Claudette (Brashear) Beaird, 103 Highpoint Dr, Bullard, TX 75757
Boyce Brashear, Rt 1, Box 1142, Cherino, TX 75937: 409/362-2314
Linda (Brashear) Metteauer, Box 32, Cherino, TX 75937; 409/362-2990
William W. Brashear, 1317 Ponderosa Pine Lane, Carrollton, TX 75007; 972/492-9236; brashear1@home.com
Larry Pleasants <lcp47@aol.com>

Some Texas Strays:

M.E. Brashear, b. 29 Sept 1853, d. 4 May 1908, bur Ryan Chapel Cem, between Diboll and Burke, Angelina Co, TX
Tolbert Brashears, b. Dec 1873, TX, parents b. AL (boarder in hh #644-651, Josephine Simms and family, in 1900 Census, Angelina Co, TX, with 5 others). Some researchers say he is a son of John M. Brashears and Nancy Clementine Treadwell, but he does not appear in any of the family censuses.
Elmore Brashears, b. 29 Dec 1897, d. 17 May 1967, bur Fielder Cem, Homer, Angelina Co, TX

(? Death Cert. #47784, Angelina Co, TX: **Doyle Brashears**, d. 30 Oct 1936.)
(? Death Cert. #12258, Angelina Co, TX: **John C. Brashears**, d. 24 March 1936.)

Arthur Brashear Jr, m. in Freestone Co, TX, ***Marjorie Miller***, d/o Randall Miller and Katherine Talbot

(re: Stephanie Tally-Frost, *Cemetery Records of Leon Co, TX*, 1967, p.81)
C.P. Brashear,* b. 23 March 1846, d. 10 March 1913, bur

Evan's Chapel Cem, Leon Co, TX

J.B. Brashear,* b. 24 Aug 1836, d. 18 Nov 1904, bur Evan's Chapel Cem, Leon Co, TX

James E. Brashear*, b. 6 Nov 1871, d. 3 Feb 1903, bur Evan's Chapel Cem, Leon Co, TX

Violet Brashear, b. 29 Sept 1901, d. 7 Jan 1906, bur Evan's Chapel Cem, Leon Co, TX

C.G. Brashear, b. 12 Aug 1898, d. 1 Sept 1957, bur Hopewell Cem, Leon Co, TX

Billy L. Brashear, b. & d. after 1900, bur Hopewell Cem, Leon Co, TX

Tommy Brashear, b. & d. after 1900, bur Hopewell Cem, Leon Co, TX

The J.B. Brashear, b. 1836, above, is John B. Brashear, s/o George Washington Brashear and his wife, Candace Pierson, of Crawford Co, IL, who moved from Crawford Co, IL to Leon Co, TX c1840-42. C.P. Brashear, b. 1846, above, was his wife; they were married in 1868.

James E. Brashear, 1871, is another son of George Washington Brashear, who was a son of Ithra Brashear Sr, of Spartanburg Co, SC; Christian Co, KY; and Crawford Co, IL. See new vol 7 for data on these families.

The others in the list above are unidentified.

INDEX

Note: I have made an effort to index names as they appear in documents. Where the surname is spelled in more than one way, e.g. both Brashear and Brashears in the same document, you will find that person indexed both ways. Also, check under variant spellings for the object of your search: Breshear(s), Boshears, Beshears, Brasher, Brashers, Brashier(s), etc.

Boshers

ISBN 0-933362-17-x

APPENDIX (some advertisements for my books)

Plan for a 9-volume "A BRASHEAR(S) FAMILY HISTORY"

by **Charles Brashear**
1718 Arroyo Sierra Circle
Santa Rosa, CA 95405-7762
e-mail: brashear@mail.sdsu.edu
phone: 707/545-3903

I am and have been for 40-something years actively engaged in research on the Brashear(s) Family, in all its branches, in all spellings of the surname. Some years ago, Troy Back and Leon Brashear gave me their blessing and permission to "update" their book, *THE BRASHEAR STORY, A FAMILY HISTORY*, but the more data I collected, the more I realized that this family history will never again fit into one volume, especially if you include the amount and kind of detail that I like to include. I now have published six of a planned nine volumes.

Vol 1. ***The First 200 Years of Brashear(s) in America*** *and Some Descendants in Maryland* (this one was published in Nov 1998 and is still available at $35 for hardcover, $25 for paperback, plus $3 postage and packaging; CA residents add 8% sales tax. See also pricing schedule, below.)

Vol 2. ***Robert C. Brashear of North Carolina*** *and Some Descendants in TN, KY, MO, TX, etc.* (Published 1 Sep 1999. Available only in hardback. $35, plus $3 p&p and 8% CA tax, if applicable.)

Vol 3. ***Robert Samuel Brashear(s)*** *and Some Descendants in TN and KY* (Published early in 2001; $40, plus $3 p&p and CA tax, if applicable.

Vol 4. ***Brashear(s) Families of the Ohio Valley*** (Published 20 April 2002. 676 pages (xx + 576) with a 59-page index, about 50 pictures, and 7 maps. $40 + $3 p&p and CA tax, if applicable.)

Vol 5. ***Two Brashear(s) Families of the Lower Mississippi Valley*** *and their Choctaw and Other Descendants.* (Published in 2002, 700 pages, including introduction, index, pictures, maps, etc; $40 + $3p&p and CA tax, if applicable.)

Vol 6. ***Brashears/ Breshears Families of TN, MO, ID, WA, OK, etc*** *including Beshears, Boshears and Other Descendants.* (The data for Vol 6 got so big, I had to divide the book. This "half" is close to 700 pages and was published in Dec, 2004, with about 100 pictures, 8 maps and scanned documents; $40 + $3 p&p and CA tax, if applicable.)

Vol 7. ***Brashears Families of SC, MO, IL, etc.*** (This one will include William Brashears and Sarah _____ of Spartanburg, SC, and their sons, William Brashears (m. Mary Elizabeth Clayton) of MO and Ithra Brashears (m. Hannah Elizabeth Middleton) of Crawford Co, IL; Scott and Campbell Co, TN Boshears Families; and Jeremiah and Isaac Beshears of Christian and Hopkins Co, KY.

Vol 8. ***Brashear(s) Families West of the Mississippi River*** (Have been collecting chapters for this one, but it's not very well formed yet. My family will finally get its space in this one!!)

Vol 9. ***Brashear Additions, Corrections, Strays, and Non-Brashear(s) Families*** (Plenty of stray data, and plenty of non-Brashears families; the problem is how to organize it all. And then who would want it? Send your data anyway; I'm keeping files as if I wanted to print a volume of miscellaneous data.)

Order published books from me: Charles Brashear, 1718 Arroyo Sierra Circle, Santa Rosa, CA 95405-7762 (please add $3 postage and packaging for the first book, $1 each for each additional book sent to the same address at the same time; CA residents add 8% sales tax). **Please do not** order books that have not yet been published.

Prices are as follows; CA residents please add 8% sales tax
vol. 1 (hardback)$38 ($35 + $3 p&p)
vol. 1 (paperback)$28 ($25 + $3 p&p)
vol. 2 (hardback only) $38 ($35 + $3 p&p)
. . . . . (v.1 hardback & v.2 together$65 + $5 p&p)
vol. 3 (hardback only) $43 ($40 + $3 p&p)
. . . . . (v.1, 2, & 3 together$100 + $5 p&p)
vol. 4 (hardback only) $43 ($40 + $3 p&p)
. . . . . (v.1 & v.4 together$70 + $5 p&p)
vol. 5 (hardback only) $43 ($40 + $3 p&p)
. . . . . (v.1 & v.5 together$70 + $5 p&p)
. . . . . (v.1, 2, & 5 together$100 + $5 p&p)
. . . . . (v.1, 2, 3, 4, & 5 together$170 + $7 p&p)
Vol. 6 (hardback only) $43 ($40 + $3 p&p)
. . . . . (v.1 & v.6 together$70 + $5 p&p)
. . . . . (v.1, 2, & 6 together$100 + $6 p&p)
. . . . . (v.1, 2, 3, 4, 5 & 6 together$200 + $10 p&p)

The other volumes (7, 8, & 9) are yet to be finished.
. . . I also have copies of A BRAZIER/BRASHER SAGA, 300 Years of the Brasher, Brazier, Brasier, Brashier Family in America. Which is an altogether different family: Descendants of William B. Brashier Sr, who died at age 34 in Old Baltimore Co (now Harford Co), MD in 1708, leaving four orphans, whom the courts took care of. This SAGA is available only in 8.5"x11" paperback and sells for $28 ($25 + $3 p&p).
. . . I'm working on the other Brashear books.

To order the printed volumes (please do NOT order the volumes not yet printed!), send a note, saying which volume(s) you want (so I won't get confused) and where you want it/them sent, along with a check or money order, to

Charles Brashear,
1718 Arroyo Sierra Circle,
Santa Rosa, CA 95405-7762

Phone: 707/545-3903

I'll mail the books as soon as I can put them into the mailing boxes and get to the Post Office.

. . . If any of you want to order a gift copy for your favorite library, I'll knock $10 off the price (that is, you pay $25 for the hardbacks of v.1 & v.2, $30 for the others, plus p&p), and I'll send it to the library in your name. Just tell me which library, or let me pick one. (Some 30 libraries already have gift copies of vol 1, not so many of the other volumes.)

MORE DETAILS

Here are some more detailed descriptions of the contents of the printed volumes, as well as some of my other writings:

Vol 1: THE FIRST 200 YEARS OF BRASHEAR(S) IN AMERICA

and Some Descendants in Maryland

WARNING! Don't mistake this for something it isn't. (Some people bought the Brazier/Brasher book and then complained that their Brashear family was not in it; these are two wholly different families.) This is a volume about the first five generations of the descendants of Robert and Benois Brasseur, French Huguenot immigrants to Virginia, c1635, whose surname was Anglicized as Brashear. Over the years, many branches of the family added an "s" to make it Brashears. Benois Brasseur was naturalized in Calvert Co, MD, in 1662, and became known as Benjamin Brashear; he is the progenitor of virtually all Americans with surnames Brashear, Brashears, Brashares, Breshear(s), Breashear(s), Broshear(s), Beshear(s), Boshear(s), Beshires, often Brasher, Brashers, Brashier, Brashiers, sometimes Brazier, and about 35 other spellings. Also, this volume only treats the first 200 years of the family, mainly in Virginia and Maryland, from about 1635 to about 1835, except that the Western Maryland chapter comes up to the last few years. I'm working on other volumes that will bring many of the Brashear(s) lines down to more recent times.

. . . The volume is 7" by 10", 336 pages long (16 pages of front matter, including contents and a review of the deBrassier Family of Carpentras, France; 300 pages of text (see contents below); and 20 pages of 4-column index--about 3500 entries).

Abbreviated CONTENTS of Vol 1:

Vol 2: ROBERT C. BRASHEAR OF NORTH CAROLINA and Some Descendants in TN, KY, MO, TX, etc,

The 1740s were an economically rough time in Maryland (some of our family lost their land and/or spent time in debtors' prison). Newly opened land in the Granville District of North Carolina was an invitation to a new start. Three Brashear brothers--Robert C., Basil, and Otho--migrated to NC in the late 1740s/ early 1750s, where Robert and Basil got land grants.

Basil went broke again and left about 1766, and Otho simply disappeared, but Robert C. Brashear and his wife, Charity Dowell, stayed on and (we think) prospered. They were patriots during the Revolutionary War, after which newly opening land in western places beckoned again, and the family succumbed to wanderlust or land-hunger; they became part of the American westward movement. This volume traces Robert C. Brashear in North Carolina and the families of sons Philip, Asa, and Zaza, and daughter, Ann (Brashear) Ball; Robert Samuel Brashear and Jesse Brashears have to wait for vol. 3 and vol. 5, respectively.

. . . The volume is 7" by 10", 316 pages (290 pages of text, about 50 illustrations, and 24 pages of 4-column index--over 4000 entries).

Abbreviated CONTENTS of Vol 2

Vol 3: Robert Samuel Brashears, "The Rolling Stone," and Some Descendants in TN and KY.

Very early in the Revolution (or maybe even before), several of the Guilford Co Brashear(s) again got wanderlust, or they had worn out the land. At any rate, Robert Samuel Brashears and all of his children migrated to the frontier, first to Sullivan Co, NC (it would become Sullivan Co, TN), then to Roane Co, TN. RSB's son, Isaac Brashears, went on to Perry/Decatur Co, TN, and his son, Capt. Samuel Brashear (he dropped the "s" on his surname), moved on to Perry Co, KY. RSB's son, Basil, stayed on in Roane Co. This volume is about these families.
. . . The volume is 7" x 10", 496 pages, including 41 pages of index and about 40 maps, pictures, or other documents. I have to charge $40 per copy. Sorry.

Abbreviated CONTENTS of Vol 3:

Vol 4. Brashear(s) Families of the Ohio Valley

Well before the Revolution, a burgeoning population made new land necessary. If you have a family of 12 children, there is no way in the world those 12 families can live on the same land as the parents, especially when the parents' land is already old, nearly worn-out. As early as the 1750s, Americans began crowding Western Maryland, the Monongahela River valley in southwestern Pennsylvania, and by about 1775, the Ohio River Valley. A fair number of Brashear(s) families and their relatives were among these emigrants— the Elder and Younger William Brashears; Otho Brashear and his wife Ruth Brown (along with two of her brothers who had married two of Otho's sisters); Ignatius "Nacy" Brashear; Marsham Brashear (and his father, Benjamin, and brothers, who soon moved on to Mississippi); remnants of older Maryland families, like Lt. Rezin Brashears, Nathan Brashears/Brashares Jr, Zachariah Brashears/Broshars; and strays like Joseph M. Brashears of Steubenville. This volume is about these people and their families.

. . . The volume is 6" x 9", hardbound, 676 pages (xx + 656), with 59 pages of index, about 50 pictures and seven maps. $40, plus $3 postage and packaging.

Abbreviated CONTENTS of Vol 4:

Vol 5. Two Brashears Families of the Lower Mississippi Valley, their Choctaw, and other Descendants.

700 pages (xvi + 686) and hard backed.$40 per copy, plus $3 postage and packaging for the first volume, $1 p&p for each additional volume.

. . . By the late 1770s, American and European immigrants were already moving into the lower Mississippi Valley in search of new land, even though much of that territory was under Spanish control. Some of them came by ship to Pensacola, Mobile, New Orleans, Baton Rouge, and Natchez, all of which were developed ports under French and Spanish administrations. Others came by flatboat down the Cherokee (Tennessee) River, then proceeded down an ancient, Indian trading path, soon to be known as The Natchez Trace. Still others began floating down the Ohio and Mississippi Rivers to find new land.

. . . Two branches of the Brashear(s) family were among these early immigrants: 1. Benjamin Brashear and all his children, except Marsham (who stayed in Louisville, KY) and 2. Jesse Brashears and all of his children. In both cases, one or more members of the family married into the Choctaw tribe and founded large families that are still traceable today. Other of their brothers and cousins founded large, non-Indian families.

Abbreviated CONTENTS of Vol 5:

Vol. 6 Brashears/Breshears (Beshears, Boshears)
Families of TN, MO, ID, WA, OK, etc,

almost 700 pages (xx + 666, including 80 pp of 3-col index) and hard backed. $40 per copy, plus $3 postage and packaging.

In the 1830s, the old restlessness overtook the Brashears/Breshears families of Lawrence Co, TN (besides the land was wearing pretty thin), and they started looking for new land in the west. Several brothers and cousins from Lawrence Co— Middleton, the Younger; Nathan Turner; Alexander; John (m. Naoma Hogg); Henry Breshears Jr; Berry Boshears; and many of their grown children headed west in 1832, 1838, 1842, etc and found new lives in Benton, Polk, Dallas, and neighboring Counties, MO; White and Saline Co, AR, etc.

These were all probably descendants of Basil Brashears, b. 1714, MD, m. Anne Belt; and their son, Middleton Brashears "The elder." After hardly a generation, many Brashears/ Breshears moved to Boise, ID, Omak, WA, Indian Territory, TX, and other neighboring counties in MO.

MY HISTORICAL FICTION:

I also write fiction (mainly historical fiction about American Indians) and books about the writing process. If any of you are interested, here are the titles. For more information, go to my website (www.CharlesBrashear.com) or to www.Amazon.com and search for my name in "books":

Killing Cynthia Ann, a novel, published 1999 by Texas Christian University Press; ISBN: 0-87565-209-3. $21.50.

Comeuppance at Kicking Horse Casino, and Other Stories, published in 2000 by American Indian Studies Center, UCLA, ISBN:0-935626-51-4. $15.

Brain, Brawn, and Will: The Turmoils and Adventures of Jeff Ross. Published in 2001 by 1stbooks Library. 6x9 Paperback, ISBN: 0-75963-364-9: $19.95.

Contemporary Insanities: Short Fictions, Published in 1990 by **The Press of MacDonald & Reinecke**, P.O.Box 840, Arroyo Grande, CA 93421-0840. $9.95 (mail orders add $2 postage) ISBN: 1-877947-11-3. Ask at your bookstore, or order from the publisher. (I also have a supply of these books.)

FIVE BOOKS ON WRITING

On Creativity in General and Creative Writing in Particular (No. 1 in "The Elements of Writing" Series; ISBN: 0-75963-362-2; $19.95)

. . . "Brashear has done something amazing in pulling together so many strands in the web of creativity. Simply the best book on the subject." (pre-pub review)

Elements of Dialog, Dialect, and Conversational Style (No. 2 in "The Elements of Writing" Series; **ISBN: 0-75963-372-X; $17.95**)

"Many current books on writing devote a chapter or a few paragraphs to writing dialog, but there is a lack of books zeroing in on the subject. Here, at last, is a good one. The author's approach is a new one, and he shows great familiarity with linguistics. He covers the subject well, including non-verbal language, explaining how it supplements words as part of dialog. His down-to-earth analyses and examples of dialects and accent can be quite useful. I have never seen the subject covered so thoroughly. His arguments contrasting academic, journalistic, and conversational style were coherent and logical.

"I believe this book will become at least moderately significant among publications for writers. I would, indeed, want it in my personal library." —U.N. Tejano

Elements of the Novel: an Update on Forster (No. 3 in "The Elements of Writing" Series; **ISBN: 0-75963-370-3; $19.95**)

. . . "Whether you think the novel is a vehicle for character study, or a vehicle for story and plot, or for some more "poetic" elements, like aesthetic design and structure, this book is for you. The depth of discussion at every phase is notable and rare in this sort of book. Brashear knows what he's talking about—and does it with clarity and economy." —Joel Black

"Brashear is a modernist, who finds much in Post-Modernism simply nonsense. For those of us who have resisted the waves of absurdities over the last fifty years, he's a breath of cleansing sea-breeze." —Bill Baeddekker

A Writer's Toolkit: Elements of Writing Personal Essays, Poems, Stories. (No. 4 in "The Elements of Writing" Series; **ISBN: 0-75963-368-1; $23.95**)

"Good book! You'll want it on your shelf. Every beginning writer should know what's in this book. And every experienced writer should be reminded of it once in a while."—Jane Wall

Elements of Form and Style in Expository Essays (No. 5 in "The Elements of Writing" Series; **ISBN: 0-75963-365-7; $17.95**)

"This author makes essay writing seem simple, rather than the arduous task I remember it being. Where was he when I needed him? And his examples, especially those on Washo and Koko, the Ameslan "talking" chimpanzee and ape, are a treat in themselves. Highly recommended!" —Howard Koppolo

All of the above books are currently available.

Cheers, Charlie Brashear

www.ingramcontent.com/pod-product-compliance
Lightning Source LLC
Chambersburg PA
CBHW030942150426
42812CB00062B/2704
9780933362178